Edward Eggleston

The schoolmaster in literature

containing selections from the writings of Ascham, Molière, Fuller, Rousseau,

Shenstone, Cowper, Goethe, Pestalozzi, Page, Mitford, Bronté, Hughes, Dickens,

Thackeray, Irving, George Eliot, Eggleston, Thompson, and others

Edward Eggleston

The schoolmaster in literature

containing selections from the writings of Ascham, Molière, Fuller, Rousseau, Shenstone, Cowper, Goethe, Pestalozzi, Page, Mitford, Brontë, Hughes, Dickens, Thackeray, Irving, George Eliot, Eggleston, Thompson, and others

ISBN/EAN: 9783741101465

Manufactured in Europe, USA, Canada, Australia, Japa

Cover: Foto ©Andreas Hilbeck / pixelio.de

Manufactured and distributed by brebook publishing software (www.brebook.com)

Edward Eggleston

The schoolmaster in literature

THE SCHOOLMASTER

IN

LITERATURE

CONTAINING SELECTIONS FROM THE WRITINGS OF ASCHAM,
MOLIÈRE, FULLER, ROUSSEAU, SHENSTONE, COWPER,
GOETHE, PESTALOZZI, PAGE, MITFORD, BRONTÉ,
HUGHES, DICKENS, THACKERAY, IRVING,
GEORGE ELIOT, EGGLESTON,
THOMPSON, AND OTHERS

WITH AN INTRODUCTION
BY
EDWARD EGGLESTON

NEW YORK ·:· CINCINNATI ·:· CHICAGO
AMERICAN BOOK COMPANY

	PAGE
INTRODUCTION	5
Roger Ascham	13
Extracts from Toxophilus	15
Extracts from the Scholemaster	18
Quick's Adaptation from the Scholemaster	20
Jean-Baptiste Poquelin Molière	25
The Education of M. Jourdain	26
Jean Jacques Rousseau	41
Quick's Adaptation and Summary of Émile	43
William Shenstone	64
The Schoolmistress	65
Thomas Fuller	74
The Good Schoolmaster	74
Of Memory	76
Johann Heinrich Pestalozzi	78
Gertrude at Home	83
The School in Bonnal	92
A Chapter from Christopher and Eliza	111
William Cowper	118
Tirocinium; or, a Review of Schools	120
The Sage Called "Discipline"	139
Johann Wolfgang von Goethe	143
Selections from Wilhelm Meister's Wanderjahre	144
Mary Russell Mitford	187
The Village Schoolmistress	188
Dr. Courtly's School	199
Charlotte Brontë	203
Lowood School	204

CONTENTS

	PAGE
David Perkins Page	230
The Schoolmaster	232
William Makepeace Thackeray	242
Miss Pinkerton's School	243
Dr. Swishtail's Academy	258
Mr. Veal's School	270
Thomas Hughes	278
Chapters from Tom Brown's School-Days at Rugby	279
Daniel Pierce Thompson	312
The School in the Horn of the Moon	312
The Examination at Mill Town Emporium	336
Charles Dickens	352
Dr. Blimber's School	353
The School at Salem House	395
Dr. Strong's School	422
Dotheboys Hall	425
William Mathews	456
Judge Story as a Teacher	457
George Eliot	465
The Night School and the Schoolmaster	467
Tom's First Half	472
Washington Irving	495
Ichabod Crane	496
George MacDonald	504
Extracts from Malcolm	505
Edward Eggleston	551
A Struggle for the Mastery	552
Some Western Schoolmasters	556
D'Arcy Wentworth Thompson	570
Day-Dreams of a Schoolmaster	571

INTRODUCTION

It is my office only to stand in the portico and open the door of the present edifice, which has been builded right skillfully by another. If the delight of the intelligent reader were the only purpose in view, hardly anything could be better than such a compilation as the present one, showing the part played by the schoolmaster in the literature of diverse ages and of different nations. It is quite worth while, for example, to take the ideal of a good schoolmaster constructed by quaint old Thomas Fuller and put it alongside the Blimbers, and to place Shenstone's village school,

"where sits the dame disguised in look profound,
And eyes her fairy throng, and turns her wheel around,"

in juxtaposition with the immaculate Miss Pinkerton's most respectable seat of learning on Chiswick Mall, or with quaint old Bartle Massey's night school for full-grown men. Here we have the schoolmaster under many lights, and literature in widely varying moods. As a means of cultivating a taste for literature and a discriminating taste *in* literature, I know of no better collection than this, particularly for the use of teachers, whose relish is certain to be quickened by professional interest in the subject.

But literary interest and literary culture are by no means the only ends served by such a collation of representative delineations of the schoolmaster. Some phases of truth are not easily communicated in didactic form; they are seen best in the delicate shading of artistic literature. This is what Charles Lamb calls the "twilight of truth." Perhaps Dickens's Dr. Blimber, with his everlasting iteration of "Bring him on, Cornelia, bring him on," has done more than the soberest treatises on pedagogy to discourage the ancient mode of education by cramming—the only sort of infanticide permitted in civilized countries. A whole board of education of the unprogressive sort, once so common, seems to be wrapped up in Dr. Blimber, with his stolid ignorance of the higher uses of learning and his stupid demand for a visible "bringing on" of the poor little Dombey. Cornelia Blimber is but the conductor through which Dr. Blimber works his "bringing on," propelled as many another teacher has found herself propelled by the force behind her to push those who ought not to be pushed. But behind the unintelligent board of Blimbers are innumerable other Blimbers in the unintelligent parents, who also demand that Cornelia shall "bring him on."

The maker of this collection has sought by means of literary cross-lights to give the teacher, not direct instruction in method, but something quite as valuable. Here the schoolmaster sees his profession in the light of literary culture and literary art, and, in some cases, he sees it illuminated by the light of genius. From such treatment of the subject the teacher gains broader views of his calling in its relation to life. This enlightenment is quite as necessary as special instruction to produce the real teacher. The real teacher is in turn the very leaven that leavens the whole lump of modern civilization.

An estimable gentleman said to me recently, "In all my life at school it was my misfortune not to encounter one real teacher." I was not surprised at the tone of regret in which this was spoken. But the man who has been so unhappy as never, during his period of plasticity, to have fallen into the shaping hands of a real teacher, is hardly capable of estimating the extent of his irreparable loss.

The real teacher is by no means a modern invention. One cannot be sure that we have now a larger proportion of men and women answering that description than there were centuries ago. The good and great Moravian brother Comenius, with his admirable spirit and methods, lived away·back in the sixteenth century. And was Roger Ascham the only good English "Scholemaster" in the days of Queen Elizabeth? There can be no doubt that we know better than the generality of old masters what to teach, and it would be a pity indeed if, with all our philosophizing and experimenting, with all our normal schooling and our teachers' institutes innumerable, we had not found out some things about method that our forefathers did not know. It is even possible that we have put too much stress upon methods of instruction, and that in our conceit of system we have hardly left standing space for the living teacher. The individuality of the real teacher sometimes unfits him to serve well as a cog-wheel in the clock-work of a complicated school system. His very originality is sometimes laid against him for a fault by the austere method-ist in pedagogy.

Far be it from me to affirm that we can count fewer real teachers in the hundred now than there were formerly. That would be to deny that we have made any real progress, for the best school systems and the most admirable of teaching methods would be a thousand times worse than useless if they should render the production of real teachers impossible. But we may have exaggerated the relative importance of method in teaching. There are signs that we are entering on a new epoch, in which men will count for more than prescribed methods, and in which the production of genuine teachers will be the objective.

Do not expect me to define the term. The best things elude definition. Words are not subtle enough to describe things that are priceless. If I were to say that the real teacher is devoted to his work, manifests a lively and intelligent sympathy with his pupils, evinces tact in management and ingenuity in conveying information, and has the sort of enthusiasm that gives him a momentum communicable to those under his care, I should have enumerated enough of his qualities to enable one to classify him. But how far short of filling the measure of his description is this list of qualities. Put these things together, and you will still have something less than the man.

This is partly because men and women who are capable of shaping others have something about them that cannot be set down in a catalogue. A lady said to me the other day, that while qualities were valuable, *quality* was something much greater. A good expression of a profound truth! Count the standard virtues on your fingers, and you can recall estimable people who possess them all, but who, nevertheless, do not go for much. That which my friend called quality—that something blending all these qualities into one harmonious and potent whole, is lacking. You do not think of the qualities of a man like Arnold of Rugby, or of a man like the revered but unfortunate Pestalozzi. One could not pick either the one or the other to pieces, and make any recognizable catalogue of his parts. There is an integrity, a wholeness about the efficient man or woman of any sort, that defies analysis.

The test of the teacher is efficiency. Not the showing he is able to make in an examination, but the final result he can produce in the character of those who come from under his hand. This efficiency is not of the sort that can be counted upon always to work an increase of salary. But the ability **to** leave a lasting mark on the mind and character of a pupil, is the unmistakable sign of the real teacher. And the source of this power lies not in the teacher's acquirements, but deeper in the very fiber of his character. "Words have weight, when there is a man behind them," said the prophet of Concord. It is the man or woman behind the instruction that makes the real teacher a great deal more than a mere instructor.

Examinations for license to teach do not get at what is most valuable in the teacher. A touch of mental enlightenment, or the possession of the least bit of the real teaching quality is worth more than expertness in extracting cube-roots. Unhappily we have no means of measuring character with precision, no accurate test for a teacher's aptitude. The owner of a creamery buys all his milk by the gallon. He pays at the same rate for the thinnest sky-tinted product that he does for the butter-laden contribution of a Jersey herd. I went through an exhibition of dairy appliances recently, and was interested most of all in a method newly devised for testing the butter-making qualities of milk. By the addition of an acid to a sample of milk, the butter oils were made to rise to the surface in a little bottle with a slender neck, graded like a thermometer. You can read on the scale the quality of the milk expressed in millimeters. But we measure the qualifications of our teachers in the old-fashioned way; we buy their grammar and arithmetic by the gallon. It is a question of quantity. "How much of each branch of study are you loaded up with?" demands the examiner. Now there are some experts in grammar and arithmetic who have no power to communicate even their technical knowledge to the pupil. How much less can they perform any of those higher services that the real teacher renders to the mind and heart of a pupil! Shall we ever devise a delicate scale for gauging the quality that gives the better teacher his superiority?

"Born, not made," is true of the great teacher as of the great man of every sort. But it is not with the great schoolmaster that we have to do. A man may be real without being great, and it can do no harm to fix the attention of the teacher of average gifts on this ideal of genuineness. Every man and woman is to be accounted a real teacher who establishes a vital relation between himself and the developing pupil; who is, to a greater or less extent, a living force in the formation of character and the enlargement of mind. In this class the mere hearer of recitations and keeper of grade marks has no place whatever.

Real teachers are of various magnitudes, and the humblest mistress of a country school, who manages to inspire her pupils with a thirst for knowledge and an aspiration for veracity in character is in the class of real teachers as truly as Socrates, the first great professor of the divine art of molding youthful character and pushing the human mind in the direction of truth. Blessed be the humble teacher who, without any chance for the great rewards of fame or money, renders noble service and leaves the impress of a genuine and generous character in one little corner of the world. No cyclopædia or dictionary of notables ever mentions that wonderful old Pennsylvania Dutchman, Christopher Dock. But, in the obscurity of the Pennsylvania back country in the last century, he did some of the noblest and most enlightened teaching the world has ever seen. He was a schoolmaster, indeed, not a master of the school in any merely outward sense, but master of the very souls of his rustic pupils.

Even of the humblest real teacher the words of Fuller are true, perhaps: "His genius inclines him with delight to the profession." I should despair of the success of any teacher who found no ground of pleasure in the work. But all such sources of enlightenment as the present work add greatly to the efficiency of the teacher. They make the light places in the teacher's work brighter, and shed some rays of illuminating humor and fancy upon the darker parts.

The kingdom of heaven is not the only good thing that cometh without observation. Great movements rarely make much stir at the outset. It is only by the harvest that we are able to measure the value of the seed-time. I suppose that this book had its origin in the Teachers' Reading Circles, which are one of "the new things under the sun." I do not know any better new fashion in these last years of a great century than the reading circles. Certain obscure religious and reformatory societies that came into being in England, nobody knows how, as the Seventeenth Century drew to its end, proved to be the very germs of some of the greatest movements that characterized the Eighteenth Century. Just now, as the Nineteenth Century is handing over the legacy of our age to the next, the public interested in education has come suddenly to realize that the culture of the teacher must be progressive. Perhaps in the Twentieth Century schoolmasters will no longer be accused of having minds rendered dry and uninteresting by unbroken contact with undeveloped intellects, and by a ceaseless repetition of the same instruction. The true antidote to what may be called the teacher's palsy is a constant acquisition of fresh knowledge or a continual whetting of the mental appetite by means of good literature. I know of no other means by which may be acquired and retained that perennial freshness of mind so necessary to success in teaching.

On one point the greatest masters are agreed—that knowledge

should be given in cheerful and delightful ways. Comenius so long ago as the Sixteenth Century insisted upon a cheerful environment, a pleasant schoolroom, and cheerful objects in association with study. And his contemporary, Ascham, had a similar notion; he would have learning "mingled with honest mirth and comely exercises." Long afterward, Pestalozzi went deeper, and sought to make the very exercises of learning agreeable by having them accord with the child's nature, and not cross it. His pupil, Froebel, even sought with ingenuity to bring to his aid child-plays, dancing, and music. All the masters, however they may have differed as to the means, agreed in desiring to make learning delightful, in trying to rob school toil of its irksomeness. I may venture to suggest that good as was Comenius's notion of a cheerful schoolroom, Ascham's alloy of honest mirth and comely exercises, and Froebel's ingenious play-work, there is one means of rendering the pursuit of study delightful that transcends all of these. That is fresh-mindedness in the teacher. The master whose mind is refreshed by his own delight in literature, whose zest for fresh knowledge remains keen, will do more than all else to render the pathway of the industrious pupil delightsome.

If, then, the Teachers' Reading Circles are to give us circles of reading teachers, hail to that which will do much to deliver us from the dry teacher and from insipid teaching!

But if literature be so good a thing, why do I stand so long in the gap, and detain the wistful reader from the green pastures that lie beyond? To borrow a stock phrase from the old playwrights, "Masters, let us within."

EDWARD EGGLESTON.

THE
SCHOOLMASTER IN LITERATURE

ROGER ASCHAM
1515-1568

ROGER ASCHAM was born in 1515, and took his degree at the university of Cambridge at the age of nineteen. That he was preëminently skilled in the Greek language is evident from the fact that, a few years after he left the university, he was invited by Sir John Cheke to become preceptor in the learned languages to Elizabeth, which office he discharged for two years with great credit and satisfaction to himself, as well as to his illustrious pupil. Soon after this he went abroad, and remained about three years in Germany. On his return, he was selected to fill the office of Latin secretary to Edward VI., but on the death of the king he returned to the university. On the accession of Elizabeth, he was immediately distinguished, and read with the queen some hours every day in the Latin and Greek languages. In this office, and in that of Latin secretary, he continued at court for the remainder of his life. He died in 1568, at the age of fifty-three.

Characterization

It would perhaps have surprised Roger Ascham, the scholar of a learned age, and a Greek professor, that the history of English literature might open with his name; for in his English writings he had formed no premeditated work designed for posterity as well as his own times. The subjects he has written on were solely suggested by the occasion, and incurred the slight of the cavilers of his day, who had not yet learned that humble titles may conceal performances which exceed their promise, and that trifles cease to be trivial in the workmanship of genius. An apology for a favorite recreation, that of archery, for his indulgence in which his enemies, and sometimes his friends, reproached the truant of academic Greek; an account of affairs of Germany, while employed as secretary to the English embassy; and the posthumous treatise of the "Scholemaster," originating in an accidental conversation at table—constitute the whole of the claims of Ascham to the rank of an English classic, a degree much higher than was obtained by the learning of Sir Thomas Elyot and the genius of Sir Thomas More. . . .

The mind of Ascham was stored with all the wealth of ancient literature the nation possessed. Ascham was proud, when alluding to his master, the learned Cheke, and to his royal pupil, Queen Elizabeth, of having been the pupil of the greatest scholar, and a preceptor to the greatest pupil in England; but we have rather to admire the intrepidity of his genius which induced him to avow the noble design of setting an example of composing in our vernacular idiom. He tells us in his "Toxophilus," "I write this English matter in the English language, for Englishmen." He introduced an easy and natural style in English prose, instead of the pedantry of the unformed taste of his day, and adopted, as he tells us, the counsel of Aristotle, "to speak as the common people do, to think as the wise men do."

"The Scholemaster," with its humble title, "to teach children to understand, write, and speak the Latin tongue," conveys an erroneous notion of the delight and the knowledge which may be drawn from this treatise, notwithstanding that the work remains incomplete, for there are references to parts which do not appear in the work itself. "The Scholemaster" is a classical production in English, which may be placed by the side of its great Latin rivals, the Orations of Cicero and the Institutes of Quintilian. It is enlivened by interesting details. The first idea of the work was started in a real conversation at table, among some eminent personages, on occasion of the flight of some scholars from Eton College, driven away by the iron rod of the master. "Was the school-house to be a house of bondage and fear, or a house of play and pleasure?" During the progress of the work the author lost his patron and incurred other disappointments. He has consigned all his variable emotions to this volume. The accidental interview with Lady Jane Grey; his readings with Queen Elizabeth, in their daily intercourse with the fine writers of antiquity, and their recreations at the regal game of chess—for such was the seduction of Attic learning, that the queen on the throne felt a happiness in again becoming a pupil of her old master—these and similar instances present those individual touches of the writer which give such a reality to an author's feelings.

The works of Ascham, which are collected in a single volume, remain for the gratification of those who preserve a pure taste for the pristine simplicity of our ancient writers. His native English, that English which we have lost, but which we are ever delighted to recover after nearly three centuries, is still critical without pedantry, and beautiful without ornament ; and (which cannot be said of the writings of Sir Thomas Elyot and Sir Thomas More) the volume of Ascham is indispensable in every English library whose possessor in any way aspires to connect together the progress of taste and of opinion in our country. ISAAC D'ISRAELI.

The "Toxophilus"[1] is, as its name imports, a treatise upon archery; and the main design of Ascham in writing it was to apologize for the zeal with which he studied and practiced the art of shooting, and to show the honor and dignity of the art in all nations and at all times, and its acknowledged utility not only in matters of war, but as an innocent and engaging pastime in times of peace. The whole work is in the dialogue form, the speakers being Toxophilus, a lover of archery, and Philologus, a student.

The work goes fully into the practical part of the art, so that the "Schole for Shootinge" is a complete manual of archery, containing not only a learned history of the art, and the highest encomiums on its excellence and utility, but likewise the most minute practical details, even down to the species of goose from the wing of which the best feathers are to be plucked for the shaft.

CHARLES D. CLEVELAND.

Extracts from "Toxophilus"

1. THE VALUE OF RECREATION

PHILOLOGUS. How much is to be given to the authority either of Aristotle or Tully[2] I cannot tell.; this I am sure, which thing this fair wheat (God save it) maketh me remember, that those husbandmen which rise earliest, and come latest home, and are content to have their dinner and other drinkings brought into the field to them, for fear of losing of time, have fatter barns in harvest than they which will either sleep at noon-time of the day, or else make merry with their neighbors

---

[1] From *toxon* (τοξον), a bow, and *philos* (φιλος), a friend. The original title runs thus : "Toxophilus, the Schole of Shootinge, conteyned In II Bookes. To all Gentlemen and Yomen of Englande, pleasaunte for theyr pastyme to rede, and profitable for theyr use to follow ; both in War and Peace."

[2] Cicero

at the ale. And so a scholar that purposeth to be a good husband,[1] and desireth to reap and enjoy much fruit of learning, must till and sow thereafter. Our best seed time, which be scholars, as it is very timely and when we be young, so it endureth not over long, and therefore it may not be let slip one hour.

TOXOPHILUS. For contrariwise, I heard myself a good husband at his book once say, that to omit study some time of the day, and some time of the year, made as much for the increase of learning, as to let the land lie some time fallow maketh for the better increase of corn. This we see, if the land be ploughed every year, the corn cometh thin up; the ear is short, the grain is small, and when it is brought into the barn and threshed, giveth very evil fall.[2] So those who never leave poring on their books have oftentimes as thin invention as other poor men have, and as small wit and weight in it as in other men's. And thus your husbandry, methinks, is more like the life of a covetous snudge that oft very evil proves, than the labor of a good husband, that knoweth well what he doth. And surely the best wits to learning must needs have much recreation and ceasing from their book, or else they mar themselves; when base and dumpish wits can never be hurt with continual study; as ye see in luting, that a treble minikin string must always be let down, but at such time as when a man must needs play, when[3] the base and dull string needeth never to be moved out of his place.

2. IN PRAISE OF THE GOOSE

TOXOPHILUS. Yet well fare the gentle goose, which bringeth to a man so many exceeding commodities! For the goose is man's comfort in war and in peace, sleeping and waking. What praise soever is given to shooting, the goose may challenge the best part of it. *How well doth she make a man fare at his table!* How easily doth she make a man lie in his bed! How fit, even as her feathers be only for shooting, so be her quills for writing.

[1] husbandman [2] produce [3] whereas

PHILOLOGUS. Indeed, Toxophile, that is the best praise you gave to a goose yet, and surely I would have said you had been to blame if you had overskipt it.

TOXOPHILUS. The Romans, I trow, Philologe, not so much because a goose with crying saved their capitolium, with their golden Jupiter did make a golden goose, and set her in the top of the capitolium, and appointed also the censors to allow, out of the common batch, yearly stipends for the finding of certain geese; the Romans did not, I say, give all this honor to a goose for that good deed only, but for other infinite mo,[1] which come daily to a man by geese; and surely if I should declaim in the praise of any manner of beast living, I would choose a goose. But the goose hath made us flee too far from our matter.

3. HIS APOLOGY FOR WRITING IN ENGLISH

If any man would blame me either for taking such a matter in hand, or else for writing it in the English tongue, this answer I may make him, that when the best of the realm think it honest for them to use, I, one of the meanest sort, ought not to suppose it vile for me to write: and though to have written it in another tongue had been both more profitable for my study, and also more honest for my name, yet I can think my labor well bestowed, if with a little hinderance of my profit and name may come any furtherance to the pleasure or commodity of the gentlemen and yeomen of England, for whose sake I took this matter in hand. And as for the Latin or Greek tongue, everything is so excellently done in them, that none can do better; in the English tongue, contrary, everything in a manner so meanly, both for the matter and handling, that no man can do worse. For therein the least learned, for the most part, have been always most ready to write. And they which had least hope in Latin have been most bold in English: when surely every man that is most ready to talk is not most able to write. He that will write well in any tongue, must follow this counsel of Aristotle, to speak as the common people do, to think

[1] more

as wise men do: as so should every man understand him, and the judgment of wise men allow him. Many English writers have not done so, but, using strange words, as Latin, French, and Italian, do make all things dark and hard. Once I communed with a man which reasoned the English tongue to be enriched and increased thereby, saying, "Who will not praise that feast where a man shall drink at a dinner both wine, ale, and beer?" "Truly (quoth I) they be all good, every one taken by himself alone, but if you put malmsey and sack, red wine and white, ale and beer, and all in one pot, you shall make a drink neither easy to be known, nor yet wholesome for the body."

Extracts from the "Scholemaster"

1. Intermixture of Study and Exercise

I would wish, that beside some good time, fitly appointed, and constantly kept, to increase by reading the knowledge of the tongues, and learning, young gentlemen should use, and delight in all courtly exercises and gentlemanlike pastimes. And good cause why: for the self-same noble city of Athens, justly commended of me before, did wisely, and upon great consideration, appoint the muses, Apollo and Pallas, to be patrons of learning to their youth. For the muses, besides learning, were also ladies of dancing, mirth, and minstrelsy: Apollo was god of shooting, and author of cunning playing upon instruments; Pallas also was lady mistress in wars. Whereby was nothing else meant, but that learning should be always mingled with honest mirth and comely exercises; and that war also should be governed by learning and moderated by wisdom; as did well appear in those captains of Athens named by me before, and also in Scipio and Cæsar, the two diamonds of Rome. And Pallas was no more feared in wearing *Ægida*, than she was praised for choosing *Olivani;* whereby shineth the glory of learning, which thus was governor and mistress, in the noble city of Athens, both of war and peace.

2. The Consequences of Neglected Education

It is pity that, commonly, more care is had, yea, and that among very wise men, to find out rather a cunning man for their horse, than a cunning man for their children. They say nay in word, but they do so in deed. For to the one they will gladly give a stipend of two hundred crowns by year, and loath to offer to the other two hundred shillings. God, that sitteth in heaven, laugheth their choice to scorn, and rewardeth their liberality as it should; for he suffereth them to have tame and well-ordered horse, but wild and unfortunate children; and, therefore, in the end, they find more pleasure in their horse than comfort in their children.

3. Dangers of Foreign Travel

I know divers noble personages, and many worthy gentlemen of England, whom all the siren songs of Italy could never untwine from the mast of God's word; nor no enchantment of vanity overturn them from the fear of God and love of honesty.

But I know as many, or mo, and some, sometime my dear friends (for whose sake I hate going into that country the more), who, parting out of England fervent in the love of Christ's doctrine, and well furnished with the fear of God, returned out of Italy worse transformed than ever was any in Circe's[1] court. I know divers, that went out of England men of innocent life, men of excellent learning, who returned out of Italy, not only with worse manners, but also with less learning; neither so willing to live orderly, nor yet so able to speak learnedly, as they were at home, before they went abroad. . . .

But I am afraid that over many of our travelers into Italy do not eschew the way to Circe's court, but go, and ride, and run, and fly thither; they make great haste to come to her; they make great suit to serve her; yea, I could point out some

---

[1] an enchantress of ancient fable, who first charmed her victims and then changed them to beasts

with my finger, that never had gone out of England, but only to serve Circe in Italy. . . . If you think we judge amiss, and write too sore against you, hear what the Italian saith of the Englishman; what the master reporteth of the scholar, who uttereth plainly what is taught by him, and what is learned by you, saying, *Inglese Italianato, è un diabolo incarnato:* that is to say, "you remain men in shape and fashion, but become devils in life and condition."

R. H. Quick's Adaptation from the "Scholemaster"

If *laudari a laudatis*[1] is any test of merit, we may assume that this book is still deserving of attention. "It contains, perhaps," says Dr. Johnson, "the best advice that was ever given for the study of languages." And Mr. J. E. B. Mayor (no mean authority) ventures on a still stronger assertion. "This book sets forth," says he, "*the only sound method of acquiring a dead language.*" Mr. George Long has also borne witness on the same side.

And yet, I believe, few teachers of the dead languages have read Ascham's book, or know the method he proposes. I will, therefore, give an account of it, as nearly as I can in Ascham's own words.

Latin is to be taught as follows: First, let the child learn the eight parts of speech, and then the right joining together of substantives with adjectives, the noun with the verb, the relative with the antecedent. After the concords are learned, let the master take Sturm's selection of Cicero's Epistles, and read them after this manner: "First, let him teach the child, cheerfully and plainly, the cause and matter of the letter; then, let him construe it into English so oft as the child may easily carry away the understanding of it; lastly, parse it over perfectly. This done, then let the child by and by both construe and parse it over again; so that it may appear that the child doubteth in nothing that his master has taught him before.

[1] to be praised by those who are themselves praised

"After this, the child must take a paper book, and sitting in some place where no man shall prompt him, by himself let him translate into English his former lesson. Then showing it to his master, let the master take from him his Latin book, and pausing an hour at the least, then let the child translate his own English into Latin again in another paper book. When the child bringeth it turned into Latin, the master must compare it with Tully's book, and lay them both together, and where the child doth well, praise him, where amiss point out why Tully's use is better.

"Thus the child will easily acquire a knowledge of grammar, and also the ground of almost all the rules that are so busily taught by the master, and so hardly learned by the scholar in all common schools."

"We do not contemn rules, but we gladly teach rules; and teach them more plainly, sensibly, and orderly than they be commonly taught in common schools. For when the master shall compare Tully's book with the scholar's translation, let the master at the first lead and teach the scholar to join the rules of his grammar book with the examples of his present lesson, until the scholar by himself be able to fetch out of his grammar every rule for every example; and let the grammar book be ever in the scholar's hand, and also used by him as a dictionary for every present use. This is a lively and perfect way of teaching of rules; where the common way used in common schools to read the grammar alone by itself is tedious for the master, hard for the scholar, cold and uncomfortable for them both."

And elsewhere Ascham says: "Yea, I do wish that all rules for young scholars were shorter than they be. For, without doubt, *grammatica*[1] itself is sooner and surer learned by examples of good authors than by the naked rules of grammarians."

"As you perceive your scholar to go better on away, first, with understanding his lesson more quickly, with parsing more readily, with translating more speedily and perfectly than he was wont; after, give him longer lessons to translate, and,

[1] Grammar

withal, begin to teach him, both in nouns and verbs, what is *proprium*,[1] and what is *translatum*,[2] what *synonymum*,[3] what *diversum*,[4] which be *contraria*,[5] and which be most notable *phrases*, in all his lectures." . . . .

Every lesson is to be thus carefully analyzed, and entered under these headings in a third MS. book.

All this time, though the boy is to work over some Terence, he is to speak no Latin. Subsequently the master must translate easy pieces from Cicero into English, and the boy, without having seen the original passage, is required to put the English into Latin. His translation must then be carefully compared with the original, for "of good heed-taking springeth chiefly knowledge."

In the Second Book of the "Scholemaster," Ascham discusses the various branches of the study then common, viz.: 1. *Translatio linguarum*;[6] 2. *Paraphrasis*;[7] 3. *Metaphrasis*;[8] 4. *Epitome*;[9] 5. *Imitatio*;[10] 6. *Declamatio*.[11] He does not lay much stress on any of these, except *translatio* and *imitatio*. Of the last he says: "All languages, both learned and mother-tongue, be gotten, and gotten only by imitation. For, as ye use to hear, so ye use to speak; if ye hear no other, ye speak not yourself; and whom ye only hear, of them ye only learn." But translation was his great instrument for all kinds of learning. "The translation," he says, "is the most common and most commendable of all other exercises for youth; most common, for all your constructions in grammar schools be nothing else but translations, but because they be not *double* translations (as I do require) they bring forth but simple and single commodity; and because also they lack the daily use of writing, which is the only thing that breedeth deep root, both in the wit for good understanding and in the memory for sure keeping of all that is learned;

[1] grammatical property
[2] that which is translated
[3] that which is synonymous
[4] that which is different in meaning
[5] expressions directly opposed in meaning
[6] translation of languages
[7] free translation
[8] verbal translation
[9] brief summary
[10] imitation
[11] vocal rendering

most commendable also, and that by the judgment of all authors which entreat of these exercises."

After quoting Pliny, he says: "You perceive how Pliny teacheth that by this exercise of double translating is learned easily, sensibly, by little and little, not only all the hard congruities of grammar, the choice of ablest words, the right pronouncing of words and sentences, comeliness of figures, and forms fit for every matter and proper for every tongue; but, that which is greater also, in marking daily and following diligently thus the footsteps of the best authors, like invention of arguments, like order in disposition, like utterance in elocution, is easily gathered up; and hereby your scholar shall be brought not only to like eloquence, but also to all true understanding and rightful judgment, both for writing and speaking."

Again he says: "For speedy attaining, I durst venture a good wager if a scholar in whom is aptness, love, diligence, and constancy, would but translate after this sort, some little book in Tully (as '*De Senectute*,' with two Epistles, the first '*Ad Quintum Fratrem*,' the other '*Ad Lentulum*') that scholar, I say, should come to a better knowledge in the Latin tongue than the most part do that spend from five to six years in tossing all the rules of grammar in common schools." After quoting the instance of Dion Prussæus, who came to great learning and utterance by reading and following only two books, the "*Phædo*" and Demosthenes' "*De Falsa Legatione*," he goes on: "And a better and nearer example herein may be our most noble Queen Elizabeth, who never took yet Greek nor Latin grammar in her hand after the first declining of a noun and a verb; but only by this double translating of Demosthenes and Isocrates daily, without missing, every forenoon, and likewise some part of Tully every afternoon, for the space of a year or two, hath attained to such a perfect understanding in both the tongues, and to such a ready utterance of the Latin, and that with such a judgment, as there be few now in both universities or elsewhere in England that be in both tongues comparable with Her Majesty." Ascham's authority is indeed not conclusive on this point, as he, in praising the queen's attainments, was vaunting his own success as a teacher, and, moreover, if he flattered her he could plead prevailing custom. But we have, I believe, abundant evidence that Elizabeth was an accomplished scholar.

Before I leave Ascham I must make one more quotation, to which I shall more than once have occasion to refer. Speaking of the plan of double translation, he says: "Ere the scholar have construed, parsed, twice translated over by good advisement, marked out his six points by skilful judgment, he shall have necessary occasion to read over every lecture a *dozen times at the least;* which because he shall do always in order, he shall do it always with pleasure. . . . And pleasure allureth love; love hath lust to labor; labor always obtaineth his purpose."

When we compare Ratich's method with that of Ascham, we find that they have much in common. Ratich began the study of a language with one book, which he worked over with the pupil a great many times. Ascham did the same. Each lecture, he says, would, according to his plan, be gone over a dozen times at the least. Both construed to the pupil, instead of requiring him to make out the sense for himself. Both taught grammar, not independently, but in connection with the model book. So far as the two methods differed, I have no hesitation in pronouncing Ascham's the better. It gave the pupil more to do, and contained the very important element, *writing*. By this means there was a chance of the interest of the pupil surviving the constant repetition, but Ratich's pupils must have been bored to death. His plan of making them familiar with the translation first, was subsequently advocated by Comenius, and may have advantages, but in effect the pupil would be tired of the play before he began to translate it. Then Ratich's plan of going through and through seems very inferior to that of thoroughly mastering one lesson before going on to the next. I should say that whatever merit there was in Ratich's plan, lay in its insisting on complete knowledge of a single book, and that this knowledge would be much better attained by Ascham's practice of double translation.

JEAN-BAPTISTE POQUELIN MOLIÈRE

1622-1672

JEAN-BAPTISTE POQUELIN was born at Paris in 1622. From childhood he was drawn irresistibly toward the stage. When scarcely more than an infant, he found his chief delight in accompanying his grandfather to witness the plays of Corneille, at the Hôtel de Bourgogne. Poquelin was destined by his parents for the legal profession. He entered college, and was an enthusiastic and ambitious student. With great self-reliance he organized a theatrical company, when his college days were ended, and opened the *Théâtre Illustre* in his native city. It was a mortifying failure, and Poquelin was imprisoned for debt. On regaining his freedom he disappeared from view at the capital. Twelve years later he returned under a new name—Molière—destined to be imperishable in letters. In the interval he had learned much of wisdom and of the art of the playwright. His star was now in the ascendant. He wrote, in all, about thirty plays, nearly all of which enjoyed a high measure of success.

His best productions are "The Misanthrope" (*Le Misanthrope*), "Learned Women" (*Les Femmes Savantes*), "The Miser" (*L'Avare*), and "The Hypocrite" (*Le Tartufe*), which are regarded as models of high comedy. "The Shopkeeper turned Gentleman" (*Le Bourgeois*) is one of his most popular dramas. Mr. Charles Heron Wall, the translator of Molière, says of this play: "*Le Bourgeois Gentilhomme* was acted before the king for the first time at Chambord, on October 14, 1670, and on November 23, at the Palais Royal. After the second representation, Louis XIV. said to Molière: 'You have never written anything which amused me more, and your play is excellent.' But it obtained a still greater success in Paris, where the *bourgeois* willingly and good-humoredly laughed at what they deemed their neighbors' weaknesses. The first three acts are the best; Louis XIV. hurried Molière so with the last that they degenerated into burlesque. Molière acted the part of Bourgeois."

Molière died in 1672.

Characterization

Molière, the noblest heart, the most illustrious soul, the greatest writer, the grandest philosopher of France, in the seventeenth century, and of the whole world in all time; Molière, whose life was so beautiful, whose knowledge was so wide, whose benevolence was so deep; Molière, the first literary man of France who realized his worth, and lived and was enriched by his genius, has been dead a hundred and fifty years, yet he remains the most youthful, the liveliest, the truest of the great writers of France.

JULES JANIN.

Molière is the most distinguished comic poet of modern times. While he is the complete embodiment of the spirit of his people, he yet rises, independent of all prejudices of nation and age, to the plane of the true great author. His bust, standing in the hall of the French Academy, bears the triumphant inscription:

"*Rien ne manque à sa gloire; il manquait à la notre.*" [1]

PROF. A. H. MIXER.

The Education of M. Jourdain

Scenes from "Le Bourgeois"—"The Shopkeeper turned Gentleman"

DRAMATIS PERSONÆ

M. JOURDAIN, the Shop-keeper turned Gentleman.
Professor of Philosophy.
Dancing Master.
Fencing Master.
Music Master.
Servants.
MADAME JOURDAIN.
Nicole, a Female Servant.

The Scene is in Paris, in the Residence of M. Jourdain.

ACT II

SCENE III.—M. JOURDAIN, FENCING MASTER, MUSIC MASTER, DANCING MASTER, A SERVANT HOLDING TWO FOILS.

FEN. MAS. (*Taking the two foils from the hands of the servant, and giving one to M. Jourdain.*) Now, sir, the salute. The body upright, resting slightly on the left thigh. The legs not so far

---

[1] "Nothing is lacking in his glory; he is lacking to ours."

apart; the feet in a line. The wrist in a line with the thigh. The point of the foil opposite the shoulder. The arm not quite so much extended. The left hand as high as the eye. The left shoulder more squared. The head erect; the look firm. Advance, the body steady. Engage my blade in quart, and retain the engagement. One, two. As you were. Once more, with the foot firm. One, two; a step to the rear. When you make an attack, sir, the sword should move first, and the body be well held back. One, two. Engage my blade in tierce, and retain the engagement. Advance; the body steady. Advance; one, two. Recover. Once more. One, two. A step to the rear. On guard, sir; on guard. (*The Fencing Master delivers two or three attacks, calling out,* " On guard!")

M. Jour. Ah!

Mus. Mas. You are doing wonders.

Fen. Mas. As I have already told you, the whole art of fencing consists of one or two things—in giving and not receiving; and, as I showed you the other day by demonstrative reason, it is impossible for you to receive if you know how to turn aside your adversary's weapon from the line of your body; and this again depends only on a slight movement of the wrist to the inside or the out.

M. Jour. So that a man, without having any courage, is sure of killing his man and of not being killed himself.

Fen. Mas. Exactly. Did you not see plainly the demonstration of it?

M. Jour. Yes.

Fen. Mas. And this shows you of what importance we must be in a state; and how much the science of arms is superior to all the other useless sciences, such as dancing, music——

Dan. Mas. Gently, Mr. Fencing Master; speak of dancing with respect, if you please.

Mus. Mas. Pray learn to treat more properly the excellence of music.

Fen. Mas. Just see the man of importance!

Dan. Mas. A fine animal, to be sure, with his plastron.

Fen. Mas. Take care, my little dancing master, or I shall make you dance in fine style. And you, my little musician, I'll teach you to sing out.

Dan. Mas. And you, my beater of iron, I'll teach you your trade.

M. Jour. (*To the Dancing Master.*) Are you mad, to go and quarrel with a man who understands tierce and quart, and knows how to kill another by demonstrative reason?

Dan. Mas. I don't care a straw for his demonstrative reason, and his tierce and quart.

M. Jour. (*To the Dancing Master.*) Gently, I tell you.

Fen. Mas. (*To the Dancing Master.*) How, you little impudent fellow!

M. Jour. Ah, my Fencing Master!

Dan. Mas. (*To the Fencing Master.*) How, you great carthorse!

M. Jour. Stop, my Dancing Master!

Fen. Mas. If I once begin with you——

M. Jour. (*To the Fencing Master.*) Gently.

Dan. Mas. If I lay my hand upon you——

M. Jour. Softly.

Fen. Mas. I will beat you after such a fashion——

M. Jour. (*To the Fencing Master.*) For goodness sake!

Dan. Mas. I'll thrash you in such a style——

M. Jour. (*To the Dancing Master.*) I beg of you——

Mus. Mas. Let us teach him a little how to behave himself.

M. Jour. (*To the Music Master.*) Gracious heavens! Do stop.

Scene IV.—Professor of Philosophy, M. Jourdain, Music Master, Dancing Master, Fencing Master, a Servant.

M. Jour. Oh! you are in the very nick of time with your philosophy. Pray come here and restore peace among these people.

Prof. Phil. What is going on? What is the matter, gentlemen?

M. Jour. They have got themselves into such a rage about the importance that ought to be attached to their different professions, that they have almost come to blows over it.

Prof. Phil. For shame, gentlemen; how can you thus forget yourselves? Have you not read the learned treatise which Seneca composed on anger? Is there anything more base and more shameful than the passion which changes a man into a savage beast, and ought not reason to govern all our actions?

Dan. Mas. How, sir! He comes and insults us both in our professions; he despises dancing, which I teach, and music, which is *his* occupation (*pointing to Music Master*).

Prof. Phil. A wise man is above all the insults that can be offered him; and the best and noblest answer one can make to all kinds of provocation is moderation and patience.

Fen. Mas. They have both the impertinence to compare their professions to mine!

Prof. Phil. Why should this offend you? It is not for vainglory and rank that men should strive among themselves. What distinguishes one man from another is wisdom and virtue.

Dan. Mas. I maintain that dancing is a science which we cannot honor too much.

Mus. Mas. And I that music is a science which all ages have revered.

Fen. Mas. And I maintain against them both that the science of attack and defence is the best and most necessary of all sciences.

Prof. Phil. And for what, then, do you count philosophy? I think you are all three very bold fellows, to dare to speak before me with this arrogance, and impudently to give the name of science to things which are not even to be honored with the name of art, but which can only be classed with the trades of prize-fighter, street-singer, and mountebank.

Fen. Mas. Get out, you dog of a philosopher!

Mus. Mas. Get along with you, you beggarly pedant!

Dan. Mas. Begone, you empty-headed college scout!

PROF. PHIL. How, scoundrels that you are!

(*The Philosopher rushes upon them, and they all three belabor him.*)

M. JOUR. Mr. Philosopher!
PROF. PHIL. Infamous villains!
M. JOUR. Mr. Philosopher!
FEN. MAS. Plague take the animal!
M. JOUR. Gentlemen!
PROF. PHIL. Impudent cads!
M. JOUR. Mr. Philosopher!
DAN. MAS. Deuce take the saddled donkey!
M. JOUR. Gentlemen!
PROF. PHIL. Scoundrels!
M. JOUR. Mr. Philosopher!
MUS. MAS. Perdition take the insolent fellow!
M. JOUR. Gentlemen!
PROF. PHIL. Knaves, beggars, wretches, impostors!
M. JOUR. Mr. Philosopher! Gentlemen! Mr. Philosopher! Gentlemen! Mr. Philosopher!

SCENE V.—M. JOURDAIN, A SERVANT.

M. JOUR. Well! fight as much as you like, I can't help it; but don't expect me to go and spoil my dressing-gown to separate you. I should be a fool indeed to trust myself among them, and receive some blow or other that might hurt me.

SCENE VI.—PROFESSOR OF PHILOSOPHY, M. JOURDAIN, A SERVANT.

PROF. PHIL. (*Setting his collar in order.*) Now for our lesson.

M. JOUR. Ah, sir, how sorry I am for the blows they have given you!

PROF. PHIL. It is of no consequence. A Philosopher knows how to receive things calmly, and I shall compose against them a satire, in the style of Juvenal, which will cut them up in proper fashion. Let us drop this subject. What do you wish to learn?

M. JOUR. Everything I can, for I have the greatest desire in the world to be learned; and it vexes me more than I can tell that my father and mother did not make me learn thoroughly all the sciences when I was young.

PROF. PHIL. This is a praiseworthy feeling. *Nam sine doctrina vita est quasi mortis imago.* You understand this, and you have, no doubt, a knowledge of Latin?

M. JOUR. Yes; but act as if I had none. Explain to me the meaning of it.

PROF. PHIL. The meaning of it is this, that without science life is an image of death.

M. JOUR. That Latin is quite right.

PROF. PHIL. Have you any principles, any rudiments of science?

M. JOUR. Oh, yes; I can read and write.

PROF. PHIL. With what would you like to begin? Shall I teach you logic?

M. JOUR. And what may this logic be?

PROF. PHIL. It is that which teaches us the three operations of the mind.

M. JOUR. What are they, those three operations of the mind?

PROF. PHIL. The first, the second, and the third. The first is to conceive well by means of universals; the second, to judge well by means of categories; and the third, to draw a conclusion aright by means of the figures *Barbara, Celarent, Darii, Baralipton,* etc.

M. JOUR. Pooh! what repulsive words. This logic does not by any means suit me. Teach me something more enlivening.

PROF. PHIL. Will you learn moral philosophy?

M. JOUR. Moral philosophy?

PROF. PHIL. Yes.

M. JOUR. What does it say, this moral philosophy?

PROF. PHIL. It treats of happiness, teaches men to moderate their passions, and——

M. JOUR. No, none of that. I am infernally hot-tempered, and, morality or no morality, I like to give full vent to my anger whenever I have a mind to it.

Prof. Phil. Would you like to learn physics?

M. Jour. And what have physics to say for themselves?

Prof. Phil. Physics are that science which explains the principles of natural things and the properties of bodies, which discourses of the nature of the elements of metals, minerals, stones, plants, and animals; which teaches us the cause of all the meteors, the rainbow, the *ignis fatuus*, comets, lightning, thunder, thunderbolts, rain, snow, hail, wind, and whirlwinds.

M. Jour. There is too much hullaballoo in all that; too much riot and rumpus.

Prof. Phil. What would you have me teach you, then?

M. Jour. Teach me spelling.

Prof. Phil. Very good.

M. Jour. Afterward you will teach me the almanac, so that I may know when there is a moon, and when there isn't one.

Prof. Phil. Be it so. In order to give a right interpretation of your thought, and to treat this matter philosophically, we must begin, according to the order of things, with an exact knowledge of the nature of the letters, and the different way in which each is pronounced. And on this head, I must tell you that letters are divided into vowels, so called because they express the voice, and into consonants, so called because they are sounded with the vowels, and only mark the different articulations of the voice. There are five vowels,[1] or voices, *a, e, i, o, u*.

M. Jour. I understand all that.

Prof. Phil. The vowel *a* is formed by opening the mouth wide; *a*.

M. Jour. *A, a;* yes.

Prof. Phil. The vowel *e* is formed by drawing the lower jaw a little nearer to the upper; *a, e*.

M. Jour. *A, e; a, e;* to be sure. Ah! how beautiful that is!

Prof. Phil. And the vowel *i* by bringing the jaws still

---

[1] The vowels here described are the French vowels. The descriptions do not apply to the English sounds of the letters.

closer to one another, and stretching the two corners of the mouth toward the ears ; *a, e, i.*

M. JOUR. *A, e, i, i, i, i.* Quite true. Long live science!

PROF. PHIL. The vowel *o* is formed by opening the jaws and drawing in the lips at the two corners, the upper and the lower; *o.*

M. JOUR. *O, o.* Nothing can be more correct; *a, e, i, o, i, o.* It is admirable! *I, o, i, o.*

PROF. PHIL. The opening of the mouth exactly makes a little circle, which resembles an *o.*

M. JOUR. *O, o, o.* You are right. *O!* Ah, what a fine thing it is to know something!

PROF. PHIL. The vowel *u* is formed by bringing the teeth near each other without entirely joining them, and thrusting out both the lips, whilst also bringing them near together without joining them; *u.*

M. JOUR. *U, u.* There is nothing more true; *u.*

PROF. PHIL. Your two lips lengthen as if you were pouting; so that, if you wish to make a grimace at anybody, and to laugh at him, you have only to *u* him.

M. JOUR. *U, u.* It's true. Oh, that I had studied when I was younger, so as to know all this!

PROF. PHIL. To-morrow we will speak of the other letters, which are the consonants.

M. JOUR. Is there anything as curious in them as in these?

PROF. PHIL. Certainly. For instance, the consonant *d* is pronounced by striking the tip of the tongue above the upper teeth ; *da.*

M. JOUR. *Da, da.* Yes. Ah, what beautiful things, what beautiful things!

PROF. PHIL. The *f*, by pressing the upper teeth upon the lower lip; *fa.*

M. JOUR. *Fa, fa.* 'Tis the truth. Ah, my father and my mother, how angry I feel with you!

PROF. PHIL. And the *r*, by carrying the tip of the tongue up to the roof of the palate, so that, being grazed by the air which comes out by force, it yields to it, and, returning to the same place, causes a sort of tremor; *r, ra.*

M. Jour. *R-r-ra; r-r-r-r-r-ra.* That's true. Ah, what a clever man you are, and what time I have lost! *R-r-ra.*

Prof. Phil. I will fully explain all these curiosities to you.

M. Jour. Pray do. And now I want to intrust you with a great secret. I am in love with a lady of quality, and I should be glad if you will help me to write something to her in a short letter which I mean to drop at her feet.

Prof. Phil. Very well.

M. Jour. That will be gallant; will it not?

Prof. Phil. Undoubtedly. Is it verse you wish to write to her?

M. Jour. Oh, no; not verse.

Prof. Phil. You only wish for prose?

M. Jour. No. I wish for neither verse nor prose.

Prof. Phil. It must be one or the other.

M. Jour. Why?

Prof. Phil. Because, sir, there is nothing by which we can express ourselves, except prose or verse.

M. Jour. There is nothing but prose or verse?

Prof. Phil. No, sir. Whatever is not prose is verse; and whatever is not verse is prose.

M. Jour. And when we speak, what is that, then?

Prof. Phil. Prose.

M. Jour. What! When I say, "Nicole, bring me my slippers, and give me my night-cap," is that prose?

Prof. Phil. Yes, sir.

M. Jour. Upon my word, I have been speaking prose these forty years without being aware of it; and I am under the greatest obligation to you for informing me of it. Well, then, I wish to write to her in a letter, *Fair Marchioness, your beautiful eyes make me die of love;* but I would have this worded in a genteel manner, and turned prettily.

Prof. Phil. Say that the fire of her eyes has reduced your heart to ashes; that you suffer day and night for her tortures——

M. Jour. No, no, no; I don't want any of that. I simply wish for what I tell you. *Fair Marchioness, your beautiful eyes make me die of love.*

Prof. Phil. Still, you might amplify the thing a little.

M. Jour. No, I tell you, I will have nothing but those words in the letter; but they must be put in a fashionable way, and arranged as they should be. Pray show me a little, so that I may see the different ways in which they may be put.

Prof. Phil. They may be put, first of all, as you have said, *Fair Marchioness, your beautiful eyes make me die of love;* or else, *Of love die make me, fair Marchioness, your beautiful eyes;* or, *Your beautiful eyes of love make me, fair Marchioness, die;* or, *Die of love your beautiful eyes, fair Marchioness, make me;* or else, *Me make your beautiful eyes die, fair Marchioness, of love.*

M. Jour. But of all these ways which is the best?

Prof. Phil. The one you said. *Fair Marchioness, your beautiful eyes make me die of love.*

M. Jour. Yet I have never studied, and I did all that right off at the first shot. I thank you with all my heart, and I beg of you to come to-morrow morning early.

Prof. Phil. I shall not fail.

ACT III

Scene I.—M. Jourdain, two Lackeys.

M. Jour. Follow me, that I may go and show my clothes about the town; and be very careful, both of you, to walk close to my heels, so that people may see that you belong to me.

Lack. Yes, sir.

M. Jour. Just call Nicole. I have some orders to give her. You need not move; here she comes.

Scene II.—M. Jourdain, Nicole, two Lackeys.

M. Jour. Nicole!

Nic. What is it, sir?

M. Jour. Listen.

Nic. (*Laughing.*) Hi, hi, hi, hi, hi!

M. Jour. What are you laughing at?

Nic. Hi, hi, hi, hi, hi, hi!

M. Jour. What does the hussy mean?

Nic. Hi, hi, hi! What a figure you cut! Hi, hi, hi!

M. Jour. Eh? What?

Nic. Ah, ah! My goodness! Hi, hi, hi, hi, hi!

M. Jour. What an impertinent jade! Are you laughing at me?

Nic. Oh, no, sir! I should be very sorry to do so. Hi, hi, hi, hi, hi!

M. Jour. I'll slap your face if you laugh again.

Nic. I can't help it, sir. Hi, hi, hi, hi, hi, hi!

M. Jour. Will you leave off?

Nic. Sir; I beg your pardon, sir; but you are so very comical that I can't help laughing. Hi, hi, hi, hi!

M. Jour. Did you ever see such impudence?

Nic. You are so odd, like that. Hi, hi!

M. Jour. I'll——

Nic. I beg of you to excuse me. Hi, hi, hi, hi!

M. Jour. Look here; if you laugh again, ever so little, I swear I will give you a box on the ears such as you never had before in your life.

Nic. Well, sir, I have done. I won't laugh any more.

M. Jour. Mind you don't. You must for this afternoon clean——

Nic. Hi, hi!

M. Jour. You must clean thoroughly——

Nic. Hi, hi!

M. Jour. You must, I say, clean the drawing-room, and——

Nic. Hi, hi!

M. Jour. Again?

Nic. (*Tumbling down with laughing.*) There, sir, beat me rather, but let me laugh to my heart's content. I am sure it will be better for me. Hi, hi, hi, hi, hi!

M. Jour. I am boiling with rage.

Nic. For pity's sake let me laugh. Hi, hi, hi!

M. Jour. If I begin——

Nic. Si-r-r, I shall bur-r-st if I d-don't laugh. Hi, hi, hi!

M. Jour. But did you ever see such a hussy? She comes and laughs at me to my face, instead of tending to my orders.

Nic. What is it you wish me to do, sir?

M. Jour. I want you to get this house ready for the company which is to come here by and by.

Nic. (*Getting up.*) Ah, well! All my wish to laugh is gone now; your company brings such disorder here that what you say is quite sufficient to put me out of temper.

M. Jour. I suppose that, to please you, I ought to shut my door against everybody?

Nic. You would do well to shut it against certain people, sir.

SCENE III.—MME. JOURDAIN, M. JOURDAIN, NICOLE, TWO SERVANTS.

Mme. Jour. Ah, me! Here is some new vexation! Why, husband, what do you possibly mean by this strange get-up? Have you lost your senses, that you go and deck yourself out like this, and do you wish to be the laughing-stock of everybody, wherever you go?

M. Jour. Let me tell you, my good wife, that no one but a fool will laugh at me.

Mme. Jour. No one has waited until to-day for that; and it is now some time since your ways of going on have been the amusement of everybody.

M. Jour. And who may everybody be, please?

Mme. Jour. Everybody is a body who is in the right, and who has more sense than you. For my part, I am quite shocked at the life you lead. I don't know our home again. One would think, by what goes on, that it was one everlasting carnival here; and as soon as day breaks, for fear we should have any rest in it, we have a regular din of fiddles and singers, that are a positive nuisance to all the neighborhood.

Nic. What mistress says is quite right. There is no longer any chance of having the house clean, with all that heap of people you bring in. Their feet seem to have gone purposely to pick up the mud in the four quarters of the town, in order to bring it here afterward; and poor Françoise is almost off her legs with the constant scrubbing of the floors, which your masters come and dirty every day as regular as clockwork.

M. Jour. I say, there, our servant Nicole, you have a pretty sharp tongue of your own for a country wench.

Mme. Jour. Nicole is right, and she has more sense by far than you have. I should like to know, for instance, what do you mean to do with a dancing master at your age?

Nic. And with that big fencing master who comes here stamping enough to shake the whole house down, and to tear up the floor tiles of our rooms.

M. Jour. Gently, my servant and my wife.

Mme. Jour. Do you mean to learn dancing for the time when you can't stand on your legs any longer?

Nic. Do you intend to kill anybody?

M. Jour. Hold your tongues, I say. You are only ignorant women, both of you, and understand nothing concerning the prerogative of all this.

Mme. Jour. You would do much better to think of seeing your daughter married, for she is now of an age to be provided for.

M. Jour. I shall think of seeing my daughter married when a suitable match presents itself; but in the mean time, I wish to think of acquiring fine learning.

Nic. I have heard say also, mistress, that, to go the whole hog, he has now taken a professor of philosophy.

M. Jour. To be sure I have. I wish to be clever, and reason concerning things with people of quality.

Mme. Jour. Had you not better go to school one of these days, and get the birch, at your age?

M. Jour. Why not? Would to Heaven I were flogged this very instant, before all the world, so that I might know all they learn at school.

Nic. Yes, to be sure. That would much improve the shape of your leg.

M. Jour. Of course.

Mme. Jour. And all this is very necessary for the management of your house?

M. Jour. Certainly. You both speak like donkeys, and I am ashamed of your ignorance. (*To Mme. Jourdain.*) Let me see, for instance, if you know what you are speaking this very moment.

Mme. Jour. Yes, I know that what I speak is rightly spoken; and that you should think of leading a different life.

M. Jour. I do not mean that. I ask you what the words are that you are now speaking.

Mme. Jour. They are sensible words, I tell you, and that is more than your conduct is.

M. Jour. I am not speaking of that. I ask you what it is that I am now saying to you. That which I am now speaking to you, what is it?

Mme. Jour. Rubbish.

M. Jour. No, no! I don't mean that. What we both speak; the language we are speaking this very moment.

Mme. Jour. Well?

M. Jour. How is it called?

Mme. Jour. It is called whatever you like to call it.

M. Jour. It is PROSE, you ignorant woman!

Mme. Jour. Prose?

M. Jour. Whatever is prose is not verse, and whatever is not verse is prose. There! you see what it is to study. (*To Nicole.*) And you, do you even know what you must do to say u?

Nic. Eh? What?

M. Jour. Yes. What do you do when you say u?

Nic. What I do?

M. Jour. Say u a little, to try.

Nic. Well, u.

M. Jour. What is it you do?

Nic. I say u.

M. Jour. Yes; but when you say *u*, what is it you do?

Nic. I do what you ask me to do.

M. Jour. Oh, what a strange thing it is to have to do with dunces! You pout your lips outwards, and bring your upper jaw near your lower jaw like this, *u;* I make a face; *u.* Do you see?

Nic. Yes, that's beautiful.

Mme. Jour. It's admirable.

M. Jour. What would you say then if you had seen *o*, and *da, da,* and *fa, fa?*

Mme. Jour. What is all this absurd stuff?

Nic. And what are we the better for all this?

M. Jour. I have no patience with such ignorant women.

JEAN JACQUES ROUSSEAU

1712-1778

JEAN JACQUES ROUSSEAU, a paradox of moralists, a strange compound of the best and the worst in human nature, was born in Geneva, Switzerland, in 1712. He was the son of a barber and dancing master, and was bereaved of his mother soon after his birth. Running away, at the age of sixteen, from the master to whom he was apprenticed, he wandered about for a time, and then found a home with an eccentric widow, Madame de Warens, at Auncey, in whose household he remained for a number of years. Rousseau was a teacher of music, successively at Lyons and in Paris. In the latter city he joined his fortunes with those of Louise le Vasseur, a coarse and ignorant seamstress. He soon became famous at Paris as a critic and essayist. He sent his children at birth to the hospital for foundlings. Years later, repenting of their conduct, he and Louise sought in vain to find them.

In 1754, Rousseau returned to Geneva, and became again a Protestant (for he had embraced Catholicism while in France), but soon returned to the vicinity of Paris, where a home had been presented to him by a friend. Here he wrote three famous books—"The New Heloise," "The Social Contract," and "Émile." The last-named work was condemned by the authorities, both in Catholic France and in Protestant Geneva, and an order was issued for the author's arrest. He fled to Germany, but was there in imminent danger. He repaired to England, where he was well received. Here he wrote his first "Confessions" (which alienated most of his remaining friends); and he then became a wanderer. He died suddenly, near Paris, in 1778, and is believed by many to have committed suicide.

Characterization

In education, as in politics, no school of thinkers has succeeded or can succeed in engrossing all truth to itself. No party, no individual even, can take up a central position between the conservatives and radicals, and, judging everything on its own merits, try to preserve that only which is worth preserving, and to destroy just that which is worth destroying. Nor do we find that judicial minds often exercise the greatest influence in these matters. The only force which can overcome the *vis inertiæ*[1] of use and wont is enthusiasm, and this, springing from the discovery of new truths and hatred of old abuses, can hardly exist with due respect for truth that has become commonplace, and usage which is easily confounded with corruptions that disfigure it. So advances are made somewhat after this manner: the reformer, urged on by his enthusiasm, attacks use and wont with more spirit than discretion; those who are wedded to things as they are, try to draw attention from the weak points of their system to the mistakes or extravagances of the reformer. In the end, both sides are benefited by the encounter; and when their successors carry on the contest, they differ as much from those whose causes they espouse as from each other.

In this way we have already made great progress. Compare, for instance, our present teaching of grammar with the ancient method, and our short and broken school-time with the old plan of keeping boys in for five consecutive hours twice a day. Our conservatives and reformers are not so much at variance as their predecessors. To convince ourselves of this we have only to consider the state of parties in the second half of the last century. On the one side, we find the schoolmasters who turned out the courtiers of Louis XV.; on the other, the most extravagant, the most eloquent, the most reckless of innovators—J. J. Rousseau.

Rousseau has told us that he resolved on having fixed principles by the time he was forty years old. Among the principles of which he accordingly laid in a stock, were these: 1st, Man, as he might be, is perfectly good; 2d, Man, as he is, is utterly bad. To maintain these opinions, Rousseau undertook to show not only the rotten state of the existing society, which he did with notable success, but also the proper method of rearing children so as to make them all that they ought to be—an attempt at construction which was far more difficult and hazardous than his philippics.

This was the origin of the "Émile," perhaps the most influential book ever written on the subject of education. R. H. QUICK.

R. H. Quick's Adaptation and Summary of "Émile"

The school to which Rousseau belonged may be said, indeed, to have been founded by Montaigne, and to have met with a champion, though not a very enthusiastic champion, in Locke. But it was reserved for Rousseau to give this theory of educa-

[1] inertia

tion its complete development, and to expound it in the clearest and most eloquent language. In the form in which Rousseau left it the theory greatly influenced Basedow and Pestalozzi, and still influences many educational reformers who differ from Rousseau as much as our schoolmasters differ from those of Louis XV.

Of course, as man was corrupted by ordinary education, the ideal education must differ from it in every respect. "Take the road directly opposite to that which is in use, and you will almost always do right." This was the fundamental maxim. So thorough a radical was Rousseau, that he scorned the idea of half measures. "I had rather follow the established practice entirely," says he, "than adopt a good one by halves."

In the society of that time everything was artificial; Rousseau therefore demanded a return to nature. Parents should do their duty in rearing their own offspring. "Where there is no mother, there can be no child." The father should find time to bring up the child whom the mother has suckled. No duty can be more important than this. But although Rousseau seems conscious that family life is the natural state, he makes his model child an orphan, and hands him over to a governor, to be brought up in the country without companions.

This governor is to devote himself, for some years, entirely to imparting to his pupil these difficult arts—the art of being ignorant and of losing time. Till he is twelve years old Émile is to have no direct instruction whatever. "At that age he shall not know what a book is," says Rousseau; though elsewhere we are told that he will learn to read of his own accord by the time he is ten, if no attempt is made to teach him. He is to be under no restraint, and is to do nothing but what he sees to be useful.

Freedom from restraint is, however, to be apparent, not real. As in ordinary education the child employs all his faculties in duping the master, so in education "according to nature," the master is to devote himself to duping the child. "Let him always be his own master in appearance, and do you take care to be so in reality. There is no subjection so complete as that which preserves the appearance of liberty; it is by this means even the will itself is led captive."

"The most critical interval of human nature is that between the hour of our birth and twelve years of age. This is the time wherein vice and error take root without our being possessed of any instrument to destroy them."

Throughout this season the governor is to be at work inculcating the art of being ignorant and losing time. "This first part of education ought to be purely negative. It consists neither in teaching virtue nor truth, but in guarding the heart from vice, and the mind from error. If you could do nothing and let nothing be done; if you could bring up your pupil healthy and robust to the age of twelve years, without his being able to distinguish his right hand from his left, the eyes of his understanding would be open to reason at your first lesson; void both of habit and prejudice, he would have nothing in him to operate against your endeavors; soon, under your instructions, he would become the wisest of men. Thus, by setting out with doing nothing, you would produce a prodigy of education."

"Exercise his body, his senses, faculties, powers, but keep his mind inactive as long as possible. Distrust all the sentiments he acquires previous to the judgment which should enable him to scrutinize them. Prevent or restrain all foreign impressions; and in order to hinder the rise of evil, be not in too great a hurry to instill good; for it is only such when the mind is enlightened by reason. Look upon every delay as an advantage: it is gaining a great deal to advance without losing anything. Let childhood ripen in children. In short, whatever lesson becomes necessary for them, take care not to give them to-day, if it may be deferred without danger till tomorrow."

"Do not, then, alarm yourself much about this apparent idleness. What would you say of the man who, in order to make the most of life, should determine never to go to sleep?

You would say, the man is mad; he is not enjoying the time; he is depriving himself of it; to avoid sleep he is hurrying toward death. Consider, then, that it is the same here, and that childhood is the sleep of reason."

Such is the groundwork of Rousseau's educational scheme. His ideal boy of twelve years old is to be a thoroughly well-developed animal, with every bodily sense trained to its highest perfection. " His ideas," says Rousseau, " are confined, but clear; he knows nothing by rote, but a great deal by experience. If he reads less well than another child in our books, he reads better in the book of nature. His understanding does not lie in his tongue, but in his brain; he has less memory than judgment; he can speak only one language, but then he understands what he says; and, although he may not talk of things so well as others, he will do them much better. He knows nothing at all of custom, fashion, or habit; what he did yesterday has no influence on what he is to do to-day; he follows no formula, is influenced by no authority or example, but acts and speaks just as it suits him. Do not, then, expect from him set discourses or studied manners, but always the faithful expression of his ideas, and the conduct which springs naturally from his inclinations."

This model child looks upon all men as equal, and will ask assistance from a king as readily as from a foot-boy. He does not understand what a command is, but will readily do anything for another person, in order to place that person under an obligation, and so increase his own rights. He knows, also, no distinction between work and play. As a climax to this list of wonders, I may add that his imagination has remained inactive, and he only sees what is true in reality.

The reader will probably have concluded by this time, that no child can possibly be so educated as to resemble Émile, and, perhaps, further, that no wise father would so educate his son, if it were possible. A child who does not understand what a command is, and who can be induced to do anything for another only by the prospect of laying that person under an obligation; who has no habits, and is guided merely by his inclinations—such a child as this is, fortunately, nothing but a dream of Rousseau's.

But fantastical as Rousseau often is, the reader of his "Émile" is struck again and again, not more by the charm of his language than by his insight into child-nature, and the wisdom of his remarks upon it. The "Émile" is a large work, and the latter part is interesting rather from a literary and philosophical point of view, than as it is connected with education. I purpose, therefore, confining my attention to the earlier portion of the book, and giving some of the passages, of which a great deal since said and written on education has been a comparatively insipid decoction.

"All things are good as their Creator made them, but everything degenerates in the hands of man." These are the first words of the "Émile," and the keynote of Rousseau's philosophy. "We are born weak, we have need of strength; we are born destitute of everything, we have need of assistance; we are born stupid, we have need of understanding. All that we are not possessed of at our birth, and which we require when grown up, is bestowed on us by education.

"This education we receive from nature, from men, or from things. The internal development of our organs and faculties is the education of nature; the use we are taught to make of that development is the education given us by men; and in the acquisitions made by our own experience on the objects that surround us, consists our education from things." "Since the concurrence of these three kinds of education is necessary to their perfection, it is by that one which is entirely independent of us we must regulate the two others." "To live is not merely to breathe; it is to act, it is to make use of our organs, our senses, our faculties, and of all those parts of ourselves which give us the feeling of our existence. The man who has lived most, is not he who has counted the greatest number of years, but he who has most thoroughly felt life."

The aim of education, then, must be complete living. But

ordinary education (and here for a moment I am expressing my own conviction, and not simply reporting Rousseau), instead of seeking to develop the life of the child, sacrifices childhood to the acquirement of knowledge, or rather the semblance of knowledge, which it is thought will prove useful to the youth, or the man. Rousseau's great merit lies in his having exposed this fundamental error. He says, very truly:

"People do not understand childhood. With the false notions we have of it, the further we go the more we blunder. The wisest apply themselves to what it is important to *men* to know, without considering what *children* are in a condition to learn. They are always seeking the *man* in the *child*, without reflecting what he is before he can be a man. This is the study to which I have applied myself most; so that, should my practical scheme be found useless and chimerical, my observation will always turn to account. I may possibly have taken a very bad view of what ought to be done, but I conceive I have taken a good one of the subject to be wrought upon. Begin, then, by studying your pupils better; for most assuredly you do not at present understand them. So if you read my book with that view, I do not think it will be useless to you."

"Nature requires children to be children before they are men. If we will pervert this order, we shall produce forward fruits, having neither ripeness nor taste, and sure soon to become rotten; we shall have young professors and old children. Childhood has its manner of seeing, perceiving, and thinking, peculiar to itself; nothing is more absurd than our being anxious to substitute our own in its stead."

"We never know how to put ourselves in the place of children; we do not enter into their ideas, we lend them our own: and following always our own train of thought, we fill their heads, even while we are discussing incontestable truths, with extravagance and error." "I wish some judicious hand would give us a treatise on the art of studying children; an art of the greatest importance to understand, though fathers and preceptors know not as yet even the elements of it."

The governor, then, must be able to sympathize with his pupil, and, on this account, Rousseau requires that he should be *young*. "The governor of a child should be young, even as young as possible, consistent with his having attained necessary discretion and sagacity. I would have him be himself a child, that he might become the companion of his pupil, and gain his confidence by partaking of his amusements. There are not things enough in common between childhood and manhood to form a solid attachment at so great a distance. Children sometimes caress old men, but they never love them."

The governor's functions are threefold: 1st, that of keeping off hurtful influences—no light task in Rousseau's eyes, as he regarded almost every influence from the child's fellow-creatures as hurtful; 2d, that of developing the bodily powers, especially the senses; 3d, that of communicating the one science for children—moral behavior. In all these, even in the last, he must be governor rather than preceptor, for it is less his province to instruct than to conduct. He must not lay down precepts, but teach his pupil to discover them. "I preach a difficult art," says Rousseau, "the art of guiding without precepts, and of doing everything by doing nothing."

The most distinctive characteristic of childhood is vitality. "In the heart of the old man the failing energies concentrate themselves: in that of the child they overflow and spread outward; he is conscious of life enough to animate all that surrounds him. Whether he makes or mars, it is all one to him; he is satisfied with having changed the state of things, and every change is an action." This vitality is to be allowed free scope. Swaddling-clothes are to be removed from infants; the restraints of school and book-learning, from children. Their love of action is to be freely indulged.

The nearest approach to teaching which Rousseau permitted was that which became afterward, in the hands of Pestalozzi, the system of object lessons. "As soon as a child begins to distinguish objects, a proper choice should be made in those which are presented to him." "He must learn to feel heat and cold, the hardness, softness, and weight of bodies; to judge of their magnitude, figure, and other sensible qualities, by looking, touching, hearing, and particularly by comparing the sight with the touch, and judging, by means of the eye, of the sensation acquired by the fingers." These exercises should be continued through childhood. "A child has neither the strength nor the judgment of a man; but he is capable of feeling and hearing as well, or at least nearly so. His palate also is as sensible, though less delicate: and he distinguishes odors as well, though not with the same nicety. Of all our faculties, the senses are perfected the first: these, therefore, are the first we should cultivate; they are, nevertheless, the only ones that are usually forgotten, or the most neglected."

"Observe a cat the first time she comes into a room; she looks and smells about; she is not easy a moment; she distrusts everything till everything is examined and known. In the same manner does a child examine into everything, when he begins to walk about, and enters, if I may so say, the apartment of the world. All the difference is, that the sight, which is common to both the child and the cat, is in the first assisted by the feeling of the hands, and in the latter by the exquisite scent which nature has bestowed on it. It is the right or wrong cultivation of this inquisitive disposition that makes children either stupid or expert, sprightly or dull, sensible or foolish. Since the primary impulses of man urge him to compare his forces with those of the objects about him, and to discover the sensible qualities of such objects as far as they relate to him, his first study is a sort of experimental philosophy relative to self-preservation, from which it is the custom to divert him by speculative studies before he has found his place on this earth. During the time that his supple and delicate organs can adjust themselves to the bodies on which they should act, while his senses are as yet exempt from illusions, this is the time to exercise both the one and the other in their proper functions; this is the time to learn the sensuous relations which things have with us. As everything that enters the human understanding is introduced by the senses, the first reason in man is a sensitive reason; and this serves as the basis of his intellectual reason. Our first instructors in philosophy are our feet, hands, and eyes. Substituting books for all this is not teaching us to reason, but teaching us to use the reasoning of others; it is teaching us to believe a great deal, and never to *know* anything."

"To exercise any art, we must begin by procuring the necessary implements; and to employ those implements to any good purpose, they should be made sufficiently solid for their intended use. To learn to think, therefore, we should exercise our limbs, and our organs, which are the instruments of our intelligence; and in order to make the best use of those instruments, it is necessary that the body furnishing them should be robust and hearty. Thus, so far is a sound understanding from being independent of the body, that it is owing to a good constitution that the operations of the mind are effected with facility and certainty."

"To exercise the senses is not merely to make use of them; it is to learn rightly to judge by them; to learn, if I may so express myself, to perceive; for we know how to touch, to see, to hear, only as we have learned. Some exercises are purely natural and mechanical, and serve to make the body strong and robust, without taking the least hold on the judgment; such are those of swimming, running, leaping, whipping a top, throwing stones, etc. All these are very well; but have we only arms and legs? Have we not also eyes and ears; and are not these organs necessary to the expert use of the former? Exercise, therefore, not only the strength, but also all the senses that direct it; make the best possible use of each, and let the impressions of one confirm those of another. Measure, reckon, weigh, compare." According to the present system, "the lessons which schoolboys learn of each other in playing about their bounds, are a hundred times more useful to them than all those which the master teaches in the school."

He also suggests experiments in the dark, which will both train the senses and get over the child's dread of darkness.

Émile, living in the country and being much in the open air, will acquire a distinct and emphatic way of speaking. He will also avoid a fruitful source of bad pronunciation among the children of the rich, viz., saying lessons by heart. These lessons the children gabble when they are learning them, and afterward, in their efforts to remember the words, they drawl, and give all kinds of false emphasis. Declamation is to be shunned as *acting*. If Émile does not understand anything, he will be too wise to pretend to understand it.

Rousseau seems perhaps inconsistent, in not excluding music and drawing from his curriculum of ignorance; but as a musician, he naturally relaxed toward the former; and drawing he would have his pupil cultivate, not for the sake of the art itself, but only to give him a good eye and supple hand. He should, in all cases, draw from the objects themselves, "my intention being, not so much that he should know how to imitate the objects, as to become fully acquainted with them."

The instruction given to ordinary school-boys was, of course, an abomination in the eyes of Rousseau. "All the studies imposed on these poor unfortunates tend to such objects as are entirely foreign to their minds. Judge, then, of the attention they are likely to bestow on them." "The pedagogues, who make a great parade of the instructions they give their scholars, are paid to talk in a different strain : one may see plainly, however, by their conduct, that they are exactly of my opinion, for, after all, what is it they teach them? Words, still words, and nothing but words. Among the various sciences they pretend to teach, they take particular care not to fall upon those which are really useful ; because there would be the sciences of things, and in them they would never succeed ; but they fix on such as appear to be understood when their terms are once gotten by rote, viz., geography, chronology, heraldry, the languages, etc., all studies so foreign to the purposes of man, and particularly to those of a child, that it is a wonder if ever he may have occasion for them as long as he lives." "In any study whatever, unless we possess the ideas of the things represented, the signs representing them are of no use or consequence. A child is, nevertheless, always confined to these signs, without our being capable of making him comprehend any of the things which they represent. What is the world to a child? It is a globe of pasteboard."

"As no science consists in the knowledge of words, so there is no study proper for children. As they have no certain ideas, so they have no real memory; for I do not call that so which is retentive only of mere sensations. What signifies imprinting on their minds a catalogue of signs which to them represent nothing? Is it to be feared that, in acquiring the knowledge of things, they will not acquire also that of signs? Why, then, shall we put them to the unnecessary trouble of learning them twice? And yet what dangerous prejudices do we not begin to instill, by making them take for knowledge words which to them are without meaning?

"In the very first unintelligible sentence with which a child sits down satisfied, in the very first thing he takes upon trust, or learns from others without being himself convinced of its utility, he loses part of his understanding; and he may figure long in the eyes of fools before he will be able to repair so considerable a loss. No; if nature has given to the child's brain that pliability which renders it fit to receive all impressions, it is not with a view that we should imprint thereon the names of kings, dates, terms of heraldry, of astronomy, of geography, and all those words, meaningless at his age, and useless at any age, with which we weary his sad and sterile childhood; but that all the ideas which he can conceive, and which are useful to him, all those which relate to his happiness, and will one day make his duty plain to him, may trace themselves there in characters never to be effaced, and may assist him in conducting himself through life in a manner appropriate to his nature and his faculties."

"That kind of memory which is possessed by children, may be fully employed without setting them to study books. Everything they see, or hear, appears striking, and they commit it to memory. A child keeps in his mind a register of the actions and conversation of those who are about him; every scene he is engaged in is a book from which he insensibly enriches his memory, treasuring up his store till time shall ripen his judgment and turn it to profit. In the choice of these scenes and objects, in the care of presenting those constantly to his view which he ought to be familiar with, and in hiding from him such as are improper, consists the true art of cultivating this primary faculty of a child. By such means, also, it is, that we should endeavor to form that magazine of knowledge which should serve for his education in youth, and to regulate his conduct afterward. This method, it is true, is not productive of little prodigies of learning, nor does it tend to the glorification of the governess or preceptor; but it is the way to form robust and judicious men, persons sound in body and mind, who, without being admired while children, know how to make themselves respected when grown up."

As for reading and writing, if you can induce a *desire* for them the child will be sure to learn them. "I am almost certain that Émile will know perfectly well how to read and write before he is ten years old, because I give myself very little trouble whether he learn it or not before he is fifteen; but I had much rather he should never learn to read at all, than to acquire that knowledge at the expense of everything that would render it useful to him; and of what service will the power of reading be to him when he has renounced its use forever?"

The following passage is perhaps familiar to Mr. Lowe: "If, proceeding on the plan I have begun to delineate, you follow rules directly contrary to those which are generally received; if, instead of transporting your pupil's mind to what is remote, if, instead of making his thoughts wander unceasingly in other places, in other climates, in other centuries, to the ends of the earth, and to the very heavens, you apply yourself to keeping him always at home and attentive to that which comes in immediate contact with him, you will then find him capable of perception, of memory, and even of reason: this is the order of nature. In proportion as the sensitive becomes an active being, he acquires a discernment proportional to his bodily powers; when he possesses more of the latter, also, than are necessary for his preservation, it is with that redundancy, and not before, that he displays those speculative faculties which are adapted to the employment of such abilities to other purposes. Are you desirous, therefore, to cultivate the understanding of your pupil? Cultivate those abilities on which it depends. Keep him in constant exercise of body; bring him up robust and healthy, in order to make him reasonable and wise; let him work, let him run about, let him make a noise, in a word, let him be always active and in motion; let him be once a man in vigor, and he will soon be a man in understanding."

Let us now examine what provision was made, in Rousseau's system, for teaching the one science for children, that of moral behavior (*des devoirs de l'homme*). His notions of this science were by no means those to which we are accustomed. As a believer in the goodness of human nature, he traced all folly, vanity, and vice to ordinary education, and he would therefore depart as widely as possible from the usual course. "Examine the rules of the common method of education," he writes, "and you will find them all wrong, particularly those which relate to virtue and manners."

A simple alteration of method, however, would not suffice. Rousseau went further than this. He discarded all received notions of goodness, and set up one of his own in their stead. "The only lesson of morality proper for children, and the most important to persons of all ages, is never to do an injury to any one. Even the positive precept of doing good, if not made subordinate to this, is dangerous, false, and contradictory. Who is there that does not do good? All the world does good, the wicked man as well as others: he makes one person happy at the expense of making a hundred miserable; hence arise all our calamities. The most sublime virtues are negative; they are also the most difficult to put in practice, because they are attended with no ostentation, and are even above the pleasure, so sweet to the heart of man, of sending away others satisfied with our benevolence. O how much good must that man necessarily do his fellow-creatures, if such a man there be, who never did any of them harm! What intrepidity of soul, what constancy of mind are necessary here! It is not, however, by reasoning on this maxim, but by endeavoring to put it in practice, that all its difficulty is to be discovered."

"The precept of never doing another harm, implies that of having as little to do as possible with human society; for in the social state the good of one man necessarily becomes the evil of another. This relation is essential to the thing itself, and cannot be changed. We may inquire, on this principle, which is best, man in a state of society or in a state of solitude?"

"A certain noble author has said, none but a wicked man might exist alone: for my part, I say, none but a good man might exist alone."

This passage fully explains Rousseau's enthusiasm for Robinson Crusoe, for he must have regarded him as the best and most beneficent of mortals. "Happy are the people among whom goodness requires no self-denial, and men may be just without virtue." And the fortunate solitary had one half of goodness ready made for him. "That which renders man essentially good is to have few wants, and seldom to compare himself with others; that which renders him essentially wicked is to have many wants, and to be frequently governed by opinion." Rousseau, however, did not vaunt the merits of negation with absolute consistency. Elsewhere he says, "He who wants nothing will love nothing, and I cannot conceive that he who loves nothing can be happy."

As Rousseau found the root of all evil in the action of man upon man, he sought to dissever his child of nature as much as possible from his fellow-creatures, and to assimilate him to Robinson Crusoe. Anything like rule and obedience was abomination to Rousseau, and he confounds the wise rule of superior intelligence with the tyranny of mere caprice. He writes: "We always either do that which is pleasing to the child, or exact of him what pleases ourselves; either submitting to his humors or obliging him to submit to ours. There is no medium; he must either give orders or receive them. Hence the first ideas he acquires are those of absolute rule and servitude." The great panacea for all evils was, then, "liberty," by which Rousseau understood independence. "He only performs the actions of his own will, who stands in no need of the assistance of others to put his designs in execution; and hence it follows that the greatest of all blessings is not authority, but liberty. A man truly free wills only that which he can do, and does only that which pleases him. This is my fundamental maxim. It need only be applied to childhood, and all the rules of education will naturally flow from it." "Whosoever does what he will is happy, provided he is capable of doing it himself; this is the case with man in a state of nature."

But a very obvious difficulty suggests itself. A child is necessarily the most dependent creature in the world. How, then, can he be brought up in what Rousseau calls liberty? Rousseau sees this difficulty, and all he can say is, that as real liberty is impossible for a child, you must give him sham liberty instead. "Let him always be his own master in appearance, and do you take care to be so in reality. There is no subjection so complete as that which preserves the appearance of liberty; it is by this means even the will itself is led captive. The poor child, who knows nothing, who is capable of nothing, is surely sufficiently at your mercy. Don't you dispose, with regard to him, of everything about him? Are not you capable of affecting him just as you please? His employment, his sports, his pleasures, his pains, are they not all in your power, without his knowing it? Assuredly, he ought not to be compelled to do anything contrary to his inclinations; but then he ought not to be inclined to do anything contrary to yours; he ought not to take a step which you had not foreseen, nor open his lips to speak without your knowing what he is about to say. When you have once brought him under such regulations, you may indulge him freely in all those corporeal exercises which his age requires, without running the hazard of blunting his intellects. You will then see, that instead of employing all his subtle arts to shake off a burdensome and disagreeable tyranny, he will be busied only in making the best use of everything about him. It is in this case you will have reason to be surprised at the subtilty of his invention, and the ingenuity with which he makes everything that is in his power contribute to his gratification, without being obliged to prepossession or opinion. In thus leaving him at liberty to follow his own will, you will not augment his caprice. By being accustomed only to do that which is proper for his state and condition he will soon do nothing but what he ought; and though he should be in continual motion of body, yet, while he is employed only in the pursuit of his present and apparent interest, you will find his reasoning faculties display themselves better, and in a manner more peculiar to himself, than if he were engaged in studies of pure speculation."

After this astonishing passage the reader will probably consider Rousseau's opinions of moral behavior mere matters of curiosity. Yet some of his advice is well worth considering.

Although children should be made happy, they should by no means be shielded from every possible hurt. "The first thing we ought to learn, and that which it is of the greatest consequence for us to know, is to suffer. It seems as if children were formed little and feeble to learn this important lesson without danger." "Excessive severity, as well as excessive indulgence, should be equally avoided. If you leave children to suffer, you expose their health, endanger their lives, and make them actually miserable; on the other hand, if you are too anxious to prevent their being sensible of any kind of pain and inconvenience, you only pave their way to feel much greater: you enervate their constitutions, make them tender and effeminate; in a word, you remove them out of their situation as human beings, into which they must hereafter return in spite of all your solicitude."

His advice on firmness is also good. "When the child desires what is necessary, you ought to know and immediately comply with his request; but to be induced to do anything by his tears, is to encourage him to cry; it is to teach him to doubt your goodwill, and to think you are influenced more by importunity than benevolence. Beware of this, for if your child once comes to imagine you are not of a good disposition, he will soon be of a bad one; if he once thinks you complain, he will soon grow obstinate. You should comply with his request immediately if you do not intend to refuse it. Mortify him not with frequent denials, but never revoke a refusal once made him." Caprice, whether of the governor or of the child, is carefully to be shunned.

"There is an innate sense of right and wrong implanted in the human heart." In proof of this, he gives an anecdote of an infant who almost screamed to death on receiving a blow from the nurse. "I am very certain," he says, "had a burning coal fallen by accident on the hand of the child, it would have been less agitated than by this slight blow, given with a manifest intention to hurt it."

For punishments he gives a hint which has been worked out by Mr. H. Spencer. "Oppose to his indiscreet desires only physical obstacles, or *the inconveniences naturally arising from the actions themselves;* these he will remember on a future occasion."

Even in the matter of liberty, about which no one disagrees more heartily with Rousseau than I do, we may, I think, learn a lesson from him. "Émile acts from his own thoughts, and not from the dictation of others." "If your head always directs your pupil's hands, his own head will become useless to him." There is a great truth in this. While differing so far from Rousseau, that I should require the most implicit obedience from boys, I feel that we must give them a certain amount of independent action and freedom from restraint, as a means of education. In many of our private schools, a boy is hardly called upon to exercise his will all day long. He rises in the morning when he must; at meals, he eats till he is obliged to stop; he is taken out for exercise like a horse; he has all his indoor work prescribed for him, both as to time and quantity.

Thus a boy grows up without having any occasion to think or act for himself. He is therefore without self-reliance. So much care is taken to prevent his doing wrong, that he gets to think only of checks from without. He is therefore incapable of self-restraint. Our public schools give more "liberty," and turn out better *men*.

We will now suppose the child to have reached the age of twelve, a proficient in ignorance. His education must at this period alter entirely. The age for learning has arrived. "Give me a child of twelve years of age, who knows nothing at all, and at fifteen I will return him to you as learned as any that you may have instructed earlier; with this difference, that the knowledge of yours will be only in his memory, and that of mine will be in his judgment." "To what use is it proper a child should put that redundancy of abilities, of which he is at present possessed, and which will fail him at another age? He should employ it on those things which may be of utility in time to come. He should throw, if I may so express myself, the superfluity of his present being into the future. The robust child should provide for the subsistence of the feeble man; not in laying up his treasure in coffers whence thieves may steal, nor by intrusting it to the hands of others; but by keeping it in his own. To appropriate his acquisitions to himself he will secure them in the strength and dexterity of his own arms, and in the capacity of his own head. This, therefore, is the time for employment, for instruction, for study. Observe, also, that I have not arbitrarily fixed on this period for that purpose; nature itself plainly points it out to us."

The education of Émile was to be, to use the language of the present day, scientific, not literary. Rousseau professed a hatred of books, which he said kept the student so long engaged upon the thoughts of other people as to have no time to make a store of his own. "The abuse of reading is destructive to knowledge. Imagining ourselves to know everything we read, we conceive it unnecessary to learn it by other means. Too much reading, however, serves only to make us presumptuous blockheads. Of all the ages in which literature has flourished, reading was never so universal as in the present, nor were men in general ever so ignorant."

Even science was to be studied, not so much with a view to knowledge as to intellectual vigor. "You will remember it is my constant maxim, not to teach the boy a multiplicity of things, but to prevent his acquiring any but clear and precise ideas. His knowing nothing does not much concern me, provided he does not deceive himself."

Again he says: "Émile has but little knowledge; but what he has is truly his own; he knows nothing by halves. Among the few things he knows, and knows *well*, the most important is, that there are many things which he is now ignorant of, and which he may one day know; that there are many more which some men know and he never will; and that there is an infinity of others which neither he nor anybody else will ever know. He possesses a universal capacity, not in point of actual knowledge, but in the faculty of acquiring it; an open, intelligent genius, adapted to everything, and, as Montaigne says, if not instructed, capable of receiving instruction. It is sufficient for me that he knows how to discover the utility of his actions, and the reason for his opinions. Once again, I say, my object is not to furnish his mind with knowledge, but to teach him the method of acquiring it when he has occasion for it; to instruct him how to hold it in estimation, and to inspire him, above all, with a love for truth. By this method, indeed, we make no great advances; but then we never take a useless step, nor are we obliged to turn back again."

The method of learning, therefore, was to be chosen with the view of bringing out the pupil's powers; and the subjects of instruction were to be sufficiently varied to give the pupil a notion of the connection between various branches of knowledge, and to ascertain the direction in which his taste and talent would lead him.

The first thing to be aimed at is to excite a desire for knowledge. "Direct the attention of your pupil to the phenomena of nature, and you will soon awaken his curiosity; but to keep that curiosity alive, you must be in no haste to satisfy it. Put questions to him adapted to his capacity, and leave him to resolve them. He is not to know anything because you have told it to him, but because he has himself comprehended it; he should not' learn, but discover science. If ever you substitute authority in the place of argument, he will reason no longer; he will be ever afterward bandied like a shuttlecock between the opinions of others."

Curiosity, when aroused, should be fostered by suspense, and the tutor must, above all things, avoid what Mr. Wilson, of Rugby, has lately called "didactic teaching." "I do not at all admire explanatory discourses," says Rousseau; "young people give little attention to them, and never retain them in memory. The things themselves are the best explanations. I can never enough repeat it, that we make words of too much consequence; with our prating modes of education we make nothing but praters."

The grand thing to be educed was *self-teaching*. "Obliged to learn of himself, the pupil makes use of his own reason, and not of that of others; for to give no influence to opinion, no weight should be given to authority; and it is certain that our errors arise less from ourselves than from others. From this continual exercise of the understanding will result a vigor of mind, like that which we give the body by labor and fatigue. Another advantage is, that we advance only in proportion to our strength. The mind, like the body, carries that only which it can carry. But when the understanding appropriates everything before it commits it to the memory, whatever it afterward draws from thence is properly its own; whereas, in overcharging the mind without the knowledge of the understanding, we expose ourselves to the inconvenience of never drawing out anything which belongs to us."

Again he writes: "We acquire, without doubt, notions more

clear and certain of things we thus learn of ourselves than of those we are taught by others. Another advantage also resulting from this method is, that we do not accustom ourselves to a servile submission to the authority of others; but, by exercising our reason, grow every day more ingenious in the discovery of the relations of things, in connecting our ideas and in the contrivance of machines; whereas, by adopting those which are put into our hands, our invention grows dull and indifferent, as the man who never dresses himself, but is served in everything by his servants, and drawn about everywhere by his horses, loses by degrees the activity and use of his limbs. Boileau boasted that he had taught Racine to rhyme with difficulty. Among the many admirable methods taken to abridge the study of the sciences, we are in great want of one to make us learn them with *effort*."

Following in the steps of Locke, Rousseau required his model pupil to learn a trade. But this was not to be acquired as a mere amusement. First, Rousseau required it to secure the self-dependence of his pupil, and secondly, to improve his head as well as his hands. "If, instead of keeping a boy poring over books, I employ him in a workshop, his hands will be busied to the improvement of his understanding; he will become a philosopher, while he thinks himself only an artisan."

I hope the quotations I have now given will suffice to convey to the reader some of Rousseau's main ideas on the subject of education. The "Émile" was once a popular book in this country. In David Williams's lectures (dated 1789) we read, "Rousseau is in full possession of public attention. . . . To be heard on the subject of education it is expedient to direct our observations to his works." But now the case is different. In the words of Mr. Herman Merivale, "Rousseau was dethroned with the fall of his extravagant child, the Republic." Perhaps we have been less influenced by both father and child than any nation of Europe; and if so, we owe this to our horror of extravagance. The English intellect is eminently decorous, and Rousseau's disregard for "appearances," or rather his evident purpose of making an impression by defying "appearances" and saying just the opposite of what is expected, simply distresses it. Hence, the "Émile" has long ceased to be read in this country, and the only English translation I have met with was published in the last century, and has not been reprinted. So Rousseau now works upon us only through his disciples, especially Pestalozzi; but the reader will see from the passages I have selected that we have often listened to Rousseau unawares.

The truths of the "Émile" will survive the fantastic forms which are there forced upon them. Of these truths, one of the most important, to my mind, is the distinction drawn between childhood and youth. I do not, of course, insist with Rousseau that a child should be taught nothing till the day on which he is twelve years old, and then that instruction should begin all at once. There is no hard and fast line that can be drawn between the two stages of development; the change from one to the other is gradual and, in point of time, differs greatly with the individual. But, as I have elsewhere said, I believe the difference between the child and the youth to be greater than the difference between the youth and the man; and I believe, further, that this is far too much overlooked in our ordinary education. Rousseau, by drawing attention to the sleep of reason and to the activity and vigor of the senses in childhood, became one of the most important educational reformers, and a benefactor of mankind.

WILLIAM SHENSTONE
1714-1763

WILLIAM SHENSTONE was born at the Leasowes, in Shropshire, England, in 1714. His school-days were passed in his native village, amid scenes which he has described in poems of much grace and beauty. For ten years he studied at Pembroke College, Oxford. Here, from time to time, he published small books of lyrics, which were well received. In 1745 he took up his permanent residence on his ancestral estate of the Leasowes, which he embellished with every adjunct of beauty and taste. Dr. Samuel Johnson, referring to the return of Shenstone to the Leasowes, says: "Now was excited his delight in real pleasures, and his ambition of rural elegance. He began from this time to point his prospects, to diversify his surface, to entangle his walks, and to wind his waters; which he did with such judgment and such fancy, as made his little domain the envy of the great and the admiration of the skillful, a place to be visited by travelers and copied by designers." Unfortunately, Shenstone did not calculate the cost of the work he had undertaken until he found himself hopelessly involved in debt. The estate was sacrificed to pay for its adornment, and the last days of the poet were clouded with care and sorrow, which doubtless hastened his end. He died in 1763.

Characterization

The inimitable "Schoolmistress" of Shenstone is one of the felicities of genius; but the purpose of this poem has been entirely misconceived. Johnson, acknowledging this charming effusion to be "the most pleasing of Shenstone's productions," observes, "I know not what claim it has to stand among the *moral* works." The truth is, that it was intended for quite a different purpose by the author, and Dodsley, the editor of his works, must have strangely blundered in designating it "a moral poem." It may be classed with a species of poetry till recently rare in our language, and which we sometimes find among the Italians in their *rime piacevoli*, or *poesie burlesche*, which does not always consist of low humor in a facetious style, with jingling rhymes, to which form we attach our idea of a burlesque poem. There is a refined species of ludicrous poetry which is comic yet tender, lusory yet elegant, and with such a blending of the serious and the facetious that the result of such a poem may often, among its other pleasures, produce a sort of ambiguity; so that we do not always know whether the writer is laughing at his subject, or whether he is to be laughed at. The admirable Whistlecraft[1] met this fate. "The Schoolmistress" of Shenstone has been admired for its exquisitely ludicrous turn. This discovery I owe to the good fortune of possessing the original edition of "The Schoolmistress," which the author printed under his own directions, and to his own fancy. To this piece of *ludicrous poetry*, as he calls it, "lest it should be mistaken," he added a *ludicrous index*, "partly to show fools that I am in jest." But "the fool," his subsequent editor, who, I regret to say, was Robert Dodsley, thought proper to suppress this amusing "Ludicrous Index," and the consequence is, as the poet foresaw, that his aim has been mistaken.

ISAAC D'ISRAELI.

But with all the beauties of the Leasowes in our minds, it may still be regretted that, instead of devoting his whole soul to clumping beeches and projecting mottoes for summer-houses, he had not gone more into living nature for subjects, and described her interesting realities with the same fond and natural touches which give so much delightfulness to his portrait of "The Schoolmistress."

THOMAS CAMPBELL.

The Schoolmistress[2]

I.

Ah me! full sorely is my heart forlorn,
To think how modest worth neglected lies;
While partial fame doth with her blasts adorn
Such deeds alone as pride and pomp disguise;

---

[1] "Whistlecraft," the *nom de plume* of J. Hookham Frere (1769-1846), an English diplomatist and poet, author of exquisite humorous compositions, comic and serious by turns.

[2] The schoolmistress portrayed is Dame Sarah Lloyd, the "school-dame" of the poet in his early years. Shenstone designed to have for an illustration of the poem a comic portrait of this since-famous personage.

The veritable schoolhouse of Dame Sarah, with its thatched roof, formed the frontispiece of the original edition of the poem. The "birch tree" in front was gilded by the rays of the setting sun. Shenstone was disgusted with the picture and with his artist, and declared the "setting sun" to be "a falling monster."

Deeds of ill sort, and mischievous emprize:
Lend me thy clarion, goddess! let me try
To sound the praise of merit, ere it dies;
Such as I oft have chancèd to espy,
Lost in the dreary shades of dull obscurity.

II.

In every village mark'd with little spire,
Embower'd in trees and hardly known to fame,
There dwells, in lowly shed and mean attire,
A matron old, whom we schoolmistress name;
Who boasts unruly brats with birch to tame;
They grieven sore, in piteous durance pent,
Awed by the pow'r of this relentless dame;
And oft-times, on vagaries idly bent,
For unkempt hair, or task unconn'd, are sorely shent.

III.

And all in sight doth rise a birchen tree,
Which learning near her little dome did stow;
Whilom a twig of small regard to see,
Tho' now so wide its waving branches flow;
And work the simple vassals mickle woe;
For not a wind might curl the leaves that blew
But their limbs shudder'd, and their pulse beat low;
And as they look'd they found their horror grew,
And shaped it into rods, and tingled at the view.

. . . .

V.

Near to this dome is found a patch so green,
On which the tribe their gambols do display;
And at the door impris'ning board is seen,
Lest weakly wights of smaller size should stray;
Eager, perdie, to bask in sunny day!

The noises intermix'd, which thence resound,
Do learning's little tenement betray;
Where sits the dame, disguised in look profound,
And eyes her fairy throng, and turns her wheel around.

VI.

Her cap, far whiter than the driven snow,
Emblem right meet of decency does yield:
Her apron dyed in grain, as blue, I trow,
As is the harebell that adorns the field:
And in her hand, for scepter, she does wield
Tway birchen sprays; with anxious fear entwined
With dark distrust, and sad repentance fill'd;
And steadfast hate, and sharp affliction join'd,
And fury uncontroll'd, and chastisement unkind.

. . . .

VIII.

A russet stole was o'er her shoulders thrown;
A russet kirtle fenced the nipping air;
'Twas simple russet, but it was her own;
'Twas her own country bred the flock so fair,
'Twas her own labor did the fleece prepare:
And, sooth to say, her pupils, ranged around,
Through pious awe, did term it passing rare;
For they in gaping wonderment abound,
And think, no doubt, she been the greatest wight on ground.

IX.

Albeit ne flattery did corrupt her truth,
Ne pompous title did debauch her ear;
Goody, good-woman, gossip, n'aunt, forsooth,
Or dame, the sole additions she did hear;
Yet these she challenged, these she held right dear,

Ne would esteem him act as mought behove,
Who should not honor'd eld with these revere:
For never title yet so mean could prove,
But there was eke a mind which did that title love.

X.

One ancient hen she took delight to feed,
The plodding pattern of the busy dame:
Which, ever and anon, impell'd by need,
Into her school, begirt with chickens, came;
Such favor did her past deportment claim;
And, if neglect had lavish'd on the ground
Fragment of bread, she would collect the same;
For well she knew, and quaintly could expound,
What sin it were to waste the smallest crumb she found.

XI.

Herbs, too, she knew, and well of each could speak
That in her garden sipp'd the silv'ry dew;
Where no vain flow'r disclosed a gaudy streak;
But herbs for use, and physic, not a few,
Of grey renown, within those borders grew.
The tufted basil, pun-provoking thyme,
Fresh balm, and marygold of cheerful hue;
The lowly gill that never dares to climb;
And more I fain would sing, disdaining here to rhyme.

XII.

Yet euphrasy, may not be left unsung,
That gives dim eyes to wander leagues around;
And pungent radish biting infant's tongue;
And plantain ribb'd, that heals the reaper's wound;
And marj'ram sweet, in shepherd's posy found;

And lavender, whose spikes of azure bloom
Shall be, ere-while, in arid bundles bound,
To lurk amidst the labors of her loom,
And crown her kerchiefs clean with mickle rare perfume.

XIII.

And here trim rosemarine, that whilom crown'd
The daintiest garden of the proudest peer;
Ere, driven from its envied site, it found
A sacred shelter for its branches here;
Where edged with gold its glitt'ring skirts appear.
O wassel days! O customs meet and well!
Ere this was banish'd from his lofty sphere,
Simplicity then sought this humble cell,
Nor ever would she more with thane and lordling dwell.

. . . .

XVI.

In elbow-chair, like that of Scottish stem
By the sharp tooth of cank'ring eld defaced,
In which, when he receives his diadem,
Our sov'reign prince and liefest liege is placed,
The matron sate; and some with rank she graced
(The source of children's and of courtier's pride).
Redress'd affronts, for vile affronts there pass'd;
And warn'd them not the fretful to deride,
But love each other dear, whatever them betide.

XVII.

Right well she knew each temper to descry;
To thwart the proud, and the submiss to raise;
Some with vile copper-prize exalt on high,
And some entice with pittance small of praise;
And other some with baleful sprig she 'frays.

Ev'n absent, she the reins of power doth hold,
While with quaint arts the giddy crowd she sways,
Forewarn'd, if little bird their pranks behold,
'Twill whisper in her ear, and all the scene unfold.

XVIII.

Lo now with state she utters the command!
Eftsoons the urchins to their tasks repair;
Their books of stature small they take in hand,
Which with pellucid horn securèd are,
To save from fingers wet the letters fair.
The work so gay, that on their back is seen,
St. George's high achievements does declare;
On which thilk[1] wight that has y-gazing been
Kens the forth-coming rod, unpleasing sight, I ween!

. . . .

XX.

O ruthful scene! when, from a nook obscure,
His little sister doth his peril see.
All playful as she sate she grows demure;
She finds full soon her wonted spirits flee;
She meditates a pray'r to set him free.
Nor gentle pardon could this dame deny
(If gentle pardon could with dames agree)
To her sad grief that swells in either eye,
And wrings her so that all for pity she could die.

XXI.

No longer can she now her shrieks command;
And hardly she forbears thro' awful fear
To rushen forth, and, with presumptuous hand,
To stay hard justice in its mid career.
On thee she calls, on thee, her parent dear

[1] that, or such

(Ah! too remote to ward the shameful blow).
She sees no kind domestic visage near,
And soon a flood of tears begins to flow,
And gives a loose at last to unavailing woe.

XXII.

But ah, what pen his piteous plight may trace?
Or what device his loud laments explain
The form uncouth of his disguisèd face?
The pallid hue that dyes his looks amain?
The plenteous shower that does his cheek distain?
When he, in abject wise, implores the dame,
Ne hopeth aught of sweet reprieve to gain;
Or when from high she levels well her aim,
And through the thatch his cries each falling stroke proclaim.

XXIII.

The other tribe, aghast, with sore dismay
Attend, and con their tasks with mickle care;
By turns astonied, ev'ry twig survey,
And from their fellow's hateful wounds beware;
Knowing, I wist, how each the same may share;
Till fear has taught them a performance meet,
And to the well-known chest the dame repair;
Whence oft with sugar'd cates she doth 'em greet,
And ginger-bread y-rare; now certes doubly sweet!

. . . .

XXVI.

Behind some door, in melancholy thought,
Mindless of food, he, dreary caitiff! pines;
Ne for his fellow's joyaunce careth aught,
But to the wind all merriment resigns;
And deems it shame if he to peace inclines;

And many a sullen look askance is sent,
　Which for his dame's annoyance he designs;
And still the more to pleasure him she's bent,
　The more doth he, perverse, her 'havior past resent.

XXVII.

Ah me! how much I fear lest pride it be!
　But if that pride it be which thus inspires,
Beware, ye dames, with nice discernment see,
　Ye quench not too the sparks of nobler fires:
Ah! better far than all the muses' lyres,
　All coward arts, is valor's gen'rous heat;
The firm fixt breast which fit and right requires,
　Like Vernon's patriot soul; more justly great
Than craft that pimps for ill, or flow'ry false deceit.

XXVIII.

Yet, nursed with skill, what dazzling fruits appear!
　Ev'n now sagacious foresight points to show
A little bench of heedless bishops here,[1]
　And there a chancellor in embryo,
Or bard sublime, if bard may e'er be so,
　As Milton, Shakespeare, names that ne'er shall die!
Tho' now he crawl along the ground so low,
　Nor weeting how the muse should soar on high,
Wisheth, poor starv'ling elf! his paper kite may fly.

. . . .

---

[1] Of these lines, which contain so pleasing a picture of "genius in its infancy," Isaac D'Israeli says: "I cannot but think that the far-famed stanza in 'Gray's Elegy,' where he discovers men of genius in peasants, as Shenstone has in children, was suggested by this original conception.

　　　"'Some mute, inglorious Milton here may rest,
　　　　Some Cromwell, guiltless of his country's blood,'

is, to me, a congenial thought, with an echoed turn of expression from the lines of 'The Schoolmistress.'"

XXX.

But now Dan Phœbus gains the middle sky,
And Liberty unbars her prison-door;
And like a rushing torrent out they fly,
And now the grassy cirque han cover'd o'er
With boist'rous revel-rout and wild uproar;
A thousand ways in wanton rings they run;
Heav'n shield their short-lived pastimes, I implore!
For well may freedom, erst so dearly won,
Appear to British elf more gladsome than the sun.

THOMAS FULLER
1608-1661

Thomas Fuller, a distinguished clergyman and a voluminous writer, was born in 1608, at Aldwinkle, in Northamptonshire, England—which was, later, the birthplace of Dryden. Fuller was precocious in youth, and entered Queen's College, Cambridge, at the age of twelve years. He was a chaplain in the royal army and, after the Restoration, was appointed chaplain extraordinary to the king. Among his most valuable works are church histories and biographical sketches.

Characterization

There was in Thomas Fuller a combination of those qualities which minister to our entertainment, such as few have ever possessed in an equal degree. He was, first of all, a man of multifarious reading, of great and digested knowledge, which an extraordinary retentiveness of memory preserved ever ready for use, and considerable accuracy of judgment enabled him successfully to apply. So well does he vary his treasures of memory and observation, so judiciously does he interweave his anecdotes, quotations, and remarks, that it is impossible to conceive a more delightful checker-work of acute thought and apposite illustration of original and extracted sentiment than is presented in his works.

"Retrospective Review."

Selections

1. The Good Schoolmaster

There is scarce any profession in the commonwealth more necessary, which is so slightly performed. The reasons whereof I conceive to be these: First, young scholars make this calling their refuge; yea, perchance, before they have taken any degree in the university, commence schoolmasters in the country, as if nothing else were required to set up this profession but only a rod and a ferula. Secondly, others who are able use it only as a passage to better preferment, to patch the rents in their present fortune, till they can provide a new one, and betake themselves to some more gainful calling. Thirdly, they are disheartened from doing their best with the miserable reward which in some places they receive, being masters to their children and slaves to their parents. Fourthly, being grown rich they grow negligent, and scorn to touch the school but by the proxy of the usher. But see how well our schoolmaster behaves himself.

His genius inclines him with delight to his profession. God of his goodness hath fitted several men for several callings, that the necessity of church and state, in all conditions, may be provided for. And thus God mouldeth some for a schoolmaster's life, undertaking it with desire and delight, and discharging it with dexterity and happy success.

He studieth his scholars' natures as carefully as they their books; and ranks their dispositions into several forms. And though it may seem difficult for him in a great school to descend to all particulars, yet experienced schoolmasters may quickly make a grammar of boys' natures.

He is able, diligent, and methodical in his teaching; not leading them rather in a circle than forwards. He minces his precepts for children to swallow, hanging clogs on the nimbleness of his own soul, that his scholars may go along with him.

He is moderate in inflicting deserved correction. Many a schoolmaster better answereth the name *paidotribes*[1] than *paidagogos*,[2] rather tearing his scholars' flesh with whipping than giving them good education. No wonder if his scholars hate the muses, being presented unto them in the shapes of fiends and furies.

Such an Orbilius[3] mars more scholars than he makes. Their

[1] boy-beater
[2] He means "boy-teacher;" but the paidagogos ($\pi\alpha\iota\delta\alpha\gamma\omega\gamma o\varsigma$), "pedagogue," of the Greeks, was the servant who conducted the children from their homes to the schools, and not the instructor.
[3] a reference to the teacher of the Latin poet Horace, satirized by the latter as "Orbilius *plagosus*"—"Orbilius of the birch."

tyranny hath caused many tongues to stammer which spake plain by nature, and whose stuttering at first was nothing else but fears quavering on their speech at their master's presence; and whose mauling them about their heads hath dulled those who in quickness exceeded their master.

To conclude, let this, amongst other motives, make schoolmasters careful in their place—that the eminences of their scholars have commended the memories of their schoolmasters to posterity.

2. Of Memory

It is the treasure-house of the mind, wherein the monuments thereof are kept and preserved. Plato makes it the mother of the muses. Aristotle sets it in one degree further, making experience the mother of arts, memory the parent of experience. Philosophers place it in the rear of the head; and it seems the mine of memory lies there, because there men naturally dig for it, scratching it when they are at a loss. This again is two-fold: one, the simple retention of things; the other, a regaining them when forgotten.

Artificial memory is rather a trick than an art, and more for the gain of the teacher than profit of the learners. Like the tossing of a pike, which is no part of the postures and motions thereof, and is rather for ostentation than use, to show the strength and nimbleness of the arm, and is often used by wandering soldiers, as an introduction to beg. Understand it of the artificial rules which at this day are delivered by memory mountebanks; for sure an art thereof may be made (wherein as yet the world is defective), and that no more destructive to natural memory than spectacles are to eyes, which girls in Holland wear from twelve years of age. But till this be found out, let us observe these plain rules.

First, soundly infix in thy mind what thou desirest to remember. What wonder is it if agitation of business jog that out of thy head which was there rather tacked than fastened? It is best knocking in the nail over night, and clinching it the next morning.

Overburden not thy memory to make so faithful a servant a slave. Remember, Atlas was weary. Have as much reason as a camel, to rise when thou hast thy full load. Memory, like a purse, if it be over full that it cannot shut, all will drop out of it; take heed of a gluttonous curiosity to feed on many things, lest the greediness of the appetite of thy memory spoil the digestion thereof.

Marshal thy notions into a handsome method. One will carry twice more weight trussed and packed up in bundles, than when it lies untoward, flapping and hanging about his shoulders. Things orderly fardled up under heads are most portable.

Adventure not all thy learning in one bottom, but divide it betwixt thy memory and thy note-books. He that with Bias carries all his learning about him in his head, will utterly be beggared and bankrupt, if a violent disease, a merciless thief, should rob and strip him. I know some have a commonplace[1] against commonplace books,[2] and yet perchance will privately make use of what they publicly declaim against. A commonplace book contains many notions in garrison, whence the owner may draw out an army into the field on competent warning.

---

[1] a trite or customary remark.

[2] It is an excellent plan for every teacher to keep a commonplace book of considerable size, different portions of it being set apart for the different subjects upon which he is to give instruction. On the first twenty pages "Geography" may be the head; the next twenty pages may be set apart for "History;" twenty more may be assigned to "Reading," and a like number to "Arithmetic," "Grammar," "Spelling," "Writing," etc., reserving quite a space for "Miscellaneous Matter." This would make a large book; but when it is remembered that it is to be used for several years, it is well to have it large enough to contain a large amount of matter. Now, whenever a teacher hears a lecture on a peculiar method of teaching either of these branches, let him note the prominent parts of it under the proper head, and *especially the illustrations*. When he reads or hears an anecdote illustrating geography, history, or grammar, let it be copied under the proper head. If it illustrates geography, let the name of the place stand at its head. When he visits a school, and listens to a new explanation or a new process, let him note it under its head. In this way he may collect a thousand valuable things to be used with judgment in his school.—*Page's "Theory and Practice of Teaching."*

JOHANN HEINRICH PESTALOZZI

1746-1827

JOHANN HEINRICH PESTALOZZI, the greatest of modern educational reformers, was born at Zurich, in German Switzerland, in 1746. His family was of Italian origin and of Protestant faith. He established at his beautiful villa of Neu Hof, in the canton Aargau, an industrial school for the poor—probably the first of its kind. It was a failure. Following the military events in the canton Unterwalden, he maintained in an old convent at Stanz a school for the starving and homeless victims of war. For a time he conducted a school at Burgdorf, and afterward he established a famous institute of learning in the old castle of Yverdon, in the canton Vaud. Besides contributing frequently to the periodical literature of his time, Pestalozzi wrote, at intervals, a number of books, the chief of which were "Figures to my Spelling Book" (a collection of fables), "Leonard and Gertrude," "Christopher and Eliza," "How Gertrude Educated her Children," and "Hours of a Hermit." He died in 1827. The following estimate of the life of this wonderful man is from the pen of Professor Joseph Payne, of the College of Preceptors in London:

"At fifty-two years of age, we find Pestalozzi utterly unacquainted with the science and the art of education, and very scantily furnished even with elementary knowledge, undertaking at Stanz, in the canton Unterwalden, the charge of eighty children, whom the events of war have rendered homeless and destitute. Here he was at last in the position which, during years of sorrow and disappointment, he had eagerly desired to fill. He was now brought into immediate contact with ignorance, vice, and brutality, and had the opportunity for testing the power of his long-cherished theories. The man whose absorbing idea had been that the ennobling of the people, even of the lowest class, through education, was no mere dream, was now, in the midst of extraordinary difficulties, to struggle with the solution of the problem. And surely if any man, consciously possessing strength to fight, and only desiring to be brought face to face with his adversary, ever had his utmost wishes granted, it was Pestalozzi at Stanz. Let us try for a moment to realize the circumstances—the forces of the enemy on the one side, the single arm on the other, and the field of the combat. The house in which the eighty children were assembled, to be boarded, lodged, and taught, was an old tumble-down Ursuline convent, scarcely habitable, and destitute of all the conveniences of life. The only apartment suitable for a schoolroom was about twenty-four feet square, furnished with a few desks and forms;[1] and into this were crowded the wretched children, noisy, dirty, diseased, and ignorant, and with the manners and habits of barbarians. Pestalozzi's only helper in the management of the institution was an old woman, who cooked the food and swept the rooms; so that he was, as he tells us himself, not only the teacher, but the paymaster, the man-servant, and almost the housemaid of the children.

"'I was obliged,' he says, 'unceasingly to be everything to my children. I was alone with them from morning till night. It was from my hand that they received whatever could be of service both to their bodies and minds. All succor, all consolation, all instruction came to them immediately from myself. Their hands were in my hands; my eyes were fixed on theirs, my tears mingled with theirs, my smiles encountered theirs, my soup was their soup, my drink was their drink. I had around me neither family, friends, nor servants; I had only them. I was with them when they were in health, by their side when they were ill. I slept in their midst. I was the last to go to bed, the first to rise in the morning. When we were in bed, I used to pray with them and talk to them until they went to sleep. They wished me to do so.'

"This active, practical, self-sacrificing love, beaming on the frozen hearts of the children, by degrees melted and animated them. But it was only by degrees. Pestalozzi was at first disappointed. He had expected too much, and had formed no plan of action. He even prided himself upon his want of plan. 'I knew,' he says, 'no system, no method, no art but that which rested on the simple consequences of the firm belief of the children in my love toward them. I wished to know no other.' Before long, however, he began to see that the response which the movement of his heart toward theirs called forth was rather a response of his personal efforts, than one dictated by their own will and conscience. It excited action, but not spontaneous, independent action. This did not satisfy him. He wished to make them act from strictly moral motives.

"But he conceived—and justly—that their intellectual training was to be looked on as part of their moral training. Whatever increases our knowledge of things as they are, leads to the appreciation of the

[1] benches

truth; for truth, in the widest sense of the term, is this knowledge. But the acquisition of knowledge, as requiring mental effort, and therefore exercising the active powers, necessarily increases the capacity to form judgments on moral questions; so that, in proportion as you cultivate the intellect, you must train the moral powers which are to carry its decisions into effect. Moral and intellectual education must consequently, in the formation of the human being, proceed together, the one stimulating and maintaining the action of the other. Pestalozzi, therefore, instructed as well as educated, and indeed educated by means of instruction. In carrying out this object, he proceeded from the near, the practical, the actual, to the remote, the abstract, and the ideal."

"One of the aspects in which he has been brought before us—and it deserves every consideration—is that of an earnest, self-sacrificing, enthusiastic philanthropist, endowed with what Richter calls 'an almighty love,' of which the first and last thought was, how he might raise the debased and suffering among his countrymen to a higher level of happiness and knowledge, by bestowing upon them the blessings of education. It is right that he should be thus exhibited to the world; for never did any man better deserve to be enrolled in the noble army of martyrs who have died that others might live, than Pestalozzi. To call him the Howard of educational philanthropists, is only doing scant justice to his devoted character, and underestimates rather than overestimates the man.

"Another aspect in which Pestalozzi is sometimes presented to us is that of an unhandy, unpractical, dreamy theorist; whose views were ever extending beyond the compass of his control; who, like the *djinn* of the Eastern story, called into being forces which mastered instead of obeying him; whose 'unrivaled incapacity for governing' (this is his own confession) made him the victim of circumstances; who was utterly wanting in worldly wisdom; who, knowing man, did not know *men;* and who, therefore, is to be set down as one who promised much more than he performed. It is impossible to deny that there is substantial truth in such a representation; but this only increases the wonder that, in spite of his disqualifications, he accomplished so much. It is still true that his awakening voice, calling for reform in education, was responded to by hundreds of earnest intelligent men, who placed themselves under his banner, and were proud to follow whither the Luther of educational reform wished to lead them. A third view of Pestalozzi presents him to us as merely interested about elementary education—and this appears to many who are engaged in teaching what are called higher subjects a matter in which they have little or no concern. Those, however, who thus look down on Pestalozzi's work, only show, by their indifference, a profound want both of self-knowledge and of a knowledge of his principles and his purpose. Elementary education, in the sense in which Pestalozzi understands it, is, or ought to be, the concern of every teacher, whatever his especial subject, and whatever the age of his pupils; and when he sees that elementary education is only another expression for the forming of the character and mind of the child, he must acknowledge that this object comes properly within the sphere of his labors, and deserves, on every ground, his thoughtful attention.

"In spite, then, of Pestalozzi's patent disqualifications in many respects for the task he undertook; in spite of his ignorance of even common subjects (for he spoke, read, wrote, and ciphered badly, and knew next to nothing of classics or science); in spite of his want of worldly wisdom, of any comprehensive and exact knowledge of men and of things; in spite of his being merely an elementary teacher, —through the force of his all-conquering love, the nobility of his heart, the resistless energy of his enthusiasm, his firm grasp of a few first principles, his eloquent exposition of them in words, his resolute manifestation of them in deeds, he stands forth among educational reformers as the man whose influence on education is wider, deeper, more penetrating, than that of all the rest—the prophet and the sovereign of the domain in which he lived and labored."

Characterization

The materials for "Leonard and Gertrude" were gathered during long years of suffering and disappointment; and the work itself was the result of an intense love, which made the cause of the poor and friendless its own. He had already failed in a practical attempt to relieve the unfortunate, but he had obtained a deeper insight into the causes which perpetuated the evils of society. With a bleeding heart, he had seen that poverty, unless counterbalanced by a healthy culture of the mind and soul, was generally accompanied by moral and physical wretchedness; by intemperance, ignorance, and superstition. He was also able to trace part of the sufferings of the poor to the selfishness and hardness of the rich, many of whom derived a shameful profit from the improvidence of their unfortunate brethren. He had also, occasionally, seen in the cottages of the poor cheerfulness, peace, and comfort; and this spirit he had, with great certainty, always traced to the influence of a sound home education, conducted by an intelligent mother.

The characters of this tale, far from engaging in brilliant or dazzling actions, are great in their very simplicity and truth to nature. The principal ones are: Gertrude, a pattern of a good and intelligent wife and mother—an educator who tries to fulfill the duties of her office to their fullest extent, without troubling her head with plans of emancipation; Leonard, her husband, who, however, plays only a secondary part; Arner, the lord of the manor, who tries to effect a thorough reform in the administration of the parish intrusted to his care; Ernst, a worthy clergyman, who assists Arner, and works on the hearts and convictions, and not on the fears and prejudices, of his parishioners; Glülphy, the schoolmaster, in whose teaching and discipline Pestalozzi embodies some of the favorite ideas of education which he afterward matured; Hummel, the bailiff, chief magistrate and judge of the village—the personification of wickedness, avarice and pride—a man with a heart hardened through many years of mismanagement and crime; and Rudi, one of the victims of the bailiff, whose story forms some of the most affecting chapters of the book.

Domestic education and social reform were considered so important by Pestalozzi, that, after completing "Leonard and Gertrude," he wrote another treatise upon these subjects, entitled "Christopher and Eliza," which was published in 1782. In the preface to the first edition of this book, Pestalozzi remarks that it was written principally to supply a commentary to "Leonard and Gertrude," the moral lessons of which he wished to impress upon the convictions of the people. He concludes by saying: "I know it will appear tedious to mere novel readers, but I desire that it should be read in humble cottages, many of the inmates of which will find in it sentiments corresponding to their own experiences."

The personages who, during thirty evenings, are supposed to read and discuss as many chapters of "Leonard and Gertrude," are: Christopher, a wealthy and intelligent farmer; Eliza, his wife; Josiah, their servant; and Fritz, their son.

By a strange anomaly, which is in strong contrast with the usual order of things, Josiah is the principal speaker, and the one who deals most in abstruse reflections. Christopher is next in importance; while Eliza only occasionally makes shrewd and sensible remarks, mostly upon moral and educational questions. Fritz is a silent listener, but, at the end of each conversation, is requested to sum up all the maxims which he has gathered from the story of the discussion. The little prodigy does this with such an amount of wisdom, originality, and wit, and in such flowing language, that one is astonished at the precocity of even an imaginary child.

HERMANN KRÜSI.

Gertrude at Home

(From "Leonard and Gertrude")

There lived in Bonnal a mason. He was called Leonard, and his wife, Gertrude. He had seven children, and some property; but he had this fault—that he often let himself be tempted to the tavern. When he was once seated there he behaved like a madman, and was often led from drinking to gaming, and thus deprived of the produce of his labor. Whenever this had happened at night Leonard repented in the morning; for, when he saw his wife and children wanting bread, it went so to his heart that he trembled and cast down his eyes to conceal his tears.

Gertrude was the best wife in the village; but she and her blooming children were in danger of being robbed of their father and driven from their home, and of sinking into the greatest misery, because Leonard would not let wine alone.

Gertrude saw the approaching danger, and felt it most keenly. When she fetched grass from the meadow, when she took hay from the loft, when she set away the milk in her clean pans, whatever she was doing, she was tormented by the thought that her meadow, her haystack, and her little hut, might soon be taken away from her. When her children were standing around her, or sitting in her lap, her anguish was still greater, and the tears streamed down her cheeks.

Hitherto, however, she had been able to conceal this silent weeping from her children; but, on Wednesday before Easter, when she had waited long, and her husband did not come home, her grief overcame her, and the children saw her tears. "O mother!" exclaimed they, "you are weeping," and they pressed closer to her. Sorrow and anxiety were on every countenance. With deep sobs, heavy downcast looks, and silent tears the children surrounded the mother, and even the baby in her arms betrayed a feeling of pain hitherto unknown. All this quite broke her heart. Her anguish burst out in a loud cry, and all the children wept with her, and there was a sound of lamentation as Leonard opened the door.

Gertrude, who lay with her face on the bed, heard not the opening of the door nor the entrance of the father; neither did the children perceive him, for they saw only their weeping mother. Thus did Leonard find them.

God in heaven sees the tears of the wretched, and puts a limit to their grief. The mercy of God brought Leonard to witness this scene, which pierced his soul. The paleness of death was on his countenance, and he could scarcely articulate, "Lord Jesus, what is this!" Then the mother saw him for the first time, the children looked up, and their loud expressions of grief were hushed.

"Tell me, Gertrude," said he, "what is this dreadful trouble in which I find thee?"

"Oh, my dear," answered she, "heavy cares press upon my heart, and when thou art away, sorrow preys more keenly upon me."

"Gertrude," said Leonard, "I know why thou weepest, wretch that I am!"

Then Gertrude sent away the children, collected all her strength, and took courage to urge him not to bring any further trouble and misery upon his children. She was pious, and trusted in God; and before she spoke, she prayed silently for her husband and children; her heart was comforted, and she said: "Leonard, trust in the mercy of God, and take courage to do nothing but what is right."

"O Gertrude, Gertrude!" exclaimed Leonard, and his tears fell in torrents.

"Oh, take courage, and trust in thy Father in heaven, and all will be better with thee. It goes to my heart to make thee weep. I would gladly keep every trouble from thee. Thou knowest that, by thy side, I could be content with bread and water, and the still midnight is often to me an hour of cheerful labor for thee and the children. But, if I concealed from thee my anxiety lest I be separated from thee and these little ones, I should be no mother to them, nor true to thee. Our children are yet full of gratitude and love toward us; but if we do not continue to act as parents, their love and tenderness must needs decrease; and only think what thou wouldst feel if Nicolas had no longer a home, and must go out to service; if he and all these dear children should become poor through our fault—should cease to thank us, and begin to weep for us, their parents. Leonard, couldst thou bear to see thy children driven out of doors to seek their bread at another's table? Oh! it would kill me." So spoke Gertrude, and the tears fell down her cheeks.

Leonard, not less affected, cried: "What shall I do, miserable creature that I am? What can I do? I am more wretched than thou knowest. O Gertrude, Gertrude!" He was again silent, and wrung his hands.

"O my dear husband, do not distrust God's mercy! Whatever it be, speak, that we may consult together and comfort each other."

. . . .

Gertrude was alone with her children. The events of the week and thoughts of the approaching festival filled her heart. In thoughtful silence she prepared the supper, took from the closet the Sunday clothes for the family, and laid them out ready for the morrow. When she had completed her work she assembled her children around the table to pray with them. It was her custom on Saturdays, at the hour of evening prayer, to remind them of their faults and of such occurrences as were peculiarly calculated to interest and please them. This day she remembered, especially, the loving kindness of God toward her during the past week; and she wished, as far as possible, to impress deeply on the minds of the children the tokens which they had received of the goodness and mercy of God.

The children sat round her in silence, with their little hands folded for prayer, and the mother began thus:

"Children, I have good news to tell you. Your dear father has had very excellent work given to him this week, by which he will earn much more than he could before; and we may hope, my children, to eat our bread with less care and sorrow in future. Give thanks, therefore, unto God, our loving Father in heaven, for his goodness toward us. Remember often the old times when I was obliged, with care and anxiety, to portion out to you every mouthful of bread. Oh, it grieved my heart that many a time I could not give you enough. But our heavenly Father knew that it would be better for you, my dears, to be accustomed to poverty and patience, and learn to conquer your own desires, than to live in plenty. Oh, my children, remember, as long as you live, our days of poverty and the distress and sorrow we have endured, and if our condition is improved, henceforth be mindful of those who suffer even as you have. Will you do so?"

"Oh, yes, dear mother, we will," replied the children.

"Well, then, Nicolas, whom dost thou know that is suffering most from hunger?"

"It is little Rudi," said Nicolas. "He is almost starving. He eats grass from the ground."

"Wouldst thou like to give him thy supper now and then?"

"Oh, yes, mother. May I to-morrow?"

"Certainly, thou mayest," said the mother. Then turning to Betti, she asked: "And thou—to whom wouldst thou give thy supper?"

Betti named some poor child, and so did the other children as each was asked in turn, all being delighted in anticipation of the pleasure they would bestow. After some moments the mother remarked: "That is enough, my children. Now see what beautiful presents his lordship Arner has made you."

"Oh! the bright pennies! Will you show them to us?" cried the children.

"Yes, after prayers," said Gertrude; and the children shouted with joy.

"You are noisy, my children," chided the mother. "If something good comes to you, always think of God, the giver. I rejoice with you; but, when people are loud and violent in their joy or sorrow, peace and evenness of temper are lost. You see, children, when you thank your father for something, you do not make much noise; you fall upon his neck silently, and when you really feel it in your hearts, the tears come to your eyes. So it should be toward God. If you feel very much joy on account of the good he does you, and at the same time it touches your heart, I am sure you will not say many words or make much noise, but the tears will come to your eyes in thinking how good your heavenly Father is."

Gertrude, after giving more advice to her children, changed the subject of conversation by asking: "But, my dears, how has your conduct been this week?" The children looked at each other, but said nothing.

"Anne, hast thou been a good girl this week?" asked Gertrude.

"No, mother; thou knowest what I did with my little brother," replied Anne.

"Oh, yes, Anne. The poor child might have been very much injured. Babes left in that way have sometimes died. Besides, only think, if thou wast shut up by thyself in a room, and left to cry and to suffer thirst and hunger. Really, Anne, I should not be able to leave this house for a moment if I were not so sure that thou wouldst take care of the baby."

"Trust me, dear mother; I will not leave him again for a single moment," pleaded Anne.

"Well, I hope thou wilt not give me another such fright. Nicolas, how has it been with thee this week?"

"I know of nothing wrong," he quickly answered.

"Hast thou forgotten that thou didst throw down Kate last Monday?" said the mother.

"I did not do it on purpose, mother."

"To be sure thou didst not. To do such a thing on purpose would be wicked, indeed. Art thou not ashamed to make such an excuse?"

"I am sorry for it. I will be more careful," said Nicolas.

"Be sure not to forget it, my dear. Believe me, thy carelessness will certainly make thee unhappy. Well, Betti, how hast thou behaved this week?"

"I am sure I cannot think of anything wrong, mother," replied she.

"Art thou quite sure, Betti?"

"I am, indeed, mother, as nearly as I can recollect. I should not mind telling it if I knew."

"It is very odd that even when thou hast nothing to tell, thou answerest with as many words as another who has a great deal to say."

"Well, what have I said then?" asked Betti.

"Thou hast said nothing, I know, but thou hast given a long answer. We have told thee a thousand times that thou art too forward. Thou never thinkest what thou shouldst say, and yet thou art always talking." Gertrude here brought to Betti's recollection a piece of forwardness—giving an envious neighbor some information which brought her father into trouble.

"I am very sorry for it," replied Betti; "but neither thou nor father had said a word about not wishing me to tell of it."

"Then it will be necessary that to whatever we say in this room we must always add: Now, this is a thing which Betti may gossip about at the neighbors' door, and at the fountain; but not this, and this," replied Gertrude.

"I do beg thy pardon, mother; I did not mean it so."

"Thou hast been told once for all, that thou art not to talk of anything which is no business of thine; but it is all in vain. There is no getting thee out of that habit, except by severe means; and the very first time I overtake thee in idle gossip, I shall make use of the rod."

The tears burst from poor Betti's eyes when her mother mentioned the rod. Gertrude saw it and said: "The greatest mischief, Betti, often arises out of idle gossip, and thou must be cured of that fault."

Thus the mother discoursed with them all. Afterward, Nicolas repeated the Saturday evening prayer which Gertrude had taught him: "Dear Father in heaven, thou art always kind to men on earth. From thee all things come that our dear father and mother give us. . . . Dear Father, we that are sitting here and praying together, are brothers and sisters; therefore, we will be kind to each other, and do to each other no harm, but all the good we can. We elder ones will take care of the younger ones with all faithfulness and diligence, that our dear father and mother may go comfortably about their work for our bread. Alas! this is all we can do for them, for all the trouble and expense they have for our sakes. Reward them, O Father in heaven, for all they do for us, and make us obedient unto their commands, that we may remain dear unto them to the end of their lives."

Here Nicolas was to stop, and they prayed according to what had happened through the week, as follows: "We thank thee, O heavenly Father, that thou hast lightened the heavy burden of our parents, and the care for the bread for themselves and their children, and hast blessed our dear father with good and profitable employment. We thank thee that our lord Arner with paternal affection protects, comforts, and assists us in all our misery and distress. We thank thee for all the blessings which thou hast bestowed on us through him."

Then the mother taught Betti to pray in this manner: "Forgive me, O my God, my besetting sin, and teach me to bridle my tongue; to be silent when I ought not to speak, and to answer considerately and directly when I am asked."

And Nicolas thus: "Preserve me, O Father, from all hastiness, and teach me to be on my guard, and to see what I do, and who is about me."

And Anne: "I am sorry, good God, for leaving my dear little brother so thoughtlessly, and so frightening my dear, good mother. I will not do it again in all my life. Forgive me, I pray thee, O God."

The mother then said: "The Lord be with you; the Lord bless you; the Lord let the light of his countenance shine upon you and be merciful unto you."

After this, mother and children sat yet a little while in that solemn silence which a true prayer always imposes.

Betti interrupted this silence: "Wilt thou show us the new pennies?" said she to her mother.

"I will," replied the mother; "but thou art always the first to speak, Betti."

Nicolas now jumped from his seat, and pushed forward that he might be nearer the candle and see the new pennies better, and in doing so hurt the baby, so that he began to cry.

Then said the mother: "Nicolas, this is very bad. Thou didst promise, not more than a quarter of an hour ago, that thou wouldst be more careful, and now see what thou hast done."

"O mother," said Nicolas, "I am very sorry for it. It shall not happen any more."

"That is what thou didst just now promise to God Almighty, and yet thou hast been careless again," said the mother. "Thou shalt go to bed without thy supper."

Thus saying, she led him away into the chamber. His brothers and sisters all stood about grieved, for they were sorry that poor Nicolas should go to bed without his supper. "What a pity it is that you will not be governed by kindness," said the mother, when she came back.

"Let him come out again for once," begged the children.

"No, my dears; he must be cured of his thoughtless habits," was the mother's reply.

"Well, then, we will not see the pennies till to-morrow, that he may see them with us," said Anne.

"Well spoken, Anne," answered the mother; "he shall see them with you."

After this she gave the children their supper, and then led them to the chamber where Nicolas was still crying.

"Be very careful another time, my dear Nicolas," said the mother to him.

Nicolas answered: "Pray forgive, dear, dear mother! do forgive and kiss me!"

Gertrude kissed him, and a burning tear flowed down her cheek, when she said to him: "O Nicolas, try to become more careful."

Nicolas threw both his arms round her neck, and said: "O mother, forgive me."

Gertrude once more blessed her children, and then returned to her room, which was lighted by a small lamp.

She was now quite alone, and her heart was still in silent prayer, which inexpressibly moved her soul. The feeling of God's goodness, the hope of life everlasting, the sense of that internal joy and peace which dwells in those who trust in their Heavenly Father, all stirred her soul, and she fell on her knees, and a flood of tears flowed over her cheeks.

[The moral to be drawn from this lesson is contained in the following directions to parents in regard to their children:

First.—Observe the nature and propensities of your children, in order to be able to educate them according to their individual wants and talents.

Second.—Speak to them in a simple, intelligent manner, that your words and sentiments may be fully understood. A prayer from the heart, applied to circumstances, is better than a formal one mechanically repeated.

Third.—Do not content yourselves with preaching of love and charity; but try to make the children loving and charitable. Lead them to experience the pleasure of self-sacrifice, that they may better understand this crowning excellence of the human character.

Fourth.—Act as the mediator between your children and God; for they cannot appreciate his goodness and greatness. In order to be able to do this, become yourselves examples of love, truthfulness, and justice.

Fifth.—Be firm, and, at the same time, kind. Real love never overlooks faults: it corrects them. The ultimate gratitude of children is of more value than their temporary gratification.]

The School in Bonnal

(From "Leonard and Gertrude")

1. A Good School is Founded

Since the squire had returned from Cotton Meyer's, he had spent every moment he could spare from the lieutenant in consultation with him on the organization of a new school. They both came to the conclusion that a child is always well educated when he has learned to practice skillfully, orderly, and to the benefit of him and his, what is to be his future occupation.

This principal object of all education seemed to them at once the first requisite of a reasonable school for human beings. And they perceived that the lieutenant, and any person proposing to establish a good school for farmers' and factory children, must either himself know and understand what such children need to know and do in order to become capable farmers and factory workers; or, if he himself does not understand it, that he must inquire and learn about it, and have those at hand who do know and can show him.

They naturally thought first of Cotton Meyer himself, and immediately after this conversation and their meal they went to him.

"This is the man of whom I have said so much to you," said the squire to the lieutenant; and then, to Meyer, "and this is the gentleman who, I hope, will encourage you about your school."

Meyer did not understand; but the squire explained to him, saying that this was to be the schoolmaster of the village.

Meyer could not sufficiently wonder at this, and after a time he said, "If the gentleman is willing to take so much pains, we cannot thank him enough; but it will require time to become well acquainted with our condition and ways in the village."

Lieut. "I presume so; but one must begin some time or other; and I shall not regret any pains I take to examine, as thoroughly as possible, what is needed and what your children can properly learn, in order to be well fitted for their farming and manufacturing."

Meyer. "That will be an excellent beginning."

Lieut. "I do not know how else I ought to begin; and I shall take every opportunity of becoming acquainted with all manner of house and field labor, so as to learn correctly what training and what example your children need, in order to the right education for their vocation and circumstances."

Meyer's Mareieli was quite at home with the lieutenant. She showed him all about the house, and in the stables, what the children must do to learn to do in good order whatever was necessary for themselves and their parents; made them dig in the garden and throw earth hither and thither, to even the ground and improve its appearance, and adjust the edges; and to scatter fodder correctly. The more he saw, the more questions he asked; inquired how they measured hay, reckoned tithes, and kept account of the cotton manufacture; what was the difference in wages in the different kinds of cotton, and a hundred other things. These they explained to him as far as they could. Then they proposed to teach the children how to spin. But Mareieli said, "We take in some hundred *zentners* of yarn in a year, and I have never yet brought them to spin right well. And I cannot complain about it, either, for they have to do a good deal in the fields and about the cattle. But if you desire to see a good arrangement for the matter of spinning, you must go to see the mason's wife. With her there is something to be seen on that point; but not with us."

Lieut. "Is not the mason's wife, of whom you speak, named Gertrude?"

Mareieli. "It seems that you know her already?"

Lieut. "No; but the squire has proposed to go directly from you to her."

Mar. "Well; then you will see that I told you correctly."

2. A Good School is the Foundation of all Good Fortune

Gertrude's room was so full, when they entered, that they could scarcely pass between the wheels. Gertrude, who had not expected to see any strangers, told the children as the door opened to get up and make room. But the squire would not let one of them move, but gave his hand first to the pastor and then to the lieutenant, to lead them behind the children, next to the wall, to Gertrude's table.

You could not believe how much the scene delighted these gentlemen. What they had seen with Cotton Meyer seemed nothing, in comparison.

And very naturally. Order and comfort about a rich man do not surprise. We think hundreds of others do not do so well because they have not money. But the happiness and comfort in a poor hut, showing so unanswerably that everybody in the world could be comfortable if they could maintain good order, and were well brought up—this astonishes a well-disposed mind almost beyond power of expression.

But the gentlemen had a whole room full of such children, in the full enjoyment of such blessings, before their eyes. The squire seemed for a time to be seeing the picture of the firstborn of his future better-taught people, as if in a dream; and the falcon eyes of the lieutenant glanced hither and thither like lightning, from child to child, from hand to hand, from work to work, from eye to eye. The more he saw, the fuller did his heart grow with the thought, "She has done, and completely, what we seek; the school which we look for is in her room."

The room was for a time as still as death. The gentlemen could do nothing but gaze and gaze, and be silent. But Gertrude's heart beat at the stillness and at the marks of respect which the lieutenant showed to her during it, and which bordered on reverence. The children, however, spun away briskly, and laughed out of their eyes to each other; for they perceived that the gentlemen were there on their account, and to see their work.

The lieutenant's first words to Gertrude were, "Do these children all belong to you, mistress?"

"No," said Gertrude, "they are not all mine;" and she then pointed out, one after another, which were hers and which were Rudi's.

"Think of it, lieutenant," said the pastor; "these children who belong to Rudi could not spin one thread four weeks ago."

The lieutenant looked at the pastor and at Gertrude and answered, "Is it possible!"

GERTRUDE. "That is not remarkable. A child will learn to spin right well in a couple of weeks. I have known children to learn in two days."

SQUIRE. "It is not that which I am wondering at in this room, but quite another thing. These children of other people, since the three or four weeks ago when Gertrude received them, have come to look so differently, that in truth I scarcely knew one of them. Living death and the extremest misery spoke from their faces; and these are so gone that no trace of them is left."

The lieutenant replied in French, "But what does she do to the children, then?"

SQUIRE. "God knows!"

PASTOR. "If you stay here all day, you hear no tone, nor see any shadow of anything particular. It seems always, and in everything she does, as if any other woman could do it; and certainly the commonest wife would never imagine that Gertrude was doing, or could do, anything she herself could not."

LIEUT. "You could not say more to raise her in my estimation. That is the culmination of art, where men think there is none at all. The loftiest is so simple that children and boys think they could do much more than that."

As the gentlemen conversed in French, the children began to look at each other and laugh. Heireli and the child who sat opposite to her made mouths to each other, as if to say, "Parlen, parlen, parlen."

Gertrude only nodded, and all was still in a moment. And then the lieutenant, seeing a book lying on every wheel, asked Gertrude what they were doing with them.

GER. "Oh, they learn out of them."

LIEUT. "But not while they are spinning?"

GER. "Certainly."

LIEUT. "I want to see that."

SQUIRE. "Yes; you must show us that, Gertrude."

GER. "Children, take up your books and learn."

CHILDREN. "Loud, as we did before?"

GER. "Yes, loud, as you did before; but right."

Then the children opened their books, and each laid the appointed page before him, and studied the lesson which had been set. But the wheels turned as before, although the children kept their eyes wholly on the books.

The lieutenant could not be satisfied with seeing, and desired her to show him everything relating to her management of the children, and what she taught them.

She would have excused herself, and said that it was nothing at all but what the gentlemen knew, and a thousand times better than she.

But the squire intimated to her to proceed. Then she told the children to close their books, and she taught them, by rote, a stanza from the song:

> "How beautiful the sunbeams' play,
> And how their soft and brilliant ray
> Delights and quickens all mankind—
> The eye, the brain, and all the mind!"

The third stanza, which they were then learning, reads thus:

> "The sun is set. And thus goes down,
> Before the Lord of heaven's frown,
> The loftiness and pride of men,
> And all is dusk and night again."

She repeated one line at a time, distinctly and slowly, and the children said it after her, just as slowly, and very distinctly, and did so over and over, until one said, "I know it now." Then she let that one repeat the stanza alone; and when he knew every syllable, she permitted him to repeat it to the others, and them to repeat after him, until they knew it. Then she began with them all three of the stanzas, of which they had already learned the first two. And then she showed the gentlemen how she taught them arithmetic, and her mode was the simplest and most practical that can be imagined.

But of that I shall speak again in another place.

3. Recruiting Officer's Doings

The lieutenant was every moment more convinced that this was the right instruction for his school; but he was also convinced that he needed a woman like this, if the giving it was to be not merely possible, but actual.

A Prussian recruiting officer does not contrive so many means of getting into the service a fellow who comes up to the standard as the lieutenant contrived to decoy into his trap this woman, who came up to his standard in school teaching.

"But, mistress," he began, "could not the arrangements in your room here be introduced into a school?"

She thought a moment, and replied, "I don't know. But it seems as if what is possible with ten children is possible with forty. But it would require much; and I do not believe that it would be easy to find a schoolmaster who would permit such an arrangement in his school."

LIEUT. "But if you knew of one who desired to introduce it, would you help him?"

GER. (*Laughing.*) "Yes, indeed; as much as I could."

LIEUT. "And if I am he?"

GER. "Are what?"

LIEUT. "The schoolmaster, who would be glad to organize such a school as you have in your room."

Ger. "You are no schoolmaster."

Lieut. "Yes, I am. Ask the gentlemen."

Ger. "Yes, perhaps, in a city, and in something of which we know neither *gigs* nor *gags*."

Lieut. "No; but, honestly, in a village."

Ger. (*Pointing to the wheels.*) "Of such children?"

Lieut. "Yes, of such children."

Ger. "It is a long way from me to the place where schoolmasters for such children look like you."

Lieut. "Not so far."

Ger. "I think it is."

Lieut. "But you will help me, if I undertake to organize my school in that way?"

Ger. "If it is far away, I will not go with you."

Lieut. "I shall remain here."

Ger. "And keep school?"

Lieut. "Yes."

Ger. "Here in the room?"

Lieut. "No; in the schoolroom."

Ger. "You would be sorry if you should be taken at your word."

Lieut. "But you still more if you should have to help me."

Ger. "I will help you—and I say so three times, if you are our schoolmaster."

Here he and the other gentlemen began to laugh; and the squire said, "Yes, Gertrude; he is certainly your schoolmaster."

This perplexed her. She blushed and did not know what to say.

Lieut. "What makes you so silent?"

Ger. "I think it would have been well if I had been silent for a quarter of an hour back."

Lieut. "Why?"

Ger. "How can I help you, if you are a schoolmaster?"

Lieut. "You are looking for excuses; but I shall not let you go."

Ger. "I beg of you."

Lieut. "It will be of no use; if you had promised to marry me, you must abide by the promise."

Ger. "No, indeed!"

Lieut. "Yes, indeed!"

Ger. "It is out of the question."

Squire. "If there is anything which you know, Gertrude, do it as well as you can; he will not ask anything more; but, whatever you do to help him, you will do to help me."

Ger. "I will, very willingly; but you see my room full of children, and how I am tied down. But with regard to advice and help in matters relating to work which a gentleman naturally cannot understand, I know a woman who understands them much better than I; and she can do whatever I cannot."

Squire. "Arrange it as you can; but give him your hand on the bargain."

4. A Proud Schoolmaster

The new condition of affairs raised the courage of the pastor, who had been almost in the state of a slave under the old squire, and his acquaintance with the son contributed much toward accomplishing his ancient plans. On the next Sunday he explained to the people some chapters of the Bible, and, at the end of the service, called for whatever else was to be done. Then the squire took the lieutenant by the hand, and told him to say himself to the congregation what he desired to do for their children.

The lieutenant arose, bowed to the squire, the pastor, and the congregation, took off his hat, leaned on his stick, and said: "I have been brought up with a nobleman, and am myself a nobleman; but I am not for that reason ashamed to serve God and my fellow-men in the situation to which Providence calls me; and I thank my dear parents, now under the ground, for the good education they gave me, and which enables me now to put your school on such a footing that, if God will, your children shall all their lives be respected for having attended it. But it is not my business to make long speeches and sermons;

but if it please God, I will begin my school instruction to-morrow, and then everything will be made plain. Only, I should say that each child should bring his work, whether sewing or spinning cotton, or whatever it be, and the instruments for the same, until the squire shall purchase such for the school."

"And what will he do with spinning-wheels in the school?" said men and women to each other in all their seats, and one, behind him, so loud that he heard it.

The lieutenant turned around, and said aloud, "Nothing, except to make the children learn from one another how to read and cipher."

This the farmers could not get into their heads, how the scholars could learn from one another how to read and cipher; and many of them said, at the church door, "It will be with him as it was with the madder plants, and the beautiful sheep that the old squire had brought from two hundred leagues away, and then let them die miserably at their fodder." But some older and experienced men said, "He does not look at all like the madder plants; and has not the appearance of a man that talks carelessly."

That evening the schoolmaster went into the schoolroom and nailed up, immediately opposite where he was going to sit, a beautiful engraving. This represented an old man, with a long white beard, who, with wrinkled brow and eyes wide open, lifted up his finger.

The squire and the pastor said, "What is that for?"

LIEUT. "He is to say to me, 'Glülphi, swear not, while you sit there before me.'"

They replied, "Then we will not pull him down; he fills too important a place."

LIEUT. "I have been considering about it."

5. SCHOOL ORGANIZATION

Next morning the lieutenant began with his school. But I should not readily recommend any other schoolmaster to do what he did, and, after such a Sunday's proclamation, which was considered proud by everybody, to cause his school to be put in order by a farmer's wife. Still, if he be a Glülphi, he may do it, and it will not injure him; but I mean a real Glülphi, not a pretended one.

He let Gertrude put the children in order, just as if she had them at home.

She divided them according to age and the work they had, as they could best be put together, and placed her own and Rudi's children, who were already accustomed to her management, between others. In front, next to the table, she put those who did not know their A, B, C; next behind them, those who were to spell, then those who could read a little, and last those who could read fluently. Then, she put only three letters on the blackboard, and taught them to the first row. Whoever knew them best was to name them aloud, and the others were to repeat them after him. Then she changed the order of the letters, wrote them larger and smaller, and so left them before their eyes, all the morning. In like manner she wrote several letters for the scholars who were learning to spell, and those who could read a little had to spell with these letters. But these, as well as those who could read fluently, were to have their books always open by their spinning-wheels, and to repeat in a low tone of voice after one who read aloud. And every moment they were saying to that one, "Go on."

For the work, Gertrude had brought a woman with her named Margaret, who was to come to the school every day, as Gertrude had no time for that purpose.

This Margaret understood her business so well, that it would not be easy to find another like her. As soon as any child's hand or wheel was still she stepped up to him, and did not leave him until all was going on in good order again.

Most of the children carried home that evening so much work that their mothers did not believe they had done it alone. But many of the children answered, "Yes; it makes a difference whether Margaret shows us or you." And in like manner they praised the lieutenant, their schoolmaster.

In the afternoon he conducted the school, and Gertrude watched him, as he had her in the morning; and things went on so well that she said to him, "If I had known that I could finish all my work in helping you organize a school in a couple of hours, I should not have been so troubled on Thursday."

And he was himself pleased that things went so well.

That evening he gave to each of the children over seven years of age two pieces of paper, stitched together, and a couple of pens; and each child found his name written on the paper as beautifully as print. They could not look at it enough; and one after another asked him how it was to be used. He showed them, and wrote for them, for a quarter of an hour, such great letters that they looked as if they were printed. They would have watched him until morning, it seemed so beautiful to them, and they kept asking him if they were to learn to do the same.

He answered, "The better you learn to write the better I shall be pleased."

At dismissal he told them to take care of their paper, and to stick the points of their pens into rotten apples, for that was the very best way to keep them.

To this many of the children answered, "Yes, that would be nice, if we had any rotten apples; but it is winter now."

At this he laughed, and said, "If you have none, perhaps I can get them for you. The pastor's wife has certainly more than she wants."

But other children said, "No, no; we will get some, we have some yet."

6. School Organization—(*Continued*)

The children all ran home, in order quickly to show their beautiful writing to their parents; and they praised the schoolmaster and Margaret as much as they could. But many answered, "Yes, yes; new brooms sweep clean;" or some such singular expression, so that the children did not understand what they meant. This troubled the children, but still they did not cease to be pleased; and if their parents took no pleasure in their beautiful writing, they showed it to whomever they could, to their little brothers in the cradle and to the cat on the table, and took such care of it as they never in their lives had taken of anything before. And if the little brother reached out his hand, or the cat its paw, after it, they quickly drew it back, and said, "You must only look at it with your eyes; not touch it." Some of them put theirs away in the Bible. Others said they could not open such a big book, and put it in a chest among the most precious things they had. Their joy at going to school again was so great that the next morning many of them got up almost before day, and called their mothers to get them something to eat, so that they might get to school in good season.

On Friday, when the new writing-benches, which the squire had had made, were ready, their pleasure was very great. During the first lesson they would all sit together; but the lieutenant divided them into four classes, in order that there should not be too many of them, and that none should escape him, and none could make a single mark that he did not see.

In this study, also, most of the children did very well. Some learned so easily that it seemed to come to them by itself; and others, again, did well, because they had been more in the habit of doing things that required attention. Some, however, who had never had very much in their hands except the spoon with which they ate, found great difficulties. Some learned arithmetic very easily, who found writing very hard, and who held the pen as if their hands had been crippled. And there were some young loafers among them, who had all their lives scarcely done anything except run around the streets and fields, and who, nevertheless, learned everything far quicker than the rest.

So it is in the world. The most worthless fellows have the best natural endowments, and usually exceed in intelligence and capacity those who do not wander about so much, but sit at home at their work. And the arithmeticians among the farmers are usually to be found at the tavern.

The schoolmaster found these poor children generally much more capable, both in body and in mind, than he had expected.

For this there is also a good reason. Need and poverty make man more reflective and shrewd than riches and superfluity, and teach him to make the best use of everything that will bring him bread.

Glülphi made so much use of this fact that, in everything he did, and in almost every word he used in the school, he had the distinct purpose of making use of this basis laid down by Nature herself for the education of the poor and the countrymen. He was so strenuous even about the sweat of daily labor, that he claimed that whatever can be done for a man makes him useful, or reliable for skill, only so far as he has acquired his knowledge and skill in the sweat of his years of study; and that, where this is wanting, the art and knowledge of a man is like a mass of foam in the sea, which often looks, at a distance, like a rock rising out of the abyss, but which falls as soon as wind and wave attack it. Therefore, he said, in education, thorough and strict training to the vocation must necessarily precede all instruction by words.

He also maintained a close connection between this training to a vocation and training in manners, and asserted that the manners of every condition and trade, and even of the place or country of a man's abode, are so important to him that the happiness and peace of all his life depends on them. Training to good manners was also a chief object of his school organization. He would have his schoolroom as clean as a church. He would not even let a pane be out of the windows, or a nail be wrongly driven in the floor; and still less would he permit the children to throw anything on the floor, eat during study, or anything else of the kind. He preserved strict order, even in the least thing; and arranged so that, even in sitting down and rising up, the children would not hit against one another.

In muddy weather they were made to leave their shoes at the door, and sit in their stockings. And if their coats were muddy, they had to dry them in the sun or at the stove, as the case might be, and clean them. He himself cut their nails for many of them, and put the hair of most all the boys in good order; and whenever any one went from writing to working, he was obliged to wash his hands. They had, likewise, to rinse out their mouths at proper times, and take care of their teeth, and see that their breath was not foul. All these were things they had known nothing about.

When they came into the school and went out, they stepped up to Glülphi, one after the other, and said to him, "God be with you." Then he looked at them from head to foot, and looked at them so that they knew by his eye, without his saying a word, if there was anything wrong about them. But if this look did not serve to set things right, he spoke to them. When he saw that the parents were to blame for anything, he sent a message to them; and not uncommonly a child came home to its mother with the message, "The schoolmaster sends his respects to you, and asks whether you have no needles, or no thread; or if water is expensive with you," and the like.

Margaret acted as though she had been made on purpose to help him about these things. If a child's hair was not in good order, she placed it with its spinning wheel before her and braided it up while the child worked and studied. Most of them did not know how to fasten their shoes and stockings. All these things she showed them; adjusted their neckcloths and their aprons, if they were wrong, and, if she saw a hole in their clothes, took a needle and thread and mended it. Just before the close of the school, she went through the room, praising or blaming the children, as they had worked well, half well, or ill. Those who had done well went first up to the schoolmaster, and said to him, "God be with you," and he then held out his hand to them and replied, "God be with you, my dear child!" Those who had done only half well came then to him, and to them he said, "God be with you," without holding out his hand to them.

Lastly, those who had not done well at all had to leave the room before the others, without daring to go to him at all.

If one of them came too late, he found the door shut like the gate of a fortress that is closed. Whether then he cried or not made no difference; the master said to him, briefly, "Go home again, now; it will do you good to think a long time about it. Everything that is done must be done at the right time, or else it is as if it is not done at all."

. . . .

9. HE WHO SEPARATES THE PRINCIPLES OF ARITHMETIC AND OF SUSCEPTIBILITY TO TRUTH, PUTS ASUNDER WHAT GOD HAS JOINED

But how much soever he cared for the hearts of his children, he took as much care of their heads; and required that whatever went into them should be as clear and lucid as the silent moon in the heavens. He said, "Nothing can be called teaching which does not proceed on that principle; what is obscure, and deceives, and makes confused, is not teaching, but perverting the mind."

This perversion of the mind, in his children, he guarded against by teaching them, above all, to see and hear closely, and by laboriously and industriously teaching them habits of cool observation, and at the same time by strengthening in them the natural capacity which every man possesses. To this end he gave them much practice in arithmetic, in which he carried them so far, within a year, that they very soon yawned if any one began to talk to them about the wonderful puzzles with which Hartknopf's friends so easily astonished the rest of the people of the village.

So true it is that the way to lead men away from error is not to oppose their folly with words, but to destroy the spirit of it within them! To describe the night and the dark colors of its shadows does not help you to see; it is only by lighting a lamp that you can show what the night was; it is only by couching a cataract that you can show what the blindness has been. Correct seeing and correct hearing are the first steps towards living wisely; and arithmetic is the means by which nature guards us from error in our searches after truth—the basis of peace and prosperity, which children can secure for their manhood only by thoughtful and careful pursuit of their employments.

For such reasons, the lieutenant thought nothing so important as a right training of his children in arithmetic; and he said, "A man's mind will not proceed well unless it gains the habitude of apprehending and adhering to the truth, either by means of much experience or of arithmetical practice, which will in great part supply the place of that habitude."

But his methods of teaching them arithmetic are too extended to be given here.

10. A Sure Means against Mean and Lying Slanders

In this matter also he succeeded with the children as he desired; and it could not but happen that one who accomplished so much for them should become dear to many people. But it was far from being the case that all were satisfied with him. The chief charge against him was, that he was too proud for a schoolmaster, and would not talk with the people at all. He said one thing and another to defend himself, and tried to make them understand that he was using his time and his lungs for the children; but the farmers said that, notwithstanding all that, he might stop a moment or two when any one wanted to say something to him, and, if pride did not prevent him, he would.

All the children, to be sure, contradicted their parents in this, and said that he certainly was not proud; but they replied, "He may be good to you, and may be proud, nevertheless."

But the rainy weather, in the third week of his school-keeping, accomplished for him what the good children could not do, with all their talking.

It was an established principle in Bonnal, that an old bridge in front of the schoolhouse, which had been in a bad condition for twenty years, should not be rebuilt; and so, whenever it rained for two days together, the children had to get wetted almost to their knees to get to the school. But the first time that Glülphi found the street so deep in water he stood out in the street, in the rain, as soon as the children came, and lifted them, one after another, over the stream.

This looked very funny to a couple of men and their wives who lived just opposite the schoolhouse, and who were the very ones who had complained most that the schoolmaster's pride would scarcely let him say good-day or good-night to people. They found great pleasure in seeing him get wet through and through, in his red coat, and thought he would never keep at it a quarter of an hour, and expected every moment that he would call out to them to know whether nobody was coming to help him. But when he kept right on with his work, just as though not even a cat lived anywhere near him, to say nothing of a man, and was dripping wet, clothes and hair, and all over, and still showed no shadow of impatience, but kept carrying over one child after another, they began to say, behind their windows, "He must be a good-natured fool, after all, to keep it up so long, and we seem to have been mistaken about him. If he had been proud, he would certainly have stopped long ago."

At last they crept out of their holes and went out to him, and said: "We did not see, before, that you were taking so much trouble, or we would have come out to you sooner. Go home and dry yourself; we will carry the children over. We can bear the rain better than you. And, before school is out, we will bring a couple of planks, too, so that there shall be a bridge here, as there used to be."

This they did not *say* merely, but did it. Before eleven o'clock there was actually a bridge erected, so that after school the scholars could go dry-shod over the brook. And also the complaints about his pride ceased; for the two neighbors' wives, who had been the loudest in making them, now sang quite another song.

If this seems incredible to you, reader, make an experiment yourself, and stand out in the rain until you are dripping wet for the sake of other people's children, without being called on to do so, or receiving anything for it; and see if those people do not then willingly speak good of you, except in regard to something very evil, or something which they cannot see and understand to be otherwise than bad.

11. Foolish Words, and School Punishments

But it was not long before the people had something else to complain about, and, indeed, something worse than before. The Hartknopf party in the village, that is, discovered that the lieutenant was not a Christian, and began quietly to make good and simple people in the village believe it. One of the first to find comfort in this story, and to endeavor to propagate it, was the old schoolmaster. He could not endure the thought that all the children should so praise and love the new schoolmaster. As long as he had been schoolmaster they had hated him; and he had become so used to this, in thirty years, that he believed it must be so; and asserted that the children, not being able to understand what is good for them, naturally hate all discipline, and consequently all schoolmasters. But he did not make much progress with this theory; and he fancied people were going to tell him that the children loved their present schoolmaster because he was good to them.

This vexed him, for he could not endure all his life to have it flung at him that his own foolishness was the reason that the children did not love him, although it was the honest truth. If he observed the least thing which he disapproved, the first word was, "You are killing me, body and soul; you will bring me into my grave. If you did not deserve hell for any other reason, you deserve it on account of me;" and the like.

Such language, especially to children, does not cause good feeling; and they must have been much more than children to love a fool who spoke to them in that way at every moment. They knew whom they were dealing with, and when he was most enraged, they would say to each other, "When we kill again, and bring him some sausages and meat, we shall not go to hell any more, at least so long as he has any of them left to eat."

With the new schoolmaster the case was quite otherwise. His harshest reproofs to the children when they did wrong were, "That is not right," or "You are injuring yourself," or "In that way you will never arrive at any good," etc. Little as this was, it was effectual, because it was the truth.

Glülphi's punishments consisted mostly in exercises intended to help the faults which they were to punish. For instance, if a child was idle, he was made to carry stone for the guard-fence which the teacher was making some of the older boys construct, at the sand-meadow, or to cut firewood, etc. A forgetful one was made school-messenger, and for four or five days had to transact whatever business the teacher had in the village.

Even during his punishments he was kind to the children, and scarcely ever talked more with them than while punishing them. "Is it not better for you," he would often say to a careless one, "to learn to keep yourself attentive to what you do, than every moment to be forgetting something, and then to have to do everything over again?" Then the child would often throw himself upon him with tears, and, with his trembling hand in his, would reply, "Yes, dear schoolmaster." And he would then answer, "Good child. Don't cry, but learn better; and tell your father and mother to help you to overcome your carelessness, or your idleness."

Disobedience which was not carelessness he punished by not speaking publicly to such a child for three or four or five days, but only alone with him, intimating to him at the close of school to remain. Impertinence and impropriety he punished in the same way. Wickedness, however, and lying, he punished with the rod; and any child punished with the rod was not permitted during a whole week to join in the children's plays; and his name and his fault stood entered in the Register of Offences until he gave unmistakable evidence of improvement, when they were stricken out again.

So great was the difference between the old and the new organization of the school.

A Chapter from "Christopher and Eliza"

"That is my chapter, father," said Eliza, when Christopher had read the twelfth chapter of the book. "A pious mother, who herself teaches her children, seems to me to be the finest sight on earth."

"It is very different from any that we see in the school-room," said Josiah.

"I did not mean to say that schools are not good," interposed Eliza.

"Nor would I allow myself to think so," added Christopher.

"The schoolmaster's instruction will never reach children's hearts in the same way as the lessons their parents teach them," said Josiah; "and I am sure that in going to school there is not all the good that people fancy there is."

"I fear, Josiah," said Christopher, "that you are out of your sphere. We ought to thank God for all the good there is in the world, and as for our schools, we cannot be sufficiently thankful for them."

"Well spoken, master," answered Josiah. "It is well that there are schools; and God forbid that I should be ungrateful for any good that is done to us. Yet, I think he must be a fool who, having plenty at home, runs about begging; and that is the very thing which our villagers do, when they forget all the good lessons which they might teach their children at home, and send them every day to gather up the dry crumbs which are to be found in our miserable schools. I am sure that is not quite as it ought to be."

"Nor is it quite as you have put it," said Christopher.

"Nay, master," continued Josiah; "only look it in the face, and you will see it the same as I do. What parents can teach their children is always what they most need in life; and it is a pity that parents should neglect this, by trusting in the words which the schoolmaster makes them learn by heart. It is very true they may be good and wise words, and have an excellent meaning to them; but, after all, they are only words, and, coming from the mouth of a stranger, they do not come half so near home as a father's or a mother's words."

"I cannot see what you aim at, Josiah," said Christopher.

"Look, master. The great point in bringing up a child is that he should be well trained for his own home. He must learn to know and use those things on which his bread and happiness will depend through life; and it seems to me very plain that fathers and mothers can teach that much better at home than any schoolmaster can in his school. No doubt the schoolmaster tells the children a great many things that are right and good; but they are never worth as much from his mouth as from that of an upright father or a pious mother.

"The schoolmaster, for instance, will tell the child to fear God, and honor his father and mother, for such is the word of God; but the child understands little of what he says, and generally forgets it before he comes home. But, if at home his father gives him milk and bread, and his mother denies herself a morsel, that she may give it to him, the child feels and understands that he ought to honor his father and mother, who are so kind to him; and he will not forget his father's words, when he tells him that such is the word of God. In the same way, if the child is told at school to be merciful, and to love his neighbor as himself, he learns the text by heart, and, perhaps, thinks of it for a few days, till the nice words slip from his memory.

"At home, he sees a poor neighbor's wife, calling upon his mother, lamenting over her misery, her hunger, and nakedness; he sees her pale countenance, her emaciated and trembling figure —the very image of wretchedness; his heart throbs, his tears flow; he lifts up his eyes full of grief and anxiety to his mother, as if he were himself starving; he sees his mother bring refreshments for the poor sufferer, in whose looks the child now reads comfort and reviving hope; his anguish ceases; his tears flow no longer; he approaches her with a smiling face; the mother's gift is received with sobs of gratitude, which again draw tears to the child's eye. Here he learns what it is to be merciful, and to love one's neighbor. He learns it without the aid of words, by the real fact; he sees mercy instead of learning words about mercy."

To this Christopher replied: "I must own I begin to think that too much value is put upon the schoolmaster's teaching."

"Of course," said Josiah, "if you send your sheep up into the mountains, you rely upon their being well cared for by the shepherd, who is paid for doing it, and you do not think of running after them. It is just the same thing with the school, with this difference: it is easy to get in pastures better food than can be found in stables, but it is not easy to find a school in which the children are better taught than they might be at home. The parents' teaching is the kernel of wisdom, and the schoolmaster's business is only to make a husk over it, and even then it is a chance if it turn out well."

"Why, you make one's brain whirl," said Eliza. "I think I see now what you are after. I fancy many a poor ignorant mother, who now sends her children to school without thinking anything about it, merely because it is the custom to do so, would be very glad to be taught better."

"There is yet another part to the story," said Josiah. "If the children must be sent to school, the schoolmaster should be an open-hearted, affectionate, and kind man, who would be like a father to the children; a man made to open children's hearts and mouths, and draw forth their ideas. In most schools, however, it is just the contrary. The master seems to shut their hearts and mouths, and bury their common sense. This is the reason why healthy and cheerful children, whose hearts are full of joy and gladness, hardly ever like the school; while stupid dunces, who have no pleasure with other children, are the bright ornaments there. If there is a boy among them who has too much good sense to keep his eyes for hours fixed on a dozen letters which he hates; or a merry girl, who, while the schoolmaster discourses on spiritual life, plays with her little hands all sorts of temporal fun under the desk, the master, in his wisdom, declares these the goats who care not for their everlasting salvation."

Thus spoke the good Josiah in the overflowing of his zeal against the nonsense of the village schools, and his master and mistress gave more and more attention to what he said.

After discussing the subject more fully, the father turned to Fritz and said, " Well, Fritz, what have you gathered from this evening's conversation ? "

" That men are foolish to ask alms outside the house, when there is abundance within," answered Fritz.

" What else ? "

" That the country children ought to be educated for the field, the barn, the house, and not merely for talk."

" What more ? " asked Christopher.

" That school knowledge is to many a child like unaccustomed food upon which he will not thrive."

" Is that all ? " said his father.

" That a father's instruction is like the kernel, and the schoolmaster's, at most, like a shell protecting it, and that the common people need common sense most."

" Anything more ? "

" That the school ought to be an auxiliary to the nursery, where father and mother plant the germs of all virtue and all knowledge."

. . . .

" It has always appeared to me that cunning is not true wisdom, for only honest men can possess that," said Christopher.

" That is so," said Josiah. " True wisdom proceeds from love, and brings blessing and peace to its owner and to all those who depend on him. Cunning proceeds from selfishness and want of love, and brings trouble and suffering upon a man who acts under its influence, and to those whom he rules or serves. If you are anxious to observe the effects of such cunning in a man, go to the poor whom he uses as his tools, and they will tell you how small is his wisdom. One will tell you that he has to praise his lean ox as a fat one, in order to induce some greenhorn to buy; another has to lure a stranger into his net. They will also tell you that they have to speak highly of his honor and virtue, even when their hearts bleed from his injustice. They must cover his sins and deny his cruelty, at least within his hearing and knowledge.

"But he who indulges in such tricks, or incites others to them, feels flattered if people talk of his keen understanding, merely because he practices his wit day and night in matters with which honest people will have nothing to do. On the other hand, he shows himself often quite foolish and inexperienced in important matters with which honest men are thoroughly familiar. No scoundrel has ever been able to keep that admixture of folly and madness which characterizes vice always under his control, so that it will not ooze out when he least expects it."

. . . .

"What do you think is the reason that men live so unwisely till their last hour comes?" asked Eliza.

"The neglect of home, without doubt," answered Josiah. "Man must have for his heart a hearth, where the fire never goes out; there he must get strength, rest, and refreshment. After leaving his home, he goes to his work with new courage. Love of mankind is not nurtured in the barren regions of a vagabond life; it requires fostering care in the sanctuary of home, as the noblest and tenderest plants require the greatest care at the hand of the gardener. But when the tender plant of home-grown virtue has taken root, let it be transferred to any soil, and it will thrive. If one behaves well as father, mother, son, you may trust him anywhere, although he may change his relations; since the propelling motive of his actions will always be the same, whether you call it duty, obedience, or tender affection."

. . . .

"Heed my words, Fritz," said Eliza, "and do not scoff at anything which is sacred to thy fellow-men, and necessary to their peace and welfare; which protects good order in society, and renders the last hours of man serene."

"Yes, my son," added Christopher, "you must fear God, love

your parents, and honor your superiors, if you would wish to fare well on earth."

"Do so, my dear boy, with an innocent and simple heart," said Josiah. "Yet never be afraid to search after truth and to stand by it; to oppose him who uses arbitrary power, and wishes to circumvent you with lies in order to effect wrong. Least of all, do not suffer yourself to be blinded by priests, when, under the name of religion, you see them only intent on furthering their own interests. When they teach you immortality, then listen to them in faith and gratitude, for it is God's word. If you hope to be pious, abhor the man who weakens the simple faith of the people in immortality, and ridicules the word of God in his intercourse with the poor and helpless, who are most in want of it. Such a man is like him who despises bread and feeds on husks. Oh, flee from the insane one, who scoffs at that which refreshes and comforts so many thousands of thy brethren. The hope of immortality lies deep in the inmost soul, and he who teaches it teaches the word of God."

"The greatest thing that religion can give us is strength for all that is good and useful," said Christopher. "Religion ought to give me the conviction that on leaving earth I leave nothing, that my soul absorbs its cares, and that my hopes reach beyond this temporal abode; but for this very reason it must enable me to use my strength for the benefit of my family and my race.

"Religion does not call men away from the duties of this earth, but it gives them strength to the last moment to take care of what has been intrusted to them. Did not Christ, when on the cross, show his care for his earthly mother by recommending her to the care of his favorite disciple? I may be misunderstood, and perhaps do not express accurately my idea, when I say that man is not made for religion, but religion for man. Religion is an essence which takes possession of a man's soul, and leads him away from his own carnal tendencies; it consists rather in powers than in words; it is a storehouse full of good instruments, rather than a saloon filled with charming and fascinating images. That which presents itself to men as an idol with which to make a constant display, is not religion.

"The way to heaven is by fulfilling all our duties on earth; and the neglect of these can only be retrieved to some extent while man is well and active, but never on a sick-bed at the approach of death. Our forefathers were wiser in this respect than we. One proof of this is that they generally disposed of their property while still in health. Not only were wife and children remembered, but also servants, institutions, the poor, and everything which the dictates of humanity as well as religion had inspired in their hearts. In our days it is not so. Death is allowed to surprise many, and they are unable to do what they intended for their family and fellow-men. We often hear people say, 'If father or mother had disposed of this or the other matter, we should have been spared much care and vexation.' It is but a shallow excuse that the departed ones were so occupied with spiritual things that worldly ones were forgotten."

. . . .

"I have known people," said Christopher, "who, unsolicited, have promised to take charge of children soon to become orphans. I have also seen this sacred duty neglected. To understand these seeming contradictions, we must assume that all men have moments in which they make good resolutions; but, unless a man is thoroughly firm and honest, these good resolutions are transitory as the light of the sun when it rises in the splendor of the morning, while the sky, with the exception of a narrow strip along the horizon, is covered with rain clouds. These clouds approach from all sides; the sunlight is extinguished; the whole heavens become gray, and the finer the illumination, the more will the rain fall."

WILLIAM COWPER

1731-1800

WILLIAM COWPER, "the most popular poet of his generation and the best of English letter writers," was born in 1731, at Berkhampstead, in Bedfordshire, England. His father was rector of the parish church in the village. His mother, who was descended from the throne, was a lady of rare worth and beauty. She died when her son was six years of age. Cowper's grief at this bereavement is touchingly described in his "Lines on Receipt of his Mother's Picture." At the age of ten he was sent to Westminster School, where he remained for eight years, diligently storing his mind with the treasures of learning. For the associations of such a school he was by nature wholly unfitted. Always morbidly sensitive, he was often upon the border of insanity, and more than once in his life he seemed hopelessly deranged. The system of "fagging" at the schools, now generally abolished (though it still has in England many defenders, who regard it as a valuable means of discipline), was in Cowper's day at its height. He never recalled his school-days without disgust, and even horror. He became a vehement opponent and critic of the schools, and counseled parents to educate their sons at home.

In his "Tirocinium," which is a terrific onslaught upon the then prevailing system of education, he draws a picture of the school as it appeared to a nervous, timid, shrinking youth, who was wholly unable to comprehend the strong, lusty life and spirits of other boys. Cowper is preëminently the *home* poet of England; yet, strange to say, he can scarcely be said to have ever possessed a home. In 1765, after various failures and discouragements, and when half mad with melancholy, he went to reside with a clergyman, Mr. Unwin, at Huntingdon, where he found congenial friends and surroundings. He remained permanently with the Unwin household. Mr. Unwin died in 1767, and his family removed to the village of Olney, in Buckinghamshire, where most of Cowper's voluminous literary work was performed. Mrs. Unwin watched over him as a mother might care for an afflicted child; and Lady Austen, a most valued friend, cheered him with her light-heartedness and encouraged him to continued literary effort. At Lady Austen's solicitation he composed his greatest poem, "The Task." It was she who related to him the story of John Gilpin, which, in a moment of merriment, he retold in rhyme. Cowper translated the Iliad, with a high degree of success. He wrote a number of hymns, that are highly prized as aids to Christian worship. He died in 1800, having survived by two years his faithful friend and guardian, Mary Unwin.

Characterization

The nature of Cowper's works makes us peculiarly identify the poet and the man in perusing them. As an individual, he was retired and weaned from the vanities of the world ; and as an original writer, he left the ambitious and luxuriant subjects of fiction and passion for those of real life and simple nature, and for the development of his own earnest feelings in behalf of moral and religious truth.

His language has such a masculine, idiomatic strength, and his manner, whether he rises into grace or falls into negligence, has so much plain and familiar freedom, that we read no poetry with a deeper conviction of its sentiments having come from the author's heart; and of the enthusiasm, in whatever he describes, having been unfeigned and unexaggerated. He impresses us with the idea of a being whose fine spirit had been long enough in the mixed society of the world to be polished by its intercourse, and yet withdrawn so soon as to retain an unworldly degree of purity and simplicity. THOMAS CAMPBELL.

Tirocinium, a Latin word, signifies the first military service, or the first campaign, of a young soldier. Cowper's " Tirocinium " is perhaps the most powerful arraignment of schools that has ever been made in any nation or age. Cowper's preface to a book of his poems refers to the "Tirocinium " in the following words : " In the poem on the subject of education, he [the author] would be very sorry to stand suspected of having aimed his censure at any particular school. His objections are such as naturally apply themselves to schools in general. If there were not, as for the most part there is, willful neglect in those who manage them, and an omission even of such discipline as they are susceptible of, the objects are yet too numerous for minute attention ; and the aching hearts of ten thousand parents, mourning under the bitterest of disappointments, attest the truth of the allegation. His quarrel, therefore, is with the mischief at large, and not with any particular instance of it." Though written by the greatest English poet of his time, and by one of the most truthful of men, the descriptions are probably exaggerated as applied even to the schools of Cowper's time. Moreover, the remedy he proposes—the general substitution of private instruction for that of schools—is fallacious, and contrary to our ideas of public policy. The poem serves a valuable purpose, however, as a warning to all who have in charge the training of youth.

Tirocinium; or, a Review of Schools

1785

To the Rev. William Cawthorne Unwin, rector of Stock in Essex, the tutor of his two sons, the following poem recommending private tuition in preference to an education at school, is inscribed by his affectionate friend. WILLIAM COWPER.

OLNEY, *November* 6th, 1784.

It is not from his form, in which we trace
Strength join'd with beauty, dignity with grace,
That man, the master of this globe, derives
His right of empire over all that lives.
That form, indeed, the associate of a mind
Vast in its powers, ethereal in its kind,
That form, the labor of Almighty skill,
Framed for the service of a freeborn will,
Asserts precedence, and bespeaks control,
But borrows all its grandeur from the soul.
Hers is the state, the splendor and the throne,
An intellectual kingdom, all her own.
For her, the memory fills her ample page
With truths pour'd down from every distant age,
For her amasses an unbounded store,
The wisdom of great nations now no more,
Though laden, not encumber'd with her spoil,
Laborious, yet unconscious of her toil,
When copiously supplied then most enlarged,
Still to be fed, and not to be surcharged.
For her, the fancy, roving unconfined,
The present Muse of every pensive mind,
Works magic wonders, adds a brighter hue
To nature's scenes than nature ever knew;
At her command winds rise and waters roar;
Again she lays them slumbering on the shore;
With flower and fruit the wilderness supplies,
Or bids the rocks in ruder pomp arise.

For her, the judgment, umpire in the strife
That grace and nature have to wage through life,
Quick-sighted arbiter of good and ill,
Appointed sage preceptor to the will,
Condemns, approves, and, with a faithful voice,
Guides the decision of a doubtful choice.

Why did the fiat of a God give birth
To yon fair Sun and his attendant Earth?
And when, descending, he resigns the skies,
Why takes the gentler Moon her turn to rise,
Whom Ocean feels, through all his countless waves,
And owns her power on every shore he laves?
Why do the seasons still enrich the year,
Fruitful and young as in their first career?
Spring hangs her infant blossoms on the trees,
Rocked in the cradle of the western breeze;
Summer in haste the thriving charge receives,
Beneath the shade of her expanded leaves,
Till Autumn's fiercer heats and plenteous dews
Dye them at last in all their glowing hues.—
'Twere wild profusion all, and bootless waste,
Power misemployed, munificence misplaced,
Had not its Author dignified the plan,
And crowned it with the majesty of man.
Thus formed, thus placed, intelligent and taught,
Look where he will, the wonders God has wrought,
The wildest scorner of his Maker's laws
Finds in a sober moment time to pause,
To press the important question on his heart,
"Why form'd at all, and wherefore as thou art?"

If man be what he seems, this hour a slave,
The next, mere dust and ashes in the grave;

Endued with reason only to descry
His crimes and follies with an aching eye;
With passions, just that he may prove, with pain,
The force he spends against their fury vain;
And if, soon after having burned, by turns,
With every lust with which frail Nature burns,
His being end where death dissolves the bond,
The tomb take all, and all be blank beyond;
Then he, of all that Nature has brought forth,
Stands self-impeached the creature of least worth,
And useless while he lives, and when he dies,
Brings into doubt the wisdom of the skies.

Truths that the learned pursue with eager thought
Are not important always as dear-bought,
Proving at last, though told in pompous strains,
A childish waste of philosophic pains;
But truths on which depend our main concern,
That 'tis our shame and misery not to learn,
Shine by the side of every path we tread
With such a lustre, he that runs may read.
'Tis true, that if to trifle life away
Down to the sunset of their latest day,
Then perish on futurity's wide shore
Like fleeting exhalations, found no more,
Were all that Heaven required of human kind,
And all the plan their destiny designed,
What none could reverence all might justly blame,
And man would breathe but for his Maker's shame.
But reason heard, and nature well perused,
At once the dreaming mind is disabused.
If all we find possessing earth, sea, air,
Reflect his attributes who placed them there,
Fulfil the purpose, and appear design'd
Proofs of the wisdom of the all-seeing Mind,

'Tis plain, the creature whom he chose to invest
With kingship and dominion o'er the rest,
Received his nobler nature, and was made
Fit for the power in which he stands array'd,
That, first or last, hereafter, if not here,
He too might make his Author's wisdom clear,
Praise him on earth or, obstinately dumb,
Suffer his justice in a world to come.
This once believed, 'twere logic misapplied
To prove a consequence by none denied,
That we are bound to cast the minds of youth
Betimes into the mould of heavenly truth,
That taught of God they may indeed be wise,
Nor, ignorantly wandering, miss the skies.

In early days the conscience has, in most,
A quickness, which in later life is lost.
Preserved from guilt by salutary fears,
Or, guilty, soon relenting into tears.
Too careless, often, as our years proceed,
What friends we sort with, or what books we read,
Our parents yet exert a prudent care
To feed our infant minds with proper fare,
And wisely store the nursery by degrees
With wholesome learning, yet acquired with ease.
Neatly secured from being soiled or torn
Beneath a pane of thin translucent horn,
A book (to please us at a tender age
'Tis called a book, though but a single page)
Presents the prayer the Savior deigned to teach,
Which children use, and parsons—when they preach.
Lisping our syllables, we scramble next
Through moral narrative, or sacred text,
And learn with wonder how this world began,
Who made, who marred, and who has ransomed man;

Points which, unless the Scripture made them plain,
The wisest heads might agitate in vain.

O thou,[1] whom, borne on Fancy's eager wing
Back to the season of life's happy spring,
I pleased remember, and, while memory yet
Holds fast her office here, can ne'er forget;
Ingenious dreamer, in whose well-told tale
Sweet fiction and sweet truth alike prevail;
Whose humorous vein, strong sense, and simple style,
May teach the gayest, make the gravest smile,
Witty, and well-employed, and like thy Lord,
Speaking in parables his slighted word,
I name thee not, lest so despised a name
Should move a sneer at thy deservèd fame;
Yet e'en in transitory life's late day,
That mingles all my brown with sober gray,
Revere the man whose PILGRIM marks the road,
And guides the PROGRESS of the soul to God.
'Twere well with most, if books that could engage
Their childhood, pleased them at a riper age;
The man, approving what had charmed the boy,
Would die at last in comfort, peace, and joy,
And not with curses on his art who stole
The gem of truth from his unguarded soul.

. . . . .

Would you your son should be a sot or dunce,
Lascivious, headstrong, or all these at once;
That in good time, the stripling's finished taste
For loose expense and fashionable waste
Should prove your ruin, and his own at last,
Train him in public with a mob of boys,
Childish in mischief only and in noise,

[1] John Bunyan

Else of a mannish growth, and five in ten
In infidelity and lewdness, men.
There shall he learn, ere sixteen winters old,
That authors are most useful pawned or sold;
That pedantry is all that schools impart,
But taverns teach the knowledge of the heart;
There waiter Dick, with bacchanalian lays,
Shall win his heart, and have his drunken praise,
His counsellor and bosom-friend shall prove.

. . . . .

Schools, unless discipline were doubly strong,
Detain their adolescent charge too long;
The management of tyros of eighteen
Is difficult, their punishment obscene.
The stout, tall captain, whose superior size
The minor heroes view with envious eyes,
Becomes their pattern, upon whom they fix
Their whole attention, and ape all his tricks.
His pride, that scorns to obey or to submit,
With them is courage; his effrontery wit;
His wild excursions, window-breaking feats,
Robbery of gardens, quarrels in the streets,
His hairbreadth 'scapes, and all his daring schemes,
Transport them, and are made their favorite themes;
In little bosoms such achievements strike
A kindred spark, they burn to do the like.
Thus, half accomplished ere he yet begin
To show the peeping down upon his chin,
And as maturity of years comes on,
Made just the adept that you designed your son,
To insure the perseverance of his course,
And give your monstrous project all its force,
Send him to college. If he there be tamed,
Or in one article of vice reclaimed,
Where no regard of ordinance is shown,
Or look'd for now, the fault must be his own.

Some sneaking virtue lurks in him no doubt,
. . . nor drinking-bout,
Nor gambling practices can find it out.

Such youths of spirit, and that spirit too,
Ye nurseries of our boys, we owe to you.
Though from ourselves the mischief more proceeds,
For public schools 'tis public folly feeds.
The slaves of custom and establish'd mode,
With pack-horse constancy we keep the road
Crooked or straight, through quags or thorny dells,
True to the jingling of our leader's bells.
To follow foolish precedents, and wink
With both our eyes, is easier than to think,
And such an age as ours balks no expense
Except of caution and of common sense;
Else, sure, notorious fact and proof so plain
Would turn our steps into a wiser train.

I blame not those who with what care they can
O'erwatch the numerous and unruly clan,
Or if I blame, 'tis only that they dare
Promise a work of which they must despair.
Have ye, ye sage intendants of the whole,
An ubiquarian presence and control,
Elisha's eye, that when Gehazi stray'd
Went with him, and saw all the game he play'd?
Yes, ye are conscious; and on all the shelves
Your pupils strike upon, have struck yourselves.
Or if by nature sober, ye had then,
Boys as ye were, the gravity of men.
Ye knew at least, by constant proofs address'd
To ears and eyes, the vices of the rest,
But ye connive at what ye cannot cure,
And evils not to be endured, endure,

Lest power exerted, but without success,
Should make the little ye retain still less.
Ye once were justly famed for bringing forth
Undoubted scholarship and genuine worth,
And in the firmament of fame still shines
A glory bright as that of all the signs,
Of poets raised by you, and statesmen, and divines.
Peace to them all! those brilliant times are fled,
And no such lights are kindling in their stead.
Our striplings shine indeed, but with such rays
As set the midnight riot in a blaze,
And seem, if judged by their expressive looks,
Deeper in none than in their surgeons' books.

Say, Muse (for education made the song,
No Muse can hesitate or linger long),
What causes move us, knowing, as we must,
That these *menageries* all fail their trust,
To send our sons to scout and scamper there,
While colts and puppies cost us so much care?
Be it a weakness, it deserves some praise,
We love the play-place of our early days.
The scene is touching, and the heart is stone
That feels not at that sight, and feels at none.
The wall on which we tried our graving skill,
The very name we carved subsisting still;
The bench on which we sat while deep employed,
Though mangled, hacked, and hewed, not yet destroyed;
The little ones, unbuttoned, glowing hot,
Playing our games, and on the very spot,
As happy as we once, to kneel and draw
The chalky ring, and knuckle down at taw;
To pitch the ball into the grounded hat,
Or drive it devious with a dexterous pat;
The pleasing spectacle at once excites

Such recollection of our own delights,
That viewing it we seem almost to obtain
Our innocent sweet simple years again.
This fond attachment to the well-known place,
Whence first we started into life's long race,
Maintains its hold with such unfailing sway,
We feel it e'en in age, and at our latest day.
Hark! how the sire of chits, whose future share
Of classic food begins to be his care,
With his own likeness placed on either knee,
Indulges all a father's heart-felt glee,
And tells them, as he strokes their silver locks,
That they must soon learn Latin, and to box;
Then, turning, he regales his listening wife
With all the adventures of his early life,
His skill in coachmanship, or driving chaise,
In bilking tavern-bills, and spouting plays;
What shifts he used, detected in a scrape,
How he was flogged, or had the luck to escape;
What sums he lost at play, and how he sold
Watch, seals, and all—till all his pranks are told.
Retracing thus his *frolics* ('tis a name
That palliates deeds of folly and of shame),
He gives the local bias all its sway,
Resolves that where he play'd his sons shall play,
And destines their bright genius to be shown
Just in the scene where he display'd his own.
The meek and bashful boy will soon be taught
To be as bold and forward as he ought;
The rude will scuffle through with ease enough,
Great schools suit best the sturdy and the rough.
Ah happy designation, prudent choice,
The event is sure, expect it and rejoice!
Soon see your wish fulfilled in either child,
The pert made perter, and the tame made wild.

. . . .

Our public hives of puerile resort
That are of chief and most approved report,
To such base hopes in many a sordid soul
Owe their repute in part, but not the whole.
A principle, whose proud pretensions pass
Unquestion'd though the jewel be but glass—
That with a world not often over-nice
Ranks as a virtue, and is yet a vice,
Or rather a gross compound, justly tried,
Of envy, hatred, jealousy, and pride—
Contributes most perhaps to enhance their fame,
And *emulation* [1] is its specious name.
Boys once on fire with that contentious zeal
Feel all the rage that female rivals feel,
The prize of beauty in a woman's eyes

---

[1] But is there not a good sense and a bad sense associated with the term *emulation ?*—and have not these eager disputants fallen into the same error in this matter that the two knights committed, when they immolated each other in a contest about the question whether a shield was gold or silver, when each had seen *but one side of it ?* I incline to the opinion that this is the case, and that those who wax so warm in this contest would do well to give us at the outset a careful *definition of the term emulation*, as they intend to use it. This would perhaps save themselves a great deal of toil, and their readers a great deal of perplexity. Now, it seems to me, the truth of this question lies within a nutshell. If emulation means a *desire for improvement, progress, growth*, an ardent wish to rise above one's present condition or attainments, or even an aspiration to attain to eminence in the school or in the world, it is a laudable motive. *This is self-emulation.* It presses the individual on to surpass himself. It compares his present condition with what he would be—with what he ought to be; and, "forgetting those things which are behind, and reaching forth unto those which are before," he presses toward the mark for the prize. An ardor kindled by the praiseworthy examples of others, inciting to imitate them, or to equal or even excel them, without the desire of depressing them, is the sense in which the apostle uses the term (Romans xi. 14), when he says, "If by any means I may provoke to emulation them which are my flesh, and might save some of them." If this be the meaning of emulation, it is every way a worthy principle to be appealed to in school. This principle exists to a greater or less extent in the mind of every child, and may very safely be strengthened by being called by the teacher into lively exercise, provided, always, that the eminence is sought from a desire to be useful, and not from a desire of self-glorification.— *Page's "Theory and Practice of Teaching."*

Not brighter than in theirs the scholar's prize.
The spirit of that competition burns
With all varieties of ill by turns.
Each vainly magnifies his own success,
Resents his fellow's, wishes it were less,
Exults in his miscarriage if he fail,
Deems his reward too great if he prevail,
And labors to surpass him day and night,
Less for improvement than to tickle spite.
The spur is powerful, and I grant its force;
It pricks the genius forward in its course,
Allows short time for play, and none for sloth,
And, felt alike by each, advances both.
But judge where so much evil intervenes,
The end, though plausible, not worth the means.
Weigh, for a moment, classical desert
Against a heart depraved and temper hurt,
Hurt, too, perhaps for life, for early wrong
Done to the nobler part affects it long;
And you are staunch indeed in learning's cause
If you can crown a discipline that draws
Such mischiefs after it with much applause.

Connection formed for interest, and endeared
By selfish views, thus censured and cashiered;
And Emulation, as engendering hate,
Doomed to a no less ignominious fate:
The props of such proud seminaries fall,
The Jachin and the Boaz of them all.
Great schools rejected, then, as those that swell
Beyond a size that can be managed well,
Shall royal institutions miss the bays,
And small academies win all the praise?

Force not my drift beyond its just intent,
I praise a school as Pope a government;

So take my judgment in his language dressed,
"Whate'er is best administered is best."
Few boys are born with talents that excel,
But all are capable of living well.
Then ask not, whether limited or large?
But, watch they strictly, or neglect their charge?
If anxious only that their boys may learn,
While morals languish, a despised concern,
The great and small deserve one common blame,
Different in size, but in effect the same.
Much zeal in virtue's cause all teachers boast,
Though motives of mere lucre sway the most;
Therefore in towns and cities they abound,
For there the game they seek is easiest found;
Though there, in spite of all that care can do,
Traps to catch youth are most abundant too.

If shrewd, and of a well-constructed brain,
Keen in pursuit, and vigorous to retain,
Your son come forth a prodigy of skill,
As wheresoever taught, so formed, he will,
The pedagogue, with self-complacent air,
Claims more than half the praise as his due share;
But if, with all his genius, he betray,
Not more intelligent than loose and gay,
Such vicious habits as disgrace his name,
Threaten his health, his fortune, and his fame,
Though want of due restraint alone have bred
The symptoms that you see with so much dread,
Unenvied there, he may sustain alone
The whole reproach, the fault was all his own.

Oh! 'tis a sight to be with joy perused
By all whom sentiment has not abused,
New-fangled sentiment, the boasted grace
Of those who never feel in the right place,

A sight surpassed by none that we can show,
Though Vestris on one leg still shine below,
A father blest with an ingenuous son,
Father and friend and tutor all in one.
How? turn again to tales long since forgot,
Æsop and Phædrus and the rest?—why not?
He will not blush that has a father's heart,
To take in childish plays a childish part,
But bends his sturdy back to any toy
That youth takes pleasure in, to please his boy;
Then why resign into a stranger's hand
A task as much within your own command,
That God and nature and your interest too
Seem with one voice to delegate to you?
Why hire a lodging in a house unknown
For one whose tenderest thoughts all hover round your
  own?
This second weaning, needless as it is,
How does it lacerate both your heart and his!
The indented stick that loses day by day
Notch after notch, till all are smooth'd away,
Bears witness long ere his dismission come,
With what intense desire he wants his home.
But though the joys he hopes beneath your roof
Bid fair enough to answer in the proof,
Harmless and safe and natural as they are,
A disappointment waits him even there:
Arrived he feels an unexpected change,
He blushes, hangs his head, is shy and strange,
No longer takes, as once, with fearless ease
His favorite stand between his father's knees,
But seeks the corner of some distant seat,
And eyes the door, and watches a retreat,
And, least familiar where he should be most,
Feels all his happiest privileges lost.
Alas, poor boy!—the natural effect

TIROCINIUM; OR, A REVIEW OF SCHOOLS

Of love by absence chilled into respect.
Say, what accomplishments at school acquired
Brings he to sweeten fruits so undesired?
Thou well deservest an alienated son,
Unless thy conscious heart acknowledge—none;
None that in thy domestic snug recess,
He had not made his own with more address,
Though some perhaps that shock thy feeling mind,
And better never learn'd, or left behind.
Add too, that thus estranged thou canst obtain
By no kind arts his confidence again,
That here begins with most that long complaint
Of filial frankness lost, and love grown faint,
Which, oft neglected in life's waning years,
A parent pours into regardless ears.

Like caterpillars dangling under trees
By slender threads, and swinging in the breeze,
Which filthily bewray and sore disgrace
The boughs in which are bred the unseemly race,
While every worm industriously weaves
And winds his web about the rivell'd leaves;
So numerous are the follies that annoy
The mind and heart of every sprightly boy,
Imaginations noxious and perverse,
Which admonition can alone disperse.
The encroaching nuisance asks a faithful hand,
Patient, affectionate, of high command,
To check the procreation of a breed
Sure to exhaust the plant on which they feed.

'Tis not enough that Greek or Roman page
At stated hours his freakish thoughts engage.
E'en in his pastimes he requires a friend
To warn, and teach him safely to unbend,

O'er all his pleasures gently to preside,
Watch his emotions and control their tide,
And levying thus, and with an easy sway,
A tax of profit from his very play,
To impress a value, not to be erased,
On moments squandered else, and running all to waste.
And seems it nothing in a father's eye
That unimproved those many moments fly?
And is he well content his son should find
No nourishment to feed his growing mind,
But conjugated verbs, and nouns declined?
For such is all the mental food purveyed
By public hackneys in the schooling trade;
Who feed a pupil's intellect with store
Of syntax truly, but with little more,
Dismiss their cares when they dismiss their flock,
Machines themselves, and governed by a clock.

Perhaps a father blessed with any brains
Would deem it no abuse, or waste of pains,
To improve this diet, at no great expense,
With savory truth and wholesome common sense;
To lead his son for prospects of delight,
To some not steep, though philosophic, height,
Thence to exhibit to his wondering eyes
Yon circling worlds, their distance, and their size,
The moons of Jove, and Saturn's belted ball,
And the harmonious order of them all;
To show him in an insect or a flower,
Such microscopic proof of skill and power,
As, hid from ages past, God now displays
To combat atheists with in modern days;
To spread the earth before him and commend,
With designation of the finger's end,
Its various parts to his attentive note,
Thus bringing home to him the most remote;

To teach his heart to glow with generous flame,
Caught from the deeds of men of ancient fame;
And more than all, with commendation due,
To set some living worthy in his view,
Whose fair example may at once inspire
A wish to copy what he must admire.
Such knowledge, gained betimes, and which appears,
Though solid, not too weighty for his years,
Sweet in itself, and not forbidding sport,
When health demands it, of athletic sort,
Would make him what some lovely boys have been,
And more than one perhaps that I have seen,
An evidence and reprehension both
Of the mere schoolboy's lean and tardy growth.

Art thou a man professionally tied,
With all thy faculties elsewhere applied,
Too busy to intend a meaner care
Than how to enrich thyself and next, thine heir;
Or art thou (as though rich, perhaps thou art)
But poor in knowledge, having none to impart,—
Behold that figure, neat, though plainly clad,
His sprightly mingled with a shade of sad,
Not of a nimble tongue, though now and then
Heard to articulate like other men,
No jester, and yet lively in discourse,
His phrase well chosen, clear, and full of force,
And his address, if not quite French in ease,
Not English stiff, but frank, and form'd to please,
Low in the world because he scorns its arts,
A man of letters, manners, morals, parts,
Unpatronized, and therefore little known,
Wise for himself and his few friends alone,
In him, thy well-appointed proxy see,
Armed for a work too difficult for thee,

Prepared by taste, by learning, and true worth,
To form thy son, to strike his genius forth,
Beneath thy roof, beneath thine eye to prove
The force of discipline when back'd by love;[1]
To double all thy pleasure in thy child,
His mind informed, his morals undefiled.
Safe under such a wing, the boy shall show
No spots contracted among grooms below,
Nor taint his speech with meannesses design'd
By footman Tom for witty and refined.
There,—in his commerce with the liveried herd
Lurks the contagion chiefly to be fear'd.

. . . . .

To you, then, tenants of life's middle state,
Securely placed between the small and great,
Whose character, yet undebauched, retains
Two thirds of all the virtue that remains,
Who, wise yourselves, desire your sons should learn
Your wisdom and your ways—to you I turn.
Look round you on a world perversely blind;
See what contempt is fallen on humankind;
See wealth abused, and dignities misplaced,
Great titles, offices, and trusts disgraced,
Long lines of ancestry, renowned of old,
Their noble qualities all quenched and cold;
See Bedlam's closeted and handcuffed charge
Surpassed in frenzy by the mad at large;
See great commanders making war a trade,
Great lawyers, lawyers without study made;

---

[1] It will be seen that Cowper's plan, like Rousseau's, requires a personal mentor, rather than a school-teacher. The ideal mentor is beautifully portrayed in Fénelon's unique (French) classic, "*Télémaque*," in which the instructor of the son of Ulysses is at once a teacher, a monitor, a companion—a guardian angel. Mentor, in the story, is not a schoolmaster, yet is a type of what the ideal schoolmaster should be, in person; and it is impossible to dissociate in our minds the two ideals.

Churchmen, in whose esteem their best employ
Is odious, and their wages all their joy.
Who, far enough from furnishing their shelves
With Gospel lore, turn infidels themselves;
See womanhood despised, and manhood shamed
With infamy too nauseous to be named,
Fops at all corners, ladylike in mien,
Civeted fellows, smelt ere they are seen,
Else coarse and rude in manners, and their tongue
On fire with curses and with nonsense hung.

. . . . .

See volunteers in all the vilest arts
Men well endowed, of honourable parts,
Design'd by nature wise, but self-made fools;
All these, and more like these, were bred at schools.
And if it chance, as sometimes chance it will,
That though school bred, the boy be virtuous still,
Such rare exceptions shining in the dark,
Prove rather than impeach the just remark,
As here and there a twinkling star descried
Serves but to show how black is all beside.
Now look on him whose very voice in tone
Just echoes thine, whose features are thine own,
And stroke his polish'd cheek of purest red,
And lay thine hand upon his flaxen head,
And say,—"My boy, the unwelcome hour is come,
When thou, transplanted from thy genial home,
Must find a colder soil and bleaker air,
And trust for safety to a stranger's care.
What character, what turn thou wilt assume
From constant converse with I know not whom;
Who there will court thy friendship, with what views,
And, artless as thou art, whom thou wilt choose;
Though much depends on what thy choice shall be,
Is all chance-medley, and unknown to me."
Canst thou, the tear just trembling on thy lids,

And while the dreadful risk foreseen forbids;
Free, too, and under no constraining force,
Unless the sway of custom warp thy course;
Lay such a stake upon the losing side,
Merely to gratify so blind a guide?
Thou canst not! Nature, pulling at thine heart,
Condemns the unfatherly, the imprudent part.
Thou wouldst not, deaf to Nature's tenderest plea,
Turn him adrift upon a rolling sea,
Nor say,—"Go thither;"—conscious that there lay
A brood of asps, or quicksands, in his way;
Then, only governed by the self-same rule
Of natural pity, send him not to school.

No!—guard him better. Is he not thine own,
Thyself in miniature, thy flesh, thy bone?
And hopest thou not ('tis every father's hope)
That, since thy strength must with thy years elope,
And thou wilt need some comfort to assuage
Health's last farewell, a staff of thine old age,
That then, in recompense of all thy cares,
Thy child shall show respect to thy gray hairs,
Befriend thee, of all other friends bereft,
And give thy life its only cordial left?
Aware, then, how much danger intervenes,
To compass that good end, forecast the means.
His heart, now passive, yields to thy command;
Secure it thine, its key is in thine hand.
If thou desert thy charge, and throw it wide,
Nor heed what guests there enter and abide,
Complain not if attachments lewd and base
Supplant thee in it, and usurp thy place.
But if thou guard its sacred chambers sure
From vicious inmates and delights impure,
Either his gratitude shall hold him fast,
And keep him warm and filial to the last,

Or if he prove unkind (as who can say
But, being man, and therefore frail, he may),
One comfort yet shall cheer thine agèd heart,
Howe'er he slight thee, thou hast done thy part.

"Oh barbarous! wouldst thou with a Gothic hand
Pull down the schools—what!—all the schools i' th' land?
Or throw them up to livery-nags and grooms?
Or turn them into shops and auction rooms?"
A captious question, sir, (and yours is one),
Deserves an answer similar, or none.
Wouldst thou, possessor of a flock, employ
(Apprised that he is such) a careless boy,
And feed him well, and give him handsome pay,
Merely to sleep, and let them run astray?
Survey our schools and colleges, and see
A sight not much unlike my simile.
From education, as the leading cause,
The public character its color draws,
Thence the prevailing manners take their cast,
Extravagant or sober, loose or chaste.
And though I would not advertise them yet,
Nor write on each—*This Building to be Let*,
Unless the world were all prepared to embrace
A plan well worthy to supply their place,
Yet backward as they are, and long have been,
To cultivate and keep the morals clean,
(Forgive the crime) I wish them, I confess,
Or better managed, or encouraged less.

The Sage Called "Discipline"

(From "The Task")

In colleges and halls,[1] in ancient days,
When learning, virtue, piety and truth

---

[1] colleges in English universities, or, as in Oxford, organizations differing from colleges chiefly in being without endowment

Were precious and inculcated with care,
There dwelt a sage call'd Discipline. His head
Not yet by time completely silver'd o'er,
Bespoke him past the bounds of freakish youth,
But strong for service still, and unimpair'd.
His eye was meek and gentle, and a smile
Play'd on his lips, and in his speech was heard
Paternal sweetness, dignity and love.
The occupation dearest to his heart
Was to encourage goodness. He would stroke
The head of modest and ingenuous worth,
That blush'd at his own praise; and press the youth
Close to his side that pleased him. Learning grew,
Beneath his care, a thriving vigorous plant;
The mind was well-inform'd, the passions held
Subordinate, and diligence was choice.
If e'er it chanced, as sometimes chance it must,
That one among so many overleap'd
The limits of control, his gentle eye
Grew stern, and darted a severe rebuke;
His frown was full of terror, and his voice
Shook the delinquent with such fits of awe
As left him not till penitence had won
Lost favor back again, and closed the breach.
But Discipline, a faithful servant long,
Declined at length into the vale of years;
A palsy struck his arm; his sparkling eye
Was quench'd in rheums of age, his voice, unstrung,
Grew tremulous, and moved derision more
Than reverence, in perverse rebellious youth.

So colleges and halls neglected much
Their good old friend, and Discipline, at length,
O'erlook'd and unemploy'd, fell sick and died.
Then study languish'd, emulation slept,

And virtue fled. The schools became a scene
Of solemn farce, where ignorance in stilts,
His cap well lined with logic not his own,
With parrot-tongue perform'd the scholar's part,
Proceeding soon a graduated dunce.
Then compromise had place, and scrutiny
Became stone-blind, precedence went in truck,
And he was competent whose purse was so.
A dissolution of all bonds ensued;
The curbs invented for the mulish mouth
Of headstrong youth were broken; bars and bolts
Grew rusty by disuse, and massy gates
Forgot their office, opening with a touch;
Till gowns at length were found mere masquerade;
The tassell'd cap and the spruce band a jest,
A mockery of the world. What need of these
For gamesters, jockeys, brothellers impure,
Spendthrifts and booted sportsmen, oftener seen
With belted waist and pointers at their heels,
Than in the bounds of duty? What was learn'd,
If aught was learn'd in childhood, is forgot,
And such expense as pinches parents blue,
And mortifies the liberal hand of love,
Is squander'd in pursuit of idle sports
And vicious pleasures; buys the boy a name
That sits a stigma on his father's house,
And cleaves through life inseparably close
To him that wears it. What can after-games
Of riper joys, and commerce with the world,
The lewd vain world that must receive him soon,
Add to such erudition thus acquired
Where science and where virtue are profess'd?
They may confirm his habits, rivet fast
His folly, but to spoil him is a task
That bids defiance to the united powers
Of fashion, dissipation, taverns, stews.

Now blame we most the nurselings or the nurse?
The children crook'd and twisted and deform'd
Through want of care, or her whose winking eye
And slumbering oscitancy mars the brood?
The nurse, no doubt. Regardless of her charge,
She needs herself correction ; needs to learn
That it is dangerous sporting with the world,
With things so sacred as a nation's trust,
The nurture of her youth, her dearest pledge.

All are not such. I had a brother, once,—
Peace to the memory of a man of worth,
A man of letters, and of manners, too;
Of manners sweet as virtue always wears,
When gay good-nature dresses her in smiles.
He graced a college in which order yet
Was sacred, and was honor'd, loved and wept
By more than one, themselves conspicuous there.
Some minds are temper'd happily and mixed
With such ingredients of good sense and taste
Of what is excellent in man, they thirst
With such a zeal to be what they approve,
That no restraints can circumscribe them more
Than they themselves by choice, for wisdom's sake.
Nor can example hurt them, what they see
Of vice in others but enhancing more
The charms of virtue in their just esteem.
If such escape contagion, and emerge
Pure from so foul a pool, to shine abroad,
And give the world their talents and themselves.
Small thanks to those whose negligence or sloth
Exposed their inexperience to the snare,
And left them to an undirected choice.

JOHANN WOLFGANG VON GOETHE

1749-1832

JOHANN WOLFGANG VON GOETHE, whose name is the greatest in German literature, was born at Frankfort-on-the-Main, in 1749. His father was an imperial councilor, a man of cultivated tastes and ample wealth. Goethe passed his youth in the ancient free city of his birth, and at the age of sixteen entered college at Leipsic. In 1770 he went to the university at Strasburg, from which, a year later, he received the degree of Doctor of Jurisprudence. In 1775, already a famous author, he was invited by Charles Augustus, Grand Duke of Saxe-Weimar, to the court at Weimar, and appointed privy councilor of legation. Here he lived and died.

Goethe's writings covered so wide a range of letters, and his long life was so full of masterly work, that it is practicable to mention within the limits of a brief sketch the names of only a few of his greatest productions. Goethe's first noted work was "Götz von Berlichingen," which appeared in 1773. "The Sorrows of Werther" followed in 1774. His first important work issued from Weimar was the drama "Iphigenia at Tauris." "Wilhelm Meister's Apprenticeship" and "Wilhelm Meister's Wanderjahre" are nondescript and deeply significant productions, generally classed as romances. "Truth and Poetry" is a sort of rambling autobiography. Goethe's greatest work is "Faust," a drama of wonderful power and deep insight into human nature. Goethe has been called the sad Shakespeare of the later world. One is amazed at the universality of his genius. He died in 1832, at the height of his fame.

"A beautiful death," says Thomas Carlyle, "like that of a soldier found faithful at his post, and in the cold hand his arms still grasped! The poet's last words are a greeting of the new-awakened earth; his last movement is to work at his appointed task. Beautiful; what we might call a classic, sacred death, if it were not rather an Elijah-translation—in a chariot, not of fire and terror, but of hope and soft vernal sunbeams! . . . The unwearied workman now rests from his labors; the fruit of these is left growing and to grow. His earthly years have been numbered, and are ended; but of his activity (for it stood rooted in the eternal) there is no end. All that we mean by the higher literature of Germany, which is the higher literature of Europe, already gathers round this man as its creator; of which grand object, dawning mysteriously on a world that hoped not for it, who is there that can measure the significance and far-reaching influences?"

Characterization

The story of "Wilhelm Meister's Wanderjahre" is almost devoid of connected plot, and is used rather as a vehicle for a number of detached dissertations and apologues than as a presentation of character or an illustration of life. For this reason it has been made the subject of adverse criticism, and many of the independent sections have been valued less highly than would have been the case if they had been offered to the reader in a more artistic setting and more intelligible association. But the too evident want of coherence in the whole, and the defects for which the author more than once apologizes, do not deprive its contents of all value. The book has been severely criticised by Mr. G. H. Lewes, who speaks of its composition as "feeble" and "careless," and cites a passage from Eckermann showing that the second edition was purposely made the receptacle of various odds and ends which very possibly would otherwise have remained unprinted. But even in the siftings of Goethe's work many grains of gold may be found; and, apart from the separate interest of some of the detached pieces, there is sufficient purpose evident in the whole to give it a concrete value. The main design is apparently the promulgation of a system of education and social life, as set forth in the sections relating to the Pedagogic Province. Unpractical as this system may seem, it is not more so than plans which have been gravely propounded and set afoot in our own day, and it is safe to predict that in generations to come there will be found educational reformers who may read with profit the description of Goethe's Pedagogic Utopia.

EDWARD BELL.

Selections from "Wilhelm Meister's Wanderjahre"[1]

(Extract from a letter from Wilhelm Meister to Natalia, his wife, concerning his son Felix.) "I have to pass over many beautiful features of the common life of these virtuous and

[1] This word is commonly translated *Travels*, but has in reality no equivalent in English. It denotes the period in which, by law or custom, a German artisan is required to sojourn in different places to perfect himself in his craft, after the completion of his apprenticeship.

happy people; for how could everything be written? A few days I have spent pleasantly, but the third already warns me to bethink me of my further travels.

"To-day I had a little dispute with Felix, for he wanted almost to compel me to transgress one of the good intentions which I have promised you to keep. Now it is just a defect, a misfortune, a fatality with me, that, before I am aware of it, the company increases around me, and I charge myself with a fresh burden, under which I afterwards have to toil and to drag myself along. Now, during my travels, we must have no third person as a constant companion. We wish and intend to be and to remain two only, and it has but just now seemed as if a new, and not exactly pleasing, connection was likely to be formed.

"A poor, merry little youngster had joined the children of the house, with whom Felix had been enjoying these days in play, who allowed himself to be used or abused just as the game required, and who very soon won the favor of Felix. From various expressions I noticed already that the latter had chosen a playmate for the next journey. The boy is known here in the neighborhood; he is tolerated everywhere on account of his merriness, and occasionally receives gratuities. But he did not please me, and I begged the master of the house to send him away. This was accordingly done, but Felix was vexed about it, and there was a little scene.

"On this occasion I made a discovery which pleased me. In a corner of the chapel, or hall, there stood a box of stones, which Felix—who since our wandering through the mountain had become exceedingly fond of stones—eagerly pulled out and examined. Among them were some fine, striking specimens. Our host said that the child might pick out for himself any he liked; that these stones were what remained over from a large quantity which a stranger had sent from here a short time before. He called him Montan,[1] and you can fancy how glad

[1] This is a name supposed to be assumed by Jarno. See "Wilhelm Meister's Apprenticeship."

I was to hear this name, under which one of our best friends, to whom we owe so much, is travelling. As I inquired as to time and circumstances, I may hope soon to meet with him in my travels."

.   .   .   .

The news that Montan was in the neighborhood had made Wilhelm thoughtful. He considered that it ought not to be left merely to chance whether he should see such a worthy friend again, and therefore he inquired of his host whether it was not known in what direction this traveller had bent his way. No one had any more exact knowledge of this, and Wilhelm had already determined to pursue his route according to the first plan, when Felix exclaimed, "If father were not so obstinate, we should soon find Montan."

"In what manner?" asked Wilhelm.

Felix answered: "Little Fitz said yesterday that he would most likely follow up the gentleman who had the pretty stones with him, and knew so much about them too."

After some discussion Wilhelm at last resolved to make the attempt, and in so doing to give all the more attention to the suspicious boy. He was soon found, and when he understood what was intended, he brought a mallet and iron, and a very powerful hammer, together with a bag, and, in this miner-like equipment, ran merrily in front.

The road led sideways up the mountain again. The children ran leaping together from rock to rock, over stock and stone, and brook and stream, without following any direct path. Fitz, glancing now to his right and now to his left, pushed quickly upwards. As Wilhelm, and particularly the loaded carrier, could not follow so quickly, the boys retraced the road several times forwards and backwards, singing and whistling. The forms of certain strange trees aroused the attention of Felix, who, moreover, now made for the first time the acquaintance of the larches and stone-pines, and was attracted by the wonderful gentians. And thus the difficult travelling from place to place did not lack entertainment.

Little Fitz suddenly stood still and listened. He beckoned to the others to come.

"Do you hear the knocking?" said he. "It is the sound of a hammer striking the rock."

"We hear it," said the others.

"It is Montan," said he, "or some one who can give us news of him."

As they followed the sound, which was repeated at intervals, they struck a clearing in the forest, and beheld a steep, lofty, naked rock, towering above everything, leaving even the tall forests deep under it. On the summit they descried a person. He stood at too great a distance to be recognized. The children at once commenced to clamber up the rugged paths. Wilhelm followed with some difficulty, nay, danger; for in ascending a rock, the first one goes more safely, because he feels his way for himself; the one that follows only sees where the former has got to, but not how. The boys soon reached the top, and Wilhelm heard a loud shout of joy.

"It is Jarno!" Felix called out to his father, and Jarno at once stepped forward to a steep place, reached his hand to his friend, and pulled him up to the top. They embraced and welcomed each other with rapture under the open canopy of heaven.

. . . .

The two friends, not without care and difficulty, had descended to join the children, who had settled themselves in a shady spot below. The mineral specimens collected by Montan and Felix were unpacked almost more eagerly than the provisions. The latter had many questions to ask, and the former many names to pronounce. Felix was delighted that he could tell him the names of them all, and committed them quickly to memory. At last he produced one more stone, and said, "What is this one called?"

Montan examined it with astonishment, and said, "Where did you get it?"

Fitz answered quickly, "I found it; it comes from this country."

"It is not from this district," replied Montan.

Felix enjoyed seeing the great man somewhat perplexed.

"You shall have a ducat," said Montan, "if you take me to the place where it is found."

"It will be easy to earn," replied Fitz, "but not at once."

"Then describe to me the place exactly, so that I shall be able to find it without fail. But that is impossible, for it is a cross-stone, which comes from St. James of Compostella, and which some foreigner has lost, if indeed you have not stolen it from him, because it looks so wonderful."

"Give your ducat to your friend to take care of," said Fitz, "and I will honestly confess where I got the stone. In the ruined church at St. Joseph's there is a ruined altar as well. Among the scattered and broken stones at the top I discovered a layer of this stone, which served as a bed for the others, and I knocked down as much of it as I could get hold of. If you only lifted away the upper stones, no doubt you would find a good deal more of it."

"Take your gold piece," replied Montan; "you deserve it for this discovery. It is a pretty one. One justly rejoices when inanimate nature brings to light a semblance of what we love and venerate. She appears to us in the form of a sibyl, who sets down beforehand evidence of what has been predestined from eternity, but can only in the course of time become a reality. Upon this, as upon a miraculous, holy foundation, the priests had set their altar."

Wilhelm, who had been listening for a time, and who had noticed that many names and many descriptions came over and over again, repeated his already expressed wish that Montan would tell him so much as he had need of for the elementary instruction of the boy.

"Give that up," replied Montan. "There is nothing more terrible than a teacher who does not know more than the scholars at all events ought to know. He who wants to teach others may often indeed be silent about the best that he knows, but he must not be half instructed himself."

"But where, then, are such perfect teachers to be found?"

"You can find them very easily," replied Montan.

"Where then?" said Wilhelm, with some incredulity.

"Wherever the matter which you want to master is at home," replied Montan. "The best instruction is derived from the most complete environment. Do you not learn foreign languages best in the countries where they are at home—where only those given ones and no others strike your ear?"

"And have you then," asked Wilhelm, "attained the knowledge of mountains in the midst of mountains?"

"Of course."

"Without conversing with people?" asked Wilhelm.

"At least only with people," replied the other, "who were familiar with mountains. Wheresoever the Pygmies, attracted by the metalliferous veins, bore their way through the rock to make the interior of the earth accessible, and by every means try to solve problems of the greatest difficulty, there is the place where the thinker eager for knowledge ought to take up his station. He sees business, action; lets things follow their own course, and is glad at success and failure. What is useful is only a part of what is significant. To possess a subject completely, to master it, one has to study the thing for its own sake. But whilst I am speaking of the highest and the last, to which we raise ourselves only late in the day by dint of frequent and fruitful observation, I see the boys before me; to them matters sound quite differently. The child might easily grasp every species of activity, because everything looks easy that is excellently performed. *Every beginning is difficult!* That may be true in a certain sense, but more generally one can say that the beginning of everything is easy, and the last stages are ascended with most difficulty and most rarely."

Wilhelm, who in the meantime had been thinking, said to Montan, "Have you really adopted the persuasion that the collective forms of activity have to be separated in precept as well as in practice?"

"I know no other or better plan," replied the former. "Whatever man would achieve, must loose itself from him like a second self; and how could that be possible if his first self were not entirely penetrated therewith?"

"But yet a many-sided culture has been held to be advantageous and necessary."

"It may be so, too, in its proper time," answered the other. "Many-sidedness prepares, in point of fact, only the element in which the one-sided man can work, who just at this time has room enough given him. Yes, now is the time for the one-sided; well for him who comprehends it, and who works for himself and others in this mind. In certain things it is understood thoroughly and at once. Practice till you are an able violinist, and be assured that the director will have pleasure in assigning you a place in the orchestra. Make an instrument of yourself, and wait and see what sort of place humanity will kindly grant you in universal life. Let us break off. Whoso will not believe, let him follow his own path; he too will succeed sometimes; but I say it is needful everywhere to serve from the ranks upwards. To limit oneself to a handicraft is the best. For the narrowest heads it is always a craft; for the better ones an art; and the best, when he does one thing, does everything—or, to be less paradoxical, in the one thing, which he does rightly, he beholds the semblance of everything that is rightly done."

This conversation, which we only reproduce sketchily, lasted until sunset, which, glorious as it was, yet led the company to consider where they would spend the night.

"I should not know how to bring you under cover," said Fitz; "but if you care to sit or lie down for the night in a warm place at a good old charcoal-burner's, you will be welcome."

And so they all followed him through strange paths to a quiet spot, where any one would soon have felt at home.

In the midst of a narrow clearing in the forest there lay smoking and full of heat the round-roofed charcoal kilns; on one side the hut of pine boughs, and a bright fire close by. They sat down and made themselves comfortable; the children at once busy helping the charcoal-burner's wife, who, with hospitable anxiety, was getting ready some slices of bread, toasted with butter so as to let them be filled and soaked with it, which afforded deliciously oily morsels to their hungry appetites.

Presently, whilst the boys were playing at hide-and-seek among the dimly lighted pine stems, howling like wolves and barking like dogs, in such a way that even a courageous wayfarer might well have been frightened by it, the friends talked confidentially about their circumstances.

But now, to the peculiar duties of the Renunciants appertained also this, that on meeting they must speak neither about the past nor the future, but only occupy themselves with the present.

Jarno, who had his mind full of mining undertakings, and of all the knowledge and capabilities that they required, enthusiastically explained to Wilhelm, with the utmost exactitude and thoroughness, all that he promised himself in both hemispheres from such knowledge and capacities; of which, however, his friend, who always sought for the true treasure in the human heart alone, could hardly form any idea, but rather answered at last with a laugh:

"Thus you stand in contradiction with yourself, when beginning only in advanced years to meddle with what one ought to be instructed in from youth up."

"Not at all," replied the other, "for it is precisely this, that I was educated in my childhood at a kind uncle's, a mining officer of consequence, that I grew up with the miners' children, and with them used to swim little bark boats down the draining channel of the mine, that has led me back into this circle wherein I now feel myself again happy and contented. This charcoal smoke can hardly agree with you as with me, who from childhood up have been accustomed to swallow it as incense. I have essayed a great deal in the world, and always found the same: in habit lies the only satisfaction of man; even the unpleasant, to which we have accustomed ourselves, we miss with regret. I was once troubled a very long time with a wound that would not heal, and when at last I recovered, it was most unpleasant to me when the surgeon remained away and no longer dressed it, and no longer took breakfast with me."

"But I should like, however," replied Wilhelm, "to impart to my son a freer survey of the world than any limited handicraft can give. Circumscribe man as you will, for all that he will at last look about himself in his time, and how can he understand it all, if he does not in some degree know what has preceded him? And would he not enter every grocer's shop with astonishment if he had no idea of the countries whence these indispensable rarities have come to him?"

"What does it matter?" replied Jarno; "let him read the newspapers like every Philistine, and drink coffee like every old woman. But still, if you cannot leave it alone, and are so bent upon perfect culture, I do not understand how you can be so blind, how you need search any longer, how you fail to see that you are in the immediate neighborhood of an excellent educational institution."

"In the neighborhood?" said Wilhelm, shaking his head.

"Certainly!" replied the other; "what do you see here?"

"Where?"

"Here, just before your nose!" Jarno stretched out his forefinger, and exclaimed impatiently: "What is that?"

"Well then," said Wilhelm, "a charcoal kiln; but what has that to do with it?"

"Good, at last! a charcoal kiln. How do they proceed to erect it?"

"They place logs one on the top of the other."

"When that is done, what happens next?"

"As it seems to me," said Wilhelm, "you want to pay me a compliment in Socratic fashion—to make me understand, to make me acknowledge, that I am extremely absurd and thickheaded."

"Not at all," replied Jarno; "continue, my friend, to answer to the point. So, what happens then, when the orderly pile of wood has been arranged solidly yet lightly?"

"Why, they set fire to it."

"And when it is thoroughly alight, when the flame bursts forth from every crevice, what happens? Do they let it burn on?"

"Not at all. They cover up the flames, which keep breaking out again and again, with turf and earth, with coal dust, and anything else at hand."

"To quench them?"

"Not at all; to damp them down."

"And thus they leave it just as much air as is necessary, that all may be penetrated with the glow, so that all ferments aright. Then every crevice is shut, every outlet prevented; so that the whole by degrees is extinguished in itself, carbonized, cooled down, finally taken out separately, as marketable ware, forwarded to farrier and locksmith, to baker and cook; and when it has served sufficiently for the profit and edification of dear Christendom, is employed in the form of ashes by washer-women and soap-boilers."

"Well," replied Wilhelm, laughing, "what have you in view in reference to this comparison?"

"That is not difficult to say," replied Jarno. "I look upon myself as an old basket of excellent beech charcoal; but in addition I allow myself the privilege of burning only for my own sake; whence also I appear very strange to people."

"And me," said Wilhelm; "how will you treat me?"

"At the present moment," said Jarno, "I look on you as a pilgrim's staff, which has the wonderful property of sprouting in every corner in which it is put, but never taking root. Now draw out the comparison further for yourself, and learn to understand why neither forester nor gardener, neither charcoal-burner nor joiner, nor any other craftsman, knows how to make anything of you."

. . . .

Our pilgrims had performed the journey according to programme, and prosperously reached the frontier of the province in which they were to learn so many wonderful things. On their first entry they beheld a most fertile region, the gentle slopes of which were favorable to agriculture, its higher mountains to sheep feeding, and its broad valleys to the rearing of cattle. It was shortly before the harvest, and everything was in the greatest abundance; still, what surprised them from the outset was, that they saw neither women nor men, but only boys and youths busy getting ready for a prosperous harvest, and even making friendly preparations for a joyous harvest home. They greeted now one, and now another, and inquired about the master, of whose whereabouts no one could give an account. The address of their letter was: *To the Master or to the Three*, and this too the boys could not explain; however, they referred the inquirers to an overseer, who was just preparing to mount his horse. They explained their object; Felix's frank bearing seemed to please him; and so they rode together along the road.

Wilhelm had soon observed that a great diversity prevailed in the cut and color of the clothing, which gave a peculiar aspect to the whole of the little community. He was just on the point of asking his companion about this, when another strange sight was displayed to him: all the children, howsoever they might be occupied, stopped their work, and turned, with peculiar yet various gestures, towards the party riding past; and it was easy to infer that their object was the overseer. The youngest folded their arms crosswise on the breast, and looked cheerfully towards the sky; the intermediate ones held their arms behind them, and looked smiling upon the ground; the third sort stood erect and boldly; with arms at the side, they turned the head to the right, and placed themselves in a row, instead of remaining alone, like the others, where they were first seen.

Accordingly, when they halted and dismounted, just where several children had ranged themselves in various attitudes and were being inspected by the overseer, Wilhelm asked the meaning of these gestures.

Felix interposed, and said cheerfully: "What position have I to take, then?"

"In any case," answered the intendant, "at first the arms across the breast, and looking seriously and gladly upward, without turning your glance." He obeyed; however he soon exclaimed: "This does not please me particularly; I see nothing overhead; does it last long? But yes, indeed," he exclaimed joyfully, "I see two hawks flying from west to east; that must be a good omen!"

"It depends on how you take to it, how you behave yourself," rejoined the former; "now go and mingle with them, just as they mingle with each other."

He made a sign, the children forsook their attitudes, resumed their occupations or went on playing as before.

"Will you, and can you," Wilhelm now asked, "explain to me that which causes my wonder? I suppose that these gestures, these positions, are greetings, with which they welcome you."

"Just so," answered the other; "greetings, that tell me at once at what stage of cultivation each of these boys stands."

"But could you," Wilhelm added, "explain to me the meaning of the graduation? For that it is such, is easy to see."

"That is the part of better people than me," answered the other; "but I can assure you of this much, that they are no empty grimaces, and that, on the contrary, we impart to the children, not indeed the highest, but still a guiding and intelligible explanation; but at the same time we command each to keep and cherish for himself what we may have chosen to impart for the information of each: they may not chat about it with strangers, nor amongst themselves, and thus the teaching is modified in a hundred ways. Besides this the secrecy has very great advantages; for if we tell people immediately and perpetually the reason of everything, they think that there is nothing behind. To certain secrets, even if they may be known, we have to show deference by concealment and silence, for this tends to modesty and good morals."

"I understand you," said Wilhelm. "Why should we not also apply spiritually what is so necessary in bodily matters? But perhaps in another respect you can satisfy my curiosity. I am surprised at the great variety in the cut and color of their clothes, and yet I do not see all kinds of color, but a few only, and these in all their shades, from the brightest to the darkest. Still I observe, that in this there cannot be meant any indication of degrees of either age or merit; since the smallest and biggest boys mingled together, may be alike in cut and color, whilst those who are alike in gestures do not agree with one another in dress."

"As concerns this, too," their companion replied, "I cannot explain any further; yet I shall be much mistaken if you depart hence without being enlightened about all that you may wish to know."

They were now going in search of the master, whom they thought that they had found; but now a stranger could not but be struck by the fact, that the deeper they got into the country, the more they were met by a harmonious sound of singing. Whatsoever the boys set about, in whatever work they were found engaged, they were for ever singing, and in fact it seemed that the songs were specially adapted to each particular occupation, and in similar cases always the same. If several children were in any place, they would accompany each other in turns. Towards evening they came upon some dancing, their steps being animated and guided by choruses. Felix from his horse chimed in with his voice, and, in truth, not badly; Wilhelm was delighted with this entertainment, which made the neighborhood so lively. "I suppose," he observed to his companion, "you devote a great deal of care to this kind of instruction, for otherwise this ability would not be so widely diffused, or so perfectly developed."

"Just so," replied the other: "with us the art of singing forms the first step in education; everything else is subservient to it, and attained by means of it. With us the simplest enjoyment, as well as the simplest instruction, is enlivened and impressed by singing; and even what we teach in matters of religion and morals is communicated by the method of song. Other advantages for independent ends are directly allied; for, whilst we practice the children in writing down by symbols on the slate the notes which they produce, and then, according to the indication of these signs, in reproducing them in their throats, and moreover in adding the text, they exercise at the same time the hand, ear, and eye, and attain orthography and calligraphy quicker than you would believe; and, finally, since all this must be practiced and copied according to pure meter and accurately fixed time, they learn to understand much sooner than in other ways the high value of measure and computation. On this account, of all imaginable means, we have chosen music as the first element of our education, for from this, equally easy roads radiate in every direction."

Wilhelm sought to inform himself further, and did not hide his astonishment at hearing no instrumental music.

"We do not neglect it," replied the other, "but we practice it in a special place, inclosed in the most charming mountain valley; and then again we take care that the different instruments are taught in places lying far apart. Especially are the discordant notes of beginners banished to certain solitary spots, where they can drive no one crazy; for you will yourself confess, that in well-regulated civil society scarcely any more miserable nuisance is to be endured than when the neighborhood inflicts upon us a beginner on the flute or on the violin. Our beginners, from their own laudable notion of wishing to be an annoyance to none, go voluntarily for a longer or shorter period into the wilds, and, isolated there, vie with one another in attaining the merit of being allowed to draw nearer to the inhabited world; on which account they are, from time to time, allowed to make an attempt at drawing nearer, which seldom fails, because in these, as in our other modes of education, we venture actually to develop and encourage a sense of shame and diffidence. I am sincerely glad that your son has got a good voice; the rest will be effected all the more easily."

They had now reached a place where Felix was to remain, and make trial of his surroundings, until they were disposed to grant a formal admission. They already heard from afar a cheerful singing; it was a game, which the boys were now enjoying in their play hour. A general chorus resounded, in which each member of a large circle joined heartily, clearly, and vigorously in his part, obeying the directions of the superintendent. The latter, however, often took the singers by surprise, by suspending with a signal the chorus singing, and bidding some one or other single performer, by a touch of his baton, to adapt alone some suitable song to the expiring tune and the passing idea. Most of them already showed considerable ability; a few who failed in the performance willingly paid their forfeit, without exactly being made a laughing-stock. Felix was still child enough to mix at once among them, and came tolerably well out of the trial. Thereupon the first style of greeting was conceded to him: he forthwith folded his arms on his breast, looked upwards, and with such a droll expression withal, that it was quite plain that no hidden meaning in it had as yet occurred to him.

The pleasant spot, the kind reception, the merry games, all pleased the boy so well, that he did not feel particularly sad when he saw his father depart; he looked almost more wistfully at the horse as it was led away; yet he had no difficulty in understanding, when he was informed that he could not keep it in the present locality. On the other hand, they promised him that he should find, if not the same, at all events an equally lively and well-trained one when he did not expect it.

As the Superior could not be found, the overseer said: "I must now leave you, to pursue my own avocations; but still I will take you to the Three, who preside over holy things: your letter is also addressed to them, and together they stand in place of the Superior."

Wilhelm would have liked to learn beforehand about the holy things, but the other replied: "The Three in return for the confidence with which you have left your son with us, will certainly, in accordance with wisdom and justice, reveal to you all that is most necessary. The visible objects of veneration, which I have called holy things, are included within a particular boundary, are not mingled with anything, or disturbed by anything; only at certain times of the year, the pupils, according to the stages of their education, are admitted to them, in order that they may be instructed historically and through their senses; for in this way they carry off with them an impression, enough for them to feed upon for a long time in the exercise of their duty."

Wilhelm now stood at the entrance of a forest valley, inclosed by lofty walls; on a given signal a small door was opened, and a serious, respectable-looking man received our friend. He found himself within a large and beautifully verdant inclosure, shaded with trees and bushes of every kind, so that he could scarcely see some stately walls and fine buildings through the dense and lofty natural growth; his friendly reception by the Three, who came up by and by, ultimately concluded in a conversation, to which each contributed something of his own, but the substance of which we shall put together in brief.

"Since you have intrusted your son to us," they said, "it is our duty to let you see more deeply into our methods of proceeding. You have seen many external things, that do not carry their significance with them all at once; which of these do you most wish to have explained?"

"I have remarked certain seemly yet strange gestures and obeisances, the significance of which I should like to learn; with you no doubt what is external has reference to what is within, and *vice versâ;* let me understand this relation."

"Well-bred and healthy children possess a great deal; Nature has given to each everything that he needs for time and continuance: our duty is to develop this; often it is better developed by itself. But one thing no one brings into the world, and yet it is that upon which depends everything through which a man becomes a man on every side. If you can find it out yourself, speak out."

Wilhelm bethought himself for a short time, and then shook his head. After a suitable pause, they exclaimed: "Veneration!"

Wilhelm was startled.

"Veneration," they repeated. "It is wanting in all, and perhaps in yourself. You have seen three kinds of gestures, and we teach a threefold veneration, which when combined to form a whole, only then attains to its highest power and effect. The first is veneration for that which is above us. That gesture, the arms folded on the breast, a cheerful glance towards the sky, that is precisely what we prescribe to our untutored children, at the same time requiring witness of them that there is a God up above, who reflects and reveals Himself in our parents, tutors, and superiors. The second, veneration for that which is below us. The hands folded on the back as if tied together, the lowered, smiling glance, bespeak that we have to regard the earth well and cheerfully; it gives us an opportunity to maintain ourselves; it affords unspeakable joys; but it brings disproportionate sufferings. If one hurts oneself bodily, whether faultily or innocently; if others hurt one, intentionally or accidentally; if earthly chance does one any harm, let that be well thought of, for such danger accompanies us all our life long. But from this condition we deliver our pupil as soon as possible, directly we are convinced that the teachings of this stage have made a sufficient impression upon him; but then we bid him be a man, look to his companions, and guide himself with reference to them. Now he stands erect and bold, yet not selfishly isolated; only in a union with his equals does he present a front towards the world. We are unable to add anything further."

"I see it all," replied Wilhelm; "it is probably on this account that the multitude is so inured to vice, because it only takes pleasure in the element of ill-will and evil speech; he who indulges in this soon becomes indifferent to God, contemptuous towards the world, and a hater of his fellows; but the true, genuine, indispensable feeling of self-respect is ruined in conceit and presumption."

"Allow me, nevertheless," Wilhelm went on, "to make one objection: has it not ever been held that the fear evinced by savage nations in the presence of mighty natural phenomena, and other inexplicable foreboding events, is the germ from which a higher feeling, a purer disposition, should gradually be developed?"

To this the others replied: "Fear, no doubt, is consonant with nature, but not reverence; people fear a known or unknown powerful being: the strong one tries to grapple with it, the weak to avoid it; both wish to get rid of it, and feel happy when in a short space they have conquered it, when their nature in some measure has regained its freedom and independence. The natural man repeats this operation a million times during his life; from fear he strives after liberty, from liberty he is driven back into fear, and does not advance one step further. To fear is easy, but unpleasant; to entertain reverence is difficult, but pleasing. Man determines himself unwillingly to reverence, or rather never determines himself to it; it is a loftier sense which must be imparted to his nature, and which is self-developed only in the most exceptionally gifted ones, whom therefore from all time we have regarded as saints, as gods. In this consists the dignity, in this the function of all genuine religions, of which also there exist only three, according to the objects towards which they direct their worship."

The men paused, Wilhelm remained silent for a while in thought; as he did not feel himself equal to pointing these strange words, he begged the worthy men to continue their remarks, which too they at once consented to do.

"No religion," they said, "which is based on fear is esteemed among us. With the reverence which a man allows himself to entertain, whilst he accords honor, he may preserve his own honor; he is not at discord with himself, as in the other case. The religion which rests on reverence for that which is above us we call the ethnical one; it is the religion of nations, and the first happy redemption from a base fear; all so-called heathen religions are of this kind, let them have what names they will. The second religion, which is founded on that reverence which we have for what is like ourselves, we call the philosophic; for the philosopher, who places himself in the middle, must draw downward to himself all that is higher, and upward to himself all that is lower, and only in this central position does he deserve the name of the sage. Now, whilst he penetrates his relations to his fellows, and therefore to the whole of humanity, and his relations to all other earthly surroundings, necessary or accidental, in the cosmical sense he only lives in the truth. But we must now speak of the third religion, based on reverence for that which is below us; we call it the Christian one, because this disposition of mind is chiefly revealed in it; it is the last one which humanity could and was bound to attain. Yet what was not demanded for it? not merely to leave earth below, and claim a higher origin, but to recognize as divine even humility and poverty, scorn and contempt, shame and misery, suffering and death; nay, to revere and make lovable even sin and crime, not as hindrances but as furtherances of holiness! Of this there are indeed found traces throughout all time; but a track is not a goal, and this having once been reached, humanity cannot turn backwards; and it may be maintained that the Christian religion, having once appeared, can never disappear again; having once been divinely embodied, cannot again be dissolved."

"Which of these religions do you then profess more particularly?" said Wilhelm.

"All three," answered the others, "for, in point of fact, they together present the true religion; from these three reverences outsprings the highest reverence, reverence for oneself, and the former again develop themselves from the latter, so that man attains to the highest he is capable of reaching, in order that he may consider himself the best that God and nature have produced; nay, that he may be able to remain on this height without being drawn through conceit or egoism into what is base."

"Such a profession of faith, developed in such a manner, does not estrange me," replied Wilhelm; "it agrees with all that one learns here and there in life, only that the very thing unites you that severs the others."

To this the others replied: "This confession is already adhered to by a large part of the world, though unconsciously."

"How so, and where?" asked Wilhelm.

"In the Creed!" exclaimed the others, loudly; "for the first article is ethnical, and belongs to all nations: the second is Christian, for those struggling against sufferings and glorified in sufferings; the third finally teaches a spiritual communion of saints, to wit, of those in the highest degree good and wise: ought not therefore in fairness the three divine Persons, under whose likeness and name such convictions and promises are uttered, to pass also for the highest Unity?"

"I thank you," replied the other, "for having so clearly and coherently explained this to me—to whom, as a full-grown man, the three dispositions of mind are not new; and when I recall that you teach the children these high truths, first through material symbols, then through a certain symbolic analogy, and finally develop in them the highest interpretation, I must needs highly approve of it."

"Exactly so," replied the former; "but now you must still learn something more, in order that you may be convinced that your son is in the best hands. However, let this matter rest for the morning hours; rest and refresh yourself, so that, contented and humanly complete, you may accompany us farther into the interior to-morrow."

. . . .

Led by the hand of the eldest, our friend now entered through a handsome portal into a room, or rather, eight-sided hall, which was so richly adorned with pictures, that it caused astonishment to the visitor. He easily understood that all that he saw must have an important meaning, though he himself was not at once able to guess it. He was just on the point of asking his conductor about it, when the latter invited him to enter a side gallery, which, open on one side, surrounded a spacious, richly planted flower-garden. The wall, however, attracted the eye more than this brilliant adornment of nature, for it was painted throughout its whole length, and the visitor could not walk far along it without remarking that the sacred books of the Israelites had furnished the subjects of these pictures.

"It is here," said the eldest, "that we teach that religion which, for the sake of brevity, I have called the ethnical. Its internal substance is found in the history of the world, as its external envelope in the events themselves. In the reoccurrence of the destinies of entire nations it is, properly speaking, grasped."

"You have, I see," said Wilhelm, "conferred the honor on the Israelitish people, and made its history the foundation of this exposition, or rather you have made it the principal subject of the same."

"Just as you see," rejoined the old man, "for you will observe that in the plinths and friezes are represented not so much synchronistic as symphronistic actions and events, whilst among all nations there occur traditions of similar and equal import. Thus, while in the principal field, Abraham is visited by his gods in the form of handsome youths, you see up there in the frieze, Apollo among the shepherds of Admetus; from which we may learn that when the gods appear to men, they mostly go about unrecognized among them."

The two observers went farther. Wilhelm found for the most part well-known subjects, yet represented in a more lively and significant manner than he had been accustomed to see them before. In reference to a few matters he asked for some explanation, in doing which he could not refrain from inquiring again, why they had selected the Israelitish history before all others?

Hereupon the eldest answered: "Among all heathen religions . . . this one has great advantages, of which I shall mention only a few. Before the ethnic tribunal, before the tribunal of the God of nations, it is not the question, whether it is the best or the most excellent nation, but only whether it still exists, whether it has maintained itself. The Israelitish nation has never been worth much, as its leaders, judges, rulers, and prophets have a thousand times thrown in its teeth; it possesses few virtues, and most of the faults of other nations;

but in independence, endurance, courage, and if all that were no longer of account, in toughness, it cannot find its equal. It is the most tenacious people on the face of the earth! It is, it has been, and will be to glorify the name of Jehovah through all time. We have, therefore, set it up as a pattern, as a masterpiece, to which the others only serve as a frame."

"It is not becoming in me to argue with you," replied Wilhelm, "since you are in a position to teach me. Proceed, therefore, to explain to me the other advantages of this nation, or rather of its history, of its religion."

"One principal advantage," answered the other, "consists in the excellent collection of its sacred books. They are combined so happily, that from the most heterogeneous elements there results a deceptive unity. They are complete enough to satisfy, fragmentary enough to stimulate interest; sufficiently barbaric to excite challenge, sufficiently tender to soothe; and how many other opposing qualities might we extol in these books, in this Book!"

The series of the principal pictures, as well as the connection of the smaller ones which accompanied them above and below, gave the guest so much to think of, that he scarcely listened to the explanatory remarks by which his companion seemed rather to divert his attention from, than to fix it on the subjects.

In the meanwhile the other took occasion to say: "I must here mention one advantage of the Israelitish religion: that it does not embody its God in any given form, and therefore leaves us at liberty to give him a worthy human figure; also, on the other hand, to depict base idolatry by the forms of beasts and monsters."

Our friend, moreover, in a short stroll through these halls, had again called to mind the history of the world: there was something new to him in regard to the circumstance. Thus, through the juxtaposition of the pictures, through the reflections of his companion, fresh ideas had dawned upon his mind; and he was glad that Felix by means of a visible representation of such merit should appropriate to himself for his whole life long, as vividly as if they had actually happened in his own time, those grand, significant, and inimitable events. He looked at these pictures at last only with the eyes of the child, and in this aspect he felt perfectly satisfied with them. And so strolling on they reached those sad, confused periods, and finally the destruction of the city and the temple, the murder, banishment and slavery of whole multitudes of this obstinate nation. Its subsequent destinies were represented by discreet allegory, since a historic and real representation of them lies beyond the limits of the noble art.

Here the gallery, through which they had walked, terminated abruptly, and Wilhelm wondered at finding himself already at the end.

"I find," he said to his guide, "an omission in this historical walk. You have destroyed the Temple of Jerusalem, and scattered the nation, without introducing the Divine Man, who shortly before that very time taught in it, and to whom, too, shortly before they would give no hearing."

"To do this, as you demand, would have been a mistake. The life of that Divine Man, to whom you allude, stands in no connection with the world history of his time. His was a private life, his doctrine a doctrine for individuals. What publicly concerns the masses of the people and its members belongs to the history of the world, to the religion of the world, which we regard as the first. What inwardly concerns the individual belongs to the second religion, to the religion of the wise; such was the one that Christ taught and practiced as long as he went about on earth. Wherefore the external ends here, and I now open to you the internal."

A door opened, and they entered a similar gallery, where Wilhelm at once recognized the pictures of the second holy writings. They seemed to be by a different hand from the first; everything was gentler, forms, movements, surroundings, light, and coloring.

"You see here," said his companion, after they had walked

past a part of the pictures, "neither deeds nor events, but miracles and parables. Here is a new world; a new exterior, different from the former, and an interior, which in that is entirely lacking. By miracles and parables a new world is opened. The former make the common extraordinary, the latter make the extraordinary common."

"Have the kindness," replied Wilhelm, "to explain me these few words more circumstantially, for I do not feel equal to doing it myself."

"You possess a natural mind," replied the other, "although a deep one. Examples will open it most readily. Nothing is more common or ordinary than eating and drinking; on the other hand, it is extraordinary to ennoble a beverage, or to multiply a meal, so that it may suffice for a countless number. Nothing is commoner than illness and bodily infirmity; but to cure, to alleviate these by spiritual or spiritual-seeming means, is extraordinary: and just in this consists the marvel of the miracle—that the common and extraordinary, the possible and the impossible, become one. In the similitude, in the parable, the reverse is the case; here you have mind, insight, the idea of the sublime, the extraordinary, the unattainable. When this is embodied in a common, ordinary, intelligible image, so that it confronts us as living, present and real, so that we can appropriate, seize, retain, and converse with it as with one of our own like; that indeed becomes a second species of miracle, which is fairly associated with the first kind, nay, perhaps, is to be preferred to it. Here the living doctrine itself is pronounced, the doctrine that arouses no dispute. It is no opinion as to what is right or wrong; it is indisputably right or wrong itself."

This part of the gallery was shorter, or rather it was only the fourth part of the inclosure of the inner court-yard. But while one cared only to pass along the first, here one was glad to linger, here one liked to walk to and fro. The subjects were not so striking nor so manifold, but so much the more did they invite inquiry into their deep and quiet meaning; moreover the two wanderers turned at the end of the corridor, whilst Wilhelm expressed a fear that in fact only the last supper, the last parting of the Master from his disciples, was reached. He asked for the remaining part of the story.

"In all teaching," replied the elder one, "in all tradition, we are very willing to set apart only what it is possible to set apart, for only thereby can the notion of what is significant be developed in youth. Life otherwise mingles and mixes everything together; and thus we have here the life of that excellent Man completely separated from its end. During life he appears as a true philosopher—do not be scandalized at this expression—as a sage in the highest sense. He stands firmly to his point; he pursues his own path unflinchingly, and whilst he draws up to himself what is inferior, whilst he allows the ignorant, the poor, the sick, a share in his wisdom, wealth, and power, and thereby seems to step down to their level; still, on the other hand, he does not deny his divine origin; he dares to make himself equal to God, nay, to declare himself God. In this manner, from his youth up, he astonishes those who surround him, gains one part of them over to himself, arouses the other against himself, and shows all those to whom it is a question of a certain sublimity in doctrine and life, what they will have to expect from the world. And thus his life's journey for the noble part of humanity is more instructive and fruitful than his death; for to the one test every one is called, but to the other only a few. And in order that we may pass over all that follows from this, only look at the touching scene of the last supper! Here the sage, as always happens, leaves his followers behind, quite orphaned, so to say, and whilst he is taking thought for the good ones, he is at the same time feeding with them a traitor, who will bring him and the better ones to destruction."

With these words the elder opened a door, and Wilhelm was astonished to find himself again in the first hall of entrance. In the meantime, they had made, as he could easily see, the entire circuit of the court-yard.

"I was hoping," said Wilhelm, "that you would conduct me to the end, whilst you are taking me back to the beginning."

"This time I can show you nothing more," said the elder; "we do not let our pupils see more, we do not explain to them more than what you have so far passed through; the external and generally mundane may be imparted to each from his youth up; the internal and specially spiritual and mental, only to those who are growing up to a certain degree of thoughtfulness; and the rest, which can be disclosed only once a year, only to those of whom we are taking leave. That last form of religion, which arises from respect for what is below us, that reverence for what is repugnant, hateful, and apt to be shunned, we impart to each only by way of outfit for the world, in order that he may know where he can find the like, if need of such should stir within him. I invite you to return after the lapse of a year to attend our general festival, and to see how far your son has progressed; at which time too you shall be initiated into the holy estate of sorrow."

. . . .

Wilhelm lingered, looking over the pictures in the vestibule, wishing to have their meaning explained.

"This too," said the elder, "we shall continue to owe you until the year is over. We do not admit any strangers to the instruction which we impart to the children during the interval; but in due time come and listen to what our best speakers think fit to say publicly on these subjects."

Soon after this conversation a knock was heard at the small door. The inspector of yesterday presented himself; he had led up Wilhelm's horse. And thus our friend took leave of the Three, who at parting recommended him to the inspector in the following terms: "He is now numbered among the confidants, and what you have to answer to his questions is known to you; for he surely still wishes to be enlightened about many things that he has seen and heard with us; the measure and purport are not unknown to you." Wilhelm had still in fact a few questions on his mind, which also he expressed forthwith. Wherever they rode by, the children ranged themselves as on the day before; but to-day he saw, although rarely, a boy here and there who did not salute the inspector as he rode past, did not look up from his work, and allowed him to pass by without notice. Wilhelm now inquired the cause of this, and what this exception meant.

The other replied thereto: "It is in fact exceedingly significant, for it is the severest punishment that we inflict upon our pupils; they are declared unworthy of showing reverence, and compelled to seem rude and uncultured; but they do all that is possible to rescue themselves from this position, and apply themselves as quickly as possible to every duty. Should, however, any hardened youngster show no readiness to recant, then he is sent back to his parents with a short but conclusive report. He who does not learn to adapt himself to the laws must leave the region where they prevail."

Another sight excited to-day as yesterday the curiosity of the traveller; it was the variety of color and shape in the clothes of the pupils. In this there seemed to prevail no graduated arrangement, for some who saluted differently were dressed in uniform style, whilst those who had the same way of greeting were clad differently. Wilhelm asked for the cause of this seeming contradiction.

"It is explained thus," replied the other; "namely, that it is a means of finding out the peculiar disposition of each boy. With strictness and method in other things, in this respect we allow a certain degree of freedom to prevail. Within the scope of our stores of cloths and trimmings, the pupils are allowed to choose any favorite color, and also within moderate limits to select both shape and cut; this we scrupulously observe, for by the color you may find out people's bent of mind, and by the cut, the style of life. Yet there is one special peculiarity of human nature which makes a more accurate judgment to some extent difficult; this is the spirit of imitation—the tendency to associate. It is very seldom that a pupil lights on anything that has not occurred before; for the most part they choose something familiar, what they see just before them. Still, this consideration does not remain unprofitable to us; by means of such external signs they ally themselves to this or that party, join in here or there, and thus more general dispositions distinguish themselves; we learn to where each inclines and to what example he assimilates himself. Now, cases have been seen, in which the dispositions inclined towards the general, in which one fashion would extend itself to all, and every peculiarity tend towards losing itself in the totality. In a gentle way we try to put a stop to a tendency of this kind; we allow our stores to run short; one or other kind of stuff or ornament is no more to be had. We substitute something new, something attractive; through light colors, and short close cut we attract the cheerful ones; by somber shades and comfortable, ample suits, the thoughtful ones, and thus gradually establish a balance. For we are altogether opposed to uniform; it hides the character, and, more than any other disguise, conceals the peculiarities of the children from the sight of their superiors."

With such and other conversation Wilhelm arrived at the frontier of the district, and precisely at the point where the traveller, according to his old friend's direction, ought to leave it, in order to pursue his own private ends.

On parting, the inspector first of all observed that Wilhelm might now wait until the grand festival for all their sympathizers in various ways was announced. To this all the parents would be invited, and able pupils be dismissed to the chances of free life. After that, he was informed, he might at his leisure enter the other districts, where, in accordance with peculiar principles, special instruction amidst the most perfect surroundings was imparted and practiced.

. . . .

If we now seek out our friend again—for some time left to his own resources—we shall find him as he comes hither from the side of the level country into the Pedagogic Province. He comes across pastures and meadows, skirts on the dry down many a small lake, looks on bushy rather than wooded hills;

on all sides a free prospect over a land but little tilled. On such tracks it did not long remain doubtful that he was in the horse-breeding district, and he noticed here and there smaller and larger herds of these noble beasts of different sex and age. But all at once the horizon is covered with a fearful dust-cloud, which, rapidly looming nearer and nearer, completely conceals the whole breadth of the space, but at last, parted by a keen side-wind, is forced to disclose the tumult inside it.

A large body of the said noble beasts rushes forward in full gallop; they are guided and kept together by keepers on horseback. The tremendous hurly-burly rushes past the traveller; a fine boy, amongst the keepers in charge, looks at him in astonishment, pulls up, jumps off, and embraces his father.

Now questioning and explanation ensue. The son relates that he had had to put up with a good deal during the first probation time; dispensing with his horse and going about on foot over ploughed lands and meadows, and, as he had declared beforehand, had not shown himself to advantage in the quiet toilsome country life. The harvest-feast had pleased him well enough; but the tillage afterwards, the ploughing, digging, and waiting, not at all. He had certainly occupied himself with the necessary and useful domestic animals, but always lazily and discontentedly until he was at last promoted to the more lively business of riding. The occupation of looking after the mares and foals was tedious enough; meanwhile if one sees before one a lively little beast, that in three or four years' time will perhaps carry one about, it is quite a different sort of thing from troubling oneself about calves and sucking pigs, of which the end and aim is to be well fed and fattened, and then sold.

With the growth of his boy, who was now really reaching youth's estate, with his healthy condition, and a certain merry freedom, not to say cleverness, in his talk, his father had good reason to be content. The two now proceeded to follow quickly on horseback the speeding convoy, past remote-lying and extensive farms to the village or country town where the great market was held. There incredible confusion was in full career, and it was impossible to distinguish whether the wares or the merchants raised the more dust. From all countries would-be purchasers here meet together in order to acquire animals of fine breed and careful rearing; and one might think that one heard all the tongues of the earth. In the midst of it all, too, sounds the lively music of the most powerful wind instruments, and everything indicates movement, vigor, and life.

Our traveller now again meets the overseer already known to him of old, and falls in company with other clever men, who manage quietly and no less unnoticeably to maintain discipline and order. Wilhelm believing that here again he sees an instance of exclusive occupation, and in spite of its seeming breadth of a narrow course of life, is anxious to ascertain by what other means they are accustomed to train the pupils, in order to prevent the youth—in such a wild, and in some degree savage, occupation of rearing and training beasts—from becoming a wild beast himself. And thus it was very gratifying to him to learn that with this same violent and rough-seeming vocation was united the most delicate in the world, the practice and the learning of languages.

At this moment the father missed his son from his side; he saw him through the interstices of the crowd eagerly bargaining and arguing with a young peddler over some trifles. In a short time he altogether lost him. On the overseer's inquiring the reason of a certain embarrassment and abstraction, and hearing in reply that it was on his son's account, "Never mind that," he said, to reassure the father, "he is not lost. But to show you how we keep our charges together——" and thereupon he blew shrilly on a whistle that hung at his breast. In a moment it was answered by dozens from all sides. The man went on: "I will let this serve for the present, it is only a signal that the overseer is in the neighborhood and happens to want to know how many hear him. On a second signal they keep quiet, but make themselves ready; on the third they answer and come rushing up. Moreover, these signals are multiplied in very many ways and for special uses." A more open space had suddenly cleared itself round about them; they were able to speak more freely whilst walking towards the adjoining heights.

"We were led to this practice of languages," proceeded the overseer, "by the fact that we find here youths from all parts of the world. Now it is to prevent the people of one country from clanning together, as usually happens abroad, and forming parties asunder from the other nations, that we try by free communion of speech to bring them nearer to one another. But a universal knowledge of language is most necessary, inasmuch as at this fair every foreigner is glad to find a sufficient means of intercourse in his own sounds and expressions, and at the same time all possible convenience in bargaining and dealing. Yet in order that no Babylonish confusion, no corruption of speech shall ensue, one language only is spoken in common, month by month throughout the year, in accordance with the principle that one should learn nothing that has to be made compulsory except the rudiments.

"We look upon our scholars," said the overseer, "as so many swimmers, who in the element that threatens to swallow them feel themselves with wonder to be lighter, and are borne up and carried forward by it—and so it is with everything that man undertakes. Yet if one of our pupils shows a special inclination for this or that language, provision is made even in the midst of this tumultuous-seeming life, which affords withal very many quiet, idle, and lonely, nay, tedious hours, for true and thorough instruction. You would have some difficulty in picking out our equestrian grammarians, amongst whom there are verily a few pedants, from amidst these bearded and beardless centaurs. Your Felix has set himself to Italian, and since melodious singing, as you know already, pervades everything in our institutions, you might hear him, in the monotony of a herdsman's life, bring out many a ditty with taste and feeling. Activity and practical ability are far more reconcilable with efficient instruction than one thinks."

As every district has its own peculiar festival, the guest was led to the domain of instrumental music. Bordering on the plains, it at once exhibited pleasantly and gracefully diversified valleys, little narrow copses, gentle brooks, by the banks of which a moss-grown rock slyly peeped out here and there amidst the turf. Scattered habitations, surrounded by bushes, were to be seen upon the hills; in gentle dales the houses clustered nearer to each other. Those cottages, set gracefully apart, were so far from each other, that no musical sound either true or false could be heard from one to the other.

They now approached a wide space, built and covered round about, where men standing shoulder to shoulder seemed on the tiptoe of attention and expectation. Just as the guest entered, a powerful symphony on all the instruments commenced, the full-toned strength and tenderness of which he could not but admire.

By the side of this roomily-constructed orchestra stood a smaller one, which attracted special attention; upon it were younger and older scholars. Each held his instrument in readiness without playing on it. These were they who as yet were not able or did not venture to join in with the whole. One noticed with interest how they were standing as it were at the spring, and heard it declared that such a festival seldom passed by without a genius in some one or other being suddenly developed.

When vocal music also was brought forward in the intervals of the instrumental, there was no longer room to doubt that this too was in favor. Upon his inquiry, moreover, as to what further sort of education was joined in friendly union with this, the traveler learned that it was the art of poetry, and withal of the lyric sort. Their whole aim in this was that the two arts, each for and from itself, but at the same time in contrast to and in conjunction with each other, should be developed. The pupils learn to know one as well as the other in their special limitations: then they are taught how they mutually limit, and again mutually emancipate one another.

To the rhythm of poetry the tone-artist opposes the division and movement of time. But here the sway of music over poetry soon manifests itself—for if the latter, as is proper and necessary, always keeps its quantities as clearly as possible in view, yet for the musician few syllables are definitely long or short; he destroys at pleasure the most conscientious proceedings of the dealer in rhythm—nay, actually converts prose into song; whence ensue the most wonderful possibilities, and the poet would very soon feel himself annihilated were he not able, on his own part, to inspire the musician with reverence by means of lyric tenderness and boldness, and to call forth new feelings, at one time in the most delicate gradation, at another by the most abrupt transitions.

The singers one finds here are for the most part themselves poets. Dancing, too, is taught in its rudiments; so that all these accomplishments may diffuse themselves methodically throughout the whole of these regions.

When the guest was conducted across the next boundary he suddenly beheld quite a different style of building. The houses were no longer scattered, and no more of the cottage sort; they rather appeared to be set together with regularity—solid and handsome from without, roomy, convenient, and elegant within. Here one perceived an unconfined and well-built town, adapted to its situation. Here plastic art and its kindred crafts are at home, and a stillness quite peculiar prevails in these places.

The plastic artist, it is true, always considers himself in relation to whatever lives and moves amidst mankind; but his occupation is a solitary one, and, by the strangest contradiction, no other, perhaps, so decidedly calls for a living environment. Here, then, does each one create in silence what is soon to occupy the eyes of men forever. A Sabbath stillness reigns over the whole place, and if one did not notice here and there the chipping of the stone-mason, or the measured blows of carpenters, just now busily employed in finishing a splendid building, not a sound would disturb the air.

Our traveler was struck with the seriousness, the wonderful strictness, with which beginners, as well as the more advanced, were treated; it seemed as if no one essayed anything by his own strength and power, but as if a hidden spirit animated all throughout, guiding them to one single great end. Neither draft nor sketch was anywhere to be seen; every stroke was drawn with care. And when the traveler asked the guide for an explanation of the whole process, the latter remarked, "The imagination is of itself a vague, inconstant faculty, whilst the whole merit of the plastic artist consists in this, namely, in learning ever more and more to define and grasp it firmly, nay, even at last to elevate it to the level of the present."

He was reminded of the necessity in other arts of more certain principles. "Would the musician allow a pupil to strike wildly at the strings, or to invent intervals according to his own caprice and pleasure? Here it is remarkable that nothing is to be left to the learner's discretion. The element in which he is to work is given definitely, the tool that he has to handle is placed in his hand, the very style and method by which he is to avail himself of them (I mean the fingering) he finds prescribed, by which one member gets out of the way of another, and gets the proper road ready for its successor, by which orderly coöperation alone, the impossible becomes possible at last. But what mostly justifies us in strict demands and definite laws, is that it is precisely genius, the inborn talent, that grasps them first, and yields them the most willing obedience. Only mediocrity would fain substitute its limited specialty for the unlimited whole, and glorify its false ideas under the pretence of an uncontrollable originality and independence. This, however, we do not let pass, but we protect our pupils against all false steps, whereby a great part of life, nay, often the whole life, is confused and broken up. With the genius we love best to deal, for he is specially inspired with the good spirit of recognizing quickly what is useful to him. He sees that Art is called Art, precisely because it is not Nature; he accommodates himself to the proper respect even for that which might be called conventional, for what else is this but that the best men have agreed to regard the necessary, the inevitable, as the best? And is it not successful in every case? To the great assistance of the teachers, the three reverences and their symbols are introduced and inculcated here too, as everywhere with us, with some variation in conformity with the nature of the business that prevails."

As the traveler was led further around, he was constrained to wonder at the fact, that the city seemed to extend itself forever, streets growing out of streets, and affording numberless fine views. The exterior of the buildings expressed their object unambiguously: they were substantial and imposing, less showy than beautiful. After the nobler and more solemn one in the middle of the town came those of more cheerful aspect, until at last charming suburbs, of a graceful character, spread away towards the open country, dwindling away finally in the shape of country villas.

The traveler could not avoid remarking here that the habitations of the musicians in the preceding region were, in respect to beauty and size, in no way to be compared with the present ones in which painters, sculptors, and architects dwelt. The answer given to him was that this lay in the nature of things. The musician must always be absorbed within himself, to shape out his inmost thought and to bring it forth. He has not to flatter the sense of sight; the eye very easily supplants the ear, and tempts outward the spirit from within. The plastic artist, on the contrary, must live in the outer world, and make his inner nature manifest, as it were unconsciously, on and in the external world. Plastic artists must live like kings and gods; how otherwise would they build and adorn for kings and gods? They must at last raise themselves above the ordinary so far that the whole community may feel honored in and by their works.

Our friend then desired the explanation of another paradox—why is it that just on these festivals, which in other regions are such lively and tumultuously excited days, here the greatest quiet prevails, and work is not even exhibited?

"A plastic artist," he said, "requires no festival; to him the whole year is a festival. When he has accomplished anything excellent, it stands afterwards, as it did before, in his sight and in the sight of the whole world. In this no repetition is needed, no new effort, no fresh success, such as the musician is forever tormented by: who for that reason is not to be grudged the most splendid festival amidst the most numerous audience."

"But yet," replied Wilhelm, "on days like this one would be glad to see an exhibition in which the three years' progress of the best pupils might be examined and criticised with pleasure."

"In other places," he was told, "an exhibition may be necessary; with us it is not; our whole end and aim is exhibition. Look here at the buildings of every sort, all carried out by pupils; after plans discussed and revised, it is true, a hundred times; for one who builds must not potter about and make experiments. What has to remain standing must stand well, and suffice, if not for eternity, at any rate for a considerable time. We may commit ever so many faults, but we must not build any. With sculptors we deal a little more leniently, most leniently of all with painters; they may experiment, here and there, each in his own style. It is open to them to choose in the inside or outside spaces of buildings, in the open squares, a spot which they will decorate. They make their ideas public, and if one is in any degree worthy of approbation, the execution is agreed to; but in one of two ways—either with the privilege of taking the work away, sooner or later, should it cease to please the artist himself, or with the condition of leaving the work, when once set up irremovably in its place. The most choose the former, and reserve the privilege for themselves, in which they are always well advised. The second case seldom occurs; and it is observable that the artists then rely less upon themselves, hold long conferences with their comrades and critics, and by that means manage to produce works really worthy of being valued and made permanent."

After all this Wilhelm did not neglect to inquire what other instruction was given besides, and he was informed that this consisted of poetry, and in fact of epic poetry.

Yet it must needs appear strange to our friend when they

added that the pupils are not allowed to read or to recite the completed poems of ancient and modern poets. "Merely a series of myths, traditions, and legends is briefly imparted to them. Thus we soon recognize by pictorial or poetic expression, the special productive power of the genius devoted to one or the other art. Poets and artists both occupy themselves at the same well-spring, and each one tries to guide the stream towards his own side for his own advantage, so as to attain his end according to his requirements; at which he succeeds much better than if he set about making over again what has been made already."

The traveler had an opportunity of seeing the process himself. Several painters were busy in one room; a lively young companion was telling a quite simple story very circumstantially, so that he employed almost as many words as they did pencil-strokes to complete his exposition in the most rounded style possible.

They assured Wilhelm that in their joint work the friends entertained themselves very pleasantly, and that in this way improvisators were often developed who were able to arouse great enthusiasm in the twofold representation.

Our friend now turned his inquiries again to plastic art. "You have," he said, "no exhibition, and consequently, I suppose, no award of prizes."

"We have not, in point of fact," replied the other, "but, quite close by here, we can let you see what we regard as more useful."

They turned into a large hall, lighted with good effect from above. A large circle of busy artists was first seen, from the midst of whom a colossal group, favorably placed, reared itself. Vigorous male and female forms, in powerful poses, reminded one of that splendid fight between youthful heroes and Amazons, in which hate and animosity at last resolve themselves into mutual and faithful alliance. This remarkably involved piece of art-work was seen to equal advantage from any point around it. Artists were sitting and standing in a large circle, each occupied after his own fashion: the painter at his easel, the draughtsman at his drawing-board, some modeling in the round, some in bas-relief; architects were even making drawings for the pedestal, upon which a similar work of art was afterwards to be placed. Everyone taking part in it adopted his own method in copying. Painters and draughtsmen developed the group in the flat, carefully, indeed, so as not to spoil it, but to give as much as possible. The work in bas-relief was treated in precisely the same manner. Only one had reproduced the whole group on a smaller scale, and in certain movements and arrangement of members he really seemed to have surpassed the model.

It now appeared that this was the designer of the model, who, before its execution in marble, was now submitting it not to a critical but to a practical test; and who, by taking accurate note of everything that each of his fellow-workers, according to his own method and way of thinking, saw, preserved, or altered in it, was enabled to turn it to his own advantage; with this object, that ultimately, when the perfect work should come forth chiseled in marble, though undertaken, designed, and executed by only one, yet still it might seem to belong to all.

In this room, too, the greatest silence reigned; but the director raised his voice and cried, " Who is there here, who, in the presence of this motionless work, can so move the imagination with the excellence of his words that all that we can see transfixed here shall again become resolved without losing its character, so that we may convince ourselves that what the artist has here laid hold of is indeed the worthiest?"

Expressly called on by them all, a beautiful youth left his work, and began by delivering a quiet discourse, in which he seemed merely to describe the present work; but soon he threw himself into the peculiar region of poetry, plunged into the midst of the action, and controlled this element to a marvel. Little by little his rendering was elevated by brilliant declamation, to such a height that the rigid group seemed to turn upon its axis, and the number of the figures seemed thereby doubled and trebled. Wilhelm stood enraptured, and at last cried, "Who can longer refrain from passing on into actual song and rhythmic verse?"

"This I would beg to refuse," replied the overseer, "for if our excellent sculptor will speak sincerely, he will confess that our poet hardly pleases him, and simply because the two artists stand as far as possible from one another: on the other hand, I would wager that here and there a painter has appropriated from him certain living traits. Yet there is a gentle kindly song that I might allow our friend to hear, one that you deliver with such sweet seriousness: it relates to art as a whole, and does me good myself whenever I hear it."

After a pause, in which they beckoned to each other, and made arrangements by signs, the following fine heart-and-spirit-stirring song resounded from all sides:

> "To invent and bring to ending,
>   Artist, bide thou oft alone:
> Joy to reap from toilsome spending,
>   Gayly to thy friends begone!
> See them as a whole compacted,
>   And discern thine own career;
> Deeds in many a year enacted
>   In thy neighbor will be clear.
>
> "First conceiving, then presenting,
>   Ranging shapes in order wise,
> Each of them the rest accenting
>   Till at last they all suffice.
> Well invented, render'd neatly,
>   Feelingly and thoroughly done,
> Thus the artist hath discreetly
>   Power from everlasting won.
>
> "As the thousand forms of nature
>   Of one God alone do tell,
> So does one enduring feature
>   In Art's wide domain prevail.
> This, the sense of Truth Eternal,
>   Beauty dons as her array,
> And unharmed by light supernal
>   Gazes on the brightest day.

> "As the speaker, as the singer
>   Blithely fare in rhyme or prose,
> Fresh beneath the painter's finger
>   Must bloom forth Life's joyous rose.
> With her sisters round her closing,
>   With the fruits that autumn brings,
> Thus the mysteries disclosing
>   Of Life's deeply hidden springs.
>
> "Form from form do thou dissever,
>   Fair, in shapes a thousand fold;
> Of man's image glad forever
>   That a God it did enfold.
> Stand in brotherhood united,
>   Whatsoe'er your work may be;
> And like sacred incense lighted
>   Rise on high in melody."

Wilhelm might well have let all this pass, although it must have seemed to him very paradoxical, and, had he not seen it with his eyes, actually impossible. But when they proceeded, in beautiful sequence, to declare and make it all clear to him openly and frankly, he hardly needed to ask a single question for further information; yet he did not forbear, at last, to address his conductor as follows:

"I see that here everything desirable in life has been provided for very wisely; but tell me, besides, which region can manifest a similar solicitude for dramatic poetry, and where might I gain information on that subject? I have looked round amongst all your edifices, and find none that could be destined for such an object."

"In reply to this question we cannot deny that there is nothing of the sort to be met with in the whole of our province, for the theater presupposes an idle crowd, perhaps even a rabble, the like of which is not to be found amongst us; for such people, if they do not go away disgusted of their own accord, are conveyed across the frontier. Be assured, however, that in our universally active institution so important a point as this has been well considered; but no region could be found for it;

some weighty objection occurred in every case. Who is there amongst our pupils who would have easily made up his mind to awaken in this mass, with feigned merriment or hypocritical sorrow, an unreal emotion inconsistent with the time, and thereby produce in alterations an ever-dubious pleasure? Such foolishness we considered altogether dangerous, and could not connect it with our serious aim."

"And yet it is said," replied Wilhelm, "that this widely-encompassing art requires all the others together."

"Not at all," was the reply; "she makes use of the others, but spoils them. I do not blame the actor when he associates himself with the painter; but still the painter, in such a partnership, is lost. The actor, without any conscience, will, for his own momentary ends, and with no small profit, use up all that art and life offer him; the painter, on the other hand, who would reap some advantage again from the theater, will always find himself at a disadvantage, and the musician will be in the same case. The arts seem to me like so many sisters, of whom the greater number have been disposed to economy, but one of trivial disposition has had a mind to appropriate the possessions and property of the whole family. The theater is in this situation: it has an ambiguous origin, which, whether as art or handicraft or dilettanteism, it can never wholly disguise."

Wilhelm looked down with a deep sigh, for all the enjoyment and the sorrow that he had had from and on the stage were suddenly present to him. He blessed the good men who were wise enough to spare their pupils such pain, who, from conviction and principle, banished these perils from their circle.

His conductor, however, did not leave him long to these meditations, but proceeded: "As it is our highest and holiest principle to misdirect no disposition or talent, we cannot hide from ourselves the fact, that amongst so great a number, a natural mimetic gift may very likely be decisively displayed. This, however, shows itself in an irrepressible desire to ape the characters, figures, motion, and speech of others. This we do not encourage, it is true, but we observe the pupil carefully, and if he remains throughout true to his nature, we have put ourselves in connection with the large theaters of all nations, and thither we send any one of tried capacity, in order that, like the duck upon the pond, he may with all speed be guided on the stage to the future waddling and quacking of his life."

Wilhelm listened to this with patience, yet only with partial conviction, and perhaps with some annoyance; for so wonderfully is man minded, that whilst he is really persuaded of the worthlessness of some favorite subject or other, and will turn away from, and even execrate himself, yet still he will not bear to have it treated in the same way by any one else, and probably the spirit of contradiction which dwells in all mankind is never more vigorously and effectively excited than in such a case.

The editor of these papers may even confess that he allows this wonderful passage to pass with some reluctance. Has he not, too, in many senses devoted more than a due share of life and strength to the theater? and would it be easy to convince him that this has been an inexcusable error, a fruitless exertion?

However, we have not time to apply ourselves ill-humoredly to such recollections and underlying feelings, for our friend finds himself agreeably surprised on seeing before him, once more, one of the Three, and one especially sympathetic. A communicative gentleness, telling of the purest peace of soul, imparted itself most revivingly: the Wanderer could approach him trustfully, and feel that his trust was returned.

He now learned that the Superior was at present in the sanctuary, and was there instructing, teaching, and blessing, whilst the Three arranged severally to visit all the regions, and in every place—after obtaining the most minute information, and arranging with the subordinate overseers to carry forward what had been begun—to establish what had been newly determined, and thus faithfully fulfill their high duty.

This excellent man it was who gave him a more general view of their internal economy and external connections, as well as a knowledge of the reciprocal effect of all the different regions; nor did he fail to make clear how a pupil could be transferred from one to the other after a longer or shorter period. Enough, everything fully harmonized with what he already knew. At the same time, the account given of his son was a source of great satisfaction, and the plan on which they intended to proceed with him must needs obtain his entire approbation.

MARY RUSSELL MITFORD

1786-1855

MARY RUSSELL MITFORD was born at Alresford, in Hampshire, England, in 1786. She was highly successful as an author and as a compiler. Her fame rests chiefly upon her exquisite portraitures of English village life, in which she has scarcely a rival. In her preface to "Our Village" she says: "The writer may at least claim the merit of a hearty love of her subject, and of that local and personal familiarity which only a long residence in one neighborhood could have enabled her to attain. Her descriptions have always been written on the spot, and at the moment, and in nearly every instance with the closest and most resolute fidelity to the place and the people." Miss Mitford wrote a number of dramatic works, which were well received, and her "Recollections of a Literary Life," published in 1851, added greatly to her reputation.

Characterization

The following dialogue by Professor John Wilson, in "*Noctes Ambrosianæ*" (taken from *Blackwood's Magazine*), affords a contemporary estimate of Miss Mitford's work. Wilson himself appears in his favorite character of Christopher North, and the shepherd represents the poet, James Hogg, the author of "Kilmeny." By means of such felicitous "conversations," Professor Wilson was accustomed to review the literature of his day.

TICKLER. Master Christopher North, there's Miss Mitford, author of "Our Village," an admirable person in all respects, of whom you have never, to my recollection, taken any notice in the magazine. What is the meaning of that? Is it an oversight? Or have you omitted her name intentionally from your eulogies on our female worthies?

NORTH. I am waiting for her second volume. Miss Mitford has not, in my opinion, either the pathos or humor of Washington Irving; but she excels him in vigorous conception of character, and in the truth of her pictures of English life and manners. Her writings breathe a sound, pure, and healthy morality, and are pervaded by a genuine rural spirit—the spirit of Merry England. Every line bespeaks the lady.

SHEPHERD. I admire Miss Mitford just excessively. I dinna wunner at her being able to write sae weel as she does about drawing-rooms, wi' sofas and settees, and about the fine folk in them, seein themsels in lookin-glasses frae tap to tae; but what puzzles the like o' me is her pictures o' poachers, and tinklers, and pottery-trampers, and ither neerdoweels, and o' huts and hovels without riggin[1] by the wayside, and the cottages o' honest puir men, and byres,[2] and barns, and stackyards, and merry-makins at winter ingles, and courtship aneath trees, and at the gable ends o' farm-houses, atween lads and lasses as laigh[3] in life as the servants in her father's ha'. That's the puzzle and that's the praise.

The Village Schoolmistress

(From "Our Village")

Women, fortunately perhaps for their happiness and their virtue, have, as compared with men, so few opportunities of acquiring permanent distinction, that it is rare to find a female, unconnected with literature or with history, whose name is remembered after her monument is defaced, and the brass on her coffin-lid is corroded. Such, however, was the case with Dame Eleanor, the widow of Sir Richard Lacy, whose name, at the end of three centuries, continued to be as freshly and as frequently spoken, as "familiar" a "household word," in the little village of Aberleigh, as if she had flourished there yesterday. Her memory was embalmed by a deed of charity and of goodness. She had founded and endowed a girls' school for "the instruction" (to use the words of the deed) "of twenty poor children, and the maintenance of one discreet and godly matron;" and the school still continued to be called after its foundress, and the very spot on which the schoolhouse stood, to be known by the name of Lady Lacy's Green.

It was a spot worthy of its destination—a spot of remarkable cheerfulness and beauty. The Green was small, of irregular shape, and situate at a confluence of shady lanes. Half the roads and paths of the parish met there, probably for the convenience of crossing in that place, by a stone bridge of one arch

[1] roofs   [2] cow-sheds   [3] low

covered with ivy, the winding rivulet which intersected the whole village, and which, sweeping in a narrow channel round the school garden, widened into a stream of some consequence in the richly-wooded meadows beyond. The banks of the brook, as it wound its glittering course over the green, were set, here and there, with clumps of forest trees, chiefly bright green elms, and aspens with their quivering leaves and their pale shining bark; whilst a magnificent beech stood alone near the gate leading to the school, partly overshadowing the little court in which the house was placed. The building itself was a beautiful small structure, in the ornamented style of Elizabeth's day, with pointed roofs and pinnacles, and clustered chimneys, and casement windows; the whole house enwreathed and garlanded by a most luxuriant vine.

The date of the erection, 1563, was cut in a stone inserted in the brick-work above the porch: but the foundress had, with an unostentatious modesty, withheld her name; leaving it, as she safely might, to the grateful recollection of the successive generations who profited by her benevolence. Altogether it was a most gratifying scene to the eye and to the heart. No one ever saw Lady Lacy's schoolhouse without admiration, especially in the play-hour at noon, when the children, freed from "restraint that sweetens liberty," were clustered under the old beech-tree, reveling in their innocent freedom, running, jumping, shouting, and laughing with all their might; the only sort of riot which it is pleasant to witness. The painter and the philanthropist might contemplate that scene with equal delight.

The right of appointing both the mistress and the scholars had been originally invested in the Lacy family, to whom nearly the whole of the parish had at one time belonged. But the estates, the manor, the hall-house, had long passed into other hands and other names, and this privilege of charity was now the only possession which the heirs of Lady Lacy retained in Aberleigh. Reserving to themselves the right of nominating the matron, her descendants had therefore delegated to the vicar and the parish officers the selection of the children, and the general regulation of the school—a sort of council of regency, which, simple and peaceful as the government seems, a disputatious churchwarden or a sturdy overseer would sometimes contrive to render sufficiently stormy. I have known as much canvassing and almost as much ill-will in a contested election for one of Lady Lacy's scholarships, as for a scholarship in grander places, or even for an M. P.-ship in the next borough; and the great schism between the late Farmer Brookes and all his coadjutors, as to whether the original uniform of little green stuff gowns, with white bibs and aprons, tippets and mob, should be commuted for modern cotton frocks and cottage bonnets, fairly set the parish by the ears. Owing to the good farmer's glorious obstinacy, (which I suppose he called firmness,) the green-gownians lost the day. I believe that, as a matter of calculation, the man might be right, and that his costume was cheaper and more convenient; but I am sure that I should have been against him, right or wrong: the other dress was so pretty, so primitive, so neat, so becoming; the little lasses looked like rose-buds in the midst of their leaves: besides, it was the old traditionary dress—the dress contrived and approved by Lady Lacy. Oh! it should never have been changed, never!

Since there was so much contention in the election of pupils, it was perhaps lucky for the vestry that the exercise of the more splendid piece of patronage, the appointment of a mistress, did not enter into its duties. Mr. Lacy, the representative of the foundress, a man of fortune in a distant county, generally bestowed the situation on some old dependant of his family. During the churchwardenship of Farmer Brookes, no less than three village gouvernantes arrived at Aberleigh—a quick succession! It made more than half the business of our zealous and bustling man of office, an amateur in such matters, to instruct and overlook them. The first importation was Dame Whitaker, a person of no small importance, who had presided as head nurse over two generations of the Lacys, and was now, on the dispersion of the last set of her nurslings to their different schools, and an unlucky quarrel with a favorite lady's maid, promoted and banished to this distant government. Nobody could well be more unfit for her new station, or better suited to her old. She was a nurse from top to toe, round, portly, smiling, with a coaxing voice, and an indolent manner; much addicted to snuff and green tea, to sitting still, to telling long stories, and to humoring children. She spoiled every brat she came near, just as she had been used to spoil the little Master Edwards and Miss Julias of her ancient dominions. She could not have scolded if she would—the gift was not in her. Under her misrule the school grew into sad disorder; the girls not only learned nothing, but unlearned what they knew before; work was lost—even the new shifts of the Vicar's lady; books were torn; and for the climax of evil, no sampler[1] was prepared to carry round at Christmas, from house to house—the first time such an omission had occurred within the memory of man.

Farmer Brookes was at his wits' end. He visited the school six days in the week, to admonish and reprove; he even went nigh to threaten that he would work a sampler himself; and finally bestowed on the unfortunate ex-nurse the nick-name of Queen Log,[2] a piece of disrespect, which, together with other grievances, proved so annoying to poor Dame Whitaker, that she found the air of Aberleigh disagree with her, patched up a peace with her old enemy the lady's maid, abdicated that unruly and rebellious principality, the school, and retired with great delight to her quiet home in the deserted nursery, where, as far as I know, she still remains.

The grief of the children on losing this most indulgent non-instructress was not mitigated by the appearance or demeanor of her successor, who at first seemed a preceptress after Farmer Brookes's own heart, a perfect Queen Stork. Dame Banks was

---

[1] a collection of needle-work patterns, as letters or the like

[2] "Queen Log" and "Queen Stork" are suggested by a celebrated fable of Æsop, in which it is related that the frogs petitioned Jupiter for a king, and that they were first given a *log*, which did nothing but make a single terrifying splash in the water. In contempt for this inane monarch, they petitioned for one of another sort, when a stork was sent to devour them.

the widow of Mr. Lacy's gamekeeper; a little thin woman, with a hooked nose, a sharp voice, and a prodigious activity of tongue. She scolded all day long; and, for the first week, passed for a great teacher. After that time it began to be discovered that, in spite of her lessons, the children did not learn; notwithstanding her rating they did not mind, and in the midst of a continual bustle nothing was ever done. Dame Banks was in fact a well-intentioned, worthy woman, with a restless, irritable temper, a strong desire to do her duty, and a woeful ignorance how to set about it. She was rather too old to be taught either; at least she required a gentler instructor than the good churchwarden; and so much ill-will was springing up between them that he had even been heard to regret the loss of Dame Whitaker's quietness, when very suddenly poor Dame Banks fell ill, and died. The sword had worn the scabbard; but she was better than she seemed; a thoroughly well-meaning woman—grateful, pious, and charitable; even our man of office admitted this.

The next in succession was one with whom my trifling pen, dearly as that light and fluttering instrument loves to dally and disport over the surface of things, must take no saucy freedom; one of whom we all felt it impossible to speak or to think without respect; one who made Farmer Brookes's office of adviser a sinecure, by putting the whole school, himself included, into its proper place, setting everybody in order, and keeping them so. I don't know how she managed, unless by good sense and good humor, and that happy art of government, which seems no art at all, because it is so perfect; but the children were busy and happy, the vestry pleased, and the churchwarden contented. All went well under Mrs. Allen.

She was an elderly woman, nearer perhaps to seventy than to sixty, and of an exceedingly venerable and prepossessing appearance. Delicacy was her chief characteristic—a delicacy so complete that it pervaded her whole person, from her tall, slender figure, her fair, faded complexion, and her silver hair to the exquisite nicety of dress by which at all hours and seasons, from Sunday morning to Saturday night, she was invariably distinguished. The soil of the day was never seen on her apparel; dust would not cling to her snowy caps and handkerchiefs; such was the art magic of her neatness. Her very pins did their office in a different manner from those belonging to other people. Her manner was gentle, cheerful, and courteous, with a simplicity and propriety of expression that perplexed all listeners; it seemed so exactly what belongs to the highest birth and the highest breeding.

She was humble, very humble; but her humility was evidently the result of a truly Christian spirit, and would equally have distinguished her in any station. The poor people, always nice judges of behavior, felt, they did not know why, that she was their superior; the gentry of the neighborhood suspected her to be their equal—some clergyman's or officer's widow, reduced in circumstances; and would have treated her as such, had she not, on discovering their mistake, eagerly undeceived them. She had been, she said, all her life a servant, the personal attendant of one dear mistress, on whose decease she had been recommended to Mr. Lacy; and to his kindness, under Providence, was indebted for a home and a provision for her helpless age, and the still more helpless youth of a poor orphan, far dearer to her than herself. This avowal, although it changed the character of the respect paid to Mrs. Allen, was certainly not calculated to diminish its amount; and the new mistress of Lady Lacy's school, and the beautiful order of her house and garden, continued to be the pride and admiration of Aberleigh.

The orphan of whom she spoke was a little girl about eleven years old, who lived with her, and whose black frock bespoke the recent death of some relative. She had lately, Mrs. Allen said, lost her grandmother—her only remaining parent, and had now no friend but herself on earth; but there was One above who was a Father to the fatherless, and he would protect poor Jane! And as she said this, there was a touch of emotion, a break of the voice, a tremor on the lip, very unlike the usual cheerfulness and self-command of her manner. The child was evidently very dear to her. Jane was, indeed, a most interesting creature; not pretty—a girl of that age seldom is; the beauty of childhood is outgrown, that of youth not come; and Jane could scarcely ever have had any other pretensions to prettiness than the fine expression of her dark gray eyes, and the general sweetness of her countenance. She was pale, thin, and delicate; serious and thoughtful far beyond her years; averse from play, and shrinking from notice. Her fondness for Mrs. Allen, and her constant and unremitting attention to her health and comforts, were peculiarly remarkable. Every part of their small housewifery, that her height and strength and skill would enable her to perform, she insisted on doing, and many things far beyond her power she attempted. Never was so industrious or so handy a little maiden. Old Nelly Chun, the char-woman, who went once a week to the house, to wash and bake and scour, declared that Jane did more than herself; and to all who knew Nelly's opinion of her own doings, this praise appeared superlative.

In the schoolroom she was equally assiduous, not as a learner, but as a teacher. None so clever as Jane in superintending the different exercises of the needle, the spelling-book and the slate. From the little work-woman's first attempt to insert thread into a pocket handkerchief, the digging and plowing of cambric, miscalled hemming, up to the nice and delicate mysteries of stitching and button-holing; from the easy junction of *a b*, *ab*, and *b a*, *ba*, to that tremendous sesquipedalian word *irrefragability*, at which even I tremble as I write; from the Numeration Table to Practice, nothing came amiss to her. In figures she was particularly quick. Generally speaking, her patience with the other children, however dull or tiresome or giddy they might be, was exemplary; but a false accountant, a stupid arithmetician, would put her out of humor. The only time I ever heard her sweet, gentle voice raised a note above its natural key, was in reprimanding Susan Wheeler, a sturdy, square-made, rosy-cheeked lass, as big again as herself, the dunce and beauty of the school, who had three times cast up a sum of three figures, and three times made the total wrong. Jane ought to have admired the ingenuity evinced by such a variety of error; but she did not; it fairly put her in a passion. She herself was not only clever in figures, but fond of them to an extraordinary degree—luxuriated in Long Division, and reveled in the Rule-of-Three. Had she been a boy, she would probably have been a great mathematician, and have won that fickle, fleeting, shadowy wreath, that crown made of the rainbow, that vainest of all earthly pleasures, but which yet *is* a pleasure—Fame.

Happier, far happier was the good, the lowly, the pious child, in her humble duties! Grave and quiet as she seemed, she had many moments of intense and placid enjoyment, when the duties of the day were over, and she sat reading in the porch, by the side of Mrs. Allen, or walked with her in the meadows on a Sunday evening after church. Jane was certainly contented and happy; and yet every one that saw her thought of her with that kind of interest which is akin to pity. There was a pale, fragile grace about her, such as we sometimes see in a rose which has blown in the shade; or rather, to change the simile, the drooping and delicate look of a tender plant removed from a hothouse to the open air. We could not help feeling sure (notwithstanding our mistake with regard to Mrs. Allen) that *this* was indeed a transplanted flower; and that the village school, however excellently her habits had become inured to her situation, was not her proper atmosphere.

Several circumstances corroborated our suspicions. My lively young friend Sophia Grey, standing with me one day at the gate of the schoolhouse, where I had been talking with Mrs. Allen, remarked to me, in French, the sly, demure vanity with which Susan Wheeler, whose beauty had attracted her attention, was observing and returning her glances. The playful manner in which Sophia described Susan's "regard furtif," made me smile; and looking accidentally at Jane, I saw that she was smiling too, clearly comprehending and enjoying the full force of the pleasantry. She must understand French;

and when questioned, she confessed she did, and thankfully accepted the loan of books in that language. Another time, being sent on a message to the vicarage, and left for some minutes alone in the parlor, with a piano standing open in the room, she could not resist the temptation of touching the keys, and was discovered playing an air of Mozart, with great taste and execution. At this detection she blushed, as if caught in a crime, and hurried away in tears and without her message. It was clear that she had once learned music. But the surest proof that Jane's original station had been higher than that which she now filled, was the mixture of respect and fondness with which Mrs. Allen treated her, and the deep regret she sometimes testified at seeing her employed in any menial office.

At last, elicited by some warm praise of the charming child, our good schoolmistress disclosed her story. Jane Mowbray was the granddaughter of the lady in whose service Mrs. Allen had passed her life. Her father had been a man of high family and splendid fortune; had married beneath himself, as it was called, a friendless orphan, with no portion but beauty and virtue; and, on her death, which followed shortly on the birth of her daughter, had plunged into every kind of vice and extravagance. What need to tell a tale of sin and suffering?

Mr. Mowbray had ruined himself, had ruined all belonging to him, and finally had joined our armies abroad as a volunteer, and had fallen undistinguished in his first battle. The news of his death was fatal to his indulgent mother; and when she too died, Mrs. Allen blessed the Providence which, by throwing in her way a recommendation to Lady Lacy's school, had enabled her to support the dear object of her mistress's love and prayers. "Had Miss Mowbray no connections?" was the natural question. "Yes; one very near—an aunt, the sister of her father, richly married in India. But Sir William was a proud and a stern man, upright in his own conduct, and implacable to error. Lady Ely was a sweet, gentle creature, and doubtless would be glad to extend a mother's protection to the orphan; but Sir

William—oh! he was so unrelenting! He had abjured Mr. Mowbray, and all connected with him. She had written to inform them where the dear child was, but had no expectation of any answer from India."

Time verified this prediction. The only tidings from India, at all interesting to Jane Mowbray, were contained in the paragraph of a newspaper which announced Lady Ely's death, and put an end to all hopes of protection from that quarter. Years passed on, and found her still with Mrs. Allen at Lady Lacy's Green, more and more beloved and respected from day to day. She had now attained almost to womanhood. Strangers, I believe, called her plain; we, who knew her, thought her pretty. Her figure was tall and straight as a cypress, pliant and flexible as a willow, full of gentle grace, whether in repose or in motion. She had a profusion of light brown hair, a pale complexion, dark gray eyes, a smile of which the character was rather sweet than gay, and such a countenance! no one could look at her without wishing her well, or without being sure that she deserved all good wishes.

Her manners were modest and elegant, and she had much of the self-taught knowledge which is, of all knowledge, the surest and the best, because acquired with most difficulty, and fixed in the memory by the repetition of effort. Every one had assisted her to the extent of his power and of her willingness to accept assistance; for both she and Mrs. Allen had a pride—call it independence—which rendered it impossible, even to the friends who were most honored by their good opinion, to be as useful to them as they could have wished. To give Miss Mowbray time for improvement had, however, proved a powerful emollient to the pride of our dear schoolmistress; and that time had been so well employed that her acquirements were considerable; whilst in mind and character she was truly admirable; mild, grateful, and affectionate, and imbued with a deep religious feeling, which influenced every action and pervaded every thought. So gifted, she was deemed by her constant friends, the vicar and his lady, perfectly competent to the care and education of children; it was agreed that she should enter a neighboring family, as a successor to their then governess, early in the ensuing spring; and she, although sad at the prospect of leaving her aged protectress, acquiesced in their decision.

One fine Sunday in the October preceding this dreaded separation, as Miss Mowbray, with Mrs. Allen leaning on her arm, was slowly following the little train of Lady Lacy's scholars from church, an elderly gentleman, sickly-looking and emaciated, accosted a pretty young woman, who was loitering with some other girls at the church-yard gate, and asked her several questions respecting the school and its mistress. Susan Wheeler (for it happened to be our old acquaintance) was delighted to be singled out by so grand a gentleman, and being a kind-hearted creature in the main, spoke of the schoolhouse and its inhabitants exactly as they deserved.

"Mrs. Allen," she said, "was the best woman in the world —the very best, except just Miss Mowbray, who was better still,—only too particular about summing, which you know, sir," added Susan, "people can't learn if they can't. She is going to be a governess in the spring," continued the loquacious damsel; "and it's to be hoped the little ladies will take kindly to their tables, or it will be a sad grievance to Miss Jane."—"A governess! Where can I make inquiries concerning Miss Mowbray?"—"At the vicarage, sir," answered Susan, dropping her little courtesy, and turning away, well pleased with the gentleman's condescension, and with half a crown which he had given her in return for her intelligence. The stranger, meanwhile, walked straight to the vicarage, and in less than half an hour the vicar repaired with him to Lady Lacy's Green.

This stranger, so drooping, so sickly, so emaciated, was the proud Indian uncle, the stern Sir William Ely! Sickness and death had been busy with him and with his. He had lost his health, his wife, and his children; and softened by affliction, was returned to England a new man, anxious to forgive and to be forgiven, and, above all, desirous to repair his neglect and injustice towards the only remaining relative of the wife whom he had so fondly loved and so tenderly lamented. In this frame of mind, such a niece as Jane Mowbray was welcomed with no common joy. His delight in her, and his gratitude towards her protectress, were unbounded. He wished them both to accompany him home, and reside with him constantly. Jane promised to do so; but Mrs. Allen, with her usual admirable feeling of propriety, clung to the spot which had been to her a "city of refuge," and refused to leave it in spite of all the entreaties of uncle and of niece. It was a happy decision for Aberleigh; for what could Aberleigh have done without its good schoolmistress!

She lives there still, its ornament and its pride; and every year Jane Mowbray comes for a long visit, and makes a holiday in the school and in the whole place. Jane Mowbray, did I say? No! not Jane Mowbray now. She has changed that dear name for the only name that could be dearer—she is married—married to the eldest son of Mr. Lacy, the lineal representative of Dame Eleanor Lacy, the honored foundress of the school. It was in a voice tremulous more from feeling than from age, that Mrs. Allen welcomed the young heir, when he brought his fair bride to Aberleigh; and it was with a yet stronger and deeper emotion that the bridegroom, with his own Jane in his hand, visited the asylum which she and her venerable guardian owed to the benevolence and the piety of his ancestress, whose good deeds had thus showered down blessings on her remote posterity.

Dr. Courtly's School

(From a charade in "Our Village.")

A fashionable Morning Room.—Mr. and Mrs. Apperley at breakfast.—Mr. Apperley lays down the newspaper

MR. APP. Mrs. Apperley, my dear, I want to speak to you on a subject on which, as a mother, you have every right to be consulted; the more especially as, from your excellent sense, I have no doubt of your being entirely of my opinion. John grows a great boy.

Mrs. App. Poor fellow! Yes. He'll be ten years old the fifteenth of next month. Time slips away, Mr. Apperley.

Mr. App. Ten years old next month! It's high time that he should be taken from Mr. Lynn's. These preparatory schools are good things for little boys; but a lad of ten years old requires to be more tightly kept.

Mrs. App. Just my opinion, Mr. Apperley. The sooner you remove the poor boy from Mr. Lynn's the better. They don't take half the care of him that they ought to do. Only yesterday, when I called there, I found him playing at cricket without his hat—really without his hat!—in the middle of that wind, and so delicate as John is too!

Mr. App. Delicate! Pshaw! There never was anything the matter with the child but your coddling, Mrs. Apperley; and Eton will soon cure him of that.

Mrs. App. Eton! Do you mean to send John to Eton?

Mr. App. To be sure I do.

Mrs. App. Our sweet John, our only son, our only child, to Eton?

Mr. App. Certainly.

Mrs. App. Never with my consent, I promise you, Mr. Apperley.

Mr. App. And why not, Mrs. Apperley?

Mrs. App. Just look at the boys; that's all. Did not the Duchess tell me herself that the poor little Marquis came home with only one skirt to his jacket, and his brother Lord Edward with scarcely a shoe to his foot? There's a pretty plight for you, Mr. Apperley! Think of our John with his toes through his shoes, and half a skirt to his jacket!

Mr. App. Pshaw!

Mrs. App. Then such rude graceless pickles as they come back, with their manners more out at elbows than their clothes.

Mr. App. Pshaw!

Mrs. App. Then the dangers they run!—to be killed by a cricket-ball, or drowned in the Thames, or——

Mr. App. Pshaw! Mrs. Apperley. Where now, in your wisdom, would you send the boy?

Mrs. App. To Dr. Courtly.

Mr. App. And pray who is Dr. Courtly?

Mrs. App. Did you never hear of Dr. Courtly's establishment for young gentlemen?—never hear of Dr. Courtly!—So elegant, so comfortable, taken such care of; linen clean twice a day; hair curled every morning; almond paste to wash their hands; china dinner-service; silver forks, napkins, and finger-glasses. —Just ten miles off, only fourteen pupils, and happens to have a vacancy. Pray send John to Dr. Courtly, Mr. Apperley.

Mr. App. And so make a coxcomb of the boy before his time! Not I, truly. Leave the hair-curling and the almond-paste to the instinct of eighteen. In the meanwhile I choose that he should learn Latin and Greek; and for that purpose I shall send him to Eton.

Mrs. App. Lord, Mr. Apperley! what is a man the better for that nonsense? You are an Etonian yourself, and pray tell me now what good has your scholarship ever done you? What use have you made of it?

Mr. App. Hem! That's a point which ladies can't understand, and had better not talk about, Mrs. Apperley!

Mrs. App. Have you ever, during the eleven years that we have been married, read a single page of Greek or Latin, Mr. Apperley?

Mr. App. Hem! Why, really, my dear——

Mrs. App. Or indeed a page of anything, except the newspapers and the Waverley novels?

Mr. App. How can you say so, Mrs. Apperley!

Mrs. App. Why, what do you read?

Mr. App. Hem! The Quarterly—I generally look over the Quarterly; and Pepys—I dipped into Pepys; and the magazines, Mrs. Apperley! Don't I turn over the magazines as regularly as the month comes? And, in short, if you could but imagine the Attic zest, the classical relish, with which a sound scholar——but this, as I said before, is what you ladies can't understand, and had better not talk about. John shall go to Eton; that's my determination.

Mrs. App. He shall go to Dr. Courtly's; that's mine. How can you be so barbarous, Mr. Apperley, as to think of sending John to such a place as Eton, subject as he is to chilblains, and the winter coming on? Now the Doctor has studied surgery, and dresses——

Mr. App. Hang the Doctor, and hang John's chilblains. The boy shall go to Eton.—That's my last word, Mrs. Apperley.

Mrs. App. If he does, he'll be dead in a week. But he shan't go to Eton—that's my resolution. And we shall see who'll have the last word, Mr. Apperley—we shall see!

[*Exeunt separately.*]

CHARLOTTE BRONTÉ

1816-1855

CHARLOTTE BRONTÉ, one of the most original novelists of her time, was born at Thornton, in Yorkshire, England, in 1816. When but eight years old, Charlotte was sent with three of her sisters to a boarding-school. Two of her sisters soon died, and Charlotte returned to a home that had not many comforts; for her father was a man of eccentric and solitary habits, and withal very poor. But the sisters nobly determined to exert all their powers to make themselves and their widowed father more comfortable. In 1842, Charlotte and Emily went to Brussels, to qualify themselves for teaching foreign languages. On their return, they advertised that they would receive pupils in the parsonage, but none came.

The three sisters, Charlotte, Emily, and Anne, then ventured to publish a volume of their poems, their names being veiled under those of Currer, Ellis, and Acton Bell. This choice of names was dictated, as Charlotte writes, by "a sort of conscientious scruple at assuming Christian names positively masculine," while they did not like to declare themselves women. But the volume had little success. Charlotte's next venture was a prose tale, "The Professor," which was rejected by the London publishers; but the rejection was sweetened by the encouragement to try her hand at another book. The fruit of this advice was soon beheld in "Jane Eyre" (1847), a work of startling interest and power, which at once made the author famous. In 1849 she published "Shirley," and in 1852, "Villette," —the last work of this woman of genius. In June, 1854, she was married to her father's curate, Mr. Nicholls, but died in the following March, in her thirty-ninth year.

Characterization

The story of the Brontés is one of the saddest in the annals of literature. They were the children of a father who was both cold and violent, and of a gentle, sickly mother, early lost. They were reared amid surroundings the most gloomy and unhealthful, and cursed as they grew older with a brother who brought them shame and sorrow in return for the love they lavished upon him. Their very genius seemed a product of disease, and often their finest pages are marred with a bitter savor of its origin. In treating such subjects these three quiet, patient daughters of a country parson found themselves quite at home. . . . One spring they were all taken sick with a complication of measles and whooping-cough, and on their recovery, Mr. Bronté thought a change of air desirable for the elder ones. In July, 1824, he sent Maria and Elizabeth to a school for clergymen's daughters, at Cowan's Bridge; in September they were joined by Emily and Charlotte. To the readers of Charlotte Bronté it would be superfluous to describe this school—the "Lowood" of "Jane Eyre." Its miserable diet, unhealthy situation, long lessons, rigid discipline, low type of religion, and continual sermons upon humility—nothing is there forgotten, nor is anything exaggerated. Moreover, the descriptions of both teachers and pupils are most of them portraits. Miss Temple and Miss Scatcherd are drawn from life; and the pathetic figure of Helen Burns is a delineation of Maria Bronté, whose death from consumption was directly due to the hardships she underwent at Cowan's Bridge. JAMES PARTON.

Lowood School

(From "Jane Eyre")

My reflections were too undefined and fragmentary to merit record; I hardly yet knew where I was; Gateshead and my past life seemed floated away to an immeasurable distance; the present was vague and strange, and of the future I could form no conjecture. I looked round the convent-like garden, and then up at the house; a large building, half of which seemed gray and old, the other half quite new. The new part, containing the schoolroom and dormitory, was lit by mullioned and latticed windows, which gave it a church-like aspect; a stone tablet over the door bore this inscription:

LOWOOD INSTITUTION.

THIS PORTION WAS REBUILT A. D. ——, BY NAOMI BROCKLEHURST OF BROCKLEHURST HALL, IN THIS COUNTY.

"Let your light so shine before men, that they may see your good works, and glorify your Father which is in heaven."
—ST. MATT. v. 16.

I read these words over and over again ; I felt that an explanation belonged to them, and was unable fully to penetrate their import. I was still pondering the signification of "Institution," and endeavoring to make out a connection between the first words and the verse of Scripture, when the sound of a cough close behind me made me turn my head. I saw a girl sitting on a stone bench near; she was bent over a book, on the perusal of which she seemed intent; and from where I stood I could see the title—it was "Rasselas;" a name that struck me as strange, and consequently attractive. In turning a leaf, she happened to look up, and I said to her directly, "Is your book interesting?" I had already formed the intention of asking her to lend it to me some day.

"I like it," she answered, after a pause of a second or two, during which she examined me.

"What is it about?" I continued. I hardly know where I found the hardihood thus to open a conversation with a stranger; the step was contrary to my nature and habits; but I think her occupation touched a chord of sympathy somewhere; for I, too, liked reading, though of a frivolous and childish kind; I could not digest or comprehend the serious or substantial.

"You may look at it," replied the girl, offering me the book.

I did so; a brief examination convinced me that the contents were less taking than the title: "Rasselas" looked dull to my trifling taste; I saw nothing about fairies, nothing about genii; no bright variety seemed spread over the closely-printed pages. I returned it to her; she received it quietly, and without saying anything she was about to relapse into her former studious mood; again I ventured to disturb her: "Can you tell me what the writing on that stone over that door means? What is Lowood Institution?"

"This house where you are come to live."

"And why do they call it Institution? Is it in any way different from other schools?"

"It is partly a charity-school: you and I, and all the rest of us, are charity-children. I suppose you are an orphan: are not either your father or your mother dead?"

"Both died before I can remember."

"Well, all the girls here have lost either one or both parents, and this is called an institution for educating orphans."

"Do we pay no money? Do they keep us for nothing?"

"We pay, or our friends pay, fifteen pounds a year for each."

"Then why do they call us charity-children?"

"Because fifteen pounds is not enough for board and teaching, and the deficiency is supplied by subscription."

"Who subscribes?"

"Different benevolent-minded ladies and gentlemen in this neighborhood and in London."

"Who was Naomi Brocklehurst?"

"The lady who built the new part of this house as that tablet records, and whose son overlooks and directs everything here."

"Why?"

"Because he is treasurer and manager of the establishment."

"Then this house does not belong to that tall lady who wears a watch, and who said we were to have some bread and cheese."

"To Miss Temple? Oh no! I wish it did; she has to answer to Mr. Brocklehurst for all she does. Mr. Brocklehurst buys all our food and all our clothes."

"Does he live here?"

"No—two miles off, at a large hall."

"Is he a good man?"

"He is a clergyman, and is said to do a great deal of good."

"Did you say that tall lady was called Miss Temple?"

"Yes."

"And what are the other teachers called?"

"The one with the red cheeks is called Miss Smith; she attends to the work, and cuts out—for we make our own clothes, our frocks, and pelisses, and everything; the little one with black hair is Miss Scatcherd; she teaches history and grammar, and hears the second-class repetitions; and the one who wears a shawl, and has a pocket-handkerchief tied to her side with a yellow ribbon, is Madame Pierrot; she comes from Lisle, in France, and teaches French."

" Do you like the teachers? "

" Well enough."

" Do you like the little black one, and the Madame ——? I cannot pronounce her name as you do."

" Miss Scatcherd is hasty—you must take care not to offend her; Madame Pierrot is not a bad sort of person."

" But Miss Temple is the best—isn't she? "

" Miss Temple is very good, and very clever; she is above the rest, because she knows far more than they do."

" Have you been long here? "

" Two years."

" Are you an orphan? "

" My mother is dead."

" Are you happy here? "

" You ask rather too many questions. I have given you answers enough for the present; now I want to read."

But at the moment the summons sounded for dinner; all reëntered the house. The odor which now filled the refectory was scarcely more appetizing than that which had regaled our nostrils at breakfast; the dinner was served in two huge tin-plated vessels, whence rose a strong steam redolent of rancid fat. I found the mess to consist of indifferent potatoes and strange shreds of rusty meat, mixed and cooked together. Of this preparation a tolerably abundant plateful was apportioned to each pupil. I ate what I could, and wondered within myself whether every day's fare would be like this.

After dinner, we immediately adjourned to the schoolroom; lessons recommenced, and were continued till five o'clock.

The only marked event of the afternoon was, that I saw the girl with whom I had conversed in the veranda dismissed in disgrace by Miss Scatcherd from a history class, and sent to stand in the middle of the large schoolroom. The punishment seemed to me in a high degree ignominious, especially for so great a girl—she looked thirteen or upward. I expected she would show signs of great distress and shame; but to my surprise she neither wept nor blushed: composed, though grave, she stood the central mark of all eyes. " How can she bear it so quietly—so firmly ? " I asked of myself. " Were I in her place, it seems to me that I should wish the earth to open and swallow me up. She looks as if she were thinking of something beyond her punishment—beyond her situation: of something not round her or before her. I have heard of day-dreams—is she in a day-dream now? Her eyes are fixed on the floor, but I am sure they do not see it—her sight seems turned in, gone down into her heart: she is looking at what she can remember, I believe, not at what is really present. I wonder what sort of a girl she is—whether good or naughty?"

Soon after five P. M. we had another meal, consisting of a small mug of coffee, and half a slice of brown bread. I devoured my bread and drank my coffee with relish; but I should have been glad of as much more—I was still hungry. Half an hour's recreation succeeded, then study; then the glass of water and the piece of oat-cake, prayers and bed. Such was my first day at Lowood.

The next day commenced as before, getting up and dressing by rush light; but this morning we were obliged to dispense with the ceremony of washing: the water in the pitchers was frozen. A change had taken place in the weather the preceding evening, and a keen northeast wind, whistling through the crevices of our bedroom windows all night long, had made us shiver in our bed, and turned the contents of the ewers to ice.

Before the long hour and a half of prayers and Bible reading was over, I felt ready to perish with cold. Breakfast-time came at last, and this morning the porridge was not burned; the quality was eatable, the quantity small; how small my portion seemed! I wished it had been doubled.

In the course of the day I was enrolled a member of the fourth class, and regular tasks and occupations were assigned me; hitherto I had only been a spectator of the proceedings at

Lowood, I was now to become an actor therein. At first, being little accustomed to learn by heart, the lessons appeared to me both long and difficult: the frequent change from task to task, too, bewildered me; and I was glad when, about three o'clock in the afternoon, Miss Smith put into my hands a border of muslin two yards long, together with needle, thimble, etc., and sent me to sit in a quiet corner of the schoolroom, with directions to hem the same. At that hour most of the others were sewing likewise; but one class still stood round Miss Scatcherd's chair reading, and as all was quiet, the subject of their lessons could be heard, together with the manner in which each girl acquitted herself, and the animadversions or commendations of Miss Scatcherd on the performance. It was English history: among the readers I observed my acquaintance of the veranda: at the commencement of the lesson, her place had been at the top of the class, but for some error of pronunciation or some inattention to stops, she was suddenly sent to the very bottom. Even in that obscure position, Miss Scatcherd continued to make her an object of constant notice: she was continually addressing to her such phrases as the following:

"Burns" (such, it seems, was her name: the girls here were called by their surnames, as boys are elsewhere), "Burns, you are standing on the side of your shoe, turn your toes out immediately." "Burns, you poke your chin most unpleasantly; draw it in." "Burns, I insist on your holding your head up; I will not have you before me in that attitude," etc., etc.

A chapter having been read through twice, the books were closed and the girls examined. The lesson had comprised part of the reign of Charles I., and there were sundry questions about tonnage and poundage and ship-money, which most of them appeared unable to answer; still, every little difficulty was solved instantly when it reached Burns; her memory seemed to have retained the substance of the whole lesson, and she was ready with answers on every point. I kept expecting that Miss Scatcherd would praise her attention; but, instead of that, she suddenly called out:

"You dirty, disagreeable girl! you have never cleaned your nails this morning!"

Burns made no answer; I wondered at her silence.

"Why," thought I, "does she not explain that she could neither clean her nails nor wash her face, as the water was frozen?"

My attention was now called off by Miss Smith desiring me to hold a skein of thread: while she was winding it, she talked with me from time to time, asking whether I had ever been at school before, whether I could mark, stitch, knit, etc.; till she dismissed me, I could not pursue my observations on Miss Scatcherd's movements. When I returned to my seat, that lady was just delivering an order, of which I did not catch the import; but Burns immediately left the class, and, going into the small inner room where the books were kept, returned in half a minute, carrying in her hand a bundle of twigs tied together at one end. This ominous tool she presented to Miss Scatcherd with a respectful courtesy; then she quietly, and without being told, unloosed her pinafore, and the teacher instantly and sharply inflicted on her neck a dozen strokes with the bunch of twigs. Not a tear rose to Burns' eye; and while I paused from my sewing, because my fingers quivered at this spectacle with a sentiment of unavailing and impotent anger, not a feature of her pensive face altered its ordinary expression.

"Hardened girl!" exclaimed Miss Scatcherd; "nothing can correct you of your slatternly habits: carry the rod away."

Burns obeyed: I looked at her narrowly as she emerged from the book-closet; she was just putting back her handkerchief into her pocket, and the trace of a tear glistened on her thin cheek.

. . . .

My first quarter at Lowood seemed an age; and not the golden age either: it comprised an irksome struggle with difficulties in habituating myself to new rules and unwonted tasks. The fear of failure in these points harassed me worse than the physical hardships of my lot; though these were no trifles.

During January, February, and part of March, the deep snows, and, after their melting, the almost impassable roads, prevented our stirring beyond the garden walls, except to go to church; but within these limits we had to pass an hour every day in the open air. Our clothing was insufficient to protect us from the severe cold; we had no boots; the snow got into our shoes, and melted there; our ungloved hands became numbed and covered with chilblains, as were our feet; I remember well the distracting irritation I endured from this cause every evening, when my feet inflamed; and the torture of thrusting the swelled, raw, and stiff toes into my shoes in the morning. Then the scanty supply of food was distressing. With the keen appetites of growing children, we had scarcely sufficient to keep alive a delicate invalid. From this deficiency of nourishment resulted an abuse, which pressed hardly on the younger pupils: whenever the famished great girls had an opportunity they would coax or menace the little ones out of their portion. Many a time I have shared between two claimants the precious morsel of brown bread distributed at tea-time; and after relinquishing to a third half the contents of my mug of coffee, I have swallowed the remainder with an accompaniment of secret tears forced from me by the exigency of hunger.

Sundays were dreary days in that wintry season. We had to walk two miles to Brocklebridge Church, where our patron officiated. We set out cold, we arrived at church colder: during the morning service we became almost paralyzed. It was too far to return to dinner, and an allowance of cold meat and bread, in the same penurious proportion observed in our ordinary meals, was served round between the services.

At the close of the afternoon service we returned by an exposed and hilly road, where the bitter winter wind, blowing over a range of snowy summits to the north, almost flayed the skin from our faces.

I can remember Miss Temple walking lightly and rapidly along our drooping line, her plaid cloak, which the frosty wind fluttered, gathered close about her, and encouraging us, by precept and example, to keep up our spirits, and march forward, as she said, "like stalwart soldiers." The other teachers, poor things, were generally themselves too much dejected to attempt the task of cheering others.

How we longed for the light and heat of a blazing fire when we got back! But to the little ones at least, this was denied: each hearth in the schoolroom was immediately surrounded by a double row of great girls, and behind them the younger children crouched in groups, wrapping their starved arms in their pinafores.

A little solace came at tea-time, in the shape of a double ration of bread—a whole, instead of a half, slice—with the delicious addition of a thin scrape of butter: it was the hebdomadal treat to which we all looked forward from Sabbath to Sabbath. I generally contrived to reserve a moiety of this bounteous repast for myself; but the remainder I was invariably obliged to part with.

The Sunday evening was spent in repeating, by heart, the Church Catechism, and the fifth, sixth, and seventh chapters of St. Matthew; and in listening to a long sermon, read by Miss Miller, whose irrepressible yawns attested her weariness. A frequent interlude of these performances was the enactment of the part of Eutychus by some half dozen little girls, who, overpowered with sleep, would fall down, if not out of the third loft, yet off the fourth form, and be taken up half dead. The remedy was, to thrust them forward into the center of the schoolroom, and oblige them to stand there till the sermon was finished. Sometimes their feet failed them, and they sank together in a heap; they were then propped up with the monitors' high stools.

I have not yet alluded to the visits of Mr. Brocklehurst; and indeed that gentleman was from home during the greater part of the first month after my arrival; perhaps prolonging his stay with his friend the archdeacon; his absence was a relief to me. I need not say that I had my own reasons for dreading his coming: but come he did at last.

One afternoon (I had then been three weeks at Lowood), as I was sitting with a slate in my hand, puzzling over a sum in long division, my eyes, raised in abstraction to the window, caught sight of a figure just passing; I recognized almost instinctively that gaunt outline; and when two minutes after, all the school, teachers included, rose *en masse*, it was not necessary for me to look up in order to ascertain whose entrance they thus greeted. A long stride measured the schoolroom, and presently beside Miss Temple, who herself had risen, stood the same black column which had frowned on me so ominously from the hearth-rug at Gateshead. I now glanced sideways at this piece of architecture. Yes, I was right; it was Mr. Brocklehurst, buttoned up in a surtout, and looking longer, narrower, and more rigid than ever.

I had my own reasons for being dismayed at this apparition; too well I remembered the perfidious hints given by Mrs. Reed about my disposition, etc.; the promise pledged by Mr. Brocklehurst to apprise Miss Temple and the teachers of my vicious nature. All along I had been dreading the fulfillment of this promise—I had been looking out daily for the "coming man," whose information respecting my past life and conversation was to brand me as a bad child forever; now there he was. He stood at Miss Temple's side; he was speaking low in her ear; I did not doubt he was making disclosures of my villainy; and I watched her eye with painful anxiety, expecting every moment to see its dark orb turn on me a glance of repugnance and contempt. I listened, too; and as I happened to be seated quite at the top of the room, I caught most of what he said; its import relieved me from immediate apprehension.

"I suppose, Miss Temple, the thread I bought at Lowton will do; it struck me that it would be just of the quality for the calico chemise, and I sorted the needles to match. You may tell Miss Smith that I forgot to make a memorandum of the darning-needles, but she shall have some papers sent in next week, and she is not, on any account, to give out more than one at a time to each pupil: if they have more, they are apt to be careless and lose them. And oh, ma'am! I wish the woolen stockings were better looked to!—when I was here last, I went into the kitchen-garden and examined the clothes drying on the line; there was a quantity of black hose in a very bad state of repair: from the size of the holes in them I was sure they had not been well mended from time to time."

He paused.

"Your directions shall be attended to, sir," said Miss Temple.

"And, ma'am," he continued, "the laundress tells me some of the girls have two clean tuckers in the week: it is too much; the rules limit them to one."

"I think I can explain that circumstance, sir. Agnes and Catharine Johnstone were invited to take tea with some friends at Lowton last Thursday, and I gave them leave to put on clean tuckers for the occasion."

Mr. Brocklehurst nodded.

"Well, for once it may pass; but please not to let the circumstance occur too often. And there is another thing which surprised me: I find, in settling accounts with the housekeeper, that a lunch, consisting of bread and cheese, has twice been served out to the girls during the past fortnight. How is this? I look over the regulations, and I find no such meal as lunch mentioned. Who introduced this innovation? and by what authority?"

"I must be responsible for the circumstance, sir," replied Miss Temple: "the breakfast was so ill-prepared that the pupils could not possibly eat it; and I dared not allow them to remain fasting till dinner-time."

"Madam, allow me an instant. You are aware that my plan in bringing up these girls is, not to accustom them to habits of luxury and indulgence, but to render them hardy, patient, self-denying. Should any little accidental disappointment of the appetite occur, such as the spoiling of a meal, the under or the over dressing of a dish, the incident ought not to be neutralized by replacing with something more delicate the comfort lost, thus pampering the body and obviating the aim of this institution; it ought to be improved to the spiritual edification of the pupils, by encouraging them to evince fortitude under the temporary privation. A brief address on those occasions would not be mistimed, wherein a judicious instructor would take the opportunity of referring to the sufferings of the primitive Christians; to the torments of martyrs; to the exhortations of our blessed Lord himself, calling upon his disciples to take up their cross and follow him; to his warnings that man shall not live by bread alone, but by every word that proceedeth out of the mouth of God; to his divine consolations, 'If ye suffer hunger or thirst for my sake, happy are ye.' Oh, madam, when you put bread and cheese, instead of burned porridge, into these children's mouths, you may indeed feed their vile bodies, but you little think how you starve their immortal souls!"

Mr. Brocklehurst again paused—perhaps overcome by his feelings. Miss Temple had looked down when he first began to speak to her; but she now gazed straight before her, and her face, naturally pale as marble, appeared to be assuming also the coldness and fixity of that material; especially her mouth closed as if it would have required a sculptor's chisel to open it, and her brow settled gradually into petrified severity.

Meantime, Mr. Brocklehurst, standing on the hearth with his hands behind his back, majestically surveyed the whole school. Suddenly his eye gave a blink, as if it had met something that either dazzled or shocked its pupil; turning, he said in more rapid accents than he had hitherto used: "Miss Temple, Miss Temple, what—*what* is that girl with curled hair? Red hair, ma'am, curled—curled all over?" And extending his cane he pointed to the awful object, his hand shaking as he did so.

"It is Julia Severn," replied Miss Temple, very quietly.

"Julia Severn, ma'am! And why has she, or any other, curled hair? Why, in defiance of every precept and principle of this house, does she conform to the world so openly—here in an evangelical, charitable establishment—as to wear her hair one mass of curls?"

"Julia's nair curls naturally," returned Miss Temple, still more quietly.

"Naturally! Yes, but we are not to conform to nature: I wish these girls to be the children of Grace: and why that abundance? I have again and again intimated that I desire the hair to be arranged closely, modestly, plainly. Miss Temple, that girl's hair must be cut off entirely; I will send a barber to-morrow: and I see others who have far too much of the excrescence—that tall girl, tell her to turn round. Tell all the first form to rise up and direct their faces to the wall."

Miss Temple passed her handkerchief over her lips, as if to smooth away the involuntary smiles that curled them; she gave the order, however, and when the first class could take in what was required of them, they obeyed. Leaning a little back on my bench I could see the looks and grimaces with which they commented on this maneuver: it was a pity Mr. Brocklehurst could not see them too; he would perhaps have felt that whatever he might do with the outside of the cup and platter, the inside was further beyond his interference than he imagined.

He scrutinized the reverse of these living medals some five minutes, then pronounced sentence. These words fell like the knell of doom: "All those top-knots must be cut off."

Miss Temple seemed to remonstrate.

"Madam," he pursued, "I have a Master to serve whose kingdom is not of this world: my mission is to mortify in these girls the lusts of the flesh; to teach them to clothe themselves with shamefacedness and sobriety, not with braided hair and costly apparel; and each of the young persons before us has a string of hair twisted in plaits which vanity itself might have woven: these, I repeat, must be cut off; think of the time wasted, of——"

Mr. Brocklehurst was here interrupted: three other visitors, ladies, now entered the room. They ought to have come a little sooner to have heard his lecture on dress, for they were splendidly attired in velvet, silk, and furs. The two younger of the trio (fine girls of sixteen and seventeen) had gray beaver hats, then in fashion, shaded with ostrich plumes, and from under the brim of this graceful head-dress fell a profusion of light tresses, elaborately curled; the elder lady was enveloped in a costly velvet shawl, trimmed with ermine, and she wore a false front of French curls.

These ladies were deferentially received by Miss Temple, as Mrs. and the Misses Brocklehurst, and conducted to seats of honor at the top of the room. It seems they had come in the carriage with their reverend relative, and had been conducting a rummaging scrutiny of the rooms up-stairs, while he transacted business with the housekeeper, questioned the laundress, and lectured the superintendent. They now proceeded to address divers remarks and reproofs to Miss Smith, who was charged with the care of the linen and the inspection of the dormitories; but I had no time to listen to what they said; other matters called off and enchained my attention.

Hitherto, while gathering up the discourse of Mr. Brocklehurst and Miss Temple, I had not at the same time neglected precautions to secure my personal safety; which I thought would be effected, if I could only elude observation. To this end, I had sat well back on the form, and while seeming to be busy with my sum, had held my slate in such a manner as to conceal my face: I might have escaped notice, had not my treacherous slate somehow happened to slip from my hand, and falling with an obtrusive crash, directly drawn every eye upon me; I knew it was all over now, and, as I stooped to pick up the two fragments of slate, I rallied my forces for the worst. It came.

"A careless girl!" said Mr. Brocklehurst, and immediately after—"It is the new pupil, I perceive." And before I could draw breath, "I must not forget I have a word to say respecting her." Then aloud—how loud it seemed to me! "Let the child who broke her slate come forward!"

Of my own accord I could not have stirred: I was paralyzed: but the two great girls who sat on each side of me set me on my legs and pushed me towards the dread judge, and then Miss Temple gently assisted me to his very feet, and I caught her whispered counsel, " Don't be afraid, Jane, I saw it was an accident; you shall not be punished."

The kind whisper went to my heart like a dagger.

" Another minute, and she will despise me for a hypocrite," thought I, and an impulse of fury against Reed, Brocklehurst and Co. bounded in my pulses at the conviction. I was no Helen Burns.

" Fetch that stool," said Mr. Brocklehurst, pointing to a very high one from which a monitor had just risen; it was brought.

" Place the child upon it."

And I was placed there, by whom I don't know—I was in no condition to note particulars—I was only aware that they had hoisted me up to the height of Mr. Brocklehurst's nose, that he was within a yard of me, and that a spread of shot orange and purple silk pelisse and a cloud of silvery plumage extended and waved below me.

Mr. Brocklehurst hemmed.

" Ladies," said he, turning to his family; " Miss Temple, teachers, and children, you all see this girl?"

Of course they did; for I felt their eyes directed like burning-glasses against my scorched skin.

" You see she is yet young; you observe she possesses the ordinary form of childhood; God has graciously given her the shape that he has given to all of us; no signal deformity points her out as a marked character. Who would think that the Evil One had already found a servant and agent in her? Yet such, I grieve to say, is the case."

A pause—in which I began to study the palsy of my nerves, and feel that the Rubicon was passed; and that the trial, no longer to be shirked, must be firmly sustained.

" My dear children," pursued the black-marble clergyman, with pathos, "this is a sad, a melancholy occasion, for it becomes my duty to warn you, that this girl, who might be one of God's own lambs, is a little castaway: not a member of the true flock, but evidently an interloper and an alien. You must be on your guard against her; you must shun her example; if necessary, avoid her company, exclude her from your sports, and shut her out from your converse. Teachers, you must watch her. Keep your eyes on her movements, weigh well her words, scrutinize her actions, punish her body to save her soul, if, indeed, such salvation be possible, for (my tongue falters while I tell it) this girl, this child, the native of a Christian land, worse than many a little heathen who says its prayers to Brahma and kneels before Juggernaut—this girl is—a liar."

Now came a pause of ten minutes: during which I, by this time in perfect possession of my wits, observed all the female Brocklehursts produce their pocket-handkerchiefs and apply them to their optics, while the elderly lady swayed herself to and fro, and the two younger ones whispered, "How shocking!"

Mr. Brocklehurst resumed.

"This I learned from her benefactress; from the pious and charitable lady who adopted her in her orphan state, reared her as her own daughter, and whose kindness, whose generosity, the unhappy girl repaid by an ingratitude so bad, so dreadful, that at last her excellent patroness was obliged to separate her from her own young ones, fearful lest her vicious example should contaminate their purity. She has sent her here to be healed, even as the Jews of old sent their diseased to the troubled pool of Bethesda; and, teachers, superintendent, I beg of you not to allow the waters to stagnate round her."

With this sublime conclusion, Mr. Brocklehurst adjusted the top button of his surtout, muttered something to his family, who rose, bowed to Miss Temple, and then all the great people sailed in state from the room. Turning at the door, my judge said, "Let her stand half an hour longer on that stool, and let no one speak to her during the remainder of the day."

There was I, then, mounted aloft—I, who had said I could not bear the shame of standing on my natural feet in the middle of the room, was now exposed to general view on a pedestal of infamy. What my sensations were, no language can describe; but just as they all rose, stifling my breath and constricting my throat, a girl came up and passed me. In passing,

she lifted her eyes. What a strange light inspired them!
What an extraordinary sensation that ray sent through me!
How the new feeling bore me up! It was as if a martyr, a
hero, had passed a slave or victim, and imparted strength in the
transit. I mastered the rising hysteria, lifted up my head, and
took a firm stand on the stool. Helen Burns asked some slight
question about her work of Miss Smith, was chidden for the
triviality of the inquiry, returned to her place, and smiled at
me as she again went by. What a smile! I remember it now,
and I know that it was the effluence of fine intellect, of true courage; it lit up her marked lineaments, her thin face, her sunken
gray eye, like a reflection from the aspect of an angel. Yet
at that moment Helen Burns wore on her arm "the untidy
badge;" scarcely an hour ago I had heard her condemned by
Miss Scatcherd to a dinner of bread and water on the morrow,
because she had blotted an exercise in copying it out. Such is
the imperfect nature of man! Such spots are there on the disk
of the clearest planet; and eyes like Miss Scatcherd's can only
see those minute defects, and are blind to the full brightness of
the orb.

Ere the half-hour ended five o'clock struck; school was dismissed, and all were gone into the refectory to tea. I now ventured to descend; it was deep dusk; I retired into a corner and
sat down on the floor. The spell by which I had been so far
supported began to dissolve; reaction took place, and soon, so
overwhelming was the grief that seized me, I sank prostrate
with my face to the ground. Now I wept. Helen Burns was
not here; nothing sustained me; left to myself, I abandoned
myself, and my tears watered the boards. I had meant to be
so good, and to do so much at Lowood, to make so many
friends, to earn respect and win affection. Already I had made
visible progress; that very morning I had reached the head of
my class; Miss Miller had praised me warmly; Miss Temple had
smiled approbation; she had promised to teach me drawing,
and to let me learn French, if I continued to make similar
improvement two months longer; and then I was well received

by my fellow-pupils; treated as an equal by those of my own age, and not molested by any; now, here I lay again crushed and trodden on; and could I ever rise more?

"Never," I thought; and ardently I wished to die. While sobbing out this wish in broken accents, some one approached; I started up—again Helen Burns was near me; the fading fires just showed her coming up the long, vacant room; she brought my coffee and bread.

"Come, eat something," she said; but I put both away from me, feeling as if a drop or a crumb would have choked me in my present condition. Helen regarded me, probably with surprise. I could not now abate my agitation, though I tried hard; I continued to weep aloud. She sat down on the ground near me, embraced her knees with her arms, and rested her head upon them; in that attitude she remained silent as an Indian. I was the first who spoke: "Helen, why do you stay with a girl whom everybody believes to be a liar?"

"Everybody, Jane? Why, there are only eighty people who have heard you called so, and the world contains hundreds of millions."

"But what have I to do with millions? The eighty I know despise me."

"Jane, you are mistaken; probably not one in the school either despises or dislikes you. Many, I am sure, pity you much."

"How can they pity me after what Mr. Brocklehurst said?"

"Mr. Brocklehurst is not a god; nor is he even a great and admired man; he is little liked here; he never took steps to make himself liked. Had he treated you as an especial favorite, you would have found enemies, declared or covert, all around you. As it is, the greater number would offer you sympathy if they dared. Teachers and pupils may look coldly on you for a day or two, but friendly feelings are concealed in their hearts; and if you persevere in doing well, these feelings will ere long appear so much the more evidently for their temporary suppression. Besides, Jane——" she paused.

"Well, Helen?" said I, putting my hand into hers. She chafed my fingers gently to warm them, and went on:

"If all the world hated you, and believed you wicked, while your own conscience approved you, and absolved you from guilt, you would not be without friends."

"No; I know I should think well of myself; but that is not enough; if others don't love me, I would rather die than live— I cannot bear to be solitary and hated, Helen. Look here; to gain some real affection from you, or Miss Temple, or any other whom I truly love, I would willingly submit to have the bone of my arm broken, or to let a bull toss me, or to stand behind a kicking horse, and let it dash its hoof at my chest——"

"Hush, Jane! you think too much of the love of human beings; you are too impulsive, too vehement. The sovereign Hand that created your frame, and put life into it, has provided you with other resources than your feeble self, or than creatures feebler than you. Besides this earth, and besides the race of men, there is an invisible world and a kingdom of spirits. That world is round us, for it is everywhere; and those spirits watch us, for they are commissioned to guard us; and if we were dying in pain and shame, if scorn smote us on all sides, and hatred crushed us, angels see our tortures, recognize our innocence (if innocent we be, as I know you are of this charge which Mr. Brocklehurst has weakly and pompously repeated at second-hand from Mrs. Reed; for I read a sincere nature in your ardent eyes and on your clear front), and God waits only the separation of spirit from flesh to crown us with a full reward. Why, then, should we ever sink overwhelmed with distress, when life is so soon over, and death is so certain an entrance to happiness—to glory?"

I was silent. Helen had calmed me; but in the tranquillity she imparted there was an alloy of inexpressible sadness. I felt the impression of woe as she spoke, but I could not tell whence it came; and when, having done speaking, she breathed a little fast and coughed a short cough, I momentarily forgot my own sorrows, to yield to a vague concern for her.

Resting my head on Helen's shoulder, I put my arms round her waist; she drew me to her and we reposed in silence. We had not sat long thus when another person came in. Some heavy clouds, swept from the sky by a rising wind, had left the moon bare; and her light, streaming in through a window near, shone full both on us and on the approaching figure, which we at once recognized as Miss Temple.

"I came on purpose to find you, Jane Eyre," said she; "I want you in my room; and as Helen Burns is with you, she may come too."

We went; following the superintendent's guidance, we had to thread some intricate passages, and mount a staircase before we reached her apartment; it contained a good fire, and looked cheerful. Miss Temple told Helen Burns to be seated in a low arm-chair on one side of the hearth, and herself taking another, she called me to her side.

"Is it all over?" she asked, looking down at my face. "Have you cried your grief away?"

"I am afraid I never shall do that."

"Why?"

"Because I have been wrongly accused; and you, ma'am, and everybody else will now think me wicked."

"We shall think you what you prove yourself to be, my child. Continue to act as a good girl, and you will satisfy me."

"Shall I, Miss Temple?"

"You will," said she, passing her arm round me. "And now tell me who is the lady whom Mr. Brocklehurst called your benefactress?"

"Mrs. Reed, my uncle's wife. My uncle is dead, and he left me to her care."

"Did she not, then, adopt you of her own accord?"

"No, ma'am; she was sorry to have to do it; but my uncle, as I have often heard the servants say, got her to promise before he died that she would always keep me."

"Well, now, Jane, you know, or at least I will tell you, that when a criminal is accused, he is always allowed to speak in his own defense. You have been charged with falsehood; defend yourself to me as well as you can. Say whatever your memory suggests as true; but add nothing and exaggerate nothing."

I resolved in the depth of my heart that I would be most moderate—most correct; and, having reflected a few minutes in order to arrange coherently what I had to say, I told her all the story of my sad childhood. Exhausted by emotion, my language was more subdued than it generally was when it developed that sad theme; and mindful of Helen's warnings against the indulgence of resentment, I infused into the narrative far less of gall and wormwood than ordinary. Thus restrained and simplified, it sounded more credible. I felt as I went on that Miss Temple fully believed me.

In the course of the tale I had mentioned Mr. Lloyd as having come to see me after the fit; for I never forgot the, to me, frightful episode of the red-room; in detailing which, my excitement was sure, in some degree, to break bounds; for nothing could soften in my recollection the spasm of agony which clutched my heart when Mrs. Reed spurned my wild supplication for pardon, and locked me a second time in the dark and haunted chamber.

I had finished. Miss Temple regarded me a few minutes in silence; she then said: "I know something of Mr. Lloyd; I shall write to him; if his reply agrees with your statement, you shall be publicly cleared from every imputation. To me, Jane, you are clear now."

She kissed me, and still keeping me at her side (where I was well contented to stand, for I derived a child's pleasure from the contemplation of her face, her dress, her one or two ornaments, her white forehead, her clustered and shining curls, and beaming dark eyes), she proceeded to address Helen Burns.

"How are you to-night, Helen? Have you coughed much to-day?"

"Not quite so much, I think, ma'am."

"And the pain in your chest?"

"It is a little better."

Miss Temple got up, took her hand and examined her pulse; then she returned to her own seat. As she resumed it, I heard her sigh low. She was pensive a few minutes, then rousing herself, she said cheerfully, "But you two are my visitors to-night; I must treat you as such." She rang her bell.

"Barbara," she said to the servant who answered it, "I have not yet had tea; bring the tray, and place cups for these two young ladies."

And a tray was soon brought. How pretty, to my eyes, did the china cups and bright teapot look, placed on the little round table near the fire! How fragrant was the steam of the beverage, and the scent of the toast! of which, however, I, to my dismay (for I was beginning to be hungry), discerned only a very small portion. Miss Temple discerned it too. "Barbara," said she, "can you not bring a little more bread and butter? There is not enough for three."

Barbara went out; she returned soon. "Madam, Mrs. Harden says she has sent up the usual quantity."

Mrs. Harden, be it observed, was the housekeeper—a woman after Mr. Brocklehurst's own heart, made up of equal parts of whalebone and iron.

"Oh, very well!" returned Miss Temple; "we must make it do, Barbara, I suppose." And as the girl withdrew, she added, smiling, "Fortunately, I have it in my power to supply deficiencies for this once."

Having invited Helen and me to approach the table, and placed before each of us a cup of tea with one delicious but thin morsel of toast, she got up, unlocked a drawer, and taking from it a parcel wrapped in paper, disclosed presently to our eyes a good-sized seed-cake.

"I meant to give each of you some of this to take with you," said she; "but as there is so little toast, you must have it now," and she proceeded to cut slices with a generous hand.

We feasted that evening as on nectar and ambrosia; and not the least delight of the entertainment was the smile of gratification with which our hostess regarded us, as we satisfied our famished appetites on the delicate fare she liberally supplied. Tea over and the tray removed, she again summoned us to the fire. We sat one on each side of her; and now a conversation followed between her and Helen which it was indeed a privilege to be admitted to hear.

Miss Temple had always something of serenity in her air, of state in her mien, of refined propriety in her language, which precluded deviation into the ardent, the excited, the eager—something which chastened the pleasure of those who looked on her and listened to her, by a controlling sense of awe; and such was my feeling now; but as to Helen Burns, I was struck with wonder.

The refreshing meal, the brilliant fire, the presence and kindness of her beloved instructress, or, perhaps, more than all these, something in her own unique mind, had roused her powers within her. They woke, they kindled. First, they glowed in the bright tint of her cheek, which till this hour I had never seen but pale and bloodless; then they shone in the liquid luster of her eyes, which had suddenly acquired a beauty more singular than that of Miss Temple's—a beauty neither of fine color nor long eyelashes, nor penciled brow, but of meaning, of movement, of radiance. Then her soul sat on her lips, and language flowed, from what source I cannot tell. Has a girl of fourteen a heart large enough, vigorous enough, to hold the swelling spring of pure, full, fervid eloquence? Such was the characteristic of Helen's discourse on that, to me, memorable evening; her spirit seemed hastening to live within a very brief span as much as many live during a protracted existence.

They conversed of things I had never heard of—of nations and times past; of countries far away; of secrets of nature discovered or guessed at. They spoke of books. How many they had read! What stores of knowledge they possessed! Then they seemed so familiar with French names and French authors; but my amazement reached its climax when Miss Temple asked Helen if she sometimes snatched a moment to recall the Latin her father had taught her, and taking a book from a shelf, bade her read and construe a page of "Virgil;" and Helen obeyed, my organ of veneration expanding at every sounding line. She had scarcely finished ere the bell announced bedtime. No delay could be admitted; Miss Temple embraced us both saying, as she drew us to her heart, "God bless you, my children!"

Helen she held a little longer than me; she let her go more reluctantly; it was Helen her eye followed to the door; it was for her she a second time breathed a sad sigh; for her she wiped a tear from her cheek.

On reaching the bedroom, we heard the voice of Miss Scatcherd. She was examining drawers; she had just pulled out Helen Burns', and when we entered, Helen was greeted with a sharp reprimand, and told that to-morrow she should have half a dozen of untidily-folded articles pinned to her shoulder.

"My things were indeed in shameful disorder," murmured Helen to me, in a 'low voice: "I intended to have arranged them, but I forgot."

Next morning Miss Scatcherd wrote, in conspicuous characters on a piece of pasteboard, the word "Slattern," and bound it like a phylactery round Helen's large, mild, intelligent, and benign-looking forehead. She wore it till evening, patient, unresentful, regarding it as a deserved punishment.

. . . .

But the privations, or rather the hardships of Lowood lessened. Spring drew on; she was indeed already come; the frosts of winter had ceased; its snows were melted, its cutting winds ameliorated. My wretched feet, flayed and swollen to lameness by the sharp air of January, began to heal and subside under the gentler breathings of April; the nights and mornings no longer by their Canadian temperature froze the very blood in our veins; we could now endure the play-hour passed in the garden; sometimes on a sunny day it began even to be pleasant and genial, and a greenness grew over those brown beds which, freshening daily, suggested the thought that Hope traversed them at night, and left each morning brighter

traces of her steps. Flowers peeped out among the leaves—
snowdrops, crocuses, purple auriculas, and golden-eyed pansies.
On Thursday afternoons (half holidays) we now took walks, and
found still sweeter flowers opening by the wayside, under the
hedges.

.   .   .   .   .   .

That forest dell, where Lowood lay, was the cradle of fog and
fog-bred pestilence; which, quickening with the quickening
spring, crept into the Orphan Asylum, breathed typhus through
its crowded schoolroom and dormitory, and, ere May arrived,
transformed the seminary into a hospital.

Semi-starvation and neglected colds had predisposed most
of the pupils to receive infection; forty-five out of the eighty
girls lay ill at one time. Classes were broken up, rules relaxed.
The few who continued well were allowed almost unlimited
license, because the medical attendant insisted on the necessity
of frequent exercise to keep them in health; and had it been
otherwise, no one had leisure to watch or restrain them. Miss
Temple's whole attention was absorbed by the patients. She
lived in the sick-room, never quitting it except to snatch a few
hours' rest at night. The teachers were fully occupied with
packing up and making other necessary preparations for the
departure of those girls who were fortunate enough to have
friends and relations able and willing to remove them from the
seat of contagion. Many already smitten went home only to
die. Some died at the school and were buried quietly and
quickly, the nature of the malady forbidding delay.

While disease had thus become an inhabitant of Lowood,
and death its frequent visitor; while there was gloom and fear
within its walls; while its rooms and passages steamed with
hospital smells, the drug and the pastil striving vainly to overcome the effluvia of mortality, that bright May shone unclouded
over the bold hills and beautiful woodland out of doors. Its
garden, too, glowed with flowers; hollyhocks had sprung up
tall as trees, lilies had opened, tulips and roses were in bloom;
the borders of the little beds were gay with pink thrift and

crimson double-daisies; the sweetbriers gave out, morning and evening, their scent of spice and apples; and these fragrant treasures were all useless for most of the inmates of Lowood, except to furnish now and then a handful of herbs and blossoms to put in a coffin.

But I, and the rest who continued well, enjoyed fully the beauties of the scene and season. They let us ramble in the wood like gypsies, from morning till night. We did what we liked, went where we liked. We lived better too. Mr. Brocklehurst and his family never came near Lowood now; household matters were not scrutinized into; the cross housekeeper was gone, driven away by the fear of infection; her successor, who had been matron at the Lowton Dispensary, unused to the ways of her new abode, provided with comparative liberality. Besides, there were fewer to feed; the sick could eat little; our breakfast-basins were better filled. When there was no time to prepare a regular dinner, which often happened, she would give us a large piece of cold pie, or a thick slice of bread and cheese, and this we carried away with us to the wood, where we each chose the spot we liked best, and dined sumptuously.

DAVID PERKINS PAGE
1810-1848

DAVID PERKINS PAGE was born at Epping, New Hampshire, in 1810. He was the son of a prosperous New England farmer, and passed his youth in his native village, where he was enrolled as a pupil in the public school. At the age of sixteen years he entered Hampton Academy, where he prepared himself for the profession of teaching. After an experience of two years as teacher of a private school at Newbury, he was chosen associate principal of the Newburyport High School, in which position he served for twelve years. In 1844 he was chosen to be president of the State Normal School of New York, at Albany. The appointment was made at the suggestion of Horace Mann. The Normal School was new, and was deemed an experiment. Mr. Page's administration of the institution was marvelously successful, and exerted a wide influence in favor of professional schools for the training of teachers. Mr. Page was a very busy man. He wrote much, in a fragmentary way, and delivered addresses of great power, some of which were published and extensively circulated. Doubtless he had formed plans for systematic authorship. He had completed but one book, "The Theory and Practice of Teaching," when he died, suddenly, in 1848, at the height of his usefulness.

"Never," says one, " was a career of brilliant promise more abruptly terminated. With him died his ambitious plans of authorship, of organization, of far-reaching personal influence. And yet, in view of the sequel, one is tempted to ask, what more could he have achieved had he lived ? Everywhere in the United States the schoolroom tells of Page. The pioneer in American pedagogical literature, he is now the patriarch, as he speaks through his writings." Of the remarkable interest manifested in Page's book in recent years the same writer says: "In this present Page revival, much interest has been manifested in all that pertains to that gifted teacher. His portrait has been sought in old paintings, engravings, and daguerreotypes. It is no disappointment. The features of Pestalozzi are pinched and wan. The face of Page is youthful, strong, and healthy. Anecdotes relating to the man —which linger in the legends of Newburyport and Albany; his motto, 'Succeed or die' (both of which he did); glimpses of his mode of life and thought, which we obtain from his writings (for he unconsciously mirrored himself as in a looking-glass); the old dialogues which he used to write for his school exhibitions, and which are to be found, now and then, in old books, and are keenly significant in their purport—all these the teachers are thinking about and writing about, as interesting souvenirs of the remarkable man now brought so prominently before them."

Characterization

Mr. Page's powers as an orator and debater were of a very high order. "He possessed," says Mr. Mann (himself an orator of no mean powers), "that rare quality, so indispensable to an orator, the power to think, standing on his feet and before folks." As a teacher, he exhibited two valuable qualifications, the ability to turn the attention of his pupils to the principles which explain facts, and in such a way that they could see clearly the connection; and the talent for reading the character of his pupils so accurately that he could at once discern what were their governing passions and tendencies, what in them needed encouragement, and what repression. His familiar lectures to his pupils on subjects connected with the teacher's life and duties, could they be published, would form an invaluable handbook for teachers. He possessed, beyond most men, the happy talent of always saying the right thing at the right time.

BARNARD'S "JOURNAL OF EDUCATION."

Page is one of the people. He is himself a teacher, who has filled the various places teachers are called upon to occupy in the public schools. He comes to them in a plain and matter-of-fact way, realizing all the conditions, the needs, the aims and purposes, the duties and cares pertaining to the teacher's work. And thus he becomes the personal adviser—the Mentor—of those who, perhaps more than any others in any community, feel the need of a personal adviser and Mentor. "INDIANA SCHOOL JOURNAL."

Page's dialogue, "The Schoolmaster," which was hastily written for a school entertainment at Newburyport, is valued chiefly as an interesting souvenir of its author—in fact, his portrait, unconsciously self-drawn. Some of its administrative features give it to-day a touch of archaism; and it must be remembered that the dialogue belongs to a day when teachers mended pens, and "set" copies, and kept "cowhides" in constant use. It is, however, a strong presentation of the true teacher—his earnestness, his solicitude for the school, his self-control, and manly strength of character.

The Schoolmaster

(A Dialogue)

DRAMATIS PERSONÆ

THE SCHOOLMASTER.
SQUIRE SNYDER,
MR. FOSDICK,
MR. O'CLARY,
MR. LE COMPTE,
} Patrons of the school.

JONAS SNYDER,
WILLIAM FOSDICK,
PATRICK O'CLARY,
JACQUES LE COMPTE,
ISAAC,
and others,
} Pupils of the school.

SCENE.—*Interior of a Village Schoolroom.—The Schoolmaster alone.*

MASTER. (*Setting copies.*) Well, so here I am again, after another night's sleep. But, sleep or no sleep, I feel about as much fatigued in the morning as I do at night. It is impossible to get the cares and anxieties of my profession out of my mind. It does seem to me that the parents of some of my pupils are very unfeeling; for I know I have done my very best to keep a good school, and, however I may have failed in some instances, I have the satisfaction of feeling, in my conscience, that my best endeavors have been devoted to my work. A merry lot of copies here, to be set before schooltime. (*Looking at his watch.*) But "a diligent hand will accomplish much;"—by the way, that will do for a copy for Jonas Snyder—little culprit! he was very idle yesterday.—(*Thinking and busy.*) What can that story mean, which Mr. Truetell told me this morning? Five or six!—who could they be?—five or six of the parents of my scholars dreadfully offended! Let me see; what have I done? Nothing, very lately, that I recollect. Let's see;—yesterday? no, there was nothing yesterday, except that I detained the class in geography till they got their lessons. Oh, yes, Jonas

Snyder was punished for idleness. But I spoke to him four or five times, and he would do nothing but whisper, and whittle his bench; and when at last he half eat up an apple, and threw the rest at Jacob Readslow, I thought he deserved it. Let's see; I gave him six claps—three on each hand;—well, he did not get more than his deserts. (*Enter one of the scholars, with his books under his arm, walking slowly, and eyeing the Master, to his seat. Master still busy, and thinking, by and by says,*) Isaac, you may come to me.

(*He walks along and says,*) Sir!

MASTER. Do you remember (*placing his pen over his ear, and turning earnestly and portentously round*) whether I punished any scholars yesterday?

ISAAC. Yes, sir; you feruled Jone Snyder, for playing and laughing.

MASTER. Did I punish any one else?

ISAAC. Not as I recollect.

MASTER. Think, Isaac; think carefully.

ISAAC. You kept a lot of us after school, for not saying our lessons——

MASTER. (*Quickly.*) You mean, Isaac, rather, I kept you to get your lessons, which you had neglected?

ISAAC. Yes, sir; and you made Patrick O'Clary stop and sweep, because he stayed out too late after recess.

MASTER. Oh, yes! I remember that.

ISAAC. He was as mad as a hop about it; he said he meant to tell his mother that you made him sweep for nothing.

MASTER. Hush! hush! You shouldn't tell tales! Do you remember any other punishments?

ISAAC. No, sir; not yesterday. You hit Jake Le Compte a clip across the knuckles, with the cowskin, day before yesterday;—don't you remember?—just as he stretched out his hand to hook that old rag upon Tom Willis' collar, you came along behind him, and clip went the old whip, right across his fingers, and down went the old rag. There, I never was more glad to see anything in my life! Little dirty, mean fellow!—he's always sticking things upon fellows;—I saw him once pin an old dirty rag upon a man's coat, just as he was putting a letter into the post-office;—I never saw such a fellow!

(*The other boys coming in gradually, the Master rings his little bell, and says,*) Boys, come to order and take your books. Now, boys, I wish to see if we can't have a good school to-day. Let's see; are we all here?

BOYS. No, sir! No, sir!

MASTER. Who is absent?

BOYS. Jone Snyder! Jake Le Compte! Patrick O'Clary! and——

MASTER. Speak one at a time, my boys. Don't make confusion, to begin with;—and (*looking around them,*)—oh! Will Fosdick,—only four!

ONE OF THE BOYS. Pat O'Clary is late. I saw him down in Baker Street, poking along!—he always comes late——

MASTER. Did he say he was coming?

SAME BOY. I asked him if he was coming to school, and he shook his head, and muttered out something about his mother, and I ran along and left him.

MASTER. Well, boys; now let us try to have a still school and close study to-day, and see if it is not more pleasant to learn than to play. (*Rises and walks to and fro on the stage.*) Take the geography lesson, James and Samuel, first thing this morning; and Isaac, I don't wish to detain you again to-day. (*Loud knock at the door.*)

(*Enter William Fosdick, walking consequentially up to the Master, saying,*) Here! father wants to see you at the door!

(*Master turns to go to the door, followed by William, who wishes to hear all that's said, and Mr. Fosdick, looking quite savage, steps right inside,—the Master politely bowing, with a "good-morning."*)

MR. FOSDICK. Here, sir; I want to see you about my boy! I don't like to have you keep him after school every day; I want him at home,—and I should like to have you dismiss him when school is done. If he wants lickin', lick him—that's all; but don't you keep him here an hour or two every day after school,—I don't send him here for that!

MASTER. But, my good sir, I have not often detained him; not more than twice within a fort——

MR. FOSDICK. Well, don't you do it again,—that's all!

MASTER. But, sir, I have only detained him to learn the lessons which he might learn in school; and surely, if——

MR. FOSDICK. Well, well, sir! don't you do it again!—that's all I have to say! If he behaves bad, you lick him,—only do it in reason;—but when school is done, I want him dismissed!

MASTER. Sir, I do what I conceive to be my duty; and I serve all my scholars alike; and while I would be willing to accommodate you, I shall do what I think is my duty. (*Gathering spirit and gravity, and advancing.*) Sir, do I understand you to wish me to whip your son for not getting his lesson?

MR. FOSDICK. Yes—no—yes—in reason; I don't want my children's bones broke!

MASTER. (*Taking from the desk a cowhide.*) Do you prefer your son should be whipped to being detained?

FOSDICK. I don't think not getting his lessons is such a dreadful crime. I never used to get my lessons, and old Master Peppermint never used to lick me, and I am sure he never kept me after school; but we used to have schools good for sumfin in them days. Bill, go to your seat, and behave yourself! and when school is done, you come home! That's all I have to say!

MASTER. But stop, my boy! (*Speaking to William, decidedly.*) There happen to be two sides to this question! There is something further to be said, before you go to your seat in this school.

FOSDICK. What! you don't mean to turn him out of school, do ye? (*Somebody knocks.*)

(*A boy steps to the door, and in steps Mr. O'Clary, who, approaching Mr. Fosdick, says,*) Is it you that's the schoolmaster, sure? It's I that's after spaking to the schoolmaster. (*Bowing.*)

FOSDICK. No; I'm no schoolmaster.

MASTER. What is your wish, sir?

Mr. O'Clary. I wants to spake with the schoolmaster, I do, sir. (*Bows.*)

Master. Well, sir (*rapping to keep the boys still, who are disposed to laugh,*) I am the schoolmaster. What is your wish?

Mr. O'C. Why, sir, my little spalpeen of a son goes to this school, he does; and he says he's made to swape every day, he is; and it's all for nothing, he tells me; and sure I don't like it, I don't; and I'm kim to complain to ye, I have! It's Patrick O'Clary that I'm spaking uv; and it's I that's his father, I be; his father, Paddy O'Clary from Cork, it is.

Master. Well, sir, he has never swept but once, I believe; and that, surely, was not without a good reason.

Mr. O'C. But himself tills a different story, he does; and I niver knew him till but one lie in my life, I didn't; and that was as good as none. But the little spalpeen shall be after tilling his own stowry, he shall! for it's he that's waiting in the entry, and will till ye no lie, at all, at all—upon that ye may depind! though it's his father that says it, and sure!—(*Calls.*) —Patrick! Patrick!! Patrick!!! My dear, here's your father wants ye to come in, and till Master how it's you that's kept to swape ivry day, and it's all for nothing, it is! Come in, I say, in a jiffy! (*Patrick, scratching his head, enters.*) Here's your father, dear! now till your master,—and till the truth—didn't ye till your mither that ye had to swape ivry day for nothing; and it's you that's going to be kept swaping ivry day, for a month to come, and sure?

Master. Now tell the truth, Patrick.

Patrick. (*Looking at his father.*) No; I niver said no such words, and sure! I said how I's kept to swape yisterday, for staying out too late; and that's all I said 'bout it, at all, at all.

Mr. O'C. "Cush la macree!" Little sonny, how you talk! He's frightened, he is, and sure! (*Turning to Mr. Fosdick.*) He's always bashful before company, he is. But, Master, it's I that don't like to have him made to swape the school, indade, and if you can do nothing else, I shall be in sad taking, I shall, and sure! If you should be after bating him, I should make no complaint; for I bates him myself, whenivcr he lies to his mither—a little spalpeen that he is! But I can't bear to have him made to do the humbling work of swaping, at all, at all; and it's I that shall make a " clish ma claver," an' it's not stopped—indade I shall! (*Somebody knocks.*)

(*Isaac steps to the door, and returning says,*) Esq. Snyder wishes to see you, sir.

MASTER. (*Smiling.*) Well, ask Mr. Snyder to step in;—we may as well have a regular court of it!

(*Isaac waits upon him in, leading Jonas, with his hands poulticed.*)

MASTER. (*Smiling.*) Good-morning, Mr. Snyder; walk in, sir!

MR. SNYDER. (*Rather gentlemanly.*) I hope you will excuse my interrupting your school; but I called to inquire what Jonas, here, could have done, that you bruised him up at such a' rate. Poor little fellow! he came home, taking on as if his heart would break! and both his hands swelled up bigger than mine! and he said you had been beating him, for nothing! I thought I'd come up and inquire into it; for I don't hold to this banging and abusing children, and especially when they haven't done anything; though I'm a friend to good order.

MASTER. I was not aware that I punished him very severely, sir.

MR. SNYDER. Oh! It was dreadfully severe! Why, the poor little fellow's hands pained him so that his mother had to poultice them, and sit up with him all night! and this morning she wanted to come up to school with him herself; but I told her I guessed she better let me come.—Jonas, do your hands ache now, dear?

JONAS. (*Holding them both out together.*) Oh! dreadfully! They feel as if they were in the fire!

MR. SNYDER. Well, dear, keep composed; don't cry, dear. Now, sir, (*addressing the Master,*) this was all for nothing!

MASTER. No, sir! It was for something, I am thinking!

JONAS. I say I did not do nothing! so there now! (*Somebody knocks.*)

MASTER. Gentlemen, sit down. (*Looking perplexed.*) Sit

down, sir. Give me a little time, and I'll endeavor to set the matter right. (*All sitting down but the boys.*)

Mr. Snyder. Why, I don't wish to make a serious matter of it. I shan't prosecute you. I was only going to ask if you couldn't devise some other kind of punishment than pommeling. If you'd made him stop after school, or set him to sweeping the house, or scouring the benches, or even whipped him with a cowhide or switch-stick, I should not have complained; but I don't like this beating boys! (*Knocking again.*)

Master. Isaac, go and see who is at the door.

(*Exit Isaac; enter Mr. Le Compte and Jacques.*)

Mr. Le Compte. Ha! Monsieur Tutor. I have one ver leetle complainte to make against your—vot you call him—your *discipleen.*

Master. Ah! indeed, and what is that, sir?

Mr. Le Compte. Why mys boy have not dse right in-cli-na-tshon for dse shastisement vot you give him.

Master. Very likely, sir. Very few boys have an inclination for a chastisement.

Mr. Le Compte. You see, Monsieur, de—vot you call his name—de furule vot you use on him wizout ceremun*ie*, is for certainment not so good for my boy as a leetle parswashon would be.

Master. But, sir, I cannot spend time in persuading boys to do right. I find it necessary to make them afraid to do wrong; and as your son is so full of mischievous pranks, I find that I only can restrain him by a free use of proper punishment.

Mr. Le Compte. I has not seen de mischeeve in him vot you speak of. He is von (*scratches his head to think of the word*)—von—vot you call a man vot has not drank dse wine?

Master. *Sober*, I suppose you mean.

Mr. Le Compte. Ah, dat's ze word—von ver sobar boy, and zerefore does not deserve de cas-ti-ga-tshon vot you gives him for mischeeve. (*Jacques pins an old rag upon the father's coat and steps back and laughs. The other boys point to the Frenchman and laugh.*)

Mr. Fosdick. Mr. Le Compte, what's that you have pinned to your coat?

Mr. Le Compte. On me coat? vere? (*Looks round.*) On de tail of my coat, von ver bad boy pinned him dere. Who vas it?

Fosdick. Your hopeful son, Jacques.

Mr. Le Compte. Jacques, you be von grand leetle scoundrel and deserve all the shastisement vot the tutor gives you. (*To the Master.*) If you will lend me de instrument vot you shastise with, I'll teach him to have respect for his father.

Master. Be calm, sir; be calm, sir. Be good enough to sit down and I'll endeavor to define my position. And now, gentlemen, (*bowing*) I think we may each of us begin to see the beauty of variety, especially in the matter of opinion. That you may all understand the whole case, I will state in a few words the facts, as they actually occurred. Day before yesterday, our young friend Jacques (*pointing to him*) was playing his favorite trick of hanging his rag signal upon a schoolmate, after the fashion in which he has here so filially served his father within a few minutes; and standing near him at the time, with my whip in hand, I could not resist the temptation to salute his mischievous knuckles with a well-directed stroke, which, however effectually it may have cut his own fingers and his father's sensibilities, it seems has not cut off his ruling propensity. Yesterday was emphatically a day of sinning on my part. Jonas Snyder, whose little hands have swelled to such enormous magnitude, was often reproved for constant idleness; and after all this, when he threw a portion of an apple at a more industrious boy, thus disturbing many of those well-disposed boys, he was called and feruled, receiving six strokes—three on each hand—with the rule I now show you. Little Patrick O'Clary was required to sweep the schoolroom floor, for a strong instance of tardiness at recess; and this punishment was given, because I did not wish to inflict a severer one upon so small a lad. And last, this little fellow (*pointing to William Fosdick*) was detained, in common with seven others, to learn a lesson which he neglected to learn at the proper time.

Such are the facts. And yet each of you has assured me that I have incurred your displeasure by using a punishment you disapprove, and "all for nothing." You have each one taken the trouble to come to this room, to render my task—already sufficiently perplexing—still more so, by giving parental support to childish complaints, and imparting your censure, in no measured terms, upon the instructor of your children. But this is a most interesting case. You all happen to be here together, and you thus give me the opportunity I have long wished to show you your own inconsistencies.

It is easy to complain of your teacher; but perhaps either of you, in your wisdom, would find it not quite so easy to take my place and escape censure. How would either of you have got along in the present instance? Mr. Fosdick, who is displeased with detention after school, would have, according to his own recommendation, resorted to "licking," either with ferule or whip. In this case, he would have incurred the censure of his friends, Esq. Snyder and Mr. Le Compte. The "squire," in turn, would have raised the displeasure of both his friends, by resorting to his favorite mode of detaining and cowhiding. Mr. O'Clary would give the "spalpeens" a "bating," as he says, after his own peculiar fashion, with which the squire and Mr. Le Compte could not have been over-much pleased;— and Mr. Le Compte—ay, Mr. Le Compte—if we may judge from the exhibition he has just given us, would have displeased even himself, by proving to be what he most of all things detests—a champion of the cowhide. But what is a little curious, as it appears, is, that while I have not carried out the favorite scheme of either one of you,—which we have already seen, would be objectionable to each of the others,—but have adopted a variety of punishments, and the very variety which your own collective suffrage would fix upon, I have got myself equally deep into hot water; and the grand question is now, what shall I do? If I take the course suggested by you collectively, the result is the same. I see no other way but to take my own course, performing conscientiously my duties, in their time and after their manner, and then to demand of you, and all others, the right of being sustained!

Mr. Snyder. Well, gentlemen, my opinion is, that we have been tried and condemned by our own testimony, and there is no appeal. My judgment approves the master; and hereafter I shall neither hear nor make any more complaints. Jonas, (*turning to Jonas,*) my son, if the master is willing, you may go home and tell your mother to take off those poultices, and then do you come to school and do as you are told; and if I hear of any more of your complaints, I will double the dose you may receive at school.

Mr. O'C. And sure, Master, Paddy O'Clary is not the man to resist authority in the new country; and bless your sowl, if you'll make my little spalpeen but a good boy, it's I that will kindly remember the favor, though ye make him swape until nixt Christmas! Here, Patrick, down upon the little knees of your own, and crave the master's forgiveness.

Master. No, sir; that I shall not allow. I ask no one to kneel to me. I shall only require that he correct his past faults, and obey me in future.

Mr. O'C. It's an ungrateful child he would be, if ever again he should be after troubling so kind a master. St. Patrick bless ye! (*Taking little Pat by the hand, they go out.*)

Mr. Fosdick. (*Taking the Master by the hand, pleasantly.*) Sir, I hope I shall profit by this day's lesson. I have only to say, that I am perfectly satisfied we are all wrong; and that is, perhaps, the best assurance I can give you, that I think you are right. That's all I have to say. (*Exeunt.*)

WILLIAM MAKEPEACE THACKERAY
1811-1863

WILLIAM MAKEPEACE THACKERAY, one of the greatest of modern novelists, was born at Calcutta, India, in 1811, and was the son of an English government official. He was educated in England, at the Charter House School, in London, and at Cambridge, though he did not take a degree at the University. For some years he traveled in Europe, and made a study of art, intending to be a painter. Investing his fortune in a newspaper enterprise, he lost heavily, and then turned his attention to literature for a support. In 1846 he published the first number of "Vanity Fair," which became popular at once. This was followed by "Pendennis," "Esmond," "The Newcomes," and "The Virginians." From 1860 to 1862, Thackeray was editor of the *Cornhill Magazine*. Thackeray was a pleasing lecturer, an able critic, and a favorite in the social world. He died suddenly on Christmas Eve, 1863.

"He went out Wednesday for a little, and came home at ten. He went to his room, suffering much, but declining his man's offer to sit with him. He hated to make others suffer. He was heard moaning, as if in pain, about twelve on the eve of Christmas morning. Then all was quiet, and then he must have died—in a moment. Next morning his man went in and, opening the windows, found his master dead, his arms behind his head, as if he had tried to take one more breath. We think of him as of our Chalmers, found dead in like manner; the same childlike, unspoiled, open face; the same gentle mouth; the same spaciousness and softness of nature; the same look of power. What a thing to think of—alone in the dark, in the midst of his own mighty London; his mother and his daughters asleep, and, it may be, dreaming of his goodness. God help them and us all."

JOHN BROWN.

Characterization

It was by "Vanity Fair" that Thackeray first made for himself a really great reputation. He was previously well known by many as a clever and brilliant writer in *Fraser* and in *Punch*. He had published various stories and books of sketches, and Christmas books. "Vanity

Fair" was his first long novel. It stands rather by itself; it is a compendium of Thackeray's so-called cynicism—a primer of the philosophy. No other of his novels has so much of his philosophy, pure and simple. It is little more than a study of character,—the plot is of the slightest. The constant theme seems to be, how stupid and ridiculous are the good, how clever and successful are the bad, and yet how plain it must be to everyone that the bad do not always prosper, and that the good probably enjoy being stupid and ridiculous, and so that everything is well enough. Thackeray is remorseless in "Vanity Fair." There is no good trait in Becky, only cleverness and wickedness; there is no mercy for Amelia; she must be plain and slow, though good and loving. Even the hero, who is truly good and noble, who waits and waits, patiently befriending the woman he loves, till she will marry him,—even he, because he is good, must be ridiculous; otherwise, why is he called Dobbin? The general run of the world of "Vanity Fair" is bad, and those who are good hardly get their deserts. To many this is the best of Thackeray's books.

EDWARD EVERETT HALE.

Miss Pinkerton's School on Chiswick Mall

(From "Vanity Fair")

While the present century was in its teens, and on one sunshiny morning in June, there drove up to the great iron gate of Miss Pinkerton's academy for young ladies, on Chiswick Mall, a large family coach, with two fat horses in blazing harness, driven by a fat coachman in a three-cornered hat and wig, at the rate of four miles an hour. A black servant, who reposed on the box beside the fat coachman, uncurled his bandy legs as soon as the equipage drew up opposite Miss Pinkerton's shining brass plate, and as he pulled the bell, at least a score of young heads were seen peering out of the narrow windows of the stately old brick house. Nay, the acute observer might have recognized the little red nose of good-natured Miss Jemima Pinkerton herself, rising over some geranium pots in the window of that lady's own drawing-room.

"It is Mrs. Sedley's coach, sister," said Miss Jemima. "Sambo, the black servant, has just rung the bell, and the coachman has a new red waistcoat."

"Have you completed all the necessary preparations incident to Miss Sedley's departure, Miss Jemima?" asked Miss Pinkerton herself, that majestic lady; the Semiramis of Hammersmith, the friend of Doctor Johnson, the correspondent of Mrs. Chapone herself.

"The girls were up at four this morning, packing her trunks, sister," replied Miss Jemima; "we have made her a bow-pot."

"Say a bouquet, Sister Jemima, 'tis more genteel."

"Well, a booky as big almost as a haystack. I have put up two bottles of the gillyflower water for Mrs. Sedley, and the receipt for making it, in Amelia's box."

"And I trust, Miss Jemima, you have made a copy of Miss Sedley's account. This is it, is it? Very good—ninety-three pounds, four shillings. Be kind enough to address it to John Sedley, Esq., and to seal this billet which I have written to his lady."

In Miss Jemima's eyes an autograph letter of her sister, Miss Pinkerton, was an object of as deep veneration as would have been a letter from a sovereign. Only when her pupils quitted the establishment, or when they were about to be married, and once, when poor Miss Birch died of the scarlet fever, was Miss Pinkerton known to write personally to the parents of her pupils; and it was Jemima's opinion that if anything *could* console Mrs. Birch for her daughter's loss, it would be that pious and eloquent composition in which Miss Pinkerton announced the event.

In the present instance Miss Pinkerton's "billet" was to the following effect:

"THE MALL, CHISWICK, June 15, 18—.

"MADAM,—After her six years' residence at the Mall, I have the honor and happiness of presenting Miss Amelia Sedley to her parents, as a young lady not unworthy to occupy a fitting position in their polished and refined circle. Those virtues which characterize the young English gentlewoman, those accomplishments which become her birth and station, will not be found wanting in the amiable Miss Sedley, whose *industry* and *obedience* have endeared her to her instructors, and whose delightful sweetness of temper has charmed her *aged* and her *youthful* companions.

"In music, in dancing, in orthography, in every variety of embroidery and needlework, she will be found to have realized her friends' *fondest wishes*. In geography there is still much to be desired; and a careful and undeviating use of the backboard, for four hours daily during the next three years, is recommended as necessary to the acquirement of that dignified *deportment and carriage*, so requisite for every young lady of *fashion*.

"In the principles of religion and morality, Miss Sedley will be found worthy of an establishment which has been honored by the presence of *The Great Lexicographer* and the patronage of the admirable Mrs. Chapone. In leaving the Mall, Miss Amelia carries with her the hearts of her companions, and the affectionate regards of her mistress, who has the honor to subscribe herself, madam,

"Your most obliged humble servant,
"BARBARA PINKERTON.

"P. S.—Miss Sharp accompanies Miss Sedley. It is particularly requested that Miss Sharp's stay in Russell Square may not exceed ten days. The family of distinction with whom she is engaged desire to avail themselves of her services as soon as possible."

This letter completed, Miss Pinkerton proceeded to write her own name and Miss Sedley's in the fly-leaf of a "Johnson's Dictionary"—the interesting work which she invariably presented to her scholars, on their departure from the Mall. On the cover was inserted a copy of "Lines addressed to a young lady on quitting Miss Pinkerton's school at the Mall; by the late revered Dr. Samuel Johnson." In fact the Lexicographer's name was always on the lips of this majestic woman, and a visit he had paid to her was the cause of her reputation and her fortune.

Being commanded by her elder sister to get the "Dixionary" from the cupboard, Miss Jemima had extracted two copies of the book from the receptacle in question. When Miss Pinkerton had finished the inscription in the first, Jemima, with rather a dubious and timid air, handed her the second.

"For whom is this, Miss Jemima?" said Miss Pinkerton, with awful coldness.

"For Becky Sharp," answered Jemima, trembling very much, and blushing over her withered face and neck, as she turned her back on her sister—"for Becky Sharp; she's going too."

"MISS JEMIMA!" exclaimed Miss Pinkerton, in the largest capitals. "Are you in your senses? Replace the 'dixionary' in the closet, and never venture to take such a liberty in future."

"Well, sister, it's only two and ninepence, and poor Becky will be miserable if she don't get one."

"Send Miss Sedley instantly to me," said Miss Pinkerton. And so venturing not to say another word, poor Jemima trotted off, exceedingly flurried and nervous.

Miss Sedley's papa was a merchant in London, and a man of some wealth; whereas Miss Sharp was an articled pupil, for whom Miss Pinkerton had done, as she thought, quite enough, without conferring upon her at parting the high honor of the "Dixionary."

Although schoolmistresses' letters are to be trusted no more nor less than churchyard epitaphs; yet, as it sometimes happens that a person departs this life who is really deserving of all the praises that the stone-cutter carves over his bones; who *is* a good Christian, a good parent, child, wife, or husband; who actually *does* leave a disconsolate family to mourn his loss; so in academies of the male and female sex it occurs every now and then that the pupil is fully worthy of the praises bestowed by the disinterested instructor. Now, Miss Amelia Sedley was a young lady of this singular species, and deserved not only all that Miss Pinkerton said in her praise, but had many charming qualities which that pompous old Minerva of a woman could not see, from the differences of rank and age between her pupil and herself.

For she could not only sing like a lark, or a Mrs. Billington, and dance like Hillisberg or Parisot, and embroider beautifully, and spell as well as a dictionary itself; but she had such a kindly, smiling, tender, gentle, generous heart of her own, as won the love of everybody who came near her, from Minerva down to the poor girl in the scullery, and the one-eyed tart woman's daughter, who was permitted to vend her wares once a week to the young ladies in the Mall. She had twelve intimate and bosom friends out of the twenty-four young ladies. Even envious Miss Briggs never spoke ill of her; high and mighty Miss Saltire (Lord Dexter's granddaughter) allowed that her figure was genteel; and as for Miss Swartz, the rich woolly-haired mulatto from St. Kitt's, on the day Amelia went away, she was in such a passion of tears that they were obliged to send for Dr. Floss, and half tipsify her with sal-volatile. Miss Pinkerton's attachment was, as may be supposed, from the high position and eminent virtues of that lady, calm and dignified; but Miss Jemima had already whimpered several times at the idea of Amelia's departure; and but for fear of her sister, would have gone off in downright hysterics, like the heiress (who paid double) of St. Kitt's. Such luxury of grief, however, is only allowed to parlor boarders. Honest Jemima had all the bills, and the washing, and the mending, and the puddings, and the plate and crockery, and the servants to superintend. But why speak about her? It is probable that we shall not hear of her again from this moment to the end of time, and that, when the great filigree iron gates are once closed on her, she and her awful sister will never issue therefrom into this little world of history.

But as we are to see a great deal of Amelia, there is no harm in saying, at the outset of our acquaintance, that she was a dear little creature; and a great mercy it is, both in life and in novels, which (and the latter especially) abound in villains of the most somber sort, that we are to have for a constant companion so guileless and good-natured a person. As she is not a heroine, there is no need to describe her person; indeed, I am afraid that her nose was rather short than otherwise, and her cheeks a great deal too round and red for a heroine; but her face blushed with rosy health, and her lips with the freshest of smiles, and she had a pair of eyes which sparkled with the brightest and honestest good-humor, except, indeed, when they filled with tears, and that was a great deal too often; for the silly thing would cry over a dead canary-bird; or over a mouse, that the cat haply had seized upon; or over the end of a novel, were it ever so stupid; and as for saying an unkind word to her, were any persons hard-hearted enough to do so—why, so much the worse for them. Even Miss Pinkerton, that austere and god-like woman, ceased scolding her after the first time, and though she no more comprehended sensibility than she did algebra, gave all masters and teachers particular orders to treat Miss Sedley with the utmost gentleness, as harsh treatment was injurious to her.

So that when the day of departure came, between her two customs of laughing and crying, Miss Sedley was greatly puzzled how to act. She was glad to go home, and yet most wofully sad at leaving school. For three days before, little Laura Martin, the orphan, followed her about like a little dog. She had to make and receive at least fourteen presents—to make fourteen solemn promises of writing every week: "Send my letters under cover to my grandpapa, the Earl of Dexter," said Miss Saltire (who, by the way, was rather shabby). "Never mind the postage, but write every day, you dear darling," said the impetuous and woolly-headed, but generous and affectionate Miss Swartz; and the orphan, little Laura Martin (who was just in round-hand) took her friend's hand and said, looking up in her face wistfully, "Amelia, when I write to you, I shall call you mamma." All which details, I have no doubt, JONES, who reads this book at his club, will pronounce to be excessively foolish, trivial, twaddling, and ultra-sentimental. Yes; I can see Jones at this minute (rather flushed with his joint of mutton and half-pint of wine), taking out his pencil and scoring under the words "foolish, twaddling," etc., and adding to them his own remark of "*quite true.*" Well, he is a lofty man of genius, and admires the great and heroic in life and novels, and so had better take warning and go elsewhere.

Well, then. The flowers, and the presents, and the trunks,

and bonnet boxes of Miss Sedley having been arranged by Mr. Sambo in the carriage together with a very small and weather-beaten old cow's-skin trunk, with Miss Sharp's card neatly nailed upon it, which was delivered by Sambo with a grin, and packed by the coachman with a corresponding sneer—the hour for parting came; and the grief of that moment was considerably lessened by the admirable discourse which Miss Pinkerton addressed to her pupil. Not that the parting speech caused Amelia to philosophize, or that it armed her in any way with calmness, the result of argument; but it was intolerably dull, pompous, and tedious; and having the fear of her schoolmistress greatly before her eyes, Miss Sedley did not venture, in her presence, to give way to any ebullitions of private grief. A seed-cake and a bottle of wine were produced in the drawing-room, as on the solemn occasions of the visit of parents, and these refreshments being partaken of, Miss Sedley was at liberty to depart.

"You'll go in and say good-by to Miss Pinkerton, Becky!" said Miss Jemima to a young lady of whom nobody took any notice, and who was coming down-stairs with her own band-box.

"I suppose I must," said Miss Sharp, calmly, and much to the wonder of Miss Jemima; and the latter having knocked at the door and receiving permission to come in, Miss Sharp advanced in a very unconcerned manner, and said in French, and with a perfect accent:

"Mademoiselle, je viens vous faire mes adieux."

Miss Pinkerton did not understand French; she only directed those who did; but biting her lips and throwing up her venerable and Roman-nosed head (on top of which figured a large and solemn turban), she said, "Miss Sharp, I wish you a good-morning." As the Hammersmith Semiramis spoke, she waved one hand both by way of adieu, and to give Miss Sharp an opportunity of shaking one of the fingers of the hand which was left out for that purpose.

Miss Sharp only folded her own hands with a very frigid

smile and bow, and quite declined to accept the proffered honor; on which Semiramis tossed up her turban more indignantly than ever. In fact it was a little battle between the young lady and the old one, and the latter was worsted. "Heaven bless you, my child," said she, embracing Amelia, and scowling the while over the girl's shoulder at Miss Sharp. "Come away, Becky," said Miss Jemima, pulling the young woman away in great alarm, and the drawing-room door closed upon them forever.

Then came the struggle and parting below. Words refuse to tell it. All the servants were there in the hall—all the dear friends—all the young ladies—the dancing-master who had just arrived; and there was such a scuffling, and hugging, and kissing, and crying, with the hysterical *yoops* of Miss Swartz, the parlor-boarder, from her room, as no pen can depict, and as the tender heart would fain pass over. The embracing was over; they parted—that is, Miss Sedley parted from her friends. Miss Sharp had demurely entered the carriage some minutes before. Nobody cried for leaving *her*.

Sambo of the bandy legs slammed the carriage-door on his young weeping mistress. He sprang up behind the carriage. "Stop!" cried Miss Jemima, rushing to the gate with a parcel.

"It's some sandwiches, my dear," said she to Amelia. "You may be hungry, you know; and Becky, Becky Sharp, here's a book for you that my sister—that is I—'Johnson's Dixionary,' you know; you mustn't leave us without that. Good-by. Drive on, coachman. God bless you!"

And the kind creature retreated into the garden, overcome with emotions.

But lo! and just as the coach drove off, Miss Sharp put her pale face out of the window, and actually flung the book back into the garden.

This almost caused Jemima to faint with terror. "Well, I never"—said she—"what an audacious "—emotion prevented her from completing either sentence. The carriage rolled away; the great gates were closed; the bell rang for the dancing lesson. The world is before the two young ladies; and so, farewell to Chiswick Mall.

. . . .

When Miss Sharp had performed the heroical act mentioned in the last chapter, and had seen the "Dixionary," flying over the pavement of the little garden, fall at length at the feet of the astonished Miss Jemima, the young lady's countenance, which had before worn an almost livid look of hatred, assumed a smile that perhaps was scarcely more agreeable, and she sank back in the carriage in an easy frame of mind, saying, "So much for the 'Dixionary;' and, thank God, I'm out of Chiswick."

Miss Sedley was almost as flurried at the act of defiance as Miss Jemima had been; for consider, it was but one minute that she had left school, and the impressions of six years are not got over in that space of time. Nay, with some persons those awes and terrors of youth last forever and ever. I know, for instance, an old gentleman of sixty-eight, who said to me one morning at breakfast, with a very agitated countenance, "I dreamed last night that I was flogged by Dr. Raine." Fancy had carried him back five-and-fifty years in the course of that evening. Dr. Raine and his rod were just as awful to him in his heart then at sixty-eight, as they had been at thirteen. If the doctor, with a large birch, had appeared bodily to him, even at the age of threescore and eight, and had said in awful voice, "Boy, take down your pant——" Well, well, Miss Sedley was exceedingly alarmed at this act of insubordination.

"How could you do so, Rebecca?" at last she said, after a pause.

"Why, do you think Miss Pinkerton will come out and order me back to the black hole?" said Rebecca, laughing.

"No; but——"

"I hate the whole house," continued Miss Sharp in a fury. "I hope I may never set eyes on it again. I wish it were in the bottom of the Thames, I do; and if Miss Pinkerton were there, I wouldn't pick her out, that I wouldn't. Oh, how I should like to see her floating in the water yonder, turban and all, with her train streaming after her, and her nose like the beak of a wherry!"

"Hush!" cried Miss Sedley.

"Why, will the black footman tell tales?" cried Miss Rebecca, laughing. "He may go back and tell Miss Pinkerton that I hate her with all my soul; and I wish he would; and I wish I had a means of proving it, too. For two years I have only had insults and outrage from her. I have been treated worse than any servant in the kitchen. I have never had a friend or a kind word, except from you. I have been made to tend the little girls in the lower schoolroom, and to talk French to the Misses, until I grew sick of my mother-tongue. But that talking French to Miss Pinkerton was capital fun, wasn't it? She doesn't know a word of French, and was too proud to confess it. I believe it was that which made her part with me; and so thank Heaven for French. *Vive la France! Vive l'Empereur! Vive Bonaparte!*"

"O Rebecca, Rebecca, for shame!" cried Miss Sedley; for this was the greatest blasphemy Rebecca had as yet uttered: and in those days in England to say, "Long live Bonaparte!" was as much as to say, "Long live Lucifer!" "How can you, how dare you, have such wicked, revengeful thoughts?"

"Revenge may be wicked, but it's natural," answered Miss Rebecca. "I'm no angel." And, to say the truth, she certainly was not.

For it may be remarked in the course of this little conversation (which took place as the coach rolled along lazily by the river-side) that though Miss Rebecca Sharp has twice had occasion to thank Heaven, it has been, in the first place, for ridding her of some person whom she hated, and secondly, for enabling her to bring her enemies to some sort of perplexity or confusion; neither of which are very amiable motives for religious gratitude, or such as would be put forward by persons of a kind and placable disposition. Miss Rebecca was not, then, in the least kind or placable. All the world used her ill, said this young misanthropist, and we may be pretty certain that persons whom all the world treats ill, deserve entirely the treatment they get. The world is a looking-glass, and gives back to every man the reflection of his own face. Frown at it, and it will in turn look sourly upon you; laugh at it, and with it, and it is a jolly, kind companion; and so let all young persons take their choice. This is certain, that if the world neglected Miss Sharp, she never was known to have done a good action in behalf of anybody; nor can it be expected that twenty-four young ladies should all be as amiable as the heroine of this work, Miss Sedley (whom we have selected for the very reason that she was the best-natured of all, otherwise what on earth was to have prevented us from putting up Miss Swartz, or Miss Crump, or Miss Hopkins as heroine in her place?)—it could not be expected that every one should be of the humble and gentle temper of Miss Amelia Sedley, should take every opportunity to vanquish Rebecca's hard-heartedness and ill-humor, and, by a thousand kind words and offices, overcome for once at least her hostility to her kind.

Miss Sharp's father was an artist, and in that quality had given lessons of drawing at Miss Pinkerton's school. He was a clever man, a pleasant companion, a careless student, with a great propensity for running into debt, and a partiality for the tavern. When he was drunk, he used to beat his wife and daughter; and the next morning, with a headache, he would rail at the world for its neglect of his genius, and abuse with a good deal of cleverness, and sometimes with perfect reason, the fools, his brother painters. As it was with the utmost difficulty that he could keep himself, and as he owed money for a mile round Soho, where he lived, he thought to better his circumstances by marrying a young woman of the French nation, who was by profession an opera-girl. The humble calling of her female parent Miss Sharp never alluded to, but used to state subsequently that the Entrechats were a noble family of Gascony, and took great pride in her descent from them. And curious it is that, as she advanced in life, this young lady's ancestors increased in rank and splendor.

Rebecca's mother had had some education somewhere, and her daughter spoke French with purity and a Parisian accent. It was in those days rather a rare accomplishment, and led to her engagement with the orthodox Miss Pinkerton. For her mother being dead, her father, finding himself not likely to recover, after his third attack of *delirium tremens*, wrote a manly and pathetic letter to Miss Pinkerton, recommending the orphan child to her protection, and so descended to the grave, after two bailiffs had quarreled over his corpse. Rebecca was seventeen when she came to Chiswick, and was bound over as an articled pupil; her duties being to talk French, as we have seen; and her privileges to live cost free, and, with a few guineas a year, to gather scraps of knowledge from the professors who attended the school.

She was small and slight in person; pale, sandy-haired, and with eyes habitually cast down; when they looked up, they were very large, odd, and attractive; so attractive that the Reverend Mr. Crisp, fresh from Oxford, and curate to the Vicar of Chiswick, the Reverend Mr. Flowerdew, fell in love with Miss Sharp; being shot dead by a glance of her eyes which was fired all the way across Chiswick Church from the school-pew to the reading-desk. This infatuated young man used sometimes to take tea with Miss Pinkerton, to whom he had been presented by his mamma, and actually proposed something like marriage in an intercepted note, which the one-eyed apple-woman was charged to deliver. Mrs. Crisp was summoned from Buxton, and abruptly carried off her darling boy; but the idea, even, of such an eagle in the Chiswick dovecot caused a great flutter in the breast of Miss Pinkerton, who would have sent away Miss Sharp, but that she was bound to her under a forfeit, and who never could thoroughly believe the young lady's protestations that she had never exchanged a single word with Mr. Crisp, except under her own eyes on the two occasions when she had met him at tea.

By the side of many tall and bouncing young ladies in the establishment, Rebecca Sharp looked like a child. But she had the dismal precocity of poverty. Many a dun had she talked to, and turned away from her father's door; many a tradesman had she coaxed and wheedled into good humor, and into the granting of one meal more. She sat commonly with her father, who was very proud of her wit, and heard the talk of many of his wild companions—often but ill-suited for a girl to hear. But she never had been a girl, she said; she had been a woman since she was eight years old. O, why did Miss Pinkerton let such a dangerous bird into her cage?

The fact is, the old lady believed Rebecca to be the meekest creature in the world, so admirably, on the occasions when her father brought her to Chiswick, used Rebecca to perform the part of the *ingénue;* and only a year before the arrangement by which Rebecca had been admitted into her house, and when Rebecca was sixteen years old, Miss Pinkerton majestically and with a little speech made her a present of a doll—which was, by the way, the confiscated property of Miss Swindle, discovered surreptitiously nursing it in school-hours. How the father and daughter laughed as they trudged home together after the evening party (it was on the occasion of the speeches, when all the professors were invited), and how Miss Pinkerton would have raged had she seen the caricature of herself which the little mimic, Rebecca, managed to make out of her doll! Becky used to go through dialogues with it; it formed the delight of Newman Street, Gerard Street, and the artists' quarter; and the young painters, when they came to take their gin-and-water with their lazy, dissolute, clever, jovial senior, used regularly to ask Rebecca if Miss Pinkerton was at home; she was as well known to them, poor soul, as Mr. Lawrence or President West. Once she had the honor to pass a few days at Chiswick; after which she brought back Jemima, and erected another doll as Miss Jemmy; for though that honest creature had made and given her jelly and cake enough for three children, and a seven-shilling piece at parting, the girl's sense of ridicule was far stronger than her gratitude, and she sacrificed Miss Jemmy quite as pitilessly as her sister.

The catastrophe came, and she was brought to the Mall as to

her home. The rigid formality of the place suffocated her; the
prayers and the meals, the lessons and the walks, which were
arranged with a conventual regularity, oppressed her almost
beyond endurance; and she looked back to the freedom and
the beggary of the old studio in Soho with so much regret
that everybody, herself included, fancied she was consumed
with grief for her father. She had a little room in the garret,
where the maids heard her walking and sobbing at night; but
it was with rage and not with grief. She had not been much
of a dissembler, until now her loneliness taught her to feign.
She had never mingled in the society of women; her father,
reprobate as he was, was a man of talent; his conversation was
a thousand times more agreeable to her than the talk of such
of her own sex as she now encountered. The pompous vanity
of the old schoolmistress, the foolish good-humor of her sister,
the silly chat and scandal of the elder girls, and the frigid cor-
rectness of the governesses equally annoyed her; and she had
no soft maternal heart, this unlucky girl, otherwise the prattle
and talk of the younger children, with whose care she was
chiefly intrusted, might have soothed and interested her; but
she lived among them two years, and not one was sorry that
she went away. The gentle, tender-hearted Amelia Sedley was
the only person to whom she could attach herself in the least;
and who could help attaching herself to Amelia?

The happiness, the superior advantages of the young women
round about her gave Rebecca inexpressible pangs of envy.
"What airs that girl gives herself because she is an earl's granddaughter," she said of one. "How they cringe and bow to that
Creole, because of her hundred thousand pounds! I am a
thousand times cleverer and more charming than that creature,
for all her wealth. I am as well bred as the earl's granddaughter, for all her fine pedigree; and yet every one passes
me by here. And yet, when I was at my father's, did not the
men give up their gayest balls and parties in order to pass the
evening with me?" She determined, at any rate, to get free
from the prison in which she found herself, and now began to

act for herself, and for the first time to make connected plans for the future.

She took advantage, therefore, of the means of study the place offered her; and as she was already a musician and a good linguist, she speedily went through the little course of study which was considered necessary for ladies in those days. Her music she practiced incessantly, and one day, when the girls were out and she had remained at home she was overheard to play a piece so well that Minerva thought wisely, she could spare herself the expense of a master for the juniors, and intimated to Miss Sharp that she was to instruct them in music for the future.

The girl refused; and for the first time, and to the astonishment of the majestic mistress of the school. "I am here to speak French with the children," Rebecca said, abruptly, "not to teach them music, and save money for you. Give me money, and I will teach them."

Minerva was obliged to yield, and, of course, disliked her from that day. "For five-and-thirty years," she said, and with grave justice, "I never have seen the individual who has dared in my own house to question my authority. I have nourished a viper in my bosom."

"A viper—a fiddlestick," said Miss Sharp to the old lady, almost fainting with astonishment. "You took me because I was useful. There is no question of gratitude between us. I hate this place, and want to leave it. I will do nothing here but what I am obliged to do."

It was in vain that the old lady asked her if she was aware she was speaking to Miss Pinkerton? Rebecca laughed in her face, with a horrid, sarcastic, demoniacal laughter, that almost sent the schoolmistress into fits. "Give me a sum of money," said the girl, "and get rid of me—or, if you like better, get me a good place as governess in a nobleman's family—you can do so if you please." And in their further disputes she always returned to this point. "Get me a situation—we hate each other, and I am ready to go."

Worthy Miss Pinkerton, although she had a Roman nose and a turban, and was as tall as a grenadier, and had been up to this time an irresistible princess, had no will or strength like that of her little apprentice, and in vain did battle against her, and tried to overawe her. Attempting once to scold her in public, Rebecca hit upon the before-mentioned plan of answering her in French, which quite routed the old woman. In order to maintain her authority in her school, it became necessary to remove this rebel, this monster, this serpent, this firebrand; and hearing about this time that Sir Pitt Crawley's family was in want of a governess, she actually recommended Miss Sharp for the situation, firebrand and serpent as she was. "I cannot, certainly," she said, "find fault with Miss Sharp's conduct, except to myself, and must allow that her talents and accomplishments are of a high order. As far as the head goes, at least, she does credit to the educational system pursued at my establishment."

And so the schoolmistress reconciled the recommendation to her conscience, and the indentures were canceled, and the apprentice was free.

Dr. Swishtail's Academy

(From "Vanity Fair")

Cuff's fight with Dobbin, and the unexpected issue of that contest, will long be remembered by every man who was educated at Dr. Swishtail's famous school. The latter youth (who used to be called Heigh-ho Dobbin, Gee-ho Dobbin, and by many other names indicative of puerile contempt) was the quietest, the clumsiest, and, as it seemed, the dullest of all Dr. Swishtail's young gentlemen. His parent was a grocer in the City; and it was bruited abroad that he was admitted into Dr. Swishtail's academy upon what are called "mutual principles"—that is to say, the expenses of his board and schooling were defrayed by his father in goods, not money; and he stood there—almost at the bottom of the school, in his scraggy corduroys and jacket, through the seams of which his great big bones were bursting—as the representative of so many pounds of tea, candles, sugar, mottled-soap, plums (of which a very mild proportion was supplied for the puddings of the establishment), and other commodities. A dreadful day it was for young Dobbin when one of the youngsters of the school, having run into the town upon a poaching excursion for hardbake and polonies, espied the cart of Dobbin & Rudge, Grocers and Oilmen, Thames Street, London, at the doctor's door, discharging a cargo of the wares in which the firm dealt.

Young Dobbin had no peace after that. The jokes were frightful, and merciless against him. "Hullo, Dobbin," one wag would say, "here's good news in the paper. Sugar is ris', my boy." Another would set a sum: "If a pound of mutton candles cost seven-pence-half-penny, how much must Dobbin cost?" and a roar would follow from all the circle of young knaves, usher and all, who rightly considered that the selling of goods by retail is a shameful and infamous practice, meriting the contempt and scorn of all real gentlemen.

"Your father's only a merchant, Osborne," Dobbin said in private to the little boy who had brought down the storm upon him. At which the latter replied, haughtily, "My father's a gentleman, and keeps his carriage;" and Mr. William Dobbin retreated to a remote outhouse in the playground, where he passed a half-holiday in the bitterest sadness and woe. Who amongst us is there that does not recollect similar hours of bitter, bitter childish grief? Who feels injustice, who shrinks before a slight, who has a sense of wrong so acute, and so glowing a gratitude for kindness, as a generous boy? and how many of those gentle souls do you degrade, estrange, torture, for the sake of a little loose arithmetic and miserable dog Latin?

Now, William Dobbin, from an incapacity to acquire the rudiments of the above language, as they are propounded in that wonderful book, the "Eton Latin Grammar," was compelled to remain among the very last of Dr. Swishtail's scholars, and was "taken down" continually by little fellows with pink faces and pinafores when he marched up with the lower form, a giant amongst them, with his downcast, stupefied look, his dog-eared primer, and his tight corduroys. High and low all made fun of him. They sewed up those corduroys, tight as they were. They cut his bed-strings. They upset buckets and benches, so that he might break his shins over them, which he never failed to do. They sent him parcels, which, when opened, were found to contain the paternal soap and candles. There was no little fellow but had his jeer and joke at Dobbin; and he bore everything quite patiently, and was entirely dumb and miserable.

Cuff, on the contrary, was the great chief and dandy of the Swishtail Seminary. He smuggled wine in. He fought the town boys. Ponies used to come for him to ride home on Saturdays. He had his top-boots in his room, in which he used to hunt in the holidays. He had a gold repeater; and took snuff like the doctor. He had been to the opera, and knew the merits of the principal actors, preferring Mr. Kean to Mr. Kemble. He could knock you off forty Latin verses in an hour. He could make French poetry. What else didn't he know, or couldn't he do? They said even the doctor himself was afraid of him.

Cuff, the unquestioned king of the school, ruled over his subjects and bullied them, with splendid superiority. This one blacked his shoes; that toasted his bread; others would fag out, and give him balls at cricket during whole summer afternoons. "Figs" was the fellow whom he despised most, and with whom, though always abusing him, and sneering at him, he scarcely ever condescended to hold personal communication.

One day in private the two young gentlemen had had a difference. Figs, alone in the schoolroom, was blundering over a home letter; when Cuff, entering, bade him go upon some message of which tarts were probably the subject.

"I can't," says Dobbin; "I want to finish my letter."

"You *can't?*" says Mr. Cuff, laying hold of that document (in which many words were scratched out, many were misspelt, on which had been spent I don't know how much thought, and labor, and tears; for the poor fellow was writing to his mother, who was fond of him, although she was a grocer's wife and lived in a back parlor in Thames Street)—" you *can't?* " says Mr. Cuff. " I should like to know why, pray? Can't you write to old Mother Figs to-morrow ? "

" Don't call names," Dobbin said, getting off the bench, very nervous.

" Well, sir, will you go ? " crowed the cock of the school.

" Put down the letter," Dobbin replied; " no gentleman readth letterth."

" Well, *now* will you go ? " says the other.

" No, I won't. Don't strike, or I'll *thmash* you," roars out Dobbin, springing to a leaden inkstand, and looking so wicked that Mr. Cuff paused, turned down his coat-sleeves again, put his hands into his pockets, and walked away with a sneer. But he never meddled personally with the grocer's boy after that; though we must do him the justice to say he always spoke of Mr. Dobbin with contempt behind his back.

Some time after this interview it happened that Mr. Cuff, on a sunshiny afternoon, was in the neighborhood of poor William Dobbin, who was lying under a tree in the playground, spelling over a favorite copy of the " Arabian Nights," which he had—apart from the rest of the school, who were pursuing their various sports—quite lonely, and almost happy. If people would but leave children to themselves; if teachers would cease to bully them; if parents would not insist upon directing their thoughts, and dominating their feelings—those feelings and thoughts which are a mystery to all (for how much do you and I know of each other, of our children, of our fathers, of our neighbors, and how far more beautiful and sacred are the thoughts of the poor lad or girl whom you govern likely to be, than those of the dull and world-corrupted person who rules him)—if, I say, parents and masters would leave their children alone a little more—small harm would accrue, although a less quantity of *as in præsenti* might be acquired.

Well, William Dobbin had for once forgotten the world, and was away with Sinbad the Sailor in the Valley of Diamonds, or with Prince Ahmed and the Fairy Peribanou in that delightful cavern where the prince found her, and whither we should all like to make a tour, when shrill cries, as of a little fellow weeping, woke up his pleasant reverie; and looking up he saw Cuff before him, belaboring a little boy.

It was the lad who had peached upon him about the grocer's cart; but he bore little malice, not at least toward the young and small. "How dare you, sir, break the bottle?" says Cuff to the little urchin, swinging a yellow cricket-stump over him.

The boy had been instructed to get over the playground wall (at a selected spot where the broken glass had been removed from the top, and niches made convenient in the brick); to run a quarter of a mile; to purchase a pint of rum-shrub on credit; to brave all the doctor's outlying spies, and to clamber back into the playground again; during the performance of which feat his foot had slipped, and the bottle was broken, and the shrub had been spilled, and his pantaloons had been damaged, and he appeared before his employer a perfectly guilty and trembling, though harmless, wretch.

"How dare you, sir, break it?" says Cuff; "you blundering little thief! You drank the shrub, and now you pretend to have broken the bottle. Hold out your hand, sir."

Down came the stump with a great heavy thump on the child's hand. A moan followed. Dobbin looked up. The Fairy Peribanou had fled into the inmost cavern with Prince Ahmed; the Roc had whisked away Sinbad the Sailor out of the Valley of Diamonds, out of sight, far into the clouds; and there was every-day life before honest William; and a big boy beating a little one without cause.

"Hold out your other hand, sir," roars Cuff to his little school-fellow, whose face was distorted with pain. Dobbin quivered, and gathered himself up in his narrow old clothes.

"Take that, you little devil!" cried Mr. Cuff, and down came the wicket again on the child's hand. Don't be horrified, ladies, every boy at a public school has done it. Your children will so do and be done by in all probability. Down came the wicket again, and Dobbin started up.

I can't tell what his motive was. Torture in a public school is as much licensed as the knout in Russia. It would be ungentleman-like (in a manner) to resist it. Perhaps Dobbin's foolish soul revolted against that exercise of tyranny; or perhaps he had a hankering feeling of revenge in his mind, and longed to measure himself against that splendid bully and tyrant, who had all the glory, pride, pomp, circumstance, banners flying, drums beating, guards saluting, in the place. Whatever may have been his incentive, however, up he sprang, and screamed out, " Hold off, Cuff; don't bully that child any more; or I'll——"

" Or you'll what? " Cuff asked in amazement at this interruption. " Hold out your hand, you little beast ! "

" I'll give you the worst thrashing you ever had in your life," Dobbin said, in reply to the first part of Cuff's sentence; and little Osborne, gasping and in tears, looked up with wonder and incredulity at seeing this amazing champion put up suddenly to defend him; while Cuff's astonishment was scarcely less. Fancy our late monarch, George III., when he heard of the revolt of the North American colonies; fancy brazen Goliath when little David stepped forward and claimed a meeting; and you have the feelings of Mr. Reginald Cuff when this rencontre was proposed to him.

" After school," says he, of course; after a pause and a look as much as to say, " Make your will, and communicate your best wishes to your friends between this time and that."

" As you please," Dobbin said. " You must be my bottle-holder, Osborne."

" Well, if you like," little Osborne replied ; for you see his papa kept a carriage, and he was rather ashamed of his champion.

Yes, when the hour of battle came, he was almost ashamed to say, " Go it, Figs;" and not a single other boy in the place uttered that cry for the first two or three rounds of this famous combat; at the commencement of which the scientific Cuff with a contemptuous smile on his face, and as light and as gay as if he was at a ball, planted his blows upon his adversary, and floored that unlucky champion three times running. At each fall there was a cheer; and everybody was anxious to have the honor of offering the conqueror a knee.

"What a licking I shall get when it's over!" young Osborne thought, picking up his man. "You'd best give in," he said to Dobbin; "it's only a thrashing, Figs, and you know I'm used to it." But Figs, all whose limbs were in a quiver, and whose nostrils were breathing rage, put his little bottle-holder aside, and went in for a fourth time.

As he did not in the least know how to parry the blows that were aimed at himself, and Cuff had begun the attack on the three preceding occasions, without ever allowing his enemy to strike, Figs now determined that he would commence the engagement by a charge on his own part; and accordingly, being a left-handed man, brought that arm into action, and hit out a couple of times with all his might—once at Mr. Cuff's left eye, and once on his beautiful Roman nose.

Cuff went down this time to the astonishment of the assembly. "Well hit, by Jove!" says little Osborne, with the air of a connoisseur, clapping his man on the back. "Give it him with the left, Figs, my boy."

Figs's left made terrific play during all the rest of the combat. Cuff went down every time. At the sixth round, there were almost as many fellows shouting out, "Go it, Figs!" as there were youths exclaiming, "Go it, Cuff!" At the twelfth round the latter champion was all abroad, as the saying is, and had lost all presence of mind and power of attack or defense. Figs, on the contrary, was as calm as a Quaker. His face being quite pale, his eyes shining open, and a great cut on his under lip bleeding profusely, gave this young fellow a fierce and ghastly air, which perhaps struck terror into many spectators. Nevertheless, his intrepid adversary prepared to close for the thirteenth time.

If I had the pen of a Napier, or a *Bell's Life*, I should like to describe this combat properly. It was the last charge of the Guard (that is, *it would* have been only Waterloo had not yet taken place)—it was Ney's column breasting the hill of La Haye Sainte, bristling with ten thousand bayonets, and crowned with twenty eagles—it was the shout of the beef-eating British, as, leaping down the hill, they rushed to hug the enemy in the savage arms of battle—in other words, Cuff coming up full of pluck, but quite reeling and groggy, the Fig-merchant put in his left as usual on his adversary's nose, and sent him down for the last time.

"I think *that* will do for him," Figs said, as his opponent dropped as neatly on the green as I have seen Jack Spot's ball plump into the pocket at billiards; and the fact is, when time was called, Mr. Reginald Cuff was not able, or did not choose, to stand up again.

And now all the boys set up such a shout for Figs as would make you think he had been their darling champion through the whole battle; and as absolutely brought Dr. Swishtail out of his study, curious to know the cause of the uproar. He threatened to flog Figs violently, of course; but Cuff, who had come to himself by this time, and was washing his wounds, stood up and said, "It's my fault, sir—not Figs's—not Dobbin's. I was bullying a little boy; and he served me right." By which magnanimous speech he not only saved his conqueror a whipping, but got back all his ascendency over the boys, which his defeat had nearly cost him.

Young Osborne wrote home to his parents an account of the transaction.

"SUGARCANE HOUSE, RICHMOND, March 18—.

"DEAR MAMMA—I hope you are quite well. I should be much obliged to you to send me a cake and five shillings. There has been a fight here between Cuff & Dobbin. Cuff, you know, was the Cock of the School. They fought thirteen rounds, and Dobbin Licked. So Cuff is now Only Second Cock. The fight was about me. Cuff was licking me for breaking a bottle of milk, and Figs wouldn't stand it. We call him Figs because his father is a Grocer—Figs & Rudge,

Thames St., City—I think as he fought for me you ought to buy your Tea & Sugar at his father's. Cuff goes home every Saturday, but can't this, because he has 2 Black Eyes. He has a white Pony to come and fetch him, and a groom in livery on a bay mare. I wish my Papa would let me have a Pony, and I am

Your dutiful Son,
"GEORGE SEDLEY OSBORNE.

"P. S.—Give my love to little Emmy. I am cutting her out a Coach in cardboard. Please not a seed-cake, but a plum-cake."

In consequence of Dobbin's victory, his character rose prodigiously in the estimation of all his schoolfellows, and the name of Figs, which had been a byword of reproach, became as respectable and popular a nickname as any other in use in the school. "After all, it's not his fault that his father's a grocer," George Osborne said, who, though a little chap, had a very high popularity among the Swishtail youth; and his opinion was received with great applause. It was voted low to sneer at Dobbin about this accident of birth. "Old Figs" grew to be a name of kindness and endearment; and the sneak of an usher jeered at him no longer.

And Dobbin's spirit rose with his altered circumstances. He made wonderful advances in scholastic learning. The superb Cuff himself, at whose condescension Dobbin could only blush and wonder, helped him on with his Latin verses; "coached" him in play hours, carried him triumphantly out of the little-boy class into the middle-sized form; and even there got a fair place for him. It was discovered, that although dull at classical learning, at mathematics he was uncommonly quick. To the contentment of all he passed third in algebra, and got a French prize-book, at the public midsummer examination. You should have seen his mother's face, when "Télémaque" (that delicious romance) was presented to him by the doctor in the face of the whole school and the parents and company, with an inscription to Gulielmo Dobbin. All the boys clapped hands in token of applause and sympathy. His blushes, his stumbles, his awkwardness, and the number of feet which he crushed as he went back to his place, who shall describe or calculate? Old Dobbin, his father, who now respected him for the first time, gave him two guineas publicly; most of which he spent in a general tuck out for the school; and he came back in a tail-coat after the holidays.

Dobbin was much too modest a young fellow to suppose that this happy change in all his circumstances arose from his own generous and manly disposition; he chose, from some perverseness, to attribute his good fortune to the sole agency and benevolence of little George Osborne, to whom henceforth he vowed such a love and affection as is only felt by children—such an affection as we read in the charming fairy book uncouth Orson had for splendid young Valentine his conqueror. He flung himself down at little Osborne's feet, and loved him.

Even before they were acquainted, he had admired Osborne in secret. Now he was his valet, his dog, his man Friday. He believed Osborne to be the possessor of every perfection, to be the handsomest, the bravest, the most active, the cleverest, the most generous of created boys. He shared his money with him; bought him uncountable presents of knives, pencil-cases, gold seals, toffee, Little Warblers, and romantic books, with large colored pictures of knights and robbers, in many of which latter you might read inscriptions to George Sedley Osborne, Esq., from his attached friend, William Dobbin—the which tokens of homage George received very graciously, as became his superior merit.

So that when Lieutenant Osborne, coming to Russell Square on the day of the Vauxhall party, said to the ladies, "Mrs. Sedley, ma'am, I hope you have room; I've asked Dobbin of ours to come and dine here and go with us to Vauxhall. He's almost as modest as Jos."

"Modesty! pooh!" said the stout gentleman, casting a *vainqueur* look at Miss Sharp.

"He is—but you are incomparably more graceful, Sedley," Osborne added, laughing. "I met him at the Bedford, when I went to look for you; and I told him that Miss Amelia was come home, and that we were all bent on going out for a night's pleasuring; and that Mrs. Sedley had forgiven his breaking the punch-bowl at the child's party. Don't you remember that catastrophe, ma'am, seven years ago?"

"Over Mrs. Flamingo's crimson silk gown," said good-natured Mrs. Sedley. "What a gawky it was! And his sisters are not much more graceful. Lady Dobbin was at Highbury last night with three of them. Such figures! my dears."

"The alderman's very rich, isn't he?" Osborne said archly. "Don't you think one of the daughters would be a good spec for me, ma'am?"

"You foolish creature! Who would take *you*, I should like to know, with your yellow face?"

"Mine a yellow face? Stop till you see Dobbin. Why, he had the yellow fever three times; twice at Nassau, and once at St. Kitt's."

"Well, well; yours is quite yellow enough for us. Isn't it, Emmy?" Mrs. Sedley said: at which speech Miss Amelia only made a smile and a blush; and looking at Mr. George Osborne's pale, interesting countenance, and those beautiful, black, curling, shining whiskers, which the young gentleman himself regarded with no ordinary complacency, she thought in her little heart, that in his Majesty's army, or in the wide world, there never was such a face or such a hero. "I don't care about Captain Dobbin's complexion," she said, "or about his awkwardness. *I* shall always like him, I know;" her little reason being that he was the friend and champion of George.

"There's not a finer fellow in the service," Osborne said, "nor a better officer, though he is not an Adonis, certainly." And he looked toward the glass himself with much *naïveté;* and in so doing, caught Miss Sharp's eye fixed keenly upon him, at which he blushed a little, and Rebecca thought in her heart, "*Ah, mon beau monsieur!* I think I have *your* gauge"—the little artful minx!

That evening, when Amelia came tripping into the drawing-room in a white muslin frock, prepared for conquest at Vauxhall, singing like a lark and as fresh as a rose, a very tall, ungainly gentleman, with large hands and feet, and large ears, set off by a closely cropped head of black hair, and in the hideous military frogged coat and cocked hat of those times, advanced to meet her, and made her one of the clumsiest bows that was ever performed by a mortal.

This was no other than Captain William Dobbin, of his Majesty's —— Regiment of Foot, returned from yellow fever, in the West Indies, to which the fortune of the service had ordered his regiment, whilst so many of his gallant comrades were reaping glory in the Peninsula.

He had arrived with a knock so very timid and quiet that it was inaudible to the ladies up-stairs; otherwise, you may be sure, Miss Amelia would never have been so bold as to come singing into the room. As it was, the sweet, fresh little voice went right into the captain's heart, and nestled there. When she held out her hand for him to shake, before he enveloped it in his own, he paused, and thought, "Well, is it possible—are you the little maid I remember in the pink frock, such a short time ago—the night I upset the punch-bowl, just after I was gazetted? Are you the little girl that George Osborne said should marry him? What a blooming young creature you seem, and what a prize the rogue has got!" All this he thought, before he took Amelia's hand into his own, and as he let his cocked hat fall.

His history since he left school, until the very moment when we have the pleasure of meeting him again, although not fully narrated, has yet, I think, been indicated sufficiently for an ingenious reader by the conversation in the last page. Dobbin, the despised grocer, was Alderman Dobbin—Alderman Dobbin was Colonel of the City Light Horse, then burning with military ardor to resist the French Invasion. Colonel Dobbin's corps, in which old Mr. Osborne himself was but an indifferent corporal, had been reviewed by the Sovereign and the Duke of York; and the colonel and alderman had been knighted. His son had entered the army; and young Osborne followed presently in the same regiment. They had served in the West Indies and in Canada. Their regiment had just come home, and the attachment of Dobbin to George Osborne was as warm and generous now as it had been when the two were schoolboys.

Mr. Veal's School

(From "Vanity Fair")

Georgy Osborne was now fairly established in his grandfather's mansion in Russell Square, occupant of his father's room in the house, and heir apparent of all the splendors there. The good looks, gallant bearing, and gentleman-like appearance of the boy won the grandsire's heart for him. Mr. Osborne was as proud of him as ever he had been of the elder George.

The child had many more luxuries and indulgences than had been awarded to his father. Osborne's commerce had prospered greatly of late years. His wealth and importance in the City had very much increased. He had been glad enough in former days to put the elder George to a good private school; and a commission in the army for his son had been a source of no small pride to him; for little George and his future prospects the old man looked much higher. He would make a gentleman of the little chap, was Mr. Osborne's constant saying regarding little Georgy. He saw him in his mind's eye, a collegian, a Parliament man—a baronet, perhaps. The old man thought he would die contented if he could see his grandson in a fair way to such honors. He would have none but a tip-top college man to educate him—none of your quacks and pretenders—no, no. A few years before, he used to be savage, and inveigh against all parsons, scholars, and the like—declaring that they were a pack of humbugs and quacks, that weren't fit to get their living but by grinding Latin and Greek, and a set of supercilious dogs, that pretended to look down upon British merchants and gentlemen who could buy up half a hundred of 'em. He would mourn now, in a very solemn manner, that his own education had been neglected, and repeatedly point out, in pompous orations to Georgy, the necessity and excellence of classical acquirements.

. . . .

Georgy, after breakfast, would sit in the arm-chair in the dining-room, and read the *Morning Post*, just like a grown-up man. "How he *du* dam an swear," the servants would cry, delighted at his precocity. Those who remembered the captain and his father declared Master George was his pa, every inch of him. He made the house lively by his activity, his imperiousness, his scolding, and his good nature.

George's education was confided to a neighboring scholar and pedagogue, who "prepared young noblemen and gentlemen for the universities, the senate, and the learned professions; whose system did not embrace the degrading corporal severities still practiced at the ancient places of education, and in whose family the pupils could find the elegancies of refined society and the confidence and affection of a home." It was in this way that the Reverend Lawrence Veal, of Hart Street, Bloomsbury, Bareacres, strove with Mrs. Veal, his wife, to entice pupils.

By thus advertising and pushing sedulously, the domestic chaplain and his lady generally succeeded in having one or two scholars by them who paid a high figure and were thought to be in uncommonly comfortable quarters. There was a large West Indian, whom nobody came to see, with a mahogany complexion, a woolly head, and an exceedingly dandified appearance; there was another hulking boy of three-and-twenty, whose education had been neglected, and whom Mr. and Mrs. Veal were to introduce into the polite world; there were two sons of Colonel Bangles of the East India Company's Service; these four sat down to dinner at Mrs. Veal's genteel board, when Georgy was introduced to her establishment.

Georgy was, like some dozen other pupils, only a day boy; he arrived in the morning under the guardianship of his friend Mr. Rowson, and if it was fine, would ride away in the afternoon on his pony followed by the groom. The wealth of his grandfather was reported in the school to be prodigious. The

Reverend Mr. Veal used to compliment Georgy upon it personally, warning him that he was destined for a high station; that it became him to prepare, by sedulity and docility in youth, for the lofty duties to which he would be called in mature age; that obedience in the child was the best preparation for command in the man; and that he therefore begged George would not bring toffy into the school, and ruin the health of the Master Bangles, who had everything they wanted at the elegant and abundant table of Mrs. Veal.

With respect to learning, "the Curriculum," as Mr. Veal loved to call it, was of prodigious extent; and the young gentlemen in Hart Street might learn a something of every known science. The Reverend Mr. Veal had an orrery, an electrifying machine, a turning lathe, a theater (in the wash-house), a chemical apparatus, and what he called a select library of all the works of the best authors of ancient and modern times and languages. He took the boys to the British Museum, and descanted upon the antiquities and the specimens of natural history there, so that audiences would gather round him as he spoke; and all Bloomsbury highly admired him as a prodigiously well-informed man. And whenever he spoke (which he did almost always), he took care to produce the very finest and longest words of which the vocabulary gave him the use, rightly judging that it was as cheap to employ a handsome, large, and sonorous epithet as to use a little stingy one!

Thus he would say to George in school: "I observed on my return home from taking the indulgence of an evening's scientific conversation with my excellent friend Dr. Bulders—a true archæologian—that the windows of your venerated grandfather's almost princely mansion in Russell Square were illuminated as if for the purposes of festivity. Am I right in my conjecture that Mr. Osborne entertained a society of chosen spirits round his sumptuous board last night?"

Little Georgy, who had considerable humor, and used to mimic Mr. Veal to his face with great spirit and dexterity, would reply that Mr. V. was quite correct in his surmise.

"Then those friends who had the honor of partaking of Mr. Osborne's hospitality, gentlemen, had no reason, I will lay any wager, to complain of their repast. I myself have been more than once so favored. (By the way, Master Osborne, you came a little late this morning, and have been a defaulter in this respect more than once.) I myself, I say, gentlemen, humble as I am, have been found not unworthy to share Mr. Osborne's elegant hospitality. And though I have feasted with the great and noble of the world—for I presume that I may call my excellent friend and patron, the Right Honorable George Earl of Bareacres, as one of the number—yet I assure you that the board of the British merchant was to the full as richly served, and his reception as gratifying and noble. Mr. Bluck, sir, we will resume, if you please, that passage of Eutropius which was interrupted by the late arrival of Master Osborne."

To this great man George's education was for some time intrusted. Amelia was bewildered by his phrases, but thought him a prodigy of learning. That poor widow made friends of Mrs. Veal, for reasons of her own. She liked to be in the house, and see Georgy coming to school there. She liked to be asked to Mrs. Veal's *conversazioni*, which took place once a month (as you were informed on pink cards, with $A\Theta HNH$ engraved on them), and where the professor welcomed his pupils and their friends to weak tea and scientific conversation. Poor little Amelia never missed one of these entertainments, and thought them delicious so long as she might have Georgy sitting by her. And she would walk from Brompton in any weather, and embrace Mrs. Veal with tearful gratitude for the delightful evening she had passed, when, the company having retired and Georgy gone off with Mr. Rowson, his attendant, poor Mrs. Osborne put on her cloaks and her shawls preparatory to walking home.

As for the learning which Georgy imbibed under this valuable master of a hundred sciences, to judge from the weekly reports which the lad took home to his grandfather, his progress was remarkable. The names of a score or more desirable branches of knowledge were printed on a table, and the pupil's progress in each was marked by the professor. In Greek Georgy was pronounced aristos, in Latin optimus, in French *très bien*, and so forth; and everybody had prizes for everything at the end of the year. Even Mr. Swartz, the woolly-headed young gentleman, and half-brother to the Honorable Mrs. MacMull, and Mr. Bluck, the neglected young pupil of three-and-twenty from the agricultural districts, and that idle young scapegrace of a Master Todd before mentioned, received little eighteen-penny books, with "Athene" engraved in them, and a pompous Latin inscription from the professor to his young friends.

The family of this Master Todd were hangers-on of the house of Osborne. The old gentleman had advanced Todd from being a clerk to be a junior partner in his establishment.

Mr. Osborne was the godfather of young Master Todd (who in subsequent life wrote Mr. Osborne Todd on his cards, and became a man of decided fashion), while Miss Osborne had accompanied Miss Maria Todd to the font, and gave her *protégée* a prayer-book, a collection of tracts, a volume of very low-church poetry, or some such memento of her goodness every year. Miss O. drove the Todds out in her carriage now and then; when they were ill, her footman, in large plush smalls and waistcoat, brought jellies and delicacies from Russell Square to Coram Street. Coram Street trembled and looked up to Russell Square indeed; and Mrs. Todd, who had a pretty hand at cutting paper trimmings for haunches of mutton, and could make flowers, ducks, etc., out of turnips and carrots in a very creditable manner, would go to "the Square," as it was called, and assist in the preparations incident to a great dinner, without even so much as thinking of sitting down to the banquet. If any guest failed at the eleventh hour, Todd was asked to dine. Mrs. Todd and Maria came across in the evening, slipped in with a muffled knock, and were in the drawing-room by the time Miss Osborne and the ladies under her convoy reached that apartment; and ready to fire off duets and sing until the gentlemen came up. Poor Maria Todd; poor young lady! How she had to work and thrum at these duets and sonatas in the street, before they appeared in public in the square!

Thus it seemed to be decreed by fate, that Georgy was to domineer over everybody with whom he came in contact, and that friends, relatives, and domestics were all to bow the knee before the little fellow. It must be owned that he accommodated himself very willingly to this arrangement. Most people do so. And Georgy liked to play the part of master, and perhaps had a natural aptitude for it. . . . . . .

One day as the young gentlemen were assembled in the study at the Reverend Mr. Veal's, and the domestic chaplain to the Right Honorable the Earl of Bareacres was spouting away as usual—a carriage drove up to the door decorated with the statue of Athene, and two gentlemen stepped out. The young Masters Bangles rushed to the window, with a vague notion that their father might have arrived from Bombay. The great hulking scholar of three-and-twenty, who was crying secretly over a passage of Eutropius, flattened his neglected nose against the panes, and looked at the drag, as the *laquais de place* sprang from the box and let out the persons in the carriage.

"It's a fat one and a thin one," Mr. Bluck said, as a thundering knock came to the door.

Everybody was interested, from the domestic chaplain himself, who hoped he saw the fathers of some future pupils, down to Master Georgy, glad of any pretext for laying his book down.

The boy in the shabby livery, with the faded copper buttons, who always thrusts himself into the tight coat to open the door, came into the study and said, "Two gentlemen want to see Master Osborne." The professor had had a trifling altercation in the morning with that young gentleman, owing to a difference about the introduction of crackers in school-time; but his face resumed its habitual expression of bland courtesy, as he said, "Master Osborne, I give you full permission to go and see your carriage friends—to whom I beg you to convey the respectful compliments of myself and Mrs. Veal."

Georgy went into the reception room, and saw two strangers,

whom he looked at with his head up in his usual haughty manner. One was fat, with mustachios, and the other was lean and long, in a blue frock-coat, with a brown face, and a grizzled head.

"My God, how like he is!" said the long gentleman, with a start. "Can you guess who we are, George?"

The boy's face flushed up, as it did usually when he was moved, and his eyes brightened. "I don't know the other," he said, "but I should think you must be Major Dobbin."

Indeed it was our old friend. His voice trembled with pleasure as he greeted the boy, and, taking both the other's hands in his own drew the lad to him, and said:

"Your mother has talked to you about me—has she?"

"That she has," Georgy answered, "hundreds and hundreds of times." . . . .

The first thing Mrs. Osborne showed the major was George's miniature, for which she ran up-stairs on her arrival at home. It was not half handsome enough, of course, for the boy, but wasn't it noble of him to think of bringing it to his mother? Whilst her papa was awake she did not talk much about Georgy. To hear about Mr. Osborne and Russell Square was not agreeable to the old man, who very likely was unconscious that he had been living for some months past mainly on the bounty of his richer rival; and lost his temper if allusion was made to the other. . . .

At his accustomed hour Mr. Sedley began to doze in his chair, and then it was Amelia's opportunity to commence her conversation, which she did with great eagerness; it related exclusively to Georgy. She did not talk at all about her own sufferings at breaking from him, for indeed this worthy woman, though she was half killed by the separation from the child, yet thought it was very wicked in her to repine at losing him; but everything concerning him, his virtues, talents, and prospects, she poured out. She described his angelic beauty; narrated a hundred instances of his generosity and greatness of mind whilst living with her; how a royal duchess had stopped and admired him in Kensington Gardens; how splendidly he was cared for now, and how he had a groom and a pony; what quickness and cleverness he had, and what a prodigiously well-read and delightful person the Reverend Lawrence Veal was, George's master. "He knows *everything*," Amelia said. "He has the most delightful parties. You who are so learned yourself, and have read so much, and are so clever and accomplished—don't shake your head and say no—*he* always used to say you were—you will be charmed with Mr. Veal's parties—the last Tuesday in every month. He says there is no place in the bar or the senate that Georgy may not aspire to. Look here," and she went to the piano-drawer and drew out a theme of Georgy's composition. This great effort of genius, which is still in the possession of George's mother, is as follows:

On selfishness.—Of all the vices which degrade the human character, Selfishness is the most odious and contemptible. An undue love of Self leads to the most monstrous crimes, and occasions the greatest misfortunes both in *States and Families*. As a selfish man will impoverish his family and often bring them to ruin, so a selfish king brings ruin on his people and often plunges them into war.

Example: The selfishness of Achilles, as remarked by the poet Homer, occasioned a thousand woes to the Greeks—$\mu\upsilon\rho\iota'$ $A\chi\alpha\iota o\tilde{\iota}\varsigma$ $\check{\alpha}\lambda\gamma\grave{\epsilon}$ $\check{\epsilon}\theta\eta\kappa\epsilon$ —(Hom. Il. A. 2). The selfishness of the late Napoleon Bonaparte occasioned innumerable wars in Europe, and caused him to perish, himself, on a miserable island—that of Saint Helena in the Atlantic Ocean.

We see by these examples that we are not to consult our own interest and ambition, but that we are to consider the interests of others as well as our own.

GEORGE S. OSBORNE.

ATHENE HOUSE, *April* 2d, 1823.

"Think of him writing such a hand, and quoting Greek, too, at his age," the delighted mother said. "O William," she added, holding out her hand to the major, "what a treasure Heaven has given me in that boy! He is the comfort of my life, and he is the image of—of him that's gone!"

THOMAS HUGHES, M.P.
1823.

THOMAS HUGHES, M.P., was born in the county of Berks, England, in 1823. His family is an old one, of eminent respectability. When a little boy, at Twyford school, he received the nickname of "Cadmus," or "Cad," from an amusing blunder, in which he described the ancient worthy of that name as a postman, or mail-carrier, because he "first carried *letters* from Asia to Greece." At ten years of age young Hughes went with his brother to the school of the celebrated Dr. Arnold, at Rugby, where he remained eight years. He was graduated from Oriel College, at Oxford, in 1845. He was admitted to the bar in 1848, and became a liberal in politics. He entered Parliament in 1865, and was a member for nine years. He has served also as queen's counsel, president of the Workingmen's College, chief manager of the Crystal Palace Company, colonel of a volunteer rifle company, and county judge of Cheshire. He visited America in 1870. "Tom Brown at Rugby" was written in 1858, and "Tom Brown at Oxford" appeared four years later. These, together with "The Life of Alfred the Great" and "The Manliness of Christ," are his most famous works.

Characterization

"Tom Brown" is the exact picture of the bright side of a schoolboy's experiences, told with a life, a spirit, and a fond minuteness of detail and recollection which are infinitely honorable to the author. Many have received equally strong impressions from their passage through a public school, but few would, we think, be able to paint them with so much vigor and fidelity. It requires so much courage, so much honesty, so much purity, to traverse that stage of life without doing and suffering many things which make the recollection of it painful, that a man who can honestly describe his school experience in the tone which the author of "Tom Brown" maintains throughout this volume without an effort, has a very high claim, indeed, to the respect and gratitude of his readers. It would be hard to imagine a more cheerful or a more useful lesson to a public-school boy. Every corner of the playhouse, every rule of football, every quaint school usage, almost every room in the schoolhouse, is sketched so boldly, yet so accurately, that Rugbœans will no doubt be able to realize to themselves every sentence of the book. Even the gentiles of Eton, Harrow, or Winchester, bigoted as they are sure to be in favor of their own institutions, cannot fail to see that Tom Brown was a very fine fellow, and that, although he had the misfortune to be at Rugby, they can hardly do better than to follow his examples in several particulars. "EDINBURGH REVIEW."

Chapters from "Tom Brown's School-Days at Rugby"

The chapel-bell began to ring at a quarter to eleven, and Tom got in early and took his place in the lowest row, and watched all the other boys come in and take their places, filling row after row; he tried to construe the Greek text which was inscribed over the door with the slightest possible success, and wondered which of the masters, who walked down the chapel and took their seats in the exalted boxes at the end, would be his lord. And then came the closing of the doors, and the Doctor[1] in his robes, and the service, which, however, didn't impress him much, for his feeling of wonder and curiosity was too strong. And the boy on one side of him was scratching his name on the oak paneling in front, and he couldn't help watching to see what the name was, and whether it was well scratched; and the boy on the other side went to sleep and kept falling against him; and on the whole, though many boys even in that part of the school, were serious and attentive, the general atmosphere was by no means devotional; and when he got into the close again, he didn't feel at all comfortable, or as if he had been to church.

But at afternoon chapel it was quite another thing. He had spent the time after dinner writing home to his mother, and so was in a better frame of mind; and his first curiosity was over, and he could attend more to the service. As the hymn after the prayers was being sung, and the chapel was getting a little dark, he was beginning to feel that he had been really worship-

[1] Dr. Thomas Arnold, Head-master of the school of Rugby

ing. And then came the great event in his life, as in every Rugby boy's life of that day—the first sermon from the Doctor.

More worthy pens than mine have described that scene. The oak pulpit standing out by itself above the school seats. The tall, gallant form, the kindling eye, the voice, now soft as the low notes of a flute, now clear and stirring as the call of the light infantry bugle, of him who stood there Sunday after Sunday, witnessing and pleading for his Lord, the King of righteousness and love and glory, with whose spirit he was filled, and in whose power he spoke. The long lines of young faces rising tier above tier down the whole length of the chapel, from the little boy's who had just left his mother to the young man's who was going out next week into the great world rejoicing in his strength. It was a great and solemn sight, and never more so than at this time of year, when the only lights in the chapel were in the pulpit and at the seats of the præpostors of the week, and the soft twilight stole over the rest of the chapel, deepening into darkness in the high gallery behind the organ.

But what was it, after all, which seized and held these three hundred boys, dragging them out of themselves, willing or unwilling, for twenty minutes, on Sunday afternoons? True, there always were boys scattered up and down the school who in heart and head were worthy to hear and able to carry away the deepest and wisest words there spoken. But these were a minority always, generally a very small one, often so small a one as to be countable on the fingers of your hand. What was it that moved and held us, the rest of the three hundred reckless, childish boys, who feared the Doctor with all our hearts, and very little besides in heaven or earth: who thought more of our sets in the school than of the Church of Christ, and put the traditions of Rugby and the public opinion of boys in our daily life above the laws of God? We couldn't enter into half that we heard; we hadn't the knowledge of our own hearts or the knowledge of one another, and little enough of the faith, hope, and love needed to that end. But we listened, as all boys in their better moods will listen (aye, and men too, for the matter of that), to a man whom we felt to be, with all his heart, and soul, and strength, striving against whatever was mean, and unmanly, and unrighteous in our little world. It was not the cold clear voice of one giving advice and warning from serene heights to those who were struggling and sinning below, but the warm living voice of one who was fighting for us and by our sides, and calling on us to help him and ourselves and one another. And so, wearily and little by little, but surely and steadily, on the whole, was brought home to the young boy, for the first time, the meaning of his life,—that it was no fool's or sluggard's paradise into which he had wandered by chance, but a battle-field ordained from of old, where there are no spectators, but the youngest must take his side, and the stakes are life and death.

And he who roused this consciousness in them showed them at the same time, by every word he spoke in the pulpit, and by his whole daily life, how that battle was to be fought, and stood there before them their fellow-soldier and the captain of their band. The true sort of captain, too, for a boy's army, one who had no misgivings and gave no uncertain word of command, and, let who would yield or make truce, would fight the fight out (so every boy felt) to the last gasp and the last drop of blood. Other sides of his character might take hold of and influence boys here and there, but it was this thoroughness and undaunted courage which, more than anything else, won his way to the hearts of the great mass of those on whom he left his mark, and made them believe first in him, and then in his Master.

It was this quality above all others which moved such boys as our hero, who had nothing whatever remarkable about him except excess of boyishness, by which I mean animal life in its fullest measure, good nature and honest impulses, hatred of injustice and meanness, and thoughtlessness enough to sink a three-decker. And so, during the next two years, in which it was more than doubtful whether he would get good or evil from the school, and before any steady purpose or principle grew up in him, whatever his week's sins and shortcomings might have been, he hardly ever left the chapel on Sunday evenings without a serious resolve to stand by and follow the Doctor, and a feeling that it was only cowardice (the incarnation of all other sins in such a boy's mind) which hindered him from doing so with all his heart.

The lower-fourth form,[1] in which Tom found himself at the beginning of the next half-year, was the largest form in the lower school, and numbered upwards of forty boys. Young gentlemen of all ages, from nine to fifteen, were to be found there, who expended such part of their energies as was devoted to Latin and Greek upon a book of Livy, the Bucolics of Virgil, and the Hecuba of Euripides, which were ground out in small daily portions. The driving of this unlucky fourth must have been grievous work to the unfortunate master, for it was the most unhappily constituted of any in the school. Here stuck the great stupid boys, who for the life of them could never master the accidence; the objects alternately of mirth and terror to the youngsters, who were daily taking them up, and laughing at them in lesson, and getting kicked by them for so doing in play-hours. There were no less than three unhappy fellows in tail-coats, with incipient down on their chins, whom the Doctor and the master of the form were always endeavoring to hoist into the upper school, but whose parsing and construing resisted the most well-meant shoves. Then came the mass of the form, boys of eleven and twelve, the most mischievous and reckless age of British youth, of whom East and Tom Brown were fair specimens. As full of tricks as monkeys, and of excuses as Irish women, making fun of their master, one another, and their lessons, Argus himself would have been puzzled to keep an eye on them; and as for making them steady or serious for half an hour together, it was simply hopeless. The remainder of the form consisted of young prodigies of nine and ten, who were going up the school at the rate of a form a half-year, all boys' hands and wits being against

[1] class

them in their progress. It would have been one man's work to see that the precocious youngsters had fair play; and as the master had a good deal besides to do, they hadn't, and were forever being shoved down three or four places, their verses stolen, their books inked, their jackets whitened, and their lives otherwise made a burden to them.

The lower fourth, and all the forms below it, were heard in the great school, and were not trusted to prepare their lessons before coming in, but were whipped into school three quarters of an hour before the lesson began by their respective masters; and there, scattered about on the benches, with dictionary and grammar, hammered out their twenty lines of Virgil and Euripides in the midst of Babel. The masters of the lower school walked up and down the great school together during the three quarters of an hour, or sat in their desks reading or looking over copies, and keeping such order as was possible. But the lower fourth was just now an overgrown form, too large for any one man to attend to properly, and consequently the elysium or ideal form of the young scapegraces who formed the staple of it.

Tom, as has been said, had come up from the third with a good character, but the temptations of the lower fourth soon proved too strong for him, and he rapidly fell away, and became as unmanageable as the rest. For some weeks, indeed, he succeeded in maintaining the appearance of steadiness, and was looked upon favorably by his new master, whose eyes were first opened by the following little incident:

Besides the desk which the master himself occupied, there was another large unoccupied desk in the corner of the great school, which was untenanted. To rush and seize upon this desk, which was ascended by three steps, and held four boys, was the great object of ambition of the lower fourthers; and the contentions for the occupation of it bred such disorder, that at last the master forbade its use altogether. This of course was a challenge to the more adventurous spirits to occupy it, and as it was capacious enough for two boys to lie hid there completely, it was seldom that it remained empty, notwithstanding the veto. Small holes were cut in the front, through which the occupants watched the masters as they walked up and down, and as lesson time approached, one boy at a time stole out and down the steps, as the masters' backs were turned, and mingled with the general crowd on the forms below. Tom and East had successfully occupied the desk some half-dozen times, and were grown so reckless that they were in the habit of playing small games with fives'-balls inside, when the masters were at the other end of the big school. One day as ill luck would have it, the game became more exciting than usual, and the ball slipped through East's fingers and rolled slowly down the steps, and out into the middle of the school, just as the masters turned in their walk and faced round upon the desk. The young delinquents watched their master through the look-out holes march slowly down the school straight upon their retreat, while all the boys in the neighborhood of course stopped their work to look on; and not only were they ignominiously drawn out, and caned over the head then and there, but their characters for steadiness were gone from that time. However, as they only shared the fate of some three fourths of the rest of the form, this did not weigh heavily upon them.

In fact, the only occasions on which they cared about the matter were the monthly examinations, when the Doctor came round to examine their form, for one long awful hour, in the work which they had done in the preceding month. The second monthly examination came round soon after Tom's fall, and it was with anything but lively anticipations that he and the other lower-fourth boys came into prayers on the morning of the examination day.

Prayers and calling-over seemed twice as short as usual, and before they could get construes of a tithe of the hard passages marked in the margin of their books, they were all seated round, and the Doctor was standing in the middle, talking in whispers to the master. Tom couldn't hear a word which passed, and never lifted his eyes from his book; but he knew by a sort of magnetic instinct that the Doctor's under lip was coming out, and his eye beginning to burn, and his gown getting gathered up more and more tightly in his left hand. The suspense was agonizing, and Tom knew that he was sure on such occasions to make an example of the schoolhouse boys. "If he would only begin," thought Tom, "I shouldn't mind."

At last the whispering ceased, and the name which was called out was not Brown. He looked up for a moment, but the Doctor's face was too awful; Tom wouldn't have met his eye for all he was worth, and buried himself in his book again.

The boy who was called up first was a clever, merry schoolhouse boy, one of their set; he was some connection of the Doctor's, and a great favorite, and ran in and out of his house as he liked, and so was selected for the first victim.

"*Triste lupus stabulis*,"[1] began the luckless youngster, and stammered through some eight or ten lines.

"There, that will do," said the Doctor. "Now construe."

On common occasions the boy could have construed the passage well enough probably, but now his head was gone.

"*Triste lupus*,—the sorrowful wolf," he began.

A shudder ran through the whole form and the Doctor's wrath fairly boiled over; he made three steps up to the construer, and gave him a good box on the ear. The blow was not a hard one, but the boy was so taken by surprise that he started back; the form[2] caught the back of his knees, and over he went on the floor behind. There was a dead silence over the whole school; never before and never again while Tom was at school did the Doctor strike a boy in lesson. The provocation must have been great. However, the victim had saved his form for that occasion, for the Doctor turned to the top bench, and put on the best boys for the rest of the hour; and though at the end of the lesson he gave them all such a rating as they did not forget, this terrible field-day passed over without any severe

---

[1] The wolf is fatal to the flock. The word *triste* (fatal) may also mean "*sorrowful*."

[2] bench

visitations in the shape of punishments or floggings. Forty young scapegraces expressed their thanks to the "sorrowful wolf" in their different ways before second lesson.

But a character for steadiness once gone is not easily recovered, as Tom found, and for years afterwards he went up the school without it, and the masters' hands were against him, and his against them. And he regarded them, as a matter of course, as his natural enemies.

Matters were not so comfortable, either, in the house as they had been, for old Brooke left at Christmas, and one or two others of the sixth-form boys at the following Easter. Their rule had been rough, but strong and just in the main, and a higher standard was beginning to be set up; in fact, there had been a short foretaste of the good time which followed some years later. Just now, however, all threatened to return into darkness and chaos again; for the new præpostors were either small young boys, whose cleverness had carried them up to the top of the school, while in strength of body and character they were not yet fit for a share in the government; or else big fellows of the wrong sort, boys whose friendships and tastes had a downward tendency, who had not caught the meaning of their position and work, and felt none of its responsibilities. So under this no-government the schoolhouse began to see bad times. The big fifth-form boys, who were a sporting and drinking set, soon began to usurp power, and to fag the little boys as if they were præpostors, and to bully and oppress any who showed signs of resistance. The bigger sort of sixth-form boys just described soon made common cause with the fifth, while the smaller sort, hampered by their colleagues' desertion to the enemy, could not make head against them. So the fags were without their lawful masters and protectors, and ridden over rough-shod by a set of boys whom they were not bound to obey, and whose only right over them stood in their bodily powers; and, as old Brooke had prophesied, the house by degrees broke up into small sects and parties, and lost the strong feeling of fellowship which he set so much store by, and with it much of the prowess in games, and the lead in all school matters, which he had done so much to keep up.

In no place in the world has individual character more weight than at a public school. Remember this, I beseech you, all you boys who are getting into the upper forms. Now is the time in all your lives, probably, when you may have more wide influence for good or evil on the society you live in than you ever can have again. Quit yourselves like men, then; speak up, and strike out if necessary for whatsoever is true and manly and lovely and of good report; never try to be popular, but only to do your duty and help others to do theirs, and you may leave the tone of feeling in the school higher than you found it, and so be doing good, which no living soul can measure, to generations of your countrymen yet unborn.

. . . . .

But now came on the May-fly season; the soft hazy summer weather lay sleepily along the rich meadows by Avon side, and the green and gray flies flickered with their graceful, lazy, up and down flight over the reeds and the water and the meadows, in myriads upon myriads. The May-flies must surely be the lotus-eaters of the ephemeræ—the happiest, laziest, carelessest fly that dances and dreams out his few hours of sunshiny life by English rivers.

Every little pitiful coarse fish in the Avon was on the alert for the flies, and gorging his wretched carcass with hundreds daily, the gluttonous rogues! and every lover of the gentle craft was out to avenge the poor May-flies.

So one fine Thursday afternoon Tom, having borrowed East's new rod, started by himself to the river. He fished for some time with small success; not a fish would rise at him; but, as he prowled along the bank, he was presently aware of mighty ones feeding in a pool on the opposite side, under the shade of a huge willow-tree. The stream was deep here, but some fifty yards below was a shallow for which he made off hot-foot; and forgetting landlords, keepers, solemn prohibitions of the Doctor, and everything else, pulled up his trousers, plunged across, and in three minutes was creeping along on all-fours towards the clump of willows.

It isn't often that great chub or any other coarse fish are in earnest about anything, but just then they were thoroughly bent on feeding, and in half an hour Master Tom had deposited three thumping fellows at the foot of the giant willow. As he was baiting for a fourth pounder, and just going to throw in again, he became aware of a man coming up the bank not one hundred yards off. Another look told him that it was the under-keeper. Could he reach the shallow before him? No, not carrying his rod. Nothing for it but the tree, so Tom laid his bones to it, shinning up as fast as he could, and dragging up his rod after him. He had just time to reach and crouch along upon a huge branch some ten feet up, which stretched out over the river, when the keeper arrived at the clump. Tom's heart beat fast as he came under the tree; two steps more and he would have passed, when, as ill-luck would have it, the gleam on the scales of the dead fish caught his eye, and he made a dead point at the foot of the tree. He picked up the fish one by one; his eye and touch told him that they had been alive and feeding within the hour. Tom crouched lower along the branch, and heard the keeper beating the clump. "If I could only get the rod hidden," thought he, and began gently shifting it to get it alongside him; "willow trees don't throw out straight hickory shoots twelve feet long, with no leaves, worse luck." Alas! the keeper catches the rustle, and then a sight of the rod, and then of Tom's hand and arm.

"Oh, be up thur, be 'ee?" says he running under the tree. "Now you come down this minute."

"Treed at last," thinks Tom, making no answer, and keeping as close as possible, but working away at the rod, which he takes to pieces: "I'm in for it, unless I can starve him out." And then he begins to meditate getting along the branch for a plunge and scramble to the other side; but the small branches are so thick, and the opposite bank so difficult, that the keeper will have lots of time to get round by the ford before he can get out, so he gives that up. And now he hears the keeper beginning to scramble up the trunk. That will never do; so he scrambles himself back to where his branch joins the trunk, and stands with lifted rod.

"Hullo, Velveteens! Mind your fingers if you come any higher."

The keeper stops and looks up, and then with a grin says, "Oh! be you, be it, young measter? Well, here's luck. Now I tells 'ee to come down at once, and 't'll be best for 'ee."

"Thank 'ee, Velveteens, I'm very comfortable," said Tom, shortening the rod in his hand, and preparing for battle.

"Werry well, please yourself," says the keeper, descending however to the ground again, and taking his seat on the bank; "I bean't in no hurry, so you med take your time. I'll larn 'ee to gee honest folk names afore I've done with 'ee."

"My luck as usual," thinks Tom; "what a fool I was to give him a black. If I'd called him 'keeper,' now, I might get off. The return match is all his way."

The keeper quietly proceeded to take out his pipe, fill and light it, keeping an eye on Tom, who now sat disconsolately across the branch, looking at the keeper—a pitiful sight for men and fishes. The more he thought of it the less he liked it. "It must be getting near second calling-over," thinks he. Keeper smokes on stolidly. "If he takes me up, I shall be flogged safe enough. I can't sit here all night. Wonder if he'll rise at silver."

"I say, keeper," said he meekly, "let me go for two bob?"

"Not for twenty neither," grunts his persecutor.

And so they sat on till long past second calling-over, and telling of locking-up near at hand.

"I'm coming down, keeper," said Tom at last, with a sigh, fairly tired out. "Now what are you going to do?"

"Walk 'ee up to school, and give 'ee over to the Doctor; them's my orders," says Velveteens, knocking the ashes out of his fourth pipe, and standing up and shaking himself.

"Very good," said Tom; "but hands off, you know. I'll go with you quietly, so no collaring, or that sort of thing."

Keeper looked at him a minute. "Werry good," said he at last; and so Tom descended, and wended his way drearily by the side of the keeper up to the schoolhouse, where they arrived just at locking up. As they passed the school gates, the Tadpole, and several others who were standing there, caught the state of things, and rushed out, crying, "Rescue!" but Tom shook his head, so they only followed to the Doctor's gate, and went back sorely puzzled.

How changed and stern the Doctor seemed from the last time that Tom was up there, as the keeper told the story, not omitting to state how Tom had called him blackguard names. "Indeed, sir," broke in the culprit, "it was only Velveteens." The Doctor only asked one question.

"You know the rule about the banks, Brown?"

"Yes, sir."

"Then wait for me to-morrow, after first lesson."

"I thought so," muttered Tom.

"And about the rod, sir?" went on the keeper; "Master's told we as we might have all the rods——"

"Oh, please, sir," broke in Tom, "the rod isn't mine." The Doctor looked puzzled, but the keeper, who was a good-hearted fellow, and melted at Tom's evident distress, gave up his claim. Tom was flogged next morning, and a few days afterwards met Velveteens, and presented him with half-a-crown for giving up the rod claim, and they became sworn friends; and I regret to say that Tom had many more fish from under the willow that May-fly season, and was never caught again by Velveteens.

It wasn't three weeks before Tom, and now East by his side, were again in the awful presence. This time, however, the Doctor was not so terrible. A few days before, they had been fagged at fives to fetch the balls that went off the court. While standing watching the game, they saw five or six nearly new balls hit on the top of the school. "I say, Tom," said East, when they were dismissed, "couldn't we get those balls somehow?"

"Let's try, anyhow."

So they reconnoitered the walls carefully, borrowed a coal hammer from old Stumps, bought some big nails, and after one or two attempts, scaled the school, and possessed themselves of huge quantities of fives'-balls. The place pleased them so much that they spent all their spare time there, scratching and cutting their names on the top of every tower; and at last, having exhausted all other places, finished up with inscribing, H. EAST, T. BROWN, on the minute-hand of the great clock, in the doing of which they held the minute-hand, and disturbed the clock's economy. So next morning, when master and boys came trooping down to prayers, and entered the quadrangle, the injured minute-hand was indicating three minutes to the hour. They all pulled up, and took their time. When the hour struck, doors were closed, and half the school late. Thomas being set to make inquiry, discovers their names on the minute-hand, and reports accordingly; and they are sent for, a knot of their friends making derisive and pantomimic allusions to what their fate would be, as they walk off.

But the Doctor, after hearing their story, doesn't make much of it, and only gives them thirty lines of Homer to learn by heart, and a lecture on the likelihood of such exploits ending in broken bones.

Alas! almost the next day was one of the great fairs in the town; and as several rows and other disagreeable accidents had of late taken place on these occasions, the Doctor gives out, after prayers in the morning, that no boy is to go down into the town. Wherefore East and Tom, for no earthly pleasure except that of doing what they were told not to do, start away, after second lesson, and making a short circuit through the fields, strike a back lane which leads into the town, go down it, and run plump upon one of the masters as they emerge into the High Street. The master in question, though a very clever, is not a righteous man: he has already caught several of his own pupils, and gives them lines to learn, while he sends East and Tom, who are not his pupils, up to the Doctor, who, on learning that they had been at prayers in the morning, flogs them soundly.

The flogging did them no good at the time, for the injustice of their captor was rankling in their minds; but it was just the end of the half, and on the next evening but one Thomas knocks at their door, and says the Doctor wants to see them. They look at one another in silent dismay. What can it be now? Which of their countless wrong-doings can he have heard of officially? However, it's no use delaying, so up they go to the study. There they find the Doctor, not angry, but very grave. "He has sent for them to speak very seriously before they go home. They have each been flogged several times in the half-year for direct and willful breaches of rules. This cannot go on. They are doing no good to themselves or others, and now they are getting up in the school, and have influence. They seem to think that rules are made capriciously, and for the pleasure of the masters; but this is not so—they are for the good of the whole school, and must and shall be obeyed. Those who thoughtlessly or willfully break them will not be allowed to stay at the school. He should be sorry if they had to leave, as the school might do them both much good, and wishes them to think very seriously in the holidays over what he has said. Good-night."

And so the two hurry off horribly scared: the idea of having to leave has never crossed their minds, and is quite unbearable.

As they go out, they meet at the door old Holmes, a sturdy, cheery præpostor of another house, who goes in to the Doctor; and they hear his genial hearty greeting of the new-comer, so different from their own reception, as the door closes, and return to their study with heavy hearts, and tremendous resolves to break no more rules.

Five minutes afterwards the master of their form, a late arrival and a model young master, knocks at the Doctor's study door. "Come in!" and as he enters, the Doctor goes on to Holmes—"you see I do not know anything of the case officially, and if I take any notice of it at all, I must publicly expel the boy. I don't wish to do that, for I think there is some good in him. There's nothing for it but a good sound thrashing." He paused to shake hands with the master, which Holmes does also, and then prepares to leave.

"I understand. Good-night, sir."

"Good-night, Holmes. And remember," added the Doctor, emphasizing the words, "a good sound thrashing before the whole house."

The door closed on Holmes; and the Doctor, in answer to the puzzled look of his lieutenant, explained shortly. "A gross case of bullying. Wharton, the head of the house, is a very good fellow, but slight and weak, and severe physical pain is the only way to deal with such a case; so I have asked Holmes to take it up. He is very careful and trustworthy, and has plenty of strength. I wish all the sixth had as much. We must have it here, if we are to keep order at all."

Now I don't want any wiseacres to read this book; but if they should, of course they will prick up their long ears, and howl, or rather bray, at the above story. Very good, I don't object; but what I have to add for you boys is this, that Holmes called a levy of his house after breakfast next morning, made them a speech on the case of bullying in question, and then gave the bully a "good sound thrashing;" and that years afterwards, that boy sought out Holmes, and thanked him, saying it had been the kindest act which had ever been done upon him, and the turning-point in his character; and a very good fellow he became, and a credit to his school.

After some other talk between them, the Doctor said, "I want to speak to you about two boys in your form, East and Brown: I have just been speaking to them. What do you think of them?"

"Well, they are not hard workers, and very thoughtless and full of spirits; but I can't help liking them. I think they are sound, good fellows at the bottom."

"I'm glad of it. I think so too. But they make me very uneasy. They are taking the lead a good deal amongst the fags in my house, for they are very active, bold fellows. I should be very sorry to lose them, but I shan't let them stay if I don't see them gaining character and manliness. In another year they may do great harm to all the younger boys."

"Oh, I hope you won't send them away," pleaded their master.

"Not if I can help it. But now I never feel sure, after any half-holiday, that I shan't have to flog one of them next morning, for some foolish, thoughtless scrape. I quite dread seeing either of them."

They were both silent for a minute. Presently the Doctor began again:

"They don't feel that they have any duty or work to do in the school, and how is one to make them feel it?"

"I think if either of them had some little boy to take care of, it would steady them. Brown is the more reckless of the two, I should say; East wouldn't get into so many scrapes without him."

"Well," said the Doctor, with something like a sigh, "I'll think of it." And they went on to talk of other subjects.

. . . .

Another two years have passed, and it is again the end of the summer half-year at Rugby; in fact, the school has broken up. The fifth-form examinations were over last week, and upon them have followed the speeches, and the sixth-form examinations for exhibitions; and they too are over now. The boys have gone to all the winds of heaven, except the town boys and the eleven, and the few enthusiasts besides who have asked leave to stay in their houses to see the result of the cricket matches. For this year the Wellesburn return match and the Marylebone match are played at Rugby, to the great delight of the town and neighborhood, and the sorrow of those aspiring young cricketers who have been reckoning for the last three months on showing off at Lords' ground.

The Doctor started for the Lakes yesterday morning, after an interview with the captain of the eleven, in the presence of

Thomas, at which he arranged in what school the cricket dinners were to be, and all other matters necessary for the satisfactory carrying out of the festivities; and warned them as to keeping all spirituous liquors out of the close, and having the gates closed by nine o'clock.

. . . . . .

There is much healthy, hearty, happy life scattered up and down the close; but the group to which I beg to call your especial attention is there, on the slope of the island, which looks towards the cricket-ground. It consists of three figures; two are seated on a bench, and one on the ground at their feet. The first, a tall, slight, and rather gaunt man, with a bushy eyebrow, and a dry, humorous smile, is evidently a clergyman. He is carelessly dressed, and looks rather used up, which isn't much to be wondered at, seeing that he has just finished six weeks of examination work; but there he basks, and spreads himself out in the evening sun, bent on enjoying life, though he doesn't quite know what to do with his arms and legs. Surely it is our friend the young master, whom we have had glimpses of before, but his face has gained a great deal since we last came across him.

And by his side, in white flannel shirt and trousers, straw hat, the captain's belt, and the untanned yellow cricket shoes which all the eleven wear, sits a strapping figure, nearly six feet high, with ruddy tanned face and whiskers, curly brown hair, and a laughing, dancing eye. He is leaning forward with his elbows resting on his knees, and dandling his favorite bat, with which he has made thirty or forty runs to-day, in his strong brown hands. It is Tom Brown, grown into a young man nineteen years old, a præpostor and captain of the eleven, spending his last day as a Rugby-boy, and let us hope as much wiser as he is bigger, since we last had the pleasure of coming across him.

And at their feet on the warm dry ground, similarly dressed, sits Arthur, Turkish fashion, with his bat across his knees. He too is no longer a boy, less of a boy in fact than Tom, if one may judge from the thoughtfulness of his face, which is somewhat paler, too, than one could wish; but his figure, though slight, is well-knit and active, and all his old timidity has disappeared, and is replaced by silent quaint fun, with which his face twinkles all over, as he listens to the broken talk between the other two, in which he joins every now and then.

All three are watching the game eagerly, and joining in the cheering which follows every good hit. It is pleasing to see the easy friendly footing which the pupils are on with their master, perfectly respectful, yet with no reserve and nothing forced in their intercourse. Tom has clearly abandoned the old theory of "natural enemies," in this case at any rate.

But it is time to listen to what they are saying, and see what we can gather out of it.

. . . . . .

"Oh, Brown, mayn't I go in next?" shouts the swiper.

"Whose name is next on the list?" says the captain.

"Winter's, and then Arthur's," answers the boy who carries it; "but there's only twenty-six runs to get, and no time to lose. I heard Mr. Aislabie say that the stumps must be drawn at a quarter past eight exactly."

"Oh, do let the Swiper go in," chorus the boys; so Tom yielded against his better judgment.

"I dare say now I've lost the match by this nonsense," he says, as he sits down again; "they'll be sure to get Jack's wicket in three or four minutes; however, you'll have the chance, sir, of seeing a hard hit or two," adds he, smiling, and turning to the master.

"Come, none of your irony, Brown," answers the master. "I'm beginning to understand the game scientifically. What a noble game it is too!"

"Isn't it? But it's more than a game—it's an institution," said Tom.

"Yes," said Arthur, "the birthright of British boys, old and young, as *habeas corpus* and trial by jury are of British men."

"The discipline and reliance on one another which it teaches is so valuable, I think," went on the master, "it ought to be such an unselfish game. It merges the individual in the eleven; he doesn't play that he may win, but that his side may."

"That's very true," said Tom, "and that's why football and cricket, now one comes to think of it, are so much better games than fives' or hare-and-hounds, or any other, where the object is to come in first or to win for one's self, and not that one's side may win."

"And then the captain of the eleven!" said the master, "what a post is his in our school world! almost as hard as the Doctor's; requiring skill and gentleness and firmness, and I know not what other rare qualities."

"Which don't he wish he may get?" said Tom, laughing; "at any rate, he hasn't got them yet, or he wouldn't have been such a flat to-night as to let Jack Raggles go in out of his turn."

"Ah! the Doctor never would have done that," said Arthur, demurely. "Tom, you've a great deal to learn yet in the art of ruling."

"Well, I wish you'd tell the Doctor so, then, and get him to let me stop till I'm twenty. I don't want to leave, I'm sure."

"What a sight it is," broke in the master, "the Doctor as a ruler. Perhaps ours is the only little corner of the British empire which is thoroughly, wisely, and strongly ruled just now. I'm more and more thankful every day of my life that I came here to be under him."

"So am I, I'm sure," said Tom; "and more and more sorry that I've got to leave."

"Every place and thing one sees here reminds one of some wise act of his," went on the master. "This island now—you remember the time, Brown, when it was laid out in small gardens, and cultivated by frost-bitten fags in February and March?"

"Of course I do," said Tom; "didn't I hate spending two

hours in the afternoons grubbing in the tough dirt with the stump of a fives'-bat? But turf-cart was good fun enough."

"I dare say it was, but it was always leading to fights with the townspeople; and then the stealing flowers out of all the gardens in Rugby for the Easter show was abominable."

"Well, so it was," said Tom, looking down, "but we fags couldn't help ourselves. But what has that to do with the Doctor's ruling?"

"A great deal, I think," said the master; "what brought island-fagging to an end?"

"Why, the Easter speeches were put off till midsummer," said Tom, "and the sixth had the gymnastic poles put up here."

"Well, and who changed the time of the speeches, and put the idea of gymnastic poles into the heads of their worships the sixth form?" said the master.

"The Doctor, I suppose," said Tom. "I never thought of that."

"Of course you didn't," said the master, "or else, fag as you were, you would have shouted with the whole school against putting down old customs. And that's the way that all the Doctor's reforms have been carried out when he has been left to himself—quietly and naturally, putting a good thing in the place of a bad, and letting the bad die out; no wavering and no hurry—the best thing that could be done for the time being, and patience for the rest."

"Just Tom's own way," chimed in Arthur, nudging Tom with his elbow, "driving a nail where it will go," to which allusion Tom answered by a sly kick.

"Exactly so," said the master, innocent of the allusion and by-play.

. . . .

As Tom and the rest of the eleven were turning back into the close, and everybody was beginning to cry out for another country-dance, encouraged by the success of the night before, the young master, who was just leaving the close, stopped him, and asked him to come up to tea at half-past eight, adding, "I won't keep you more than half an hour, and ask Arthur to come up too."

"I'll come up with you directly, if you'll let me," said Tom, "for I feel rather melancholy, and not quite up to the country-dance and supper with the rest."

"Do by all means," said the master; "I'll wait here for you."

So Tom went off to get his boots and things from the tent, to tell Arthur of the invitation, and to speak to his second in command about stopping the dancing and shutting up the close as soon as it grew dusk. Arthur promised to follow as soon as he had a dance. So Tom handed his things over to the man in charge of the tent, and walked quietly away to the gate where the master was waiting, and the two took their way together up the Hillmorton road.

Of course they found the master's house locked up, and all the servants away in the close, about this time, no doubt footing it away on the grass with extreme delight to themselves, and in utter oblivion of the unfortunate bachelor their master, whose one enjoyment in the shape of meals was his "dish of tea" (as our grandmothers called it) in the evening; and the phrase was apt in his case, for he always poured his out into the saucer before drinking. Great was the good man's horror at finding himself shut out of his own house. Had he been alone he would have treated it as a matter of course, and would have strolled contentedly up and down his gravel-walk until some one came home; but he was hurt at the stain on his character of host, especially as the guest was a pupil. However, the guest seemed to think it a great joke, and presently, as they poked about round the house, mounted a wall, from which he could reach a passage window: the window, as it turned out, was not bolted, so in another minute Tom was in the house and down at the front door, which he opened from inside. The master chuckled grimly at this burglarious entry, and insisted on leaving the hall-door and two of the front windows open to frighten the truants on their return; and then the two set about foraging for tea, in which operation the master was much at fault, having the faintest possible idea of where to find anything, and being, moreover, wondrously short-sighted; but Tom by a sort of instinct knew the right cupboards in the kitchen and pantry, and soon managed to place on the snuggery table better materials for a meal than had appeared there probably during the reign of his tutor, who was then and there initiated, amongst other things, into the excellence of that mysterious condiment, a dripping-cake. The cake was newly baked, and all rich and flaky; Tom had found it reposing in the cook's private cupboard, awaiting her return; and as a warning to her they finished it to the last crumb. The kettle sang away merrily on the hob of the snuggery, for, notwithstanding the time of year, they lighted a fire, throwing both the windows wide open at the same time; the heap of books and papers were pushed away to the other end of the table, and the great solitary engraving of King's College Chapel over the mantelpiece looked less stiff than usual, as they settled themselves down in the twilight to the serious drinking of tea.

After some talk on the match, and other different subjects, the conversation came naturally back to Tom's approaching departure, over which he began again to make his moan.

"Well, we shall all miss you quite as much as you will miss us," said the master. "You are the Nestor of the school now, are you not?"

"Yes, ever since East left," answered Tom.

"By the bye, have you heard from him?"

"Yes, I had a letter in February just before he started for India to join his regiment."

"He will make a capital officer."

"Ay, won't he!" said Tom brightening; "no fellow could handle boys better, and I suppose soldiers are very like boys. And he'll never tell them to go where he won't go himself. No mistake about that—a braver fellow never walked."

"His year in the sixth will have taught him a good deal that will be useful to him now."

"So it will," said Tom, staring into the fire. " Poor, dear Harry," he went on, " how well I remember the day we were put out of the twenty. How he rose to the situation, and burned his cigar-cases, and gave away his pistols, and pondered on the constitutional authority of the sixth, and his new duties to the Doctor, and the fifth form and the fags. Ay, and no fellow ever acted up to them better, though he was always a people's man—for the fags, and against constituted authorities. He couldn't help that, you know. I'm sure the Doctor must have liked him?" said Tom, looking up inquiringly.

"The Doctor sees the good in every one, and appreciates it," said the master, dogmatically; " but I hope East will get a good colonel. He won't do if he can't respect those above him. How long it took him even here to learn the lesson of obeying."

"Well, I wish I were alongside of him," said Tom. "If I can't be at Rugby, I want to be at work in the world, and not dawdling away three years at Oxford."

"What do you mean by 'at work in the world'?" said the master, pausing, with his lips close to his saucerful of tea, and peering at Tom over it.

"Well, I mean real work—one's profession; whatever one will have really to do, and make one's living by. I want to be doing some real good, feeling that I am not only at play in the world," answered Tom, rather puzzled to find out himself what he really did mean.

"You are mixing up two very different things in your head, I think, Brown," said the master, putting down the empty saucer, "and you ought to get clear about them. You talk of 'working to get your living' and 'doing some real good in the world' in the same breath. Now, you may be getting a very good living in a profession and yet doing no good at all in the world, but quite the contrary, at the same time. Keep the latter before you as your one object, and you will be right, whether you make a living or not; but if you dwell on the other, you'll very likely drop into mere money-making, and let the world take care of itself for good or evil. Don't be in a hurry about finding your work in the world for yourself; you are not old enough to judge for yourself yet, but just look about you in the place you find yourself in, and try to make things a little better and honester there. You'll find plenty to keep your hand in at Oxford, or wherever else you go. And don't be led away to think this part of the world important and that unimportant. Every corner of the world is important. No man knows whether this part or that is most so, but every man may do some honest work in his own corner." And then the good man went on to talk wisely to Tom of the sort of work which he might take up as an undergraduate, warned him of the prevalent university sins, and explained to him the many and great differences between university and school life, till the twilight changed into darkness, and they heard the truant servant stealing in by the back entrance.

"I wonder where Arthur can be," said Tom at last, looking at his watch; "why, it's nearly half-past nine already."

"Oh, he is comfortably at supper with the eleven, forgetful of his oldest friends," said the master. "Nothing has given me greater pleasure," he went on, "than your friendship for him; it has been the making of you both."

"Of me, at any rate," answered Tom; "I should never have been here now but for him. It was the luckiest chance in the world that sent him to Rugby, and made him my chum."

"Why do you talk of lucky chances?" said the master; "I don't know that there are any such things in the world; at any rate there was neither luck nor chance in that matter."

Tom looked at him inquiringly, and he went on. "Do you remember when the Doctor lectured you and East at the end of one half-year, when you were in the shell, and had been getting into all sorts of scrapes?"

"Yes, well enough," said Tom; "it was the half-year before Arthur came."

"Exactly so," answered the master. "Now, I was with him a few minutes afterwards, and he was in great distress about you two. And, after some talk, we both agreed that you in particular wanted some object in the school beyond games and mischief; for it was quite clear that you never would make the regular school work your first object. And so the Doctor, at the beginning of the next half-year, looked out the best of the new boys, and separated you and East, and put the young boy into your study, in the hope that when you had somebody to lean on you, you would begin to stand a little steadier yourself, and get manliness and thoughtfulness. And I can assure you he has watched the experiment ever since with great satisfaction. Ah! not one of you boys will ever know the anxiety you have given him, or the care with which he has watched over every step in your school lives."

Up to this time, Tom had never wholly given in to or understood the Doctor. At first he had thoroughly feared him. For some years, as I have tried to show, he had learned to regard him with love and respect, and to think him a very great and wise and good man. But, as regarded his own position in the school, of which he was no little proud, Tom had no idea of giving any one credit for it but himself, and, truth to tell, was a very self-conceited young gentleman on the subject. He was wont to boast that he had fought his own way fairly up the school, and had never made up to or been taken up by any big fellow or master, and that it was now quite a different place from what it was when he first came. And, indeed, though he didn't actually boast of it, in his secret soul he did to a great extent believe that the great reform of the school had been owing quite as much to himself as to any one else. Arthur, he acknowledged, had done him good, and taught him a good deal, so had other boys in different ways, but they had not had the same means of influence on the school in general; and as for the Doctor, why, he was a splendid master, but every one knew that masters could do very little out of school hours. In short, he felt on terms of equality with his chief, so far as the social state of the school was concerned, and thought that the Doctor would find it no easy matter to get on without him.

Moreover, his school toryism was still strong, and he looked still with some jealousy on the Doctor, as somewhat of a fanatic in the matter of change, and thought it very desirable for the school that he should have some wise person (such as himself) to look sharply after vested school-rights, and see that nothing was done to the injury of the republic without due protest.

It was a new light to him to find that, besides teaching the sixth, and governing and guiding the whole school, editing classics, and writing histories, the great head-master had found time in those busy years to watch over the career even of him, Tom Brown, and his particular friends,—and, no doubt, of fifty other boys at the same time; and all this without taking the least credit to himself, or of seeming to know, or let any one else know, that he ever thought particularly of any boy at all.

However, the Doctor's victory was complete from that moment over Tom Brown at any rate. He gave way at all points, and the enemy marched right over him, cavalry, infantry and artillery, the land transport corps, and the camp followers. It had taken eight long years to do it, but now it was done thoroughly, and there wasn't a corner of him left which didn't believe in the Doctor. Had he returned to school again, and the Doctor begun the half-year by abolishing fagging and football and the Saturday half-holiday, or all or any of the most cherished school institutions, Tom would have supported him with the blindest faith. And so, after a half confession of his previous shortcomings, and sorrowful adieus to his tutor, from whom he received two beautifully-bound volumes of the Doctor's sermons, as a parting present, he marched down to the school-house, a hero-worshiper who would have satisfied the soul of Thomas Carlyle himself.

. . . .

In the summer of 1842, our hero stopped once again at the well-known station, and leaving his bag and fishing-rod with a porter, walked slowly and sadly up towards the town. It was now July. He had rushed away from Oxford the moment that term was over, for a fishing ramble in Scotland with two college friends, and had been for three weeks living on oat-cake, mutton-hams and whisky, in the wildest parts of Skye. They had descended one sultry evening on the little inn at Kyle Rhea ferry, and while Tom and another of the party put their tackle together and began exploring the stream for a sea-trout for supper, the third strolled into the house to arrange for their entertainment. Presently he came out in a loose blouse and slippers, a short pipe in his mouth, and an old newspaper in his hand, and threw himself on the heathery scrub which met the shingle, within easy hail of the fishermen. There he lay, the picture of free-and-easy, loafing, hand-to-mouth young England, "improving his mind," as he shouted to them, by the perusal of the fortnight-old weekly paper, soiled with the marks of toddy-glasses and tobacco-ashes, the legacy of the last traveler, which he had hunted out from the kitchen of the little hostelry, and being a youth of a communicative turn of mind, began imparting the contents to the fishermen as he went on.

"What a bother they are making about these wretched Corn-laws; here's three or four columns full of nothing but sliding-scales and fixed duties. Hang this tobacco, it's always going out! Ah, here's something better—a splendid match between Kent and England, Brown! Kent winning by three wickets. Felix fifty-six runs without a chance, and not out!"

Tom, intent on a fish which had risen at him twice, answered only with a grunt.

"Anything about the Goodwood?" called out the third man.

"Rory O'More drawn. Butterfly colt amiss," shouted the student.

"Just my luck," grumbled the inquirer, jerking his flies off the water, and throwing again with a heavy, sullen splash, and frightening Tom's fish.

"I say, can't you throw lighter over there? we ain't fishing for grampuses," shouted Tom across the stream.

"Hullo, Brown! here's something for you," called out the reading man next moment. "Why, your old master, Arnold of Rugby, is dead."

Tom's hand stopped half way in his cast, and his lines and flies went all tangling round and round his rod; you might have knocked him over with a feather. Neither of his companions took any notice of him, luckily; and with a violent effort he set to work mechanically to disentangle his line. He felt completely carried off his moral and intellectual legs, as if he had lost his standing point in the invisible world. Besides which, the deep loving loyalty which he felt for his old leader made the shock intensely painful. It was the first great wrench of his life, the first gap which the angel Death had made in his circle, and he felt numbed, and beaten down, and spiritless. Well, well! I believe it was good for him, and for many others in like case, who had to learn by that loss that the soul of man cannot stand or lean upon any human prop, however strong, and wise, and good; but that He upon whom alone it can stand and lean will knock away all such props in his own wise and merciful way, until there is no ground or stay left but Himself, the Rock of Ages, upon whom alone a sure foundation for every soul of man is laid.

As he wearily labored at his line, the thought struck him, "It may all be false, a mere newspaper lie," and he strode up to the recumbent smoker.

"Let me look at the paper," said he.

"Nothing else in it," answered the other, handing it up to him listlessly.—"Hullo, Brown! what's the matter, old fellow—ain't you well?"

"Where is it?" said Tom, turning over the leaves, his hands trembling, and his eyes swimming, so that he could not read.

"What? What are you looking for?" said his friend, jumping up and looking over his shoulder.

"That—about Arnold," said Tom.

"Oh, here," said the other, putting his finger on the paragraph. Tom read it over and over again; there could be no mistake of identity, though the account was short enough.

"Thank you," said he at last, dropping the paper. "I shall go for a walk: don't you and Herbert wait supper for me."

And away he strode, up over the moor at the back of the house, to be alone, and master his grief if possible.

His friend looked after him, sympathizing and wondering, and knocking the ashes out of his pipe, walked over to Herbert. After a short parley, they walked together up to the house.

"I'm afraid that confounded newspaper has spoiled Brown's fun for this trip."

"How odd that he should be so fond of his old master," said Herbert. Yet they also were both public-school men.

The two, however, notwithstanding Tom's prohibition, waited supper for him, and had everything ready when he came back some half an hour afterwards. But he could not join in their cheerful talk, and the party was soon silent, notwithstanding the efforts of all three. One thing only had Tom resolved, and that was, that he couldn't stay in Scotland any longer; he felt an irresistible longing to get to Rugby, and then home, and soon broke it to the others, who had too much tact to oppose.

So by daylight the next morning he was marching through Ross-shire, and in the evening hit the Caledonian canal, took the next steamer, and traveled as fast as boat and railway could carry him to the Rugby station.

As he walked up to the town, he felt shy and afraid of being seen, and took the back streets; why, he didn't know, but he followed his instinct. At the school-gates he made a dead pause; there was not a soul in the quadrangle—all was lonely and silent and sad. So with another effort he strode through the quadrangle, and into the schoolhouse offices.

He found the little matron in her room in deep mourning; shook her hand, tried to talk, and moved nervously about. She was evidently thinking of the same subject as he, but he couldn't begin talking.

"Where shall I find Thomas?" said he at last, getting desperate.

"In the servants' hall, I think, sir. But won't you take anything?" said the matron, looking rather disappointed.

"No, thank you," said he, and strode off again, to find the old verger, who was sitting in his little den as of old, puzzling over hieroglyphics.

He looked up through his spectacles, as Tom seized his hand and wrung it.

"Ah! you've heard all about it, sir, I see," said he.

Tom nodded, and then sat down on the shoe-board, while the old man told his tale, and wiped his spectacles, and fairly flowed over with quaint, homely, honest sorrow.

By the time he had done, Tom felt much better.

"Where is he buried, Thomas?" said he at last.

"Under the altar in the chapel, sir," answered Thomas. "You'd like to have the key, I dare say."

"Thank you Thomas.—Yes, I should very much." And the old man fumbled among his bunch, and then got up, as though he would go with him, but after a few steps, stopped short, and said, "Perhaps you'd like to go by yourself, sir?"

Tom nodded, and the bunch of keys was handed to him, with an injunction to be sure and lock the door after him, and bring them back before eight o'clock.

He walked quickly through the quadrangle and out into the close. The longing which had been upon him and driven him thus far, like the gad-fly in the Greek legends, giving him no rest in mind or body, seemed all of a sudden not to be satisfied, but to shrivel up, and pall. "Why should I go on? It's no use," he thought, and threw himself at full length on the turf, and looked vaguely and listlessly at all the well-known objects. There were a few of the town boys playing cricket, their wicket pitched on the best piece in the middle of the big-side ground —a sin about equal to a sacrilege in the eyes of the captain of the eleven. He was very nearly getting up to go and send them off. "Pshaw! they won't remember me. They've more right there than I," he muttered. And the thought that his scepter had departed, and his mark was wearing out, came home to him for the first time, and bitterly enough. He was lying on the very spot where the fights came off; where he himself had fought six years ago his first and last battle. He conjured up the scene till he could almost hear the shouts of the ring, and East's whisper in his ear ; and looking across the close to the Doctor's private door, half expected it to open, and the tall figure in cap and gown come striding under the elm trees towards him.

No, no! that sight could never be seen again. There was no flag flying on the round tower; the schoolhouse windows were all shuttered up; and when the flag went up again, and the shutters came down, it would be to welcome a stranger. All that was left on earth of him whom he had honored was lying cold and still under the chapel floor. He would go in and see the place once more, and then leave it once for all. New men and new methods might do for other people; let those who would worship the rising star ; he, at least, would be faithful to the sun which had set. And so he got up, and walked to the chapel door and unlocked it, fancying himself the only mourner in all the broad land, and feeding on his own selfish sorrow.

He passed through the vestibule, and then paused for a moment to glance over the empty benches. His heart was still proud and high, and he walked up to the seat which he had last occupied as a sixth-form boy, and sat himself down there to collect his thoughts.

And, truth to tell, they needed collecting and setting in order not a little. The memories of eight years were all dancing through his brain, and carrying him about whither they would, while beneath them all his heart was throbbing with the dull sense of a loss that could never be made up to him. The rays of the evening sun came solemnly through the painted windows above his head, and fell in gorgeous colors on the opposite wall, and the perfect stillness soothed his spirit little by little. And he turned to the pulpit, and looked at it, and then, leaning forward with his head on his hands, groaned aloud. "If he could only have seen the Doctor again for one five minutes; have told him all that was in his heart, what he owed to him, how he loved and reverenced him, and would, by God's help, follow his steps in life and death, he could have borne it all without a murmur. But that he should have gone away forever without knowing it all, was too much to bear."—"But am I sure he does not know it all?" The thought made him start. "May he not even now be near me, in this very chapel? If he be, am I sorrowing as he would have me sorrow—as I should wish to have sorrowed when I shall meet him again?"

He raised himself up and looked round, and after a minute rose and walked humbly down to the lowest bench, and sat down on the very seat which he had occupied on his first Sunday at Rugby. And then the old memories rushed back again, but softened and subdued, and soothing him as he let himself be carried away by them. And he looked up at the great painted window above the altar, and remembered how, when a little boy, he used to try not to look through it at the elm trees and the rooks, before the painted glass came, and the subscription for the painted glass, and the letter he wrote home for money to give to it. And there, down below, was the very name of the boy who sat on his right hand on that first day, scratched rudely on the oak paneling.

And then came the thought of all his old schoolfellows, and form after form of boys, nobler and braver and purer than he, rose up and seemed to rebuke him. Could he not think of them, and what they had felt and were feeling, they who had honored and loved from the first the man whom he had taken years to know and love? Could he not think of those yet dearer to him who was gone, who bore his name and shared his blood, and were now without a husband or a father? Then the grief which he began to share with others became gentle and holy, and he rose up once more, and walked up the steps to the altar; and while the tears flowed freely down his cheeks, knelt down humbly and hopefully, to lay down there his share of the burden which had proved itself too heavy for him to bear in his own strength.

Here let us leave him—where better could we leave him, than at the altar, before which he had first caught a glimpse of the glory of his birthright, and felt the drawing of the bond which links all living souls together in one brotherhood—at the grave beneath the altar of him who had opened his eyes to see that glory, and softened his heart till it could feel that bond?

And let us not be hard on him if at that moment his soul is fuller of the tomb, and him who lies there, than of the altar and Him of whom it speaks. Such stages have to be gone through, I believe, by all young and brave souls, who must win their way through hero-worship to the worship of Him who is the King and Lord of heroes. For it is only through our mysterious human relationships, through the love and tenderness and purity of mothers, and sisters, and wives, through the strength, and courage, and wisdom of fathers, and brothers, and teachers, that we can come to the knowledge of Him in whom alone the love, and the tenderness, and the purity, and the strength, and the courage, and the wisdom of all these dwell forever and ever in perfect fullness.

DANIEL PIERCE THOMPSON
1795-1868

DANIEL PIERCE THOMPSON was born at the foot of Bunker Hill, in Boston, Mass., in 1795. He was graduated from Middlebury College at the age of twenty-five, and entered upon the practice of law at Montpelier, Vt., where he speedily rose to eminence. He served his State as clerk of the legislature, judge of probate, county clerk, and secretary of state. He compiled the laws of Vermont, contributed to the leading periodicals of his time, and wrote a number of books, which proved successful ventures. Among these were "May Martin," "The Green Mountain Boys," and "Locke Amsden; or, the Schoolmaster." Of the latter work nine editions have been published. Judge Thompson died in 1868.

Characterization

"Locke Amsden," though not sufficiently ambitious to receive much attention from critical reviews, was very favorably noticed in former years, by the educational and secular press, and was more fortunate than many contemporary stories somewhat similar in plan, since it secured a sufficient hold upon popular interest to insure its perpetuation to the present day. This it owes largely, no doubt, to the subject-matter of the book, and to the high esteem in which its author was held as an eminent citizen of spotless fame. Moreover, the style of the composition, while not exhibiting a high order of genius, is yet pleasing and creditable, and the book is one that is read with real profit, especially by those who are actively connected with educational interests.

The School in the Horn of the Moon

(From "Locke Amsden; or, the Schoolmaster")

It was near the middle of the dark and dreary season which characterizes our northern clime. Old Winter had taken his January nap. And having protracted longer than usual his cold, sweaty slumbers, he had now, as if to make amends for his remissness, aroused himself with a rage and fury which seemed to show his determination to expel the last vestige of his antagonistic element, heat, that had thus invaded and for a while disarmed him, forever from his dominions. The whole season, indeed, to drop the metaphorical for plain language, had been one of uncommon mildness. A warm and broken December had been succeeded by a still warmer and more thawy January. And so little had people been made aware of the presence of winter thus far, that their doors were often left open, and small fires only were either used or required. But the cold weather now set in with intense severity, and compelled all to keep tightly closed doors and roaring fires.

The schoolhouse, which we have been for some time making the scene of action, had been built the preceding fall; and the interior, consequently, had been freshly plastered; while the woodwork of the doors and windows, already tight before from its newness, had been swollen by the recent thawy weather: so that the whole room, by this, and the finishing operation of the frost in closing up the remaining interstices, had been made almost wholly impervious to the admission of any fresh air from without.

From this, however, no evil consequences, owing to the mildness of the season, and the attendant circumstances we have mentioned, had resulted to the school. But scarcely a week had elapsed, after the change of weather just described, before the scholars, though apparently much enjoying the contrasted comforts of their tight, stove-heated room, while the cold, savage blasts could be heard raging and howling without, became very visibly affected. A livid paleness overspread their features; while their every appearance and movement indicated great and increasing languor and feebleness. The general health of the school, in short, including that of the master, seemed to be rapidly failing. These indications were soon followed by several instances of so great illness as to confine its victims to their homes, and even to their beds. Among the latter was the case of the only son and child of a poor but pious and intelligent widow, by the name of Marvin, which excited in the bosom of Locke feelings of the deepest sorrow for the misfortune of the boy, and sympathy in the affliction of his doting parent. And it was not without reason that both teacher and parent were touched with peculiar grief on the occasion; for the boy, who was about ten years old, was not only kind and amiable in disposition, but a very excellent scholar. And now, almost for the first time, having the advantages of good instruction, and his ambition and natural love of learning having been kindled into enthusiasm by the various incitements held out to him by his instructor, with whom he had become a secret favorite, he pursued his studies with an ardor and assiduity which knew no relaxation. And having made surprising progress in grammar, during the few weeks the school had kept, he had recently solicited and obtained leave to commence arithmetic, to which he was giving his whole heart and soul, when he was thus snatched from his engrossing pursuit by the hand of sickness.

These cases of sickness, and especially the more serious one of the good and studious little Henry, the boy we have particularized, produced much sensation in the neighborhood. And the cause, not only of these instances of absolute illness, but of the altered and sickly appearance of the whole school, which now excited observation and uneasiness, began to be generally discussed. As no epidemic was prevailing in the country, and as all other schools in the vicinity, as far as could be heard from, were even unusually healthy, it was soon concluded that the present unhealthiness must be occasioned by something wrong about the schoolhouse, or in the manner of conducting the school. And as nothing amiss could possibly be perceived in the schoolhouse, which all pronounced warm and comfortable, it was settled that the fault, of course, must be looked for in the master. Some averred that the latter, by undue severity, or by some other means, had broken down the spirit of his scholars, which had caused them to become melancholy, drooping, and sickly. Others said that he had made the scholars study so hard, that it had caused their health to give way under the tasks which they were induced, through fear, or some mysterious influence he had obtained over their minds, to perform. And there were yet others who carried still farther the idea thrown out by those last named, and contended that the master must have resorted to some unlawful art or power, which he had exercised upon his pupils, not only to subjugate them, but somehow to give them an unnatural thirst for their studies, and as unnatural a power of mastering them. In proof of this, one man cited the instance of his son, who, having become half-crazed on his arithmetic, and having worked all one evening on a sum which he could not do, went to bed, leaving his slate upon the table, but rose some time in the night in his sleep, actually worked out the answer, returned to bed, wholly unconscious of what he had done, and slept till morning, when he found, to his surprise, the whole process in his own figures, upon the slate.[1]

This incident, however little it might have had to do, in the minds of others, in proving the position it was cited to sustain, seemed to go far with these people in confirming the strange notion they were beginning to conceive, that the master had brought some unnatural influence to bear upon his pupils. And when they compared the wild, thoughtless, and unstudious conduct which had ever characterized the scholars before, with their present greatly altered behavior, and the eager diligence with which many of them, both day and night, pursued their studies, particularly mathematical studies, they mysteriously shook their heads, and said, "they didn't know about these things; such a change might have come in a natural way, but they couldn't understand it." It was agreed on all hands, they further argued, that the master was deep in figures. Captain Bunker, who was considered the best natural reckoner in those parts, had confessed

[1] This incident, improbable as it may appear to some, is a true one, having occurred within the knowledge of the author, who otherwise would not have ventured in relating it.—*D. P. Thompson.*

that he couldn't hold a candle to him in that respect. They had always heard that strange things could be done with figures, if a person sought to do so. Indeed, there was a certain point in figures, they supposed, beyond which, if a person persisted in going, he was sure to have help from one who should be nameless, but who always exacted his pay for his assistance. They hoped this was not the case with their master; but if it was, and he was trying to lead his scholars into the same forbidden paths, it was no wonder that they had such strange, blue looks; nor was it at all surprising that sickness should come upon them, as a judgment. And they again shook their heads and said "it was high time that something should be done."

Let it not be inferred, that we would convey the idea, that the people of the country in which our scene is laid were generally as superstitious as some of the circumstances here represented to have taken place might seem to imply. They certainly were not so. And comparatively few locations, we presume, could have been found, where such arguments as we have put into the mouths of some of the good people of this uncultured district would have been listened to a moment. But our observations, made during considerable travel and intercourse among the common classes of people in the Middle and Northern States, have apprised us that instances of the prevalence of notions similar to those just mentioned are still to be found, and much oftener, too, than we had formerly supposed. We have often come across isolated neighborhoods, even in the heart of intelligent communities, where, to our surprise, we found all the exploded notions of witchcraft, sorcery, divination, and the like, still entertained; and to an extent, indeed, that led us almost to doubt whether we had not, by some miracle or other, been carried back a century and a half, and set down among a clan of the immediate disciples of old Cotton Mather, who spent so much time and learning in making mystery and mischief about things which have no existence, except in imagination. Such a neighborhood, with a few honorable exceptions, we are constrained to say, was that of the *Horn of the Moon.*

On the day following that during which the singular surmises and discussions, to which we have alluded, were started, two more members of the school were taken down; and the situation of Henry Marvin had become so alarming, that his agonized mother, some time in the preceding night, had dispatched a man for a physician of high reputation, residing in a large village, known by the name of *Cartersville,* nearly thirty miles distant; though she was compelled to pledge her only cow to defray the expenses of the man, and induce him to become answerable to the doctor for his pay. All this, as may be supposed, much increased the alarm in the district, and quickened into action those who had busied themselves in getting up an excitement against the master. Meanwhile, the innocent victim of these absurd imputations remained at his post, wholly ignorant of the stir that was going on about him, and thinking only of the misfortune which threatened his school. On the evening of the day last mentioned he dismissed his school early, and with a heavy heart repaired to the residence of the distressed widow, to visit his sick little favorite. On reaching the house, he entered the room ordinarily occupied by the family; when he was introduced, by a woman in attendance, to Dr. Lincoln, the physician before named, who, having arrived a short time before, was now taking some refreshment.

"Our little patient here is a pupil of yours, sir?" inquiringly said the doctor, who was a small, unostentatious, but a highly intellectual man.

"He is," replied Locke; "and I can hardly express how much anxiety I feel for his situation, which I fear you will pronounce dangerous."

"Your apprehensions, I regret to say, are but too well grounded, sir."

"What do you consider the true character of his disease?"

"Whatever it may have been at first, it is now a brain fever, threatening congestion."

"Are you prepared to assign any particular cause?"

"Of his first attack, I am not. In regard to the form the disease has now assumed, I may be better prepared, perhaps, to give an opinion after asking you a few questions. What are the boy's habits of study and scholarship?"

"He is a bright scholar—uncommonly so—very industrious and anxious to learn."

"I suspected so. And you have held up to him what to others, perhaps, would scarcely be an inducement sufficient to move them, but what, to his sensitive mind, has incited him to unwonted exertions?"

"As you say, sir, I may have said that which had the effect to incite *him;* although I am sure I have used more exertions with many others."

"I presume so. It does not require a timber chain to draw a miser to a supposed bed of gold. A bare glimpse of the loved treasure is enough to kindle his whole soul for the eager grasp. So with the youthful intellect, if bright, and united with a strong love of learning. And let me caution you, my dear sir, how you spur on such a mind, in one of tender years. The body must be permitted to grow, as well as the mind. Very bright children are said always to die first, and though the cause generally assigned for this may be false, there is yet much truth in the saying; the true cause of the fact being, that the minds of such children, by the injudiciously applied incitements of parents and teachers, are often so over-wrought, that disease, at every slight attack on other parts of the system, is prone to fly to the enfeebled brain, and, oftener than otherwise, destroy its victim. In these remarks you will read the opinion to which I incline respecting the present case."

"Ay; but are you aware that several others of my school have been taken ill, and those, too, that would be the last to whom you would think of imputing injury from undue mental exertion?"

"I have so understood, sir. There may have been some local cause for these, as well as the first attack of the poor little fellow here. Has any such cause suggested itself to your mind?"

"No! unless it be the late sudden and great change in the weather."

"That will hardly account for the manner in which your school, almost the whole of it, in some degree, as I understand, has been affected, in a time of such general health. There must be other causes, which I feel some curiosity to ascertain before I return."

The conversation was here interrupted by the entrance of a woman of the neighborhood, one of that valuable class of society who retail news, with comments.

"Do you attend the school-meeting to night, Mr. Amsden?" she soon asked; for she did not appear very bashful in claiming her right to a share in the conversation.

"School meeting, madam!" said Locke, in surprise; "I was not aware that there was to be one."

"Oh, yes, there is; why, everybody is going, they say. I supposed you, *of course*, knew it."

"This is the first I have heard of it. But what is the object of the meeting?"

"Oh, to see what's to be done about the scholars being in this sickly and malagantly way to be sure. Some say the school won't keep any more at any rate. But I tell 'em, like enough the master will clear it up, after all's said and done."

"Clear up what, pray, madam? Of what can I possibly be accused, in connection with this misfortune to my school?"

"Oh, don't ask me now—I let it pass into one ear and out the other, what I hear; because I never mean to be one of those who go about telling things to breed mischief and ill-will among people." And here the good and scrupulous lady struck off in a tangent, and asked the doctor, now while she thought of it, as she said, seeing she had heard a great many disputes about it, "whether saffron or camomile tea was, upon the whole, the best for the measles?"

As soon as the doctor, who was a man of much sly but caustic humor, had gravely delivered himself of a very learned answer, which, he said, *upon the whole*, all things carefully considered, he must conclude in the language of the great Dr. Pope,—

> "For forms of *diet drinks* let fools contest ;
> That which is best administered is best "—

as soon as he had done this, Locke, whose mind was still running upon the inexplicable news he had just heard from the woman, again turned to her, and asked if she knew whether Mr. Bunker had returned from the journey on which he had been for the last fortnight absent.

"Why, we don't certainly know yet," replied the newsmongress; " but we kinder 'spect he got home this very afternoon. Jim Walker, who was to our house about a nour ago, to borrow a sassage-filler for his wife, said he thought he saw, from his house, a creter over there, that looked like the captain's old black hoss, going to water, and rolling in the snow, as if he'd jest been onharnessed after a journey."

"Well, I am thankful for that, if he has indeed arrived," replied Locke, who felt anxious for the presence of his friend at the approaching meeting.

"Come, Mr. Amsden," said the doctor, rising, " you will of course attend the school-meeting; and I will go with you, if I can be spared ; but we will now walk into the sick-room, if you please. We cannot admit much company," he continued, as he saw the gossip turn a longing eye upon the opening door, as if waiting for an invitation to accompany them ; " but Mr. Amsden is the boy's teacher, whose presence may be a benefit, by recalling his wandering mind."

When they entered the sick-chamber, a scene of silent but touching woe presented itself. The grief-stricken mother, who scarcely heeded their approach, sat bending over the pillowed couch, intently gazing, with fixed, glazed, and watery eyes, upon the face of the little sufferer, as he lay nervously moving his restless limbs, and rolling his swathed head, in the deep and troubled slumbers which exhausted nature seemed to be strongly claiming on the one hand, and grappling disease fiercely disputing and constantly disturbing on the other. The doctor took the patient's hand, and attentively examined his pulse ; when some movement, in restoring the limb to its place, awoke him. As his dim and slowly wandering eyes fell upon the face of his beloved teacher, a single glance of intelligence slightly illumined them ; and the semblance of an affectionate smile played faintly, an instant, over his sunken and livid features, vanishing away like some struggling sunbeam that has partially burst through a stormy cloud.

The mother saw the glance, with the recognition it evinced. And the association, as her thoughts flew back to the happy days of her darling boy's health and friendly intercourse with his teacher, of which that look had so plainly spoken, and reverted to what he now was, and probably soon would be,—the association thus called up was too much for her bursting heart. She groaned aloud from the inmost recesses of her troubled spirit. Her whole frame became deeply agitated, and her bosom shook with the convulsive throes of her agony, as with indistinct, quick, whispered ejaculations, she seemed eagerly snatching for the hand of mercy from above to save her from sinking under the insupportable weight of her own feelings. Her prayers were so far answered as to bring her the temporary relief of tears, which now gushed and fell like rain from their opening fountains of bitterness.

"I am glad to see that," observed Lincoln, brushing away a tear that had started out upon his knitting brows. "It will relieve you, madam. And now let me persuade you to go out, bathe your face, and otherwise refresh yourself. We will remain, and take care of your son."

"Our profession," resumed the doctor, after the widow had retired, as she did, in silence, on the suggestion just made to her, "our profession, Mr. Amsden, is one which brings along with it many pains, but which, at the same time, is not without its gratifications. A case now, like this, an almost hopelessly sick child, with a distracted parent hanging over it—and we are daily pained with witnessing such scenes—draws hard,

hard, I confess, upon my sympathies. But again, on the other hand, if this boy should recover through my means, I shall lay up in the bosom of that mother, whether I deserve it or not, a store of gratitude which will, perhaps, often find utterance in blessings at the bare mention of my name! Yes, if he recover," continued the speaker, musingly, as he rose at some new appearance he noticed in the patient, and went to the bedside, "if he recover—and all that I can do shall be done, and that too with no charge to the poor woman, even if I knew I had got to beg my next meal. But it is a fierce and unmanageable disease, and I tremble for the crisis of this night. Here, step here, Mr. Amsden, and listen to the confused mutterings of broken thoughts and images that are whirling in the chaos of that perplexed and laboring brain."

Locke immediately complied with the request; and as he turned his ear towards the rapidly-moving lips of the delirious boy, he could soon distinguish "*six times six are thirty-six—seven times six are forty-two—eight times six are forty-eight*," and so on. Sometimes he would follow one figure in this manner through all its successive multipliers, in the usual table, and then take up another, follow it awhile, and suddenly drop it for a third, which in turn, perhaps, would be relinquished for some attempted process in subtraction or division; in all of which he seemed to be constantly meeting with troubles and perplexities, with which he would appear to contend awhile, and then return to his old starting point in the multiplication table, and with freshened impulse hurry on with "*six times six are thirty-six—seven times six are forty-two*," etc., etc., till something again occurred to turn his bewildered mind from the course it was mechanically pursuing.

"Poor, poor boy!" exclaimed Locke, as, with a sigh and starting tear, he turned away from the affecting spectacle.

The time having arrived for our hero's departure for the school-meeting, and the widow now coming in, the doctor apprised her of his intention of accompanying the former, and, giving his directions for the next hour, requested her to send for him should any considerable change occur in the patient, when they both set off together for the schoolhouse.

On reaching the place of destination, they found, with the exception of Bunker and one or two others, all the men, together with several of the older scholars of the district, already assembled, and on the point of proceeding to business. As soon as Locke had helped his friend, the doctor, to a seat, and taken one near by for himself, he cast a leisurely look round the assembly. It required neither much time nor closeness of observation to apprise him that there was a great deal of suppressed, excited feeling prevailing generally among the company. Nor was he much longer in satisfying himself, from the words which occasionally reached his ears, from little knots of eager whispers around him, and from the many cold and suspicious glances he encountered, that a great portion of this feeling was unfavorably directed against himself, the cause of which he was still unable to conjecture.

"I motion Deacon Gilchrist be Moderator of this meeting," said one, bobbing half-way up, and hastily squatting back to his seat, before the sentence was fairly out of his mouth.

"I am not so sure but they will need a *moderator* before they get through," whispered the doctor to Locke, emphasizing the word so as to give it a literal signification.

The vote having been taken, and the chairman, a short, sluggish man, whose wisdom and sanctity lay principally in his face, being duly installed in his seat, he pronounced the meeting open, and invited those present " to offer."

"I motion," again said the person who had first spoken, "I motion, Mr. Moderator, that this school come to an eend. And I've got my reasons for't."

The motion was eagerly seconded by two or three others, all speaking at once, and demanding the question, in a manner that plainly showed that a considerable portion of those present were acting in concert, and with the intention of having the vote taken before any debate could be had on the subject. And the chairman, who was evidently a secret favorer of the project, jumped up to put the question; when Locke, who had witnessed the movement with the utmost surprise, rose and demanded the reasons which the mover asserted he had for his proposed measure.

"I call for the vote—put it to vote!" was the only reply which Locke received to his reasonable demand.

"Look here now, Mr. Moderator," cried a tall, rough-looking young fellow, who rose in a different part of the room from that occupied by the combined party, "I have neither chick or child to send to school, to be sure; but I'm a voter here, and I must say I think you are for pushing the master rather hard, to vote him out without giving him your reasons, so as to allow him a chance to clear it up, if he can. And as to any blame for the sickness resting on him, I ain't so sure but what he can; for I can't say I think much of this *black art* business, or of its having anything to do in bringing on the trouble. I wouldn't give much for all the help the master or anybody else ever got that way. Now you may think as you're a mind to; but I never thought the old boy was half so much of a critter as he's cracked up to be. And I don't believe he's any great scratch at cipherin himself neither, much less to teach it to others."

The sensibilities of the good deacon received a very visible shock from this strange and irreverent speech, as it was deemed; and his zealous supporter, whom we have mentioned as taking the lead in motions thus far made, was so much outraged in his feelings, either by the sentiments of the speaker, or the opposition they implied to his plans, that he rose, and said he thought the young man ought to be rebuked for such loose discourse, in a meeting like this, where folks had so much reason to be solemn. "I wonder if he believes," continued the zealot, warming up, "what the scripture says about the power of sorcerers' getting unlawful help to do what other folks couldn't do? And I should like to ask him where he thinks the help come from, when young John Mugridge, that the master had got along so unnatural fast in figures, did a hard sum in his sleep. I want to know, too, what he thinks about widow

Marvin's boy being taken sick—in mercy, perhaps—the very next week after the master put him to ciphering. And then I wish he'd tell us what makes the whole school look so blue and ghastly, if there ain't anything wrong in the master's doings. And I call on the master himself to say whether he can deny that he understands the black art."

Locke could hardly bring himself to reply to this ridiculous charge, or even to answer the particular question that he had been thus publicly called on to answer. He did so, however, by briefly stating that he knew of no such art. He had heard, indeed, that the faculty of foretelling events, fortunes, and the like, was supposed to be attainable by figures. And he recollected, as he commenced arithmetic when a mere boy, indulging a sort of vague expectation that he should come across this art, if he went far enough. But the further he advanced, the more did he see the impossibility of acquiring any such faculty by the use of figures, which, more peculiarly than any other science, discarded all suppositions, and had to do only with certain demonstrable facts. And now, having studied or examined, as he believed, nearly all of that science that had been published, he was fully prepared to say that the belief in the faculty in question was wholly a delusion.

"I don't blame him for denying it," said the superstitious spokesman before named. "I think I should, if I was wicked enough to tamper with sich forbidden things. But I should like to hear Deacon Gilchrist the Moderator's views on this subject."

The Moderator, after sundry hems and haws, by way of getting his apparatus of speech in motion, assumed a look of wise solemnity, and observed:

"It appears to me, my beloved friends, that there's an awful responsibility on us. Duty is duty. I do think so. I don't know, nor want to, much about the hidden things of figures, except they are thought to be the instruments that Satan works by sometimes. We know there were sorcerers and workers in hidden mysteries, in the days of the apostles; and the scripter says they shall be multiplied in the latter days, which now is. I once read a book by a great and deep divine—I've eeny most forgot his name, but I think it was Woollen Marther, or some sich oncommon crissen name—who had seen, with his own eyes, a great deal of the awful doings of Satan. And he speaks of the strange looks of those that were buffeted by the adversary, and the divers maladies and sore evils that befell those who were led by his emissaries into unlawful ways. And I do think, my friends, there's something very mysterious in this 'ere school. I do think we have seen a token of displeasure, that seems to say to us, in a loud voice—yea, the voice of many thunders—*Come out, and be separate from him that bringeth the evil upon you.*"

This speech was triumphantly echoed by several of the deacon's supporters, as an unanswerable argument for the measure they were so intent on carrying. There were others, however, who were so obtuse as not to perceive the force of the argument, or the justice of its application. Among these were the intended victim of this combination, and his newly-found friend, the tall fellow, whose speech had so scandalized his opponents; both of whom made a reply to the oracular speech of our modern Solomon—the one by denying both premises and conclusions, and the other by drolly asking pardon of the old boy, the deacon, or any of their friends, if he had underrated or offended them in his former speech, and by contending that the master had cleared himself, to his mind, of the charge of ciphering his scholars into fevers, and their parents into fidgets. These replies led to a good deal of scattering debate, in which nearly all, by speech, word thrown in, or other manifestation, participated; and by which it became apparent that there were strictly three parties in the assembly: first, the deacon's trained followers, who, numbering about one third of the district, were for breaking up the school, for reasons before given; second, another portion, of about the same number, who had been induced to come into the plan of the former, through their secret fears that some contagious disease was about to break out in the school, which their children would be more likely to take if the school continued; and last, the other third, who believed the master in no way chargeable for the condition of the school, which they wished might be still continued.

The deacon's party, perceiving, by this time, that they could safely count on strength enough to carry their measure, clamored more loudly than ever for a decision of the question. Locke gave himself up as lost, and a few minutes more would, indeed, have been decisive of his doom, but for the unexpected arrival of a new personage. This was Bunker, who having reached home only a few hours before, had not heard what was in train till the evening was considerably advanced; when, accidentally learning something of the facts, he came post haste to the scene of action. This arrival very visibly disconcerted the deacon's party, and produced a dead pause in their proceedings, during which the former marched boldly up to Locke, and gave him one of those hearty and cordial shakes of the hand, which send assurance to the desponding heart, and are more gratefully felt, on some emergencies, than a thousand expressed pledges of friendship, on others. After being introduced to Dr. Lincoln, Bunker, taking a conspicuous stand before the company, immediately demanded the object of the meeting, and, by a series of sharp and rapid questions, addressed first to one, then another, soon succeeded in drawing out the whole truth, with all that had transpired.

"O ye miserable thinkers!" he exclaimed, as soon as he had satisfied himself of the true situation of affairs, "what, in the name of common sense, could have put ye up to such nonsense and folly as this? Three decent efforts for a correct idea should have told you that the master would not be caught teaching, for nothing, so valuable a secret as the black art, if that art is all you suppose it to be. Why, by foretelling the rise in the markets, or the lucky number of the ticket that is to draw the highest prize in the next lottery, he can make an independent fortune in six months, if he will keep his secret to himself; but if he goes and imparts this faculty to others, they will get away all his chances for such luck, and his art won't be worth a farthing to him. Do you believe he would do such a foolish thing? No! not a soul of you. There is thought number one for you.

"Again—what could make you think that the teaching of this art ever did, or could, bring ill-health, either upon the teacher or the taught? This was never a fact. Is there anything said in the Bible about the magicians, witches, or diviners, or their followers, being taken sickly for their practices? Did Simon Magus make anybody sick? Did the sorceress, or black-art girl, that St. Paul converted, carry disease in her train? No; for she had brought her master a good deal of money by telling folk's fortunes; when, if she had brought sickness and judgments upon them, they would have given him more money to have kept her away.

"Nor was there any such misfortunes connected with the witchcraft in the old Bay State. Doctor Mather, even in his book, don't say so; for I have heard it read. The bewitched, according to his story, only acted and appeared a little wild and devilish. But, if his book had said this, it would amount to nothing; for I don't believe, if the old Nick himself should turn book-maker to-day, and sit down, with his old yellow, brimstone-tempered steel pen, and do his best, for a month, he could get more of the real essence of falsehood between the two lids of a book, than can be found in the book I've mentioned. And if ever that learned doctor—for he was accounted pious—gets within the walls of the New Jerusalem, he will find, I fear, when he comes to see what suffering, death, and crime were brought about through his influence and example, as well as he might mean, that heaven will be rather an uneasy place for him. But, supposing the judgments of sickness, and so on, did attend such doings, what then? How would it stand in the present case? Why, the master, by the very art that was to produce the misfortune, would know that the misfortune would follow his attempt to teach it. And do you think he would try it, when he knew it would bring sickness and trouble on his school, that must break it up, cost him the loss of all his wages, and, what is more, send him off with a character that would forever prevent his getting another school? Would he be such a stupid fool as to do this? Never! and you all now see and know it. There is thought number two for you.

"Once more. In what I have said, I have taken you wholly on your own ground; so that you should not say I could meet you only on my own dunghill. I will now make you come on to my ground, and see if you can stand fire any better there. And this is my ground:—I say that this black art, as you understand it, the faculty of foretelling events, together with sorcery, magic, or witchery, and every other art that lays claim to any such faculty by the aid of figures, or anything else, is all moonshine, imposition, and falsehood. And I don't want to set before you but one single idea to make you know and feel the truth of my assertion. Now follow me. Did you ever know or hear of a rich fortune-teller, black-art-worker, or conjurer? Speak out, if you ever did. A single one that was *rich*, I say. You don't speak? No; for you can't say you ever did hear of such an one. You all well know that they are a set of poor, beggarly rascals from beginning to end. Well now, what prevents them, as I said of our master here, if they have this faculty of looking or figuring into futurity, from seeing and seizing upon every lottery ticket that is to draw a good prize; from buying every article in the markets that is about to rise greatly in price? What prevents them from doing this, and making their fortunes at a blow? Tell me, you, or you, or you. This is thought number three for you.

"Now my number first pinned an argument upon you— even allowing you your own false premises—with nothing but a wooden pin that you could not break. My number second, still giving you the same advantage, put in a board nail, that, with or without the pin, not one of you could twist or move. And my number third puts a double ten clincher upon the whole, that all of you together can never start. Now stand forth and gainsay it, ye persecutors of the best teacher we ever had in the district, or forever hold your peace! No one speaks; and I pronounce the master guiltless, and acquitted of your foolish charge.

"But although the master is no way blamable, yet that an unusual number of the scholars are sick, and nearly all drooping, if I am rightly informed, I am not going to deny. And there is some cause for it, which we must try to discover, that we may stop the evil. If it is not the starting point of some epidemic disease that is about to spread over the country, why, then it must be owing to something wrong about the schoolhouse. By taking up the possibilities, one after another, I probably could think it out myself within twenty-four hours. But here is a man," continued the speaker, turning towards the doctor, "who has been in the way of thinking of such things half of his life. Let us have his opinion. Dr. Lincoln, will you favor us with your views on the subject of inquiry?"

The doctor, who had attentively listened to the whole debate, much of which he had appeared to enjoy with the highest zest, now rose, and observed that he had already made up his mind to offer his opinion on the matter in question, before called on; and he would now proceed to do so. He had some secret suspicion of the cause of the general unhealthiness of the school, on first learning the fact; and having come to the meeting, mainly with the view of satisfying himself in relation to the matter, his attention, during the time he had been here, had been particularly directed to the subject; and he was now prepared to say, that what was before a mere suspicion with him was now a confirmed opinion. The cause, and sole cause, of this unhealthiness was the want of ventilation; and, from what he had suffered himself since in the room, although the door had been frequently opened, he was only surprised that the condition of the scholars was not infinitely worse than he understood it was. Though not wishing it to strengthen his own convictions, yet, as it might better convince others, he would proceed to set the matter in a stronger light before them.

The doctor, then, while every ear and eye were regarding his words and movements with intense interest, called on Locke to ascertain the number of cubic feet contained in the empty space of the room. A carpenter present, who happened to have a bundle of his tools with him, having called into the meeting while on his way home from some finished job, produced a rule, and took the different dimensions of the apartment with great exactness; when Locke, from the data thus furnished, quickly ascertained and told off the number of cubic feet, as required. This number, owing to the ill-advised construction of the school-room, in which the floor rose from one side at so great an angle as to take up about one sixth part of what would have been the space with a level floor, amounted only, with proper deductions for stove, seats, etc., to sixteen hundred cubic feet.

"Now let me observe," said the doctor, "that, from the latest and most accurate experiments of chemists and medical men, it has been ascertained that one person, by respiration from the lungs alone, destroys all the oxygen, or vital principle, in thirteen cubic feet of space per hour. How many scholars have you, Mr. Amsden?"

"Sixty, upon the average, perhaps more, say sixty-four."

"Ascertain, then, how many cubic feet of vital air these all will destroy in one hour."

Both Locke and Bunker, the latter of whom now began to be in his element, almost the next instant gave the same answer —eight hundred and thirty-two feet.

"How long do you generally keep them in without intermission, in which the doors would necessarily remain open a moment while they were passing out?"

"Generally an hour and a half, sometimes two."

"Then, gentlemen," said the doctor, "the true, but greatly misconceived, cause of your trouble and just alarm is now plainly before you. You see, by our calculation, that, in less than two hours, all the air that can sustain life a moment would be, in this new and almost bottle-tight room, if not renovated by opening the doors or windows, entirely consumed. And, taking into the account the quantity of this vital principle inhaled by the pores of so many persons, and the probably greater portion destroyed by the fire and reflecting surface of the stove and pipe, I presume one hour is sufficient to render the air extremely unhealthy; an hour and a half, absolutely poisonous; and two hours, so fatally so as to cause your children to drop dead on the floor."

"Thunder!" exclaimed Bunker, "can this be so? I long since knew that we were put upon our allowance, when in close rooms, for the right kind of breathing air; but I never supposed there was so much death in the pot as that comes to. But that fact which you build upon—the amount of vital air a person destroys an hour—I am afraid, doctor, you got it only out of the books, which I am rather shy in trusting for what I call gospel."

"Both from books and my own imperfect experiments," replied Lincoln, "and I am satisfied that the proportion is not rated too highly. But I have not quite done all that I propose in this case. We have now been in the room, I perceive by my watch, but three quarters of an hour, while there are not probably over thirty persons present. And yet, even in this time, and with this number, I will ask you all, if you do not feel oppressed and uneasy from the impurity of the air here?"

"I do—and I—and I too," responded several; while others, as the case was thus now brought home to their own senses, which plainly spoke in the affirmative, sprang forward in alarm to throw open the doors.

"Not yet—not yet," said the doctor, interposing. "We can live awhile longer; and I wish in some degree to satisfy you, and particularly Captain Bunker here, whose thorough mode of coming at results I much admire, that what I have said is not altogether incapable of proof, even with the means at hand. Cannot our carpenter here, with a few minutes' work, so alter the casings, that the upper sashes of these windows can be lowered some few inches?"

Locke—who felt both pained and chagrined that his inattention to this matter, in which he so well knew all the principles involved, should have so nearly led to disastrous consequences, and whose active mind, having seen through the whole subject at a glance, the moment the doctor put him on the track, had long since been engaged in devising a ready remedy for the discovered evil—here interposed, and suggested that an opening made in the centre of the ceiling would best effect the object in view.

"If it can be done?" inquiringly said the doctor.

"Be done!" said Bunker, "yes, it can. Here, carpenter, up in this chair with your tools, and make a hole through there, in no time. This business is just beginning to get through my hair."

A few moments sufficed to make an aperture about eight inches square, opening into the attic story above; the square form being adopted, as best comporting with the simple contrivance with which it was proposed to cover it—that of a mere board slide, supported by cleats, in which it would play back and forth, as the aperture required to be opened for ventilation, or shut to preserve the warmth of the room. Scarcely had the workman time to adjust the slide in its place, before every particle of impure air had apparently escaped through the opening, to pass off by the crevices in the roof. All felt and acknowledged the change with astonishment and delight. The sensations of languor and oppression that had begun to weigh heavily on the feelings and spirits of the company, had left them almost as unexpectedly and suddenly as fell the bundle of sins from the back of Bunyan's Pilgrim.

"Well, gentlemen," said Doctor Lincoln, as he looked round, and saw in the speaking countenances of the company that all were as well satisfied as they were gratified at the result; "I believe the mystery is now solved. At all events, I'll agree to cure for nothing all the scholars that are hereafter made sick from anything about the schoolhouse, or in the conduct of their master."

"Yes, the room is as clear as a horn, by George!" exclaimed Bunker, "and the thing is done—proved out as square as a brick, right in our face and eyes; and there's no getting away from it. But what sticks in my crop is, that we must have a man—and a book man, too, though he plainly don't swallow books whole, without chewing, as most of 'em do—have a man come thirty miles to think it out for us! Master, you and I ought to be trounced."

"Well, Mr. Moderator," said the deacon's tormentor, the rustic humorist, we mean, who was the first to take up for Locke in the debate, and who now seemed greatly to enjoy the triumph of the latter over the little clique of his chop-fallen foes—"Well, Mr. Moderator, how is it about the old boy and his little blue influences, now? Don't you think they've pretty much all cleared out through that hole up yonder? Ah! I was about right, deacon: if the old chap had been any great affair, he couldn't have crept out through so small a hole as that comes to, quite so quick, you may depend on 't."

But the deacon, who suddenly recollected a promise he had made to carry, that night, some thorough-wort to a jaundery neighbor, was in too much of a hurry to reply to such scoffing questions; and he, with one or two of his most zealous supporters, immediately quitted the house, leaving the rest of the vanquished party, whether superstitionists or alarmists, to join the master and his increasing number of friends, acknowledge their error, and reciprocate congratulations on the unexpectedly happy result of the whole of this singular affair. We say the whole; for, before the company broke up, word was brought by one of the larger scholars, who had gone over to Widow Marvin's during the meeting, and just returned, that the sick boy there had fallen into a quiet sleep, attended by gentle perspiration;—symptoms which the gratified doctor at once pronounced to be a plain indication that the disease was going off by what he technically termed resolution. And the result, in this case at least, went to prove the doctor's skill in prognostics. The boy, after that night, was consigned, by his departing physician, to the care only of his grateful mother, who, within a fortnight, had the unspeakable happiness of seeing her darling son restored to health and his still loved but now more temperately pursued studies.

Of the remainder of young Amsden's career in this district, little more need be added. Compared with the trials, vexations, and labors of the past, he now found but a path of flowers. The recent misfortune in his school, and the consequent infatuated movement to overthrow him, operating as all overwrought persecutions usually do, instead of injuring him, were the means of turning the popular current strongly in his favor, and of giving him a place in the estimation of nearly all around him which he otherwise would have failed to obtain.

Being no further troubled with the injudicious interference of parents, or the misbehavior of their children,—those two evils which too often require the best part of a teacher's time and attention to meet and overcome—he had nothing to do but instruct his pupils. And by no means unprofitably did the latter use the opportunity thus afforded them. From a rough, wild, unthinking set of creatures, who could appreciate nothing but animal pleasures or physical prowess, they became rational beings, ambitious for the acquisition of knowledge, and capable of intellectual pleasures. A new standard of taste and merit, in short, had been imperceptibly raised among them; and the winter that Locke Amsden kept school became an era in the district, from which commenced a visible and happy change in the whole moral and intellectual tone of its society.

Nor were the advantages which attended his exertions in this place wholly on one side. In teaching others, the master himself was often taught. Questions were daily put to him, even by children in their abs, which led him to reflection, research, and discoveries of truths, which, thorough scholar as he was, he found, to his surprise, he had before overlooked, and which otherwise might never have occurred to him;—discoveries, we repeat, of important truths, in almost every study of his school, and particularly in those of orthography, orthoepy, and etymology, those sadly neglected branches which require a philosopher to teach them understandingly, but which are yet, oftener than otherwise, intrusted to the teaching of an ignoramus!

In what is termed a physical education, also, he here received hints which led him to the adoption of much more correct and enlarged views than any he had before entertained. His attention, indeed, had never been directed to the subject; and he had therefore continued to look upon it as did others around him, either as a matter of little importance, or, at best, as one which had no legitimate connection with popular education. But the painful and alarming occurrences which we have described, as arising from the want of ventilation in his schoolhouse, taught him a lesson which could not be disregarded or easily forgotten; caused him to give an earnest consideration to this subject in all its bearings, whether in relation to ventilation, length of confinement to study, or ease of position; and forced upon his mind the conviction, that physical education, or an observance of those laws of life which can only insure the health of the body, and the consequent health of the mind, is, as truly as any other, a part of an instructor's duty, for the performance of which, before high Heaven, he will be held responsible.

The Examination at Mill Town Emporium

(From "Locke Amsden; or, the Schoolmaster")

In his journeys to and from college, at the time of his matriculation, and afterwards on his occasional brief visits to his family, young Amsden had passed through a thriving little village, which was generally known by the name of Mill Town, but which its ambitious inhabitants had recently thought to dignify by re-christening it by the more sonorous and classical appellation of Mill Town Emporium. The village, numbering perhaps two hundred souls, contained a store, a tavern, a cluster of mills, and several very spruce-looking dwelling-houses, among which the newly painted two-story house of the merchant glared in conspicuous whiteness. And, as our hero was now on his way homeward, and in search of some good situation in a winter's school, which he had neglected to secure,—though many eligible ones had been offered him, which he had declined on account of their location,—he concluded to call at this place, in order to ascertain whether he might not here obtain a situation, which for him might prove a desirable one, as the village was pleasantly located on the main road leading to and within half a day's ride from the residence of his family, with whom he wished to keep up a personal intercourse.

Upon inquiry of the bustling keeper of the inn where he stopped, Locke was told that the village school had not yet been supplied with a teacher; and that the managing committee, consisting of the merchant of the place, the tailor, and the newspaper editor (for a political newspaper called the *Blazing Star* had just been established in this miniature city), "were now on the lookout to engage a man of those splendidest qualifications which the growing importance of the place demanded."

Though somewhat startled at this pompous announcement, our candidate yet took directions to the house of the merchant, who, it was said, would probably exercise a rather controlling influence among this able board of managers. A few steps brought him to the showy white house before named, as belonging to the popular personage—as an only merchant of a little village generally is—of whom he was in quest. On applying the knocker, the door was opened by the merchant himself, who appeared with a pen behind his ear, and invited the other into his sitting-room, where it appeared he had been posting his books. He was a youngerly man, of an affectedly brisk and courteous manner. Supposing his visitor had called for the purposes of trade, he received him with all the smirks and bows of a practiced salesman, and began to talk rapidly about nothing—*i.e.*, the state of the weather, and the condition of the roads for traveling. As soon, however, as Locke announced his name and business, he suddenly became much less profuse of his bows and smiles, and, assuming a consequential air, observed:

"Why, sir, we are not over-anxious to engage a teacher just now—though, to be sure, we have so many applications pressing upon us that we shall be compelled to decide soon. But you see, sir, we have a flourishing village here. It is thought we shall have an academy soon. There are many public-spirited and genteel people in the place; and they will not be suited with anything short of a teacher of the most superfine qualifications."

"I trust to be able to answer all reasonable expectations, in that respect," remarked Amsden, scarcely able to repress a smile at the other's singular application of terms.

"Presume it—presume it—that is, can't say to the contrary. But do you bring any letters of credit with you?"

"Credentials? I have something of the kind about me, I believe; but having seen how easily they are obtained, and how little reliance the public place upon them, I thought not of offering them, preferring to be examined, and not doubting that your committee would be abundantly able to satisfy yourselves of my qualifications by such a course much better than by a dependence on the certificates of others."

"That's fair—that's fair, sir. Why, to be sure, I profess to know something myself about education, having been to an academy a quarter before entering business; and the gentlemen who are committee with me, one the editor of the *Blazing Star*, and the other the merchant tailor of our village, are both men of some parts—especially our editor, whom I consider to be a man of splendid talents. I will send for them, sir."

So saying, the merchant committee-man went out and dispatched a boy for his colleagues, who soon made their appearance, and were thereupon introduced, in due form, to our candidate for the throne of a village school. The new-comers also were both men below the middle age. He of the goose (we mean no disrespect to that honest calling, who take all the jokes and get all the money) was a man of a fair, feminine appearance, of pert, jaunty manners, and of showy dress, done in the very extremes of last year's city fashions, though recently made, and now worn as a sort of sign-board sample to display constantly before the great public of Mill Town Emporium, and its tributaries, convincing proof of his signal ability to make good the glowing professions of his standing advertisement in the *Blazing Star*, " to be always prepared to cut and make to order after the very latest New York and London fashions." The editor was a personage of quite a different appearance. He was grave and severe of look, his countenance plainly indicating how deeply he was conscious of the important responsibilities of his position, as conductor of the *Blazing Star*, on which the political destinies of the country so much depended.

The sage trio, who were to decide on our hero's qualifications in the sciences, being thus brought together, the merchant announced to his colleagues the cause of the convocation, and the progress already made in the business on hand.

" Do you teach after the latest style and fashion of teaching, sir ? " commenced the tailor; " there must be much in that, I think. There is nothing like keeping up with the improvements and latest style of the times, if one calculates to succeed, in almost anything, at this day."

" As far as I could see changes to be improvements, I certainly should follow them," replied Locke.

" Do you teach book-keeping ? " asked the merchant ; " I consider that to be of the last importance."

" Literally, so do I, sir. An understanding, and mechanical skill of execution, of the principles of penmanship, I consider of the first importance; and, these attained, it may be lastly important that the pupil be instructed in book-keeping," answered Locke, without observing the air of pique which became visible in the countenance of the interrogator at this answer.

" I feel impelled by my sense of duty to my country," said the editor, " to make a preliminary question. And I trust the gentleman will excuse my desire to know which of the two great political parties of the day he supports. This I would not consider a *sine qua non*,[1] or even very important, at some periods in our public affairs; but when, as now, I see an obnoxious party power stalking through the land, like the besom of destruction, to overthrow the sacred liberties of the country, I do hold it an imperious duty to know the principles of those we encourage; not because I should fear that one of that party, whose further increase I so much deprecate, could exercise a pernicious influence in our intelligent village, where, since the establishment of the *Blazing Star*, the political views of the people, I am proud to say, are so generally correct—no, not at all on that account, but for the inherent principle of the thing."

"I have never," replied Locke, utterly surprised that a test-question of this kind should be put to him, "I have never, till within the present year, been qualified by age for a voter. I have examined the leading principles of our government, it is true, and I much admire them; but, supposing that the opposing parties of the day were all mainly agreed in their aims to sustain those principles, and were, after all, only disputing about men, or at the worst, the different means of gaining the same end, I have so little interested myself in party questions, that I have as yet formed no decided preferences for either side."

"You are mistaken, sir," rejoined the editor. "If you suppose that both parties are for sustaining the same principles, you are most"——

The speaker was here interrupted by a smart rap of the knocker without. The merchant sprang to the door, and soon ushered into the room a personage alike unexpected and unknown to all present. His appearance at once showed him to be a person of many airs, with no lack of confidence in himself. He carried a tasseled cane, and wore a showy safety chain, with an abundance of watch seals, to say the least, dangling from his pocket, while his dress was what has significantly been termed the shabby genteel. After inquiring if the gentle-

[1] an indispensable condition

men present were the school committee, he announced his business, which, to the surprise, and, it must be confessed, somewhat to the uneasiness of our hero, proved to be the same that had prompted his own call. The committee, however, seemed very far from looking upon the visit of the stranger as an intrusion; and, apprising him that they had just commenced the examination of one candidate, they told him "the more the merrier," as it would afford them a better chance for selection, and invited him to make number two; which, being assented to, they proceeded with the examination.

"What are your views, Mr. Blake—for that, I think, you told me was your name"—said the editor, whose mind was still running on the subject on which he was about to be eloquent, when interrupted by the entrance of the new candidate; "What are your views of the propriety of instilling correct political principles into the minds of your pupils, who are the rising generation, and soon to wield the destinies of our glorious republic?"

"I hold, sir," replied Blake, who, it appeared, had cunningly inquired out the calling, politics, etc., of each of the committee, before coming near them,—"I do hold, though others may disagree with me, that it is rather important to attend to the particular you have instigated, sir. I'm always open in my politics. I read several articles in a newspaper over at the tavern, just now, while waiting for my dinner, that speaks my sentiments on that head exactly."

"What paper was it?" eagerly asked the editor.

"I didn't mind particularly," replied the other, with affected carelessness; "but I think it was the *Star*, or some such title."

"The *Blazing Star?*" said the former, with a complaisant bow.

"The same," rejoined Blake, "the very same; I now recall it."

"That is the paper, sir, which I have the honor of conducting," said the other, with another bow, and a gracious smile.

"Indeed! Why, sir," said Blake, with pretended embarrassment, "why, sir, had I supposed—but I was so struck with the able—I hope you will pardon me, sir, for introducing"——

"Oh, certainly, certainly, sir," interrupted the editor. "I feel myself both flattered and gratified by your opinions. There, gentlemen," he continued, turning with a triumphant air to his two associates, "I have done what I considered my duty with the candidates, on the point in which I feel a deep interest. I am now willing to turn them over to you, for examination in the sciences."

"I should like to hear what Mr. Blake thinks about teaching book-keeping in a school, since I have the misfortune to disagree with the other gentleman here," said the merchant.

"Book-keeping?" said Blake, instantly catching a hint from the last part of the other's observation. "Oh, book-keeping is quite essential—quite, sir, quite; I always learn it to my pupils."

"I think so; I think it's an important item in the account," responded the merchant, glancing round at his colleagues, significantly, as he threw himself back with a self-satisfied air.

"I have a boy," said the tailor, "whom is pretty cute in grammar, as all allow; and I would be pleased to hear the gentlemen explain on that department, and tell whether their mode and manner of teaching it is of the latest style?"

Mr. Blake here being not so prompt as usual in taking the lead, Amsden briefly but clearly explained the first principles of English Grammar, the object and uses of that branch, and his manner of teaching it by the text-books of Murray and others. The other candidate, after waiting till pressed to give his views in so pointed a manner, that he saw no way to avoid saying something on the subject—with some hesitation observed:

"Well, gentlemen, my notions about grammar may be different from others, perhaps yours. Now my sentiments is something like this:—the true use of grammar is to learn 'em sense. Well, in what the gentleman here calls parsing Syntax, *I*, now, should make my scholars find out the sense of a piece. And if they can do that, it is all I should require; because the only use of grammar being to learn 'em the sense, as I said, why, the work is done, ain't it? I take it so, gentlemen. But suppose they can't do this, then I should take the piece in hand myself; and if I could not make sense out of it then I should call it false grammar, that's all. So when I have my scholars write compositions, I square the grammar of their pieces upon the sense they contain; for where there's sense, there must, in course, be grammar; and visy versy. Now that's my system, gentlemen. For I have no notion of spoiling sense to make it fay in with book rules; but I make the grammar come down to the sense, not the sense give up to the grammar."

"Just my sentiments, to a shaving!" exclaimed the merchant. "I used to study grammar when at the academy, and bothered and bothered to parse by the rules; but I never could see the use of it. And now, in my business letters, I never think of trying to write by any of the rules I learnt; and yet I write grammar, because I write sense, as he says. Yes, them's my sentiments about grammar."

"Well, it does look kinder reasonable," said the tailor, "though my boy learnt the rules, Syntax, and catemology, and all; and I don't know what he would say to leaving 'em off. But perhaps this way of teaching grammar the gentleman speaks of is some new imported fashion that's soon to be all the style?" he added, inquiringly looking at the patent grammarian who had just before spoken.

"Precisely," answered the other, with a conciliating nod; "it is indeed, sir, a new system, of the very latest cut."

"I am satisfied, then, sir," rejoined the other.

"Which is the most useful rule in arithmetic, Mr. Amsden?" asked the merchant. "I profess to know something about that."

"Why, that would be nearly as difficult to tell, I imagine, as regards all the fundamental rules, as it would be to point out the most useful wheel of a watch, in which all the wheels are required to keep the whole in motion," replied Locke.

"Now I don't think so," said the questioner; "but I'll ask Mr. Blake."

"Oh, I say the rule that helps a man most to do business by, and you know quite well what that is, I fancy; for you tell what the articles you sell come to by that," observed Blake, obsequiously bowing to the merchant.

"Ay; I see you are a practical man, Mr. Blake," here chimed in the editor; "and such men are the very nerves and sinews of our republic."

"I care less about that," rejoined the merchant; "but I must say I approve the gentleman's views of grammar and arithmetic. But suppose we now pass on to geography——

"How do you bound the Polar Sea, Mr. Amsden?"

"Which Polar Sea?" asked Locke, quite innocently.

"Why, the Frozen Sea, to be sure," said the other.

"I must still ask to which Polar or Frozen Sea you refer, sir, before I can answer your question," said the former; "the Northern or Southern?"

"Well, that beats me," observed the erudite dealer; "I had supposed the Frozen Ocean was, of course, in the north; for we all know that the farther we go north, the colder it is; and the farther we go south, the warmer it is. Don't you think so, Mr. Blake?"

"Why, I had thought so, certainly," responded Blake, glancing at Amsden with a supercilious smile—"not that I have any wish to expose anybody's ignorance, by any means; but being appealed to in the matter, so, it's but civil to answer the question. And, now I am speaking on the subject of geographical literature, I may as well, gentlemen," he continued—deeming it now a favorable time to press the advantage he supposed he had gained over his rival, by an extra display of his erudition —"I may as well tell you at once that I rather pride myself on my knowledge of terrestrial geography, and my improved modes of teaching it. I teach it almost entirely by maps, and the map-making process. And it would astonish you to see how quick scholars, in this way, will become accomplished geographians. I learn 'em, in a very short time, also, to make the most splendid maps, equal, nearly, to the printed ones, of all sorts and sizes, both on Mercator's project, as they call it, and on the principle of circular latitudes. Nor is this but a small part of the embellishments I teach my scholars, when they have the proper instruments to work with. There's the problems and the circles, the squares, triangular geometry, ovals, perspective configurations, and a thousand curious things I could teach, if I only had the instruments; such as Gunter's dividers, circumflutors, and the like. And then I would teach musical psalmody, of evenings, for nothing, which, as I see you are about building a new church here, might be an object. In short, gentlemen, I should be very happy to add my best powers in accomplishing your children, and helping to build up your flourishing village. But I leave the decision to you, gentlemen, with the greatest pleasure; because I have discovered you to be men of the most ecstatic discernment."

As soon as the speaker had fairly delivered himself of this learned harangue, Amsden, who knew not which most to admire, the effrontery and ignorance of the fellow, or the ignorance and blindness of the committee who seemed so readily to swallow all he said—inquired if there was not some man of science in the place who could be called in to conduct the examination, and assist the committee in deciding upon the merits of the applicants now before them. This inquiry, as reasonable and fair as was its obvious object, produced, as a close observer might have easily seen, considerable sensation in the before well-assured mind of Locke's exulting competitor; and his uneasiness was the next moment increased into downright apprehension by a remark of the tailor, who, in a rather hesitating manner, said:

"Why, there's the minister that preaches half the time here —and he's now in the place, I guess. He's a college-learnt man, they say, and would be willing to come in, perhaps, if——"

"Why, if these gentlemen," interrupted Blake, rising in visible agitation, "if these gentlemen don't consider themselves capable of deciding on our qualifications and embellishments, then, I say, I am willing—perfectly willing, I say, too——"

"Well, I am not," interposed the luminous head of the *Blazing Star*, with much decision. "I shall most pointedly object to that measure. I should consider it as no less than involving an approach to a sanction of that never-to-be-enough reprobated doctrine of the union of church and state. And I should raise my voice——"

"Ah! I think we can get along," said the merchant, breaking in on the latter, and now rising and looking at his watch with an impatient and irritated air, "I think we can get along without the help of the minister in this business. And if the two gentlemen," he continued, with rather a discriminating gesture, "will step into the other room, or over to the tavern, we can probably come to a decision of the case without much trouble, I think."

The two candidates accordingly retired,—Blake into the adjoining room, and Amsden, as was doubtless intended, to the tavern,—to give to the astute trio of examiners an opportunity for private deliberation.

"Shall we mark, gentlemen?" said the merchant, cutting three separate slips of paper, and passing two of them to his colleagues, with a pencil, that each might write the name of the candidate he would select, and present it for comparison with those of the others, after the manner of appraising a horse.

"Well, if I was fully satisfied about Mr. Blake's grammar"— said the tailor, doubtingly, holding his pencil over his paper.

"I am satisfied about it well enough for my case," observed the merchant, dashing down the chosen name with a decisive sweep of the hand.

"And so am I," responded the editor; "and what is more, he is sound in political principles, to the core."

"Oh, I ain't strenuous, gentlemen," said the tailor, following the example of the others in filling his blank.

The three slips, with the written sides downward, were then

held up together, and turned over, bringing the name on each to view. And it was *Blake—Blake—Blake!*

"As I supposed," said the merchant; "just as I knew it must be. Boy," he continued, opening the door leading into the kitchen, "you may step over to the tavern, and say to the gentleman who just went from here, that he needn't trouble himself to call again. And, here! take this decanter, and get it filled with the best wine at the store. We will call in Mr. Blake, and settle the terms with him, over a bottle of my nice Madeira; for I feel like taking a bumper on the occasion."

Meanwhile Locke, who was traveling horseback, but too well anticipating the result of the deliberation just described, had ordered his horse to the door, and stood impatiently waiting for some sign or message from the white house, which should apprise him of the decision of the committee. The message came even sooner than he expected, and was delivered by the boy literally, and no less cavalierly than it was indited by his master. The next instant our rejected candidate was in his saddle, and leaving Mill Town Emporium at a pace which his sober steed appeared to wonder should be required by one who before had shown himself so moderate and gentle a rider.

As soon as his feelings, smarting with chagrin and vexation at his mortifying defeat, and the folly and ignorance which, he believed, alone had occasioned it,—as soon as his excited feelings had sufficiently subsided to permit of connected thought, he reined his thankful horse into a walk, to try to review the novel occurrences he had just witnessed, and bestow upon them something like sober reflection.

"What does education avail me?" he despondingly soliloquized, as he thought over his recent reception, and how he had been set aside for an ignorant coxcomb, or at best a pitiful smatterer. "The more I study, the worse I succeed. Yes, what avails all this intellectual toil, if my acquirements thereby are to be thus rewarded?" And as he pondered upon these discouraging circumstances, he almost resolved to abandon forever all thought of that noble employment to which he had so often declared his intention to devote himself. Locke had, thus far, had no acquaintance with aught but country life, with which he had been accustomed to associate ideas of comparative ignorance and degradation, while his mind had been directed to villages and cities, as the exclusive seats of intelligence and refinement. Like many another modest country lad of merit, he would have bowed in deference to the pert dashing villager or citizen, as his supposed superior, when the latter, probably, possessed not a tithe of his own worth in all that should constitute true excellence of character. For he had not learned that the people of cities and villages, as a mass, are, generally, less thinking, and often, less reading communities, than those formed of the residents of the country, who, finding themselves outshone by the former in external appearance, are thus driven to depend more on intrinsic qualities on which to base a reputation, leaving the others to dazzle by show, and, too often only,

"To measure their worth by the cloth of their coats."

It was not very strange, therefore, that with impressions and views like those just named, contracted through a limited knowledge of the world, young Amsden should have presented himself at Mill Town with a high opinion of the intelligence of its inhabitants, or that his disappointment should be great at finding things so exactly the reverse of what he had anticipated. A knowledge of the world as it is would have taught him that what he had witnessed was no miracle, even in the most favored parts of our land of boasted intelligence; and it might have taught him also, that he who would succeed must always, in some measure, adapt the means he employs to the compass of the minds of those with whom he desires success.

As Locke was slowly jogging onward, deeply engrossed in reflections which grew out of the occasion, and no less deeply dejected in spirits at the dark and discouraging prospects before him, he met a man in a sulky, who, in passing him, suddenly halted and pronounced his name. Looking up at the traveler, now for the first time, the former at once recognized him to be no other than Dr. Lincoln, the kind and gifted physician with whom he had formed so interesting an acquaintance at his school in the Horn of the Moon.

"Why, this is a singular affair, this meeting you just at this time and place," said the doctor, gayly, after the usual salutations had been exchanged. "I am almost minded to quote a homely old proverb; for I have not traveled forty rods since I was thinking of you, and really wishing that I knew where you might be found. But more of that anon. How has the world used you since I parted with you, Mr. Amsden?"

"Mainly well—quite so, indeed, if I except a little vexation of to-day's occurrence."

"And what has crossed your path to-day of an unpleasant nature? I perceived at the first glance that your countenance wore a look of dejection that did not formerly belong to it."

"Oh, it is nothing of consequence, sir."

"In one sense, it may be. I have long since observed, sir, that there is no way in which a disturbed mind can be sooner restored to its natural equilibrium than by a disclosure of its burden to others; even though it receive no sympathy in return. We are made social beings; and the law of our nature cannot be contravened with impunity here, any more than in more important matters. The cause of your trouble is none of my business to be sure; but a communication of it, I will venture to say, will lighten your heart. And it is best to enjoy all the happiness we can get, you know. So let us have your story."

Struck with the kind interest which the other seemed to take in his concerns, Locke proceeded to give him a minute detail of all the circumstances attending his application for the school in the village he had just left, his examination, and the result of the whole affair.

"And what opinion did you form of your successful rival?" asked the doctor, after indulging in a hearty laugh at some parts of the story.

"Why, that he was a pitiful ignoramus, to be sure."

"Undoubtedly; but yet a fellow of considerable tact and a pretty keen insight into the weaknesses of men, and the unworthy passions and selfish motives that too often govern them. And all this he had need of, to succeed upon pretensions so ridiculous; but with it, you see, he did succeed, and that too, at fearful odds against him. With what low cunning he first inquired the characters of the committee!—for such, as you suppose, was probably the case. And then how eagerly he seized on the first opportunity to bedaub them with flattery, rightly judging that, in this instance, the words of the poet would hold good,

>——' flattery never seems absurd—
> The flattered always take your word.'

And having thus secured the feelings and prejudices of the committee for himself, he appears fairly to have exemplified, with them, the truth of another line of the same writer, by making

> ' Impossibilities seem just.'

Indeed, sir, I think the fellow, who may be a broken-down pedler, or possibly a discarded subscription agent of catchpenny books or periodicals, managed his slender stock in trade to pretty good advantage. I see but one blunder that need at all to have endangered him with his learned examiners,—that was his mention of '*circumflutors*,' meaning, probably, to have hit on *circumferentors*, of which he might have heard from some students or surveyors with whom he chanced to fall in company, perhaps. But even that blunder, it seems, passed unnoticed. Oh, yes," continued the doctor, with an ironical smile, " this fellow managed his part to admiration. But what shall we say of that committee, who, both through ignorance and will, have thus betrayed their trust? And, furthermore, what shall we say of the people of that village, who so blindly conferred that important trust on such men? But we may spare words; for the employment of this impostor will fall as a judgment on their children, in the shape of errors imbibed, that will sufficiently punish these people for their unpardonable blindness and folly. And I will here tell you, Mr. Amsden, we have more to do in improving the condition of our common schools than to increase the number of qualified teachers. We have got to appoint managing committees who are qualified to discover and appreciate them. But enough of this; where do you think of looking for a school now, my dear sir?"

"I know not where to look, or what to do," replied Locke, despondingly. "I am poor, and need, particularly at this time, the amount of what would be respectable wages. But our country schools afford so little remuneration; and as for the villages, you see what my success is with them."

"Don't despair quite so soon, sir," said Lincoln, a little roguishly; "you may find some men in other villages of a little larger pattern than that of the learned trio you just encountered. What say you to coming to Cartersville and taking the school in the district where I live?"

"I would," replied Locke, "if you were to be the examining committee."

"Well, I shall be," rejoined the doctor, "for all the examination I shall want of you."

"How am I to take you, sir?" asked the former with a doubtful air.

"Why, that, as it strangely happens, I am sole committee myself," answered the doctor.

CHARLES DICKENS

1812-1870

CHARLES DICKENS was born at Landport, in Portsea, England, in 1812. His father was at that time a clerk in the marine service, and subsequently became a reporter of debates in Parliament. The greater part of the life of the great novelist was spent in London, and no man was ever more fully and intimately acquainted with the myriad phases of life in the world's metropolis. Glimpses of the early years of Dickens are found in his novels, particularly in "David Copperfield." In his young manhood he studied law—to please his father, but soon abandoned the attorney's office to become a reporter for the press. In this capacity he studied human life and character from observation. "Sketches by Boz," in the *Chronicle*, first brought him reputation as an author. "The Pickwick Papers," "Nicholas Nickleby," "Oliver Twist," "Old Curiosity Shop," and "Barnaby Rudge" followed; and when, in 1842, Dickens made a visit to the United States, he was a recognized star in the literary firmament. The "American Notes" and "Martin Chuzzlewit," which soon afterward appeared, were not very favorable to Americans. Mr. Dickens established in London the *Daily News*, from which he soon retired, and, later, he became the editor of *Household Words*, which developed into *All The Year Round*. In this his later novels appeared, as serials. In 1867 he re-visited America, and was cordially received. Among his greater works are "Dombey and Son," "David Copperfield," "Bleak House," "Little Dorrit," "Our Mutual Friend," "A Tale of Two Cities," and "The Mystery of Edwin Drood." The latter was unfinished when the author died, worn out by overwork. The end came in 1870.

Characterization

As for the charities of Mr. Dickens, multiplied kindnesses which he has conferred upon us all, upon our children, upon people educated and uneducated, upon the myriads who speak our common tongue, have not you, have not I, all of us, reason to be thankful to this kind friend, who soothed and charmed so many hours, brought pleasure and laughter to so many homes, made such multitudes of children happy, endowed us with such a sweet store of gracious thoughts, fair fancies, soft sympathies, hearty enjoyments? . . . I may quarrel with Mr. Dickens's art a thousand and a thousand times; I delight and wonder at his genius; I recognize in it—I speak with awe and reverence —a commission from that Divine Beneficence whose blessed task we know it will one day be to wipe every tear from every eye. Thankfully I take my share of the feast of love and kindness which this gentle and generous and charitable soul has contributed to the happiness of the world. I take and enjoy my share, and say a benediction for the meal.   WILLIAM MAKEPEACE THACKERAY.

Were all his books swept by some intellectual catastrophe out of the world, there would still exist in the world some score, at least, of people—with all those ways and sayings we are more intimately acquainted with than with those of our brothers and sisters,—who would owe to him their being. While we live and while our children live, Sam Weller and Dick Swiveller, Mr. Pecksniff and Mrs. Gamp, the Micawbers and the Squeerses, can never die. . . . They are more real than we are ourselves, and will outlive and outlast us as they have outlived their creator. This is the one proof of genius which no critic, not the most carping or dissatisfied, can gainsay.

"BLACKWOOD'S MAGAZINE."

Dr. Blimber's School

(From "Dombey and Son")

Whenever a young gentleman was taken in hand by Doctor Blimber, he might consider himself sure of a pretty tight squeeze. The Doctor only undertook the charge of ten young gentlemen, but he had, always ready, a supply of learning for a hundred, on the lowest estimate; and it was at once the business and delight of his life to gorge the unhappy ten with it.

In fact, Doctor Blimber's establishment was a great hot-house, in which there was a forcing apparatus incessantly at work. All the boys blew before their time. Mental green peas were produced at Christmas, and intellectual asparagus all the year round. Mathematical gooseberries (very sour ones too) were common at untimely seasons, and from mere sprouts of bushes, under Dr. Blimber's cultivation. Every description of Greek and Latin vegetable was got off the driest twigs of boys, under the frostiest circumstances. Nature was of no consequence at all. No matter what a young gentleman was intended to bear, Doctor Blimber made him bear to pattern, somehow or other.

This was all very pleasant and ingenious, but the system of forcing was attended with its usual disadvantages. There was not the right taste about the premature productions, and they didn't keep well. Moreover, one young gentleman, with a swollen nose and an excessively large head (the oldest of the ten, who had "gone through" everything), suddenly left off blowing one day, and remained in the establishment a mere stalk. And people did say that the Doctor had rather overdone it with young Toots, and that when he began to have whiskers he left off having brains.

There young Toots was, at any rate; possessed of the gruffest of voices and the shrillest of minds; sticking ornamental pins into his shirt, and keeping a ring in his waistcoat pocket to put on his little finger by stealth, when the pupils went out walking; constantly falling in love by sight with nursery-maids, who had no idea of his existence; and looking at the gas-lighted world over the little iron bars in the left-hand corner window of the front three pairs of stairs, after bedtime, like a greatly overgrown cherub who had sat up aloft much too long.

The Doctor was a portly gentleman in a suit of black, with strings at his knees, and stockings below them. He had a bald head, highly polished; a deep voice; and a chin so very double, that it was a wonder how he ever managed to shave into the creases. He had likewise a pair of little eyes that were always half shut up, and a mouth that was always half expanded into a grin, as if he had, that moment, posed a boy, and were waiting to convict him from his own lips. Insomuch, that when the Doctor put his right hand into the breast of his coat, and with his other hand behind him, and a scarcely perceptible wag of his head, made the commonest observation to a nervous stranger, it was like a sentiment from the Sphinx, and settled his business.

The Doctor's was a mighty fine house, fronting the sea. Not

a joyful style of house within, but quite the contrary. Sad-colored curtains, whose proportions were spare and lean, hid themselves despondently behind the windows. The tables and chairs were put away in rows, like figures in a sum; fires were so rarely lighted in the rooms of ceremony, that they felt like wells, and a visitor represented the bucket; the dining-room seemed the last place in the world where any eating or drinking was likely to occur; there was no sound through all the house but the ticking of a great clock in the hall, which made itself audible in the very garrets; and sometimes a dull crying of young gentlemen at their lessons, like the murmurings of an assemblage of melancholy pigeons.

Miss Blimber, too, although a slim and graceful maid, did no soft violence to the gravity of the house. There was no light nonsense about Miss Blimber. She kept her hair short and crisp, and wore spectacles. She was dry and sandy with working in the graves of deceased languages. None of your live languages for Miss Blimber. They must be dead—stone dead—and then Miss Blimber dug them up like a Ghoul.

Mrs. Blimber, her mamma, was not learned herself, but she pretended to be, and that did quite as well. She said, at evening parties, that if she could have known Cicero, she thought she could have died contented. It was the steady joy of her life to see the Doctor's young gentlemen go out walking, unlike all other young gentlemen, in the largest possible shirt collars and the stiffest possible cravats. It was so classical, she said.

As to Mr. Feeder, B.A., Doctor Blimber's assistant, he was a kind of human barrel-organ, with a little list of tunes at which he was continually working, over and over again, without any variation. He might have been fitted up with a change of barrels, perhaps, in early life, if his destiny had been favorable; but it had not been; and he had only one, with which, in a monotonous round, it was his occupation to bewilder the young ideas of Doctor Blimber's young gentlemen. The young gentlemen were prematurely full of carking anxieties. They knew no rest from the pursuit of stony-hearted verbs, savage noun-substantives, inflexible syntactic passages, and ghosts of exercises that appeared to them in their dreams. Under the forcing system, a young gentleman usually took leave of his spirits in three weeks. He had all the cares of the world on his head in three months. He conceived bitter sentiments against his parents or guardians in four; he was an old misanthrope in five; envied Curtius that blessed refuge in the earth in six; and at the end of the first twelvemonth had arrived at the conclusion, from which he never afterward departed, that all the fancies of the poets, and lessons of the sages, were a mere collection of words and grammar, and had no other meaning in the world.

But he went on, blow, blow, blowing, in the Doctor's hot-house, all the time; and the Doctor's glory and reputation were great when he took his wintry growth home to his relations and friends.

Upon the Doctor's door-steps, one day, Paul stood with a fluttering heart, and with his small right hand in his father's. His other hand was locked in that of Florence. How tight the tiny pressure of that one; and how loose and cold the other!

Mrs. Pipchin hovered behind the victim, with her sable plumage and her hooked beak, like a bird of ill omen. She was out of breath—for Mr. Dombey, full of great thoughts, had walked fast—and she croaked hoarsely as she waited for the opening of the door.

"Now, Paul," said Mr. Dombey exultingly, "this is the way indeed to be Dombey and Son, and have money. You are almost a man already."

"Almost," returned the child.

Even his childish agitation could not master the sly and quaint, yet touching look with which he accompanied the reply.

It brought a vague expression of dissatisfaction into Mr. Dombey's face; but, the door being opened, it was quickly gone.

"Doctor Blimber is at home, I believe?" said Mr. Dombey.

The man said yes; and, as they passed in, looked at Paul as if he were a little mouse, and the house were a trap. He was a weak-eyed young man, with the first faint streaks or early dawn of a grin on his countenance. It was mere imbecility; but Mrs. Pipchin took it into her head that it was impudence, and made a snap at him directly.

"How dare you laugh behind the gentleman's back?" said Mrs. Pipchin. "And what do you take me for?"

"I ain't a laughing at nobody, and I'm sure I don't take you for nothing, ma'am!" returned the young man in consternation.

"A pack of idle dogs!" said Mrs. Pipchin, "only fit to be turnspits. Go and tell your master that Mr. Dombey's here, or it'll be worse for you!"

The weak-eyed young man went, very meekly, to discharge himself of this commission; and soon came back to invite them to the Doctor's study.

"You're laughing again, sir," said Mrs. Pipchin, when it came to her turn, bringing up the rear, to pass him in the hall.

"I *ain't*," returned the young man, grievously oppressed. "I never see such a thing as this!"

"What is the matter, Mrs. Pipchin?" said Mr. Dombey, looking round. "Softly! Pray!"

Mrs. Pipchin, in her deference, merely muttered at the young man as she passed on, and said, "Oh! he was a precious fellow"—leaving the young man, who was all meekness and incapacity, affected even to tears by the incident. But Mrs. Pipchin had a way of falling foul of all meek people; and her friends said, who could wonder at it, after the Peruvian mines?

The Doctor was sitting in his portentous study, with a globe at each knee, books all round him, Homer over the door, and Minerva on the mantel-shelf. "And how do you do, sir?" he said to Mr. Dombey, "and how is my little friend?" Grave as an organ was the Doctor's speech; and when he ceased, the great clock in the hall seemed (to Paul at least) to take him up, and to go on saying, "How, is, my, lit, tle, friend?" How, is, my, lit, tle, friend?" over and over and over again.

The little friend being somewhat too small to be seen at all from where the Doctor sat, over the books on his table, the Doctor made several futile attempts to get a view of him round the legs: which Mr. Dombey perceiving, relieved the Doctor from his embarrassment by taking Paul up in his arms, and sitting him on another little table, over against the Doctor, in the middle of the room.

"Ha!" said the Doctor, leaning back in his chair, with his hand in his breast. "Now I see my little friend. How do you do, my little friend?"

The clock in the hall wouldn't subscribe to this alteration in the form of words, but continued to repeat "How, is, my, lit, tle, friend? how, is, my, lit, tle, friend?"

"Very well, I thank you, sir," returned Paul, answering the clock quite as much as the Doctor.

"Ha!" said Doctor Blimber. "Shall we make a man of him?"

"Do you hear, Paul?" added Mr. Dombey; Paul being silent.

"Shall we make a man of him?" repeated the Doctor.

"I had rather be a child," replied Paul.

"Indeed!" said the Doctor. "Why?"

The child sat on the table looking at him, with a curious expression of suppressed emotion in his face, and beating one hand proudly on his knee, as if he had the rising tears beneath it, and crushed them. But his other hand strayed a little way the while, a little further—further from him yet—until it lighted on the neck of Florence. "This is why," it seemed to say, and then the steady look was broken up and gone; the working lip was loosened; and the tears came streaming forth.

"Mrs. Pipchin," said his father in a querulous manner, "I am really very sorry to see this."

"Come away from him, do, Miss Dombey," quoth the matron.

"Never mind," said the Doctor, blandly nodding his head to

keep Mrs. Pipchin back. "Ne-ver mind; we shall substitute new cares and new impressions, Mr. Dombey, very shortly. You would still wish my little friend to acquire——"

"Everything, if you please, Doctor," returned Mr. Dombey firmly.

"Yes," said the Doctor, who, with his half-shut eyes and his usual smile, seemed to survey Paul with the sort of interest that might attach to some choice little animal he was going to stuff. "Yes, exactly. Ha! We shall impart a great variety of information to our little friend, and bring him quickly forward, I dare say. I dare say. Quite a virgin soil, I believe you said, Mr. Dombey?"

"Except some ordinary preparation at home, and from this lady," replied Mr. Dombey, introducing Mrs. Pipchin, who instantly communicated a rigidity to her whole muscular system, and snorted defiance beforehand, in case the doctor should disparage her; "except so far, Paul has, as yet, applied himself to no studies at all."

Doctor Blimber inclined his head, in gentle tolerance of such insignificant poaching as Mrs. Pipchin's, and said he was glad to hear it. It was much more satisfactory, he observed, rubbing his hands, to begin at the foundation. And again he leered at Paul, as if he would have liked to tackle him with the Greek alphabet on the spot.

"That circumstance, indeed, Doctor Blimber," pursued Mr. Dombey, glancing at his little son, "and the interview I have already had the pleasure of holding with you, render any further explanation, and consequently, any further intrusion on your valuable time, so unnecessary, that——"

"Now, Miss Dombey!" said the acid Pipchin.

"Permit me," said the Doctor, "one moment. Allow me to present Mrs. Blimber and my daughter, who will be associated with the domestic life of our young Pilgrim to Parnassus. Mrs. Blimber,"—for the lady, who had perhaps been in waiting, opportunely entered, followed by her daughter, that fair sexton in spectacles,—" Mr. Dombey. My daughter Cornelia, Mr. Dombey. Mr. Dombey, my love," pursued the Doctor, turning to his wife, "is so confiding as to—Do you see our little friend?"

Mrs. Blimber, in an excess of politeness, of which Mr. Dombey was the object, apparently did not, for she was backing against the little friend, and very much endangering his position on the table. But, on this hint, she turned to admire his classical and intellectual lineaments, and turning again to Mr. Dombey, said, with a sigh, that she envied his dear son.

"Like a bee, sir," said Mrs. Blimber, with uplifted eyes, "about to plunge into a garden of the choicest flowers, and sip the sweets for the first time. Virgil, Horace, Ovid, Terence, Plautus, Cicero. What a world of honey have we here! It may appear remarkable, Mr. Dombey, in one who is a wife—the wife of such a husband——"

"Hush, hush," said Doctor Blimber. "Fie for shame!"

"Mr. Dombey will forgive the partiality of a wife," said Mrs. Blimber with an engaging smile.

Mr. Dombey answered, "Not at all;" applying those words, it is to be presumed, to the partiality, and not to the forgiveness.

"—And it may seem remarkable in one who is a mother also—" resumed Mrs. Blimber.

"And such a mother," observed Mr. Dombey, bowing with some confused idea of being complimentary to Cornelia.

"But really," pursued Mrs. Blimber, "I think if I could have known Cicero, and been his friend, and talked with him in his retirement at Tusculum (beau-ti-ful Tusculum!), I could have died contented."

A learned enthusiasm is so very contagious, that Mr. Dombey half believed this was exactly his case; and even Mrs. Pipchin, who was not, as we have seen, of an accommodating disposition generally, gave utterance to a little sound between a groan and a sigh, as if she would have said that nobody but Cicero could have proved a lasting consolation under that failure of the Peruvian mines, but that he indeed would have been a very Davy-lamp of refuge.

Cornelia looked at Mr. Dombey through her spectacles as if

she would have liked to crack a few quotations with him from the authority in question. But this design, if she entertained it, was frustrated by a knock at the room-door.

"Who is that?" said the Doctor. "Oh! Come in, Toots; come in. Mr. Dombey, sir." Toots bowed. "Quite a coincidence!" said Doctor Blimber. "Here we have the beginning and the end. Alpha and Omega. Our head boy, Mr. Dombey."

The Doctor might have called him their head-and-shoulders boy, for he was at least that much taller than any of the rest. He blushed very much at finding himself among strangers, and chuckled aloud.

"An addition to our little Portico, Toots," said the Doctor; "Mr. Dombey's son."

Young Toots blushed again; and finding, from a solemn silence which prevailed, that he was expected to say something, said to Paul, "How are you?" in a voice so deep, and a manner so sheepish, that if a lamb had roared it couldn't have been more surprising.

"Ask Mr. Feeder, if you please, Toots," said the Doctor, "to prepare a few introductory volumes for Mr. Dombey's son, and to allot him a convenient seat for study. My dear, I believe Mr. Dombey has not seen the dormitories."

"If Mr. Dombey will walk upstairs," said Mrs. Blimber, "I shall be more than proud to show him the dominions of the drowsy god."

With that Mrs. Blimber, who was a lady of great suavity, and a wiry figure, and who wore a cap composed of sky-blue materials, proceeded upstairs with Mr. Dombey and Cornelia; Mrs. Pipchin following, and looking out sharp for her enemy, the footman.

While they were gone, Paul sat upon the table, holding Florence by the hand, and glancing timidly from the Doctor round and round the room, while the Doctor, leaning back in his chair, with his hand in his breast as usual, held a book from him at arm's length, and read. There was something very awful in this manner of reading. It was such a determined, unimpassioned, inflexible, cold-blooded way of going to work. It left the Doctor's countenance exposed to view; and when the Doctor smiled auspiciously at his author, or knit his brows, or shook his head and made wry faces at him as much as to say, "Don't tell me, sir; I know better," it was terrific.

Toots, too, had no business to be outside the door, ostentatiously examining the wheels in his watch, and counting his half-crowns. But that didn't last long; for Doctor Blimber, happening to change the position of his tight plump legs, as if he were going to get up, Toots swiftly vanished, and appeared no more.

Mr. Dombey and his conductress were soon heard coming down-stairs again, talking all the way; and presently they re-entered the Doctor's study.

"I hope, Mr. Dombey," said the Doctor, laying down his book, "that the arrangements meet your approval?"

"They are excellent, sir," said Mr. Dombey.

"Very fair indeed," said Mrs. Pipchin, in a low voice; never disposed to give too much encouragement.

"Mrs. Pipchin," said Mr. Dombey, wheeling round, "will, with your permission, Doctor and Mrs. Blimber, visit Paul now and then."

"Whenever Mrs. Pipchin pleases," observed the Doctor.

"Always happy to see her," said Mrs. Blimber.

"I think," said Mr. Dombey, "I have given all the trouble I need, and may take my leave. Paul, my child,"—he went close to him, as he sat upon the table,—"good-by."

"Good-by, papa."

The limp and careless little hand that Mr. Dombey took in his was singularly out of keeping with the wistful face. But he had no part in its sorrowful expression. It was not addressed to him. No, no. To Florence—all to Florence.

If Mr. Dombey, in his insolence of wealth, had ever made an enemy, hard to appease and cruelly vindictive in his hate, even such an enemy might have received the pang that wrung his proud heart then as compensation for his injury.

He bent down over his boy, and kissed him. If his sight were dimmed, as he did so, by something that for a moment blurred the little face, and made it indistinct to him, his mental vision may have been for that short time, the clearer, perhaps.

"I shall see you soon, Paul. You are free on Saturdays and Sundays, you know."

"Yes, papa," returned Paul, looking at his sister. "On Saturdays and Sundays."

"And you'll try and learn a great deal here, and be a clever man," said Mr. Dombey; "won't you?"

"I'll try," returned the child wearily.

"And you'll soon be grown up now!" said Mr. Dombey.

"Oh! very soon!" replied the child. Once more the old, old look passed rapidly across his features like a strange light. It fell on Mrs. Pipchin, and extinguished itself in her black dress. That excellent ogress stepped forward to take leave and to bear off Florence, which she had long been thirsting to do. The move on her part roused Mr. Dombey, whose eyes were fixed on Paul. After patting him on the head, and pressing his small hand again, he took leave of Doctor Blimber, Mrs. Blimber, and Miss Blimber with his usual polite frigidity, and walked out of the study.

Despite his entreaty that they would not think of stirring, Doctor Blimber, Mrs. Blimber, and Miss Blimber all pressed forward to attend him to the hall; and thus Mrs. Pipchin got into a state of entanglement with Miss Blimber and the Doctor, and was crowded out of the study before she could clutch Florence. To which happy accident Paul stood afterward indebted for the dear remembrance, that Florence ran back to throw her arms round his neck, and that hers was the last face in the doorway, turned toward him with a smile of encouragement, the brighter for the tears through which it beamed.

It made his childish bosom heave and swell when it was gone; and sent the globes, the books, blind Homer, and Minerva swimming round the room. But they stopped all of a sudden; and then he heard the loud clock in the hall still gravely inquiring, "How, is, my, lit, tle, friend? how, is, my, lit, tle, friend?" as it had done before.

He sat, with folded hands, upon his pedestal, silently listening. But he might have answered, "Weary, weary! very lonely, very sad!" And there, with an aching void in his young heart, and all outside so cold, and bare, and strange, Paul sat as if he had taken life unfurnished, and the upholsterer were never coming.

After the lapse of some minutes, which appeared an immense time to little Paul Dombey on the table, Doctor Blimber came back. The Doctor's walk was stately, and calculated to impress the juvenile mind with solemn feelings. It was a sort of march; but when the Doctor put out his right foot, he gravely turned upon his axis, with a semi-circular sweep toward the left; and when he put out his left foot, he turned in the same manner toward the right. So that he seemed, at every stride he took, to look about him as though he were saying, "Can anybody have the goodness to indicate any subject, in any direction on which I am uninformed? I rather think not."

Mrs. Blimber and Miss Blimber came back in the Doctor's company; and the Doctor, lifting his new pupil off the table, delivered him over to Miss Blimber.

"Cornelia," said the Doctor, "Dombey will be your charge at first. Bring him on, Cornelia, bring him on."

Miss Blimber received her young ward from the Doctor's hands; and Paul, feeling that the spectacles were surveying him, cast down his eyes.

"How old are you, Dombey?" said Miss Blimber.

"Six," answered Paul, wondering, as he stole a glance at the young lady, why her hair didn't grow long like Florence's, and why she was like a boy.

"How much do you know of your Latin Grammar, Dombey?" said Miss Blimber.

"None of it," answered Paul. Feeling that the answer was a shock to Miss Blimber's sensibility, he looked up at the three faces that were looking down at him, and said:

"I haven't been well. I have been a weak child. I couldn't learn a Latin Grammar when I was out, every day, with old Glubb. I wish you'd tell old Glubb to come and see me, if you please."

"What a dreadfully low name!" said Mrs. Blimber. "Unclassical to a degree! Who is the monster, child?"

"What monster?" inquired Paul.

"Glubb," said Mrs. Blimber, with a great disrelish.

"He's no more a monster than you are," returned Paul.

"What!" cried the Doctor in a terrible voice. "Ay, ay, ay? Aha! What's that?"

Paul was dreadfully frightened; but still he made a stand for the absent Glubb, though he did it trembling.

"He's a very nice old man, ma'am," he said. "He used to draw my couch. He knows all about the deep sea, and the fish that are in it, and the great monsters that come and lie on rocks in the sun, and dive into the water again when they're startled, blowing and splashing so, that they can be heard for miles. There are some creatures," said Paul, warming with his subject, "I don't know how many yards long, and I forget their names, but Florence knows, that pretend to be in distress; and when a man goes near them, out of compassion, they open their great jaws, and attack him. But all he has got to do," said Paul, boldly tendering this information to the very doctor, himself, "is to keep on turning as he runs away, and then, as they turn slowly, because they are so long, and can't bend, he's sure to beat them. And though old Glubb don't know why the sea should make me think of my mamma that's dead, or what it is that it is always saying—always saying! he knows a great deal about it. And I wish," the child concluded, with a sudden falling of his countenance, and failing in his animation, as he looked like one forlorn upon the three strange faces, "that you'd let old Glubb come here to see me, for I know him very well, and he knows me."

"Ha!" said the Doctor, shaking his head; "this is bad, but study will do much."

Mrs. Blimber opined, with something like a shiver, that he was an unaccountable child; and, allowing for the difference of visage, looked at him pretty much as Mrs. Pipchin had been used to do.

"Take him round the house, Cornelia," said the doctor, "and familiarize him with his new sphere. Go with that young lady, Dombey."

Dombey obeyed: giving his hand to abstruse Cornelia, and looking at her sideways, with timid curiosity, as they went away together. For her spectacles, by reason of the glistening of the glasses, made her so mysterious, that he didn't know where she was looking, and was not, indeed, quite sure that she had any eyes at all behind them.

Cornelia took him first to the schoolroom, which was situated at the back of the hall, and was approached through two baize doors, which deadened and muffled the young gentlemen's voices. Here there were eight young gentlemen in various stages of mental prostration, all very hard at work, and very grave indeed. Toots, as an old hand, had a desk to himself in one corner; and a magnificent man, of immense age, he looked, in Paul's young eyes behind it.

Mr. Feeder, B.A., who sat at another little desk, had his Virgil stop on, and was slowly grinding that tune to four young gentlemen. Of the remaining four, two, who grasped their foreheads convulsively, were engaged in solving mathematical problems: one with his face like a dirty window, from much crying, was endeavoring to flounder through a hopeless number of lines before dinner; and one sat looking at his task in stony stupefaction and despair—which it seemed had been his condition ever since breakfast-time.

The appearance of a new boy did not create the sensation that might have been expected. Mr. Feeder, B.A. (who was in the habit of shaving his head for coolness, and had nothing but little bristles on it), gave him a bony hand, and told him he was glad to see him—which Paul would have been very glad to have told *him*, if he could have done so with the least sincerity. Then Paul, instructed by Cornelia, shook hands with the four young gentlemen at Mr. Feeder's desk; then with the two young gentlemen at work on the problems, who were very feverish; then with the young gentleman at work against time, who was very inky; and lastly, with the young gentleman in a state of stupefaction, who was flabby and quite cold.

Paul having been already introduced to Toots, that pupil merely chuckled and breathed hard, as his custom was, and pursued the occupation in which he was engaged. It was not a severe one; for, on account of his having "gone through" so much (in more senses than one), and also of his having, as before hinted, left off blowing in his prime, Toots now had license to pursue his own course of study; which was chiefly to write long letters to himself from persons of distinction, addressed "P. Toots, Esquire, Brighton, Sussex," and to preserve them in his desk with great care.

These ceremonies passed, Cornelia led Paul upstairs to the top of the house; which was rather a slow journey, on account of Paul being obliged to land both feet on every stair before he mounted another. But they reached their journey's end at last; and there in a front room, looking over the wild sea, Cornelia showed him a nice little bed with white hangings, close to the window, on which there was already beautifully written on a card in round text—down strokes very thick, and up strokes very fine—DOMBEY; while two other little bedsteads in the same room were announced, through like means, as respectively appertaining unto BRIGGS and TOZER.

Just as they got down-stairs again into the hall, Paul saw the weak-eyed young man, who had given that mortal offense to Mrs. Pipchin, suddenly seize a very large drum-stick, and fly at a gong that was hanging up, as if he had gone mad, or wanted vengeance. Instead of receiving warning, however, or being instantly taken into custody, the young man left off unchecked, after having made a dreadful noise. Then Cornelia Blimber said to Dombey that dinner would be ready in a quarter of an hour, and perhaps he had better go into the schoolroom among his "friends."

So Dombey, deferentially passing the great clock, which was still as anxious as ever to know how he found himself, opened the schoolroom door a very little way, and strayed in like a lost boy: shutting it after him with some difficulty. His friends were all dispersed about the room except the stony friend, who remained immovable. Mr. Feeder was stretching himself in his gray gown, as if, regardless of expense, he were resolved to pull the sleeves off.

"Heigh ho hum!" cried Mr. Feeder, shaking himself like a cart-horse. "Oh dear me, dear me! Ya-a-a-ah!"

Paul was quite alarmed by Mr. Feeder's yawning; it was done on such a great scale, and he was so terribly in earnest. All the boys, too (Toots excepted), seemed knocked up, and were getting ready for dinner—some newly tying their neckcloths, which were very stiff indeed; and others washing their hands, or brushing their hair, in an adjoining ante-chamber—as if they didn't think they should enjoy it at all.

Young Toots, who was ready beforehand, and had therefore nothing to do, and had leisure to bestow upon Paul, said, with heavy good-nature:

"Sit down, Dombey."

"Thank you, sir," said Paul.

His endeavoring to hoist himself on to a very high window-seat, and his slipping down again, appeared to prepare Toots's mind for the reception of a discovery.

"You're a very small chap," said Mr. Toots.

"Yes, sir, I'm small," returned Paul. "Thank you, sir."

For Toots had lifted him into his seat, and done it kindly too.

"Who's your tailor?" inquired Toots, after looking at him for some moments.

"It's a woman that has made my clothes as yet," said Paul. "My sister's dressmaker."

"My tailor's Burgess and Co.," said Toots. "Fash'nable. But very dear."

Paul had wit enough to shake his head, as if he would have said it was easy to see *that;* and, indeed, he thought so.

"Your father's regularly rich, ain't he?" inquired Mr. Toots.

"Yes, sir," said Paul. "He's Dombey and Son."

"And which?" demanded Toots.

"And Son, sir," replied Paul.

Mr. Toots made one or two attempts, in a low voice, to fix the firm in his mind; but not quite succeeding, said he would get Paul to mention the name again to-morrow morning, as it was rather important. And, indeed, he purposed nothing less than writing himself a private and confidential letter from Dombey and Son immediately.

By this time the other pupils (always excepting the stony boy) gathered round. They were polite, but pale; and spoke low; and they were so depressed in their spirits, that, in comparison with the general tone of that company, Master Bitherstone was a perfect Miller, or complete Jest Book. And yet he had a sense of injury upon him too, had Bitherstone.

"You sleep in my room, don't you?" asked a solemn young gentleman, whose shirt collar curled up the lobes of his ears.

"Master Briggs?" inquired Paul.

"Tozer," said the young gentleman.

Paul answered yes; and Tozer, pointing out the stony pupil, said that was Briggs. Paul had already felt certain that it must be either Briggs or Tozer, though he didn't know why.

"Is yours a strong constitution?" inquired Tozer.

Paul said he thought not. Tozer replied that *he* thought not also, judging from Paul's looks, and that it was a pity, for it need be. He then asked Paul if he were going to begin with Cornelia; and, on Paul saying "Yes," all the young gentlemen (Briggs excepted) gave a low groan.

It was drowned in the tintinnabulation of the gong, which sounding again with great fury, there was a general move toward the dining-room; still excepting Briggs, the stony boy, who remained where he was, and as he was; and on its way to whom Paul presently encountered a round of bread, genteely served on a plate and napkin, and with a silver fork lying crosswise on the top of it. Doctor Blimber was already in his place in the dining-room, at the top of the table, with Miss Blimber and Mrs. Blimber on either side of him. Mr. Feeder, in a black coat, was at the bottom. Paul's chair was next to Miss Blimber; but it being found, when he sat in it, that his eyebrows were not much above the level of the table-cloth, some books were brought in from the Doctor's study, on which he was elevated, and on which he always sat from that time—carrying them in and out himself, on after occasions, like a little elephant and castle.

Grace having been said by the doctor, dinner began. There was some nice soup; also roast meat, boiled meat, vegetables, pie, and cheese. Every young gentleman had a massive silver fork, and a napkin; and all the arrangements were stately and handsome. In particular, there was a butler in a blue coat, and bright buttons, who gave quite a winy flavor to the table beer; he poured it out so superbly.

Nobody spoke, unless spoken to, except Doctor Blimber, Mrs. Blimber, and Miss Blimber, who conversed occasionally. Whenever a young gentleman was not actually engaged with his knife and fork or spoon, his eye, with an irresistible attraction, sought the eye of Doctor Blimber, Mrs. Blimber, or Miss Blimber, and modestly rested there. Toots appeared to be the only exception to this rule. He sat next Mr. Feeder, on Paul's side of the table, and frequently looked behind and before the intervening boys to catch a glimpse of Paul.

Only once during dinner was there any conversation that included the young gentlemen. It happened at the epoch of the cheese, when the Doctor, having taken a glass of port wine, and hemmed twice or thrice, said:

"It is remarkable, Mr. Feeder, that the Romans———"

At the mention of this terrible people, their implacable enemies, every young gentleman fastened his gaze upon the Doctor, with an assumption of the deepest interest. One of the number, who happened to be drinking, and who caught the

Doctor's eye glaring at him through the side of his tumbler, left off so hastily that he was convulsed for some moments, and in the sequel ruined Doctor Blimber's point.

"It is remarkable, Mr. Feeder," said the Doctor, beginning again slowly, "that the Romans, in those gorgeous and profuse entertainments of which we read in the days of the Emperors, when luxury had attained a height unknown before or since, and when whole provinces were ravaged to supply the splendid means of one imperial banquet——"

Here the offender, who had been swelling and straining, and waiting in vain for a full stop, broke out violently.

"Johnson," said Mr. Feeder in a low, reproachful voice, "take some water."

The Doctor, looking very stern, made a pause until the water was brought, and then resumed:

"And when, Mr. Feeder——"

But Mr. Feeder, who saw that Johnson must break out again, and who knew that the Doctor would never come to a period before the young gentlemen until he had finished all he meant to say, couldn't keep his eye off Johnson; and thus was caught in the fact of not looking at the Doctor, who consequently stopped.

"I beg your pardon, sir," said Mr. Feeder, reddening. "I beg your pardon, Doctor Blimber."

"And when," said the Doctor, raising his voice, "when, sir, as we read, and have no reason to doubt—incredible as it may appear to the vulgar of our time—the brother of Vitellius prepared for him a feast, in which were served, of fish, two thousand dishes——"

"Take some water, Johnson—dishes, sir," said Mr. Feeder.

"Of various sorts of fowl, five thousand dishes——"

"Or try a crust of bread," said Mr. Feeder.

"And one dish," pursued Dr. Blimber, raising his voice still higher as he looked all round the table, "called, from its enormous dimensions, the Shield of Minerva, and made, among other costly ingredients, of the brains of pheasants——"

"Ow, ow, ow!" (from Johnson).

"Woodcocks——"

"Ow, ow, ow!"

"The sounds of the fish called scari——"

"You'll burst some vessel in your head," said Mr. Feeder. "You had better let it come."

"And the spawn of the lamprey, brought from the Carpathian Sea," pursued the Doctor in his severest voice; "when we read of costly entertainments such as these, and still remember that we have a Titus——"

"What would be your mother's feelings if you died of apoplexy?" said Mr. Feeder.

"A Domitian——"

"And you're blue, you know," said Mr. Feeder.

"A Nero, a Tiberius, a Caligula, a Heliogabulus, and many more," pursued the Doctor; "it is, Mr. Feeder—if you are doing me the honor to attend—remarkable; VERY remarkable, sir——"

But Johnson, unable to suppress it any longer, burst at that moment into such an overwhelming fit of coughing, that, although both his immediate neighbors thumped him on the back, and Mr. Feeder himself held a glass of water to his lips, and the butler walked him up and down several times between his own chair and the sideboard, like a sentry, it was full five minutes before he was moderately composed, and then there was a profound silence.

"Gentlemen," said Doctor Blimber, "rise for Grace! Cornelia, lift Dombey down"—nothing of whom but his scalp was accordingly seen above the table-cloth. "Johnson will repeat to me to-morrow morning before breakfast, without book, and from the Greek Testament, the first chapter of the Epistle of St. Paul to the Ephesians. We will resume our studies, Mr. Feeder, in half an hour."

The young gentlemen bowed and withdrew. Mr. Feeder did likewise. During the half-hour, the young gentlemen, broken into pairs, loitered arm-in-arm up and down a small piece of ground behind the house, or endeavored to kindle a spark of animation in the breast of Briggs. But nothing happened so vulgar as play. Punctually at the appointed time the gong was sounded, and the studies, under the joint auspices of Doctor Blimber and Mr. Feeder, were resumed.

As the Olympic game of lounging up and down had been cut shorter than usual that day, on Johnson's account, they all went out for a walk before tea. Even Briggs (though he hadn't begun yet) partook of this dissipation; in the enjoyment of which he looked over the cliff two or three times darkly. Doctor Blimber accompanied them; and Paul had the honor of being taken in tow by the Doctor himself; a distinguished state of things, in which he looked very little and feeble.

Tea was served in a style no less polite than the dinner; and after tea, the young gentlemen, rising and bowing as before, withdrew to fetch up the unfinished tasks of that day, or to get up the already looming tasks of to-morrow. In the mean time Mr. Feeder withdrew to his own room; and Paul sat in a corner, wondering whether Florence was thinking of him, and what they were all about at Mrs. Pipchin's.

Mr. Toots, who had been detained by an important letter from the Duke of Wellington, found Paul out after a time, and having looked at him for a long while, as before, inquired if he was fond of waistcoats.

Paul said " Yes, sir."

" So am I," said Toots.

No word more spake Toots that night; but he stood looking at Paul as if he liked him; and as there was company in that, and Paul was not inclined to talk, it answered his purpose better than conversation.

At eight o'clock or so, the gong sounded again for prayers in the dining-room, where the butler afterward presided over a side-table, on which bread and cheese and beer were spread for such young gentlemen as desired to partake of those refreshments. The ceremonies concluded by the Doctor's saying, " Gentlemen, we will resume our studies at seven to-morrow : " and then, for the first time, Paul saw Cornelia Blimber's eye, and saw that it was upon him. When the Doctor had said these words, "Gentlemen, we will resume our studies at seven to-morrow," the pupils bowed again, and went to bed.

In the confidence of their own room upstairs, Briggs said his head ached ready to split, and that he should wish himself dead if it wasn't for his mother, and a blackbird he had at home. Tozer didn't say much, but he sighed a good deal, and told Paul to look out, for his turn would come to-morrow. After uttering those prophetic words, he undressed himself moodily, and got into bed. Briggs was in his bed too, and Paul in his bed too, before the weak-eyed young man appeared to take away the candle, when he wished them good-night and pleasant dreams. But his benevolent wishes were in vain as far as Briggs and Tozer were concerned; for Paul, who lay awake for a long while, and often woke afterward, found that Briggs was ridden by his lesson as a nightmare; and that Tozer, whose mind was affected in his sleep by similar causes, in a minor degree, talked unknown tongues, or scraps of Greek and Latin—it was all one to Paul—which, in the silence of night, had an inexpressibly wicked and guilty effect.

Paul had sunk into a sweet sleep, and dreamed that he was walking hand in hand with Florence through beautiful gardens, when they came to a large sunflower which suddenly expanded itself into a gong, and began to sound. Opening his eyes, he found that it was a dark, windy morning, with a drizzling rain; and that the real gong was giving dreadful note of preparation down in the hall.

So he got up directly, and found Briggs with hardly any eyes, for nightmare and grief had made his face puffy, putting his boots on; while Tozer stood shivering and rubbing his shoulders in a very bad humor. Poor Paul couldn't dress himself easily, not being used to it, and asked them if they would have the goodness to tie some strings for him; but, as Briggs merely said "Bother!" and Tozer, "Oh yes!" he went down, when he was otherwise ready, to the next story, where he saw a pretty young woman in leather gloves, cleaning a stove.

The young woman seemed surprised at his appearance, and asked him where his mother was. When Paul told her she was dead, she took her gloves off, and did what he wanted; and furthermore rubbed his hands to warm them; and gave him a kiss; and told him whenever he wanted anything of that sort—meaning in the dressing way—to ask for 'Melia; which Paul, thanking her very much, said he certainly would. He then proceeded softly on his journey down-stairs, toward the room in which the young gentlemen resumed their studies, when, passing by a door that stood ajar, a voice from within cried, "Is that Dombey?" On Paul replying, "Yes, ma'am;" for he knew the voice to be Miss Blimber's: Miss Blimber said, "Come in, Dombey." And in he went.

Miss Blimber presented exactly the appearance she had presented yesterday, except that she wore a shawl. Her little light curls were as crisp as ever, and she had already her spectacles on, which made Paul wonder whether she went to bed in them. She had a cool little sitting-room of her own up there, with some books in it, and no fire. But Miss Blimber was never cold, and never sleepy.

"Now, Dombey," said Miss Blimber, "I'm going out for a constitutional."

Paul wondered what that was, and why she didn't send the footman out to get it in such unfavorable weather. But he made no observation on the subject; his attention being devoted to a little pile of new books, on which Miss Blimber appeared to have been recently engaged.

"These are yours, Dombey," said Miss Blimber.

"All of 'em, ma'am?" said Paul.

"Yes," returned Miss Blimber; "and Mr. Feeder will look you out some more very soon, if you are as studious as I expect you will be, Dombey."

"Thank you, ma'am," said Paul.

"I am going out for a constitutional," resumed Miss Blimber; "and while I am gone, that is to say, in the interval between this and breakfast, Dombey, I wish you to read over what I have marked in these books, and to tell me if you quite understand what you have got to learn. Don't lose time, Dombey, for you have none to spare, but take them down-stairs, and begin directly."

"Yes, ma'am," answered Paul.

There were so many of them, that although Paul put one hand under the bottom book, and his other hand and his chin on the top book, and hugged them all closely, the middle book slipped out before he reached the door, and then they all tumbled down on the floor. Miss Blimber said, "Oh, Dombey, Dombey, this is really very careless!" and piled them up afresh for him; and this time, by dint of balancing them with great nicety, Paul got out of the room, and down a few stairs, before two of them escaped again. But he held the rest so tight, that he only left one more on the first floor, and one in the passage; and when he had got the main body down into the schoolroom, he set off upstairs again to collect the stragglers. Having at last amassed the whole library, and climbed into his place, he fell to work, encouraged by a remark from Tozer to the effect that he "was in for it now;" which was the only interruption he received till breakfast-time. At that meal, for which he had no appetite, everything was quite as solemn and genteel as at the others; and when it was finished he followed Miss Blimber upstairs.

"Now, Dombey," said Miss Blimber, "how have you got on with those books?"

They comprised a little English, and a deal of Latin—names of things, declensions of articles and substantives, exercises thereon, and preliminary rules—a trifle of orthography, a glance at ancient history, a wink or two at modern ditto, a few tables, two or three weights and measures, and a little general information. When poor Paul had spelt out number two, he found he had no idea of number one; fragments whereof afterward obtruded themselves into number three, which slided into number four, which grafted itself on to number two. So that whether twenty Romuluses made a Remus, or *hic hæc hoc* was troy weight, or a verb always agreed with an ancient Briton, or three times four was Taurus a bull, were open questions with him.

"Oh, Dombey, Dombey!" said Miss Blimber, "this is very shocking."

"If you please," said Paul, "I think, if I might sometimes talk a little to old Glubb, I should be able to do better."

"Nonsense, Dombey," said Miss Blimber. "I couldn't hear of it. This is not the place for Glubbs of any kind. You must take the books down, I suppose, Dombey, one by one, and perfect yourself in the day's installment of subject A, before you turn at all to subject B. And now take away the top book, if you please, Dombey, and return when you are master of the theme."

Miss Blimber expressed her opinions on the subject of Paul's uninstructed state with a gloomy delight, as if she had expected this result, and were glad to find that they must be in constant communication. Paul withdrew with the top task, as he was told, and labored away at it down below: sometimes remembering every word of it, and sometimes forgetting it all, and everything else besides: until at last he ventured upstairs again to repeat the lesson, when it was nearly all driven out of his head before he began, by Miss Blimber's shutting up the book, and saying, "Go on, Dombey!" a proceeding so suggestive of the knowledge inside of her, that Paul looked upon the young lady with consternation, as a kind of learned Guy Fawkes, or artificial Bogie, stuffed full of scholastic straw.

He acquitted himself very well, nevertheless; and Miss Blimber, commending him as giving promise of getting on fast, immediately provided him with subject B; from which he passed to C, and even D before dinner. It was hard work, resuming his studies soon after dinner: and he felt giddy and confused, and drowsy and dull. But all the other young gentlemen had similar sensations, and were obliged to resume their studies too, if there were any comfort in that. It was a wonder that the great clock in the hall, instead of being constant to its first inquiry, never said, "Gentlemen, we will now resume our studies," for that phrase was often enough repeated in its neighborhood. The studies went round like a mighty wheel, and the young gentlemen were always stretched upon it.

After tea there were exercises again, and preparations for next day by candle-light. And in due course there was bed; where, but for that resumption of the studies which took place in dreams, were rest and sweet forgetfulness.

Oh, Saturdays! Oh, happy Saturdays! when Florence always came at noon, and never would, in any weather, stay away, though Mrs. Pipchin snarled and growled, and worried her bitterly. Those Saturdays were Sabbaths for at least two little Christians among all the Jews, and did the holy Sabbath work of strengthening and knitting up a brother's and a sister's love.

Not even Sunday nights—the heavy Sunday nights, whose shadow darkened the first waking burst of light on Sunday mornings—could mar those precious Saturdays. Whether it was the great sea-shore, where they sat and strolled together; or whether it was only Mrs. Pipchin's dull back room, in which she sang to him so softly, with his drowsy head upon her arm; Paul never cared. It was Florence. That was all he thought of. So, on Sunday nights, when the Doctor's dark door stood agape to swallow him up for another week, the time was come for taking leave of Florence; no one else.

Mrs. Wickam had been drafted home to the house in town, and Miss Nipper, now a smart young woman, had come down. To many a single combat with Mrs. Pipchin did Miss Nipper gallantly devote herself; and if ever Mrs. Pipchin in all her life had found her match, she had found it now. Miss Nipper threw away the scabbard the first morning she arose in Mrs. Pipchin's house. She asked and gave no quarter. She said it must be war, and war it was; and Mrs. Pipchin lived from that time in the midst of surprises, harassings, and defiances; and skirmishing attacks that came bouncing in upon her from the passage, even in unguarded moments of chops, and carried desolation to her very toast.

Miss Nipper had returned one Sunday night with Florence, from walking back with Paul to the Doctor's, when Florence took from her bosom a little piece of paper, on which she had penciled down some words.

"See here, Susan," she said. "These are the names of the little books that Paul brings home to do those long exercises with, when he is so tired. I copied them last night while he was writing."

"Don't show 'em to me, Miss Floy, if you please," returned Nipper; "I'd as soon see Mrs. Pipchin."

"I want you to buy them for me, Susan, if you will, to-morrow morning. I have money enough," said Florence.

"Why, goodness gracious me, Miss Floy," returned Miss Nipper, "how can you talk like that, when you have books upon books already, and masterses and misses a teaching of you everything continual, though my belief is that your pa, Miss Dombey, never would have learnt you nothing, never would have thought of it, unless you'd asked him—when he couldn't well refuse; but giving consent when asked, and offering when unasked, miss, is quite two things; I may not have any objections to a young man's keeping company with me, and when he puts the question, may say 'Yes,' but that's not saying, 'Would you be so kind as like me?'"

"But you can buy me the books, Susan; and you will, when you know I want them."

"Well, miss, and why do you want 'em?" replied Nipper; adding, in a lower voice, "If it was to fling at Mrs. Pipchin's head, I'd buy a cart-load."

"I think I could perhaps give Paul some help, Susan, if I had these books," said Florence, "and make the coming week a little easier to him. At least I want to try. So buy them for me, dear, and I will never forget how kind it was of you to do it!"

It must have been a harder heart than Susan Nipper's that could have rejected the little purse Florence held out with these words, or the gentle look of entreaty with which she seconded her petition. Susan put the purse in her pocket without reply, and trotted out at once upon her errand.

The books were not easy to procure; and the answer at several shops was, either that they were just out of them, or that they never kept them, or that they had had a great many last month, or that they expected a great many next week. But Susan was not easily baffled in such an enterprise; and having entrapped a white-haired youth, in a black calico apron, from a library where she was known, to accompany her in her quest, she led him such a life in going up and down, that he exerted himself to the utmost, if it were only to get rid of her; and finally enabled her to return home in triumph.

With these treasures, then, after her own daily lessons were over, Florence sat down at night to track Paul's footsteps through the thorny ways of learning; and being possessed of a naturally quick and sound capacity, and taught by that most wonderful of masters, love, it was not long before she gained upon Paul's heels, and caught and passed him.

Not a word of this was breathed to Mrs. Pipchin; but many a night when they were all in bed, and when Miss Nipper, with her hair in papers and herself asleep in some uncomfortable attitude, reposed unconscious by her side; and when the chinking ashes in the grate were cold and gray; and when the candles were burnt down and guttering out; Florence tried so hard to be a substitute for one small Dombey, that her fortitude and perseverance might have almost won her a free right to bear the name herself.

And high was her reward, when one Saturday evening, as little Paul was sitting down as usual to "resume his studies," she sat down by his side, and showed him all that was so rough, made smooth, and all that was so dark, made clear and plain, before him. It was nothing but a startled look in Paul's wan face—a flush—a smile—and then a close embrace—but God knows how her heart leaped up at this rich payment for her trouble.

"Oh, Floy!" cried her brother, "how I love you! How I love you, Floy!"

"And I you, dear!"

"Oh! I am sure of that, Floy!"

He said no more about it, but all that evening sat close by her, very quiet; and in the night he called out from his little room within hers, three or four times, that he loved her.

Regularly, after that, Florence was prepared to sit down with Paul on Saturday night, and patiently assist him through so much as they could anticipate together of his next week's work. The cheering thought that he was laboring on where Florence had just toiled before him would, of itself, have been a stimulant to Paul in the perpetual resumption of his studies; but, coupled with the actual lightening of his load, consequent on this assistance, it saved him, possibly, from sinking underneath the burden which the fair Cornelia Blimber piled upon his back.

It was not that Miss Blimber meant to be too hard upon him, or that Doctor Blimber meant to bear too heavily on the young gentlemen in general. Cornelia merely held the faith in which she had been bred; and the Doctor, in some partial confusion of his ideas, regarded the young gentlemen as if they were all Doctors, and were born grown up. Comforted by the applause of the young gentlemen's nearest relations, and urged on by their blind vanity and ill-considered haste, it would have been strange if Doctor Blimber had discovered his mistake, or trimmed his swelling sails to any other tack.

Thus in the case of Paul. When Doctor Blimber said he made great progress, and was naturally clever, Mr. Dombey was more bent than ever on his being forced and crammed. In the case of Briggs, when Doctor Blimber reported that he did not make great progress yet, and was not naturally clever, Briggs senior was inexorable in the same purpose. In short, however high and false the temperature at which the Doctor kept his hot-house, the owners of the plants were always ready to lend a helping hand at the bellows, and to stir the fire.

Such spirits as he had in the outset, Paul soon lost, of course. But he retained all that was strange, and old, and thoughtful in his character; and, under circumstances so favorable to the development of those tendencies, became even more strange, and old, and thoughtful than before.

The only difference was, that he kept his character to himself. He grew more thoughtful and reserved every day; and had no such curiosity in any living member of the Doctor's household as he had had in Mrs. Pipchin. He loved to be alone; and, in those short intervals when he was not occupied with his books, liked nothing so well as wandering about the house by himself, or sitting on the stairs, listening to the great clock in the hall. He was intimate with all the paper-hanging in the house; saw things that no one else saw in the patterns; found out miniature tigers and lions running up the bedroom walls, and squinting faces leering in the squares and diamonds of the floor-cloth.

The solitary child lived on, surrounded by this arabesque work of his musing fancy, and no one understood him. Mrs. Blimber thought him "odd," and sometimes the servants said among themselves that little Dombey "moped;" but that was all.

Unless young Toots had some idea on the subject, to the expression of which he was wholly unequal. Ideas, like ghosts (according to the common notion of ghosts), must be spoken to a little before they will explain themselves; and Toots had long left off asking any questions of his own mind. Some mist there may have been, issuing from that leaden casket, his cranium, which, if it could have taken shape and form, would have become a genie; but it could not; and it only so far followed the example of the smoke in the Arabian story as to roll out in a thick cloud, and there hang and hover. But it left a little figure visible upon a lonely shore, and Toots was always staring at it.

"How are you?" he would say to Paul fifty times a day.

"Quite well, sir, thank you," Paul would answer.

"Shake hands," would be Toots's next advance.

Which Paul, of course, would immediately do. Mr. Toots generally said again, after a long interval of staring and hard breathing, "How are you?" To which Paul again replied, "Quite well, sir, thank you."

One evening Mr. Toots was sitting at his desk, oppressed by correspondence, when a great purpose seemed to flash upon him. He laid down his pen, and went off to seek Paul, whom he found at last, after a long search, looking through the window of his little bedroom.

"I say!" cried Toots, speaking the moment he entered the room, lest he should forget it; "what do you think about?"

"Oh! I think about a great many things," replied Paul.

"Do you, though?" said Toots, appearing to consider that fact in itself surprising.

"If you had to die—" said Paul, looking up into his face.

Mr. Toots started, and seemed much disturbed.

"—Don't you think you would rather die on a moonlight night, when the sky was quite clear, and the wind blowing, as it did last night?"

Mr. Toots said, looking doubtfully at Paul, and shaking his head, that he didn't know about that.

"Not blowing, at least," said Paul, "but sounding in the air like the sea sounds in the shells. It was a beautiful night. When I had listened to the water for a long time, I got up and looked out. There was a boat over there, in the full light of the moon; a boat with a sail."

The child looked at him so steadfastly, and spoke so earnestly that Mr. Toots, feeling himself called upon to say something about this boat, said, "Smugglers." But, with an impartial remembrance of there being two sides to every question, he added, "or Preventive."

"A boat with a sail," repeated Paul, "in the full light of the moon. The sail like an arm, all silver. It went away into the distance, and what do you think it seemed to do as it moved with the waves?"

"Pitch," said Mr. Toots.

"It seemed to beckon," said the child, "to beckon me to come! There she is! There she is!"

Toots was almost beside himself with dismay at this sudden exclamation, after what had gone before, and cried, "Who?"

"My sister Florence!" cried Paul, "looking up here, and waving her hand. She sees me—she sees me! Good-night, dear, good-night, good-night!"

His quick transition to a state of unbounded pleasure, as he stood at his window, kissing and clapping his hands, and the way in which the light retreated from his features as she passed out of his view, and left a patient melancholy on the little face, were too remarkable wholly to escape even Toots's notice. Their interview being interrupted at this moment by a visit from Mrs. Pipchin, who usually brought her black skirts to bear upon Paul just before dusk, once or twice a week, Toots had no opportunity of improving the occasion: but it left so marked an impression on his mind, that he twice returned, after having exchanged the usual salutations, to ask Mrs. Pipchin how she did. This the irascible old lady conceived to be a deeply-devised and long-meditated insult, originating in the diabolical invention of the weak-eyed young man down-stairs, against whom she accordingly lodged a formal complaint with Doctor Blimber that very night; who mentioned to the young man that if he ever did it again, he should be obliged to part with him.

The evenings being longer now, Paul stole up to his window every evening to look out for Florence. She always passed and repassed at a certain time until she saw him; and their mutual recognition was a gleam of sunshine in Paul's daily life. Often, after dark, one other figure walked alone before the Doctor's house. He rarely joined them on the Saturday now. He could not bear it. He would rather come unrecognized, and look up at the windows where his son was qualifying for a man; and wait, and watch, and plan, and hope.

Oh! could he but have seen, or seen as others did, the slight, spare boy above, watching the waves and clouds at twilight with his earnest eyes, and breasting the window of his solitary cage when birds flew by, as if he would have emulated them, and soared away!

. . . . . .

When the Midsummer vacation approached, no indecent manifestations of joy were exhibited by the leaden-eyed young gentlemen assembled at Doctor Blimber's. Any such violent expression as "breaking-up" would have been quite inapplicable to that polite establishment. The young gentlemen oozed away, semi-annually, to their own homes; but they never broke up. They would have scorned the action.

. . . .

They were within two or three weeks of the holidays, when, one day, Cornelia Blimber called Paul into her room, and said, "Dombey, I am going to send home your analysis."

"Thank you, ma'am," returned Paul.

"You know what I mean, do you, Dombey?" inquired Miss Blimber, looking hard at him through the spectacles.

"No, ma'am," said Paul.

"Dombey, Dombey," said Miss Blimber, "I begin to be afraid you are a sad boy. When you don't know the meaning of an expression, why don't you seek for information?"

"Mrs. Pipchin told me I wasn't to ask questions," returned Paul.

"I must beg you not to mention Mrs. Pipchin to me on any account, Dombey," returned Miss Blimber. "I couldn't think of allowing it. The course of study here is very far removed from anything of that sort. A repetition of such allusions would make it necessary for me to request to hear without a mistake, before breakfast-time to-morrow morning, from *Verbum personale* down to *simillima cygno*."

"I didn't mean, ma'am—" began little Paul.

"I must trouble you not to tell me that you didn't mean, if you please, Dombey," said Miss Blimber, who preserved an awful politeness in her admonitions. "That is a line of argument I couldn't dream of permitting."

Paul felt it safest to say nothing at all, so he only looked at Miss Blimber's spectacles. Miss Blimber, having shaken her head at him gravely, referred to a paper lying before her.

"'Analysis of the character of P. Dombey.' If my recollection serves me," said Miss Blimber, breaking off, "the word analysis, as opposed to synthesis, is thus defined by Walker: 'The resolution of an object, whether of the senses or of the intellect, into its first elements.' As opposed to synthesis, you observe. *Now* you know what analysis is, Dombey."

Dombey didn't seem to be absolutely blinded by the light let in upon his intellect, but he made Miss Blimber a little bow.

"'Analysis,'" resumed Miss Blimber, casting her eye over the paper, "'of the character of P. Dombey. I find that the natural capacity of Dombey is extremely good: and that his general disposition to study may be stated in an equal ratio. Thus, taking eight as our standard and highest number, I find these qualities in Dombey stated at six three-fourths!'"

Miss Blimber paused to see how Paul received this news. Being undecided whether six three-fourths meant six pounds fifteen, or sixpence three farthings, or six foot three, or three-quarters past six, or six somethings that he hadn't learnt yet, with three unknown something else's over, Paul rubbed his hands and looked straight at Miss Blimber. It happened to answer as well as anything else he could have done; and Cornelia proceeded:

"'Violence two. Selfishness two. Inclination to low company, as evinced in the case of a person named Glubb, originally seven, but since reduced. Gentlemanly demeanor four, and improving with advancing years.' Now, what I particularly wish to call your attention to, Dombey, is the general observation at the close of this analysis."

Paul set himself to follow it with great care.

"'It may be generally observed of Dombey,'" said Miss Blimber, reading in a loud voice, and at every second word directing her spectacles toward the figure before her: "'that his abilities and inclinations are good, and that he has made as much progress as under the circumstances could have been expected. But it is to be lamented of this young gentleman that he is singular (what is usually termed old-fashioned) in his character and conduct, and that, without presenting anything in either which distinctly calls for reprobation, he is often very unlike other young gentlemen of his age and social position.' Now, Dombey," said Miss Blimber, laying down the paper, "do you understand that?"

"I think I do, ma'am," said Paul.

"This analysis, you see, Dombey," Miss Blimber continued, "is going to be sent home to your respected parent. It will naturally be very painful to him to find that you are singular in your character and conduct. It is naturally painful to us; for we can't like you, you know, Dombey, as well as we could wish."

She touched the child upon a tender point. He had secretly become more and more solicitous from day to day, as the time of his departure drew more near, that all the house should like him. For some hidden reason, very imperfectly understood by himself—if understood at all—he felt a gradually increasing impulse of affection toward almost everything and everybody in the place. He could not bear to think that they would be quite indifferent to him when he was gone. He wanted them to remember him kindly; and he had made it his business even to conciliate a great, hoarse, shaggy dog, chained up at the back of the house, who had previously been the terror of his life, that even he might miss him when he was no longer there.

Little thinking that in this he only showed again the difference between himself and his compeers, poor tiny Paul set it forth to Miss Blimber as well as he could, and begged her, in despite of the official analysis, to have the goodness to try and like him. To Mrs. Blimber, who had joined them, he preferred the same petition; and when that lady could not forbear, even in his presence, from giving utterance to her often-repeated opinion, that he was an odd child, Paul told her that he was sure she was quite right; that he thought it must be his bones, but he didn't know; and that he hoped she would overlook it, for he was fond of them all.

"Not so fond," said Paul, with a mixture of timidity and perfect frankness, which was one of the most peculiar and most engaging qualities of the child, "not so fond as I am of Florence, of course; that could never be. You couldn't expect that, could you, ma'am?"

"Oh! the old-fashioned little soul!" cried Mrs. Blimber in a whisper.

"But I like everybody here very much," pursued Paul, "and I should grieve to go away, and think that any one was glad that I was gone, or didn't care."

Mrs. Blimber was now quite sure that Paul was the oddest child in the world; and when she told the Doctor what had passed, the Doctor did not controvert his wife's opinion. But he said, as he had said before, when Paul first came, that study would do much; and he also said, as he had said on that occasion, "Bring him on, Cornelia! Bring him on!"

Cornelia had always brought him on as vigorously as she could; and Paul had had a hard life of it. But, over and above the getting through his tasks, he had long had another purpose always present to him, and to which he still held fast. It was, to be a gentle, useful, quiet little fellow, always striving to secure the love and attachment of the rest; and though he was yet often to be seen at his old post on the stairs, or watching the waves and clouds from his solitary window, he was oftener found, too, among the other boys, modestly rendering them some little voluntary service. Thus it came to pass that, even among those rigid and absorbed young anchorites who mortified themselves beneath the roof of Doctor Blimber, Paul was an object of general interest; a fragile little plaything that they all liked, and that no one would have thought of treating roughly. But he could not change his nature, or rewrite the analysis; and so they all agreed that Dombey was old-fashioned.

. . . .

Paul had never risen from his little bed. He lay there, listening to the noises in the street, quite tranquilly; not caring much how the time went, but watching it and watching everything about him, with observing eyes.

When the sunbeams struck into his room through the rustling blinds, and quivered on the opposite wall like golden water, he knew that evening was coming on, and that the sky was red and beautiful. As the reflection died away, and a gloom went creeping up the wall, he watched it deepen, deepen, deepen into night. Then he thought how the long streets were dotted with lamps, and how the peaceful stars were shining overhead. His fancy had a strange tendency to wander to the river, which he knew was flowing through the great city: and now he thought how black it was, and how deep it would look, reflecting the hosts of stars—and more than all, how steadily it rolled away to meet the sea.

As it grew later in the night, and footsteps in the street became so rare that he could hear them coming, count them as they paused, and lose them in the hollow distance, he would lie and watch the many-colored ring about the candle, and wait patiently for day. His only trouble was, the swift and rapid river. He felt forced, sometimes, to try to stop it—to stem it with his childish hands—or choke its way with sand—and when he saw it coming on, resistless, he cried out. But a word from Florence, who was always at his side, restored him to himself; and leaning his poor head upon her breast, he told Floy of his dream, and smiled.

When day began to dawn again, he watched for the sun; and when its cheerful light began to sparkle in the room, he pictured to himself—pictured! he saw—the high church tower rising up into the morning sky, the town reviving, waking, starting into life once more, the river glistening as it rolled (but rolling fast as ever), and the country bright with dew. Familiar sounds and cries came by degrees into the street below; the servants in the house were roused and busy; faces looked in at the door, and voices asked his attendants softly how he was. Paul always answered for himself, "I am better. I am a great deal better, thank you! Tell papa so!"

By little and little, he got tired of the bustle of the day, the noise of carriages and carts, and people passing and re-passing; and would fall asleep, or be troubled with a restless and uneasy sense again—the child could hardly tell whether this were in his sleeping or his waking moments—of that rushing river. "Why, will it never stop, Floy?" he would sometimes ask her. "It is bearing me away, I think!"

But Floy could always soothe and reassure him; and it was his daily delight to make her lay her head down on his pillow, and take some rest.

"You are always watching me, Floy. Let me watch *you*, now!"

They would prop him up with cushions in a corner of his bed, and there he would recline the while she lay beside him, bending forward oftentimes to kiss her, and whispering to those who were near that she was tired, and how she had sat up so many nights beside him.

Thus, the flush of the day, in its heat and light, would gradually decline; and again the golden water would be dancing on the wall.

He was visited by as many as three grave doctors—they used to assemble down-stairs, and come up together—and the room was so quiet, and Paul was so observant of them (though he never asked of anybody what they said), that he even knew the difference in the sound of their watches. But his interest centered in Sir Parker Peps, who always took his seat on the side of the bed. For Paul had heard them say, long ago, that that gentleman had been with his mamma when she clasped Florence in her arms, and died. And he could not forget it, now. He liked him for it. He was not afraid.

The people round him changed as unaccountably as on that first night at Doctor Blimber's—except Florence; Florence never changed—and what had been Sir Parker Peps was now his father, sitting with his head upon his hand. Old Mrs.

Pipchin, dozing in an easy-chair, often changed to Miss Tox, or his aunt; and Paul was quite content to shut his eyes again, and see what happened next without emotion. But this figure with its head upon its hand returned so often, and remained so long, and sat so still and solemn, never speaking, never being spoken to, and rarely lifting up its face, that Paul began to wonder languidly if it were real; and in the night-time saw it sitting there with fear.

"Floy!" he said. "What *is* that?"

"Where, dearest?"

"There! at the bottom of the bed."

"There's nothing there, except papa!"

The figure lifted up its head, and rose, and coming to the bedside, said: "My own boy! Don't you know me?"

Paul looked it in the face, and thought, was this his father? But the face, so altered to his thinking, thrilled while he gazed, as if it were in pain; and before he could reach out both his hands to take it between them, and draw it toward him, the figure turned away quickly from the little bed, and went out at the door.

Paul looked at Florence with a fluttering heart, but he knew what she was going to say, and stopped her with his face against her lips. The next time he observed the figure sitting at the bottom of the bed, he called to it.

"Don't be so sorry for me, dear papa! Indeed, I am quite happy!"

His father coming, and bending down to him—which he did quickly, and without first pausing by the bedside—Paul held him round the neck, and repeated those words to him several times, and very earnestly; and Paul never saw him in his room again at any time, whether it were day or night, but he called out, "Don't be so sorry for me! Indeed, I am quite happy!" This was the beginning of his always saying in the morning that he was a great deal better, and that they were to tell his father so.

How many times the golden water danced upon the wall;

how many nights the dark, dark river rolled toward the sea in spite of him; Paul never counted, never sought to know. If their kindness, or his sense of it, could have increased, they were more kind, and he more grateful, every day; but whether they were many days or few, appeared of little moment now to the gentle boy.

One night he had been thinking of his mother, and her picture in the drawing-room down-stairs, and had thought she must have loved sweet Florence better than his father did, to have held her in her arms when she felt that she was dying—for even he, her brother, who had such dear love for her, could have no greater wish than that. The train of thought suggested to him to inquire if he had ever seen his mother; for he could not remember whether they had told him yes or no, the river running very fast, and confusing his mind.

"Floy, did I ever see mamma?"

"No, darling: why?"

"Did I never see any kind face, like mamma's, looking at me when I was a baby, Floy?"

He asked incredulously, as if he had some vision of a face before him.

"Oh yes, dear!"

"Whose, Floy?"

"Your old nurse's. Often."

"And where is my old nurse?" said Paul. "Is she dead too? Floy, are we *all* dead, except you?"

There was a hurry in the room for an instant—longer, perhaps; but it seemed no more—then all was still again; and Florence, with her face quite colorless, but smiling, held his head upon her arm. Her arm trembled very much.

"Show me that old nurse, Floy, if you please!"

"She is not here, darling. She shall come to-morrow."

"Thank you, Floy!"

Paul closed his eyes with those words, and fell asleep. When he awoke the sun was high, and the broad day was clear and warm. He lay a little, looking at the windows, which were open, and the curtains, rustling in the air, and waving to and fro: then he said, "Floy, is it to-morrow? Is she come?"

Some one seemed to go in quest of her. Perhaps it was Susan. Paul thought he heard her telling him, when he had closed his eyes again, that she would soon be back; but he did not open them to see. She kept her word—perhaps she had never been away—but the next thing that happened was a noise of footsteps on the stairs, and then Paul woke—woke, mind and body—and sat upright in his bed. He saw them now about him. There was no gray mist before them, as there had been sometimes in the night. He knew them every one, and called them by their names.

"And who is this? Is this my old nurse?" said the child, regarding with a radiant smile a figure coming in.

Yes, yes. No other stranger would have shed those tears at sight of him, and called him her dear boy, her pretty boy, her own poor blighted child. No other woman would have stooped down by his bed, and taken up his wasted hand, and put it to her lips and breast, as one who had some right to fondle it. No other woman would have so forgotten everybody there but him and Floy, and been so full of tenderness and pity.

"Floy! this is a kind, good face!" said Paul. "I am glad to see it again. Don't go away, old nurse! Stay here!"

His senses were all quickened, and he heard a name he knew.

"Who was that who said 'Walter'?" he asked, looking round. "Some one said 'Walter.' Is he here? I should like to see him very much."

Nobody replied directly; but his father soon said to Susan, "Call him back, then: let him come up!" After a short pause of expectation, during which he looked with smiling interest and wonder on his nurse, and saw that she had not forgotten Floy, Walter was brought into the room. His open face and manner, and his cheerful eyes, had always made him a favorite with Paul; and when Paul saw him, he stretched out his hand, and said, "Good-by!"

"Good-by, my child!" cried Mrs. Pipchin, hurrying to his bed's head. "Not good-by?"

For an instant Paul looked at her with the wistful face with which he had so often gazed upon her in his corner by the fire. "Ah, yes," he said placidly, "good-by! Walter dear, good-by!"—turning his head to where he stood, and putting out his hand again. "Where is papa?"

He felt his father's breath upon his cheek before the words had parted from his lips.

"Remember Walter, dear papa," he whispered, looking in his face. "Remember Walter. I was fond of Walter." The feeble hand waved in the air as if it cried "Good-by!" to Walter once again.

"Now lay me down," he said, "and, Floy, come close to me, and let me see you!"

Sister and brother wound their arms around each other, and the golden light came streaming in, and fell upon them, locked together.

"How fast the river runs, between its green banks and the rushes, Floy! But it's very near the sea. I hear the waves! They always said so."

Presently he told her that the motion of the boat upon the stream was lulling him to rest. How green the banks were now, how bright the flowers growing on them, and how tall the rushes! Now the boat was out at sea, but gliding smoothly on. And now there was a shore before him. Who stood on the bank?——

He put his hands together, as he had been used to do at his prayers. He did not remove his arms to do it; but they saw him fold them so, behind her neck.

"Mamma is like you, Floy. I know her by the face! But tell them that the print upon the stairs at school is not divine enough. The light about the head is shining on me as I go!"

The golden ripple on the wall came back again, and nothing else stirred in the room. The old, old fashion! The fashion that came in with our first garments, and will last unchanged until our race has run its course, and the wide firmament is rolled up like a scroll. The old, old fashion—Death!

Oh, thank GOD, all who see it, for that older fashion yet, of Immortality! And look upon us, angels of young children, with regards not quite estranged when the swift river bears us to the ocean!

The School at Salem House

(From "David Copperfield")

A short walk brought us—I mean the Master and me—to Salem House, which was inclosed within a high brick wall, and looked very dull. Over a door in this wall was a board with SALEM HOUSE upon it; and through a grating in this door we were surveyed, when we rang the bell, by a surly face, which I found, on the door being opened, belonged to a stout man with a bull-neck, a wooden leg, overhanging temples, and his hair cut close all round his head.

"The new boy," said the Master.

The man with the wooden leg eyed me all over—it didn't take long, for there was not much of me—and locked the gate behind us and took out the key. We were going up to the house, among some dark heavy trees, when he called after my conductor.

"Hallo!"

We looked back, and he was standing at the door of a little lodge, where he lived, with a pair of boots in his hand.

"Here! The cobbler's been," he said, "since you've been out, Mr. Mell, and he says he can't mend 'em any more. He says there ain't a bit of the original boot left, and he wonders you expect it."

With these words he threw the boots toward Mr. Mell, who went back a few paces to pick them up, and looked at them (very disconsolately, I was afraid) as we went on together. I observed then, for the first time, that the boots he had on were a good deal the worse for wear, and that his stocking was just breaking out in one place, like a bud.

Salem House was a square brick building with wings, of a bare and unfurnished appearance. All about it was so very quiet, that I said to Mr. Mell I supposed the boys were out; but he seemed surprised at my not knowing that it was holiday-time. That all the boys were at their several homes. That Mr. Creakle, the proprietor, was down by the sea-side with Mrs. and Miss Creakle. And that I was sent in holiday-time as a punishment for my misdoing. All of which he explained to me as we went along.

I gazed upon the schoolroom into which he took me, as the most forlorn and desolate place I had ever seen. I see it now. A long room, with three long rows of desks, and six of forms, and bristling all round with pegs for hats and slates. Scraps of old copy-books and exercises litter the dirty floor. Some silkworms' houses, made of the same materials, are scattered over the desks. Two miserable little white mice, left behind by their owner, are running up and down in a fusty castle made of pasteboard and wire, looking in all the corners with their red eyes for anything to eat. A bird, in a cage very little bigger than himself, makes a mournful rattle now and then in hopping on his perch, two inches high, or dropping from it; but neither sings nor chirps. There is a strange unwholesome smell upon the room, like mildewed corduroys, sweet apples wanting air, and rotten books. There could not well be more ink splashed about it, if it had been roofless from its first construction, and the skies had rained, snowed, hailed, and blown ink through the varying seasons of the year.

Mr. Mell having left me while he took his irreparable boots upstairs, I went softly to the upper end of the room, observing all this as I crept along. Suddenly I came upon a pasteboard placard, beautifully written, which was lying on the desk, and bore these words: "*Take care of him. He bites.*"

I got upon the desk immediately, apprehensive of at least a great dog underneath. But, though I looked all round with anxious eyes, I could see nothing of him. I was still engaged in peering about when Mr. Mell came back and asked me what I did up there.

"I beg your pardon, sir," says I; "if you please, I'm looking for the dog."

"Dog?" says he. "What dog?"

"Isn't it a dog, sir?"

"Isn't what a dog?"

"That's to be taken care of, sir; that bites?"

"No, Copperfield," says he, gravely, "that's not a dog. That's a boy. My instructions are, Copperfield, to put this placard on your back.[1] I am sorry to make such a beginning with you, but I must do it."

With that he took me down, and tied the placard, which was neatly constructed for the purpose, on my shoulders like a knapsack; and wherever I went afterward, I had the consolation of carrying it.

What I suffered from that placard nobody can imagine. Whether it was possible for people to see me or not, I always fancied that somebody was reading it. It was no relief to turn round and find nobody; for wherever my back was, there I imagined somebody always to be. That cruel man with the wooden leg aggravated my sufferings. He was in authority, and if he ever saw me leaning against a tree, or a wall, or the house, he roared out from his lodge-door in a stupendous voice, "Hallo, you sir! You Copperfield! Show that badge conspicuous, or I'll report you." The playground was a bare graveled yard, open to all the back of the house and the offices; and I knew that the servants read it, and the butcher read it, and the baker read it; that everybody, in a word, who came backward and forward to the house of a morning when I was ordered to walk there, read that I was to be taken care of, for I bit. I recollect that I positively began to have a dread of myself as a kind of wild boy who did bite.

[1] The boy had bitten the finger of his step-father, while being cruelly punished by the latter.

There was an old door in this playground, on which the boys had a custom of carving their names. It was completely covered with such inscriptions. In my dread of the end of the vacation and their coming back, I could not read a boy's name without inquiring in what tone and with what emphasis *he* would read, "Take care of him. He bites." There was one boy —a certain J. Steerforth—who cut his name very deep and very often, who, I conceived, would read it in a rather strong voice, and afterward pull my hair. There was another boy, one Tommy Traddles, who I dreaded would make game of it, and pretend to be dreadfully frightened of me. There was a third, George Demple, who I fancied would sing it. I have looked, a little shrinking creature, at that door, until the owners of all the names—there were five-and-forty of them in the school then, Mr. Mell said—seemed to send me to Coventry by general acclamation, and to cry out, each in his own way, "Take care of him. He bites!"

It was the same with the places at the desks and forms. It was the same with the groves of deserted bedsteads I peeped at, on my way to, and when I was in, my own bed. I remember dreaming night after night, of being with my mother as she used to be, or of going to a party at Mr. Peggotty's, or of traveling outside the stage coach, or of dining again with my unfortunate friend the waiter, and in all these circumstances making people scream and stare, by the unhappy disclosure that I had nothing on but my little nightshirt and that placard.

In the monotony of my life, and in my constant apprehension of the re-opening of the school, it was such an insupportable affliction! I had long tasks every day to do with Mr. Mell; but I did them, there being no Mr. and Miss Murdstone here, and got through them without disgrace. Before, and after them, I walked about—supervised, as I have mentioned, by the man with the wooden leg. How vividly I call to mind the damp about the house, the green cracked flagstone in the court, an old leaky water-butt, and the discolored trunks of some of the grim trees, which seemed to have dripped more in the rain than other trees, and to have blown less in the sun! At one we dined, Mr. Mell and I, at the upper end of a long bare dining-room, full of deal-tables, and smelling of fat. Then, we had more tasks until tea, which Mr. Mell drank out of a blue tea-cup, and I out of a tin pot. All day long, and until seven or eight in the evening Mr. Mell, at his own detached desk in the schoolroom, worked hard with pen, ink, ruler, books, and writing-paper, making out the bills (as I found) for last half-year. When he had put up his things for the night, he took out his flute, and blew at it, until I almost thought he would gradually blow his whole being into the large hole at the top, and ooze away at the keys.

I picture my small self in the dimly-lighted rooms, sitting with my head upon my hand, listening to the doleful performance of Mr. Mell, and conning to-morrow's lessons. I picture myself with my books shut up, still listening to the doleful performance of Mr. Mell, and listening through it to what it used to be at home, and to the blowing of the wind on Yarmouth flats, and feeling very sad and solitary. I picture myself going up to bed, among the unused rooms, and sitting on my bedside crying for a comfortable word from Peggotty. I picture myself coming down-stairs in the morning, and looking through a long ghastly gash of a staircase window at the school-bell hanging on the top of an outhouse with a weather-cock above it, and dreading the time when it shall ring J. Steerforth and the rest to work. Such time is only second, in my foreboding apprehensions, to the time when the man with the wooden leg shall unlock the rusty gate to give admission to the awful Mr. Creakle. I cannot think I was a very dangerous character in any of these aspects, but in all of them I carried the same warning on my back. Mr. Mell never said much to me, but he was never harsh to me. I suppose we were company to each other, without talking. I forgot to mention that he would talk to himself sometimes, and grin, and clinch his fist, and grind his teeth, and pull his hair in an unaccountable manner. But he had these peculiarities. At first they frightened me, though I soon got used to them.

We led this life about a month, when the man with the wooden leg began to stump about with a mop and bucket of water, from which I inferred that preparations were making to receive Mr. Creakle and the boys. I was not mistaken, for the mop came into the schoolroom before long, and turned out Mr. Mell and me, who lived where we could, and got on how we could, for some days, during which we were always in the way of two or three young women, who had rarely shown themselves before, and were so continually in the midst of dust that I sneezed almost as much as if Salem House had been a great snuff-box.

One day I was informed by Mr. Mell that Mr. Creakle would be home that evening. In the evening, after tea, I heard that he was come. Before bed-time I was fetched by the man with the wooden leg to appear before him.

Mr. Creakle's part of the house was a good deal more comfortable than ours, and he had a snug bit of garden that looked pleasant after the dusty playground, which was such a desert in miniature that I thought no one but a camel or a dromedary could have felt at home in it. It seemed to me a bold thing even to take notice that the passage looked comfortable, as I went on my way, trembling, to Mr. Creakle's presence, which so abashed me, when I was ushered into it, that I hardly saw Mrs. Creakle or Miss Creakle (who were both there, in the parlor), or anything but Mr. Creakle, a stout gentleman, with a bunch of watch-chain and seals, in an arm-chair, with a tumbler and bottle beside him.

"So!" said Mr. Creakle. "This is the young gentleman whose teeth are to be filed! Turn him round."

The wooden-legged man turned me about so as to exhibit the placard; and having afforded time for a full survey of it, turned me about again, with my face to Mr. Creakle, and posted himself at Mr. Creakle's side. Mr. Creakle's face was fiery, and his eyes were small and deep in his head; he had thick veins in his forehead, a little nose, and a large chin. He was bald on the top of his head, and had some thin wet-looking hair, that was just turning gray, brushed across each temple, so that the two sides interlaced on his forehead. But the circumstance about him which impressed me most, was that he had no voice, but spoke in a whisper. The exertion this cost him, or the consciousness of talking in that feeble way, made his angry face so much more angry, and his thick veins so much thicker, when he spoke, that I am not surprised, on looking back, at this peculiarity striking me as his chief one.

"Now," said Mr. Creakle, "what's the report of this boy?"

"There's nothing against him yet," returned the man with the wooden leg. "There has been no opportunity."

I thought Mr. Creakle was disappointed. I thought that Mrs. Creakle and Miss Creakle (at whom I now glanced for the first time, and who were, both, thin and quiet) were not disappointed.

"Come here, sir!" said Mr. Creakle, beckoning to me.

"Come here!" said the man with the wooden leg, repeating the gesture.

"I have the happiness of knowing your father-in-law," whispered Mr. Creakle, taking me by the ear; "and a worthy man he is, and a man of a strong character. He knows me, and I know him. Do *you* know me? Hey?" said Mr. Creakle, pinching my ear with ferocious playfulness.

"Not yet, sir," I said, flinching with the pain.

"Not yet? Hey?" repeated Mr. Creakle. "But you will soon. Hey?"

"You will soon. Hey?" repeated the man with the wooden leg. I afterward found that he generally acted, with his strong voice, as Mr. Creakle's interpreter to the boys.

I was very much frightened, and said I hoped so, if he pleased. I felt, all this while, as if my ear were blazing; he pinched it so hard.

"I'll tell you what I am," whispered Mr. Creakle, letting it go at last, with a screw at parting that brought the water into my eyes. "I'm a Tartar."

"A Tartar," said the man with the wooden leg.

"When I say I'll do a thing, I do it," said Mr. Creakle; "and when I say I will have a thing done, I will have it done."

"Will have a thing done, I will have it done," repeated the man with the wooden leg.

"I am a determined character," said Mr. Creakle. "That's what I am. I do my duty; that's what *I* do. My flesh and blood," he looked at Mrs. Creakle as he said this, "when it rises against me, is not my flesh and blood. I discard it. Has that fellow," to the man with the wooden leg, "been here again?"

"No," was the answer.

"No," said Mr. Creakle. "He knows better. He knows me. Let him keep away. I say let him keep away," said Mr. Creakle, striking his hand upon the table, and looking at Mrs. Creakle, "for he knows me. Now you have begun to know me, too, my young friend, and you may go. Take him away."

I was very glad to be ordered away, for Mrs. and Miss Creakle were both wiping their eyes, and I felt as uncomfortable for them as I did for myself. But I had a petition on my mind which concerned me so nearly, that I couldn't help saying, though I wondered at my own courage:

"If you please, sir——"

Mr. Creakle whispered: "Hah! What's this?" and bent his eyes upon me, as if he would have burnt me up with them.

"If you please, sir," I faltered, "if I might be allowed (I am very sorry, indeed, sir, for what I did) to take this writing off, before the boys came back."

Whether Mr. Creakle was in earnest, or whether he only did it to frighten me, I don't know, but he made a burst out of his chair, before which I precipitately retreated, without waiting for the escort of the man with the wooden leg, and never once stopped until I reached my own bedroom, where, finding I was not pursued, I went to bed, as it was time, and lay quaking, for a couple of hours.

Next morning Mr. Sharp came back. Mr. Sharp was the first master, and superior to Mr. Mell. Mr. Mell took his meals with the boys, but Mr. Sharp dined and supped at Mr. Creakle's table. He was a limp, delicate-looking gentleman, I thought, with a good deal of nose, and a way of carrying his head on one side, as if it were a little too heavy for him. His hair was very smooth and wavy; but I was informed by the very first boy who came back that it was a wig (a second-hand one *he* said), and that Mr. Sharp went out every Saturday afternoon to get it curled.

It was no other than Tommy Traddles who gave me this piece of intelligence. He was the first boy who returned. He introduced himself by informing me that I should find his name on the right-hand corner of the gate, over the top bolt; upon that I said "Traddles?" to which he replied, "The same," and then he asked me for a full account of myself and family.

It was a happy circumstance for me that Traddles came back first. He enjoyed my placard so much, that he saved me from the embarrassment of either disclosure or concealment, by presenting me to every other boy who came back, great or small, immediately on his arrival, in this form of introduction, "Look here! Here's a game!" Happily, too, the greater part of the boys came back low spirited, and were not so boisterous at my expense as I had expected. Some of them certainly did dance about me like wild Indians, and the greater part could not resist the temptation of pretending that I was a dog, and patting and smoothing me, lest I should bite, and saying, "Lie down, sir!" and calling me Towser. This was naturally confusing, among so many strangers, and cost me some tears, but on the whole, it was much better than I had anticipated.

I was not considered as being formally received into the school, however, until J. Steerforth arrived. Before this boy, who was reputed to be a great scholar, and was very good-looking, and at least half a dozen years my senior, I was carried as before a magistrate. He inquired, under a shed in the playground, into the particulars of my punishment, and was pleased to express his opinion that it was a "jolly shame," for which I became bound to him ever afterward.

"What money have you got, Copperfield?" he said, walking aside with me when he had disposed of my affair in these terms.

I told him seven shillings.

"You had better give it to me to take care of," he said. "At least you can if you like. You needn't if you don't like."

I hastened to comply with his friendly suggestion, and opening Peggotty's purse, turned it upside down into his hand.

"Do you want to spend anything now?" he asked me.

"No, thank you," I replied.

"You can, if you like, you know," said Steerforth. "Say the word."

"No, thank you, sir," I repeated.

"Perhaps you'd like to spend a couple of shillings or so, in a bottle of currant wine by and by, up in the bedroom?" said Steerforth. "You belong to my bedroom, I find."

It certainly had not occurred to me before, but I said, Yes, I should like that.

"Very good," said Steerforth. "You'll be glad to spend another shilling or so, in almond cakes, I dare say?"

I said, Yes, I should like that, too.

"And another shilling or so in biscuits, and another in fruits, eh?" said Steerforth. "I say, young Copperfield, you're going it!"

I smiled because he smiled, but I was a little troubled in my mind, too.

"Well!" said Steerforth, "We must make it stretch as far as we can; that's all. I'll do the best in my power for you. I can go out when I like, and I'll smuggle the prog in." With these words he put the money in his pocket, and kindly told me not to make myself uneasy; he would take care it should be all right.

He was as good as his word, if that were all right which I had a secret misgiving was nearly all wrong—for I feared it was a waste of my mother's two half-crowns—though I had preserved the piece of paper they were wrapped in, which was a precious saving. When we went upstairs to bed, he produced the whole seven shillings' worth, and laid it out on my bed in the moonlight, saying:

"There you are, young Copperfield, and a royal spread you've got."

I couldn't think of doing the honors of the feast, at my time of life, while he was by; my hand shook at the very thought of it. I begged him to do me the favor of presiding; and my request being seconded by the other boys who were in that room, he acceded to it, and sat upon my pillow, handing round the viands—with perfect fairness, I must say—and dispensing the currant-wine in a little glass without a foot, which was his own property. As to me, I sat on his left hand, and the rest were grouped about us, on the nearest beds and on the floor.

How well I recollect our sitting there, talking in whispers; or their talking, and my respectfully listening, I ought rather to say; the moonlight falling a little way into the room, through the window, painting a pale window on the floor, and the greater part of us in shadow, except when Steerforth dipped a match into a phosphorus box, when he wanted to look for anything on the board, and shed a blue glare over us that was gone directly! A certain mysterious feeling, consequent on the darkness, the secrecy of the revel, and the whisper in which everything was said, steals over me again, and I listen to all they tell me with a vague feeling of solemnity and awe, which makes me glad that they are all so near, and frightens me (though I feign to laugh) when Traddles pretends to see a ghost in the corner.

I heard all kinds of things about the school and all belonging to it. I heard that Mr. Creakle had not preferred his claim to being a Tartar without reason; that he was the sternest and most severe of masters; that he laid about him right and left every day of his life, charging in among the boys like a trooper, and slashing away unmercifully. That he knew nothing himself, but the art of slashing, being more ignorant (J. Steerforth said) than the lowest boy in the school; that he had been, a good many years ago, a small hop dealer in the Borough, and had taken to the schooling business after being bankrupt in hops, and making away with Mrs. Creakle's money. With a good deal more of that sort, which I wondered how they knew.

I heard that the man with the wooden leg, whose name was Tungay, was an obstinate barbarian who had formerly assisted in the hop business, but had come into the scholastic line with Mr. Creakle, in consequence, as was supposed among the boys, of his having broken his leg in Mr. Creakle's service, and having done a deal of dishonest work for him, and knowing his secrets. I heard that with the single exception of Mr. Creakle, Tungay considered the whole establishment, masters and boys, as his natural enemies, and that the only delight of his life was to be sour and malicious. I heard that Mr. Creakle had a son, who had not been Tungay's friend, and who, assisting in the school, had once held some remonstrance with his father on an occasion when its discipline was very cruelly exercised, and was supposed, besides, to have protested against his father's usage of his mother. I heard that Mr. Creakle had turned him out of doors in consequence, and that Mrs. and Miss Creakle had been in a sad way ever since.

But the greatest wonder that I heard of Mr. Creakle was, there being one boy in the school on whom he never ventured to lay a hand, and that boy being J. Steerforth. Steerforth himself confirmed this when it was stated, and said that he should like to begin to see him do it. On being asked by a mild boy (not me) how he would proceed if he did begin to see him do it, he dipped a match into his phosphorus box on purpose to shed a glare over his reply, and said he would commence by knocking him down with a blow on the forehead from his seven-and-sixpenny ink bottle that was always on the mantelpiece. We sat in the dark for some time breathless.

I heard that Mr. Sharp and Mr. Mell were both supposed to be wretchedly paid; and that when there was hot and cold meat for dinner at Mr. Creakle's table, Mr. Sharp was always expected to say he preferred cold; which was again corroborated by J. Steerforth, the only parlor-boarder. I heard that Mr. Sharp's wig didn't fit him; and that he needn't be so "bounceable"—somebody else said "bumptious"—about it, because his own red hair was very plainly to be seen behind.

I heard that one boy, who was a coal merchant's son, came as a set-off against the coal bill, and was called on that account, "Exchange or Barter"—a name selected from the arithmetic-book, as expressing this arrangement. I heard that the table-beer was a robbery of parents, and the pudding an imposition. I heard that Miss Creakle was regarded by the school in general as being in love with Steerforth; and I am sure, as I sat in the dark, thinking of his nice voice, and his fine face, and his easy manner, and his curling hair, I thought it very likely. I heard that Mr. Mell was not a bad sort of fellow, but hadn't a sixpence to bless himself with; and that there was no doubt that old Mrs. Mell, his mother, was as poor as Job. I thought of my breakfast then, and what had sounded like "My Charlie!" but I was, I am glad to remember, as mute as a mouse about it.

The hearing of all this, and a good deal more, outlasted the banquet some time. The greater part of the guests had gone to bed as soon as the eating and drinking were over; and we, who had remained whispering and listening, half undressed, at last betook ourselves to bed, too.

"Good-night, young Copperfield," said Steerforth. "I'll take care of you."

"You're very kind," I gratefully returned. "I am very much obliged to you."

"You haven't got a sister, have you?" said Steerforth, yawning.

"No," I answered.

"That's a pity," said Steerforth. "If you had had one, I should think she would have been a pretty, timid, little bright-eyed sort of a girl. I should have liked to know her. Good-night, young Copperfield."

"Good-night, sir," I replied.

I thought of him very much after I went to bed, and raised myself, I recollect, to look at him where he lay in the moonlight, with his handsome face turned up, and his head reclining easily on his arm. He was a person of great power in my eyes; that was, of course, the reason of my mind running on him. No veiled future dimly glanced upon him in the moonbeams. There was no shadowy picture of his footsteps in the garden that I dreamed of walking in all night.

School began in earnest next day. A profound impression was made upon me, I remember, by the roar of voices in the schoolroom suddenly becoming hushed as death when Mr. Creakle entered after breakfast, and stood in the doorway looking round upon us like a giant in a story-book surveying his captives.

Tungay stood at Mr. Creakle's elbow. He had no occasion, I thought, to cry out "Silence!" so ferociously, for the boys were all struck speechless and motionless.

Mr. Creakle was seen to speak, and Tungay was heard, to this effect:

"Now, boys, this is a new half. Take care what you're about in this new half. Come fresh up to the lessons, I advise you, for I come fresh up to the punishment. I won't flinch. It will be of no use you rubbing yourselves; you won't rub the marks out, that I shall give you. Now get to work, every boy."

When this dreadful exordium was over, and Tungay had stumped out again, Mr. Creakle came to where I sat, and told me that if I were famous for biting, he was famous for biting, too. He then showed me the cane, and asked me what I thought of *that* for a tooth? Was it a sharp tooth, hey? Was it a double tooth, hey? Had it a deep prong, hey? Did it bite, hey? Did it bite? At every question he gave me a fleshy cut with it that made me writhe; so I was very soon made free of Salem House (as Steerforth said), and was very soon in tears also.

Not that I mean to say these were special marks of distinction, which only I received. On the contrary, a large majority of the boys (especially the smaller ones) were visited with similar instances of notice, as Mr. Creakle made the round of the schoolroom. Half the establishment was writhing and crying, before the day's work began; and how much of it had writhed and cried before the day's work was over, I am really afraid to recollect, lest I should seem to exaggerate.

I should think there never can have been a man who enjoyed his profession more than Mr. Creakle did. He had a delight in cutting at the boys, which was like the satisfaction of a craving appetite. I am confident that he couldn't resist a chubby boy, especially; that there was a fascination in such a subject, which made him restless in his mind until he had scored and marked him for the day. I was chubby myself, and ought to know. I am sure when I think of the fellow now, my blood rises against him with the disinterested indignation I should feel if I could have known all about him without having ever been in his power; but it rises hotly, because I know him to have been an incapable brute, who had no more right to be possessed of the great trust he held than to be Lord High Admiral, or Commander-in-chief—in either of which capacities, it is probable, that he would have done infinitely less mischief.

Miserable little propitiators of a remorseless Idol, how abject we were to him! What a launch in life I think it now, on looking back, to be so mean and servile to a man of such parts and pretensions!

Here I sit at the desk again, watching his eye—humbly watching his eye, as he rules a ciphering book for another victim whose hands have just been flattened by that identical ruler, and who is trying to wipe the sting out with a pocket handkerchief. I have plenty to do. I don't watch his eye in idleness, but because I am morbidly attracted to it, in a dread desire to know what he will do next, and whether it will be my turn to suffer or somebody else's. A lane of small boys beyond me, with the same interest in his eye, watch it too. I think he knows it, though he pretends he don't. He makes dreadful mouths as he rules the ciphering book; and now he throws his eye sideways down our lane, and we all droop over our books and tremble. A moment afterward we are again eying him. An unhappy culprit, found guilty of imperfect exercise, approaches at his command. The culprit falters, excuses, and professes a determination to do better to-morrow. Mr. Creakle cuts a joke before he beats him, and we laugh at it—miserable little dogs, we laugh, with our visages as white as ashes, and our hearts sinking into our boots.

Here I sit at the desk again on a drowsy summer afternoon. A buzz and a hum go up around me, as if the boys were so many blue bottles. A cloggy sensation of the luke-warm fat of meat is upon me (we dined an hour or two ago) and my head is as heavy as so much lead. I would give the world to go to sleep. I sit with my eye on Mr. Creakle, blinking at him like a young owl; when sleep overpowers me for a minute, he still looms through my slumber, ruling those ciphering books, until he softly comes behind me and wakes me to plainer perception of him with a red ridge across my back.

Here I am in the playground, with my eye still fascinated by him, though I can't see him. The window at a little distance from which I know he is having his dinner, stands for him, and I eye that instead. If he shows his face near it, mine assumes an imploring and submissive expression. If he looks out through the glass, the boldest boy (Steerforth excepted) stops in the middle of a shout or yell, and becomes contemplative. One day, Traddles (the most unfortunate boy in the world) breaks that window accidentally with a ball. I shudder at this moment with the tremendous sensation of seeing it done, and feeling that the ball has bounded on to Mr. Creakle's sacred head.

Poor Traddles! In a tight sky-blue suit that made his arms and legs like German sausages or roly-poly puddings, he was the merriest and most miserable of all the boys. He was always being caned—I think he was caned every day that half-year, except one holiday Monday when he was only ruler'd on both hands—and was always going to write to his uncle about it, and never did. After laying his head on the desk for a little while, he would cheer up somehow, begin to laugh again, and draw skeletons all over his slate, before his eyes were dry. I used at first to wonder what comfort Traddles found in drawing skeletons; and for some time looked upon him as a sort of hermit, who reminded himself of those symbols of mortality that caning couldn't last for ever. But I believe he only did it because they were easy, and didn't want any features.

He was very honorable, Traddles was, and held it as a solemn duty in the boys to stand by one another. He suffered for this on several occasions; and particularly once, when Steerforth laughed in church, and the Beadle thought it was Traddles, and took him out. I see him now going away in custody, despised by the congregation. He never said who was the real offender, though he smarted for it next day, and was imprisoned so many hours that he came forth with a whole churchyardful of skeletons swarming all over his Latin dictionary. But he had his reward. Steerforth said there was nothing of the sneak in Traddles, and we all felt that to be the highest praise. For my part, I could have gone through a good deal (though I was much less brave than Traddles, and nothing like so old) to have won such a recompense.

To see Steerforth walk to church before us, arm-in-arm with Miss Creakle, was one of the great sights of my life. I didn't think Miss Creakle equal to little Em'ly in point of beauty, and I didn't love her (I didn't dare); but I thought her a young lady of extraordinary attractions, and in point of gentility not to be surpassed. When Steerforth, in white trousers, carried her parasol for her, I felt proud to know him; and believed that she could not choose but adore him with all her heart. Mr. Sharp and Mr. Mell were both notable personages in my eyes; but Steerforth was to them what the sun was to two stars.

Steerforth continued his protection of me, and proved a very useful friend, since nobody dared to annoy one whom he honored with his countenance. He couldn't—or at all events he didn't—defend me from Mr. Creakle, who was very severe with me; but whenever I had been treated worse than usual, he always told me that I wanted a little of his pluck, and that he wouldn't have stood it himself; which I felt he intended for encouragement, and considered to be very kind of him. There was one advantage, and only one that I knew of, in Mr. Creakle's severity. He found my placard in his way when he came up or down behind the form on which I sat, and wanted to make a cut at me in passing; for this reason it was soon taken off, and I saw it no more.

An accidental circumstance cemented the intimacy between Steerforth and me, in a manner that inspired me with great pride and satisfaction, though it sometimes led to inconvenience. It happened on one occasion, when he was doing me the honor of talking to me in the playground, that I hazarded the observation that something or somebody—I forgot what now—was like something or somebody in "Peregrine Pickle." He said nothing at the time; but when I was going to bed at night, asked me if I had got that book? I told him no, and explained how it was that I had read it, and all those other books of which I have made mention.

"And do you recollect them?" Steerforth said.

"Oh, yes;" I replied, I had a good memory, and I believed I recollected them very well.

"Then I tell you what, young Copperfield," said Steerforth, "you shall tell 'em to me. I can't get to sleep very early at night, and I generally wake rather early in the morning. We'll go over 'em one after another. We'll make some regular 'Arabian Nights' of it."

I felt extremely flattered by this arrangement, and we commenced carrying it into execution that very evening. What ravages I committed on my favorite authors in the course of my interpretation of them, I am not in a condition to say, and should be very unwilling to know; but I had a profound faith in them, and I had, to the best of my belief, a simple earnest manner of narrating what I did narrate; and these qualities went a long way.

The drawback was, that I was often sleepy at night, or out of spirits and indisposed to resume the story, and then it was rather hard work, and it must be done; for to disappoint or to displease Steerforth was, of course, out of the question. In the morning, too, when I felt weary, and should have enjoyed another hour's repose very much, it was a tiresome thing to be roused, like the Sultana Scheherazade, and forced into a long story before the getting-up bell rang; but Steerforth was resolute; and as he explained to me, in return, my sums and exercises, and anything in my tasks that was too hard for me, I was no loser by the transaction. Let me do myself justice, however. I was moved by no interest or selfish motive, nor was I moved by fear of him. I admired and loved him, and his approval was return enough. It was so precious to me, that I look back on these trifles, now, with an aching heart.

Steerforth was considerate, too, and showed his consideration, in one particular instance in an unflinching manner, and was a little tantalizing, I suspect, to poor Traddles and the rest. Peggotty's promised letter—what a comfortable letter it was!— arrived before "the half" was many weeks old, and with it a cake in a perfect nest of oranges, and two bottles of cowslip wine. This treasure, as in duty bound, I laid at the feet of Steerforth, and begged him to dispense.

"Now, I tell you what, young Copperfield," said he: "the wine shall be kept to wet your whistle when you are story-telling."

I blushed at the idea, and begged him, in my modesty, not to think of it. But he said he had observed I was sometimes hoarse—a little roopy was his exact expression—and it should be, every drop, devoted to the purpose he had mentioned. Accordingly, it was locked up in his box, and drawn off by himself in a vial, and administered to me through a piece of quill in the cork, when I was supposed to be in want of a restorative. Sometimes to make it a more sovereign specific, he was so kind as to squeeze orange juice into it, or to stir it up with ginger, or dissolve a peppermint drop in it; and although I cannot assert that the flavor was improved by these experiments, or that it was exactly the compound one would have chosen for a stomachic, the last thing at night and the first thing in the morning, I drank it gratefully, and was very sensible of his attention.

We seem to me to have been months over "Peregrine," and months more over the other stories. The institution never flagged for want of a story, I am certain, and the wine lasted out almost as well as the matter. Poor Traddles—I never think of that boy but with a strange disposition to laugh, and with tears in my eyes—was a sort of chorus, in general, and affected to be convulsed with mirth at the comic parts, and to be overcome with fear when there was any passage of an alarming character to the narrative. This rather put me out very often. It was a great jest of his, I recollect, to pretend that he couldn't keep his teeth from chattering whenever mention was made of an Alguazil in connection with the adventures of Gil Blas; and I remember that when Gil Blas met the captain of the robbers in Madrid, this unlucky joker counterfeited such an ague of terror that he was overheard by Mr. Creakle, who was prowling about the passage, and handsomely flogged for disorderly conduct in the bedroom.

Whatever I had within me that was romantic and dreamy, was encouraged by so much story-telling in the dark; and in that respect the pursuit may not have been very profitable to me. But the being cherished as a kind of plaything in my room, and the consciousness that this accomplishment of mine was bruited about among the boys, and attracted a good deal of notice to me, though I was the youngest there, stimulated me to exertion. In a school carried on by sheer cruelty, whether it is presided over by a dunce or not, there is not likely to be much learned. I believe our boys were, generally, as ignorant a set as any schoolboys in existence; they were too much troubled and knocked about to learn; they could no more do that to advantage than any one can do anything to advantage in a life of constant misfortune, torment, and worry.

But my little vanity, and Steerforth's help, urged me on somehow; and without saving me from much, if anything, in the way of punishment, made me, for the time I was there, an exception to the general body, insomuch that I did steadily pick up some crumbs of knowledge.

In this I was much assisted by Mr. Mell, who had a liking for me that I am grateful to remember. It always gave me pain to observe that Steerforth treated him with systematic disparagement, and seldom lost an occasion of wounding his feelings, or inducing others to do so. This troubled me the more for a long time, because I had soon told Steerforth, from whom I could no more keep such a secret than I could keep a cake or any other tangible possession, about the two old women Mr. Mell had taken me to see; and I was always afraid that Steerforth would let it out, and twit him with it.

We little thought, any one of us, I dare say, when I ate my breakfast that first morning, and went to sleep under the shadow of the peacock's feathers to the sound of the flute, what consequences would come of the introduction into those almshouses of my insignificant person. But the visit had its unforeseen consequences; and of a serious sort, too, in their way.

One day when Mr. Creakle kept the house from indisposition, which naturally diffused a lively joy through the school, there was a good deal of noise in the course of the morning's work. The great relief and satisfaction experienced by the boys made them difficult to manage; and though the dreaded Tungay brought his wooden leg in twice or thrice, and took notes of the principal offenders' names, no great impression was made by it, as they were pretty sure of getting into trouble to-morrow, do what they would, and thought it wise, no doubt, to enjoy themselves to-day.

It was, properly, a half holiday, being Saturday. But as the noise in the playground would have disturbed Mr. Creakle, and the weather was not favorable for going out walking, we were ordered into school in the afternoon, and set some lighter tasks than usual, which were made for the occasion. It was the day of the week on which Mr. Sharp went out to get his wig curled; so Mr. Mell, who always did the drudgery, whatever it was, kept school by himself.

If I could associate the idea of a bull or a bear with any one so mild as Mr. Mell, I should think of him in connection with that afternoon when the uproar was at its height, as of one of those animals, baited by a thousand dogs. I recall him bending his aching head, supported on his bony hand over the book on his desk, and wretchedly endeavoring to get on with his tiresome work amidst an uproar that might have made the Speaker of the House of Commons giddy. Boys started in and out of their places playing at puss-in-the-corner with other boys; there were laughing boys, singing boys, talking boys, dancing boys, howling boys; boys shuffled with their feet, boys whirled about him, grinning, making faces, mimicking him behind his back and before his eyes; mimicking his poverty, his boots, his coat, his mother, everything belonging to him that they should have had consideration for.

"Silence!" cried Mr. Mell, suddenly rising up, and striking his desk with the book. "What does this mean? It's impossible to bear it. It's maddening. How can you do it to me, boys?"

It was my book that he struck his desk with; and as I stood beside him, following his eye as it glanced round the room, I saw the boys all stop, some suddenly surprised, some half afraid, and some sorry, perhaps.

Steerforth's place was at the bottom of the school at the opposite end of the long room. He was lounging with his back against the wall, and his hands in his pockets, and looked at Mr. Mell with his mouth shut up as if he were whistling, when Mr. Mell looked at him.

"Silence, Mr. Steerforth!" said Mr. Mell.

"Silence yourself," said Steerforth, turning red. "Whom are you talking to?"

"Sit down," said Mr. Mell.

"Sit down yourself," said Steerforth, "and mind your business."

There was a titter, and some applause; but Mr. Mell was so white that silence immediately succeeded; and one boy, who had darted out behind him to imitate his mother again, changed his mind, and pretended to want a pen mended.

"If you think, Steerforth," said Mr. Mell, "that I am not acquainted with the power you can establish over any mind here"—he laid his hand, without considering what he did (as I supposed), upon my head—" or that I have not observed you, within a few minutes, urging your juniors on to every sort of outrage against me, you are mistaken."

"I don't give myself the trouble of thinking at all about you," said Steerforth, coolly; "so I'm not mistaken, as it happens."

"And when you make use of your position of favoritism here sir," pursued Mr. Mell, with his lip trembling very much, "to insult a gentleman——"

"A what?—where is he?" said Steerforth.

Here somebody cried out, "Shame, J. Steerforth! Too bad!" It was Traddles; whom Mr. Mell instantly discomfited by bidding him hold his tongue.

—"To insult one who is not fortunate in life, sir, and who never gave you the least offense, and the many reasons for not insulting whom you are old enough and wise enough to understand," said Mr. Mell, with his lip trembling more and more, "you commit a mean and base action. You can sit down or stand up as you please, sir. Copperfield, go on."

"Young Copperfield," said Steerforth, coming forward up the room, "stop a bit. I tell you what, Mr. Mell, once for all. When you take the liberty of calling me mean or base, or anything of that sort, you are an impudent beggar. You are always a beggar, you know; but when you do that, you are an impudent beggar."

I am not clear whether he was going to strike Mr. Mell, or Mr. Mell was going to strike him, or there was any such intention on either side. I saw a rigidity come upon the whole school as if they had been turned into stone, and found Mr. Creakle in the midst of us, with Tungay at his side, and Mrs. and Miss Creakle looking on at the door as if they were frightened. Mr. Mell, with his elbows on his desk and his face in his hands, sat, for some moments, quite still.

"Mr. Mell," said Mr. Creakle, shaking him by the arm; and his whisper was so audible now, that Tungay felt it unnecessary to repeat his words; "you have not forgotten yourself, I hope?"

"No, sir, no," returned the Master, showing his face and shaking his head, and rubbing his hands in great agitation. "No, sir, no. I have remembered myself, I—no, Mr. Creakle, I have not forgotten myself, I—I have remembered myself, sir. I—I—could wish you had remembered me a little sooner, Mr. Creakle. It—it—would have been more kind, sir, more just, sir. It would have saved me something, sir."

Mr. Creakle, looking hard at Mr. Mell, put his hand on Tungay's shoulder, and got his feet upon the form close by, and sat upon the desk. After still looking hard at Mr. Mell from this throne, as he shook his head and rubbed his hands, and remained in the same state of agitation, Mr. Creakle turned to Steerforth, and said:

"Now, sir, as he don't condescend to tell me, what is this?"

Steerforth evaded the question for a little while; looking in scorn and anger on his opponent, and remaining silent. I could not help thinking even in that interval, I remember, what a noble fellow he was in appearance, and how homely and plain Mr. Mell looked opposed to him.

"What did he mean by talking about favorites, then?" said Steerforth, at length.

"Favorites!" repeated Mr. Creakle, with the veins in his forehead swelling quickly. "Who talked about favorites?"

"He did," said Steerforth.

"And pray what did you mean by that, sir?" demanded Mr. Creakle, turning angrily on his assistant.

"I meant, Mr. Creakle," he returned in a low voice, "as I said; that no pupil had a right to avail himself of his position of favoritism to degrade me."

"To degrade *you?*" said Mr. Creakle. "My stars. But give me leave to ask you, Mr. What's-your-name;" and here Mr. Creakle folded his arms, cane and all, upon his chest, and made such a knot of his brows that his little eyes were hardly visible below them; "whether, when you talked about favorites, you showed proper respect to me? To me, sir," said Mr. Creakle, darting his head at him suddenly, and drawing it back again, "the principal of this establishment, and your employer."

"It was not judicious, sir, I am willing to admit," said Mr. Mell. "I should not have done so, if I had been cool."

Here Steerforth struck in.

"Then he said I was mean, and then he said I was base, and then I called him a beggar. If I had been cool, perhaps I shouldn't have called him a beggar. But I did, and I am ready to take the consequences of it."

Without considering, perhaps, whether there were any consequences to be taken, I felt quite in a glow at this gallant speech. It made an impression on the boys, too, for there was a low stir among them, though no one spoke a word.

"I am surprised, Steerforth—although your candor does you honor, certainly—I am surprised, Steerforth, I must say, that you should attach such an epithet to any person employed and paid in Salem House, sir."

Steerforth gave a short laugh.

"That's not an answer, sir," said Mr. Creakle, "to my remark. I expect more than that from you, Steerforth."

If Mr. Mell looked homely, in my eyes, before the handsome boy, it would be quite impossible to say how homely Mr. Creakle looked.

"Let him deny it," said Steerforth.

"Deny that he is a beggar, Steerforth!" cried Mr. Creakle. "Why, where does he go a-begging?"

"If he is not a beggar himself, his near relation's one," said Steerforth. "It's all the same."

He glanced at me, and Mr. Mell's hand gently patted me upon the shoulder. I looked up with a flush upon my face and remorse in my heart, but Mr. Mell's eyes were fixed on Steerforth. He continued to pat me kindly on the shoulder, but he looked at him.

"Since you expect me, Mr. Creakle, to justify myself," said Steerforth, "and to say what I mean—what I have to say is, that his mother lives on charity in an almshouse."

Mr. Mell still looked at him, and still patted me kindly on the shoulder and said to himself in a whisper, if I heard right, "Yes, I thought so."

Mr. Creakle turned to his assistant, with a severe frown and labored politeness :

"Now you hear what this gentleman says, Mr. Mell. Have the goodness, if you please, to set him right before the assembled school."

"He is right, sir, without correction," returned Mr. Mell, in the midst of a dead silence; "what he has said is true."

"Be so good, then, as to declare publicly, will you," said Mr. Creakle, putting his head on one side, and rolling his eyes round the school, "whether it ever came to my knowledge until this moment?"

"I believe not directly," he returned.

"Why, you know not," said Mr. Creakle. "Don't you, man?"

"I apprehend you never supposed my worldly circumstances to be very good," replied the assistant. "You know what my position is, and always has been here."

"I apprehend, if you come to that," said Mr. Creakle, with his veins swelling again bigger than ever, "that you've been in a wrong position altogether, and mistook this for a charity school. Mr. Mell, we'll part, if you please. The sooner the better."

"There is no time," answered Mr. Mell, rising, "like the present."

"Sir, to you!" said Mr. Creakle.

"I take my leave of you, Mr. Creakle, and all of you," said Mr. Mell, glancing round the room, and again patting me gently on the shoulder. "James Steerforth, the best wish I can leave you is that you may come to be ashamed of what you have done to-day. At present I would prefer to see you anything rather than a friend, to me, or to any one in whom I feel an interest."

Once more he laid his hand upon my shoulder; and, then taking his flute and a few books from his desk, and leaving the key in it for his successor, he went out of the school, with his property under his arm. Mr. Creakle then made a speech, through Tungay, in which he thanked Steerforth for asserting (though perhaps too warmly) the independence and respectability of Salem House; and which he wound up by shaking hands with Steerforth, while we gave three cheers—I did not quite know what for, but I supposed for Steerforth, and so joined in them ardently, though I felt miserable. Mr. Creakle then caned Tommy Traddles for being discovered in tears, instead of cheers, on account of Mr. Mell's departure; and went back to his sofa, or his bed, or wherever he had come from.

We were all left to ourselves now, and looked very blank, I recollect, on one another. For myself, I felt so much self-reproach and contrition for my part in what had happened, that nothing would have enabled me to keep back my tears but the fear that Steerforth, who often looked at me, I saw, might think it unfriendly—or, I should rather say, considering our relative ages, and the feeling with which I regarded him, undutiful—if I showed the emotion which distressed me. He was very angry with Traddles, and said he was glad he had caught it.

Poor Traddles, who had passed the stage of lying with his head upon the desk, and was relieving himself as usual with a burst of skeletons, said he didn't care. Mr. Mell was ill-used.

"Who has ill-used him, you girl?" said Steerforth.

"Why, you have," returned Traddles.

"What have I done?" said Steerforth.

"What have you done?" retorted Traddles. "Hurt his feelings and lost him his situation."

"His feelings!" repeated Steerforth disdainfully. "His feelings will soon get the better of it, I'll be bound. His feelings are not like yours, Miss Traddles. As to his situation—which was a precious one, wasn't it?—do you suppose I am not going to write home, and take care that he gets some money, Polly?"

We thought this intention very noble in Steerforth, whose mother was a widow, and rich, and would do almost anything, it was said, that he asked her. We were all extremely glad to see Traddles so put down, and exalted Steerforth to the skies; especially when he told us, as he condescended to do, that what he had done had been done expressly for us, and for our cause, and that he had conferred a great boon upon us by unselfishly doing it.

But I must say that when I was going on with a story in the dark that night, Mr. Mell's old flute seemed more than once to sound mournfully in my ears; and that when at last Steerforth was tired, and I lay down in my bed, I fancied it playing so sorrowfully somewhere that I was quite wretched.

I soon forgot him in the contemplation of Steerforth, who, in an easy amateur way, and without any book (he seemed to me to know everything by heart), took some of his classes until a new master was found. The new master came from a grammar school, and before he entered on his duties, dined in the parlor one day, to be introduced to Steerforth. Steerforth approved of him highly, and told us he was a Brick. Without exactly understanding what learned distinction was meant by this, I respected him greatly for it, and had no doubt whatever of his superior knowledge; though he never took the pains with me —not that *I* was anybody—that Mr. Mell had taken.

Dr. Strong's School

(From "David Copperfield")

Doctor Strong's was an excellent school; as different from Mr. Creakle's as good is from evil. It was very gravely and decorously ordered, and on a sound system; with an appeal in everything to the honor and good faith of the boys, and an avowed intention to rely on their possession of those qualities unless they proved themselves unworthy of it, which worked wonders. We all felt that we had a part in the management of the place, and in sustaining its character and dignity. Hence, we soon became warmly attached to it—I am sure I did, for one, and I never knew, in all my time, of any other boy being otherwise—and learned with a good will, desiring to do it credit. We had noble games out of hours, and plenty of liberty; but even then, as I remember, we were well spoken of in the town, and rarely did any disgrace, by our appearance or manner, to the reputation of Doctor Strong and Doctor Strong's boys.

Some of the higher scholars boarded in the Doctor's house, and through them I learned, at second hand, some particulars of the Doctor's history. As how he had not yet been married twelve months to the beautiful young lady I had seen in the study, whom he had married for love; for she had not a sixpence, and had a world of poor relations (so our fellows said) ready to swarm the Doctor out of house and home. Also, how the Doctor's cogitating manner was attributable to his being always engaged in looking out for Greek roots, which, in my innocence and ignorance, I supposed to be a botanical furor on the Doctor's part, especially as he always looked at the ground when he walked about until I understood that they were roots of words, with a view to a new Dictionary which he had in contemplation. Adams, our head boy, who had a turn for mathematics, had made a calculation, I was informed, of the time this Dictionary would take in completing, on the Doctor's plan, and at the Doctor's rate of going. He considered that it might be done in one thousand six hundred and forty-nine years, counting from the Doctor's last, or sixty-second birthday.

But the Doctor himself was the idol of the whole school, and it must have been a badly composed school if he had been anything else, for he was the kindest of men, with a simple faith in him that might have touched the stone hearts of the very urns upon the wall. As he walked up and down that part of the court-yard which was at the side of the house, with the stray rooks and jackdaws looking after him with their heads cocked slyly, as if they knew how much more knowing they were in worldly affairs than he, if any sort of vagabond could only get near enough to his creaking shoes to attract his attention to one sentence of a tale of distress, that vagabond was made for the next two days. It was so notorious in the house that the masters and head boys took pains to cut these marauders off at angles, and to get out of windows and turn them out of the court-yard, before they could make the Doctor aware of their presence, which was sometimes happily effected within a few yards of him, without his knowing anything of the matter, as he jogged to and fro. Outside of his own domain, and unprotected, he was a very sheep for the shearers. He would have taken his gaiters off his legs to give away.

In fact, there was a story current among us (I have no idea, and never had, on what authority, but I have believed it for so many years that I feel quite certain it is true), that on a frosty day, one winter-time, he actually did bestow his gaiters on a beggar-woman, who occasioned some scandal in the neighborhood by exhibiting a fine infant from door to door, wrapped in those garments, which were universally recognized, being as well known in the vicinity as the Cathedral. The legend added that the only person who did not identify them was the Doctor himself, who, when they were shortly afterward displayed at the door of a little second-hand shop of no very good repute, where such things were taken in exchange for gin, was more than once observed to handle them approvingly, as if admiring some curious novelty in the pattern, and considering them an improvement on his own.

It was very pleasant to see the Doctor with his pretty young wife. He had a fatherly, benignant way of showing his fondness for her, which seemed in itself to express a good man. I often saw them walking in the garden where the peaches were, and I sometimes had a nearer observation of them in the study or the parlor. She appeared to me to take great care of the Doctor, and to like him very much, though I never thought her vitally interested in the Dictionary; some cumbrous fragments of which work the Doctor always carried in his pockets, and in the lining of his hat, and generally seemed to be expounding to her as they walked about.

Dotheboys Hall

(From "Nicholas Nickleby")

"Are you cold, Nickleby?" inquired Squeers, after they had traveled some distance in silence.

"Rather, sir, I must say."

"Well, I don't find fault with that," said Squeers; "it's a long journey this weather."

"Is it much further to Dotheboys Hall, sir?" asked Nicholas.

"About three mile from here," replied Squeers. "But you needn't call it a Hall down here."

Nicholas coughed, as if he would like to know why.

"The fact is, it ain't a Hall," observed Squeers, dryly.

"Oh, indeed!" said Nicholas, whom this piece of intelligence much astonished.

"No," replied Squeers. "We call it a Hall up in London, because it sounds better, but they don't know it by that name in these parts. A man may call his house an island if he likes; there's no act of Parliament against that, I believe."

"I believe not, sir," rejoined Nicholas.

Squeers eyed his companion slyly, at the conclusion of this little dialogue, and finding that he had grown thoughtful and appeared in nowise disposed to volunteer any observations, contented himself with lashing the pony until they reached their journey's end.

"Jump out," said Squeers. "Hallo there! come and put this horse up. Be quick, will you?"

While the schoolmaster was uttering these and other impatient cries, Nicholas had time to observe that the school was a long, cold-looking house, one story high, with a few straggling out-buildings behind, and a barn and stable adjoining. After the lapse of a minute or two, the noise of somebody unlocking the yard-gate was heard, and presently a tall lean boy, with a lantern in his hand, issued forth.

"Is that you, Smike?" cried Squeers.

"Yes, sir," replied the boy.

"Then why the devil didn't you come before?"

"Please, sir, I fell asleep over the fire," answered Smike, with humility.

"Fire! what fire? Where's there a fire?" demanded the schoolmaster, sharply.

"Only in the kitchen, sir," replied the boy. "Missus said as I was sitting up, I might go in there for a warm."

"Your Missus is a fool," retorted Squeers. "You'd have been a deuced deal more wakeful in the cold, I'll engage."

By this time Mr. Squeers had dismounted; and after ordering the boy to see to the pony, and to take care that he hadn't any more corn that night, he told Nicholas to wait at the front door a minute while he went round and let him in.

A host of unpleasant misgivings, which had been crowding upon Nicholas during the whole journey, thronged upon his mind with redoubled force when he was left alone. His great distance from home and the impossibility of reaching it, except on foot, should he feel ever so anxious to return, presented itself to him in the most alarming colors; and as he looked up at the dreary house and dark windows, and upon the wild country round, covered with snow, he felt a depression of heart and spirit which he had never experienced before.

. . . . . .

A ride of two hundred and odd miles in severe weather is one of the best softeners of a hard bed that ingenuity can devise. Perhaps it is even a sweetener of dreams, for those which hovered over the rough couch of Nicholas, and whispered their airy nothings in his ear, were of an agreeable and happy kind. He was making his fortune very fast indeed, when the faint glimmer of an expiring candle shone before his eyes, and a voice he had no difficulty in recognizing as part and parcel of Mr. Squeers, admonished him that it was time to rise.

"Past seven, Nickleby," said Mr. Squeers.

"Has morning come already?" asked Nicholas, sitting up in bed.

"Ah! that has it," replied Squeers, "and ready iced too. Now, Nickleby, come! tumble up, will you?"

Nicholas needed no further admonition, but "tumbled up" at once, and proceeded to dress himself by the light of the taper which Mr. Squeers carried in his hand.

"Here's a pretty go," said that gentleman; "the pump's froze."

"Indeed!" said Nicholas, not much interested in the intelligence.

"Yes," replied Squeers. "You can't wash yourself this morning."

"Not wash myself!" exclaimed Nicholas.

"No, not a bit of it," rejoined Squeers, tartly. "So you must be content with giving yourself a dry polish till we break the ice in the well, and can get a bucketful out for the boys. Don't stand staring at me, but do look sharp, will you?"

Offering no further observation, Nicholas huddled on his clothes. Squeers, meanwhile, opened the shutters and blew the candle out; when the voice of his amiable consort was heard in the passage, demanding admittance.

"Come in, my love," said Squeers.

Mrs. Squeers came in, still habited in the primitive nightjacket which had displayed the symmetry of her figure on the previous night, and further ornamented with a beaver bonnet of some antiquity, which she wore, with much ease and lightness, on the top of the nightcap before mentioned.

"Drat the things," said the lady, opening the cupboard: "I can't find the school-spoon anywhere."

"Never mind it, my dear," observed Squeers, in a soothing manner; "it's of no consequence."

"No consequence, why, how you talk!" retorted Mrs. Squeers, sharply; "isn't it brimstone morning?"

"I forgot, my dear," rejoined Squeers; "yes, it certainly is. We purify the boys' blood now and then, Nickleby."

"Purify fiddlesticks' ends," said his lady. "Don't think, young man, that we go to the expense of flower of brimstone and molasses, just to purify them; because if you think we carry on the business in that way, you'll find yourself mistaken, and so I tell you plainly."

"My dear," said Squeers, frowning. "Hem!"

"Oh! nonsense," rejoined Mrs. Squeers. "If the young man comes to be a teacher here, let him understand at once that we don't want any foolery about the boys. They have the brimstone and treacle, partly because if they hadn't something or other in the way of medicine they'd be always ailing and giving a world of trouble, and partly because it spoils their appetites and comes cheaper than breakfast and dinner. So it does them good and us good at the same time, and that's fair enough, I'm sure."

Having given this explanation, Mrs. Squeers put her hand into the closet and instituted a stricter search after the spoon in which Mr. Squeers assisted. A few words passed between them while they were thus engaged, but as their voices were partially stifled by the cupboard, all that Nicholas could distinguish was that Mr. Squeers said what Mrs. Squeers had said was injudicious, and that Mrs. Squeers said what Mr. Squeers said was "stuff."

A vast deal of searching and rummaging ensued, and it proving fruitless, Smike was called in, and pushed by Mrs. Squeers, and boxed by Mr. Squeers; which course of treatment brightening his intellects, enabled him to suggest that possibly Mrs. Squeers might have the spoon in her pocket, as indeed turned out to be the case. As Mrs. Squeers had previously protested, however, that she was quite certain she had not got it, Smike received another box on the ear for presuming to contradict his mistress, together with a promise of a sound thrashing if he were not more respectful in future; so that he took nothing very advantageous by his motion.

"A most invaluable woman, that, Nickleby," said Squeers, when his consort had hurried away, pushing the drudge before her.

"Indeed, sir!" observed Nicholas.

"I don't know her equal," said Squeers; "I do not know her equal. That woman, Nickleby, is always the same—always the same bustling, lively, active, saving creetur that you see her now."

Nicholas sighed involuntarily at the thought of the agreeable domestic prospect thus opened to him; but Squeers was, fortunately, too much occupied with his own reflections to perceive it.

"It's my way to say, when I am up in London," continued Squeers, "that to them boys she is a mother. But she is more than a mother to them: ten times more. She does things for them boys, Nickleby, that I don't believe half the mothers going would do for their own sons."

"I should think they would not, sir," answered Nicholas.

Now, the fact was, that both Mr. and Mrs. Squeers viewed the boys in the light of their proper and natural enemies; or, in other words, they held and considered that their business and profession was to get as much from every boy as could by possibility be screwed out of him. On this point they were both agreed, and behaved in unison accordingly. The only difference between them was, that Mrs. Squeers waged war against the enemy openly and fearlessly, and that Squeers covered his rascality, even at home, with a spice of his habitual deceit; as if he really had a notion of some day or other being able to take himself in, and persuade his own mind that he was a very good fellow.

"But come," said Squeers, interrupting the progress of some thoughts to this effect in the mind of his usher, "let's go into the schoolroom; and lend me a hand with my school-coat, will you?"

Nicholas assisted his master to put on an old fustian shooting-jacket, which he took down from a peg in the passage; and

Squeers, arming himself with his cane, led the way across a yard, to a door in the rear of the house.

"There," said the schoolmaster, as they stepped in together, "this is our shop, Nickleby!"

It was such a crowded scene, and there were so many objects to attract attention, that at first Nicholas stared about him, really without seeing anything at all. By degrees, however, the place resolved itself into a bare and dirty room, with a couple of windows, whereof a tenth part might be of glass, the remainder being stopped up with old copybooks and paper. There were a couple of long old rickety desks, cut and notched, and inked, and damaged in every possible way; two or three forms; a detached desk for Squeers, and another for his assistant. The ceiling was supported, like that of a barn, by cross-beams and rafters; and the walls were so stained and discolored, that it was impossible to tell whether they had ever been touched with paint or whitewash.

But the pupils—the young noblemen! How the last faint traces of hope, the remotest glimmering of any good to be derived from his efforts in this den, faded from the mind of Nicholas as he looked in dismay around! Pale and haggard faces, lank and bony figures, children with the countenances of old men, deformities with irons upon their limbs, boys of stunted growth, and others whose long meager legs would hardly bear their stooping bodies, all crowded on the view together; there were the bleared eye, the hare lip, the crooked foot, and every ugliness or distortion that told of unnatural aversion conceived by parents for their offspring, or of young lives which, from the earliest dawn of infancy, had been one horrible endurance of cruelty and neglect. There were little faces which should have been handsome, darkened with the scowl of sullen, dogged suffering; there was childhood with the light of its eye quenched, its beauty gone, and its helplessness alone remaining; there were vicious-faced boys, brooding, with leaden eyes, like malefactors in a jail; and there were young creatures on whom the sins of their frail parents had descended, weeping even for the mercenary nurses they had known, and lonesome even in their loneliness. With every kindly sympathy and affection blasted in its birth, with every young and healthy feeling flogged and starved down, with every revengeful passion that can fester in swollen hearts, eating its evil way to their core in silence, what an incipient Hell was breeding here!

And yet this scene, painful as it was, had its grotesque features, which, in a less interested observer than Nicholas, might have provoked a smile. Mrs. Squeers stood at one of the desks, presiding over an immense basin of brimstone and treacle, of which delicious compound she administered a large installment to each boy in succession, using for the purpose a common wooden spoon, which might have been originally manufactured for some gigantic top, and which widened every young gentleman's mouth considerably; they being all obliged, under heavy corporal penalties, to take in the whole of the bowl at a gasp. In another corner, huddled together for companionship, were the little boys who had arrived on the preceding night, three of them in very large leather breeches, and two in old trousers, a somewhat tighter fit than drawers are usually worn; at no great distance from these was seated a juvenile son and heir of Mr. Squeers—a striking likeness of his father—kicking with great vigor under the hands of Smike, who was fitting upon him a pair of new boots that bore almost suspicious resemblance to those which the least of the little boys had worn on the journey down—as the little boy himself seemed to think, for he was regarding the appropriation with a look of most rueful amazement. Besides these, there was a long row of boys waiting, with countenances of no pleasant anticipation, to be treacled; and another file, who had just escaped from the infliction, making a variety of wry mouths, indicative of anything but satisfaction. The whole were attired in such motley, ill-sorted, extraordinary garments, as would have been irresistibly ridiculous, but for the foul appearance of dirt, disorder, and disease, with which they were associated.

"Now," said Squeers, giving the desk a great rap with his

cane, which made half the little boys nearly jump out of their boots, " is that physicking over?"

"Just over," said Mrs. Squeers, choking the last boy in her hurry, and tapping the crown of his head with the wooden spoon to restore him. " Here, you Smike; take this away now. Look sharp!"

Smike shuffled out with the basin, and Mrs. Squeers, having called up a little boy with a curly head and wiped her hands upon it, hurried out after him into a species of wash-house, where there was a small fire and a large kettle, together with a number of little wooden bowls which were arranged upon a board.

Into these bowls, Mrs. Squeers, assisted by the hungry servant, poured a brown composition, which looked like diluted pincushions without the covers, and was called porridge. A minute wedge of brown bread was inserted in each bowl, and when they had eaten the porridge by means of the bread, the boys ate the bread itself, and had finished their breakfast; whereupon Mr. Squeers said, in a solemn voice: " For what we have received, may the Lord make us truly thankful!"—and went away to his own.

Nicholas distended his stomach with a bowl of porridge, for much the same reason which induces some savages to swallow earth—lest they should be inconveniently hungry when there is nothing to eat. Having further disposed of a slice of bread and butter, allotted to him in virtue of his office, he sat himself down to wait for school time.

He could not but observe how silent and sad the boys all seemed to be. There was none of the noise and clamor of a schoolroom; none of its boisterous play or hearty mirth. The children sat crouching and shivering together, and seemed to lack the spirit to move about. The only pupil who evinced the slightest tendency toward locomotion or playfulness was Master Squeers, and as his chief amusement was to tread upon the other boys' toes, in his new boots, his flow of spirits was rather disagreeable than otherwise.

After some half hour's delay, Mr. Squeers reappeared, and the boys took their places and their books, of which latter commodity the average might be about one to eight learners. A few minutes having elapsed, during which Mr. Squeers looked very profound, as if he had a perfect apprehension of what was inside all the books, and could say every word of their contents by heart if he only chose to take the trouble, that gentleman called up the first class.

Obedient to this summons, there ranged themselves in front of the schoolmaster's desk half a dozen scarecrows, out at knees and elbows, one of whom placed a torn and filthy book beneath his learned eye.

"This is the first class in English spelling and philosophy, Nickleby," said Squeers, beckoning Nicholas to stand beside him. "We'll get up a Latin one, and hand that over to you. Now, then, where's the first boy?"

"Please, sir, he's cleaning the back parlor window," said the temporary head of the philosophical class.

"So he is, to be sure," rejoined Squeers. "We go upon the practical mode of teaching, Nickleby; the regular education system. C-l-e-a-n, clean, verb active, to make bright, to scour. W-i-n, win, d-e-r, winder, a casement. When the boy knows this out of book, he goes and does it. It's just the same principle as the use of the globes. Where's the second boy?"

"Please, sir, he's weeding the garden," replied a small voice.

"To be sure," said Squeers, by no means disconcerted. "So he is. B-o-t, bot, t-i-n, bottin, n-e-y, ney, bottinney, noun substantive, a knowledge of plants. When he has learned that bottinney means a knowledge of plants, he goes and knows 'em. That's our system, Nickleby; what do you think of it?"

"It's a very useful one, at any rate," answered Nicholas.

"I believe you," rejoined Squeers, not remarking the emphasis of his usher. "Third boy, what's a horse?"

"A beast, sir," replied the boy.

"So it is," said Squeers. "Ain't it, Nickleby?"

"I believe there is no doubt of that, sir," answered Nicholas.

"Of course there isn't," said Squeers. "A horse is a quadruped, and quadruped's Latin for beasts, as everybody that's gone through the grammar knows, or else where's the use of having grammars at all?"

"Where, indeed!" said Nicholas, abstractedly.

"As you're perfect in that," resumed Squeers, turning to the boy, "go and look after *my* horse, and rub him down well, or I'll rub you down. The rest of the class go and draw water up, till somebody tells you to leave off, for it's washing-day to-morrow, and they want the coppers filled."

So saying, he dismissed the first class to their experiments in practical philosophy, and eyed Nicholas with a look, half cunning and half doubtful, as if he were not altogether certain what he might think of him by this time.

"That's the way we do it, Nickleby," he said, after a pause.

Nicholas shrugged his shoulders in a manner that was scarcely perceptible, and said he saw it was.

"And a very good way it is, too," said Squeers. "Now, just take them fourteen little boys and hear them some reading, because, you know, you must begin to be useful. Idling about here won't do."

Mr. Squeers said this, as if it suddenly occurred to him either that he must not say too much to his assistant, or that his assistant did not say enough to him in praise of the establishment. The children were arranged in a semicircle round their new master, and he was soon listening to their dull, drawling, hesitating recital of those stories of engrossing interest which are to be found in the more antiquated spelling-books.

In this exciting occupation, the morning lagged heavily on. At one o'clock, the boys, having previously had their appetites thoroughly taken away by stirabout and potatoes, sat down in the kitchen to some hard salt beef, of which Nicholas was graciously permitted to take his portion to his own solitary desk, to eat it there in peace. After this, there was another hour of crouching in the schoolroom and shivering with cold, and then school began again.

It was Mr. Squeers's custom to call the boys together, and make a sort of report, after every half yearly visit to the metropolis, regarding the relations and friends he had seen, the news he had heard, the letters he had brought down, the bills which had been paid, the accounts which had been left unpaid, and so forth. This solemn proceeding always took place in the afternoon of the day succeeding his return; perhaps, because the boys acquired strength of mind from the suspense of the morning, or, possibly, because Mr. Squeers himself acquired greater sternness and inflexibility from certain warm potations in which he was wont to indulge after his early dinner. Be this as it may, the boys were recalled from house-window, garden, stable, and cow-yard, and the school were assembled in full conclave, when Mr. Squeers, with a small bundle of papers in his hand, and Mrs. S. following with a pair of canes, entered the room and proclaimed silence.

"Let any boy speak a word without leave," said Mr. Squeers, mildly, "and I'll take the skin off his back."

This special proclamation had the desired effect, and a deathlike silence immediately prevailed, in the midst of which Mr. Squeers went on to say:

"Boys, I have been to London, and have returned to my family and you, as strong and well as ever."

According to half-yearly custom, the boys gave three feeble cheers at this refreshing intelligence. Such cheers! Sighs of extra strength with the chill on.

"I have seen the parents of some boys," continued Squeers, turning over his papers, "and they're so glad to hear how their sons are getting on, that there's no prospect at all of their going away, which of course is a very pleasant thing to reflect upon, for all parties."

Two or three hands went to two or three eyes when Squeers said this, but the greater part of the young gentlemen having no particular parents to speak of, were wholly uninterested in the thing one way or other.

"I have had disappointments to contend against," said

Squeers, looking very grim; "Bolder's father was two pound ten short. Where is Bolder?"

"Here he is, please sir," rejoined twenty officious voices. Boys are very like men to be sure.

"Come here, Bolder," said Squeers.

An unhealthy-looking boy, with warts all over his hands, stepped from his place to the master's desk, and raised his eyes imploringly to Squeers's face; his own, quite white from the rapid beating of his heart.

"Bolder," said Squeers, speaking very slowly, for he was considering, as the saying goes, where to have him. "Bolder, if your father thinks that because—why, what's this, sir?"

As Squeers spoke he caught up the boy's hand by the cuff of his jacket, and surveyed it with an edifying aspect of horror and disgust.

"What do you call this, sir?" demanded the schoolmaster, administering a cut with the cane to expedite the reply.

"I can't help it, indeed, sir," rejoined the boy, crying. "They will come; it's the dirty work, I think, sir—at least I don't know what it is, sir, but it's not my fault."

"Bolder," said Squeers, tucking up his wristbands, and moistening the palm of his right hand to get a good grip of the cane, "you are an incorrigible young scoundrel, and as the last thrashing did you no good we must see what another will do toward beating it out of you."

With this, and wholly disregarding a piteous cry for mercy, Mr. Squeers fell upon the boy and caned him soundly; not leaving off, indeed, until his arm was tired out.

"There," said Squeers, when he had quite done; "rub away as hard as you like you won't rub that off in a hurry. Oh! you won't hold that noise, won't you? Put him out, Smike."

The drudge knew better, from long experience, than to hesitate about obeying, so he bundled the victim out by a side door, and Mr. Squeers perched himself again on his own stool, supported by Mrs. Squeers, who occupied another at his side.

"Now let us see," said Squeers. "A letter for Cobbey. Stand up, Cobbey."

Another boy stood up, and eyed the letter very hard while Squeers made a mental abstract of the same.

"Oh!" said Squeers; "Cobbey's grandmother is dead, and his uncle John has took to drinking, which is all the news his sister sends, except eighteenpence, which will just pay for that broken square of glass. Mrs. Squeers, my dear, will you take the money?"

The worthy lady pocketed the eighteenpence with a most business-like air, and Squeers passed on to the next boy, as coolly as possible.

"Graymarsh," said Squeers, "he's the next. Stand up, Graymarsh."

Another boy stood up, and the schoolmaster looked over the letter as before.

"Graymarsh's maternal aunt," said Squeers, when he had possessed himself of the contents, "is very glad to hear he's so well and happy, and sends her respectful compliments to Mrs. Squeers, and thinks she must be an angel. She likewise thinks Mr. Squeers is too good for this world; but hopes he may long be spared to carry on the business. Would have sent the two pair of stockings as desired, but is short of money, so forwards a tract instead, and hopes Graymarsh will put his trust in Providence. Hopes, above all, that he will study in everything to please Mr. and Mrs. Squeers, and look upon them as his only friends; and that he will love Master Squeers; and not object to sleeping five in a bed, which no Christian should. Ah!" said Squeers, folding it up, "a delightful letter. Very affecting indeed."

It was affecting in one sense, for Graymarsh's maternal aunt was strongly supposed, by her more intimate friends, to be no other than his maternal parent: Squeers, however, without alluding to this part of the story (which would have sounded immoral before boys), proceeded with the business by calling out "Mobbs," whereupon another boy rose, and Graymarsh resumed his seat.

"Mobbs's mother-in-law," said Squeers, "took to her bed on hearing that he wouldn't eat fat, and has been very ill ever since. She wishes to know, by an early post, where he expects to go to if he quarrels with his vittles; and with what feelings he could turn up his nose at the cow's liver broth, after his good master had asked a blessing on it. This was told her in the London newspapers—not by Mr. Squeers, for he is too kind and too good to set anybody against anybody—and it has vexed her so much, Mobbs can't think. She is sorry to find he is discontented, which is sinful and horrid, and hopes Mr. Squeers will flog him into a happier state of mind; with this view, she has also stopped his half penny a week pocket money, and given a double-bladed knife with a corkscrew in it to the Missionaries, which she had bought on purpose for him."

"A sulky state of feeling," said Squeers after a terrible pause, during which he had moistened the palm of his right hand again, "won't do. Cheerfulness and contentment must be kept up. Mobbs, come to me!"

Mobbs moved slowly toward the desk, rubbing his eyes in anticipation of good cause for doing so; and he soon afterward retired by the side door, with as good cause as a boy need have.

Mr. Squeers then proceeded to open a miscellaneous collection of letters; some inclosing money, which Mrs. Squeers "took care of;" and others referring to small articles of apparel, as caps and so forth, all of which the same lady stated to be too large, or too small, and calculated for nobody but young Squeers, who would appear indeed to have had most accommodating limbs, since everything that came into the school fitted him to a nicety. His head, in particular, must have been singularly elastic, for hats and caps of all dimensions were alike to him.

The business dispatched, a few slovenly lessons were performed, and Squeers retired to his fireside, leaving Nicholas to take care of the boys in the schoolroom, which was very cold, and where a meal of bread and cheese was served out shortly after dark.

There was a small stove at that corner of the room which

was nearest to the master's desk, and by it Nicholas sat down, so depressed and self-degraded by the consciousness of his position, that if death could have come upon him at that time, he would have been almost happy to meet it. The cruelty of which he had been an unwilling witness, the coarse and ruffianly behavior of Squeers, even in his best moods, the filthy place, the sights and sounds about him, all contributed to this state of feeling; but when he recollected that, being there as an assistant, he actually seemed—no matter what unhappy train of circumstances had brought him to that pass—to be the aider and abettor of a system which filled him with honest disgust and indignation, he loathed himself, and felt, for the moment, as though the mere consciousness of his present situation must, through all time to come, prevent his raising his head again.

But, for the present, his resolve was taken, and the resolution he had formed on the preceding night remained undisturbed. He had written to his mother and sister, announcing the safe conclusion of his journey, and saying as little about Dothèboys Hall, and saying that little as cheerfully, as he possibly could. He hoped that by remaining where he was, he might do some good, even there; at all events, others depended too much on his uncle's favor, to admit of his awakening his wrath just then.

One reflection disturbed him far more than any selfish consideration arising out of his own position. This was the probable destination of his sister Kate. His uncle had deceived him, and might he not consign her to some miserable place where her youth and beauty would prove a far greater curse than ugliness and decrepitude? To a caged man, bound hand and foot, this was a terrible idea; but no, he thought, his mother was by; there was the portrait-painter, too—simple enough, but still living in the world and of it. He was willing to believe that Ralph Nickleby had conceived a personal dislike to himself. Having pretty good reason, by this time, to reciprocate it, he had no great difficulty in arriving at this conclusion, and tried to persuade himself that the feeling extended no further than between them.

As he was absorbed in these meditations, he all at once encountered the upturned face of Smike, who was on his knees before the stove, picking a few stray cinders from the hearth and planting them on the fire. He had paused to steal a look at Nicholas, and when he saw that he was observed, shrunk back as if expecting a blow.

"You need not fear me," said Nicholas, kindly. "Are you cold?"

"N-n-o."

"You are shivering."

"I am not cold," replied Smike, quickly. "I am used to it."

There was such an obvious fear of giving offence in his manner, and he was such a timid, broken-spirited creature, that Nicholas could not help exclaming, "Poor fellow!"

If he had struck the drudge, he would have slunk away without a word. But now he burst into tears.

"Oh, dear, oh, dear!" he cried, covering his face with his cracked and horny hands. "My heart will break. It will, it will!"

"Hush!" said Nicholas, laying his hand upon his shoulder. "be a man; you are nearly one by years, God help you!"

"By years!" cried Smike. "Oh, dear, dear, how many of them! How many of them since I was a little child, younger than any that are here now! Where are they all?"

"Whom do you speak of?" inquired Nicholas, wishing to rouse the poor half-witted creature to reason. "Tell me."

"My friends," he replied, "myself—my—oh! what sufferings mine have been!"

"There is always hope," said Nicholas; he knew not what to say.

"No," rejoined the other; "no, none for me. Do you remember the boy that died here?"

"I was not here, you know," said Nicholas, gently; "but what of him?"

"Why," replied the youth, drawing closer to his questioner's side, "I was with him at night, and when it was all silent he cried no more for friends he wished to come and sit with him, but began to see faces round his bed that came from home; he said they smiled and talked to him; and he died at last lifting his head to kiss them. Do you hear?"

"Yes, yes," rejoined Nicholas.

"What faces will smile on me when I die?" cried his companion, shivering. "Who will talk to me in those long nights? They cannot come from home; they would frighten me if they did, for I don't know what it is, and shouldn't know them. Pain and fear, pain and fear for me, alive or dead. No hope, no hope!"

The bell rang to bed; and the boy, subsiding at the sound into his usual listless state, crept away as if anxious to avoid notice. It was with a heavy heart that Nicholas soon afterward —no, not retired; there was no retirement there—followed, to his dirty and crowded dormitory.

. . . .

The wretched creature, Smike, since the night Nicholas had spoken kindly to him in the schoolroom, had followed him to and fro, with an ever restless desire to serve or help him; anticipating such little wants as his humble ability could supply, and content only to be near him. He would sit beside him for hours, looking patiently into his face; and a word would brighten up his careworn visage, and call into it a passing gleam, even of happiness. He was an altered being; he had an object now; and that object was, to show his attachment to the only person—that person a stranger—who had treated him, not to say with kindness, but like a human creature.

Upon this poor being, all the spleen and ill-humor that could not be vented on Nicholas were unceasingly bestowed. Drudgery would have been nothing—Smike was well used to that. Buffetings inflicted without cause, would have been equally a matter of course; for to them also he had served a long and weary apprenticeship; but it was no sooner observed that he had become attached to Nicholas, than stripes and blows, stripes and blows, morning, noon, and night, were his only portion.

Squeers was jealous of the influence which his man had so soon acquired, and his family hated him, and Smike paid for both. Nicholas saw it, and ground his teeth at every repetition of the savage and cowardly attack.

He had arranged a few regular lessons for the boys; and one night as he paced up and down the schoolroom, his swollen heart almost bursting to think that his protection and countenance should have increased the misery of the wretched being whose peculiar destitution had awakened his pity, he paused mechanically in a dark corner where sat the object of his thoughts.

The poor soul was poring hard over a tattered book, with the traces of recent tears still upon his face, vainly endeavoring to master some task which a child of nine years old, possessed of ordinary powers, could have conquered with ease, but which, to the addled brain of the crushed boy of nineteen, was a sealed and hopeless mystery. Yet there he sat, patiently conning the page again and again, stimulated by no boyish ambition, for he was the common jest and scoff even of the uncouth objects that congregated about him, but inspired by the one eager desire to please his solitary friend.

Nicholas laid his hand upon his shoulder.

"I can't do it," said the dejected creature, looking up with bitter disappointment in every feature. "No, no."

"Do not try," replied Nicholas.

The boy shook his head, and, closing the book with a sigh, looked vacantly round, and laid his head upon his arm. He was weeping.

"Do not, for God's sake," said Nicholas, in an agitated voice; "I cannot bear to see you."

"They are more hard with me than ever," sobbed the boy.

"I know it," rejoined Nicholas. "They are."

"But for you," said the outcast, "I should die. They would kill me; they would; I know they would."

"You will do better, poor fellow," replied Nicholas, shaking his head mournfully, "when I am gone."

"Gone!" cried the other, looking intently in his face.

"Softly!" rejoined Nicholas. "Yes."

"Are you going?" demanded the boy, in an earnest whisper.

"I cannot say," replied Nicholas. "I was speaking more to my own thoughts than to you."

"Tell me," said the boy, imploringly, "oh, do tell me, *will* you go—*will* you?"

"I shall be driven to that at last!" said Nicholas. "The world is before me, after all."

"Tell me," urged Smike, "is the world as bad and dismal as this place?"

"Heaven forbid!" replied Nicholas, pursuing the train of his own thoughts. "Its hardest, coarsest toil were happiness to this."

"Should I ever meet you there?" demanded the boy, speaking with unusual wildness and volubility.

"Yes," replied Nicholas, willing to soothe him.

"No, no!" said the other, clasping him by the hand. "Should I—should I—tell me that again. Say I should be sure to find you."

"You would," replied Nicholas, with the same humane intention, "and I would help and aid you, and not bring fresh sorrow on you, as I have done here."

The boy caught both the young man's hands passionately in his, and, hugging them to his breast, uttered a few broken sounds, which were unintelligible. Squeers entered, at the moment, and he shrank back into his old corner. . . .

The cold, feeble dawn of a January morning was stealing in at the windows of the common sleeping-room, when Nicholas, raising himself on his arm, looked among the prostrate forms which on every side surrounded him, as though in search of some particular object.

It needed a quick eye to detect, from among the huddled mass of sleepers, the form of any given individual. As they lay closely packed together, covered, for warmth's sake, with their patched and ragged clothes, little could be distinguished but the sharp outlines of pale faces, over which the somber light shed the same dull heavy color; with here and there a gaunt arm thrust forth; its thinness hidden by no covering, but fully exposed to view, in all its shrunken ugliness. There were some who, lying on their backs with upturned faces and clinched hands, just visible in the leaden light, bore more the aspect of dead bodies than of living creatures; and there were others coiled up into strange and fantastic postures, such as might have been taken for the uneasy efforts of pain to gain some temporary relief, rather than the freaks of slumber. A few—and these were among the youngest of the children—slept peacefully on, with smiles upon their faces, dreaming perhaps of home; but ever and again a deep and heavy sigh, breaking the stillness of the room, announced that some new sleeper had awakened to the misery of another day; and, as morning took the place of night, the smiles gradually faded away, with the friendly darkness which had given them birth.

Dreams are the bright creatures of poem and legend, who sport on earth in the night season, and melt away in the first beam of the sun, which lights grim care and stern reality on their daily pilgrimage through the world.

Nicholas looked upon the sleepers; at first, with the air of one who gazes upon a scene which, though familiar to him, has lost none of its sorrowful effect in consequence; and afterward, with a more intense and searching scrutiny, as a man would who missed something his eye was accustomed to meet, and had expected to rest upon. He was still occupied in this search, and had half risen from his bed in the eagerness of his quest, when the voice of Squeers was heard, calling from the bottom of the stairs.

"Now, then," cried that gentleman, "are you going to sleep all day up there——"

"You lazy hounds!" added Mrs. Squeers, finishing the sentence, and producing at the same time a sharp sound, like that which is occasioned by the lacing of stays.

"We shall be down directly, sir," replied Nicholas.

"Down directly!" said Squeers. "Ah! you had better be down directly, or I'll be down upon some of you in less. Where's that Smike?"

Nicholas looked hurriedly round again, but made no answer.

"Smike!" shouted Squeers.

"Do you want your head broke in a fresh place, Smike?" demanded his amiable lady, in the same key.

Still there was no reply, and still Nicholas stared about him, as did the greater part of the boys, who were by this time roused.

"Confound his impudence!" muttered Squeers, rapping the stair-rail impatiently with his cane. "Nickleby!"

"Well, sir?"

"Send that obstinate scoundrel down; don't you hear me calling?"

"He is not here, sir," replied Nicholas.

"Don't tell me a lie!" retorted the schoolmaster. "He is."

"He is not," retorted Nicholas, angrily; "don't tell me one."

"We shall soon see that," said Mr. Squeers, rushing upstairs. "I'll find him, I warrant you."

With which assurance Mr. Squeers bounced into the dormitory, and, swinging his cane in the air ready for a blow, darted into the corner where the lean body of the drudge was usually stretched at night. The cane descended harmlessly upon the ground. There was nobody there.

"What does this mean?" said Squeers, turning round, with a very queer face. "Where have you hid him?"

"I have seen nothing of him since last night," replied Nicholas.

"Come," said Squeers, evidently frightened, though he endeavored to look otherwise, "you won't save him this way. Where is he?"

"At the bottom of the nearest pond for aught I know," rejoined Nicholas in a low voice, and fixing his eyes full on the master's face.

"D—n you, what do you mean by that?" retorted Squeers

in great perturbation. Without waiting for a reply, he inquired of the boys whether any one among them knew anything of their missing schoolmate.

There was a general hum of anxious denial, in the midst of which, one shrill voice was heard to say (as indeed, everybody thought):

"Please, sir, I think Smike's run away, sir."

"Ha!" cried Squeers, turning sharp round. "Who said that?"

"Tomkins, please, sir," rejoined a chorus of voices. Mr. Squeers made a plunge into the crowd, and at one dive, caught a very little boy, habited still in his night gear, and the perplexed expression of whose countenance as he was brought forward, seemed to intimate that he was as yet uncertain whether he was about to be punished or rewarded for the suggestion. He was not long in doubt.

"You think he has run away, do you, sir?" demanded Squeers.

"Yes, please, sir," replied the little boy.

"And what, sir," said Squeers, catching the little boy suddenly by the arms and whisking up his drapery in a most dexterous manner; "what reason have you to suppose that any boy would want to run away from this establishment? Eh, sir?"

The child raised a dismal cry, by way of answer, and Mr. Squeers, throwing himself into the most favorable attitude for exercising his strength, beat him until the little urchin in his writhings actually rolled out of his hands, when he mercifully allowed him to roll away, as best he could.

"There," said Squeers. "Now, if any other boy thinks Smike has run away, I should be glad to have a talk with him."

There was, of course, a profound silence, during which Nicholas showed his disgust as plainly as looks could show it.

"Well, Nickleby," said Squeers, eyeing him maliciously. "*You* think he has run away, I suppose?"

"I think it extremely likely," replied Nicholas, in a quiet manner.

"Oh, you do, do you?" sneered Squeers. "Maybe you know he has?"

"I know nothing of the kind."

"He didn't tell you he was going, I suppose, did he?" sneered Squeers.

"He did not," replied Nicholas; "I am very glad he did not, for it would then have been my duty to have warned you in time."

"Which no doubt you would have been devilish sorry to do," said Squeers, in a taunting fashion.

"I should, indeed," replied Nicholas. "You interpret my feelings with great accuracy."

Mrs. Squeers had listened to this conversation from the bottom of the stairs, but, now losing all patience, she hastily assumed her night-jacket, and made her way to the scene of action.

"What's all this here to do?" said the lady, as the boys fell off right and left, to save her the trouble of clearing a passage with her brawny arms. "What on earth are you talking to him for, Squeery?"

"Why, my dear," said Squeers, "the fact is, that Smike is not to be found."

"Well I know that," said the lady, "and where's the wonder? If you get a parcel of proud-stomached teachers that set the young dogs a rebelling, what else can you look for? Now, young man, you just have the kindness to take yourself off to the schoolroom, and take the boys off with you, and don't you stir out of there till you have leave given you, or you and I may fall out in a way that'll spoil your beauty, handsome as you think yourself, and so I tell you."

"Indeed!" said Nicholas.

"Yes; and indeed and indeed again, Mister Jackanapes," said the excited lady; "and I wouldn't keep such as you in the house another hour, if I had my way."

"Nor would you if I had mine," replied Nicholas. "Now, boys!"

"Ah! Now, boys," said Mrs. Squeers, mimicking, as nearly

as she could, the voice and manner of the usher. "Follow your leader, boys, and take pattern by Smike, if you dare. See what he'll get for himself, when he is brought back; and, mind! I tell you that you shall have as bad and twice as bad, if you so much as open your mouths about him."

"If I catch him," said Squeers, "I'll only stop short of flaying him alive. I give you notice, boys."

"*If* you catch him," retorted Mrs. Squeers, contemptuously, "you are sure to; you can't help it, if you go the right way to work! Come! Away with you!"

With these words, Mrs. Squeers dismissed the boys, and after a little light skirmishing with those in the rear who were pressing forward to get out of the way, but were detained for a few moments by the throng in front, succeeded in clearing the room, when she confronted her spouse alone.

"He is off!" said Mrs. Squeers. "The cow-house and stable are locked up, so he can't be there; and he's not down-stairs anywhere, for the girl has looked. He must have gone York way, and by a public road, too."

"Why must he?" inquired Squeers.

"Stupid!" said Mrs. Squeers, angrily. "He hadn't any money, had he?"

"Never had a penny of his own in his whole life, that I know of," replied Squeers.

"To be sure," rejoined Mrs. Squeers, "and he didn't take anything to eat with him; that I'll answer for. Ha! ha! ha!"

"Ha! ha! ha!" laughed Squeers.

"Then, of course," said Mrs. S., "he must beg his way, and he could do that, nowhere, but on the public road."

"That's true," exclaimed Squeers, clapping his hands.

"True! Yes; but you would never have thought of it, for all that, if I hadn't said so," replied his wife. "Now, if you take the chaise and go one road, and I borrow Swallow's chaise and go the other, what with keeping our eyes open, and asking questions, one or other of us is pretty certain to lay hold of him."

The worthy lady's plan was adopted and put in execution without a moment's delay. After a very hasty breakfast, and the prosecution of some inquiries in the village, the result of which seemed to show that he was on the right track, Squeers started forth in the pony-chaise, intent upon discovery and vengeance. Shortly afterward, Mrs. Squeers, arrayed in the white top-coat, and tied up in various shawls and handkerchiefs, issued forth in another chaise and another direction, taking with her a good-sized bludgeon, several odd pieces of strong cord, and a stout laboring man—all provided and carried upon the expedition, with the sole object of assisting in the capture, and (once caught) insuring the safe custody of the unfortunate Smike.

Nicholas remained behind, in a tumult of feeling, sensible that whatever might be the upshot of the boy's flight, nothing but painful and deplorable consequences were likely to ensue from it. Death, from want and exposure to the weather, was the best that could be expected from the protracted wandering of so poor and helpless a creature, alone and unfriended, through a country of which he was wholly ignorant. There was little, perhaps, to choose between this fate and a return to the tender mercies of the Yorkshire school; but the unhappy being had established a hold upon his sympathy and compassion, which made his heart ache at the prospect of the suffering he was destined to undergo. He lingered on in restless anxiety, picturing a thousand possibilities, until the evening of the next day, when Squeers returned alone and unsuccessful.

"No news of the scamp!" said the schoolmaster, who had evidently been stretching his legs, on the old principle, not a few times during the journey. "I'll have consolation for this out of somebody, Nickleby, if Mrs. Squeers don't hunt him down. So I give you warning."

"It is not in my power to console you, sir," said Nicholas. "It is nothing to me."

"Isn't it?" said Squeers, in a threatening manner. "We shall see!"

"We shall," rejoined Nicholas.

"Here's the pony run right off his legs, and me obliged to come home with a hack cob, that'll cost fifteen shillings besides other expenses," said Squeers; "who's to pay for that, do you hear?"

Nicholas shrugged his shoulders, and remained silent.

"I'll have it out of somebody, I tell you," said Squeers, his usual harsh, crafty manner changed to open bullying. "None of your whining vaporings here, Mr. Puppy; but be off to your kennel, for it's past your bed-time! Come, get out!"

Nicholas bit his lip and knit his hands involuntarily, for his finger-ends tingled to avenge the insult; but remembering that the man was drunk, and that it could come to little but a noisy brawl, he contented himself with darting a contemptuous look at the tyrant, and walked, as majestically as he could, upstairs; not a little nettled, however, to observe that Miss Squeers, and Master Squeers, and the servant girl, were enjoying the scene from a snug corner; the two former indulging in many edifying remarks about the presumption of poor upstarts, which occasioned a vast deal of laughter, in which even the most miserable of all miserable servant girls joined; while Nicholas, stung to the quick, drew over his head such bed-clothes as he had, and sternly resolved that the outstanding account between himself and Mr. Squeers should be settled rather more speedily than the latter anticipated.

Another day came, and Nicholas was scarcely awake when he heard the wheels of a chaise approaching the house. It stopped. The voice of Mrs. Squeers was heard, and in exultation, ordering a glass of spirits for somebody, which was in itself a sufficient sign that something extraordinary had happened. Nicholas hardly dared to look out of the window; but he did so, and the very first object that met his eyes was the wretched Smike so bedabbled with mud and rain, so haggard, and worn, and wild, that, but for his garments being such as no scarecrow was ever seen to wear, he might have been doubtful, even then, of his identity.

"Lift him out," said Squeers, after he had literally feasted his eyes in silence upon the culprit. "Bring him in; bring him in!"

"Take care," cried Mrs. Squeers, as her husband proffered his assistance. "We tied his legs under the apron and made 'em fast to the chaise, to prevent him giving us the slip again."

With hands trembling with delight, Squeers unloosened the cord; and Smike, to all appearance more dead than alive, was brought into the house and securely locked up in a cellar, until such time as Mr. Squeers should deem it expedient to operate upon him, in presence of the assembled school.

Upon a hasty consideration of the circumstances it may be matter of surprise to some persons that Mr. and Mrs. Squeers should have taken so much trouble to repossess themselves of an incumbrance of which it was their wont to complain so loudly; but their surprise will cease when they are informed that the manifold services of the drudge, if performed by anybody else, would have cost the establishment some ten or twelve shillings per week in the shape of wages; and, furthermore, that all runaways were, as a matter of policy, made severe examples of at Dotheboys Hall, inasmuch as, in consequence of the limited extent of its attractions, there was but little inducement beyond the powerful impulse of fear, for any pupil, provided with the usual number of legs, and the power of using them, to remain.

The news that Smike had been caught and brought back in triumph ran like wild-fire through the hungry community, and expectation was on tiptoe all the morning. On tiptoe it was destined to remain, however, until afternoon; when Squeers, having refreshed himself with his dinner, and further strengthened himself by an extra libation or so, made his appearance (accompanied by his amiable partner) with a countenance of portentous import, and a fearful instrument of flagellation, strong, supple, wax-ended, and new—in short, purchased that morning expressly for the occasion.

"Is every boy here?" asked Squeers, in a tremendous voice.

Every boy was there, but every boy was afraid to speak; so

Squeers glared along the lines to assure himself; and every eye drooped, and every head cowered down, as he did so.

"Each boy keep his place," said Squeers, administering his favorite blow to the desk, and regarding with gloomy satisfaction the universal start which it never failed to occasion. "Nickleby! to your desk, sir."

It was remarked by more than one small observer that there was a very curious and unusual expression in the usher's face; but he took his seat without opening his lips in reply. Squeers, casting a triumphant glance at his assistant and a look of most comprehensive despotism on the boys, left the room, and shortly afterward returned, dragging Smike by the collar—or rather by that fragment of his jacket which was nearest the place where his collar would have been, had he boasted such a decoration.

In any other place, the appearance of the wretched, jaded, spiritless object would have occasioned a murmur of compassion and remonstrance. It had some effect even there; for the lookers-on moved uneasily in their seats, and a few of the boldest ventured to steal looks at each other, expressive of indignation and pity.

They were lost on Squeers, however, whose gaze was fastened on the luckless Smike, as he inquired, according to custom in such cases, whether he had anything to say for himself.

"Nothing, I suppose?" said Squeers, with a diabolical grin.

Smike glanced round, and his eye rested, for an instant, on Nicholas, as if he had expected him to intercede; but his look was riveted on his desk.

"Have you anything to say?" demanded Squeers again; giving his right arm two or three flourishes to try its power and suppleness. "Stand a little out of the way, Mrs. Squeers, my dear; I've hardly got room enough."

"Spare me, sir!" cried Smike.

"Oh! that's all, is it?" said Squeers. "Yes, I'll flog you within an inch of your life, and spare you that."

"Ha, ha, ha!" laughed Mrs. Squeers, "that's a good 'un!"

"I was driven to do it," said Smike, faintly; and casting another imploring look about him.

"Driven to do it, were you?" said Squeers. "Oh! it wasn't your fault; it was mine, I suppose—eh?"

"A nasty, ungrateful, pig-headed brutish, obstinate, sneaking dog," exclaimed Mrs. Squeers, taking Smike's head under her arm, and administering a cuff at every epithet; "what does he mean by that?"

"Stand aside, my dear," replied Squeers. "We'll try and find out."

Mrs. Squeers being out of breath with her exertions, complied. Squeers caught the boy firmly in his grip; one desperate cut had fallen on his body—he was wincing from the lash and uttering a scream of pain—it was raised again, and again about to fall—when Nicholas Nickleby suddenly starting up, cried, "Stop!" in a voice that made the rafters ring.

"Who cried stop?" said Squeers, turning savagely round.

"I," said Nicholas, stepping forward. "This must not go on."

"Must not go on!" cried Squeers, almost in a shriek.

"No!" thundered Nicholas.

Aghast and stupefied by the boldness of the interference, Squeers released his hold of Smike, and, falling back a pace or two, gazed upon Nicholas with looks that were positively frightful.

"I say must not," repeated Nicholas, nothing daunted; "shall not. I will prevent it."

Squeers continued to gaze upon him, with his eyes starting out of his head; but astonishment had actually for the moment bereft him of speech.

"You have disregarded all my quiet interference in the miserable lad's behalf," said Nicholas; "you have returned no answer to the letter in which I begged forgiveness for him, and offered to be responsible that he would remain quietly here. Don't blame me for this public interference. You have brought it upon yourself; not I."

"Sit down, beggar!" screamed Squeers, almost beside himself with rage, and seizing Smike as he spoke.

"Wretch," rejoined Nicholas, fiercely, "touch him at your peril! I will not stand by and see it done. My blood is up, and I have the strength of ten such men as you. Look to yourself, for by Heaven I will not spare you, if you drive me on!"

"Stand back!" cried Squeers, brandishing his weapon.

"I have a long series of insults to avenge," said Nicholas, flushed with passion; "and my indignation is aggravated by the dastardly cruelties practiced on helpless infancy in this foul den. Have a care; for if you do raise the devil within me, the consequences shall fall heavily upon your own head!"

He had scarcely spoken, when Squeers, in a violent outbreak of wrath, and with a cry like the howl of a wild beast, spat upon him, and struck him a blow across the face with his instrument of torture, which raised up a bar of livid flesh as it was inflicted. Smarting with the agony of the blow and concentrating into that one moment all his feelings of rage, scorn and indignation, Nicholas sprang upon him, wrested the weapon from his hand, and pinning him by the throat, beat the ruffian till he roared for mercy.

The boys—with the exception of Master Squeers, who, coming to his father's assistance, harassed the enemy in the rear—moved not, hand or foot; but Mrs. Squeers, with many shrieks for aid, hung on to the tail of her partner's coat, and endeavored to drag him from his infuriated adversary; while Miss Squeers who had been peeping through the key-hole in the expectation of a very different scene, darted in at the very beginning of the attack, and after launching a shower of ink-stands at the usher's head, beat Nicholas to her heart's content, animating herself, at every blow, with the recollection of his having refused her proffered love, and thus imparting additional strength to an arm which (as she took after her mother in this respect) was, at no time, one of the weakest.

Nicholas, in the full torrent of his violence, felt the blows no more than if they had been dealt with feathers; but, becoming tired of the noise and uproar, and feeling that his arm grew weak besides, he threw all his remaining strength into half-a-dozen finishing cuts, and flung Squeers from him, with all the force he could muster. The violence of his fall precipitated Mrs. Squeers completely over an adjacent form; and Squeers, striking his head against it in his descent, lay at his full length on the ground, stunned and motionless.

Having brought affairs to this happy termination, and ascertained, to his thorough satisfaction, that Squeers was only stunned, and not dead (upon which point he had had some unpleasant doubts at first), Nicholas left his family to restore him, and retired to consider what course he had better adopt. He looked anxiously round for Smike, as he left the room, but he was nowhere to be seen.

After a brief consideration, he packed up a few clothes in a small leathern valise, and, finding that nobody offered to oppose his progress, marched boldly out by the front door, and, shortly afterward, struck into the road which led to Greta Bridge.

WILLIAM MATHEWS

1818

WILLIAM MATHEWS was born in Waterville, Maine, in 1818. He was a precocious pupil, and entered Waterville College (now Colby University), at the age of thirteen. Here he was graduated in 1835. He studied law at Harvard University, but abandoned the legal practice after a brief experience as an attorney. He established at Waterville a famous literary paper, the *Yankee Blade*, which was subsequently transferred to Boston.

Dr. Mathews removed in 1856 to Chicago, where he engaged in literary work. For twelve years or more he was professor of literature in the University of Chicago. Having published two books which had an extraordinary sale, he resigned his chair in order to devote himself wholly to literature. In 1880 Dr. Mathews removed to Boston, where he has since resided.

His principal works are "Getting on in the World" (which has been reproduced in London and in Canada, and translated into Swedish, Norwegian and Magyar); "The Great Conversers;" "Words: their Use and Abuse;" "Hours with Men and Books;" "Monday Chats: a Translation of Selections from Saint Beuve's 'Causeries du Lundi;'" "Orators and Oratory;" "Literary Style, and other Essays;" "Men, Places and Things," and "Wit and Humor: their Use and Abuse."

Characterization

It is not every one who has been able to be useful when aiming to amuse, or so sensible while amusing, as has Dr. Mathews. Humor and good sense have gone to the making of this volume ("Hours with Men and Books"). A book that encourages the love of letters is so rare in this country that it is impossible not to be grateful to Dr. Mathews for one that is so kindly and attractive.

"ATLANTIC MONTHLY."

Dr. Mathews appears to have known everybody worth knowing, to have seen everything worth seeing, to have read everything worth

reading, and to have forgotten nothing worth remembering. Without the garb or the rod of the teacher, he allures to the bright realms of literature, and leads the way through smooth and delightful paths.
"NEW YORK TRIBUNE."

Judge Story as a Teacher

(From "Hours with Men and Books")

In the year 1836 the writer entered the Law School at Cambridge, and saw, for the first time, Judge Story, whose pupil he was for some two years to be. Rarely has the physiognomy of a distinguished man whose looks we had previously pictured to ourself contrasted so strikingly as in this instance with our ideal. Instead of a man "severe and stern to view," with an awe-inspiring countenance in every hue and lineament of which justice was legibly written, and whose whole demeanor manifested a fearful amount of stiffness, starch, and dignity,—in short, an incarnation of law, bristling all over with technicalities and subtleties,—a walking Coke upon Littleton,—we saw before us a sunny, smiling face which bespoke a heart full of kindness, and listened to a voice whose musical tones imparted interest to everything it communicated, whether dry subtleties of the law or reminiscences of the "giants in those days," when he was a practitioner at the bar, and of which he was so eloquent a panegyrist.

Further acquaintance deepened our first impressions; we found that he was the counselor, guide, philosopher, and friend of all his pupils; that without the slightest forfeiture of self-respect he could chat, jest, and laugh with all; and that if he never looked the Supreme Court judge, or assumed the airs of a Sir Oracle, it was simply because he had a real dignity and inward greatness of soul which rendered it needless that he should protect himself from intrusion by any *chevaux-de-frise*[1] of formalities,—still less by the frizzled, artificial locks, black robes, and portentous seals of a British judge, who without the insignia

[1] dread-naught cavalry—main dependence

of his office would almost despise himself. Overflowing as the judge was with legal lore, which bubbled up as from a perennial fountain, he made no display of learning; in this matter, as in the other, he never led one to suspect the absence of the reality by his over-preciseness and niceness about the shadow. His pupil did not pass many hours in his presence before he learned, too, that the same fertile mind that could illumine the depths of constitutional law and solve the knottiest and most puzzling problems of commercial jurisprudence could also enliven the monotony of recitation by a keen witticism or a sparkling pun. Though thirty years and more have elapsed since the time of which we speak, we can yet see him in fancy as plainly as we see his portrait hanging before us. It is two o'clock, P.M.; he walks briskly into the recitation-room, his face wreathed with smiles, and, laying down his white hat, takes his seat at the table, puts on his spectacles, and, with a semi-quizzical look, inquires as he glances about the room:

"Where do I begin to-day? Ah! Mr. L——, I believe you *dodged out*, yesterday, just before I reached you; so we'll begin with you."

This sally provokes a laugh, in which the judge joins as heartily as the students; and then begins perhaps an examination in "Long on Sales," a brief treatise, which suggests the remark that "Long is short, and short because he *is* Long; a writer who can condense into a small book what others would spin out into volumes."

Probably no two teachers of equal ability were ever associated who were more unlike in the constitution of their minds, and who conducted a recitation in modes more dissimilar, than Judge Story and Professor Greenleaf. The latter, the *beau ideal*[1] of a lawyer in his physique, was severe and searching in the class-room, probing the student to the quick, accepting no half answers or vague general statements for accurate replies; showing no mercy to laziness; and when he commented on the

---

[1] a conception or image of consummate beauty, formed in the mind, free from all the deformities, defects, and blemishes which nature exhibits

text, it was always in the fewest, pithiest words that would convey the ideas. Language in his mouth seemed to have proclaimed a sumptuary law, forbidding that it should in any case overstep the limits of the thought. Indolent students who had skimmed over the lesson dreaded his scrutiny, for they knew that an examination by him was a literal weighing of their knowledge—that they could impose on him by no shams. Judge Story's *forte*, on the other hand, was in lecturing, not in questioning; in the communication of information, not in ascertaining the exact sum of the pupil's knowledge. In most cases his questions were put in such a way as to suggest the answer. For example, having stated two modes of legal proceeding under certain circumstances, he would ask the student:

"Would you adopt the former course, or would you *rather* adopt the latter?"

"I would rather adopt the latter," the student would reply, who perhaps had not looked at the lesson.

"You are right," would be the comment of the kind-hearted Dane professor; "Lord Mansfield himself could not have answered more correctly." Whether he was too good-natured to put the student on the rack, or thought the time might be more profitably spent, we know not; but no one feared to recite because he was utterly ignorant of the lesson.

The manner of the judge, when lecturing, was that of an enthusiast rather than of a professional teacher. The recitation—if recitation it could be called, where the professor was questioned on many days nearly as often as the student—was not confined to the text-book; but everything that could throw light on the subject in hand—all the limitations or modifications of the principles laid down by the author—were fully stated and illustrated by numerous apt examples. The book was merely the starting point whence excursions were made into all the cognate provinces of the law, from which the *opima spolia*[1] of a keen and searching intellect and a capacious memory could be gathered. His readiness of invention, as his son

[1] the richest booty

has remarked in the biography of his father, was particularly exhibited in the facility and exhaustless ingenuity with which he supplied fictitious cases to illustrate a principle, and shaped the circumstances so as to expose and make prominent the various exceptions to which it was subject. Often his illustrations were drawn from incidents of the day, and the listless student whose ears had been pricked up by some amusing tale or anecdote, found that all this was but the gilding of the pill, and that he had been cheated into swallowing a large dose of legal wisdom. Thus "he attracted the mind along, instead of driving it. Alive himself, he made the law alive. His lectures were not bundles of dried fagots, but budding scions. Like the Chinese juggler, he planted the seed, and made it grow before the eyes of his pupils into a tree."

Few men have ever been less subject to moods. He had no fits of enthusiasm. Of those alternations of mental sunshine and gloom—of buoyancy and depression—to which most men, and especially men of genius, are subject, he seemed to know nothing. Nor did he, even when most overwhelmed with work, manifest any sense of weariness. After having tried a tedious and intricate case in the United States Court-room in Boston, he was as fresh, elastic, and vivacious in the recitation room as if he had taken a mountain walk or some other bracing exercise. He had that rare gift, the faculty of communicating; and loved, above all things else, to communicate knowledge. The one ruling passion of his mind was what the French writer calls "*un goût dominant d'instruire et documenter quelqu'un.*"[1] Few men with equal stores of learning have had a more perfect command of their acquisitions. All his knowledge, whether gathered from musty black-letter folios or from modern octavos, was at the tip of his tongue. He had no unsmelted gold or bullion, but kept his intellectual riches in the form of current coin, as negotiable as it was valuable. His extraordinary fluency, his vast acquirements, his sympathy with the young, and especially his personal magnetism, eminently fitted him to be a teacher. To

---

[1] a ruling desire to instruct and *to document* somebody

smooth the pathway of the legal learner, to give a clew by which to thread the labyrinths of jurisprudence, to hold a torch by which to light his way through its dark passages—above all, to kindle in his breast some of his own ever-burning enthusiasm—was to the judge a constant joy. We doubt if ever a dull hour was known in his lecture-room. His perennial liveliness; his frankness and *abandon;* his " winning smile, that played lambent as heat-lightning around his varying countenance ; " his bubbling humor; his contagious, merry and irresistible laugh ; his exhaustless fund of incident and anecdote, with which he never failed to give piquancy and zest to the driest and most crabbed themes—all won not only the attention, but the love of his pupils, and he who could have yawned amid such stimulants to attention, must have been dull indeed. Only a dunce or a beatified intelligence could listen uninterested to such a teacher.

Judge Story was fond of telling that Mr. Webster, on one or two occasions, after grumbling at a legal decision of the former, had afterwards the magnanimity to acknowledge that he was wrong. We are sure that when the judge himself was in error, he was frank, on discovering it, to avow the fact. One day in the Moot Court, as a student, arguing a case before him, said : " My next authority will be one which Your Honor will not be disposed to question—a decision by Mr. Justice Story, of the United States Supreme Court—"   "I beg your pardon," said the judge, bowing, " but that opinion by Mr. Justice Story is *not* law."

It was well observed by Charles Sumner, in his eulogy of Judge Story, that any just estimate of the man and his works must have regard to his three different characters—as a judge, as an author, and as a teacher. When we look at his books only, we are astonished at his colossal industry : it seems almost incredible that a single mind, in a single life, should have been able to accomplish so much. His written judgments on his own circuit, and his various commentaries, occupy twenty-seven volumes, and his judgments in the Supreme Court of the

United States form an important part of thirty-four volumes. Rightly does Mr. Sumner characterize him as the Lope de Vega, or the Walter Scott, of the Common Law. With far more truth might it be said of him, than was said by Dryden of one of the greatest British lawyers:

> "Our law, that did a boundless ocean seem,
> Was coasted all, and fathomed all by him."

Besides all his legal labors he delivered many discourses on literary and scientific subjects, wrote many biographical sketches of his contemporaries, elaborated reviews for the *North American*, drew up learned memorials to Congress, made long speeches in the Massachusetts Legislature, contributed largely to the "Encyclopædia Americana," prepared Reports on Codification, etc., and drafted some of the most important Acts of Congress. The secret of these vast achievements was ceaseless, methodical industry, frequent change of labor, and concentration of mind. He economized odd moments, bits and fragments of time, never overworked, and, when he worked, concentrated upon the subject all the powers of his intellect. Add to this that his knowledge did not lie in undigested heaps in his mind, but was thoroughly assimilated, so as to become a part of his mental constitution. His brain was a vast repository of legal facts and principles, each one of which had its cell or pigeon-hole, from which it was always forthcoming whenever it was wanted.

No other American lawyer or jurist has so wide-spread a European fame. His legal works, republished in England, are recognized as of the highest authority in all the courts of that country; and his "Conflict of Laws"—embodying the essence of all similar works, as well as the fruits of his own deep thinking—a work of enormous labor upon a most intricate and perplexing theme—has been translated into many European languages, and is cited as the most inexhaustible discussion of the subject. Yet—such is fame—this man, whose name has crossed the Atlantic, and was on the lips of the most profound jurists of the Old World, had comparatively little reputation in his lifetime among his own countrymen. Men immeasurably inferior to him, intellectually and morally, overshadowed him in the public mind. And yet no man was more susceptible to merited praise than he. While he despised flattery and could detect the least taint of it with the quickness of an instinct, his heart was yet as fresh and tender as a child's, and he felt neglect as keenly as the bud the frost. Not soon shall we forget the good humor, mingled with a sensibility that could not be concealed, with which he told the following story of himself, illustrating the saying that "a prophet is not without honor, save in his own country":

"One day I was called suddenly to Boston to attend to some business matters, and on my way thither I discovered that I had forgotten my pocket-book. It was too late to return, and so, when the omnibus halted at the Port (Cambridgeport, half way between Old Cambridge, the judge's residence, and Boston), I ran hastily into the neighboring bank, and asked to be accommodated with a hundred dollars. The cashier stared at me as if he thought me insane; but I noticed that he particularly scrutinized my feet; and then he coldly informed me that he had not the pleasure of recognizing me. I immediately told him my name, supposing that it might have reached, at least, the limits of my own place of residence. He still kept his eyes upon my feet, and finally, as I was about to leave, more chagrined than disappointed, he requested me to step back, adding that he would be pleased to accommodate me. Upon my inquiring the reason of his delay, he replied: 'Sir, I have never heard your name before, but I know you must be a gentleman, *from the looks of your boots.*'" The unction and perfect good humor with which the judge told this anecdote, and the joyous laugh with which he concluded it—aside from the absurdity that such a man should be judged of by the *material understanding*—were irresistible. We need not add that his pupils laughed, as Falstaff says, "without intervellums"—till their faces were "like a wet cloak ill laid up."

We doubt if any teacher ever loved his pupils more deeply,

or was more universally loved by them, than the subject of this article. In the success of his "boys," as he called them, both at the school and in their after life, he felt a profound interest; their triumphs were his triumphs, and their failures caused him the keenest pain. The tact with which he adapted himself to the various temperaments and idiosyncrasies of his pupils, and the patience with which he bore any one's dullness, were also remarkable. We remember that one day a somewhat eccentric and outspoken student from Tennessee came to the judge in the library of the Law School, and, holding up an old folio, said: "Judge, what do you understand by this here rule in Shelley's Case? I've been studying it three days, and can't make anything out of it." "Shelley's Case! Shelley's Case!" exclaimed the judge, with a look of astonishment as he took the volume and held it up before his eyes. "Do you expect to understand that in three days? Why, it took *me* three weeks!"

. . . .

Within the lifetime of Judge Story, a volume of "Miscellanies" from his pen was published, containing his literary orations, contributions to reviews, and his beautiful address at the consecration of Mount Auburn Cemetery. There, under the trees that overshadow the lovely dell in which he spoke, lie his remains; and in the chapel, near the entrance to this home of the dead, stands a marble statue of the great jurist, executed by his son, W. W. Story, the sculptor and poet,—an exquisite work of art, in which all the characteristic qualities of the original are idealized, yet most faithfully reproduced and preserved.

GEORGE ELIOT

1819-1880

GEORGE ELIOT was the *nom de plume* assumed by Mary Ann Evans, one of the greatest novelists of our times. She was born at Arbury Farm, in the parish of Colton, Warwickshire, in 1819. Her father was Robert Evans, a carpenter, whose character is portrayed with more or less truth in the person of Adam Bede. At an early age she attended the village free school, and in 1828 she was sent to a boarding-school at Nuneaton. In 1832 she attended a school at Coventry, where she remained until December, 1835. Shortly after her return from school, in 1836, her mother died, and she assumed the care of her father's household. In 1841 they removed to Coventry, where she made the acquaintance of the family of Charles Bray, with whom she became very intimate. This connection had a marked effect upon her religious opinions, and led to an abandonment of her orthodox views. At about this time she began her literary work by a translation of Strauss's "Life of Jesus."

In 1849 her father died, and soon afterwards she went abroad. Upon her return to England, in 1850, she became assistant editor of the *Westminster Review*. She now found herself in the center of a large literary circle which included George Henry Lewes, with whom she fell in love. In 1854 she entered into a connection with Mr. Lewes, which was in every sense a marriage, though without legal sanction.

In 1856, urged by Mr. Lewes, she wrote her first novel, "Amos Barton," which, included in the "Scenes of Clerical Life," was published in *Blackwood's Magazine*. This was followed by "Adam Bede," the success of which was unprecedented.

From this time to the year of her death George Eliot wrote indefatigably, and she has contributed some of the finest novels to be found in English literature.

In 1878, Mr. Lewes died. In April, 1880, George Eliot married Mr. John Walter Cross, but their married life was of brief duration, as she died in December of the same year.

Her most important writings are: "Adam Bede;" "The Mill on the Floss;" "Silas Marner;" "Romola;" "Felix Holt, the Radical;" "Middlemarch;" "Daniel Deronda;" "Scenes from Clerical Life;" "The Spanish Gypsy;" "The Legend of Jubal," and "Theophrastus Such."

Characterization

It is at this point that we touch the secret spring of George Eliot's art: her whole work is imbued with ethical notions. The novel is, no less than the poem, a criticism of life; and the remarkable influence of George Eliot's novels has been mainly due to the consistent application of moral ideas to the problems set by each novel. Their stimulative effect was due to the fact that her ethical views were in consonance with some of the most advanced ideas of the age. The three chief principles which dominated her thinking were the reign of law in human affairs, the solidarity of society, and the constitution of society as incarnate history (the phrase is Riehl's). Flowing from these were the ethical laws which rule the world of her novels, the principle summed up in Novalis's words, "Character is Fate," the radiation of good and evil deeds throughout society, and the supreme claims of family or race. Add to these the scientific tone of impartiality, with its moral analogue, the extension of sympathy to all, and we have exhausted the *idées mères* of George Eliot's ethical system, which differentiates her novels from all others of the age.

JOSEPH JACOBS.

There can be no doubt that George Eliot touched the highest point which, in a woman, has been reached in our literature. . . . The remarkable thing about George Eliot's genius is that though there is nothing at all unfeminine in it—if we except a certain touch of scientific pedantry which is not pedantry in *motive*, but due only to a rather awkward manipulation of somewhat unfeminine learning—its greatest qualities are not the least the qualities in which women have usually surpassed men, but rather the qualities in which, till George Eliot's time, women had always been notably deficient. Largeness of mind, largeness of conception, was her first characteristic, as regards both matters of reason and matters of imagination. . . . Her own nature was evidently sedate and rather slow-moving, with a touch of Miltonic stateliness in it, and a love of elaboration at times even injurious to her genius. Yet no characters she ever drew were more powerful than those at the very opposite pole to her own. . . . Her greatest stories lose in form by their too wide reflectiveness, and especially by an engrafted mood of artificial reflectiveness not suitable to her genius. . . . No novelist, however, in the whole series of English novelists, has combined so much power of painting external life on a broad canvas with so wonderful an insight into the life of the soul.

"SPECTATOR."

The Night-School and the Schoolmaster
(From "Adam Bede")

Bartle Massey's was one of a few scattered houses on the edge of a common which was divided by the road to Treddleston. Adam reached it in a quarter of an hour after leaving the Hall Farm; and when he had his hand on the door latch, he could see, through the curtainless window, that there were eight or nine heads bending over the desks, lighted by thin dips.

When he entered, a reading lesson was going forward, and Bartle Massey merely nodded, leaving him to take his place where he pleased. He had not come for the sake of a lesson to-night, and his mind was too full of personal matters, too full of the first two hours he had passed in Hetty's presence, for him to amuse himself with a book till school was over; so he sat down in a corner, and looked on with an absent mind. It was a sort of scene which Adam had beheld almost weekly for years; he knew by heart every arabesque flourish in the framed specimen of Bartle Massey's handwriting which hung over the schoolmaster's head, by way of keeping a lofty ideal before the minds of his pupils; he knew the backs of all the books on the shelf running along the whitewashed wall above the pegs for the slates; he knew exactly how many grains were gone out of the ear of Indian-corn that hung from one of the rafters; he had long ago exhausted the resources of his imagination in trying to think how the bunch of feathery seaweed had looked and grown in its native element; and from the place where he sat he could make nothing of the old map of England that hung against the opposite wall, for age had turned it of a fine yellow-brown, something like that of a well-seasoned meerschaum. The drama that was going on was almost as familiar as the scene; nevertheless habit had not made him indifferent to it, and even in his present self-absorbed mood, Adam felt a momentary stirring of the old fellow-feeling as he looked at the rough men painfully holding pen or pencil with their cramped hands, or humbly laboring through their reading lesson.

The reading class now seated on the form in front of the schoolmaster's desk, consisted of the three most backward pupils. Adam would have known it, only by seeing Bartle Massey's face as he looked over his spectacles, which he had shifted to the ridge of his nose, not requiring them for present purposes. The face wore its mildest expression; the grizzled bushy eyebrows had taken their more acute angle of compassionate kindness, and the mouth, habitually compressed with a pout of the lower lip, was relaxed so as to be able to speak a hopeful word or syllable in a moment. This gentle expression was the more interesting because the schoolmaster's nose, an irregular aquiline twisted a little on one side, had rather a formidable character; and his brow, moreover, had that peculiar tension which always impresses one as a sign of a keen impatient temperament; the blue veins stood out like cords under the transparent yellow skin, and this intimidating brow was softened by no tendency to baldness, for the gray bristly hair, cut down to about an inch in length, stood round it in as close ranks as ever.

"Nay, Bill, nay," Bartle was saying, in a kind tone, as he nodded to Adam, "begin that again, and then, perhaps, it'll come to you what d, r, y, spells. It's the same lesson you read last week, you know."

"Bill" was a sturdy fellow, aged four-and-twenty, an excellent stone-sawyer, who could get as good wages as any man in the trade of his years; but he found a reading lesson in words of one syllable a harder matter to deal with than the hardest stone he had ever had to saw. The letters, he complained, were so "uncommon alike, there was no tellin' 'em one from another," the sawyer's business not being concerned with minute differences such as exist between a letter with its tail turned up and a letter with its tail turned down. But Bill had a firm determination that he would learn to read, founded chiefly on two reasons: first, that Tom Hazelow, his cousin, could read anything "right off," whether it was print or writing, and Tom had sent him a letter from twenty miles off, saying how he was prospering in the world, and had got an overlooker's place; secondly, that Sam Philips, who sawed with him, had learned to read when he was turned twenty; and what could be done by a little fellow like Sam Philips, Bill considered, could be done by himself, seeing that he could pound Sam into wet clay if circumstances required it. So here he was, pointing his big finger toward three words at once, and turning his head on one side that he might keep better hold with his eye of the one word which was to be discriminated out of the group. The amount of knowledge Bartle Massey must possess was something so dim and vast that Bill's imagination recoiled before it; he would hardly have ventured to deny that the schoolmaster might have something to do in bringing about the regular return of daylight and the changes in the weather.

The man seated next to Bill was of a very different type; he was a Methodist brickmaker, who, after spending thirty years of his life in perfect satisfaction with his ignorance, had lately "got religion," and along with it the desire to read the Bible. But with him, too, learning was a heavy business, and on his way out to-night he had offered as usual a special prayer for help, seeing that he had undertaken this hard task with a single eye to the nourishment of his soul—that he might have a greater abundance of texts and hymns wherewith to banish evil memories and the temptations of old habits; or, in brief language, the devil. For the brickmaker had been a notorious poacher, and was suspected, though there was no good evidence against him, of being the man who had shot a neighboring gamekeeper in the leg. However that might be, it is certain that shortly after the accident referred to, which was coincident with the arrival of an awakening Methodist preacher at Treddleston, a great change had been observed in the brickmaker; and though he was still known in the neighborhood by his old sobriquet of "Brimstone," there was nothing he held in so much horror as any farther transactions with that evil-smelling element. He was a broad-chested fellow with a fervid temperament, which helped him better in imbibing religious ideas than in the dry process of acquiring the mere human knowledge of the alphabet. Indeed, he had been already a little shaken in his resolution by a brother Methodist, who assured him that the letter was a mere obstruction to the Spirit, and expressed a fear that Brimstone was too eager for the knowledge that puffeth up.

The third beginner was a much more promising pupil. He was a tall but thin and wiry man, nearly as old as Brimstone, with a very pale face, and hands stained a deep blue. He was a dyer, who, in the course of dipping home-spun wool and old women's petticoats, had got fired with the ambition to learn a great deal more about the strange secrets of color. He had already a high reputation in the district for his dyes, and he was bent on discovering some method by which he could reduce the expense of crimsons and scarlets. The druggist at Treddleston had given him a notion that he might save himself a great deal of labor and expense if he could learn to read, and so he had begun to give his spare hours to the night-school, resolving that his "little chap" should lose no time in coming to Mr. Massey's day-school as soon as he was old enough.

It was touching to see these three big men, with the marks of their hard labor upon them, anxiously bending over the worn books, and painfully making out, "The grass is green," "The sticks are dry," "The corn is ripe"—a very hard lesson to pass to after columns of single words all alike except in the first letter. It was almost as if three rough animals were making humble efforts to learn how they might become human. And it touched the tenderest fiber in Bartle Massey's nature, for such full-grown children as these were the only pupils for whom he had no severe epithets, and no impatient tones. He was not gifted with an imperturbable temper, and on music nights it was apparent that patience could never be an easy virtue to him; but this evening, as he glances over his spectacles at Bill Downes, the sawyer, who is turning his head on one side with a desperate sense of blankness before the letters, d, r, y, his eyes shed their mildest and most encouraging light.

After the reading class, two youths, between sixteen and nineteen, came up with imaginary bills of parcels, which they had been writing out on their slates, and were now required to calculate "off-hand"—a test which they stood with such imperfect success that Bartle Massey, whose eyes had been glaring at them ominously through his spectacles for some minutes, at length burst out in a bitter high-pitched tone, pausing between every sentence to rap the floor with a knobbed stick which rested between his legs.

"Now, you see, you don't do this thing a bit better than you did a fortnight ago; and I'll tell you what's the reason. You want to learn accounts; that's well and good. But you think all you need do to learn accounts is to come to me and do sums for an hour or so, two or three times a week; and no sooner do you get your caps on and turn out of doors again, than you sweep the whole thing clean out of your mind. You go whistling about, and take no more care what you're thinking of than if your heads were gutters for any rubbish to swill through that happened to be in the way; and if you get a good notion in 'em, it's pretty soon washed out again. You think knowledge is to be got cheap—you'll come and pay Bartle Massey sixpence a week, and he'll make you clever at figures without your taking any trouble. But knowledge isn't to be got by paying sixpence, let me tell you; if you're to know figures, you must turn 'em over in your own heads, and keep your thoughts on 'em. There's nothing you can't turn into a sum, for there's nothing but what's got number in it—even a fool. You may say to yourselves, 'I'm one fool and Jack's another; if my fool's head weighed four pound, and Jack's three pound three ounces and three quarters, how many pennyweights heavier would my head be than Jack's? A man that has got his heart in learning figures would make sums for himself, and work 'em in his head; when he sat at his shoemaking, he'd count his stitches by fives, and then put a price on his stitches, say half a farthing, and then see how much money he could get in an hour; and then ask himself how much money he'd get in a day at that rate; and then how much ten workmen would get working three, or twenty, or a hundred years at that rate—and all the while his needle would be going just as fast as if he left his head empty for the devil to dance in. But the long and the short of it is—I'll have nobody in my night-school that doesn't strive to learn what he came to learn, as hard as if he was striving to get out of a dark hole into broad daylight. I'll send no man away because he is stupid; if Billy Taft, the idiot, wanted to learn anything, I'd not refuse to teach him. But I'll not throw away good knowledge on people who think they can get it by the sixpenn'orth, and carry it away with them as they would an ounce of snuff. So never come to me again, if you can't show that you have been working with your own heads, instead of thinking you can pay mine to work for you. That's the last word I've got to say to you."

With this final sentence, Bartle Massey gave a sharper rap than ever with his knobbed stick, and the discomfited lads got up with a sulky look.

Tom's "First Half"

(From "The Mill on the Floss")

Tom Tulliver's sufferings during the first quarter he was at King's Lorton, under the distinguished care of the Rev. Walter Stelling, were rather severe. At Mr. Jacobs's academy, life had not presented itself to him as a difficult problem: there were plenty of fellows to play with, and Tom being good at all active games—fighting especially—had that precedence among them which appeared to him inseparable from the personality of Tom Tulliver. Mr. Jacobs himself, familiarly known as Old Goggles, from his habit of wearing spectacles, imposed no painful awe; and if it was the property of snuffy old hypocrites like him to write like copper-plate and surround their signatures with arabesques, to spell without forethought, and to spout "My Name is Norval" without bungling, Tom, for his part, was rather glad he was not in danger of those mean accomplishments.

He was not going to be a snuffy schoolmaster—he; but a substantial man like his father, who used to go hunting when he was younger, and rode a capital black mare—as pretty a bit of horse-flesh as ever you saw. Tom had heard what her points were a hundred times. *He* meant to go hunting too, and to be generally respected. When people were growing up, he considered, nobody inquired about their writing and spelling; when he was a man, he should be master of everything and do just as he liked. It had been very difficult for him to reconcile himself to the idea that his school-time was to be prolonged, and that he was not to be brought up to his father's business, which he had always thought extremely pleasant, for it was nothing but riding about, giving orders, and going to market; and he thought that a clergyman would give him a great many Scripture lessons, and probably make him learn the Gospel and Epistle on a Sunday, as well as the Collect.

But in the absence of specific information it was impossible for him to imagine that school and a schoolmaster would be something entirely different from the academy of Mr. Jacobs. So, not to be at a deficiency, in case of his finding genial companions, he had taken care to carry with him a small box of percussion caps; not that there was anything particular to be done with them, but they would serve to impress strange boys with a sense of his familiarity with guns. Thus poor Tom, though he saw very clearly through Maggie's illusions, was not without illusions of his own, which were to be cruelly dissipated by his enlarged experience at King's Lorton.

He had not been there a fortnight before it was evident that life, complicated not only with the Latin grammar, but with a new standard of English pronunciation, was a very difficult business, made all the more obscure by a thick mist of bashfulness. Tom, as you have observed, was never an exception among boys for ease of address; but the difficulty of enunciating a monosyllable in reply to Mr. and Mrs. Stelling was so great, that he even dreaded to be asked at the table whether he would have more pudding. As to the percussion-caps, he had almost resolved, in the bitterness of his heart, that he would throw them into a neighboring pond; for not only was he the solitary pupil, but he began to have a certain skepticism about guns, and a general sense that his theory of life was undermined. For Mr. Stelling thought nothing of guns, or horses either, apparently; and yet it was impossible for Tom to despise Mr. Stelling as he had despised Old Goggles. If there was anything that was not thoroughly genuine about Mr. Stelling, it lay quite beyond Tom's power to detect it; it is only by a wide comparison of facts that the wisest full-grown man can distinguish well-rolled barrels from more supernal thunder.

Mr. Stelling was a well-sized, broad-chested man, not yet thirty, with flaxen hair standing erect, and large lightish-gray eyes, which were always very wide open; he had a sonorous bass voice, and an air of defiant self-confidence inclining to brazenness. He had entered on his career with great vigor, and intended to make a considerable impression on his fellow-men. The Rev. Walter Stelling was not a man who would remain among the "inferior clergy" all his life. He had a true British determination to push his way in the world. As a schoolmaster, in the first place; for there were capital masterships of grammar-schools to be had, and Mr. Stelling meant to have one of them. But as a preacher also, for he meant always to preach in a striking manner, so as to have his congregation swelled by admirers from neighboring parishes, and to produce a great sensation whenever he took occasional duty for a brother clergyman of minor gifts. The style of preaching he had chosen was the extemporaneous, which was held little short of the miraculous in rural parishes like King's Lorton. Some passages of Massillon and Bourdaloue, which he knew by heart, were really very effective when rolled out in Mr. Stelling's deepest tones; but as comparatively feeble appeals of his own were delivered in the same manner, they were often thought quite as striking by his hearers. Mr. Stelling's doctrine was of no particular school; if anything, it had a tinge of evangelicalism, for that was "the telling thing" just then in the diocese to which King's Lorton belonged.

In short, Mr. Stelling was a man who meant to rise in his profession, and to rise by merit, clearly, since he had no interest beyond what might be promised by a problematic relationship to a great lawyer who had not yet become Lord Chancellor. A clergyman who has such vigorous intentions naturally gets a little into debt at starting; it is not to be expected that he will live in the style of a man who means to be a poor curate all his life, and if the few hundreds Mr. Timpson advanced toward his daughter's fortune did not suffice for the purchase of handsome furniture, together with a stock of wine, a grand piano, and the laying out of a superior flower-garden, it followed in the most rigorous manner, either that these things must be procured by some other means, or else that the Rev. Mr. Stelling must go without them—which last alternative would be an absurd procrastination of the fruits of success, where success was certain.

Mr. Stelling was so broad-chested and resolute that he felt equal to anything; he would become celebrated by shaking the consciences of his hearers, and he would by-and-by edit a Greek play, and invent several new readings. He had not yet selected the play, for having been married little more than two years, his leisure time had been much occupied with attentions to Mrs. Stelling; but he had told that fine woman what he meant to do some day, and she felt great confidence in her husband, as a man who understood everything of that sort.

But the immediate step to future success was to bring on Tom Tulliver during this first half-year; for, by a singular coincidence, there had been some negotiation concerning another pupil from the same neighborhood, and it might further a decision in Mr. Stelling's favor, if it were understood that young Tulliver, who, Mr. Stelling observed in conjugal privacy, was rather a rough cub, had made prodigious progress in a short time. It was on this ground that he was severe with Tom about his lessons: he was clearly a boy whose powers would never be developed through the medium of the Latin grammar, without the application of some sternness. Not that Mr. Stelling was a harsh-tempered or unkind man—quite the contrary; he was jocose with Tom at table, and corrected his provincialisms and his deportment in the most playful manner; but poor Tom was only the more cowed and confused by this double novelty, for he had never been used to jokes at all like Mr. Stelling's; and for the first time in his life he had a painful sense that he was all wrong somehow. When Mr. Stelling said, as the roast-beef was being uncovered, "Now, Tulliver! which would you rather decline, roast-beef, or the Latin for it?"—Tom, to whom in his coolest moment a pun would have been a hard nut, was thrown into a state of embarrassed alarm that made everything dim to him except the feeling that he would rather not have anything to do with Latin; of course he answered, "Roast-beef," whereupon there followed much laughter and some practical joking with the plates, from which Tom gathered that he had in some mysterious way refused beef, and, in fact, made himself appear "a silly."

If he could have seen a fellow-pupil undergo these painful operations and survive them in good spirits, he might sooner have taken them as a matter of course. But there are two expensive forms of education, either of which a parent may procure for his son by sending him as solitary pupil to a clergyman: one is, the enjoyment of the reverend gentleman's undivided neglect; the other is, the endurance of the reverend gentleman's undivided attention. It was the latter privilege for which Mr. Tulliver paid a high price in Tom's initiatory months at King's Lorton.

That respectable miller and malster had left Tom behind, and driven homeward in a state of great mental satisfaction. He considered that it was a happy moment for him when he had thought of asking Riley's advice about a tutor for Tom. Mr. Stelling's eyes were so wide open, and he talked in such an off-hand, matter-of-fact way—answering every difficult slow remark of Mr. Tulliver's with, " I see, my good sir, I see ; " " To be sure, to be sure ; " " You want your son to be a man who will make his way in the world,"—that Mr. Tulliver was delighted to find in him a clergyman whose knowledge was so applicable to the every-day affairs of this life. Except Counselor Wylde, whom he had heard at the last sessions, Mr. Tulliver thought the Rev. Mr. Stelling was the shrewdest fellow he had ever met with—not unlike Wylde, in fact ; he had the same way of sticking his thumbs in the armholes of his waistcoat. Mr. Tulliver was not by any means an exception in mistaking brazenness for shrewdness : most laymen thought Stelling shrewd, and a man of remarkable powers generally ; it was chiefly by his clerical brethren that he was considered rather a dull fellow. But he told Mr. Tulliver several stories about " Swing " and incendiarism, and asked his advice about feeding pigs in so thoroughly secular and judicious a manner, with so much polished glibness of tongue, that the miller thought here was the very thing he wanted for Tom. He had no doubt this first-rate man was acquainted with every branch of information, and knew exactly what Tom must learn in order to become a match for the lawyers—which poor Mr. Tulliver himself did *not* know, and so was necessarily thrown for self-direction on this wide kind of inference. It is hardly fair to laugh at him, for I have known much more highly instructed persons than he make inferences quite as wide, and not at all wiser.

As for Mrs. Tulliver—finding that Mrs. Stelling's views as to the airing of linen and the frequent recurrence of hunger in a growing boy, entirely coincided with her own ; moreover, that Mrs. Stelling, though so young a woman, and only anticipating her second confinement, had gone through very nearly the same experience as herself with regard to the behavior and fundamental character of the monthly nurse—she expressed great contentment to her husband, when they drove away, at leaving Tom with a woman who, in spite of her youth, seemed quite sensible and motherly, and asked advice as prettily as could be.

"They must be very well off, though," said Mrs. Tulliver, "for everything's as nice as can be all over the house, and that watered silk she had on cost a pretty penny. Sister Pullet has got one like it."

"Ah," said Mr. Tulliver, "he's got some income besides the curacy, I reckon. Perhaps her father allows 'em something. There's Tom 'ull be another hundred to him, and not much trouble either, by his own account; he says teaching comes natural to him. That's wonderful, now," added Mr. Tulliver, turning his head on one side, and giving his horse a meditative tickling on the flank.

Perhaps it was because teaching came naturally to Mr. Stelling, that he set about it with that uniformity of method and independence of circumstances which distinguish the actions of animals understood to be under the immediate teaching of nature. Mr. Broderip's amiable beaver, as that charming naturalist tells us, busied himself as earnestly in constructing a dam, in a room up three pairs of stairs in London, as if he had been laying his foundation in a stream or lake in Upper Canada. It was "Binny's" function to build: the absence of water or of possible progeny was an accident for which he was not accountable. With the same unerring instinct Mr. Stelling set to work at his natural method of instilling the Eton Grammar and Euclid into the mind of Tom Tulliver. This, he considered, was the only basis of solid instruction: all other means of education were mere charlatanism, and could produce nothing better than smatterers. Fixed on this firm basis, a man might observe the display of various or special knowledge made by irregularly educated people, with a pitying smile; all that sort of thing was very well, but it was impossible these people could form sound opinions.

In holding this conviction Mr. Stelling was not biased, as some tutors have been, by the excessive accuracy or extent of his own scholarship; and as to his views about Euclid, no opinion could have been freer from personal partiality. Mr. Stelling was very far from being led astray by enthusiasm, either religious or intellectual; on the other hand, he had no secret belief that everything was humbug. He thought religion was a very excellent thing and Aristotle a great authority, and deaneries and prebends useful institutions, and Great Britain the providential bulwark of Protestantism, and faith in the unseen a great support to afflicted minds: he believed in all these things as the Swiss hotel-keeper believes in the beauty of the scenery around him, and in the pleasure it gives to artistic visitors. And in the same way Mr. Stelling believed in his method of education; he had no doubt that he was doing the very best thing for Mr. Tulliver's boy. Of course, when the miller talked of "mapping" and "summing" in a vague and diffident manner, Mr. Stelling had set his mind at rest by an assurance that he understood what was wanted; for how was it possible the good man could form any reasonable judgment about the matter? Mr. Stelling's duty was to teach the lad in the only right way—indeed, he knew no other; he had not wasted his time in the acquirement of anything abnormal.

He very soon set down poor Tom as a thoroughly stupid lad; for though by hard labor he could get particular declensions into his brain, anything so abstract as the relation between cases and terminations could by no means get such a lodgment there as to enable him to recognize a chance genitive or dative. This struck Mr. Stelling as something more than natural stupidity; he suspected obstinacy, or at any rate, indifference, and lectured Tom severely on his want of thorough application. "You feel no interest in what you're doing, sir," Mr. Stelling would say, and the reproach was painfully true. Tom had never found any difficulty in discerning a pointer from a setter, when once he had been told the distinction, and his perceptive powers were not at all deficient.

I fancy they were quite as strong as those of the Rev. Mr. Stelling; for Tom could predict with accuracy what number of horses were cantering behind him; he could throw a stone right into the center of a given ripple; he could guess to a fraction how many lengths of his stick it would take to reach across the playground, and could draw almost perfect squares on his slate without any measurement. But Mr. Stelling took no note of these things; he only observed that Tom's faculties failed him before the abstractions hideously symbolized to him in the pages of the Eton Grammar, and that he was in a state bordering on idiocy with regard to the demonstration that two given triangles must be equal—though he could discern with great promptitude and certainty the fact that they *were* equal. Whence Stelling concluded that Tom's brain, being peculiarly impervious to etymology and demonstrations, was peculiarly in need of being ploughed and harrowed by these patent implements. It was his favorite metaphor, that the classics and geometry constituted that culture of the mind which prepared it for the reception of any subsequent crop.

I say nothing against Mr. Stelling's theory: if we are to have one regimen for all minds, his seems to be as good as any other. I only know it turned out as uncomfortably for Tom Tulliver as if he had been plied with cheese in order to remedy a gastric weakness which prevented him from digesting it. It is astonishing what a different result one gets by changing the metaphor! Once call the brain an intellectual stomach, and one's ingenious conception of the classics and geometry as plows and harrows seems to settle nothing. But then it is open to some one else to follow great authorities, and call the mind a sheet of white paper or a mirror, in which case one's knowledge of the digestive process becomes quite irrelevant. It was doubtless an ingenious idea to call the camel the ship of the desert, but it would hardly lead one far in training that useful beast. O Aristotle! if you had had the advantage of being "the freshest modern" instead of the greatest ancient, would you not have mingled your praise of metaphorical speech, as a sign of high intelligence, with a lamentation that intelligence so rarely shows itself in speech without metaphor—that we can so seldom declare what a thing is, except by saying it is something else.

Tom Tulliver, being abundant in no form of speech, did not use any metaphor to declare his views as to the nature of Latin:

he never called it an instrument of torture; and it was not until he had got on some way in the next half year, and in the Delectus, that he was advanced enough to call it a "bore" and "beastly stuff." At present, in relation to this demand that he should learn Latin declensions and conjugations, Tom was in a state of as blank unimaginativeness concerning the cause and tendency of his sufferings as if he had been an innocent shrew-mouse imprisoned in the split trunk of an ash tree, in order to cure lameness in cattle.

It is doubtless almost incredible to instructed minds of the present day that a boy of twelve, not belonging strictly to "the masses," who are now understood to have the monopoly of mental darkness, should have had no distinct idea how there came to be such a thing as Latin on this earth; yet so it was with Tom. It would have taken a long while to make conceivable to him that there ever existed a people who bought and sold sheep and oxen, and transacted the every-day affairs of life, through the medium of this language, and still longer to make him understand why he should be called upon to learn it, when its connection with those affairs had become entirely latent. So far as Tom had gained any acquaintance with the Romans at Mr. Jacob's academy, his knowledge was strictly correct, but it went no farther than the fact that they were "in the New Testament;" and Mr. Stelling was not the man to enfeeble and emasculate his pupil's mind by simplifying and explaining, or to reduce the tonic effect of etymology by mixing it with smattering, extraneous information, such as is given to girls.

Yet, strange to say, under this vigorous treatment Tom became more like a girl than he had ever been in his life before. He had a large share of pride, which had hitherto found itself very comfortable in the world, despising Old Goggles, and reposing in the sense of unquestioned rights; but now this same pride met with nothing but bruises and crushings. Tom was too clear-sighted not to be aware that Mr. Stelling's standard of things was quite different, was certainly something higher in the eyes of the world than that of the people he had been living amongst, and that, brought in contact with it, he, Tom Tulliver, appeared uncouth and stupid; he was by no means indifferent to this, and his pride got into an uneasy condition which quite nullified his boyish self-satisfaction, and gave him something of the girl's susceptibility. He was of a very firm, not to say obstinate disposition, but there was no brute-like rebellion and recklessness in his nature; the human sensibilities predominated, and if it had occurred to him that he could enable himself to show some quickness at his lessons, and so acquire Mr. Stelling's approbation, by standing on one leg for an inconvenient length of time, or rapping his head moderately against the wall, or any voluntary action of that sort, he would certainly have tried it. But no—Tom had never heard that these measures would brighten the understanding or strengthen the verbal memory; and he was not given to hypothesis and experiment.

It did occur to him that he could perhaps get some help by praying for it; but as the prayers he said every evening were forms learned by heart, he rather shrank from the novelty and irregularity of introducing an extempore passage on a topic of petition for which he was not aware of any precedent. But one day, when he had broken down, for the fifth time, in the supines of the third conjugation, and Mr. Stelling, convinced that this must be carelessness, since it transcended the bounds of possible stupidity, had lectured him very seriously, pointing out that if he failed to seize the present golden opportunity of learning supines, he would have to regret it when he became a man— Tom, more miserable than usual, determined to try his sole resource; and that evening, after his usual form of prayer for his parents and "little sister" (he had begun to pray for Maggie when she was a baby), and that he might be able always to keep God's commandments, he added, in the same low whisper, "and please to make me always remember my Latin." He paused a little to consider how he should pray about Euclid— whether he should ask to see what it meant, or whether there was any other mental state which would be more applicable to the case. But at last he added—" And make Mr. Stelling say I shan't do Euclid any more. Amen."

The fact that he got through his supines without mistake next day encouraged him to persevere in this appendix to his prayers, and neutralized any skepticism that might have arisen from Mr. Stelling's continued demand for Euclid. But his faith broke down under the apparent absence of all help when he got into the irregular verbs. It seemed clear that Tom's despair under the caprices of the present tense did not constitute a *nodus* worthy of interference, and since this was the climax of his difficulties, where was the use of praying for help any longer? He made up his mind to this conclusion in one of his dull, lonely evenings, which he spent in the study, preparing his lessons for the morrow. His eyes were apt to get dim over the page—though he hated crying, and was ashamed of it. He couldn't help thinking with some affection even of Spouncer, whom he used to fight and quarrel with; he would have felt at home with Spouncer, and in a condition of superiority. And then the mill, and the river, and Yap pricking up his ears, ready to obey the least sign when Tom said, "Hoigh!" would all come before him in a sort of calenture, when his fingers played absently in his pocket with his great knife and his coil of whipcord, and other relics of the past.

Tom, as I said, had never been so much like a girl in his life before, and at that epoch of irregular verbs his spirit was further depressed by a new means of mental development which had been thought of for him out of school hours. Mrs. Stelling had lately had her second baby, and as nothing could be more salutary for a boy than to feel himself useful, Mrs. Stelling considered she was doing Tom a service by setting him to watch the little cherub Laura while the nurse was occupied with the sickly baby. It was quite a pretty employment for Tom to take little Laura out in the sunniest hour of the autumn day— it would help to make him feel that Lorton Parsonage was a home for him, and that he was one of the family. The little cherub Laura, not being an accomplished walker at present, had a ribbon fastened round her waist, by which Tom held her as if she had been a little dog during the minutes in which she chose to walk; but as these were rare, he was for the most part carrying this fine child round and round the garden, within sight of Mrs. Stelling's window—according to orders.

If any one considers this unfair and even oppressive toward Tom, I beg him to consider that there are feminine virtues which are with difficulty combined, even if they are not incompatible. When the wife of a poor curate contrives, under all her disadvantages, to dress extremely well and to have a style of coiffure which requires that her nurse shall occasionally officiate as lady's-maid—when, moreover, her dinner-parties and her drawing-room show that effort of elegance and completeness of appointment to which ordinary women might imagine a large income necessary, it would be unreasonable to expect of her that she should employ a second nurse, or even act as a nurse herself. Mr. Stelling knew better; he saw that his wife did wonders already, and was proud of her; it was certainly not the best thing in the world for young Tulliver's gait to carry a heavy child, but he had plenty of exercise in long walks with himself, and next half-year Mr. Stelling would see about having a drilling-master. Among the many means whereby Mr. Stelling intended to be more fortunate than the bulk of his fellow-men, he had entirely given up that of having his own way in his own house. What then?—he had married "as kind a little soul as ever breathed," according to Mr. Riley, who had been acquainted with Mrs. Stelling's blonde ringlets and smiling demeanor throughout her maiden life, and on the strength of that knowledge would have been ready any day to pronounce that whatever domestic differences might arise in her married life must be entirely Mr. Stelling's fault.

If Tom had had a worse disposition, he would certainly have hated the little cherub, Laura; but he was too kind-hearted a lad for that—there was too much in him of the fiber that turns to true manliness, and to protecting pity for the weak. I am afraid he hated Mrs. Stelling, and contracted a lasting dislike to pale blonde ringlets and broad plaits, as directly associated with haughtiness of manner, and a frequent reference to other people's "duty." But he couldn't help playing with little Laura, and liking to amuse her; he even sacrificed his percussion caps for her sake, in despair of their ever serving a greater purpose—thinking the small flash and bang would delight her, and thereby drawing down on himself a rebuke from Mrs. Stelling for teaching her child to play with fire. Laura was a sort of playfellow—and oh, how Tom longed for playfellows! In his secret heart he yearned to have Maggie with him, and was almost ready to dote on her exasperating acts of forgetfulness; though, when he was at home, he always represented it as a great favor on his part to let Maggie trot by his side on his pleasure excursions.

And before this dreary half-year was ended, Maggie actually came. Mrs. Stelling had given a general invitation for the little girl to come and stay with her brother; so when Mr. Tulliver drove over to King's Lorton late in October, Maggie came, too, with the sense that she was taking a great journey, and beginning to see the world. It was Mr. Tulliver's first visit to see Tom, for the lad must learn not to think too much about home.

"Well, my lad," he said to Tom, when Mr. Stelling left the room to announce the arrival to his wife, and Maggie had begun to kiss Tom freely, "you look rarely! School agrees with you."

Tom wished he had looked rather ill.

"I don't think I *am* well, father," said Tom; "I wish you'd ask Mr. Stelling not to let me do Euclid—it brings on the toothache, I think."

(The toothache was the only malady to which Tom had ever been subject.)

"Euclid, my lad—why, what's that?" said Mr. Tulliver.

"Oh, I don't know; it's definitions, and axioms and, triangles, and things. It's a book I've got to learn in—there's no sense in it."

"Go, go!" said Mr. Tulliver, reprovingly, "you mustn't say

so. You must learn what your master tells you. He knows what is right for you to learn."

"*I'll* help you now, Tom," said Maggie, with a little air of patronizing consolation. "I've come to stay ever so long, if Mrs. Stelling asks me. I've brought my box and my pinafores, haven't I, father?"

"*You* help me, you little silly thing!" said Tom, in such high spirits at this announcement that he quite enjoyed the idea of confounding Maggie by showing her a page of Euclid. "I should like to see you doing one of *my* lessons! Why, I learn Latin, too! Girls never learn such things. They're too silly."

"I know what Latin is very well," said Maggie, confidently. "Latin's a language. There are Latin words in the dictionary. There's bonus, a gift."

"Now, you're just wrong there, Miss Maggie!" said Tom, secretly astonished. "You think you're very wise! But 'bonus' means 'good,' as it happens—*bonus, bona, bonum.*"

"Well, that's no reason why it shouldn't mean 'gift,'" said Maggie, stoutly. "It may mean several things—almost every word does. There's 'lawn,'—it means the grass-plot, as well as the stuff pocket-handkerchiefs are made of."

"Well done, little 'un," said Mr. Tulliver, laughing, while Tom felt rather disgusted with Maggie's knowingness, though beyond measure cheerful at the thought that she was going to stay with him. Her conceit would soon be overawed by the actual inspection of his books.

Mrs. Stelling, in her pressing invitation, did not mention a longer time than a week for Maggie's stay; but Mr. Stelling, who took her between his knees, and asked her where she stole her dark eyes from, insisted that she must stay a fortnight. Maggie thought Mr. Stelling was a charming man, and Mr. Tulliver was quite proud to leave his little wench where she would have an opportunity of showing her cleverness to appreciating strangers. So it was agreed that she should not be fetched home till the end of the fortnight.

"Now, then, come with me into the study, Maggie," said Tom, as their father drove away. "What do you shake and toss your head now for, you silly?" he continued; for though her hair was now under a new dispensation, and was brushed smoothly behind her ears, she seemed still in imagination to be tossing it out of her eyes. "It makes you look as if you were crazy."

"Oh, I can't help that," said Maggie, impatiently. "Don't tease me, Tom. Oh, what books!" she exclaimed, as she saw the book-cases in the study, "How I should like to have as many books as that!"

"Why, you couldn't read one of 'em," said Tom, triumphantly. "They're all Latin."

"No, they aren't," said Maggie. "I can read the back of this—'History of the Decline and Fall of the Roman Empire.'"

"Well, what does that mean? *You* don't know," said Tom, wagging his head.

"But I could soon find out," said Maggie, scornfully.

"Why, how?"

"I should look inside, and see what it was about."

"You'd better not, Miss Maggie," said Tom, seeing her hand on the volume. "Mr. Stelling lets nobody touch his books without leave, and *I* shall catch it, if you take it out."

"Oh, very well! Let me see all *your* books, then," said Maggie, turning to throw her arms round Tom's neck, and rub his cheek with her small round nose.

Tom, in the gladness of his heart at having dear old Maggie to dispute with and crow over again, seized her round the waist, and began to jump with her round the large library table. Away they jumped with more and more vigor, till Maggie's hair flew from behind her ears, and twirled about like an animated mop. But the revolutions round the table became more and more irregular in their sweep, till at last reaching Mr. Stelling's reading-stand, they sent it thundering down with its heavy lexicons to the floor. Happily it was the ground-floor, and the study was a one-storied wing to the house, so that the downfall made no alarming resonance, though Tom stood dizzy and aghast for a few minutes, dreading the appearance of Mr. or Mrs. Stelling.

"Oh, I say, Maggie," said Tom at last, lifting up the stand, "we must keep quiet here, you know. If we break anything, Mrs. Stelling 'll make us cry peccavi."

"What's that?" said Maggie.

"Oh, it's the Latin for a good scolding," said Tom, not without some pride in his knowledge.

"Is she a cross woman?" said Maggie.

"I believe you!" said Tom, with an emphatic nod.

"I think all women are crosser than men," said Maggie. "Aunt Glegg's a great deal crosser than Uncle Glegg, and mother scolds me more than father does."

"Well, *you'll* be a woman some day," said Tom, "so *you* needn't talk."

"But I shall be a *clever* woman," said Maggie, with a toss.

"Oh, I dare say, and a nasty conceited thing. Everybody 'll hate you."

"But you oughtn't to hate me, Tom; it 'll be very wicked of you, for I shall be your sister."

"Yes, but if you're a disagreeable thing, I *shall* hate you."

"Oh, but, Tom, you won't! I shan't be disagreeable. I shall be very good to you—and I shall be good to everybody. You won't hate me really, will you, Tom?"

"Oh, bother! never mind! Come, it's time for me to learn my lessons. See here! what I've got to do," said Tom, drawing Maggie toward him and showing her his theorem, while she pushed her hair behind her ears, and prepared herself to prove her capability of helping him in Euclid. She began to read with full confidence in her own powers, but presently, becoming quite bewildered, her face flushed with irritation. It was unavoidable—she must confess her incompetency, and she was not fond of humiliation.

"It's nonsense!" she said, "and very ugly stuff—nobody need want to make it out."

"Ah, there now, Miss Maggie!" said Tom, drawing the book away, and wagging his head at her, "you see you're not so clever as you thought you were."

"Oh," said Maggie, pouting, "I dare say I could make it out, if I'd learned what goes before, as you have."

"But that's what you just couldn't, Miss Wisdom," said Tom. "For it's all the harder when you know what goes before; for then you've got to say what definition 3 is, and what axiom V. is. But get along with you now. I must go on with this. Here's the Latin Grammar. See what you can make of that."

Maggie found the Latin Grammar quite soothing after her mathematical mortification; for she delighted in new words, and quickly found that there was an English Key at the end, which would make her very wise about Latin, at slight expense. She presently made up her mind to skip the rules in the Syntax —the examples became so absorbing. These mysterious sentences, snatched from an unknown context,—like strange horns of beasts, and leaves of unknown plants, brought from some far-off region,—gave boundless scope to her imagination, and were all the more fascinating because they were in a peculiar tongue of their own, which she could learn to interpret. It was really very interesting—the Latin Grammar that Tom had said no girls could learn; and she was proud because she found it interesting. The most fragmentary examples were her favorites. *Mors omnibus est communis* would have been jejune, only she liked to know the Latin; but the fortunate gentleman whom every one congratulated because he had a son "endowed with *such* a disposition" afforded her a great deal of pleasant conjecture, and she was quite lost in the "thick grove penetrable by no star," when Tom called out:

"Now, then, Magsie, give us the grammar!"

"Oh, Tom, it's such a pretty book!" she said, as she jumped out of the large arm-chair to give it him; "it's much prettier than the dictionary. I could learn Latin very soon. I don't think it's at all hard."

"Oh, I know what you've been doing," said Tom, "you've

been reading the English at the end. Any donkey can do that."

Tom seized the book and opened it with a determined and business-like air, as much as to say that he had a lesson to learn which no donkeys would find themselves equal to. Maggie, rather piqued, turned to the book-cases, to amuse herself with puzzling out the titles.

Presently Tom called to her: "Here, Magsie, come and hear if I can say this. Stand at that end of the table, where Mr. Stelling sits when he hears me."

Maggie obeyed, and took the open book.

"Where do you begin, Tom?"

"Oh, I begin at '*Appellativa arborum*,' because I say all over again what I've been learning this week."

Tom sailed along pretty well for three lines; and Maggie was beginning to forget her office of prompter in speculating as to what *mas* could mean, which came twice over, when he stuck fast at *Sunt etiam volucrum*.

"Don't tell me, Maggie; *Sunt etiam volucrum—Sunt etiam volucrum—ut ostrea, cetus———*"

"No," said Maggie, opening her mouth and shaking her head.

"*Sunt etiam volucrum*," said Tom, very slowly, as if the next words might be expected to come sooner when he gave them this strong hint that they were waited for.

"C, e, u," said Maggie, getting impatient.

"Oh, I know—hold your tongue," said Tom. "*Ceu passer, hirundo; Ferarum—ferarum—*" Tom took his pencil and made several hard dots with it on his book-cover—"*ferarum———*"

"Oh dear, oh dear, Tom," said Maggie, "what a time you are! *Ut———*"

"*Ut ostrea———*"

"No, no," said Maggie, "*ut tigris———*"

"Oh, yes, now I can do," said Tom; "it was *tigris, vulpes*, I'd forgotten: *ut tigris, vulpes; et Piscium.*"

With some further stammering and repetition, Tom got through the next few lines.

"Now, then," he said, "the next is what I've just learned for to-morrow. Give me hold of the book a minute."

After some whispered gabbling, assisted by the beating of his fist on the table, Tom returned the book.

"*Mascula nomina in a,*" he began.

"No, Tom," said Maggie, "that doesn't come next. It's *Nomen non creskens genittivo*——"

"*Creskens genittivo!*" exclaimed Tom, with a derisive laugh, for Tom had learned this omitted passage for his yesterday's lesson, and a young gentleman does not require an intimate or extensive acquaintance with Latin before he can feel the pitiable absurdity of a false quantity. "*Creskens genittivo!* What a little silly you are, Maggie!"

"Well, you needn't laugh, Tom, for you didn't remember it at all. I'm sure it's spelled so; how was I to know?"

"Phee-e-e-h! I told you girls couldn't learn Latin. It's *Nomen non crescens genitivo*——"

"Very well, then," said Maggie, pouting. "I can say that as well as you can. And you don't mind your stops. For you ought to stop twice as long at a semicolon as you do at a comma, and you make the longest stops where there ought to be no stop at all."

"Oh, well, don't chatter. Let me go on."

They were presently fetched to spend the rest of the evening in the drawing-room, and Maggie became so animated with Mr. Stelling, who, she felt sure, admired her cleverness, that Tom was rather amazed and alarmed at her audacity. But she was suddenly subdued by Mr. Stelling's alluding to a little girl of whom he had heard that she once ran away to the gypsies.

"What a very odd little girl that must be!" said Mrs. Stelling, meaning to be playful—but a playfulness that turned on her supposed oddity was not at all to Maggie's taste. She feared that Mr. Stelling, after all, did not think much of her, and went to bed in rather low spirits. Mrs. Stelling, she felt, looked at her as if she thought her hair was very ugly because it hung down straight behind.

Nevertheless it was a very happy fortnight to Maggie, this visit to Tom. She was allowed to be in the study while he had his lessons, and in her various readings got very deep into the examples in the Latin Grammar. The astronomer who hated women generally, caused her so much puzzling speculation that she one day asked Mr. Stelling if all astronomers hated women, or whether it was only this particular astronomer. But forestalling his answer, she said:

"I suppose it's all astronomers; because, you know, they live up in high towers, and if the women came there, they might talk and hinder them from looking at the stars."

Mr. Stelling liked her prattle immensely, and they were on the best terms. She told Tom she should like to go to school to Mr. Stelling, as he did, and learn just the same things. She knew she could do Euclid, for she had looked into it again, and she saw what A B C meant: they were the names of the lines.

"I'm sure you couldn't do it now," said Tom; "and I'll just ask Mr. Stelling if you could."

"I don't mind," said the little conceited minx. "I'll ask him myself."

"Mr. Stelling," she said, that same evening when they were in the drawing-room, "couldn't I do Euclid, and all Tom's lessons, if you were to teach me instead of him?"

"No; you couldn't," said Tom, indignantly. "Girls can't do Euclid; can they, sir?"

"They can pick up a little of everything, I dare say," said Mr. Stelling. "They've a great deal of superficial cleverness; but can't go far into anything. They're quick and shallow."

Tom, delighted with this verdict, telegraphed his triumph by wagging his head at Maggie, behind Mr. Stelling's chair. As for Maggie, she had hardly ever been so mortified. She had been so proud to be called "quick" all her little life, and now it appeared that this quickness was the brand of inferiority. It would have been better to be slow, like Tom.

"Ha, ha! Miss Maggie!" said Tom, when they were alone; "you see it's not such a fine thing to be quick. You'll never go far into anything, you know."

And Maggie was so oppressed by this dreadful destiny that she had no spirit for a retort.

But when this small apparatus of shallow quickness was fetched away in the gig by Luke, and the study was once more quite lonely for Tom, he missed her grievously. He had really been brighter, and had got through his lessons better, since she had been there; and she had asked Mr. Stelling so many questions about the Roman Empire, and whether there really ever was a man who said in Latin, "I would not buy it for a farthing or a rotten nut," or whether that had only been turned into Latin, that Tom had actually come to a dim understanding of the fact that there had once been people upon the earth who were so fortunate as to know Latin without learning it through the medium of the Eton Grammar. This luminous idea was a great addition to his historical acquirements during this half-year, which were otherwise confined to an epitomized history of the Jews.

But the dreary half-year *did* come to an end. How glad Tom was to see the last yellow leaves fluttering before the cold wind! The dark afternoons, and the first December snow, seemed to him far livelier than the August sunshine; and that he might make himself the surer about the flight of days that were carrying him homeward, he stuck twenty-one sticks deep in a corner of the garden, when he was three weeks from the holidays, and pulled one up every day with a great wrench, throwing it to a distance with a vigor of will which would have carried it to limbo, if it had been in the nature of sticks to travel so far.

But it was worth purchasing, even at the heavy price of the Latin Grammar—the happiness of seeing the bright light in the parlor at home, as the gig passed noiselessly over the snow-covered bridge; the happiness of passing from the cold air to the warmth and the kisses and the smiles of that familiar hearth, where the pattern of the rug and the grate and the fire-irons were "first-ideas" that it was no more possible to criticise than the solidity and extension of matter. There is no sense of ease like the ease we felt in those scenes where we were born, where objects became dear to us before we had known the labor of choice, and where the outer world seemed only an extension of our own personality: we accepted and loved it as we accepted our own sense of existence and our own limbs.

Very common-place, even ugly, that furniture of our early home might look if it were put up at auction; an improved taste in upholstery scorns it; and is not the striving after something better and better in our surroundings, the grand characteristic that distinguishes man from the brute—or, to satisfy a scrupulous accuracy of definition, that distinguishes the British man from the foreign brute? But Heaven knows where that striving might lead us, if our affections had not a trick of twining round those old inferior things—if the loves and sanctities of our life had no deep immovable roots in memory. One's delight in an elderberry bush overhanging the confused leafage of a hedgerow bank, as a more gladdening sight than the finest cistus or fuchsia spreading itself on the softest undulating turf, is an entirely unjustifiable preference to a nursery-gardener, or to any of those severely regulated minds who are free from the weakness of any attachment that does not rest on a demonstrable superiority of qualities. And there is no better reason for preferring this elderberry bush than that it stirs an early memory—that it is no novelty in my life, speaking to me merely through my present sensibilities to form and color, but the long companion of my existence, that wove itself into my joys when joys were vivid.

WASHINGTON IRVING
1783-1859

No name in our literary annals is more fondly cherished than that of Washington Irving, one of the earliest and most distinguished of American writers. He was born in New York in 1783, and died at Sunnyside, his home on the Hudson, in 1859. He began his literary career by contributing to the columns of the *Morning Chronicle*, of which his brother, Dr. Peter Irving, was editor. His health failing, he went to Europe, where he remained two years. On his return he was admitted to the Bar, but gave little attention to his profession. In 1807 appeared the first number of *Salmagundi; or, the Whim Whams and Opinions of Launcelot Langstaff and Others*,—a semi-monthly periodical of light and agreeable character, which was very popular during its existence of less than two years. In 1809 the famous "History of New York, by Diedrich Knickerbocker," was published, and had a most cordial reception. The next year Washington Irving became a partner in the mercantile business conducted by his brothers; but in 1812 the firm failed, and the young author returned to literary labors.

"The Sketch-Book" appeared in 1819, and established his fame in England and America. "Bracebridge Hall," "The Conquest of Granada," "The Life of Columbus," and other works, were issued at intervals prior to 1832. In 1842 he was appointed United States Minister to Spain, and held that office four years. After his return he wrote a "Life of Goldsmith," "The Life of Washington," and "Mahomet and his Successors." It is safe to say that no American author has been so generally and heartily loved as Washington Irving, and he was as popular in Great Britain as at home. His style is a model of ease, grace, and refinement.

Characterization

Other writers may no doubt arise in the course of time, who will exhibit in verse or prose a more commanding talent, and soar a still loftier flight in the empyrean sky of glory. Some western Homer, Shakespeare, Milton, Corneille, or Calderon, may irradiate our literary

world with a flood of splendor that shall throw all other greatness
into the shade. This, or something like it may or may not happen;
but even if it should, it can never be disputed that the mild and beautiful genius of Mr. Irving was the Morning Star that led up the march
of our heavenly host; and that he has a fair right, much fairer certainly than the great Mantuan, to assume the proud device, "*Primus
ego in patriam.*"

ALEXANDER H. EVERETT.

Ichabod Crane

(From "The Legend of Sleepy Hollow")

In the bosom of one of those spacious coves which indent
the eastern shore of the Hudson, at that broad expansion of
the river denominated by the ancient Dutch navigators the
Tappan Zee, and where they always prudently shortened sail,
and implored the protection of Saint Nicholas when they
crossed, there lies a small market-town or rural port, which by
some is called Greensburgh, but which is more generally and
properly known by the name of Tarry Town. This name was
given, we are told, in former days, by the good housewives of
the adjacent country, from the inveterate propensity of their
husbands to linger about the village tavern on market-days.
Be that as it may, I do not vouch for the fact, but merely
advert to it, for the sake of being precise and authentic. Not
far from this village, perhaps about two miles, there is a little
valley, or rather lap of land, among high hills, which is one of
the quietest places in the whole world. A small brook glides
through it, with just murmur enough to lull one to repose; and
the occasional whistle of a quail, or tapping of a woodpecker,
is almost the only sound that ever breaks in upon the uniform
tranquillity.

I recollect that, when a stripling, my first exploit in squirrel
shooting was in a grove of tall walnut trees that shades one
side of the valley. I had wandered into it at noon-time, when
all nature is peculiarly quiet, and was startled by the roar of
my own gun as it broke the Sabbath stillness around, and was

prolonged and reverberated by the angry echoes. If ever I should wish for a retreat, whither I might steal from the world and its distractions, and dream quietly away the remnant of a troubled life, I know of none more promising than this little valley.

From the listless repose of the place, and the peculiar character of its inhabitants, who are descendants from the original Dutch settlers, this sequestered glen has long been known by the name of SLEEPY HOLLOW, and its rustic lads are called the Sleepy Hollow Boys throughout all the neighboring country. A drowsy, dreamy influence seems to hang over the land, and to pervade the very atmosphere. Some say that the place was bewitched by a high German doctor, during the early days of the settlement; others, that an old Indian chief, the prophet or wizard of his tribe, held his powwows there before the country was discovered by Master Hendrick Hudson. Certain it is, the place still continues under the sway of some witching power, that holds a spell over the minds of the good people, causing them to walk in a continual revery. They are given to all kinds of marvelous beliefs; are subject to trances and visions; and frequently see strange sights, and hear music and voices in the air. The whole neighborhood abounds with local tales, haunted spots, and twilight superstitions; stars shoot and meteors glare oftener across the valley than in any other part of the country, and the nightmare, with her whole nine fold, seems to make it the favorite scene of her gambols.

The dominant spirit, however, that haunts this enchanted region, and seems to be commander-in-chief of all the powers of the air, is the apparition of a figure on horseback without a head. It is said by some to be the ghost of a Hessian trooper, whose head had been carried away by a cannon-ball, in some nameless battle during the Revolutionary War; and who is ever and anon seen by the country folk, hurrying along in the gloom of night, as if on the wings of the wind. His haunts are not confined to the valley, but extend at times to the adjacent roads, and especially to the vicinity of a church at no great distance. Indeed, certain of the most authentic historians of those parts, who have been careful in collecting and collating the floating facts concerning this specter, allege that, the body of the trooper having been buried in the church-yard, the ghost rides forth to the scene of battle in nightly quest of his head; and that the rushing speed with which he sometimes passes along the Hollow, like a midnight blast, is owing to his being belated, and in a hurry to get back to the church-yard before daybreak.

Such is the general purport of this legendary superstition, which has furnished materials for many a wild story in that region of shadows; and the specter is known, at all the country firesides, by the name of the Headless Horseman of Sleepy Hollow.

It is remarkable that the visionary propensity I have mentioned is not confined to the native inhabitants of the valley, but is unconsciously imbibed by every one who resides there for a time. However wide-awake they may have been before they entered that sleepy region, they are sure, in a little time, to inhale the witching influence of the air, and begin to grow imaginative,—to dream dreams and see apparitions.

I mention this peaceful spot with all possible laud; for it is in such little retired Dutch valleys, found here and there embosomed in the great state of New York, that population, manners, and customs remain fixed; while the great torrent of migration and improvement which is making such incessant changes in other parts of this restless country sweeps by them unobserved. They are like those little nooks of still water which border a rapid stream; where we may see the straw and bubble riding quietly at anchor, or slowly revolving in their mimic harbor, undisturbed by the rush of the passing current. Though many years have elapsed since I trod the drowsy shades of Sleepy Hollow, yet I question whether I should not still find the same trees and the same families vegetating in its sheltered bosom.

In this by-place of Nature there abode, in a remote period of

American history, that is to say, some thirty years since, a worthy wight of the name of Ichabod Crane; who sojourned, or, as he expressed it, "tarried," in Sleepy Hollow, for the purpose of instructing the children of the vicinity. He was a native of Connecticut—a state which supplies the Union with pioneers for the mind as well as for the forest, and sends forth yearly its legions of frontier woodsmen and country schoolmasters. The cognomen of Crane was not inapplicable to his person. He was tall, but exceedingly lank, with narrow shoulders, long arms and legs, hands that dangled a mile out of his sleeves, feet that might have served for shovels, and his whole frame most loosely hung together. His head was small, and flat at top, with huge ears, large green glassy eyes, and a long snipe nose, so that it looked like a weather-cock perched upon his spindle neck to tell which way the wind blew. To see him striding along the profile of a hill on a windy day, with his clothes bagging and fluttering about him, one might have mistaken him for the genius of famine descending upon the earth, or some scarecrow eloped from a cornfield.

His schoolhouse was a low building of one large room, rudely constructed of logs; the windows partly glazed, and partly patched with leaves of old copy-books. It was most ingeniously secured at vacant hours by a withe twisted in the handle of the door, and stakes set against the window-shutters; so that, though a thief might get in with perfect ease, he would find some embarrassment in getting out—an idea most probably borrowed by the architect, Yost Van Houten, from the mystery of an eel-pot. The schoolhouse stood in a rather lonely but pleasant situation, just at the foot of a woody hill, with a brook running close by, and a formidable birch-tree growing at one end of it. From hence the low murmur of his pupils' voices, conning over their lessons, might be heard in a drowsy summer's day, like the hum of a beehive, interrupted now and then by the authoritative voice of the master, in the tone of menace or command; or, peradventure, by the appalling sound of the birch, as he urged some tardy loiterer along the flowery path of knowledge. Truth to say, he was a conscientious man, and ever bore in mind the golden maxim, "Spare the rod, and spoil the child." Ichabod Crane's scholars certainly were not spoiled.

I would not have it imagined, however, that he was one of those cruel potentates of the school who joy in the smart of their subjects; on the contrary, he administered justice with discrimination rather than severity; taking the burden off the backs of the weak, and laying it on those of the strong. Your mere puny stripling that winced at the least flourish of the rod, was passed by with indulgence; but the claims of justice were satisfied by inflicting a double portion on some little tough, wrong-headed, broad-skirted Dutch urchin, who sulked and swelled and grew dogged and sullen beneath the birch. All this he called "doing his duty by their parents;" and he never inflicted a chastisement without following it by the assurance, so consolatory to the smarting urchin, that "he would remember it, and thank him for it, the longest day he had to live."

When school-hours were over he was even the companion and playmate of the larger boys; and on holiday afternoons would convoy some of the smaller ones home who happened to have pretty sisters, or good housewives for mothers, noted for the comforts of the cupboard. Indeed, it behooved him to keep on good terms with his pupils. The revenue arising from his school was small, and would have been scarcely sufficient to furnish him with daily bread, for he was a huge feeder, and, though lank, had the dilating powers of an anaconda; but to help out his maintenance, he was, according to country custom in those parts, boarded and lodged at the houses of the farmers whose children he instructed. With these he lived successively a week at a time; thus going the rounds of the neighborhood, with all his worldly effects tied up in a cotton handkerchief.

That all this might not be too onerous on the purses of his rustic patrons, who are apt to consider the costs of schooling a grievous burden, and schoolmasters as mere drones, he had various ways of rendering himself both useful and agreeable. He assisted the farmers occasionally in the lighter labors of

their farms; helped to make hay; mended the fences; took
the horses to water; drove the cows from pasture; cut wood for
the winter fire. He laid aside, too, all the dominant dignity
and absolute sway with which he lorded it in his little empire,
the school, and became wonderfully gentle and ingratiating.
He found favor in the eyes of the mothers by petting the children, particularly the youngest; and like the lion bold, which
whilom so magnanimously the lamb did hold, he would sit
with a child on one knee, and rock a cradle with his foot for
whole hours together.

In addition to his other vocations, he was the singing-master
of the neighborhood, and picked up many bright shillings by
instructing the young folks in psalmody. It was a matter of
no little vanity to him, on Sundays, to take his station in front
of the church gallery, with a band of chosen singers; where, in
his own mind, he completely carried away the palm from the
parson. Certain it is, his voice resounded far above all the
rest of the congregation; and there are peculiar quavers still to
be heard in that church, and which may even be heard half a
mile off, quite to the opposite side of the mill-pond, on a still
Sunday morning, which are said to be legitimately descended
from the nose of Ichabod Crane. Thus by divers little make-
shifts in that ingenious way which is commonly denominated
"by hook and by crook," the worthy pedagogue got on tolerably enough, and was thought, by all who understood nothing
of the labor of head-work, to have a wonderfully easy life of it.

The schoolmaster is generally a man of some importance in
the female circle of a rural neighborhood, being considered a
kind of idle gentleman-like personage, of vastly superior taste
and accomplishments to the rough country swains, and, indeed,
inferior in learning only to the parson. His appearance, therefore, is apt to occasion some little stir at the tea-table of a farm-
house, and the addition of a supernumerary dish of cakes or
sweetmeats, or, peradventure, the parade of a silver tea-pot.
Our man of letters, therefore, was peculiarly happy in the smiles
of all the country damsels. How he would figure among them

in the church-yard, between services on Sundays! gathering grapes for them from the wild vines that overran the surrounding trees; reciting for their amusement all the epitaphs on the tombstones; or sauntering, with a whole bevy of them, along the banks of the adjacent mill-pond; while the more bashful country bumpkins hung sheepishly back, envying his superior elegance and address.

From his half itinerant life, also, he was a kind of traveling gazette, carrying the whole budget of local gossip from house to house; so that his appearance was always greeted with satisfaction. He was, moreover, esteemed by the women as a man of great erudition, for he had read several books quite through, and was a perfect master of Cotton Mather's "History of New England Witchcraft"—in which, by the way, he most firmly and potently believed.

He was, in fact, a mixture of small shrewdness and simple credulity. His appetite for the marvelous, and his powers of digesting it, were equally extraordinary; and both had been increased by his residence in this spell-bound region. No tale was too gross or monstrous for his capacious swallow. It was often his delight, after his school was dismissed in the afternoon, to stretch himself on the rich bed of clover bordering the little brook that whimpered by his schoolhouse, and there con over old Mather's direful tales until the gathering dusk of the evening made the printed page a mere mist before his eyes. Then, as he wended his way, by swamp and stream and awful woodland, to the farm-house where he happened to be quartered, every sound of nature, at that witching hour, fluttered his excited imagination,—the moan of the whippoorwill from the hill-side; the boding cry of the tree-toad, that harbinger of storm; the dreary hooting of the screech-owl, or the sudden rustling in the thicket of birds frightened from their roost. The fire-flies, too, which sparkled most vividly in the darkest places, now and then startled him, as one of uncommon brightness would stream across his path; and if, by chance, a huge blockhead of a beetle came winging his blundering flight against him, the poor varlet was ready to give up the ghost, with the idea that he was struck with a witch's token. His only resource on such occasions, either to drown thought or drive away evil spirits, was to sing psalm-tunes; and the good people of Sleepy Hollow, as they sat by their doors of an evening, were often filled with awe at hearing his nasal melody, in " linked sweetness long drawn out," floating from the distant hill, or along the dusky road.

Another of his sources of fearful pleasure was, to pass long winter evenings with the old Dutch wives as they sat spinning by the fire, with a row of apples roasting and spluttering along the hearth, and listen to their marvelous tales of ghosts and goblins, and haunted fields, and haunted brooks, and haunted bridges, and haunted houses, and particularly of the headless horseman, or Galloping Hessian of the Hollow, as they sometimes called him. He would delight them equally by his anecdotes of witchcraft, and of the direful omens and portentous sights and sounds in the air which prevailed in the earlier times of Connecticut; and would frighten them wofully with speculations upon comets and shooting stars; and with the alarming fact that the world did absolutely turn round; and that they were half the time topsy-turvy!

GEORGE MacDONALD
1824

GEORGE MACDONALD, a descendant of the MacDonalds of Glencoe, and a son of a wealthy Scotch manufacturer, was born at Huntley, in Aberdeenshire, Scotland, in 1824. His college days were passed at the University of Aberdeen; and after graduation he studied theology at Owen's College, in Manchester. For some years he was an independent minister in Surrey and Sussex counties, England. Later he became a layman of the established English Church. In 1855, Mr. MacDonald issued a volume of poetry, entitled "Within and Without." This was followed in the succeeding year by another book of "Poems," and in 1858 by "Phantastes, a Fairy Romance."

In 1863 appeared the author's first novel, "David Elginbrod," a work of powerful and dramatic interest, peculiarly tinged with his speculative tendency and mystic significance. The success of the book demonstrated that the writer had found his true vocation. Other prose works followed in quick succession, maintaining the high standard of the first, and revealing an untiring energy, and an inexhaustible invention which recalled the career of Sir Walter Scott. In 1872-3 Mr. MacDonald visited the United States, and made a lecturing tour of leading American cities, in which he was most cordially received. He has long resided alternately in London and at Hastings. Among his best novels are "The Portent," "David Elginbrod," "Robert Falconer," "Wilfred Cumbermede," "Malcolm," and "Sir Gibbie."

Characterization

Certain qualities of Mr. MacDonald's writings lie so immediately upon the surface that it can scarcely be said that you notice them. Upon reflection, you recall them; but it would hardly strike you to say that he is singularly pure, elevated, and tender, or that he wrote beautiful English. Yet, of course, all this is true; and the transparency or lucidity of his style appears to be closely connected with, perhaps, the first peculiarity that an attentive reader can be said to notice. It reminds you of running water; and so, also, does the course of the author's thought. . . . We can see that he is primarily a poet; he sometimes reaches the perfection of poetic form which carries with it the infinite suggestion that may make a small poem more valuable than a big prose book, however good. Yet the superiority in point of force and profusion, rests with his prose works. . . . It may be a hazardous thing to say, but he reminds us more of Mendelssohn than of any writer. We have already hinted that we take his genius to be, on the whole, the flower of certain spiritual tendencies of our time, and a very beautiful and fragrant flower it is. In the dainty little casket which shuts over these ten volumes there is more of a talismanic virtue than the reader will appropriate in a lifetime.

"CONTEMPORARY REVIEW."

Extracts from "Malcolm"

The sea-town of Portlossie was as irregular a gathering of small cottages as could be found on the surface of the globe. They faced every way, turned their backs and gables every way —only of the roofs could you predict the position; were divided from each other by every sort of small, irregular space and passage, and looked like a national assembly debating a constitution. Close behind the Seaton, as it was called, ran a highway, climbing far above the chimneys of the village to the level of the town above. Behind this road, and separated from it by a high wall of stone, lay a succession of heights and hollows covered with grass. In front of the cottages lay sand and sea. The place was cleaner than most fishing-villages, but so closely built, so thickly inhabited, and so pervaded with "a very ancient and fish-like smell," that but for the besom of the salt north wind it must have been unhealthy. Eastward the houses could extend no further for the harbor, and westward no further for a small river that crossed the sands to find the sea—discursively and merrily at low water, but with sullen, submissive mingling when banked back by the tide.

Avoiding the many nets extended long and wide on the grassy sands, the youth Malcolm walked through the tide-swollen mouth of the river, and passed along the front of the village until he arrived at a house, the small window in the seaward gable of which was filled with a curious collection of things for sale—dusty-looking sweets in a glass bottle; ginger-bread cakes in the shape of large hearts, thickly studded with sugar-plums of rainbow colors, invitingly poisonous; strings of tin covers for tobacco-pipes, over-lapping each other like fish-scales; toys, and tapes, and needles, and twenty other kinds of things, all huddled together.

Turning the corner of this house, he went down the narrow passage between it and the next, and in at its open door. But the moment it was entered it lost all appearance of a shop, and the room with the tempting window showed itself only as a poor kitchen with an earthen floor.

"Weel, hoo did the pipes behave themsels the day, daddy?" said the youth as he strode in.

"Och, she'll pe peing a coot poy to-day," returned the tremulous voice of a gray-headed old man, who was leaning over a small peat-fire on the hearth, sifting oatmeal through the fingers of his left hand into a pot, while he stirred the boiling mess with a short stick held in his right.

It had grown to be understood between them that the pulmonary conditions of the old piper should be attributed not to his internal, but his external lungs—namely, the bag of his pipes. Both sets had of late years manifested strong symptoms of decay, and decided measures had had to be again and again resorted to in the case of the latter to put off its evil day, and keep within it the breath of its musical existence. The youth's question, then, as to the behavior of the pipes, was in reality an inquiry after the condition of his grandfather's lungs, which, for their part, grew yearly more and more asthmatic: notwithstanding which Duncan MacPhail would not hear of resigning the dignity of town-piper.

"That's fine, daddy," returned the youth. "Wull I mak oot the parritch? I'm thinkin' ye've had eneuch o' hangin' ower the fire this het mornin'." . . .

Malcolm lifted the pot from the table and set it on the hearth; put the plates together and the spoons, and set them on a chair, for there was no dresser; tilted the table, and wiped it hearthward—then from a shelf took down and laid upon it a Bible, before which he seated himself with an air of reverence. The old man sat down on a low chair by the chimney corner, took off his bonnet, closed his eyes and murmured some almost inaudible words; then repeated in Gaelic the first line of the hundred and third psalm:

> O m' anam, beannuich thus' a nis—

and raised a tune of marvelous wail. Arrived at the end of the line, he repeated the process with the next, and so went on, giving every line first in the voice of speech and then in the voice of song, through three stanzas of eight lines each. And no less strange was the singing than the tune—wild and wailful as the wind of his native desolations, or as the sound of his own pipes borne thereon; and apparently all but lawless, for the multitude of so-called grace-notes, hovering and fluttering endlessly around the center-tone like the comments on a text, rendered it nearly impossible to unravel from them the air even of a known tune. It had in its kind the same liquid uncertainty of confluent sound which had hitherto rendered it impossible for Malcolm to learn more than a few of the common phrases of his grandfather's mother-tongue.

The psalm over, during which the sightless eye-balls of the singer had been turned up toward the rafters of the cottage—a sign surely that the germ of light, "the sunny seed," as Henry Vaughan calls it, must be in him, else why should he lift his *eyes* when he thought upward?—Malcolm read a chapter of the Bible, plainly the next in an ordered succession, for it could never have been chosen or culled; after which they kneeled together, and the old man poured out a prayer, beginning in a low, scarcely audible voice, which rose at length to a loud, modulated chant. Not a sentence, hardly a phrase of the utterance did his grandson lay hold of; but there were a few inhabitants of the place who could have interpreted it, and it was commonly believed that one part of his devotions was invariably a prolonged petition for vengeance on Campbell of Glenlyon, the main instrument in the massacre of Glencoe.

He *could* have prayed in English, and then his grandson might have joined in his petitions, but the thought of such a thing would never have presented itself to him. Nay, although, understanding both languages, he used that which was unintelligible to the lad, he yet regarded himself as the party who had the right to resent the consequent schism. Such a conversation as now followed was no new thing after prayers.

"I could fery well wish, Malcolm, my son," said the old man, "tat you would be learnin' to speak your own lancuach. It is all fery well for ta Sassenach (*Saxon, i.e., non-Celtic*) podies to read ta Piple in English, for it will be pleasing ta Maker not to make tem cawpable of ta Gaelic, no more tan monkeys; but for all tat it's not ta vord of God. Ta Gaelic is ta lancuach of ta carden of Aiden, and no doubt but it pe ta lancuach in which ta Shepherd calls his sheep on ta everlastin' hills. You see, Malcolm, it must be so, for how can a mortal man speak to his God in *anything put* Gaelic? When Mr. Craham—no, not Mr. Craham, ta coot man; it was ta new minister—he speak an' say to her: 'Mr. MacPhail, you ought to make your prayers in Enclish,' I was fery wrathful, and I answered and said: 'Mr. Downey, do you tare to suppose tat God doesn't prefer ta Gaelic to ta Sassenach tongue?'—'Mr. MacPhail,' says he, 'it'll pe for your poy I mean it. How's ta lad to learn ta way of salvation if you speak to your God in his presence in a strange tongue?' So I was opedient to his vord, and ta next efening I tid kneel town in Sassenach and I tid make begin. But, ochone! she wouldn't go; her tongue would be cleafing to ta roof of her mouth; ta claymore woold be sticking rusty in ta scappard; for her heart she was ashamed to speak to ta Hielan'man's Maker in ta Sassenach tongue. You must pe learning ta Gaelic, or you'll not pe peing worthy to pe her nain son, Malcolm."

.   .   .   .   .   .

As soon as his grandfather left the house, Malcolm went out also, closing the door behind him, and turning the key, but leaving it in the lock. He ascended to the upper town, only, however, to pass through its main street, at the top of which he turned and looked back for a few moments, apparently in contemplation. The descent to the shore was so sudden that he could see nothing of the harbor or of the village he had left —nothing but the blue bay and the filmy mountains of Sutherlandshire, molten by distance into cloudy questions, and looking, betwixt blue sea and blue sky, less substantial than either. After gazing for a moment, he turned again, and held on his way, through fields which no fence parted from the road. The morning was still glorious, the larks right jubilant, and the air filled with the sweet scents of cottage flowers. Across the fields came the occasional low of an ox, and the distant sounds of children at play. But Malcolm saw without noting, and heard without seeing, for his mind was full of speculation concerning the lovely girl whose vision appeared already far off:—who might she be?—whence had she come?—whither could she have vanished? That she did not belong to the neighborhood was certain, he thought; but there was a farmhouse near the sea-town where they let lodgings; and, although it was early in the season, she might belong to some family which had come to spend a few of the summer weeks there; possibly his appearance had prevented her from having her bath that morning. If he should have the good fortune to see her again, he would show her a place far fitter for the purpose —a perfect arbor of rocks, utterly secluded, with a floor of deep sand, and without a hole for crab or lobster.

His road led him in the direction of a few cottages lying in a hollow. Beside them rose a vision of trees, bordered by an ivy-grown wall, from amidst whose summits shot the spire of the church; and from beyond the spire, through the trees, came golden glimmers as of vane and crescent and pinnacled ball, that hinted at some shadowy abode of enchantment within; but as he descended the slope towards the cottages the trees gradually rose and shut in everything.

These cottages were far more ancient than the houses of the town; were covered with green thatch; were buried in ivy, and would soon be radiant with roses and honeysuckles. They were gathered irregularly about a gate of curious old iron-work, opening on the churchyard, but more like an entrance to the grounds behind the church, for it told of ancient state, bearing on each of its pillars a great stone heron with a fish in its beak.

This was the quarter whence had come the noises of children, but they had now ceased, or rather sunk into a gentle murmur, which oozed like the sound of bees from a straw-covered beehive, out of a cottage rather larger than the rest, which stood close by the churchyard gate. It was the parish school, and these cottages were all that remained of the old town of Portlossie, which had at one time stretched in a long, irregular street almost to the shore. The town cross yet stood, but away solitary on a green hill that overlooked the sands.

During the summer the long walk from the new town to the school and to the church was anything but a hardship; in winter it was otherwise, for then there were days in which few would venture the single mile that separated them.

The door of the school, bisected longitudinally, had one of its halves open, and by it outflowed the gentle hum of the honey-bees of learning. Malcolm walked in and had the whole of the busy scene at once before him. The place was like a barn, open from wall to wall, and from floor to rafters and thatch, browned with the peat smoke of vanished winters. Two thirds of the space were filled with long desks and forms; the other had only the master's desk, and thus afforded room for standing classes. At the present moment it was vacant, for the prayer was but just over, and the Bible-class had not been called up: there Alexander Graham, the schoolmaster, descending from his desk, met and welcomed Malcolm with a kind shake of the hand. He was a man of middle height, but very thin; and about five and forty years of age, but looked older, because of his thin gray hair and a stoop in the shoulders. He was dressed in a shabby black tail-coat, and clean white neck-cloth; the rest of his clothes were of parson gray, noticeably shabby also. The quiet sweetness of his smile, and a composed look of submission were suggestive of the purification of sorrow, but were attributed by the townsfolk to disappointment; for he was still but a schoolmaster, whose aim they thought must be a pulpit and a parish. But Mr. Graham had been early released from such an ambition, if it had ever possessed him, and had for many years been more than content to give himself to the hopefuller work of training children for the true ends of life. He lived the quietest of studious lives, with an old housekeeper.

Malcolm had been a favorite pupil, and the relation of master and scholar did not cease when the latter saw that he ought to do something to lighten the burden of his grandfather, and so left the school and betook himself to the life of a fisherman —with the slow leave of Duncan, who had set his heart on making a scholar of him, and would never, indeed, had Gaelic been amongst his studies, have been won by the most laborsome petition. He asserted himself perfectly able to provide for both for ten years to come at least, in proof of which he roused the inhabitants of Portlossie, during the space of a whole month, a full hour earlier than usual, with the most terrific blasts of the bagpipes, and this notwithstanding complaint and expostulation on all sides, so that at length the provost had to interfere; after which outburst of defiance to time, however, his energy had begun to decay so visibly that Malcolm gave himself to the pipes in secret, that he might be ready, in case of sudden emergency, to take his grandfather's place; for Duncan lived in constant dread of the hour when his office might be taken from him and conferred on a mere drummer, or, still worse, on a certain ne'er-do-weel cousin of the provost, so devoid of music as to be capable only of ringing a bell.

"I've had an invitation to Miss Campbell's funeral—Miss Horn's cousin, you know," said Mr. Graham, in a hesitating and subdued voice. "Could you manage to take the school for me, Malcolm?"

"Yes, sir. There's naething to hinner me. What day is 't upo'?"

"Saturday."

"Verra weel, sir. I s' be here in guid time."

This matter settled, the business of the school, in which, as he did often, Malcolm had come to assist, began. Only a pupil of his own could have worked with Mr. Graham, for his mode was very peculiar. But the strangest fact in it would have been the last to reveal itself to an ordinary observer. This was, that he rarely contradicted anything. He would call up the opposing truth, set it face to face with the error, and leave the two to fight it out. The human mind and conscience were, he said, the plains of Armageddon, where the battle of good and evil was forever raging; and the one business of a teacher was to rouse and urge this battle by leading fresh forces of the truth into the field—forces composed as little as might be of the hireling troops of the intellect, and as much as possible of the native energies of the heart, imagination, and conscience. In a word, he would oppose error only by teaching the truth.

In early life he had come under the influence of the writings of William Law, which he read as one who pondered every doctrine in that light which only obedience to the truth can open upon it. With a keen eye for the discovery of universal law in the individual fact, he read even the marvels of the New Testament practically. Hence, in training his soldiers, every lesson he gave them was a missile; every admonishment of youth or maiden was as the mounting of an armed champion, and the launching of him with a *God-speed* into the thick of the fight.

He now called up the Bible-class, and Malcolm sat beside and listened. That morning they had to read one of the chapters in the history of Jacob.

"Was Jacob a good man?" he asked, as soon as the reading (each of the scholars in turn taking a verse) was over.

An apparently universal expression of assent followed; halting in its wake, however, came the voice of a boy near the bottom of the class:

"Wasna he some dooble, sir?"

"You are right, Sheltie," said the master; "he *was* double.

I must, I find, put the question in another shape: Was Jacob a bad man?"

Again came such a burst of yeses that it might have been taken for a general hiss. But limping in the rear came again the half-dissentient voice of Jamie Joss, whom the master had just addressed as Sheltie:

"Pairtly, sir."

"You think, then, Sheltie, that a man may be both bad and good?"

"I dinna ken, sir. I think he may be whiles ane an' whiles the ither, an' whiles maybe it wad be ill to say whilk. Oor collie's whiles in twa min's whether he'll du what he's telled or no."

"That's the battle of Armageddon, Sheltie, my man. It's aye ragin', ohn gun roared or bagonet clashed. Ye maun up an' do yer best in't, my man. Gien ye dee fechtin' like a man, ye'll flee up wi' a quaiet face an' wide-open een; an' there's a great Ane 'at 'll say to ye, 'Weel dune, laddie!' But gien ye gie in to the enemy, he'll turn ye intill a creepin' thing 'at eats dirt; an' there'll no be a hole in a' the crystal wa' o' the New Jerusalem near eneuch to the grun' to lat ye creep throu'."

As soon as ever Alexander Graham, the polished thinker and sweet-mannered gentleman, opened his mouth concerning the things he loved best, that moment the most poetic forms came pouring out in the most rugged speech.

"I reckon, sir," said Sheltie, "Jacob hadna fouchten oot his battle."

"That's jist it, my boy. And because he wouldna get up and fecht manfully, God had to tak him in han'. Ye've heard tell o' generals, when their troops war rinnin' awa', haein' to cut this man doon, shute that ane, and lick anither, till he turned them a' richt face aboot and drave them on to the foe like a spate! And the trouble God took wi' Jacob wasna lost upon him at last."

"An' what cam o' Esau, sir?" asked a pale-faced maiden with blue eyes. "He wasna an ill kin' o' a chield—was he, sir?"

"No, Mappy," answered the master; "he was a fine chield, as you say; but he nott (*needed*) mair time and gentler treatment to mak onything o' him. Ye see he had a guid hert, but was a duller kin' o' cratur a'thegither, and cared for naething he could na see or han'le. He never thoucht muckle aboot God at a'. Jacob was anither sort—a poet kin' o' a man, but a sneck-drawin' cratur for a' that. It was easier, hooever, to get the slyness oot o' Jacob, than the dullness oot o' Esau. Punishment tellt upo' Jacob like upon a thin-skinned horse, whauras Esau was mair like the minister's powny, that can hardly be made to unnerstan' that ye want him to gang on. But o' the ither han', dullness is a thing that can be borne wi': there's nay hurry aboot that; but the deceitfu' tricks o' Jacob war na to be endured, and sae the tawse (*leather-strap*) cam doon upo' him."

"An' what for didna God mak Esau as clever as Jacob?" asked a wizened-faced boy near the top of the class.

"Ah, my Peery!" said Mr. Graham, "I canna tell ye that. A' that I can tell is, that God hadna dune makin' at him, an' some kin' o' fowk tak langer to mak oot than ithers. An' ye canna tell what they're to be till they're made oot. But whether what I tell ye be richt or no, God maun hae the verra best o' rizzons for 't, ower guid maybe for us to unnerstan'—the best o' rizzons for Esau himsel', I mean, for the Creator luiks efter his cratur first ava' (*of all*). And now," concluded Mr. Graham, resuming his English, "go to your lessons; and be diligent, that God may think it worth while to get on faster with the making of you."

In a moment the class was dispersed and all were seated. In another, the sound of scuffling arose, and fists were seen storming across a desk.

"Andrew Jamieson and Poochy, come up here," said the master in a loud voice.

"*He* hittit me first," cried Andrew, the moment they were within a respectful distance of the master, whereupon Mr. Graham turned to the other with inquiry in his eyes.

"He had nae business to ca' me Poochy."

"No more he had; but you had just as little right to punish him for it. The offense was against me; he had no right to use my name for you, and the quarrel was mine. For the present, you are Poochy no more. Go to your place, William Wilson."

The boy burst out sobbing, and crept back to his seat with his knuckles in his eyes.

"Andrew Jamieson," the master went on, "I had almost got a name for you, but you have sent it away. You are not ready for it yet, I see. Go to your place."

With downcast looks Andrew followed William, and the watchful eyes of the master saw that, instead of quarreling any more during the day, they seemed to catch at every opportunity of showing each other a kindness.

Mr. Graham never used bodily punishment; he ruled chiefly by the aid of a system of individual titles, of the mingled characters of pet-name and nickname. As soon as the individuality of a boy had attained to signs of blossoming—that is, had become such that he could predict not only an upright but a characteristic behavior in given circumstances, he would take him aside and whisper in his ear that henceforth, so long as he deserved it, he would call him by a certain name—one generally derived from some object in the animal or vegetable world, and pointing to a resemblance which was not often patent to any eye but the master's own. He had given the name of *Poochy*, for instance, to William Wilson, because, like the kangaroo, he sought his object in a succession of awkward, yet not the less availing leaps —gulping his knowledge and pocketing his conquered marble after a like fashion. *Mappy*, the name which thus belonged to a certain flaxen-haired, soft-eyed girl, corresponds to the English *bunny*. *Sheltie* is the small Scotch mountain-pony, active and strong. *Peery* means *pegtop*. But not above a quarter of the children had pet names. To gain one was to reach the highest honor of the school; the withdrawal of it was the severest of punishments, and the restoring of it the sign of perfect reconciliation. The master permitted no one else to use it, and was seldom known to forget himself so far as to utter it while its owner was in disgrace. The hope of gaining such a name, or the fear of losing it, was in the pupil the strongest ally of the master, the most powerful enforcement of his influences. It was a scheme of government by aspiration. But it owed all its operative power to the character of the man who had adopted rather than invented it—for the scheme had been suggested by a certain passage in the book of the Revelation.

Without having read a word of Swedenborg, he was a believer in the absolute correspondence of the inward and outward; and, thus long before the younger Darwin arose, had suspected a close relationship—remote identity, indeed, in nature and history, between the animal and human worlds. But photographs from a good many different points would be necessary to afford anything like a complete notion of the character of this country schoolmaster.

Towards noon, while he was busy with an astronomical class, explaining, by means partly of the blackboard, partly of two boys representing the relation of the earth and the moon, how it comes that we see but one half of the latter, the door gently opened and the troubled face of the mad laird peeped slowly in. His body followed as gently, and at last—sad symbol of his weight of care—his hump appeared, with a slow half-revolution as he turned to shut the door behind him. Taking off his hat, he walked up to Mr. Graham, who, busy with his astronomy, had not perceived his entrance, touched him on the arm, and, standing on tip-toe, whispered softly in his ear, as if it were a painful secret that must be respected:

"I dinna ken whaur I cam frae. I want to come to the school."

Mr. Graham turned and shook hands with him, respectfully addressing him as Mr. Stewart, and got down for him the armchair which stood behind his desk. But with the politest bow the laird declined it, and mournfully repeating the words, "I dinna ken whaur I cam frae," took a place readily yielded him in the astronomical circle surrounding the symbolic boys.

This was not by any means his first appearance there; for every now and then he was seized with a desire to go to school, plainly with the object of finding out where he came from. This always fell in his quieter times, and for days together he would attend regularly; in one instance he was not absent an hour for a whole month. He spoke so little, however, that it was impossible to tell how much he understood, although he seemed to enjoy all that went on. He was so quiet, so sadly gentle, that he gave no trouble of any sort, and after the first few minutes of a fresh appearance, the attention of the scholars was rarely distracted by his presence.

The way in which the master treated him awoke like respect in his pupils. Boys and girls were equally ready to make room for him on their forms, and any one of the latter who had by some kind attention awakened the watery glint of a smile on the melancholy features of the troubled man, would boast of her success. Hence it came that the neighborhood of Portlossie was the one spot in the county where a person of weak intellect or peculiar appearance might go about free of insult.

The peculiar sentence the laird so often uttered was the only one he invariably spoke with definite clearness. In every other attempt at speech he was liable to be assailed by an often recurring impediment, during the continuance of which he could compass but a word here and there, often betaking himself, in the agony of suppressed utterance, to the most extravagant gestures, with which he would sometimes succeed in so supplementing his words as to render his meaning intelligible.

The two boys representing the earth and the moon had returned to their places in the class, and Mr. Graham had gone on to give a description of the moon, in which he had necessarily mentioned the enormous height of her mountains as compared with those of the earth. But in the course of asking some questions, he found a need of further explanation, and therefore once more required the services of the boy-sun and boy-moon.

The moment the latter, however, began to describe his circle around the former, Mr. Stewart stepped gravely up to him, and laying hold of his hand, led him back to his station in the class; then, turning first one shoulder, then the other to the company, so as to attract attention to his hump, uttered the single word *Mountain*, and took on himself the part of the moon, proceeding to revolve in the circle which represented her orbit. Several of the boys and girls smiled, but no one laughed, for Mr. Graham's gravity maintained theirs. Without remark, he used the mad laird for a moon to the end of his explanation.

Mr. Stewart remained in the school all the morning, stood up with every class Mr. Graham taught, and in the intervals sat, with book or slate before him, still as a Brahmin on the fancied verge of his reabsorption, save that he murmured to himself now and then:

"I dinna ken whaur I cam frae."

When his pupils dispersed for dinner, Mr. Graham invited him to go to his house and share his homely meal; but with polished gesture and broken speech, Mr. Stewart declined, walked away towards the town, and was seen no more that afternoon.

. . . .

The next day, the day of the Resurrection, rose glorious from its sepulcher of sea-fog and drizzle. It had poured all night long, but at sunrise the clouds had broken and scattered, and the air was the purer for the cleansing rain, while the earth shone with that peculiar luster which follows the weeping which has endured its appointed night. The larks were at it again, singing as if their hearts would break for joy as they hovered in brooding exultation over the song of the future; for their nests beneath hoarded a wealth of larks for summers to come. Especially about the old church—half buried in the ancient trees of Lossie House, the birds that day were jubilant; their throats seemed too narrow to let out the joyful air that filled all their hollow bones and quills; they sang as if they must sing, or choke with too much gladness. Beyond the short spire and its shining cock, rose the balls and stars and arrowy vanes of the House, glittering in gold and sunshine.

The inward hush of the resurrection, broken only by the prophetic birds, the poets of the groaning and travailing creation, held time and space as in a trance; and the center from which radiated both the hush and the caroling expectation seemed to Alexander Graham to be the churchyard in which he was now walking in the cool of the morning. It was more carefully kept than most Scottish churchyards, and yet was not too trim: Nature had a word in the affair—was allowed her part of mourning, in long grass and moss and the crumbling away of stone. The wholesomeness of decay, which both in nature and humanity is but the miry road back to life, was not unrecognized here; there was nothing of the hideous attempt to hide death in the garments of life. The master walked about gently, now stopping to read some well-known inscription and ponder for a moment over the words; and now wandering across the stoneless mounds, content to be forgotten by all but those who loved the departed. At length he seated himself on a slat by the side of the mound that rose but yesterday; it was sculptured with symbols of decay—needless surely where the originals lay about the mouth of every newly opened grave, and as surely ill-befitting the precincts of a church whose indwelling gospel is of life victorious over death!

"What are these stones," he said to himself, "but monuments to oblivion? They are not memorials of the dead, but memorials of the forgetfulness of the living. How vain it is to send a poor forsaken name, like the title-page of a lost book, down the careless stream of time! Let me serve my generation, and let God remember me!"

The morning wore on; the sun rose higher and higher. He drew from his pocket the *Nosce Teipsum* of Sir John Davies, and was still reading, in quiet enjoyment of the fine logic of the lawyer-poet, when he heard the church key, in the trembling hand of Jonathan Auld, the sexton, jar feebly battling with the reluctant lock. Soon the people began to gather, mostly in groups and couples. At length came solitary Miss Horn, whom the neighbors, from respect to her sorrow, had left to walk alone. But Mr. Graham went to meet her, and accompanied her into the church.

It was a cruciform building, as old as the vanished monastery, and the burial place of generations of noble blood; the dust of royalty even lay under its floor. A knight of stone reclined cross-legged in a niche with an arched Norman canopy in one of the walls, the rest of which was nearly encased in large tablets of white marble, for at his foot lay the ashes of barons and earls whose title was extinct, and whose lands had been inherited by the family of Lossie. Inside as well as outside of the church the ground had risen with the dust of generations, so that the walls were low; and heavy galleries having been erected in parts, the place was filled with shadowy recesses and haunted with glooms.

From a window in the square pew where he sat, so small and low that he had to bend his head to look out of it, the schoolmaster could see a rivulet of sunshine streaming through between two upright grave-stones, and glorifying the long grass of a neglected mound that lay close to the wall under the wintry drip from the eaves; when he raised his head, the church looked very dark. The best way there to preach the Resurrection, he thought, would be to contrast the sepulchral gloom of the church, its dreary psalms and drearier sermons, with the sunlight on the graves, the lark-filled sky, and the wind blowing where it listed. But although the minister was a young man of the commonest order, educated to the church that he might eat bread, hence a mere willing slave to the beck of his lord and master the patron, and but a parrot in the pulpit, the schoolmaster not only endeavored to pour his feelings and desires into the mold of his prayers, but listened to the sermon with a countenance that revealed no distaste for the weak and unsavory broth ladled out to him to nourish his soul withal. When, however, the *service*—though whose purposes the affair could be supposed to *serve* except those of Mr. Cairns himself, would have been a curious question—was over, he did breathe a sigh of relief; and when he stepped out into the sun and wind which had been shining and blowing all the time of the dreary ceremony, he wondered whether the larks might not have had the best of it in the God-praising that had been going on for two slow-paced hours. Yet, having been so long used to the sort of thing, he did not mind it half so much as his friend Malcolm, who found the Sunday observances an unspeakable weariness to both flesh and spirit.

On the present occasion, however, Malcolm did not find the said observances dreary, for he observed nothing but the vision which radiated from the dusk of the small gallery forming Lossie pew, directly opposite the Norman canopy and stone crusader. Unconventional, careless girl as Lady Florimel had hitherto shown herself to him, he saw her sit that morning like the proudest of her race, alone, and, to all appearance, unaware of a single other person's being in the church besides herself. She manifested no interest in what was going on, nor indeed felt any—how could she?—never parted her lips to sing; sat during the prayer; and throughout the sermon seemed to Malcolm not once to move her eyes from the carved crusader. When all was over, she still sat motionless—sat until the last old woman had hobbled out. Then she rose, walked slowly from the gloom of the church, flashed into the glow of the churchyard, gleamed across it to a private door in the wall, which a servant held for her, and vanished. If, a moment after, the notes of a merry song invaded the ears of those who yet lingered, who could dare suspect that proudly sedate damsel thus suddenly breaking the ice of her public behavior?

For a mere schoolgirl she had certainly done the lady's part well. What she wore I do not exactly know; nor would it perhaps be well to describe what might seem grotesque to such prejudiced readers as have no judgment beyond the fashions of the day. But I will not let pass the opportunity of reminding them how sadly old-fashioned we of the present hour also look in the eyes of those equally infallible judges who have

been in dread procession toward us ever since we began to
be—our posterity—judges who perhaps will doubt with a smile
whether we even knew what love was, or ever had a dream of
the grandeur they are on the point of grasping. But at least
bethink yourselves, dear posterity; we have not ceased because
you have begun.

Out of the church the blind Duncan strode with long, confident strides. He had no staff to aid him, for he never carried one when in his best clothes; but he leaned proudly on Malcolm's arm, if one who walked so erect could be said to lean. He had adorned his bonnet the autumn before with a sprig of the large purple heather, but every bell had fallen from it, leaving only the naked spray, pitiful analogue of the whole withered exterior of which it formed part. His sporran, however, hid the stained front of his kilt, and his Sunday coat had been new within ten years—the gift of certain ladies of Portlossie, some of whom, to whose lowland eyes the kilt was obnoxious, would have added a pair of trousers, had not Miss Horn stoutly opposed them, confident that Duncan would regard the present as an insult. And she was right; for rather than wear anything instead of the philibeg, Duncan would have plaited himself one with his own blind fingers out of an old sack. Indeed, although the *trews* were never at any time unknown in the Highlands, Duncan had always regarded them as effeminate, and especially in his lowland exile would have looked upon the wearing of them as a disgrace to his highland birth.

"Tat wass a fery coot sairmon to-day, Malcolm," he said, as they stepped from the churchyard upon the road.

Malcolm, knowing well whither conversation on the subject would lead, made no reply. His grandfather, finding him silent, iterated his remark, with the addition:

"Put how could it pe a paad one, you'll pe thinking, my poy, when he'd pe hafing such a text to keep him straight."

Malcolm continued silent, for a good many people were within hearing whom he did not wish to see amused with the remarks certain to follow any he could make. But Mr. Graham, who happened to be walking near the old man on the other side, out of pure politeness made a partial response.

"Yes, Mr. MacPhail," he said, "it was a grand text."

"Yes, and it wass'll pe a cran' sairmon," persisted Duncan. "'Fenchence is mine—I will repay.' Ta Lord loves fenchence. It's a fine thing, fenchence. To make ta wicked know tat tey'll pe peing put men! Yes; ta Lord will slay ta wicked. Ta Lord will gif ta honest man fenchence upon his enemies. It *wass* a cran' sairmon!"

"Don't you think vengeance a very dreadful thing, Mr. MacPhail?" said the schoolmaster.

"Yes, for ta von tat'll pe in ta wrong—I wish ta fenchence was mine!" he added with a loud sigh.

"But the Lord doesn't think any of *us* fit to be trusted with it, and so keeps it to himself, you see."

"Yes; and tat'll pe pecause it'll pe too coot to be gifing to another. And some people would be waik of heart, and be letting teir enemies co."

"I suspect it's for the opposite reason, Mr. MacPhail: we would go much too far, making no allowances, causing the innocent to suffer along with the guilty, neither giving fair play nor avoiding cruelty—and indeed——"

"No fear!" interrupted Duncan, eagerly—"no fear, when ta wrong wass as larch as Morven!"

In the sermon there had not been one word as to St. Paul's design in quoting the text. It had been but a theatrical setting forth of the vengeance of God upon sin, illustrated with several common tales of the discovery of murder by strange means—a sermon after Duncan's own heart; and nothing but the way in which he now snuffed the wind, with head thrown back and nostrils dilated, could have given an adequate idea of how much he enjoyed the recollection of it.

Mr. Graham had for many years believed that he must have some personal wrongs to brood over—wrongs, probably, to which were to be attributed his loneliness and exile; but of such

Duncan had never spoken, uttering no maledictions except against the real or imagined foes of his family.

The master placed so little value on any possible results of mere argument, and had indeed so little faith in any words except such as came hot from the heart, that he said no more, but, with an invitation to Malcolm to visit him in the evening, wished them good day, and turned in at his own door.

. . . . . .

On Sundays, Malcolm was always more or less annoyed by the obtrusive presence of his arms and legs, accompanied by a vague feeling that, at any moment, and no warning given, they might, with some insane and irrepressible flourish, break the Sabbath on their own account, and degrade him in the eyes of his fellow-townsmen, who seemed all silently watching how he bore the restraints of the holy day. It must be conceded, however, that the discomfort had quite as much to do with his Sunday clothes as with the Sabbath day, and that it interfered but little with an altogether peculiar calm which appeared to him to belong in its own right to the Sunday, whether its light flowed in the sunny cataracts of June, or oozed through the spongy clouds of November.

As he walked again to the Alton, or Old Town, in the evening, the filmy floats of white in the lofty blue, the droop of the long dark grass by the side of the short brown corn, the shadows pointing like all lengthening shadows toward the quarter of hope, the yellow glory filling the air and paling the green below, the unseen larks hanging aloft—like air-pitcher-plants that overflowed in song—like electric jars emptying themselves of the sweet thunder of bliss in the flashing of wings and the trembling of melodious throats; these were indeed of the summer—but the cup of rest had been poured out upon them; the Sabbath brooded like an embodied peace over the earth, and under its wings they grew sevenfold peaceful—with a peace that might be felt, like the hand of a mother pressed upon the half-sleeping child. The rusted iron cross on the eastern gable of the old church stood glowing lusterless in the westering sun;

while the gilded vane, whose business was the wind, creaked radiantly this way and that, in the flaws from the region of the sunset; its shadow flickered soft on the new grave, where the grass of the wounded sod was drooping. Again seated on a neighboring stone, Malcolm found his friend.

"See," said the schoolmaster as the fisherman sat down beside him, "how the shadow from one grave stretches like an arm to embrace another! In this light the churchyard seems the very birthplace of shadows. See them flowing out of the tombs as from fountains, to overflow the world! Does the morning or the evening light suit such a place best, Malcolm?"

The pupil thought for a while.

"The evenin' licht, sir," he answered at length; "for ye see the sun's decin' like, an' deith's like a fa'in' asleep, an' the grave's the bed, an' the sod's the bed-claes, an' there's a long nicht to the fore."

"Are ye sure o' that, Malcolm?"

"It's the wye folk thinks an' says aboot it, sir."

"Or maybe doesna think, an' only says?"

"Maybe, sir; I dinna ken."

"Come here, Malcolm," said Mr. Graham, and took him by the arm, and led him towards the east end of the church, where a few tombstones were crowded against the wall, as if they would press close to a place they might not enter.

"Read that," he said, pointing to a flat stone, where every hollow letter was shown in high relief by the growth in it of a lovely moss. The rest of the stone was rich in gray and green and brown lichens, but only in the letters grew the bright moss: the inscription stood as it were in the hand of Nature herself—
"*He is not here; he is risen.*"

While Malcolm gazed, trying to think what his master would have him think, the latter resumed.

"If he is risen—if the sun is up, Malcolm—then the morning and not the evening is the season for the place of tombs; the morning when the shadows are shortening and separating, not the evening when they are growing all into one. I used to love

the churchyard best in the evening, when the past was more to
me than the future; now I visit it almost every bright summer
morning, and only occasionally at night."

"But, sir, isna deith a dreidfu' thing?" said Malcolm.

"That depends on whether a man regards it as his fate, or as
the will of a perfect God. Its obscurity is its dread; but if God
be light, then death itself must be full of splendor—a splendor
probably too keen for our eyes to receive."

"But there's the deein' itsel'; isna that fearsome? It's that
I wad be fleyed at."

"I don't see why it should be. It's the want of a God that
makes it dreadful, and *you* will be greatly to blame, Malcolm,
if you haven't found your God by the time you have to
die."

. . . . .

The next morning rose as lovely as if the mantle of the
departing Resurrection-day had fallen upon it. Malcolm rose
with it, hastened to his boat, and pulled out into the bay for an
hour or two's fishing. Nearly opposite the great conglomerate
rock at the western end of the dune, called the Bored Craig
(*Perforated Crag*) because of a large hole that went right through
it, he began to draw in his line. Glancing shoreward as he
leaned over the gunwale, he spied at the foot of the rock, near
the opening, a figure in white, seated, with bowed head. It was
of course the mysterious lady, whom he had twice before seen
thereabout at this unlikely, if not untimely hour; but with yesterday fresh in his mind, how could he fail to see in her an
angel of the resurrection waiting at the sepulcher to tell the
glad news that the Lord was risen?

Many were the glances he cast shoreward as he re-baited his
line, and, having thrown it again into the water, sat waiting
until it should be time to fire the swivel. Still the lady sat on,
in her whiteness a creature of the dawn, without even lifting
her head. At length, having added a few more fishes to the
little heap in the bottom of his boat, and finding his watch bear
witness that the hour was at hand, he seated himself on his

thwart, and rowed lustily to the shore, his bosom filled with the hope of yet another sight of the lovely face, and another hearing of the sweet English voice and speech. But the very first time he turned his head to look, he saw but the sloping foot of the rock sink bare into the shore. No white-robed angel sat at the gate of the resurrection; no moving thing was visible on the far-vacant sands. When he reached the top of the dune, there was no living creature beyond but a few sheep feeding on the thin grass. He fired the gun, rowed back to the Seaton, ate his breakfast, and set out to carry the best of his fish to the House. . . .

The garden was a curious, old-fashioned place with high hedges, and close alleys of trees, where two might have wandered long without meeting, and it was some time before he found any hint of the presence of the marquis. At length, however, he heard voices, and following the sound, walked along one of the alleys till he came to a little arbor, where he discovered the marquis seated, and, to his surprise, the white-robed lady of the sands beside him. A great deer-hound at his master's feet was bristling his mane, and baring his eye-teeth with a growl, but the girl had a hold of his collar.

"Who are *you*?" asked the marquis rather gruffly, as if he had never seen him before.

"I beg yer lordship's pardon," said Malcolm, "but they telled me yer lordship wantit to see me, and sent me to the flooer-garden. Will I gang, or will I bide?"

The marquis looked at him for a moment, frowningly, and made no reply. But the frown gradually relaxed before Malcolm's modest but unflinching gaze, and the shadow of a smile slowly usurped its place. He still kept silent, however.

"Am I to gang or bide, my lord?" repeated Malcolm.

"Can't you wait for an answer?"

"As lang's yer lordship likes. Will I gang an' walk aboot, mem—my leddy, till his lordship's made up his min'? Wad that please him, duv ye think?" he said, in the tone of one who seeks advice.

But the girl only smiled, and the marquis said, "Go to the devil."

"I maun luik to yer lordship for the necessar' directions," rejoined Malcolm.

"Your tongue's long enough to inquire as you go," said the marquis.

A reply in the same strain rushed to Malcolm's lips, but he checked himself in time, and stood silent, with his bonnet in his hand, fronting the two. The marquis sat gazing as if he had nothing to say to him, but after a few moments the lady spoke—not to Malcolm, however.

"Is there any danger in boating here, papa?" she said.

"Not more, I daresay, than there ought to be," replied the marquis listlessly. "Why do you ask?"

"Because I should so like a row! I want to see how the shore looks to the mermaids."

"Well, I will take you some day, if we can find a proper boat."

"Is yours a proper boat?" she asked, turning to Malcolm with a sparkle of fun in her eyes.

"That depen's on my lord's definition o' *proper*."

"Definition!" repeated the marquis.

"Is 't ower lang a word, my lord?" asked Malcolm.

The marquis only smiled.

"I ken what ye mean. It's a strange word in a fisher-lad's mou', ye think. But what for should na a fisher-lad hae a smatterin' o' loagic, my lord? For Greek or Laitin there's but sma' opportunity o' exerceese in oor pairts; but for loagic, a fisher-body may aye haud his han' in i' that. He can aye be tryin' 't upo' 's wife, or 's guid-mother, or upo' 's boat, or upo' the fish whan they winna tak. Loagic wad save a heap o' cursin' an' ill words—amo' the fisher-fowk, I mean, my lord."

"Have you been to college?"

"Na, my lord—the mair's the pity! But I've been to the school sin' ever I can min'."

"Do they teach logic there?"

"A kin' o' 't. Mr. Graham sets us to try oor han' whiles—jist to mak 's a bit gleg (*quick and keen*), ye ken."

"You don't mean you go to school still?"

"I dinna gang reg'lar; but I gang as aften as Mr. Graham wants me to help him, an' I aye gether something."

"So it's schoolmaster you are as well as fisherman? Two strings to your bow!—Who pays you for teaching?"

"Ow! naebody. Wha wad pay me for that?"

"Why, the schoolmaster."

"Na, but that wad be an affront, my lord!"

"How can you afford the time for nothing?"

"The time comes to little, compairt wi' what Mr. Graham gies me i' the lang forenichts—i' the winter time, ye ken, my lord, whan the sea's whiles ower contumahcious to be meddlet muckle wi'."

"But you have to support your grandfather."

"My gran'father wad be ill-pleased to hear ye say 't, my lord. He's terrible independent; an' what wi' his pipes, an' his lamps, an' his shop, he could keep's baith. It's no muckle the likes o' us wants. He winna lat me gang far to the fishin', so that I hae the mair time to read an' gang to Mr. Graham."

As the youth spoke, the marquis eyed him with apparently growing interest.

"But you haven't told me whether your boat is a proper one," said the lady.

"Proper eneuch, mem, for what's required o' her. She taks guid fish."

"But is it a proper boat for me to have a row in?"

"No wi' that goon on, mem, as I telled ye afore."

"The water won't get in, will it?"

"No more than's easy gotten oot again."

"Do you ever put up a sail?"

"Whiles—a wee bit o' a lug-sail."

"Nonsense, Flory!" said the marquis. "I'll see about it." Then, turning to Malcolm:

"You may go," he said. "When I want you I will send for you."

Malcolm thought with himself that he had sent for him this time before he wanted him; but he made his bow, and departed—not without disappointment, for he had expected the marquis to say something about his grandfather going to the house with his pipes, a request he would fain have carried to the old man to gladden his heart withal.

Lord Lossie had been one of the boon companions of the Prince of Wales—considerably higher in type, it is true, yet low enough to accept usage for law, and measure his obligation by the custom of his peers. Duty merely amounted to what was expected of him, and honor, the flitting shadow of the garment of truth, was his sole divinity. Still he had a heart, and it would speak—so long at least as the object affecting it was present. But alas! it had no memory. Like the unjust judge, he might redress a wrong that cried to him, but out of sight and hearing it had for him no existence. To a man he would not have told a deliberate lie—except, indeed, a woman was in the case; but to women he had lied enough to sink the whole ship of fools. Nevertheless, had the accusing angel himself called him a liar, he would have instantly offered him his choice of weapons.

There was in him by nature, however, a certain generosity which all the vice he had shared in had not quenched. Overbearing, he was not yet too overbearing to appreciate a manly carriage, and had been pleased with what some would have considered the boorishness of Malcolm's behavior—such not perceiving that it had the same source as the true aristocratic bearing—namely, a certain unselfish confidence which is the mother of dignity.

He had, of course, been a spendthrift—and so much the better, being otherwise what he was; for a cautious and frugal voluptuary is about the lowest style of man. Hence he had never been out of difficulties, and when, a year or so agone, he succeeded to his brother's marquisate, he was, notwithstanding his enlarged income, far too much involved to hope any immediate rescue from them. His new property, however, would afford him a refuge from troublesome creditors; there he might also avoid expenditure for a season, and perhaps rally the forces of a dissolute life; the place was not new to him, having, some twenty years before, spent nearly twelve months there, of which time the recollections were not altogether unpleasant. Weighing all these things he had made up his mind, and here he was at Lossie House.

The marquis was about fifty years of age, more worn than his years would account for, yet younger than his years in expression, for his conscience had never bitten him very deep. He was middle-sized, broad-shouldered but rather thin, with fine features of the aquiline Greek type, light-blue hazy eyes, and fair hair, slightly curling and streaked with gray. His manners were those of one polite for his own sake. To his remote inferiors he was kind—would even encourage them to liberties, but might in turn take greater with them than they might find agreeable. He was fond of animals—would sit for an hour stroking the head of Demon, his great Irish deerhound; but at other times would tease him to a wrath which touched the verge of dangerous. He was fond of practical jokes, and would not hesitate to indulge himself even in such as were incompatible with any genuine refinement: the sort had been in vogue in his merrier days, and Lord Lossie had ever been one of the most fertile in inventing and loudest in enjoying them. For the rest, if he was easily enraged, he was readily appeased; could drink a great deal, but was no drunkard; and held as his creed that a God had probably made the world and set it going, but that he did not care a brass farthing, as he phrased it, how it went on, or what such an insignificant being as a man did or left undone in it. Perhaps he might amuse himself with it, he said, but he doubted it. As to men, he believed every man loved himself supremely, and therefore was in natural warfare with every other man. Concerning women, he professed himself unable to give a definite utterance of any sort—and yet, he would add, he had had opportunities.

The mother of Florimel had died when she was a mere child, and from that time she had been at school until her father brought her away to share his fresh honors. She knew little; that little was not correct, and, had it been, would have yet been of small value. At school she had been under many laws, and had felt their slavery; she was now in the third heaven of delight with her liberty. But the worst of foolish laws is, that when the insurgent spirit casts them off, it is but too ready to cast away with them the genial self-restraint which these fretting trammels have smothered beneath them.

Her father regarded her as a child of whom it was enough to require that she should keep out of mischief. He said to himself now and then that he must find a governess for her; but as yet he had not begun to look for one. Meantime he neither exercised the needful authority over her, nor treated her as a companion. His was a shallow nature, never very pleasantly conscious of itself except in the whirl of excitement and the glitter of crossing lights; with a lovely daughter by his side, he neither sought to search into her being, nor to aid its unfolding, but sat brooding over past pleasures, or fancying others yet in store for him—lost in the dull flow of life along the lazy reach to whose mire its once tumultuous torrent had now descended. But, indeed, what could such a man have done for the education of a young girl? How many of the qualities he understood and enjoyed in women could he desire to see developed in his daughter? There was yet enough of the father in him to expect those qualities in her to which in other women he had been an insidious foe; but had he not done what in him lay to destroy his right of claiming such from her?

So Lady Florimel was running wild, and enjoying it. As long as she made her appearance at meals, and looked happy, her father would give himself no trouble about her. How he himself managed to live in those first days without company—what he thought about or speculated upon, it were hard to say. All he could be said to do was to ride here and there over the estate with his steward, Mr. Crathie, knowing little and caring less about farming, or crops, or cattle. He had by this time, however, invited a few friends to visit him, and expected their arrival before long.

"How do you like this dull life, Flory?" he said, as they walked up the garden to breakfast.

"Dull, papa!" she returned. "You never were at a girls' school, or you wouldn't call this dull. It is the merriest life in the world. To go where you like, and have miles of room! And such room! It's the loveliest place in the world, papa!"

He smiled a small, satisfied smile, and, stooping, stroked his Demon.

.   .   .   .

The home season of the herring-fishery was to commence a few days after the occurrences last recorded. The boats had all returned from other stations, and the little harbor was one crowd of stumpy masts, each with its halyard, the sole cordage visible, rove through the top of it, for the hoisting of a lug sail, tanned to a rich red brown. From this underwood towered aloft the masts of a coasting schooner, discharging its load of coal at the little quay. Other boats lay drawn up on the beach in front of the Seaton, and beyond it on the other side of the burn. Men and women were busy with the brown nets, laying them out on the short grass of the shore, mending them with netting-needles like small shuttles, carrying huge burdens of them on their shoulders in the hot sunlight; others were mending, calking, or tarring their boats, and looking to their various fittings. All was preparation for the new venture in their own waters, and everything went merrily and hopefully. Wives who had not accompanied their husbands now had them home again, and their anxieties would henceforth endure but for a night—joy would come with the red sails in the morning; lovers were once more together, the one great dread broken into a hundred little questioning fears; mothers had their sons again, to watch with loving eyes as they swung their slow limbs at their labor, or in the evenings sauntered about, hands in pockets, pipe in mouth, and blue bonnet cast carelessly on the head; it was almost a single family, bound together by a network of intermarriages so intricate as to render it impossible for any one who did not belong to the community to follow the threads or read the design of the social tracery.

And while the Seaton swarmed with "the goings on of life," the town of Portlossie lay above it still as a country hamlet, with more odors than people about; of people it was seldom, indeed, that three were to be spied at once in the wide street, while of odors you would always encounter a smell of leather from the saddler's shop, and a mingled message of bacon and cheese from the very general dealer's—in whose window hung what seemed three hams, and only he who looked twice would discover that the middle object was no ham, but a violin—while at every corner lurked a scent of gillyflowers and southernwood. Idly supreme, Portlossie, the upper, looked down in condescension, that is in half-concealed contempt, on the ant-heap below it.

The evening arrived on which the greater part of the boats was to put off for the first assay. Malcolm would have made one in the little fleet, for he belonged to his friend Joseph Mair's crew, had it not been found impossible to get the new boat ready before the following evening; whence, for this once more, he was still his own master, with one more chance of a pleasure for which he had been on the watch ever since Lady Florimel had spoken of having a row in his boat. True, it was not often she appeared on the shore in the evening; nevertheless he kept watching the dune with his keen eyes, for he had hinted to Mrs. Courthope that perhaps her young lady would like to see the boats go out.

Although it was the fiftieth time his eyes had swept the links in vague hope, he could hardly believe their testimony when now at length he spied a form, which could only be hers, looking seaward from the slope, as still as a sphinx on Egyptian sands.

He sauntered slowly towards her by the landward side of the dune, gathering on his way a handful of the reddest daisies he could find; then, ascending the sand-hill, approached her along the top.

"Saw ye ever sic gowans in yer life, my leddy?" he said, holding out his posy.

"Is that what you call them?" she returned.

"Ow ay, my leddy—daisies *ye* ca' them. I dinna ken but yours is the bonnier name o' the twa—gien it be what Mr. Graham tells me the auld poet Chaucer maks o' 't."

"What is that?"

"Ow, jist the een o' the day—the *day's eyes*, ye ken. They're sma' een for sic a great face, but syne there's a lot o' them to mak up for that. They've begun to close a'ready, but the mair they close the bonnier they luik, wi' their bits o' screwed-up mooies (*little mouths*). But saw ye ever sic reid anes, or ony sic a size, my leddy?"

"I don't think I ever did. What is the reason they are so large and red?"

"I dinna ken. There canna be muckle nourishment in sic a thin soil, but there maun be something that agrees wi' *them*. It's the same a' roon' aboot here."

Lady Florimel sat looking at the daisies, and Malcolm stood a few yards off, watching for the first of the red sails, which must soon show themselves, creeping out on the ebb tide. Nor had he waited long before a boat appeared, then another and another—six huge oars, ponderous to toil withal, urging each from the shelter of the harbor out into the wide weltering plain. The fishing-boat of that time was not decked as now, and each, with every lift of its bows, revealed to their eyes a gaping hollow, ready, if a towering billow should break above it, to be filled with sudden death. One by one the whole fleet crept out, and ever as they gained the breeze, up went the red sails, and filled: aside leaned every boat from the wind, and went dancing away over the frolicking billows towards the sunset, its sails, deep-dyed in oak-bark, shining redder and redder in the growing redness of the sinking sun.

Nor did Portlossie alone send out her boats, like huge sea-

birds warring on the live treasures of the deep; from beyond
the headlands east and west, out they glided on slow red wing
—from Scaurnose, from Sandend, from Clamrock, from the villages all along the coast—spreading as they came, each to its
work apart through all the laborious night, to rejoin its fellows
only as home drew them back in the clear gray morning, laden
and slow with the harvest of the stars. But the night lay between, into which they were sailing over waters of heaving
green that forever kept tossing up roses—a night whose curtain was a horizon built up of steady blue, but gorgeous with
passing purple and crimson, and flashing with molten gold.

Malcolm was not one of those to whom the sea is but a pond
for fish, and the sky a storehouse of wind and rain, sunshine
and snow; he stood for a moment gazing, lost in pleasure. Then
he turned to Lady Florimel; she had thrown her daisies on the
sand, appeared to be deep in her book, and certainly caught
nothing of the splendor before her beyond the red light on her
next page.

"Saw ye ever a bonnier sicht, my leddy?" said Malcolm.

She looked up, and saw, and gazed in silence. Her nature
was full of poetic possibilities; and now a formless thought
foreshadowed itself in a feeling she did not understand. Why
should such a sight as this make her feel sad? The vital connection between joy and effort had begun from afar to reveal
itself with the question she now uttered.

"What is it all for?" she asked dreamily, her eyes gazing
out on the calm ecstasy of color, which seemed to have broken
the bonds of law and ushered in a new chaos, fit matrix of
new heavens and new earth.

"To catch herrin'," answered Malcolm, ignorant of the mood
that prompted the question, and hence mistaking its purport.

But a falling doubt had troubled the waters of her soul, and
through the ripple she could descry it settling into form. She
was silent for a moment.

"I want to know," she resumed, "why it looks as if some
great thing were going on. Why is all this pomp and show?

Something ought to be at hand. All I see is the catching of a few miserable fish! If it were the eve of a glorious battle, now, I could understand it—if those were the little English boats rushing to attack the Spanish Armada, for instance. But they are only gone to catch fish. Or if they were setting out to discover the Isles of the West, the country beyond the sunset!—but this jars."

"I canna answer ye a' at ance, my leddy," said Malcolm; "I maun tak time to think aboot it. But I ken brawly what ye mean."

Even as he spoke he withdrew, and, descending the mound, walked away beyond the bored craig, regardless now of the far-lessening sails and the sinking sun. The motes of the twilight were multiplying fast as he returned along the shore side of the dune, but Lady Florimel had vanished from its crest. He ran to the top; thence, in the dim of the twilight, he saw her slow retreating form, phantom-like, almost at the grated door of the tunnel, which, like that of a tomb, appeared ready to draw her in, and yield her no more.

"My leddy, my leddy," he cried, "winna ye bide for 't?"

He went bounding after her like a deer. She heard him call, and stood holding the door half open.

"It's the battle o' Armageddon, my leddy," he cried, as he came within hearing distance.

"The battle of what?" she exclaimed, bewildered. "I really can't understand your savage Scotch."

"Hoot, my leddy! the battle o' Armageddon's no ane o' the Scots battles; it's the battle atween the richt and the wrang, 'at ye read aboot i' the buik o' the Revelations."

"What on earth are you talking about?" returned Lady Florimel in dismay, beginning to fear that her squire was losing his senses.

"It's jist what ye was sayin', my leddy; sic a pomp as yon bude to hing abune a gran' battle some gait or ither."

"What *has* the catching of fish to do with a battle in the Revelations?" said the girl moving a little within the door.

"Weel, my leddy, gien I took in han' to set it furth to ye, I wad hae to tell ye a' that Mr. Graham has been learnin' me sin' ever I can min'. He says 'at the whole economy o' natur is fashiont unco like that o' the kingdom o' haven: its jist a gradation o' services, an' the highest en' o' ony animal is to contreebute to the life o' ane higher than itsel'; sae that it's the gran' preevilege o' the fish we tak, to be aten by human bein's, an' uphaud what's abune them."

"That's a poor consolation to the fish," said Lady Florimel.

"Hoo ken ye that, my leddy? Ye can tell nearhan' as little aboot the hert o' a herrin'—sic as it has—as the herrin' can tell aboot yer ain, whilk, I'm thinkin', maun be o' the largest size."

"How should you know anything about my heart, pray?" she asked, with more amusement than offense.

"Jist by my ain," answered Malcolm.

Lady Florimel began to fear she must have allowed the fisher lad more liberty than was proper, seeing he dared avow that he knew the heart of a lady of her position by his own. But indeed Malcolm was wrong, for in the scale of hearts, Lady Florimel's was far below his. She stepped quite within the door, and was on the point of shutting it, but something about the youth restrained her, exciting at least her curiosity; his eyes glowed with a deep, quiet light, and his face, even grand at the moment, had a greater influence upon her than she knew. Instead, therefore, of interposing the door between them, she only kept it poised, ready to fall-to the moment the sanity of the youth should become a hair's-breadth more doubtful than she already considered it.

"It's a' pairt o' ae thing, my leddy," Malcolm resumed. "The herrin' 's like the fowk' at cairries the mate an' the pooder an' sic like for them 'at does the fechtin'. The hert o' the leevin' man's the place whaur the battle's foucht, an' it's aye gaein' on an' on there atween God an' Sawtan; an' the fish they haud fowk up till 't——"

"Do you mean that the herrings help you to fight for God?" said Lady Florimel with a superior smile.

"Aither for God or for the deevil, my leddy—that depen's upo' the fowk themsel's. I say it hauds them up to fecht, an' the thing maun be fouchten oot. Fowk to fecht maun live, an' the herrin' hauds the life i' them, an' sae the catchin' o' the herrin' comes in to be a pairt o' the battle."

"Wouldn't it be more sensible to say that the battle is between the fishermen and the sea, for the sake of their wives and children?" suggested Lady Florimel supremely.

"Na, my leddy, it wadna be half sae sensible, for it wadna justifee the grandur that hings over the fecht. The battle wi' the sea 's no sae muckle o' an affair. An', 'deed, gien it warna that the wives an' the verra weans hae themsel's to fecht i' the same battle o' guid an' ill, I dinna see the muckle differ there wad be atween them an' the fish, nor what for they sudna ate ane anither as the craturs i' the water du. But gien 't be the battle I say, there can be no pomp o' sea or sky ower gran' for 't; an' it's a' weel waured (*expended*) gien it but haud the gude anes merry an' strong, an' up to their wark. For that, weel may the sun shine a celestial rosy reid, an' weel may the boatie row, an' weel may the stars luik doon, blinkin' an' luikin' again—ilk ane duin' its bonny pairt to mak a man a richt-hetit guid-willed sodger!"

.   .   .   .

Before Malcolm was awake, his lordship had sent for him. When he re-entered the sick-chamber, Mr. Glennie had vanished, the table had been removed, and instead of the radiance of the wax lights, the cold gleam of a vapor dimmed sun, with its sickly blue-white reflex from the widespread snow, filled the room. The marquis looked ghastly, but was sipping chocolate with a spoon.

"What w'y are ye the day, my lord?" asked Malcolm.

"Nearly well," he answered; "but those cursed carrion-crows are set upon killing me." (Here he uttered a curse.)

"We'll hae Leddy Florimel sweirin' awfu' gien ye gang on that gait, my lord," said Malcolm.

The marquis laughed feebly.

"An' what's mair," Malcolm continued, "I doobt they're some partic'lar aboot the turn o' their phrases up yonner, my lord."

The marquis looked at him keenly.

"You don't anticipate that inconvenience for me?" he said. "I'm pretty sure to have my billet where they're not so precise."

"Dinna brak my hert, my lord!" cried Malcolm, the tears rushing to his eyes.

"I should be sorry to hurt you, Malcolm," rejoined the marquis gently, almost tenderly. "I won't go there if I can help it. I shouldn't like to break any more hearts. But how the devil am I to keep out of it? Besides, there are people up there I don't want to meet; I have no fancy for being made ashamed of myself. The fact is I'm not fit for such company, and I don't believe there is any such place. But if there be I trust in God there isn't any other, or it will go badly with your poor master, Malcolm. It doesn't look *like* true—now does it? Only such a multitude of things I thought I had done with forever, keep coming up and grinning at me! It nearly drives me mad, Malcolm—and I would fain die like a gentleman, with a cool bow and a sharp face-about."

"Wadna ye hae a word wi' somebody 'at kens, my lord?" said Malcolm, scarcely able to reply.

"No," answered the marquis fiercely. "That Cairns is a fool."

"He's a' that an' mair, my lord. I didna mean *him*."

"They're all fools together."

"Ow, na, my lord! There's a heap o' them no muckle better, it may be; but ther's guid men and true amang them, or the kirk wad hae been wi' Sodom and Gomorrha by this time. But it's no a minister I wad hae yer lordship confair wi'."

"Who then, Mrs. Courthope? Eh?"

"Ow na, my lord—no Mistress Coorthoup! She's a guid body, but she wadna believe her ain een gien onybody ca'd a minister said contrar' to them."

"Who the devil do you mean then?"

"Nae deevil, but an honest man 'at's been his warst enemy sae lang's I hae kent him; Maister Graham, the schuilmaister."

"Pooh!" said the marquis with a puff. "I'm too old to go to school."

"I dinna ken the man 'at isna a bairn till *him*, my lord."

"In Greek and Latin?"

"I' richteousness an' trouth, my lord; in what's been an' what is to be."

"What! has he the second sight, like the piper?"

"He *has* the second sight, my lord—but ane 'at gangs a sicht farther than my auld daddy's."

"He could tell me then what's going to become of me?"

"As weel's ony man, my lord."

"That's not saying much, I fear."

"Maybe mair nor ye think, my lord."

"Well, take him my compliments, and tell him I should like to see him," said the marquis, after a pause.

"He'll come direckly, my lord."

"Of course he will," said the marquis.

"Jist as readily, my lord, as he wad gang to ony tramp 'at sent for 'im at sic a time," returned Malcolm, who did not relish either the remark or its tone.

"What do you mean by that? *You* don't think it such a serious affair—do you?"

"My lord, ye haena a chance."

The marquis was dumb. He had actually begun once more to buoy himself up with earthly hopes.

Dreading a recall of his commission, Malcolm slipped from the room, sent Mrs. Courthope to take his place, and sped to the schoolmaster. The moment Mr. Graham heard the marquis's message, he rose without a word, and led the way from the cottage. Hardly a sentence passed between them as they went, for they were on a solemn errand.

"Mr. Graham's here, my lord," said Malcolm.

"Where? Not in the room?" returned the marquis.

"Waitin' at the door, my lord."

"Bah! You needn't have been so ready. Have you told the sexton to get a new spade? But you may let him in. And leave him alone with me."

Mr. Graham walked gently up to the bedside.

"Sit down, sir," said the marquis courteously—pleased with the calm, self-possessed, unobtrusive bearing of the man. "They tell me I'm dying, Mr. Graham."

"I'm sorry it seems to trouble you, my lord."

"What! wouldn't it trouble you, then?"

"I don't think so, my lord."

"Ah! you're one of the elect, no doubt!"

"That's a thing I never did think about, my lord."

"What do you think about, then?"

"About God."

"And when you die you'll go straight to heaven, of course!"

"I don't know, my lord. That's another thing I never trouble my head about."

"Ah! you're like me then! *I* don't care much about going to heaven! What do you care about?"

"The will of God. I hope your lordship will say the same."

"No, I won't. I want my own will."

"Well, that is to be had, my lord."

"How?"

"By taking his for yours, as the better of the two, which it must be every way."

"That's all moonshine."

"It *is* light, my lord."

"Well, I don't mind confessing, if I am to die, I should prefer heaven to the other place; but I trust I have no chance of either. Do you now honestly believe there are two such places?"

"I don't know, my lord."

"You don't know! And you come here to comfort a dying man!"

"Your lordship must first tell me what you mean by 'two *such* places.' And as to comfort, going by my notions, I cannot tell which you would be more or less comfortable in; and that, I presume, would be the main point with your lordship."

"And what, pray sir, would be the main point with you?"

"To get nearer to God."

"Well, I can't say *I* want to get nearer to God. It's little he's ever done for me."

"It's a good deal he has tried to do for you, my lord."

"Well, who interfered? Who stood in his way, then?"

"Yourself, my lord."

"I wasn't aware of it. When did he ever try to do anything for me, and I stood in his way?"

"When he gave you one of the loveliest of women, my lord," said Mr. Graham, with solemn, faltering voice, "and you left her to die in neglect, and the child to be brought up by strangers."

The marquis gave a cry. The unexpected answer had roused the slowly gnawing death, and made it bite deeper.

"What have *you* to do," he almost screamed, "with my affairs? It was for *me* to introduce what I chose of them. You presume."

"Pardon me, my lord; you led me to what I was bound to say. Shall I leave you, my lord?"

The marquis made no answer.

"God knows I loved her," he said, after a while, with a sigh.

"You loved her, my lord?"

"I did."

"Love a woman like that, and come to this?"

"Come to this! We must all come to this, I fancy, sooner or later. Come to what, in the name of Beelzebub?"

"That, having loved a woman like her, you are content to lose her. In the name of God, have you no desire to see her again?"

"It would be an awkward meeting," said the marquis.

His was an old love, alas! He had not been capable of the

sort that defies change. It had faded from him until it seemed one of the things that are not! Although his being had once glowed in its light, he could now speak of a meeting as awkward!

"Because you wronged her?" suggested the schoolmaster.

"Because they lied to me."

"Which they dared not have done, had you not lied to them first."

"Sir!" shouted the marquis, with all the voice he had left—"O God, have mercy! I *cannot* punish the scoundrel."

"The scoundrel is the man who lies, my lord."

"Were I anywhere else——"

"There would be no good in telling you the truth, my lord. You showed her to the world not as the honest wife she was. What *kind* of a lie was that, my lord? Not a white one, surely?"

"You are a coward to speak so to a man who cannot even turn on his side to curse you for a base hound. You would not dare it but that you know I cannot defend myself."

"You are right, my lord; your conduct is indefensible."

"If I could but get this cursed leg under me, I would throw you out of the window."

"I shall go by the door, my lord. While you hold by your sins, your sins will hold by you. If you should want me again, I shall be at your lordship's command."

He rose and left the room, but had not reached his cottage before Malcolm overtook him with a second message from his master. He turned at once, saying only, "I expected it."

"Mr. Graham," said the marquis, looking ghastly, "you must have patience with a dying man. I was very rude to you, but I was in horrible pain."

"Don't mention it, my lord. It would be a poor friendship that gave way for a rough word."

"How can you call yourself my friend?"

"I should be your friend, my lord, if it were only for your wife's sake. She died loving you. I want to send you to her, my lord. You will allow that, as a gentleman, you at least owe her an apology."

"By Jove, you are right, sir! Then you really and positively believe in the place they call heaven?"

"My lord, I believe that those who open their hearts to the truth, shall see the light on their friends' faces again, and be able to set right what was wrong between them."

"It's a week too late to talk of setting right!"

"Go and tell her you are sorry, my lord—that will be enough to her."

"Ah! but there's more than her concerned."

"You are right, my lord. There is another—one who cannot be satisfied that the fairest works of his hands, or rather the loveliest children of his heart, should be treated as you have treated women."

"But the Deity you talk of——"

"I beg your pardon, my lord. I talked of no deity; I talked of a living Love that gave us birth and calls us his children. Your deity I know nothing of."

"Call him what you please—*he* won't be put off so easily!"

"He won't be put off one jot or one tittle. He will forgive anything, but he will pass nothing. Will your wife forgive you?"

"She will—when I explain."

"Then why should you think the forgiveness of God, which created her forgiveness, should be less?"

Whether the marquis could grasp the reasoning, may be doubtful.

"Do you really suppose God cares whether a man comes to good or ill?"

"If he did not, he could not be good himself."

"Then you don't think a good God would care to punish poor wretches like us?"

"Your lordship has not been in the habit of regarding himself as a poor wretch. And, remember, you can't call a child a poor wretch without insulting the father of it."

"That's quite another thing."

"But on the wrong side for your argument—seeing the relation between God and the poorest creature is infinitely closer than that between any father and his child."

"Then he can't be so hard on him as the parsons say."

"He will give him absolute justice, which is the only good thing. He will spare nothing to bring his children back to himself—their sole well-being. What would you do, my lord, if you saw your son strike a woman?"

"Knock him down and horsewhip him."

It was Mr. Graham who broke the silence that followed.

"Are you satisfied with yourself, my lord?"

"No, by God!"

"You would like to be better?"

"I would."

"Then you are of the same mind with God."

"Yes; but I'm not a fool! It won't do to say I should like to be. I must be, and that's not so easy. It's hard to be good. I would have a fight for it, but there's no time. How is a poor devil to get out of such an infernal scrape?"

"Keep the commandments."

"That's it, of course; but there's no time, I tell you—at least so those cursed doctors will keep telling me."

"If there were but time to draw another breath, there would be time to begin."

"How am I to begin? Which am I to begin with?"

"There is one commandment which includes all the rest."

"Which is that?"

"To believe on the Lord Jesus Christ."

"That's cant."

"After thirty years' trial of it, it is to me the essence of wisdom. It has given me a peace which makes life or death all but indifferent to me, though I would choose the latter."

"What am I to believe about him, then?"

"You are to believe *in* him, not about him."

"I don't understand."

"He is our Lord and Master, Elder Brother, King Saviour, the divine Man, the human God; to believe in him is to give ourselves up to him in obedience, to search out his will and do it."

"But there's no time, I tell you again," the marquis almost shrieked.

"And I tell you, there is all eternity to do it in. Take him for your master, and he will demand nothing of you which you are not able to perform. This is the open door to bliss. With your last breath you can cry to him, and he will hear you, as he heard the thief on the cross who cried to him dying beside him. 'Lord, remember me when thou comest into thy kingdom.' 'To-day shalt thou be with me in paradise.' It makes my heart swell to think of it, my lord! No cross-questioning of the poor fellow! No preaching to him! He just took him with him where he was going, to make a man of him."

"Well, you know something of my history. What would you have me do now? At once, I mean. What would the person you speak of have me do?"

"That is not for me to say, my lord."

"You could give me a hint."

"No. God is telling you himself. For me to presume to tell you, would be to interfere with him. What he would have a man do, he lets him know in his mind."

"But what if I had not made up my mind before the last came?"

"Then I fear he would say to you—'Depart from me, thou worker of iniquity.'"

"That would be hard when another minute might have done it."

"If another minute would have done it, you would have had it."

A paroxysm of pain followed, during which Mr. Graham silently left him.

. . . .

The marquis would not have the doctor come near him, and when Malcolm entered there was no one in the room but Mrs.

Courthope. The shadow had crept far along the dial. His face had grown ghastly, the skin had sunk to the bones, and his eyes stood out as if from much staring into the dark. They rested very mournfully on Malcolm for a few moments, and then closed softly.

"Is she come yet?" he murmured, opening them wide, with sudden stare.

"No, my lord."

The lids fell again, softly, slowly.

"Be good to her, Malcolm," he murmured.

"I wull, my lord," said Malcolm solemnly.

Then the eyes opened and looked at him; something grew in them—a light as of love, and drew up after it a tear; but the lips said nothing. The eyelids fell again, and in a minute more, Malcolm knew by his breathing that he slept.

The slow night waned. He woke sometimes, but soon dozed off again. The two watched by him till the dawn. It brought a still gray morning, without a breath of wind, and warm for the season. The marquis appeared a little revived, but was hardly able to speak. Mostly by signs he made Malcolm understand that he wanted Mr. Graham, but that some one else must go for him. Mrs. Courthope went.

As soon as she was out of the room, he lifted his hand with effort, laid feeble hold on Malcolm's jacket, and drawing him down, kissed him on the forehead. Malcolm burst into tears, and sank weeping by the bedside.

Mr. Graham, entering a little after, and seeing Malcolm on his knees, knelt also, and broke into a prayer.

"O blessed Father!" he said, "who knowest this thing, so strange to us, which we call death, breathe more life into the heart of thy dying son, that in the power of life he may front death. O Lord Christ, who diedst thyself, and in thyself knowest it all, heal this man in his sore need—heal him with strength to die."

Came a faint *Amen* from the marquis.

"Thou didst send him into the world; help him out of it. O

God, we belong to thee utterly. We dying men are thy children, O living Father! Thou art such a father, that thou takest our sins from us and throwest them behind thy back. Thou cleanest our souls, as thy Son did wash our feet. We hold our hearts up to thee; make them what they must be, O Love, O Life of men, O Heart of hearts! Give thy dying child courage, and hope, and peace—the peace of him who overcame all the terrors of humanity, even death itself, and liveth for evermore, sitting at thy right hand, our God-brother, blessed to all ages—amen."

"Amen!" murmured the marquis, and slowly lifting his hand from the coverlid, he laid it on the head of Malcolm, who did not know it was the hand of his father, blessing him ere he died.

"Be good to her," said the marquis once more.

But Malcolm could not answer for weeping, and the marquis was not satisfied. Gathering all his force he said again:

"Be good to her."

"I wull, I wull," burst from Malcolm in sobs, and he wailed aloud.

The day wore on, and the afternoon came. Still Lady Florimel had not arrived, and still the marquis lingered.

As the gloom of the twilight was deepening into the early darkness of the winter night, he opened wide his eyes, and was evidently listening. Malcolm could hear nothing; but the light in his master's face grew, and the strain of his listening diminished. At length Malcolm became aware of the sound of wheels, which came rapidly nearer, till at last the carriage swung up to the hall door. A moment, and Lady Florimel was flitting across the room.

"Papa! papa!" she cried, and, throwing her arm over him, laid her cheek to his.

The marquis could not return her embrace; he could only receive her into the depths of his shining tearful eyes.

"Flory!" he murmured, "I'm going away. I'm going—I've got—to make an—apology. Malcolm, be good——"

The sentence remained unfinished. The light paled from his countenance—he had to carry it with him. He was dead.

Lady Florimel gave a loud cry. Mrs. Courthope ran to her assistance.

"My lady's in a dead faint!" she whispered, and left the room to get help.

Malcolm lifted Lady Florimel in his great arms, and bore her tenderly to her own apartment. There he left her to the care of her women, and returned to the chamber of death.

Meantime Mr. Graham and Mr. Soutar had come.

When Malcolm re-entered, the schoolmaster took him kindly by the arm and said:

"Malcolm, there can be neither place nor moment fitter for the solemn communication I am commissioned to make to you; I have, as in the presence of your dead father, to inform you that you are now Marquis of Lossie; and God forbid you should be less worthy as marquis than you have been as fisherman!"

EDWARD EGGLESTON

1837

EDWARD EGGLESTON was born of Virginia lineage, in Vevay, Indiana, on the 10th of December, 1837. His father, a man of fine education, scholarly tastes and acquirements, and locally prominent as a lawyer and in public life, died when Edward was but nine years of age. One of his last acts was to direct in his will that his law library should be exchanged for works of general literature for the cultivation of his children's tastes.

Edward's health was delicate and his education very irregular, but he early showed a strong bent for a literary life. He removed to Minnesota in 1857, having already entered the Methodist ministry. He served as pastor of churches in several of the leading towns of Minnesota, but he gave up the ministry on account of ill health in 1866, and became successively editor of *The Little Corporal*, and *The National Sunday School Teacher*, at Chicago.

In 1870 he removed to New York, to become literary editor of the *Independent*, and at the close of that year he became the chief editor of the same paper. In 1871 he retired from the *Independent*, to take charge for more than a year of *Hearth and Home*, and he signalized the change by producing his first novel, "The Hoosier Schoolmaster," in the columns of the latter paper. Its popularity was very great and its sale continues large to the present time. Pirated editions appeared in England and in several of the British colonies, and it was translated into French, German, and Danish.

Other novels have followed with varying success. Some of these have rivaled "The Hoosier Schoolmaster" in persistent popularity. In 1889, Mr. Eggleston published his "History of the United States and its People, for the Use of Schools," and in 1890 his "First Book in American History," both of which have been very successful.

Mr. Eggleston worked unremittingly in favor of international copyright, and it was largely due to his efforts and untiring zeal that this law was finally passed in 1891. His brother authors, in grateful appreciation of the service he rendered them in this respect, insisted that his book, "The Faith Doctor," should be the first to be copyrighted under the new law. This has proved to be one of the most popular of his works.

For many years Mr. Eggleston has led a purely literary life, devoting himself to historical study and to the production of an occasional novel.

Characterization

Mr. Eggleston's stories have held from the beginning a great popularity with a large circle of readers, and it has been in many ways well deserved. They are full of incident; all of these rapid events occur amid scenes almost entirely new to the Eastern reader and the new generation of Westerners; and they have in a high degree the element of dialectic speech, which confers upon the personages of the story that appearance of reality and individuality for which the novel-writer has to watch so keenly and work so hard.

"THE NATION."

With each new novel the author of "The Hoosier Schoolmaster" enlarges his audience and surprises old friends by reserve forces unsuspected. Sterling integrity of character and high moral motives illuminate Dr. Eggleston's fiction and assure its place in the literature of America, which is to stand as a worthy reflex of the best thought of this age. "NEW YORK WORLD."

Mr. Eggleston's merits as a writer are fairly well known. He has a very pleasant and slightly cynical humor; he writes with restraint, without undue emphasis or exaggeration. He knows the strong side of human nature well, and the weak side exceedingly well.

"LONDON SPEAKER."

A Struggle for the Mastery[1]

(From "The Hoosier Schoolmaster")

The school closed on Monday evening, as usual. The boys had been talking in knots all day. Nothing but the bull-dog in the slender resolute young master had kept down the rising storm. Let a teacher lose moral support at home, and he cannot long govern a school. Ralph had effectually lost his popularity in the district; and the worst of it was that he could not

[1] By permission of the publishers, Orange Judd Company.

divine from just what quarter the ill wind came, except that he felt sure of Small's agency in it somewhere. Even Hannah had slighted him when he called at Means's, on Monday morning, to draw the pittance of pay that was due him.

He had expected a petition for a holiday on Christmas day. Such holidays were deducted from the teacher's time, and it was customary for the boys to "turn out" the teacher who refused to grant them, by barring him out of the schoolhouse on Christmas and New Year's morning. Ralph had intended to grant a holiday if it should be asked, but it was not asked. Hank Banta was the ringleader in the disaffection, and he had managed to draw the surly Bud, who was present this morning, into it. It is but fair to say that Bud was in favor of making a request before resorting to extreme measures, but he was overruled. He gave it as his solemn opinion that the master was mighty pert, and they would be beat anyhow some way, but he would lick the master fer two cents ef he warn't so slim that he'd feel like he was fighting a baby.

And all that day things looked black. Ralph's countenance was cold and hard as stone, and Shocky trembled where he sat in front of him. Betsey Short tittered rather more than usual. A riot or a murder would have seemed amusing to her.

School was dismissed, and Ralph, instead of returning to the Squire's, set out for the village of Clifty, a few miles away. No one knew what he went for, and some suggested that he had "sloped." But Bud said "he warn't that air kind. He was one of them air sort as died in ther tracks, was Mr. Hartsook. They'd find him on the ground nex' morning, and he 'lowed the master war made of air sort of stuff as would burn the dogon'd ole schoolhouse to ashes, or blow it into splinters, but what he'd beat. Howsumdever he'd said he was a-goin' to help, and help he would; but all the sinnoo in Golier wouldn' be no account agin the cute they was in the head of the master."

But Bud, discouraged as he was with the fear of Ralph's "cute," went like a martyr to the stake and took his place with the rest in the schoolhouse, at nine o'clock at night. It may have been Ralph's intention to have preoccupied the schoolhouse, for at ten o'clock Hank Banta was set shaking from head to foot at seeing a face that looked like the master's at the window. He waked up Bud and told him about it.

"Well, what are you a-tremblin' about, you coward?" growled Bud. "He won't shoot you; but he'll beat you at this game, I'll bet a hoss, and me, too, and make us both as 'shamed of ourselves as dogs with tin-kittles to their tails. You don't know the master, though he did duck you. But he'll larn you a good lesson this time, and me too, like as not." And Bud soon snored again, but Hank shook with fear every time he looked at the blackness outside the windows. He was sure he heard footfalls. He would have given anything to have been at home.

When morning came, the pupils began to gather early. A few boys who were likely to prove of service in the coming siege were admitted through the window, and then everything was made fast, and a " snack " was eaten.

"How do you 'low he'll git in?" said Hank, trying to hide his fear.

"How do I 'low?" said Bud. "I don't 'low nothin' about it. You might as well ax me where I 'low the nex' shootin' star is a-goin' to drap. Mr. Hartsook's mighty onsartin. But he'll git in though, and tan your hide fer you, you see ef he don't. *Ef* he don't blow up the schoolhouse with gunpowder!" This last was thrown in by way of alleviating the fears of the cowardly Hank, for whom Bud had a great contempt.

The time for school had almost come. The boys inside were demoralized by waiting. They began to hope that the master had " sloped." They dreaded to see him coming.

"I don't believe he'll come," said Hank, with a cold shiver. "It's past school-time."

"Yes, he will come, too," said Bud. " And he 'lows to come in here mighty quick. I don't know how. But he'll be a-standin' at that air desk when it's nine o'clock. I'll bet a thousand dollars on that. *Ef* he don't take it into his head to blow us up!" Hank was now white.

Some of the parents came along, accidentally of course, and stopped to see the fun, sure that Bud would thrash the master if he tried to break in. Small, on the way to see a patient, perhaps, reined up in front of the door. Still no Ralph. It was just five minutes before nine. A rumor now gained currency that he had been seen going to Clifty the evening before, and that he had not come back; in fact, Ralph had come back, and had slept at Squire Hawkins's.

"There's the master," cried Betsey Short, who stood out in the road, shivering and giggling alternately. For Ralph at that moment emerged from the sugar-camp by the schoolhouse, carrying a board.

"Ho! ho!" laughed Hank, "he thinks he'll smoke us out. I guess he'll find us ready." The boys had let the fire burn down, and there was now nothing but hot hickory coals on the hearth.

"I tell you he'll come in. He didn't go to Clifty fer nothin'," said Bud, who sat on one of the benches which leaned against the door. "I don't know how, but they's lots of ways of killing a cat besides chokin' her with butter. He'll come in—*ef* he don't blow us all sky-high!"

Ralph's voice was now heard, demanding that the door be opened.

"Let's open her," said Hank, turning livid with fear at the firm confident tone of the master.

Bud straightened himself up. "Hank, you're a coward. I've got a mind to kick you. You got me into this blamed mess, and now you want to flunk. You just tech one of these ere fastenings, and I'll lay you out flat of your back afore you can say Jack Robinson."

The teacher was climbing to the roof, with the board in his hand.

"That air won't win," laughed Pete Jones, outside. He saw that there was no smoke. Even Bud began to hope that Ralph would fail, for once. The master was now on the ridge-pole of the schoolhouse. He took a paper from his pocket, and deliberately poured the contents down the chimney.

Mr. Pete Jones shouted "Gunpowder!" and started down the road, to be out of the explosion. Dr. Small remembered, probably, that his patient might die while he sat there, and started on.

But Ralph emptied the paper, and laid the board over the chimney. What a row there was inside! The benches that were braced against the door were thrown down, and Hank Banta rushed out, rubbing his eyes, coughing frantically, and sure that he had been blown up. All the rest followed, Bud bringing up the rear sulkily, but coughing and sneezing for dear life. Such a smell of sulphur as came from that schoolhouse!

Betsey had to lean against the fence to giggle.

As soon as all were out, Ralph threw the board off the chimney, leaped to the ground, entered the schoolhouse, and opened the windows. The school soon followed him, and all was still.

"Would he thrash?" This was the important question in Hank Banta's mind. And the rest looked for a battle with Bud.

"It is just nine o'clock," said Ralph, consulting his watch, "and I'm glad to see you all here promptly. I should have given you a holiday, if you had asked me like gentlemen, yesterday. On the whole, I think I shall give you a holiday, anyhow. The school is dismissed."

And Hank felt foolish.

And Bud secretly resolved to thrash Hank or the master, he didn't care which.

And Mirandy looked the love she could not utter.

And Betsey giggled.

Some Western Schoolmasters[1]

In a ragged little frontier village, where the smoky wigwams of the savage and thriftless Sioux still lingered among the

[1] By permission of the Century Company.

unpainted board cottages of the settlers, there was a schoolmaster who published a little sheet, at the close of his school term, filled with the essays of his pupils. For a motto over this weakly paper he told the printer to set:

> "No pent-up continent contracts our powers,
> But the whole boundless universe is ours."

The printer thought that the little school was staking out rather too large a preëmption claim; he suggested to the teacher that

> "No pent-up Utica contracts our powers,
> But the whole boundless continent is ours,"

was the correct version, and was sufficiently broad for the size of the sheet.

"Oh, that isn't right," said the master, contemptuously. "I suppose some of them Utica papers had it that way."

It seems just possible that this teacher, on the edge of civilization, was a sort of embodiment of our modern spirit. Is the present system of cramming a great advance on older and simpler methods of teaching? In the curriculum of our time, neither Utica nor the continent will serve our turn. We attempt the whole boundless universe, forgetful of Hosea Biglow's wise couplet:

> "For it strikes me ther's sech a thing ez sinnin'
> By overloadin' children's underpinnin'."

As I recall the old-time school, I cannot but think that, if its discipline was somewhat more brutal than the school discipline of to-day, its course of study was far less so. Children did not often die of the severity of the old masters, though many perish from the hard requirements of the modern system.

To a nervous child the old discipline was, indeed, very terrible. The long beech switches hanging on hooks against the wall haunted me night and day, from the time I entered one of the old schools. And whenever there came an outburst between master and pupils, the thoughtless child often got the beating that should have fallen upon the malicious mischief-maker. As the master was always quick to fly into a passion, the fun-loving boys were always happy to stir him up. It was an exciting sport, like bull-baiting, or like poking sticks through a fence at a cross dog. Sometimes the ferocious master showed an ability on his own part to get some fun out of the conflict, as when on one occasion in a school in Ohio, the boys were forbidden to attend a circus. Five or six of them went, in spite of the prohibition. The next morning the schoolmaster called them out on the floor and addressed them:

"So you went to the circus, did you?"

"Yes, sir."

"Well, the others did not get a chance to see the circus. I want you boys to show them what it looked like, and how the horses galloped around the ring. You will join your hands in a circle about the stove. Now start!"

With that he began whipping them, as they trotted around and around the stove. This story is told, I believe, in a little volume of "Sketches," by Erwin House, now long forgotten, like many other good books of the Western literature of a generation ago. I think the author was one of the boys who "played horse" in the master's circus.

It was fine sport for the more daring boys to plant a handful of coffee-nuts in the ashes just before the master's entrance. It is the nature of these coffee-nuts to lie quietly in the hot ashes for about half an hour, and then to explode with a sharp report, scattering the live coals in an inspiring way. Nothing could be funnier than the impotent wrath of the schoolmaster, as he went poking in the embers to find the remaining nuts, which generally eluded his search and popped away like torpedoes under his very nose.

The teaching in these schools was often quite absurd. I was made to go through Webster's spelling-book five times before I was thought fit to begin to read, and my mother, twenty years earlier, spelled it through nine times before she was allowed to begin Lindley Murray's "English Reader." It was by mere chance of the survival of some of the tougher old masters that I knew the old school in its glory. The change for the better was already beginning thirty or forty years ago. The old masters taught their pupils to "do sums," the new ones had already begun to teach arithmetic. In one of the schools in the generation before me was one Jim Garner; he must be an old man now, if he is yet living, and he will pardon my laughing at the boy of fifty years ago. One day he sat for a long time tapping his slate with his pencil.

"Jeems," cried the master, "what are you doing?"

"I'm a-tryin' to think, and I can't," said Jim, "if you take three from one, how many there is left."

It was in the same old Bethel schoolhouse, about the same time, that the master, one Benefiel, called out the spelling class of which my mother, then a little girl, was usually at the head. The word given out was "onion." I suppose the scholars at the head of the class had not recognized the word by its spelling in studying their lessons. They all missed it widely, spelling it in the most ingeniously incorrect fashions. Near the foot of the class stood a boy who had never been able to climb up toward the head. But of the few words he did know how to spell, one was "onion." When the word was missed at the head he became greatly excited, twisting himself into the most ludicrous contortions as it came nearer and nearer to him. At length the one just above the eager boy missed, the master said "next," whereupon he exultingly swung his hand above his head and came out with: "O-n, un, i-o-n, yun, *ing-un*,—I'm head, by gosh!" and he marched to the head while the master hit him a blow across the shoulders for swearing.

The beginning of "educational reform" in my childhood took on curious forms. We had one grown man in Benefiel's school who got his tuition free of charge in consideration of his teaching the master and some of the older pupils geography by the new method of singing it, which he had learned somewhere. At the noon recess he and the master, with others, would sit with Smith's Atlas open before them, singing away in the most earnest and sentimental sing-song such refrains as this, pointing to the state capitals while they sang:

"Maine, Au—gusta! Maine, Au—gusta!
  New Hampshire, Concord, *New* Hampshire, Concord."

and so on down to the newly annexed state of Texas.

The "Rule of Three" was the objective point of all study, and he who had ciphered through that had well-nigh exhausted human knowledge. The illiteracy of the up-country regions was very great, and, during the six years which my father, on account of declining health, passed in a country place, our experience with schools was not a happy one. There came at one time to our district an old Irish master who also claimed to be a doctor. Some years before, in a lawsuit in which my father was retained, the old man persisted in writing his own deposition, wherein he related that he had studied "medesin" in Ireland. The old man was very much enraged when my father declined to send us to his school. He had been known to spend a solid hour in family devotions and then, rising from his knees, to walk across the floor and kick his son for going to sleep during prayers. He was afterward tried for poisoning his wife, but acquitted through the eloquence of that unsurpassed orator, Joseph G. Marshall.

Of course, it often came to pass in such a state of things that men rose to prominence who had little education. A rich distiller, who represented us in Congress some years later, wrote a letter, full of blunders, that fell into the hands of his opponents. They published it, and he suffered much ridicule. "F——," said one of his friends, "*did* you write that letter?" "Yes," said he, "but it wasn't so bad as that—they mucilated it."

In all the period of darkness and insufficient schools that preceded my childhood, there were here and there good teachers in some of the villages, and to the lucky village that had a good master came boys and girls from near and far—sometimes from fifty miles away. There was never a period of indifference to education in the Ohio River region—never a time when a good school was not accounted a thing of the greatest value; but the sparse settlement made schools scarce—the great demand for men of education in other walks of life always makes good teachers scarce in a new country—and the excess of demand over supply in the matter of women left no unmarried young women of education to serve as schoolmistresses.

The earliest female teachers that I remember, with one exception, were the thrifty wives of New England settlers, who knew how to mind their children and turn an honest dollar by teaching the children of their neighbors. But we were particularly warned against New England provincialisms; my father, who was a graduate of William and Mary in Virginia, even threatened us with corporal punishment if we should ever give the peculiar vowel sound heard in some parts of New England in such words as "roof" and "root." After our return to the village, I had the good fortune to have some teachers whom I remember with gratitude. One was a Presbyterian minister from New England, who, with his wife—a woman of fine ability—taught an excellent school. In this school we first saw blackboards and similar devices for teaching in an intelligent way. The minister's wife kept good books to lend to thoughtful pupils, and her influence on the village was a very beneficent one. Another was Jesse Williams, also a New Englander, who became afterward a Methodist minister. These two were the only men that I knew in my boyhood who could teach school without beating their pupils like oxen. There was another New England minister whose pupil I was in one of the Indiana cities, who kept his school in a state of continual terror. This is a cheap sort of discipline, quite possible to men who have not tact enough to govern otherwise than brutally.

So great was the desire for education in Indiana, even at this early date, that before my memory of the place our old town of Vevay was adorned by a "county seminary." It was proposed to educate by counties, and a seminary was to be built at the county's expense; but the old jealousy between town and country flamed up. The people of the country were not going to pay taxes to build a seminary in town, so the seminary was built outside the corporation line in a commanding position on the top of a steep hill, at least three hundred feet high. This high school always reminded me of the temple of fame which did duty as frontispiece to Webster's spelling book in that day, the temple being situated on an inaccessible mountain, at the foot of which an ambitious school-boy stood looking wistfully up. For one or two winters, the village youth and the country children boarding in town walked a mile, and then scrambled up this hard hill; but the school was soon abandoned for better schools in the town, and the old brick "seminary" stands there yet, I believe, a monument of educational folly. Many an ambitious modern device is like our seminary, useless from inaccessibility.

While the good Presbyterian minister was teaching in our village, he was waked up one winter morning by a poor bound boy, who had ridden a farm horse many miles to get the "master" to show him how to "do a sum" that had puzzled him. The fellow was trying to educate himself, but was required to be back at home in time to begin his day's work as usual. The good master, chafing his hands to keep them warm, sat down by the boy and expounded the "sum" to him so that he understood it. Then the poor boy straightened himself up and, thrusting his hard hand into the pocket of his blue jeans trowsers, pulled out a quarter of a dollar, explaining, with a blush, that it was all he could pay, for it was all he had. Of course the master made him put it back, and told him to come whenever he wanted any help. I remember the huskiness of the minister's voice when he told us about it in school that morning. When I recall how eagerly the people sought for opportunities of education, I am not surprised to hear that Indiana, of all the states, has to-day one of the largest, if not the largest, school fund.

We had one teacher who was, so far as natural genius for teaching goes, the best of all I have ever known. Mrs. Julia L.

Dumont is, like all our Western writers of that day, except Prentice, almost entirely forgotten. But in the time, before railways, when the West, shut in by the Alleghanies, had an incipient literature, Mrs. Dumont occupied no mean place as a writer of poetry and prose tales. Eminent *littérateurs* of the time, from Philadelphia and Cincinnati, used to come to Vevay to see her; but they themselves—these great lights of ancient American literature away back in the forties—are also forgotten. Who remembers Gallagher and the rest to-day? Dear brethren, who like myself scratch away to fill up magazine pages, and who, no doubt, like myself are famous enough to be asked for an autograph, or a "sentiment" in an album sometimes, let us not boast ourselves. Why, indeed, should the spirit of mortal be proud? We also shall be forgotten—the next generation of school-girls will get their autographs from a set of upstarts who will smile at our stories and poems as out-of-date puerilities. Some industrious Allibone, making a cemetery of dead authors, may give us, in his dictionary, three lines apiece as a sort of head-stone. Oh, let us be humble and pray that even the Allibone that is to come may not forget us. For I look in vain in Allibone for some of the favorite names in our Western Parnassus. It was not enough that the East swallowed that incipient literature, it even obliterated the memory of it. Let us hope that the admirable Mr. Tyler, who has made to live again the memories of so many colonial writers, will revive also the memory of some of the forgotten authors of the Mississippi Valley.

Among those who have been so swiftly forgotten as not even to have a place in Allibone, is my old and once locally famous teacher, Mrs. Dumont. We thought her poem on "The Retreat of the Ten Thousand" admirable, but we were partial judges. Her story of "Boonesborough" was highly praised by the great lights of the time. But her book of stories is out of print, and her poems are forgotten, and so also are the great lights who admired them. I do not pretend that there was enough in these writings to have made them deserve a different fate.

Ninety-nine hundredths of all good literary production must of necessity be forgotten; if the old trees endured forever, there would be no room for the new shoots.

But as a schoolmistress, Mrs. Dumont deserves immortality. She knew nothing of systems, but she went unerringly to the goal by pure force of native genius. In all her early life she taught because she was poor; but after her husband's increasing property relieved her from necessity, she still taught school from love of it. When she was past sixty years old, a schoolroom was built for her alongside her residence, which was one of the best in the town. It was here that I first knew her, after she had already taught two generations· in the place. The "graded" schools had been newly introduced, and no man was found who could, either in acquirements or ability, take precedence of the venerable schoolmistress; so the high school was given to her.

I can see the wonderful old lady now, as she was then, with her cape pinned awry, rocking her splint-bottom chair nervously while she talked. Full of all manner of knowledge, gifted with something very like eloquence in speech, abounding in affection for her pupils and enthusiasm in teaching, she moved us strangely. Being infatuated with her, we became fanatic in our pursuit of knowledge, so that the school hours were not enough, and we had a "lyceum" in the evening for reading "compositions," and a club for the study of history. If a recitation became very interesting, the entire· school would sometimes be drawn into the discussion of the subject; all other lessons went to the wall, books of reference were brought out of her library, hours were consumed, and many a time the school session was prolonged until darkness forced us reluctantly to adjourn.

Mrs. Dumont was the ideal of a teacher because she succeeded in forming character. She gave her pupils unstinted praise, not hypocritically, but because she lovingly saw the best in every one. We worked in the sunshine. A dull but industrious pupil was praised for diligence, a bright pupil for ability, a good one for general excellence. The dullards got more than their share, for knowing how easily such an one is disheartened, Mrs. Dumont went out of her way to praise the first show of success in a slow scholar. She treated no two alike. She was full of all sorts of knack and tact, a person of infinite resource for calling out the human spirit. She could be incredibly severe when it was needful, and no overgrown boy whose meanness had once been analyzed by Mrs. Dumont ever forgot it.

I remember one boy with whom she had taken some pains. One day he wrote an insulting word about one of the girls of the school on the door of a deserted house. Two of us were deputized by the other boys to defend the girl by complaining of him. Mrs. Dumont took her seat and began to talk to him before the school. The talking was all there was of it, but I think I never pitied any human being more than I did that boy as she showed him his vulgarity and his meanness, and, as at last in the climax of her indignation, she called him "a miserable hawbuck." At another time when she had picked a piece of paper from the floor with a bit of profanity written on it, she talked about it until the whole school detected the author by the beads of perspiration on his forehead.

When I had written a composition on "The Human Mind" based on Combe's Phrenology, and adorned with quotations from Pope's "Essay on Man," she gave me to read the old Encyclopedia Britannica containing an article expounding the Hartleian system of mental philosophy, and followed this with Locke on the "Conduct of the Understanding." She was the only teacher I have known who understood that school studies were entirely secondary to general reading as a source of culture, and who put the habit of good reading first in the list of acquirements.

There was a rack for hats and cloaks so arranged as to cut off a portion of the school from the teacher's sight. Some of the larger girls who occupied this space took advantage of their concealed position to do a great deal of talking and tittering which did not escape Mrs. Dumont's watchfulness. But in the extreme corner of the room was the seat of the excellent Drusilla H——, who had never violated a rule of the school. To reprimand the others, while excepting her, would have excited jealousy and complaints. The girls who sat in that part of the room were detained after school and treated to one of Mrs. Dumont's tender but caustic lectures on the dishonorableness of secret ill-doing. Drusilla bore silently her share of the reproof. But at the last the schoolmistress said:

"Now, my dears, it may be that there is some one among you not guilty of misconduct. If there is I know I can trust you to tell me who is not to blame."

"Drusilla never talks," they all said at once, while Drusilla, girl like, fell to crying.

But the most remarkable illustration of Mrs. Dumont's skill in matters of discipline was shown in a case in which all the boys of the school were involved, and were for a short time thrown into antagonism to a teacher whose ascendancy over them had been complete.

We were playing "town-ball" on the common at a long distance from the schoolroom. Town-ball is one of the old games from which the more scientific but not half so amusing "national game" of base-ball has since been evolved. In that day the national game was not thought of. Eastern youth played field-base, and Western boys town-ball in a free and happy way, with soft balls, primitive bats, and no nonsense. There were no scores, but a catch or a cross-out in town-ball put the whole side out, leaving the others to take the bat or "paddle" as it was appropriately called. The very looseness of the game gave opportunity for many ludicrous mischances and surprising turns which made it a most joyous play.

Either because the wind was blowing adversely or because the play was more than commonly interesting, we failed to hear the ringing of Mrs. Dumont's hand-bell at one o'clock. The afternoon wore on until more than an hour of school-time had passed, when some one suddenly bethought himself. We dropped the game and started, pell-mell, full of consternation for the schoolroom. We would at that moment have preferred to face an angry schoolmaster with his birchen rod than to have offended one whom we reverenced so much.

The girls all sat in their places; the teacher was sitting silent and awful in her rocking-chair; in the hour and a half no lessons had been recited. We shuffled into our seats and awaited the storm. It was the high school, and the boys were mostly fifteen or sixteen years of age, but the schoolmistress had never a rod in the room. Such weapons are for people of fewer resources than she. Very quietly she talked to us, but with great emphasis. She gave no chance for explanation or apology. She was hopelessly hurt and affronted. We had humiliated her before the whole town, she said. She should take away from us the morning and afternoon recess for a week. She would demand an explanation from us to-morrow.

It was not possible that a company of boys could be kept for half an hour in such a moral sweat-box as that to which she treated us without growing angry. When school was dismissed we held a running indignation meeting as we walked toward home. Of course we all spoke at once. But after awhile the more moderate saw that the teacher had some reason. Nevertheless, one boy was appointed to draft a written reply that should set forth our injured feelings. I remember in what perplexity that committee found himself. With every hour he felt more and more that the teacher was right and the boys wrong, and that by the next morning the reviving affection of the scholars for the beloved and venerated schoolmistress would cause them to appreciate this. So that the address which was presented for their signatures did not breathe much indignation. I can almost recall every word of that somewhat pompous but very sincere petition. It was about as I give it here:

"HONORED MADAM:

In regard to our offence of yesterday we beg that you will do us the justice to believe that it was not intentional. We do not ask you to remit the punishment you have inflicted in taking away our recess, but we do ask you to remit the heavier penalty we have incurred, your own displeasure."

The boys all willingly signed this except one, who was perhaps the only conscious offender in that party. He confessed that he had observed that the sun was "getting a little slanting" while we were at play, but as his side "had the paddles" he did not say anything until they were put out. The unwilling boy wanted more indignation in the address, and he wanted the recess back. But when all the others had signed he did not dare leave his name off, but put it at the bottom of the list.

With trembling hands we gave the paper to the schoolmistress. How some teachers would have used such a paper as a means of further humiliation to the offenders! How few could have used it as she did! The morning wore on without recess. The lessons were heard as usual. As the noon hour drew near, Mrs. Dumont rose from her chair and went into the library. We all felt that something was going to happen. She came out with a copy of Shakspere, which she opened at the fourth scene of the fourth act of the second part of "King Henry IV." Giving the book to my next neighbor and myself she bade us read the scene, alternating with the change of speaker. You remember the famous dialogue in that scene between the dying king and the prince who has prematurely taken the crown from the bedside of the sleeping king. It was all wonderfully fresh to us and to our schoolmates, whose interest was divided between the scene and a curiosity as to the use the teacher meant to make of it. At length the reader who took the king's part read:

"O my son!
Heaven put it in thy mind to take it hence,
That thou mightst win the more thy father's love,
Pleading so wisely in excuse of it."

Then she took the book and closed it. The application was evident to all, but she made us a touching little speech full of affection, and afterward restored the recess. She detained the girls when we had gone to read to them the address, that she might "show them what noble brothers they had." Without doubt she made overmuch of our nobleness. But no one knew better than Mrs. Dumont that the surest way of evoking the best in man or boy, is to make the most of the earliest symptoms of it. From that hour our schoolmistress had our whole hearts; we loved her and reverenced her; we were thoughtless enough, but for the most of us, her half-suspected wish was a supreme law.

So, after all, it does not matter that the world no longer reads her stories or remembers her poems. Her life always seemed to me a poem, or something better than a poem. It does not matter, fellow-scribblers, that the generation to come shall forget us and go to upstart fellows of another generation for autograph verses for church fairs and charity bazaars. It does not matter greatly, dear, aspiring young reader, whether you ever succeed in getting your poetry embalmed in "Scribner" or not. I cannot read an old magazine of forty years ago without a laugh—and almost a tear—over the airs those notabilities of a day gave themselves. How sure they were of immortality, and how utterly forgotten are the most of them, like last year's burdock, that boasted itself so proudly in the fence-row! But whether you print your story or poem or not, blessed are you if you put heroism into your life, so that the memory of it shall refresh some weary wayfarer long after the fickle public has forgotten your work.

D'ARCY WENTWORTH THOMPSON

1829

D'ARCY WENTWORTH THOMPSON was born in County Cumberland, in North England, in 1829. He received his early education at a famous school in London, known as the Hospital. His college days were passed at the University of Cambridge. For twelve years or more he was classical master in the Edinburgh Academy. In 1864 he was appointed professor of Greek in Queen's College, in Galway, Ireland, which position he still holds.

While at Edinburgh, Professor Thompson wrote the "Day-dreams of a Schoolmaster," which was well received, and early attracted attention in America, for its expression of radical views on the teaching of ancient languages. In 1867 he was invited to deliver a series of lectures on education at the Lowell Institute, in Boston. He complied, and the lectures were subsequently published under the title, "Wayside Thoughts." Among other works by Professor Thompson are "Ancient Leaves," "Sales Attici; or, the Wit and Wisdom of the Athenian Drama," and "Scalæ Novæ; or, A Ladder to Latin."

Characterization

Professor D'Arcy Thompson has several first-rate qualifications for the work which he has undertaken. He knows the nature of boys, and is in full sympathy with them. He also knows Latin thoroughly, thinks in it, and writes it with great elegance. He has also thought with original power on the philosophy of language, is always in search of explanations, and is eager to bring everything out of the realms of unreason. All these qualities make themselves visible in the book before us. At the same time, great moderation is shown in hazarding explanations or dismissing irrational rules.

"ENGLISH JOURNAL OF EDUCATION."

Day-Dreams of a Schoolmaster

(Abbreviated)

I.

THE UNDER FORM AT ST. EDWARD'S, AND THE THEORY OF ELEMENTARY UNINTELLIGIBILITY

This day—October 10th, 1863—my Junior Class, in the Schola Nova[1] of Dunedin,[2] had its first lesson in Greek; put aside its frock and linen pants, and donned its breeches, intellectually. No transition state is agreeable to the subject, or graceful in the eyes of a looker-on. These little fellows will all waddle, duck-like, for a considerable period in their new clothes: some will never habituate themselves thereto; but will by and by discard them and return to the frock and linen pants; affording, it may be, a passing laugh to the unphilosophic bystander, but themselves deriving permanent comfort and unrestricted swing of limb.

The step these innocents take to-day is, of course, a step into the dark. Will the darkness, into which they so confidingly plunge, be to them perpetual and Cimmerian? or will it duly break into a clear, bright dawn? Within three years the majority of them will have probably passed from within these walls. What an opportunity is meanwhile afforded of wreaking upon their little heads summary vengeance for the wrongs done me by a past generation!—of doing to them as I was done by! Not only should I thus be giving vent to my indignation for past ill-usage; but, strange to say, I should actually be carrying out the wishes of the parents of my victims; for, in general, those parents dread new-fangled ways, and cling piously to old scholastic superstitions. Well, for three years, then, let me lead this little flock, blind-folded, by curiously sinuous and zigzag ways; so that, always in motion, they may never progress;

[1] new school   [2] a poetic name for Edinburgh

and at the close of the triennium, remove the bandage from their eyes, and show them, to their wonderment, that they are standing by the starting-post; that they have been dancing their Greek hornpipe on a plate.

This first lesson has turned back the dial-hand of my days, and for a passing hour I am standing in the dawn of my own most dreary, weary boyhood.

I was not quite seven and a half years old when my dear mother was presented with a free admission for myself, her eldest son, to the Grammar School of St. Edward. The offer was too valuable an one to admit of refusal. I was accordingly prepared for admission to my new home, by having my hair somewhat closely shorn, and by being clothed in a long, blue gown, not of itself ungraceful, but opening in front so as to disclose the ridiculous spectacle of knee-breeched, yellow-stockinged legs. After some laughter at my disguise, and much weeping at my banishment, I bade good-bye to my dear mother. We little thought at the time that school was to be my home for twelve long years.

The day after my entry into this colossal institution, a Latin grammar was placed into my hands. It was a bulky book of its kind: considering the diminutiveness of the new student, a portentously bulky book. It was bulky in consequence of its comprehensiveness. It gave all imaginable rules, and all imaginable exceptions. It had providentially stored within it the requisite gear for whatever casualty might befall us. The syntax rules, in the edition presented to me, were, for the first time, rendered mercifully in English: those for gender and quantity remained in the old Latin; and the Latin was communicated in a hideously discordant rhythm. Over a space of years we went systematically through and through that book; page after page, chapter after chapter. It was all unintelligible; all obscure; but some spots were wrapt in more than ordinary gloom. Our chronic bewilderment was varied from time to time by shooting pains, brought on by some passage or expression unusually indigestible. We read of creatures, happily few in number, that went about in the *Epicæne Gender*. Were they fish, flesh or fowl? Would the breed be ever extinct? Under certain desperate circumstances a participle and a noun together were bound hand and foot, and put into the *Ablative Absolute*. What had they done to be treated in a manner thus peremptory, unreasonable, crotchety? Did they ever get out after being once put in? Then there were gerunds in *Di, Do,* and *Dum*. How they recalled to us the old *Fee, Fi, Fo, Fum,* and the smell of English blood! And supines in *Um* and *U*. What was the meaning of these cabalistic names? I did not know then; and I do not know now. And yet I have been behind the scholastic curtain for twelve long years.

There was no entire chapter in the book more broken with pitfalls than that, composed in doggerel, which treated of the rules for gender. Not one word, I am sure, of an exceptionable kind had escaped the diabolic ken of the compiler. String upon string of jangling, unmusical lines could we repeat with a singular rapidity; understanding nothing; asking no questions. Oh, the sweet, simple faith of childhood! We had been told to commit those lines to memory, and we committed them. They would, doubtless, do us good in the latter days. We should, at all events, be flogged there and then, unless we sang them like caged birds. It was the will of Allah: Allah was good.

Many of the words in that puzzling liturgy I have never fallen in with since, though I have been a student of its dialect for twenty-seven years. Some of the words I have since discovered to be grossly indecent in their naked English meaning. Well, well: they might have all been so, without doing more harm to our morality, than they did good to our understandings. I can vividly recollect one circumstance, that broke in a startling manner to me the dull monotony of these years. It was a hot and sultry afternoon. My wits were wandering, I suppose in green fields. So, in class-time when my turn came round, my brain was a *tabula rasa:*[1] the inscription was clean

---

[1] a blank tablet

wiped out, that had been carefully written there but half an hour before. The master, a clergyman, had broken his cane upon a previous delinquent; his riding-whip was sent for, and I received ten lashes on my two hands. I was then under nine years of age. For a passing bewilderment I was treated as though I had broken into an orchard. Our master was shortly after, if I mistake not, presented to a vicarage; he was in appearance almost effeminately genteel; in dress, scrupulously neat; with fingers tapering and delicate as a lady's.

The round-shot of a Latin grammar had been, I believe, tied to our legs, to prevent our intellectually straying. However, in course of time we became habituated to the incumbrance, and ceased to feel it as a serious check upon our movements. The hour at length arrived in which it was considered wise to attach another round-shot to our other legs. This was done accordingly in the shape of a Greek grammar, written entirely in Latin. This extra weight answered the purpose effectually: we were all brought to an immediate standstill.

I have sometimes thought, in a charitable mood, that the compiler of this book—Heaven forgive him! to word it mildly—composed it originally for such students as might be familiar with the tongue in which it was written. My comrades and I were not in that condition. We had to grapple with the difficulties of one unknown tongue through the medium of another tongue almost equally unknown. We were, in fact, required to give a determinate solution to an indeterminable problem. We had set us the equation:

$$x + y = 0;$$

and were called upon to give the values of x and y in terms of constants to be manufactured by ourselves. It was the old, old story. Bricks without straw. "Ye are idle," said the taskmasters. So they took away our scanty wisps; but diminished naught of the tale of bricks as heretofore.

I have heard the system casuistically defended by men who,

old prejudices apart, were intelligent and sagacious. "The abstract rules of grammar," said they, "are at first above the comprehension of all children. Even if they be worded in the mother-tongue, it will be long before their true and full significance is apprehended. If, then, these rules be communicated in a strange language, the very difficulty surmounted in committing them to memory will imprint them the more lastingly on their understandings."

Now it would occur to me—but my simplicity may be to blame—that if subjects, concrete or abstract, be beyond a boy's comprehension, the less he has to do with them the better. We never ask an errand-boy to *carry* a weight we know he cannot *lift*. Might not the communication of such subjects be deferred to a period when, by a process of training, a boy's intellect were rendered capable of grasping them? Or, again, at the expense of a little time and trouble, might not the majority of grammatical rules be so simply worded and so familiarly illustrated, as to be brought home to the intelligence of boys of ordinary capacity? I grant the difficulty, if we persist in using unintelligible terms, as *Gerunds, Supines, Aorists*, and the like; and rules that would be awkwardly enough worded, even if they were correct in substance.

But for the sake of argument, let us admit the defense put forward for the old system of Elementary Unintelligibility. Then, surely, we may push it to its logical issues. All will allow morality to be higher than grammar. It is, consequently, a more important task to imprint upon the minds of our children the rules of the former than the rules of the latter. But what will serve to imprint indelibly the rules of one science, will serve also to imprint the rules of another; supposing that, for the time, it be unnecessary that either set of rules be understood. Then why not communicate the Ten Commandments through the medium of Chinese? Or, if that method be found insufficiently irksome and tedious, why not improve upon the method, by rendering it physically painful? Might we not inculcate each portion of the Decalogue with the aid of a pin, and imprint it upon the memory of childhood by associating it with pricks upon some sensitive portion of the frame? In this simple manner, we might literally fasten a whole system of ethics and grammar upon the bodies as well as the brains of our little ones. The system might be extended to our university course; and a petty domestic instrument might prove a weapon of power in the hands of an energetic professor of chemistry, logic, or metaphysics! Our academic youth would go out into the world, tattooed with the records of their education. A man's own skin—and sometimes even that would be of the old material—would be his portable diploma.

But to return to our Greek grammar written in Latin. Day after day our clerical Sphinx propounded the mysterious enigma. *When is a door not a door?* was the simple conundrum that confounded us. It was set us in the language of the Cumæan Sibyl, and the solution was to be given in that of the Pythian Apollo. Day after day a victim fell;

αἰεὶ δὲ πυραὶ νεκύων καίοντο θαμειαί.¹

When I escaped from Thebes, no Œdipus had appeared. I wonder if the Sphinx is at the old work still.

For five years—and five years make a hole in one's schooltime, not to say in one's life—for five dreary years the process went on. We committed daily to memory some page or half-page of the sacred but unintelligible book. We revised it, and we re-revised it again and again. To lisp its contents seemed as natural as respiration. We could repeat glibly most perplexing declensions and conjugations; contracts of all kinds; changes Attic, Ionic, and Æolic; verbs in ω and verbs in μι; rules of syntax, prosody, and construction, which no one seemed called upon to understand at the time, and to which, in their Latin form, no one was, to my knowledge, ever referred afterwards.

So far did Greek accommodate itself to ordinary views, that we occasionally caught glimpses of such familiar friends as

[1] And ever the crowded pyres of the dead kept burning. (From the "Iliad.")

nouns, and *verbs*, and *prepositions*, and the like. But here the condescension ceased. Ever and anon came looming through the Latin fog strange forms, gigantic, spectral; Heteroclites, Paradigms, Asynartetuses, Syzygies; Augments, temporal and syllabic. The former seemed to embody some dim records of a pre-Adamite state; mystic allusions to bygone Mammoths, Behemoths, Ichthyosauri; under the latter twain seemed to lurk an allegory of the connection between Church and State.

It is a grand thing to be conversant with a noble language, unknown to all around us, to our nearest kin. It conveys an undefined idea of wealth and power. We travel where they cannot travel. We visit at great houses, and leave them standing at the door. We stand in sunlight on the hill-top, while they are groping in the valley. We wield with ease a mighty flail of thought, which they cannot uplift with both hands. Yes, we may reasonably be proud of the capability of speaking, maybe of thinking in a foreign tongue. But it is either superlatively sublime, or superlatively ridiculous, to speak for years a language unintelligible to one's self.

But before quitting forever the old Under Form, let me say that my quarrel has been with a system and not with persons. The only unfeeling man under whom I had been placed was the genteel clergyman of the riding-whip. My other masters were good and kindly men, who went according to order through a dull routine, believing in it most probably, and quite powerless from their position, if not also from their abilities, to modify it to any material extent. One of them, before passing further, I must specially recall. He was the only classical usher; the only classical authority not in orders; a tall, gigantically tall and muscular Scotchman, of the name of Ramsay. *He was also the only classical teacher without a cane.* He used a strap; *Scoticè*,[1] *the tawse.* Was it because he was only an usher and a layman?—or was it a kindly record of his own more merciful training in his dear native land? Good soul: even in the using of this innocuous instrument he kept his elbow on the

[1] in Scotch

desk, to spare us the full sweep of his tremendous arm. There was a silly legend current among us, founded only on his physical strength, that the cane had been denied him, after his having once cut unintentionally through a boy's hand—an idle myth, that wrapped a possibility in specious falsehood. To see the huge *torso* towering above the comparatively puny desk, it was like the figure-head of a man-of-war. Why, with a cane the man could have hewn a beadle to the chine, and with a birch have minced us mannikins to collops. I wonder if he had an ancestor at Bannockburn: such an one, I could imagine, with a great two-handed sword, would have chopped off English heads like turnips. I have an indistinct idea of there having been something very soft and tender in the domestic relations of that biggest and best of ushers.

But, farewell! good, kindly usher! and farewell! good gentlemen of the Under Form!—ye deserved a better fate than the fate of Sisyphus Æolides.

III.

The Hellenists

I have been dubbed Hellenist. Nay, never start, reader: I am too proud to be conceited. There: you need not stand uncovered. I am invested with the Latin Order of the Garter, and the Greek Order of the Golden Fleece. I am standing on a peak in Darien, and staring at a new Pacific, broad and blue, wherein lie happy islands. I have reached the zenith of all boyish hopes; surely, henceforth my path will slope downwards to the grave. I am self-poised, self-centered. All pettiness of vanity is swallowed up in an absorbing contentment and pride. For three years I shall pace the old, shadowy cloisters; then for as many years shall I walk the garden of Academus; and then pass into the great world by one of two roads; and at the end of one road I can dimly see men with gray wigs and silk gowns; and at the end of the other, a circle of reverend elders with white lawn sleeves. O Phaëton, Phaëton, your head is turning giddy!

To descend, then, from my dizzy flight. I am in the middle of my seventeenth year. *I have had nine years of classical drilling.* All that I have as yet learnt might very easily, indeed, have been acquired, had I commenced in my thirteenth instead of in my eighth year, and had the system of instruction been natural and easy instead of being unnatural and difficult. This I state unhesitatingly, after having twice carried a class through the whole of a school curriculum of seven years.

Had it been my lot now to leave school, I should have carried away a rather pleasant remembrance of my first usher, and an affectionate remembrance of but one master, Delille. It was only in the Hellenist class that I came to love and venerate Rice, to love and admire Webster. Speaking from the light of subsequent experience, I believe no school in the world ever had, or ever will have, a trio of masters to surpass the trio I here mention. Let me pause for a moment, to portray them in few but loving words.

Delille, our master of French, was a tall and powerfully built man, with a fresh and ruddy complexion, and a manly carriage. His temper was imperturbably good, his sense of humor infectious. He had no vulgar instrument of punishment; but by his noble presence and the unseen force of his character, he could maintain the strictest order in classes numbering above a hundred pupils. He spoke our language without a flaw of accent; it was only by an occasional hyper-correctness of *hither* for *here* that one could detect the foreigner. His classes were held out of the usual school-hours, sometimes even on half-holidays; and for all that, they were the pleasantest classes in the under school. His severest mode of punishment was to set a fable of La Fontaine to be committed to memory. You were not released until it had been repeated without one single break; and you generally left him, exasperated a little at the loss of play, but laughing perforce at some grave piece of badinage with which he had dismissed you.

I knew him afterwards as a friend, and guest, and host. And what a companion he was at table or over a cigar! He was, like his compatriots, *bon vivant;* [1] and as good a judge of wine as any member of a London club. He had a splendid voice for declamation or singing; was an admirable after-dinner speaker in either French or English; could sing a song of Lover's with a rich Irish brogue; a song of Burns' with all the subtlety of its pure, sweet accent; and roll out a sea-song of Dibdin's like a sailor! Had I never esteemed him as a master, I should have liked him as an accomplished man of the world and a delightful companion. With a number of university friends, I once dined with him at his house in Ely Place. I still remember the four kinds of champagne that were broached at dinner; the Chambertin that flowed freely afterwards with the flow of wit and good-humor; the music in the drawing-room, and the singing from ballad, opera, and oratorio; the hour at midnight in the snug library; a fuming bowl and irreproachable cigars; and I remember, as my cab drove me to the Tavistock, that the lamps of Holborn showed through the window like mad and merry dancing stars. Alas! I am writing of one whose hand I shall never grasp again, for cordial welcome or regretful farewell.

Of Webster I cannot speak at such length; and happily, for the best of reasons: he is not, like his two colleagues, a memory alone. But I shall never forget how contagious was his zeal for work; how impetuously chivalrous was his character; how thorough his respect for industry; how unmistakable his abhorrence of shuffling and sloth. And I remember thinking, at times, when I looked up from a remarkably white hand on the desk to a handsome and proud and almost haughty face before me, that my clerical master should have been a courtly abbé, and have " set in hall with prince and gentle ladye."

And *Burney*—dear old Burney, as we used to call our headmaster—how feeble would be any words to describe our fondness for that dear, white head! The doctor was a noble type

[1] one who lives well

of the old-fashioned English headmaster. He had a loathing for all scientific study; was utterly ignorant of modern languages: indeed, I believe, he looked upon Delille as the only Frenchman that had ever been reclaimed from greasy cookery and sour claret to a repentant but honest appreciation of roast beef and port wine. English literature of the day to him was non-existent; his lectures smacked of the last century, with their long undulating periods, and pauses Ciceronian. He was the fellow-student rather than the master of his Hellenists. Patiently would he pore over their exercises, in the lightest study that sent a melancholy gleam into the long, dark schoolroom. All information, historical, antiquarian, geographical, or philosophic, as connected with the classics, he regarded with contempt: any dunderhead, he considered, might cram that at his leisure; but it pained him to the quick if a senior pupil violated the Porsonian pause, or trifled with a subjunctive. "A word in your ear, doctor," said an Oxford examiner once to him; "your captain yesterday could not tell me where Elis was!" "I looked horrified," said the doctor, in repeating the circumstance; "I looked horrified, of course; but, on my word, I did not know it myself. But," continued he, "these Oxford fellows like this kind of thing; but I'll wager you'd get few of them to write a good Porson."

Like all simple and unworldly natures, he was generous to a fault. He would have given anything, forgiven anything to a good Greek scholar. The boys of the under school feared him as a strict and resolute and severe disciplinarian. We, his Hellenists, knew that, while he followed, unquestioningly, old Draconian laws, his heart was of the kindest and softest and tenderest. How the old man, that could look so stern at times, would weep, when an old pupil went wrong at college; with what unreproaching kindness he would help him out of difficulties, into which idleness or extravagance or misfortune might have plunged him. How like a father he would welcome him, when all errors had been retrieved by the winning of an honorable place in the list of final honors. "You must remember, sir, that my place is due to you; that but for your help last summer, I could not have returned for long-vacation reading." "Nonsense," replied the doctor; "I remember nothing of the kind; but I'll remember long enough the place you held in the classical Tripos."

And he, to whom he thus spoke, and I, who am now writing, and all who had the honor of belonging to the class of his Hellenists, will remember him with love and gratitude and reverence to the end; ay, to the end.

And now, reader, why should I give a description of the Hellenist class? With three such masters, and a set of comrades most of whom were enthusiastic students, and all of whom were pleasant fellows, how could a triennium fail to be an industrious and a happy one?—It was the reign of Antoninus Pius in my school-life, and needs no chronicling.

X.

Place aux Dames[1]

. . . .

The only grammar taught to girls below the age of twelve should be that of their own language; and its terms should be made as plain and intelligible as possible. Perhaps no subject is better taught than this latter one in our schools. But to girls of superior intelligence, even English is not the language upon which to found general and comprehensive ideas of grammar, such as may facilitate the after-acquisition of any modern language. You may never inculcate ideas of filial duty on a child, by continually obtruding upon him impertinent mention of his own parents. You would tell him amusing and instructive stories of *other* children and *other* parents. Even so with grammar.

In the education of boys, it has been agreed, perhaps truly,

[1] Room for the Ladies

that Latin is the best instrument for inculcating the general laws of language. Are there genders in educational systems, like as in Latin or French nouns? Is there anything in Latin grammar peculiarly *male?* How did they talk at dinner-time in ancient Rome? Did the men speak only masculine nouns; the ladies, feminine ones; and the servants, *common* ones? We have no warrant for such a conclusion. I believe the Latin language to have been, and still to be, incapable of such partitioning. It is not of the masculine gender; nor of the feminine; nor of the neuter or neither; but, like other languages, of *the either gender*. And, if properly taught, it would be found a far easier language than German; considerably easier than French; and a little easier in its old form than in its slightly altered form of modern Italian, which is very easy indeed.

Heaven forbid that our girls should be taught Latin with the grammars now in use, and those annotated books that may help an incompetent master over an occasional stile, but can only enervate a pupil's brain, and transfer coin from the pocket of an exasperated parent to the pocket of an undeserving publisher.

. . . .

Girls might, with great advantage, pass through two or even three years of Latin teaching, if that language were taught on an easy, simple, and natural method.

Although a schoolmaster of boys, reader, I have still a touch of gallantry. Smile at my proposal. I would undertake to teach Latin to a class of girls twelve years of age, without the use of pedantic and expensive books, or of pedantic and meaningless grammar rules.

My pronunciation would be Italian, as nearly Tuscan as I could make it. I would never forget that I was training children, not to be schoolmistresses, but gentle ladies in a drawing-room, and gentler mothers in a nursery. I would so teach a young class, that if a master of a great English school were to interrupt us in our work, he would say: "Ah! they are engaged in a lesson of trumpery Italian." And I would, perhaps, mildly quiz him to my pupils in correct Latinity, which, from being rapidly and musically spoken, he would not understand. And in two years, perhaps; and in three years, most certainly; I would have girls in my class, who would speak an old language, not unlike the language of modern Tuscany, in a way that would shame their brothers and cousins, who had been five years at any grammar school in the kingdom, and trained on the old system of Elementary Unintelligibility. And I would teach them Latin in such a way that very soon they would read a parable in either Italian or Spanish without stumbling over either word of construction. And I would engage to say that my pupils would like their work, and would not dislike their master.

And consider the collateral effects of so bracing and healthful an education of our girls. Boy-classics would be forced, in emulation, to dispense with much of their dull pedantry and youths would be ashamed to continue ignorant of modern tongues that their sisters spoke with elegance and ease. We have now a smattering of youth that cram reluctantly some knowledge of French, German, Italian, or Spanish, to win marks in our Chinese examinations. What a vulgar and profane usage of the dialects of Corneille, Goethe, Dante, and Cervantes!

But, reader, you are alarmed. You are afraid that such a system would make blue-stockings of our girls. Prejudice, reader—unmanly, unchivalrous prejudice. The ladies of the Russian noblesse can speak almost every language of Europe; but they are exquisitely feminine. My brother sat for a week opposite a fair creature at a *table d'hôte*[1] in Venice; and perhaps he never eat less, or enjoyed dinner more, for a week together. He heard her speak all the languages he knew; and some that he did not know. But for her linguistic powers he would have taken her for an English girl, from her English accent and her blonde beauty. Of course, she was a Russian. She had no appearance of the blue. If she was one—then I could wish

[1] a common table for guests at a hotel

that all were even as that sweet, young, blue-eyed polyglot. 'Twas a lucky fellow, I should think, that caught that little Tartar.

Do, reader, disabuse your reasonable mind of unreasonable crotchets. Women have just as keen intelligence as men; less powers, maybe, of abstract reasoning; but far finer perceptive and linguistic faculties. They need not be trained to exhaustive scholarship; but refinement of mental culture suits them, perhaps, even more than it does our own sex.

I imagine that the Lady Jane, who read her Phædo when the horn was calling, had as pretty a mouse-face as you ever saw in a dream; and I am sure that gentle girl was a better scholar than any lad of seventeen is now in any school of England or Scotland.

And once upon a time, reader—a long, long while ago—I knew a schoolmaster, and that schoolmaster had a wife. And she was young, and fair, and learned; like that princess-pupil of old Ascham; fair and learned as Sydney's sister, Pembroke's mother. And her voice was ever soft, gentle, and low, reader—an excellent thing in woman. And her fingers were quick at needlework, and nimble in all a housewife's cunning. And she could draw sweet music from the ivory board; and sweeter, stranger music from the dull life of her schoolmaster-husband. And she was slow at heart to understand mischief, but her feet ran swift to do good. And she was simple with the simplicity of girlhood, and wise with the wisdom that cometh only of the Lord,—cometh only to the children of the Kingdom. And her sweet young life was as a Morning Hymn, sung by child-voices to rich organ-music. Time shall throw his dart at Death, ere Death has slain such another.

For she died, reader: a long, long while ago. And I stood once by her grave; her green grave, not far from dear Dunedin. Died, reader, for all she was so fair, and young, and learned, and simple, and good. And I am told it made a great difference to that schoolmaster.

XXI.

Suum Cuique[1]

Nascitur, non fit,[2] may be said as truly of the schoolmaster as of the poet. The popular but mistaken idea is, that any young man, who at the age of twenty-one is well enough educated for a learned profession, but lacks the means or spirit to push his way in the world of law or medicine, may subside into a teacher of the classics. Many young Englishmen think so themselves, and take clerical orders at the time of entering the despised profession, that they may escape from it, if on any white day a vicarage should fall from the clouds. These are they that are not born schoolmasters, but are made schoolmasters of men.

In the matter of education, Scotland is, in many points, in advance of her southern neighbor. The middle-class preparatory schools of Dunedin are unapproachably superior to anything of the kind—if there be anything of the kind—in England. The teaching of the elementary classes in our high school and Schola Nova is even at present far superior to that of similar classes in any public schools in England with which I have been directly or indirectly acquainted; and that includes almost all the public schools of importance in the country. With a few, but I must own, very important modifications, our training of junior classes might be made almost perfect of its kind.

In our high school is still retained much of the beautiful vowel-music of Italian-Latin. The Greek professor of our Dunedin University—faithful among the faithless, in *this* respect—can read a simile of Homer, without marring rhythm or ignoring accent.

In Scotland, also, the profession of teaching, though not sufficiently honored from a social point of view, is rightly considered as *specific*, and calling for *specific qualifications*. When Adam and

---

[1] His own   [2] He is born, he is not made

Carson of our high school, Melvin of Aberdeen, and Carmichael of our own Schola Nova, first apprenticed themselves to their craft, they left no plank behind them for recrossing at a favorable opportunity to ease or affluence in an extraneous calling. They put their hands to the plough, these simple men; and there was no looking back. They devoted themselves to the business of classical instruction as single-heartedly as did the Apostles to the dissemination of Christian doctrine. They knew well enough that spiritual darkness abounded, but they left its enlightenment to another calling—the only one that in the dignity of usefulness takes precedence of their own.

And one of them lived too short a life; but they all lived lives laborious and useful and honorable. From dawn to sunset of their day of toil they sowed the seed, or drave the plow, or brake with harrows the obstructive glebe. And when at length it *was growing dark*, these husbandmen dismissed their little reapers and gleaners; and gat them home, wearied; and turned to; and fell on sleep. No foretaste of earthly glory sweetened the bitterness of the last cup. From modest homes they were borne, unnoticed, to modest graves. But the statues of these Cincinnatus-teachers stand, not unwreathed with laurel, in the Valhalla of great and good and single-hearted schoolmasters, with all the other good men and true. And the Valhalla is not in Dunedin, reader; but in a great and distant city; a city not built with hands; a city more beautiful by far than beautiful Dunedin.

About a furlong from my own lodgings, in a room as near to heaven,[1] burns the midnight lamp of one who could read a play of Sophocles ere I could inarticulately scream. He has read more of ancient literature than many literary men have read of English. He has purified his Greek seven times in the fire. He has resuscitated many Aorists, that for centuries had lain dormant under mossy stones. He has passed, alone and fearless, through waste places, where no footfall had echoed for a hundred years. In England, nothing but a special inter-

[1] an allusion to the very tall buildings of Edinburgh

position of Providence could have saved this scholar from the Bench of Bishops; in Scotland, nothing short of personal violence could have pushed him into a Professorial Chair. The fact is, this man, with all his learning, is bowed down with the weight of a most unnational modesty. Indeed, of this quality, as of erudition, there is as much contained in his well as would serve to irrigate his native country. Heaven knows what he might have been had he consented in earlier life to play in public the cymbals of claptrap and the tom-tom of self-conceit. But his voice was never heard in the Palaverium of Dunedin. My friend, in fact, was ostracized by his fellow-citizens of the modern Athens. You may hear of him at Jena, Göttingen, or Heidelberg; but, in perusing the list of doctors of our own universities, after running your finger down some columns of mediocre Rabbis, you will experience a sensation of relief in missing the name of Veitch.

In day-schools, like the two great institutions of Dunedin, where the boys only give a morning and noon attendance for five days in the week, there is no call for the clerical element whatsoever. Their pupils combine the advantages of a public school with the inestimable and civilizing influences of home life. As their parents and guardians may reasonably be supposed to be in all cases Christian, there would seem to be no need for religious instruction in their school-hours; and it might be thought sufficient, if such institutions opened the work of each day with the reverent reading of some chapter of the New Testament, and a short and appropriate prayer; and if a weekly lesson were given from the historical portions of the older Scriptures. Not to speak of the heterogeneous admixture of doctrinal lessons with those in Latin syntax and Rule of Three, the boys are supposed to hear family prayers each morning and evening; to attend Divine Service regularly; and to hear the Bible read and expounded by a devout father or mother. The hearing of one parable from the gentle voice of the latter is worth all the religious instruction that a master can impart in class, where in the hearts of boys the spirit of gentleness is too apt to succumb to the sterner spirit of class ambition.

However, the question is different in regard to large schools where children are, with questionable propriety, removed entirely from home. Here I can perfectly understand how well the moral and religious training of pupils might be intrusted to discreet clerical hands; and would allow to the chaplain of such an institution *preëminence in rank and emolument*, as due to the sacredness of his calling. There would be some studies, also, in which he could give valuable help; as in that of Biblical, and even secular history; and over all he might exert a wholesome influence. But I am wholly at a loss to account for the fact that in England, the teaching of the classical languages should be considered as almost necessarily devolving upon the clergy. Why should it require Holy Orders to fit a man to teach the heathen tongues of Athens and Rome, any more than to teach the Christian tongues of France, Germany or Italy?—or, indeed, any more than to teach drawing or music or dancing? Greek and Latin are important elements in the education of a gentleman, but they enter very indirectly into the training of a Christian. They may lead a man part of the way to the woolsack; but they cannot carry him one step on the road that leads to the Everlasting Gates. No: many children have gone in thereat, that never stumbled through a declension; or that stumbled through one, and nothing more: many men, that in boyhood fell through the Asses' Bridge, have, in spite of corpulence, passed safely over the suspended camel's hair, that breaks only beneath iniquity: many dear illiterate old saints have outstripped wits and critics and scholars and theologians on their journey to an unaspirated Heaven.

.   .   .   .

Not many years ago the patrons of a large proprietary school in the West of England offered their headmastership to a very distinguished scholar, a friend of my own, on condition that he would take Holy Orders. It was more than insinuated that these Orders would merely affect the fashion of his neck-tie, and the prejudices of an enlightened public. My friend was a man of middle age, with habits and character thoroughly formed, and with as much idea of turning clergyman as of buying the practice of a dentist. Consequently the offer, though pecuniarily a very tempting one, was not accepted. My friend is prosecuting his journey heavenwards with a well-stored brain; a rather ill-stored scrip; a white conscience; and a black tie. For my own part I regard such martyrdom as utterly out of place in a practical age. When the headmastership is next vacant, I trust the patrons will make a similar offer to me. They have merely to name their salary—and their bishop.

XXII.

The Social Position of Schoolmasters

Many of my school vacations I passed in Bruges and Brussels, and made the acquaintance from time to time of boys of my own age attending the *Athénées*, or public schools of these towns. Indeed, my own brother received at such schools the greater part of his education. The masters were laymen; in a country next to Spain perhaps the most bigotedly Catholic in Europe. The means of coercion at their disposal seemed to my young English ideas barbarously simple. No birch; no cane; not even the ridiculously mild strap. How on earth could pupils learn Latin versification, or any other useful accomplishment, without such obviously requisite stimulants? However, their classes of rhetoric, or senior classes, *did* turn out well-educated and most gentlemanly-mannered men. But the strangest thing to me was that the masters were never spoken of as occupying any peculiar or comical position in society. It never seemed to strike a boy to speak in terms of ridicule of his schoolmaster any more than of his clergyman or medical attendant. In fact, society at large seemed unconsciously to regard the master of an Athénée as *an ordinary gentleman,* neither more nor less.

One of the most polished and accomplished men I have ever had the honor of knowing was my brother's music-master, whose lessons were given at a rate that would appear to us ludicrously small. He associated on terms of perfect intimacy with families of very ancient lineage in the neighborhood of Bruges. He used to describe in the most humorous fashion the treatment he occasionally met with in English *salons*, whose occupants, of undoubtedly high position at home, were temporarily residing abroad for reasons of financial retrenchment.

I have had many relatives educated entirely in Florence, and have heard that the masters, who visited the leading schools there, held a social position in that not unaristocratic city quite equal to that of an ordinary barrister amongst ourselves. And these masters had no ecclesiastical title to raise them in the social scale.

In England, at a very early period, the birch and cane were engrafted upon our educational system. They naturally made the position of a schoolmaster odious in the sight of children, and somewhat ludicrous in the eyes of the world, and especially so in the eyes of women. Now the English character is essentially practical, but by no means bigoted to logic. Their political Constitution might be theoretically assailed on many points; but it works satisfactorily as a whole. In the matter of education, England shows an equal disregard of logic and an equal determination of working good ends by any practical means. The position of a schoolmaster needed backing up, it seemed, in some way. Then make the schoolmaster a clergyman. Never mind the absurdity of calling upon a man to swear that he will spend and be spent in preaching the Glad Tidings, when *he* knows, and everybody knows, that he will pass his life in teaching the rudiments of Greek and Latin. With a practical people such obligations are generally understood in a practical way; and the practical way of understanding them seems, in this one instance, to lie in ignoring them partially or altogether.

There can be little doubt that, without the aid of clerical prestige, no body of men could have continued to command public respect in spite of the odium and ridicule attached to such flagrantly cruel implements as the cane and birch. The former of these, as I know to my cost, is painful in the extreme; and the infliction of the latter is always brutal, and very often abominably indecent.

Now, in Scotland, whatever our faults may be—and *Scottish* writers on the London press purge us from time to time of our conceit—we are acknowledged to be a logical race. Consequently we call a schoolmaster a schoolmaster. We no more think of allowing him to take fictitious orders, than we should think of giving a haberdasher the fictitious title of M.D., and yet a schoolmaster in Scotland has certainly need of any aid that could be rendered for the improvement of his social status. The latter is far below that of any other professional body. Yet, low as is comparatively the social position of the Scottish schoolmaster, he can point to his ridiculous but almost innocuous leather strap, and boast that he has contrived therewith to maintain discipline and stimulate to exertion, while a wealthier body, with rich endowments and ecclesiastical prestige, have made unsparing use of two instruments, whose barbarity as far exceeds that of his own strap, as the income of an Eton provost exceeds that of a rector of our high school.

But to revert to the consideration of the social rank of a master in a Scottish grammar-school. The rectors of the two chief Edinburgh schools are exceptions to the ordinary rule. They enjoy a social rank befitting the dignity of their official duties. But how is it that the masters of classics, mathematics, and modern languages, in these and similar institutions, take by general consent a lower place at feasts than a medical man of little practice, and an advocate of few briefs?

In the social estimate of a whole order of men, I am inclined to think the world at large cannot be *altogether* wrong. There is generally fault on both sides. If, then, we schoolmasters *are* at fault, it would be of use if we could only hit upon our weak point. We might then give it a fair and serious consideration; and use means, if they could be suggested, for remedying the evil.

I have heard it said by a gentleman of very high position, and of reputed scholarship, that the subordinate master in a great Scottish school is only expected by a Scottish public to be a man of ordinary attainments, who can drill his pupils well in the rudiments, and just keep pace with them in their higher reading. While such melancholy opinions are generally entertained of our craft, it is especially incumbent upon us to endeavor by our teaching and our lives to belie them. It is because we too often give in, for want of courage or proper pride, to such a condemnation of our order that we continue to be members of a Pariah profession. We are too often contented with the limited intellectual stores that were laid in at college. We too often go uninquiringly through a dull routine; caring little whether or no we carry the inclinations and sympathies of our boys along with us, so long as we get through the prescribed work, and preserve a mechanical discipline. We are not impressed with the fact that a schoolmaster cannot be too learned, too accomplished. Under any circumstances, something of the tedious must creep into the routine of school-work, and it will need a wide field of continual reading to enable one to illustrate and vivify daily lessons, that vary from the declension of *penna* to the study of the Agamemnon.

The pupils at our chief public schools study German and French. Should a master of the two great ancient languages be ignorant of linguistic studies, in which his pupils may be proficient? No; he should outstrip them immeasurably in every department of study that bears upon his own. He should be so impressed with the dignity of his calling,—and what calling, save the cure of souls is more dignified?—so full of chastened respect for himself, as to command the respect of his pupils, though he may fail for a while to command that of the more unthinking of the public. If we could only work ourselves up to some such standard we might then gradually dispense with that little leathern instrument, that still keeps a burr of ridicule attached to our black gowns.

But, stop: am I again traveling to Utopia? Let me turn my hobby's head, and gallop back to dear Dunedin. When a man's liver is out of order what on earth is the use of his doctor's telling him to keep early hours; to use a cold tub; to live temperately, and take frequent outdoor exercise? Why, his grandmother might have suggested that. What the man wants is a blue pill or two. They can be taken in a minute; and he need not materially change his dietetics. Could not some such violent but easy remedy be suggested for the cure of our social abasement? Certainly. Why should barring-out be confined to boys?—or strikes to artisans? A fig for political economy! Let us form ourselves into a league and proclaim a general STRIKE OF SCHOOLMASTERS! There will be some sneaking recusants among us; but we will brain them with their own dictionaries.

Some summer morning Scotland will awake and find every grammatical fountain frozen. What fun it will be for the boys! For a week the parents may outface the inconvenience; but in a month the animal, always latent in boyhood, will be growing rampant and outrageous. Gradually will it develop, unsoothed by the influences of grammar, unchecked by the sterner influences of our magic leather. No father will be safe in his own house. The smaller boys will be smoking brown paper in the drawing-room, and the older boys wallowing in Bass and cavendish in the lower kitchen.

Meanwhile, calmly reposing in the stillness of his back parlor, M'Gillicuddy will be putting the finishing stroke to that folio edition of "Cornelius Nepos," on which his fame in after ages is to rest; and I, in my aërial lodgings, shall be setting to Greek iambics the moral aphorisms of the great Tupper, whose terseness and originality are the wonder of a grateful people.

Our hospitable provost, like his predecessor in olden days

when the English were marching north, will hold a meeting of troubled citizens. They will meet in arms; each father will be provided with his life-preserver of cut leather. One speaker will tell how nouns are at a fabulous premium; that an adjective may not be had for love or money. Another will tell the horrible tale, how whole families have for weeks subsisted on the smallest prepositions. They will attempt a compromise. We shall decline treating on such terms. They will surrender unconditionally; and our terms—monstrous as they may seem—shall be as follows:

A schoolmaster, who shall have graduated at an university, shall hereafter be addressed, personally or epistolarily, with the courtesy usually shown to a second-rate solicitor or a briefless advocate.

Whosoever shall wittingly and willfully offend against the above decree, let him for the first offense be dismissed after due admonition; but, on a second offense being proven, let him be sentenced to parse *verbatim* the folio edition of M'Gillicuddy's "Nepos," declining all nouns, conjugating all verbs, and repeating all syntax rules, *usque ad Rei ipsius et totius Curiæ nauseam.*[1]

XXIII

TINT, TINT, TINT [2]

It is now twelve years ago that I was for the first time brought face to face with a class, some fifty in number, of little Latin novices. They all regarded me with sensations of wonderment and awe; they had but a faint idea, luckily, of the terror with which I regarded them. I had, certainly, the recollections of my own long elementary training to guide me in my proceedings; and I had the traditions of the school, to which I had been recently appointed as master, to direct my uncertain steps. But the recollections of my own training

---

[1] even to disgust for the thing itself and for the whole tribe
[2] Lost, Lost, Lost. (Scotch.)

were all tinged with melancholy; and with the traditions of my new sphere of duty I was but imperfectly acquainted.

In the middle of my class-room stood a machine, somewhat resembling a patent engine for the simultaneous polishing of many knives; and I was desired to take a firm grasp of its wooden handle, and to turn it with vigor and rapidity. And an implement of simple leather was put into my hands, by the dexterous application of which I was to quicken the apprehensions of such children as might be uninfluenced by the monotonous music of my gerund-stone.

And for many a day, obedient to tradition and to my orders, I turned rapidly the wooden handle, and flourished vigorously the simple implement to the very best of my ability. But, strange to say, although I was then youthful and strong, and eaten up with a superfluous zeal for my calling, I could never turn the machine without its creaking painfully; and whenever I applied my leathern implement to a child's palm, I was immediately conscious of a thrill, as of electricity, that ran from my finger-tips to the very center of my nervous system; and sometimes, after the performance of such an ordinary act of duty, I would find myself standing before my pupils with a heightened color upon my face, and a tingling in my ears; and to a looker-on I should have appeared as one ashamed of having done some questionable deed.

Finding all my efforts unavailing to work smoothly and noiselessly my mechanical engine of instruction, I at length relinquished it altogether; and it has been now standing for years in a side-room adjoining my place of business, and is covered over with cobwebs, and rusted at the juncture of the stone and handle.

To supply the place of its simple mechanism, I brought to bear upon my pupils all the moral and intellectual means at my disposal. I spared myself neither in the matter of time nor trouble in my endeavors to educe the dormant faculties of my charges; and enjoying as I did for many years a bodily health impervious to fatigue, and having a keen sympathy with boyhood, I succeeded more and more until I almost ceased at length to regret the disappearance of my gerund-stone.

But the more I gave satisfaction to myself, the less I gave satisfaction to the majority of my so-called patrons—the guardians of my young pupils. From time to time, when I was indulging in a dream of appreciated toil, I heard of complaints being circulated by such as were favorers of mechanism in instruction. Pupils in whose progress I had begun to take a keen interest were from time to time removed without a word of explanation or the civility of a farewell. "They were not *grounded*," said these waggish but unmannerly guardians; meaning all the while, " They were not *ground.*"

I had almost begun to despair of my system, and to think that I had mistaken my calling, and was casting about my eyes for some honest trade to which I might apprentice myself, when one afternoon my class was honored with a lengthened visit from a gentleman of acknowledged rank and worth and judgment. After the lesson was over I complained to this distinguished visitor that my system of conveying instruction, as being natural and philosophic, was popularly considered a more difficult one for a pupil than the ancient turning of a piece of mechanism. My visitor, who had a son under my charge, stated his firm conviction that my system was not only likely to produce better results, but was also in its operation far more easy and interesting for a young pupil to follow. For that moment I felt reassured, and determined never again to regret the absence of my gerund-stone.

And now to treat of the loss of my other auxiliary implement. The application of this latter, I can honestly say, was never made excepting with the view of stimulating ever-dormant energies, and of repressing tendencies to chronic negligence or misconduct. I considered myself as an abstraction; as the embodied representative of the class; and used the implement only to protect the interests of the latter, which suffered, to my mind, whenever one of its members, by carelessness or lack of study, turned upon himself that stream of time and energy that should have run uninterruptedly to the irrigation of the body corporate. In fact I made myself the dividend in a long division sum, whose divisor was *duty;* the quotient, I found, was *teacher* + *superintendent*, and the remainder, *personal identity*, which was very small in comparison with the divisor, and might practically be ignored. So, when a little fellow walked after me for a few days at the striking of the bell, with his hands beneath imaginary coat-tails in imitation of my gait, I considered him as only joking with me in my capacity of *remainder;* and I merely asked him to desist, as otherwise I should make fun of him in revenge; and he desisted. And when a boy wrote my name upon the desk, I was contented with showing him how he had misspelled it; and he rubbed it out at my request. And when a boy, years ago, put his tongue into his cheek after an admonition, I showed his comrades what little control he had over that organ; knowing as I did that he intended to protrude it on the side that would have been invisible to me. And I may state that such trifling incidents were of so rare occurrence that I could enumerate them all upon the fingers of one hand.

But still, although I was conscious that I used the implement with good intent, and aware that it was similarly used by men who were my superiors in age, and certainly not my inferiors in kindliness and sympathy with boyhood, I was haunted with an idea that the use of it was founded on an error in our system of instruction, and I was long pondering where the error could lie; and I found the subject far more difficult than I had at first supposed, and I confess it still to be a problem difficult of solution.

I was in this frame of mind one day, when, according to an unalterable rule, there came under the influence of the electric implement a little, quiet, well-behaved, and intelligent foreigner. The application had scarce been made when a young comrade—bless the lad!—gave vent to an unmistakable hiss! Order, of course, was immediately and energetically re-established. But in my walk that afternoon by the sea, and in many a lonely walk afterwards, I thought about that little foreigner and his courageous comrade. And I thought how that little foreigner, returning to his own land, the ancient home of courtesy and gentle manners, would tell his friends of our rude, northern ways. And I tremble at the idea of my usage of the Electric Leather being narrated in the hearing of one of those terrible colonels, whom their emperor holds with difficulty on the leash. For I thought if ever our great metropolis were in their hands, how ill it would fare with all therein that turned the gerund-stone, and with those therein that bare my hapless surname. And the name of these is Legion. And knowing that the comrade was no vulgar and low-natured boy, I felt sure in my heart that there was at least something right in the impulse that had pushed him into danger and disobedience. But still I was afraid of allowing sentimentalism or impulsiveness on my part to take the place of duty, however stern and unpalatable.

I was standing not alone one morning in the lobby of my own home, just before leaving for the day's work. A greatcoat of mine was hanging from the wall. My companion, in a playful mood, put a small white hand into one of its pockets, and drew a something out; then thrust it back hurriedly as though it had been a something venomous. And over a very gentle face passed a look of surprise not unmingled with reproof; but the reproof gave way almost momently to the wonted smile. But I long remembered the mild reproof upon that gentle face, for it was an expression very seldom seen there; and it came afterwards to be numbered with other sad and sweet memories.

Meanwhile, at the end of the last bench upon my class sat a boy who was very backward in his learning. He was continually absent upon what seemed to me frivolous pretenses. These absences entailed upon me much additional trouble. I had occasionally to keep him and a little remnant in the room when the others had gone out to play; to make up to him and them for lost time. And on one occasion my look was very cross, and my speech very short; for it seemed to me provoking that children should be so backward in their Latin. And when the work was over and we two were left alone, he followed me to my desk, and said, " You have no idea, sir, how weak I am." And I said, " Why, my boy, you look stout enough." But he answered, " I am really very weak, sir; far weaker than I look ! " and there was a pleading earnestness in his words that touched me to the heart; and, afterwards, there was an unseen chord of sympathy that bound the master to the pupil, who was still very dull at Latin.

And still he would be absent; at times, for a day or two together. But it excited no surprise. For the boy seemed to sit almost a stranger among his fellows, and in play-hours seemed to take no interest in boyish games. And by and by he had been absent for some weeks together. But I was afraid to ask concerning him; thinking he might have been removed, as many boys had been, without a letter of explanation, or his shaking me by the hand. And one morning I received a letter with a broad black edge, telling me that he had died the day previously of a virulent contagious fever.

So when school was over I made my way to his whilom lodging, and stood at the door, pondering. For the fever, of which the child had died, had been to me a Death-in-life, and had passed like the Angel of old over my dwelling; but, unlike that angel, had spared my first-born, and only-born. And because the latter sat each evening on my knee, I was afraid of the fever, and intended only to leave my card, as a mark of respectful sympathy. But the good woman of the house said, " Nay, nay, sir, but ye'll see the laddie ; " and I felt drawn by an influence of fatherhood more constraining than a father's fears, and followed the good woman into the small and dim chamber where my pupil was lying. And, as I passed the threshold, my masterhood slipped off me like a loose robe; and I stood, very humble and pupil-like, in that awful Presence, that teacheth a wisdom to babes and sucklings, to which our treasured lore is but a jingling of vain words. And, when left alone, I drew near the cheerless and dismantled bed, on which my pupil lay asleep in his early coffin. And he looked very calm and happy, as though there had been to him no pain in passing from a world where he had had few companions and very little pleasure. And I knew that his boyhood had been as dreary as it had been short; and I thought that the good woman of his lodging had perhaps been his only sympathizing friend at hand. And I communed with myself whether aught I had done could have made his dullness more dull. And I felt thankful for the chord of sympathy that had united us, unseen, for a little while. But, in a strange and painful way, I stood rebuked before the calm and solemn and unrebuking face of the child on whom I had frowned for his being backward in his Latin.

That evening, as usual, my own child was seated on my knee, making sunrise out of sunset for myself and his mother's mother. And the table was alive with moo-cows, and bow-wows, and silly sheep. And we sang snatches of impossible songs, or hid ourselves behind chairs and curtains in a barefaced and undeceitful manner. And the penates at my hearth, that were chipped and broken, blinked merrily by the fire-light; and the child was taken to his tiny bed; and the chipped penates, thereupon, slowly faded out of view, and disappeared among the cinders.

And I sat, musing; alone. And yet not all alone. For in the chair, where recently had been sitting the mother of my child's mother, there sat a gray transparent shape. And the shape and I were familiar friends. He had sat with me many a time from midnight until when the morning had come peeping through the green lattice. And he had peopled all the chambers of my house with sad thoughts and black-stoled memories. So, never heeding my familiar friend, I sat, staring in the fire, and thinking.

And I thought, sadly and almost vindictively, of the dreary years of my own early boyhood, with their rope of sand, and the mill-wheel that had ground no corn. And I remembered how at times there would come to me in my exile the sound of my brother's laugh, and the sweeter music of my mother's voice. But I remembered, thankfully, that through years of monotonous work and rough usage I had enjoyed sound health, and had had companions with whom I had walked and talked, and romped and fought, cheerily.

And I wondered whether I should be spared to see my own child grow to be a merry and frank-hearted little fellow; to hear the music of his ringing laugh; to see his face flushed with rude but healthful sport; to hear of him as beloved for many boyish virtues, and reproved, not unlovingly, for his share of boyish faults. And I longed to be climbing with him the hill of difficulty, and lightening the ascent for him with varied converse; resting now and then to look down upon the valley, or to let him gather blue-bells that grew on the hillside.

And then I thought of a boy who had sat of late on the last bench in my class-room, with a timid and scared look, beside his bluff and bold companions; who had stood in the noisy play-ground, lonely as in a wilderness; whom I had seen that afternoon in his early coffin, with the seal upon his forehead of everlasting peace; the peace that passeth all understanding.

So I determined—from the recollections of my own dreary boyhood; for the mild reproof that once had clouded momently very gentle eyes; for the love I bear my own little one; and for the calm and unrebuking face I had seen that afternoon—that I would do as little as possible in the exercise of my stern duties to make of life a weariness to young children; and especially to such as should be backward in their Latin.

XXIV

The Pressure of Gentleness

A close relation of my own was for twelve years an officer in almost the severest of all continental services. In that chivalric army is conserved a traditional discipline whose details would appall a democrat, and the exactions of which could only be endured by an obedient and military race. He tells me that, in his long experience, he only met with one captain who, in dealing with his company, avowedly ignored all means of physical coercion. On this captain's breast were the orders of two kingdoms and two empires. After one well-fought day he had been voted by acclamation as a candidate for the Order of the Iron Crown, which he would have obtained had he added his own signature to those of all his brother officers; and yet so softhearted was this *chevalier sans peur*[1] that any slattern beggarwoman could draw from him an ill-spared florin. In a village where a portion of the regiment were once quartered, the good *curé*,[2] at the close of a sermon on Christian character, told his flock that if they wished to see Christianity in action, they might see it in a captain of Grenadiers, who clothed their poorest children with his pocket-money, and whose closest companion was ignorant of his good deeds. This captain's company was noted as being the best dressed and the best conducted in the regiment. There were at Solferino (and there are, alas! such cases in all engagements) cases of gallant but stern officers that fell by a traitorous bullet from behind. There was not one man in the company of this captain that would not have taken in his stead a bullet aimed at him from the front.

A year and a half ago I met in Yorkshire an invalid young sailor. From his smooth face, short stature, and attenuated form, I should have taken him for a senior midshipman. To my complete astonishment I found he was commander of a Pacific liner, with a numerous crew under his orders, and in receipt of a splendid income. He had been third in command, when the two seniors had taken fever, and his gallantry under trying circumstances of all kinds had procured his unusually early promotion. I discussed with him the theory of discipline. He considered physical chastisement as brutal; swearing as unChristian; and hectoring as unmanly. "The man who cannot control himself is not fit to command a crew," he said, tritely and truly. I looked in wonder at this shrimp of a man, that was speaking with such calm confidence. "I never," he continued, "raise my voice above its usual tone to enforce an order." He was worn to skin and bone by a chest disorder of

[1] a knight without fear   [2] curate

long continuance, which he considered would close his life at no distant date. I could have pushed him over with a rude jostle of my elbow. But there was something in his face that told you unmistakably he was not the man with whom to take a liberty. He gave me a remarkable anecdote of himself. His ship was alongside of an American liner in the Liverpool docks. The Yankee captain was dining with him, and the conversation fell upon the means of maintaining order in a crew. The Yankee scouted all means but the stick. He and his mates used on principle the most brutal means of coercion. During their argument the steward came to announce that the English crew were fighting the Yankees on the neighboring vessel. The captains went on deck, and the Englishman, slinging himself by a rope, alighted in the midst of an uproarious crowd. "Well, my men," said he, "so you are making beasts of yourselves, and disgracing your captain." And the big fellows slunk off without a word to their own vessel, and one or two of the ringleaders were set for an hour or two to swab the decks. But of the quarreling tars there was not a man but could have lifted his wee captain and dropped him overboard without an effort. I trust to God he may yet be living, and may long be spared, as a specimen of a quiet, resolute English Christian skipper.

My chiefest friend at school was a man of widest mental culture, of even temper, and of sound judgment. Among his friends and my own at Trinity I knew a few men of a similarly high stamp. I remember one man, in particular, in whom the scholar and the Christian so curiously blended, that it would be difficult to say where his Latin ended and his religion began. He was a spiritual and mental merman. But if I were called upon to name the Aristides of my life-acquaintance, I should name a man whom I never knew till I had crossed the Tweed. I believe it would be as hard to warp a Carlyle into sentimental or religious cant, and a prophet-Cumming into common-sense and modesty, as to twist the nature of my friend into petty words or illiberal action.

He was once the superintendent of a public educational institution. He had been present one day in the drill-ground, where an honest sergeant with a good deal of superfluous bluster was putting a little regiment through its facings. When the boys were dismissed the sergeant approached his superior, and said: "Excuse the liberty, sir; but really, when you are more used to boys, you'll find that you must put more pepper into what you do and say." "Well," said my friend, "every man has his own way; for my own part, I don't believe in pepper."

A few weeks afterwards the principal was in his library, when the sergeant was ushered in. "I've come, sir," said the latter, "to ask a favor. Those boys are a little troublesome at times. If you'd be kind enough just to stand at your drawing-room window for a few minutes when drill was going on, it would do a deal of good; if you'd only stand for a few minutes, reading a newspaper."

Ah! worthy sergeant, your pepper won't do, after all. No, friend, keep it for your vegetables, and use it then in moderation.

I hold that men may be called of God to more offices than the holy one of the Christian ministry. There was an under-officer at my old school, who to me seemed always to partake largely of some of the finest attributes of the gentleman. He had failed, through continued ill-health, in business as a bookseller, and was a well-read man. He was uniformly civil and respectful to us senior scholars; but, while we could tip and bribe others, we could never venture on the liberty of an unadorned surname with him. This man was called to the humble office of maintaining order in the school-yard. So there are men called to command men on the field of battle, and boys in the schoolroom. I have met with a schoolmaster in Scotland who could govern a crowd of boys in one room, though they might be divided into scattered groups, and engaged in varied work; and his only implements of discipline were a word or two of good-natured banter or kindly encouragement, and occasionally a calm and stern rebuke. I have been much struck by the expression of his opinion, that physical coercion cannot be dispensed with altogether. In defiance, however, of a kindness, a sagacity, and a judgment that I respect, I do most firmly believe that the necessity for physical chastisement rests mainly upon two blemishes in our ordinary school system: the mechanical nature of our routine of work, and the crowding of our class-rooms. In the latter respect, we are more at fault than our English brethren; in the former, we are far less sinning. In the teaching of our elementary classes we employ far more spirit, and far less wood; and I wish I could add, *no leather*. There is less of a gulf between pupil and master. The severest means of physical chastisement at the disposal of the latter is almost innocuous. But mild as our implement may be from the point of view of physical pain inflicted, its employment is of necessity associated with some degree of odium, and a more formidable amount of ridicule. I am convinced that many children imagine that we schoolmasters were as naturally born with tawse, as foxes with tails. Did you ever see children in a nursery play at school? The rule seems to be for the elder brother to play our part; and that part is limited to the fun or business of flogging all his little sisters.

We have gone a great way already in Scotland in the way of civilized teaching, in forbearing to use an instrument of acute pain and an instrument of indecent brutality. Let us make a further advance, and if we can invent some intellectual and moral substitute for our ridiculous scourges, let us send the latter in bundles to the public schools of England, to be there adopted when their system is sufficiently ripened by a few extra centuries of Christianity. Let us clothe their scholastic nakedness with the last rags of our barbarism. Our boys will be none the less manly and respectful. Flogging can never instil courage into a child, but it has helped to transform many an one into a sneak. And sneakishness is a vice more hard to eradicate than obduracy. So far from curing an ill-conditioned boy of rude and vulgar ways, it is calculated rather to render inveterate in him a distaste for study, and a solid hatred of our craft.

Let us be less careful of the mere number of our classes, and more careful of their intellectual culture. Let us care more for what we think of ourselves, than what the public think of us. The respect of others follows upon self-respect. Let us not care to be called of men, *Rabbi, Rabbi.* Let us be content with classes of limited numbers, every member of which can keep pace with a properly advancing curriculum. Let us aim at a broad and invigorating culture, not a narrow and pedantic one; let us ignore examinations of College or Civil service, and aim only at the great and searching examination of actual life. Let our aims be high and generous, irrespective of the exactions of unreasoning parents and well-meaning but unqualified intermeddlers; let our means of coercion be dignified, in spite of the trials to which our tempers may be exposed. Let us endeavor to make our pupils love their work without fearing us. They may live—God knows—to love *us.* Whether they ever love us or not perhaps matters but little, if we do our work singleheartedly. The *mens conscia recti*[1] is of itself no mean reward. I am, perhaps, an enthusiast; but I have an idea that, ere a generation is passed away, the last sound of the last tawse will be heard in the leading grammar-schools of Scotland. Her scholars will be none the worse taught, and her schoolmasters none the less respected, when instruction has been made less rugged in her aspect, and discipline is maintained by the more than hydraulic pressure of a persistent and continuous gentleness.

And, O brother schoolmaster, remember evermore the exceeding dignity of our calling. It is not the holiest of all callings; but it runs near and parallel to the holiest. The lawyer's wits are sharpened, and his moral sense not seldom blunted, by a life-long familiarity with ignorance, chicanery, and crime. The physician, in the exercise of a more beneficent craft, is sad-

---

[1] mind conscious of right

dened continually by the spectacle of human weakness and human pain. We have usually to deal with fresh and unpolluted natures. A noble calling, but a perilous! We are dressers in a moral and mental vineyard. We are undershepherds of the Lord's little ones; and our business it is to lead them into green pastures, by the sides of refreshing streams. Let us into our linguistic lessons introduce cunningly and imperceptibly all kinds of amusing stories; stories of the real kings of earth, that have reigned in secret, crownless and unsceptred; leaving the vain show of power to gilded toy-kings and make-believe statesmen; of the angels that have walked the earth in the guise of holy men and holier women; of the seraph-singers, whose music will be echoing forever; of the cherubim of power, that with the mighty wind of conviction and enthusiasm have winnowed the air of pestilence and superstition.

Yes, friend, throw a higher poetry than all this into your linguistic work; the poetry of pure and holy motive. Then, in the coming days, when you are fast asleep under the green grass, they will not speak lightly of you over their fruit and wine, mimicking your accent, and retailing dull, insipid boy-pleasantries. Enlightened by the experience of fatherhood, they will see with a clear remembrance your firmness in dealing with their moral faults, your patience in dealing with their intellectual weakness. And, calling to mind the old schoolroom, they will think: "Ah! it was good for us to be there. For, unknown to us, were made therein three tabernacles; one for us, and one for our schoolmaster, and one for Him that is the Friend of all children, and the Master of all schoolmasters."

Ah! believe me, brother mine, where two or three children are met together, unless He, who is the Spirit of gentleness, be in the midst of them, then our Latin is but sounding brass, and our Greek a tinkling cymbal.

www.ingramcontent.com/pod-product-compliance
Lightning Source LLC
Chambersburg PA
CBHW021228300426
44111CB00007B/461